Books by James Thomas Flexner

AMERICAN PAINTING
I. First Flowers of Our Wilderness
II. The Light of Distant Skies
III. That Wilder Image

AMERICA'S OLD MASTERS

THE POCKET HISTORY OF AMERICAN PAINTING
(also published as *A Short History of American Painting*)

JOHN SINGLETON COPLEY

GILBERT STUART

THE WORLD OF WINSLOW HOMER
(with the editors of Time-Life Books)

NINETEENTH CENTURY AMERICAN PAINTING

THE FACE OF LIBERTY

DOCTORS ON HORSEBACK:
Pioneers of American Medicine

STEAMBOATS COME TRUE
(also published as *Inventors in Action*)

THE TRAITOR AND THE SPY
(also published as *The Benedict Arnold Case*)

LORD OF THE MOHAWKS:
A Biography of Sir William Johnson
(previously published as *Mohawk Baronet*)

WILLIAM HENRY WELCH AND THE HEROIC AGE
OF AMERICAN MEDICINE
(with Simon Flexner)

GEORGE WASHINGTON
I. The Forge of Experience (1732–1775)
II. In the American Revolution (1775–1783)
III. And the New Nation (1783–1793)
IV. Anguish and Farewell (1793–1799)

WASHINGTON: THE INDISPENSABLE MAN

THE YOUNG HAMILTON

STATES DYCKMAN
American Loyalist

AN AMERICAN SAGA
The Story of Helen Thomas and Simon Flexner

AN
AMERICAN
SAGA

JAMES THOMAS FLEXNER

AN AMERICAN SAGA

The Story of Helen Thomas and Simon Flexner

LITTLE, BROWN AND COMPANY · BOSTON · TORONTO

FIRST EDITION

The author is grateful to Simon & Schuster for permission to reprint excerpts from *I Remember* by Abraham Flexner. Copyright 1940 by Abraham Flexner; Copyright © 1960 by Jean
Flexner Lewison and Eleanor Flexner.

Library of Congress Cataloging in Publication Data

Flexner, James Thomas, 1908–
  An American saga.

  Bibliography: p.
  Includes index.
  1. Flexner, Helen Thomas, 1871–1956. 2. Feminists—
United States—Biography. 3. Flexner, Simon, 1863–1946.
4. Pathologists—United States—Biography. 5. Johns
Hopkins University—History. I. Title.
HQ1412.F57   1983   616'.07'0924 [B]   83-19918
ISBN 0-316-28611-7

MV

Published simultaneously in Canada
by Little, Brown & Company (Canada) Limited

PRINTED IN THE UNITED STATES OF AMERICA

To
Helen Hudson Flexner
and
Beatrice Hudson Flexner

Contents

VII

APPROACHING LIVES

VIII

JOINING TOGETHER

IX

CONCLUSION

List of Illustrations

(between pages 238–239)

Prologue

AN author who is writing on the history of his own family has in equalitarian America, so I quickly discovered, two strikes against him. It is automatically assumed that he is engaged in unworthy self-aggrandizement. Reluctance to face such reproaches has been among the reasons why I have postponed for so long picking up the treasure-trove of historical and biographical materials scattered about my home ground. Had I happened on such material in another family domain, I would at once have pled for its use. And now that I have turned to my own family history, I have endeavored — while not neglecting my own memories — to write such an unbiased factual narrative as in all my books I have wished to achieve.

This book is in essence the account of how a man and a woman, nurtured at opposite poles of the American historical, economic, and social spheres, came at last together to form a matrimonial alliance that was to have a profound effect on life in the United States and, indeed, the world. It is a deeply American saga since Simon Flexner and Helen Thomas could hardly in any other land have been led to each other and then united into so harmonious a whole.

My father, Simon Flexner, was the son of impoverished German-speaking Jewish immigrants who appeared in Louisville, Kentucky, shortly before the Civil War. Brought up in the most humble circumstances, Simon became a sullen delinquent who dropped out of school during the eighth grade, and thereafter lost job after job. His father led him through the local jail to show him where he would probably end up. But then, at a drugstore where he came to be employed, he found a mi-

xvi   Prologue

croscope normally used for routine tests. The instrument became for the isolated nineteen-year-old an open sesame to one of the most fruitful advances ever engaged in by the human race.

This was the time when a progression of experiments and findings in Europe were setting in motion modern scientific medicine. The new techniques and discoveries were just beginning to filter into the United States when Simon carried the microscope home. Under the one gaslight the family could afford, while his mother sewed and his smaller brothers and sisters played around him, he struggled to teach himself, from what books he could procure and using his own experimental ingenuity, the new sciences of pathology and bacteriology.

Still with no formal training worth consideration, having borrowed $500 from his brother Abraham who was a school teacher, Simon journeyed in 1890 to the brand-new university that was to go furthest in bringing scientific medicine to America. Simon appeared at the Johns Hopkins even before its celebrated medical school had opened. Gaining access to brilliant teachers and sophisticated apparatus, he almost instantly began making original discoveries. By the time he met Helen Thomas in 1900, he was, although still naive in most aspects of life, considered the most distinguished younger medical scientist in the United States.

Helen's ancestral lines stretched for the most part back in America to the 1600's. Her forebears had prospered. The one great economic fall was due to the Quaker idealism of Helen's great-grandparents. During 1810, they banished the Thomas family from Maryland plantation life by freeing their some hundred slaves. After a period of hardship, the Thomases reestablished themselves in Baltimore, where their fortunes rapidly revived. In family-proud Maryland, Helen's father, James Carey Thomas, was considered a leading aristocrat. Only partially dependent on his earnings as a practicing physician, he concerned himself with Quaker good works and the furtherance of education. He played significant roles in the founding of Bryn Mawr College, the Johns Hopkins University, and the Johns Hopkins Medical School.

Helen's maternal family, the Whitalls (pronounced "Whytle") of West Jersey and Philadelphia, were particularly characterized by religious fervor and feminine power. Helen's mother, Mary Whitall Thomas, and more conspicuously her aunt, Hannah Whitall Smith, were triumphant evangelists. The "Whitall Women" prided themselves on the tradition founded by their ancestress Ann. While a battle of the American Revolution was progressing on her farm, Ann gave her

Quaker "testimony against war" by defying the cannonballs from her seat at her spinning wheel. A family male, the author Logan Pearsall Smith, wrote in 1936, "Even now, in the American and English nurseries of her descendants, Ann Whitall seems to stir in some cradle, and her plangent voice makes itself heard. The husband of a niece of mine once told me that after his marriage he found that his wife was an Ogress, was the daughter and granddaughter of Ogresses, and had become the mother of a fourth of the species."

Although untroubled by financial or cultural privations, Helen's path towards maturity was more dangerous than Simon's. Once he had grasped a microscope, he had found a direction he could resolutely follow. But Helen, as the youngest girl in a large family, aware of a long tradition behind her, surrounded with elders engaged in multitudinous and often important matters, was prevented by the complications of her environment from finding directions of her own. All she could do was look and listen and try to puzzle out the meaning and the values of what she saw and heard. Passionately eager to understand, she became ever broader in knowledge and sensibility — and ever more unsure of herself. Being by nature gentle, she was dominated by the three Ogresses in her family circle: her mother and her aunt and her much older sister, M. Carey Thomas. Then, at the age of sixteen, she was assaulted by a family catastrophe that almost destroyed her. Long periods of illness followed.

Helen found solace in literature. She came to teach English at Bryn Mawr, but her ambition was to demonstrate women's ability by becoming a great writer. However, in the turmoil of her thoughts and feelings, specific subject matter eluded her.

According to Helen's eldest sister, who was by then president of Bryn Mawr, women who were determined to make their mark in the world should not marry. Helen grew to be handsome, gloriously crowned with golden red hair, but she found it not difficult to follow Carey's prescription. She was bored by male admirers who were less powerful than the powerful women among whom she had been brought up. In her entire life, Helen was romantically interested in only two men, both of tremendous strength and ability. But Bertrand Russell was out of bounds because he was married to her cousin. And Simon Flexner seemed to her, at first, a puzzling stranger from a different and lower sphere.

When Helen and Simon finally met, he was thirty-seven and she twenty-nine. During the almost three years that elapsed before their marriage, they wrote each other hundreds of letters. The more than a thousand pages that remain reveal an interweaving, often tortuous, of their widely varying backgrounds, experiences, intellectual interests, and characters. During the same period, preliminary plans for the Rockefeller Institute for Medical Research were in progress, and Simon, in accepting the directorship of what was in itself a revolutionary experiment, pointed the way that led to its epoch-making success.

Slowly Simon and Helen joined together like the two halves of a circle. He brought to her a strength of purpose which was to help her literary efforts to flower. She brought to him the broadness of knowledge and feeling he had yearned for during his restricted rise. Together they formed a team that created one of the world's great scientific institutions. Simon continued to make important discoveries, particularly the "Flexner serum" for cerebrospinal meningitis. And Helen's deeper understanding of human nature helped him become the almost unchallenged leader of American scientific medicine.

In so wide-ranging a drama, many characters walk the stage. Among the best known are Helen's sister M. Carey Thomas; Simon's brother Abraham, who reformed medical schools and founded the Institute for Advanced Study in Princeton; Helen's English cousins Logan Pearsall Smith, Alys and Bertrand Russell, Mary and Bernard Berenson. Also present are the scientists who brought modern medicine to the United States — William H. Welch, William Osler, and many others; the John D. Rockefellers, Senior and Junior; the evangelist Dwight Lyman Moody; and Walt Whitman.

I

New Americans

I

---◈◈◈◈◈◈---

Bohemia — Strasbourg — Kentucky

D URING the mid-nineteenth century, travelers through the countryside behind Louisville, Kentucky, might see approaching them a
cart loaded with peddler's wares and pulled by an ancient horse. At
every forward step, one of the horse's legs missed the ground altogether,
protruding sidewise into the road. The driver, a spare man in his early
thirties, with a long face and black beard, drew his equipage up in the
gutter so that the protruding leg would not get caught in approaching
wheels. Moritz Flexner was grateful for the infirmity that had enabled
him to buy the horse for what he could pay: four dollars. Before that, he
had carried a pack on his back.[1]

The progenitor of the Flexner family was still unmarried. Probably in
1854, when a little over thirty years of age, he had hobbled on crutches
off an Ohio riverboat to that newcomer among large cities, Louisville.[2]

The phoenixlike rise of Simon and Abraham Flexner to commanding
positions in American life has engendered considerable interest in the
humble, impoverished immigrant nest in Kentucky from which they
sprang so amazingly upward. To what extent did the culture their parents had brought from Europe explain? Simon Flexner's principal me-
morialist, Peyton Rous, who had been his intimate disciple and was to
win a Nobel Prize in medicine, conventionally attributed much of
Simon's success to an "erudite" Jewish background.[3]

Simon, as he grew older, sifted for clues through what he could remember of his parents and of their relatives who also came to Louisville.
He persuaded his mother, Esther Abraham Flexner, to write down what
she knew of her own and her husband's European roots and experiences.

Concerning Moritz Flexner's forebears she was extremely brief. His paternal grandfather, whose name was subsequently anglicized to Philip, had been rabbi-in-chief of Moravia and Bohemia. His father, Michael, became a tutor in "one of the best families of Bohemia, people of large means, and married a daughter of the house."* He was taken into the business, but continued his studies to be a rabbi. However, "learning served him no purpose as a man of affairs, and one night through fire [he] lost all his goods and chattels, and nothing had been insured." In 1820, before the catastrophe, Moritz was born at Neumark (Všeruby), Bohemia.[4]

A second, more detailed account is to be found in the Flexner family papers. On the typescript Simon wrote, "This was prepared, I think, by the mother of Szigeti. I wonder how accurate it is?" (The internationally celebrated violinist, Joseph Szigeti, was a Flexner cousin.)[5]

The "Szigeti Manuscript" backs up the statement that Moritz's grandfather had been chief rabbi by stating that he had been the rabbi at Brünn (Brno), the capital of Moravia. Moritz's father, Michael Flexner, was born at Brünn in 1789. Although destined to become also a rabbi, Michael expressed "a decided preference for philosophy." Philip Flexner grudgingly agreed to his son's undertaking such studies, but only on condition that he not abandon rabbinical preparations. Michael received little support from his father, and failed to make much money by teaching. Determining, "after a hard struggle with himself," to seek a position as a tutor in a prosperous household, "he succeeded in attaining an excellent position."

Michael Flexner entered the home of Leopold Klauber, "the brewer who lived on the Bavarian-Bohemian border, and who was called the Bavarian Hop King because of his wealth. The young man [so the Szigeti Manuscript claims] entered the very center of the best society, which consisted in the main of property owners, officers, and the remaining elite." As the Klauber children grew up, Michael instructed them one after the other. Years passed without his finding time to complete his studies.

Finally, the youngest child, Therese, flowered into young womanhood. The tutor became so fascinated that he could not keep his mind on his books, and her eyes seemed to be perpetually resting on him. When she was seventeen, her father decided it was time for her to get married.

---

* In passages from this and other sources quoted in the book, the spelling and punctuation have been modernized.

Wealthy young men, "in accord with her social status, were called to her attention, but no: she was haughty to them all."

Finally, the truth came out! She was in love with the tutor. Her parents were both astonished and "unpleasantly disturbed." However, as Therese remained obdurate, the match was finally agreed to on condition that Michael give up his impractical studies and join the business. "Michael, who had long perceived the futility of realizing his bosom ambition, assented with great joy. So the nuptials of the young couple were celebrated with great pomp" during 1818. Soon, Moritz was born.

The couple had had three more children when misfortune struck. Klauber, the businessman of the family, died. Shortly thereafter, when Moritz was about ten, there was a great light in the sky, much rushing around of anguished people, and then the smoldering ruins of the brewery. The Klauber family decided to pool their assets and re-create the business. The brewery rose up again — but alas! Another great light in the sky, again anguished shouts, and again smoldering ashes. The Klaubers, and with them Michael Flexner, were "completely ruined."

Michael resolved to revive his old skills and concerns. After a crash course of study, he passed the necessary rabbinical examinations. He became a district rabbi at "Pjestice" (Pschestitz?) and was then called to Bischop-Ternitz, a neighborhood center that, like Pschestitz, was near the scene of his prosperity. The Szigeti Manuscript assures us that he "issued several theological works and compiled the first Hebrew-Latin dictionary." When he died in 1871, his funeral "was attended by a stream of admirers from all parts of the country." His widow survived him by about fourteen years. Here the Szigeti Manuscript ends.[6]

The expunging of Jewish records, first under Hitler and then by the Czechoslovak government, has prevented the discovery of any original records concerning the Flexner background in Moravia and Bohemia. That the two family manuscripts in no way contradict each other is a hopeful sign. A direct Klauber-Flexner connection is confirmed by the record in one of Simon's diaries that two Klauber girls, freshly arrived from Europe, stayed for a while with the Louisville household. The Szigeti Manuscript statement that the Klaubers lived on the Bavarian-Bohemian border is verified by Esther Flexner's information that Moritz was born at Neumark (Všeruby). That border — it still separates Czechoslovakia from Germany — is dictated by a long, narrow (mean width twenty-five miles) chain of mountains (peaks up to 4,780 feet)

known as the Bohemian Forest. The major pass, four miles from Neumark, is waterless, but Neumark is beside a small river called the Cham,
which flows southwest, into Bavaria, to meet a larger river that eventually joins the Danube. In an era when bulky and heavy produce could
be transported any distance only by water, the Cham almost miracu-
lously erased the intervening mountains, joining western Bohemia with
much of Germany and all the territory washed by the Danube. Furthermore, that part of Bohemia is famous for its hop fields and thus celebrated for its beer. Neumark is not far from what were then called
Pilsen and Budweis; hence it was an ideal location for a brewery — and
it was also a most grateful one for a Jewish businessman. The few miles
that separated Moritz's birthplace from Bavaria were of the greatest significance: the legal restrictions on Jews were much less stringent in Bohemia than in Bavaria.

Although their underlying account of the Flexner background in Europe may be accepted, the family manuscripts, particularly that attributed to Mrs. Szigeti, are surely not innocent of engrandizement.
Simon's suspicions were incited by his own inability to recall, in relation to his father or his father's many younger brothers, traits that
would indicate an impressive background. There was not a touch of
faded grandeur in the household where Simon was brought up, no hint
that his father's parents and his father when a child had lived lux-
uriously "in the center of the best society." Although the Klauber brewery had undoubtedly existed, the "Bavarian Hop King" may not have
been so much of a king after all.

Of greater concern to the American Flexner family was the question
of cultural influences. The statement that Michael had in the mid-nineteenth century compiled the first Hebrew-Latin lexicon is on the face of
it ridiculous. What of the theological publications so erudite that admirers flocked "from all parts of the country" to his funeral? Simon
could not remember any intellectual culture that had come with his father across the ocean. Moritz was, it is true, separated from his presumably learned father at an early age, but there were the younger brothers
who had grown to manhood in Michael's household. "None of the
brothers," Simon remembered, "were devout or educated men in any
real sense." In Louisville, "they did not amount to much. . . . They were
all in some kind of business in a small way."[7]

At the time of the second brewery burning, Moritz was, so his son
Abraham tells us, about thirteen.[8] To relieve pressure on the suddenly
impoverished family, the boy's uncle, Joseph Flexner, who was living in

Strasbourg, assumed responsibility for his upbringing. The family story in Louisville made Joseph a rabbi, but the official birth and death records in Strasbourg put him down sometimes as a teacher, sometimes as a merchant. In May, 1850, the signature "Moritz Flexner" appears, very interestingly, as a witness on the death certificate of an infant child named Simon.

Moritz eventually became a "regular teacher" in the public school of Herlisheim, a small community on the outskirts of Strasbourg. Such a position would not have been open to him either in Bohemia or in Germany, where Jews were allowed to teach only in their own schools. This part of Alsace was largely bilingual, but public instruction had to be in French. In spending almost twenty years in Strasbourg and its environs, Moritz came to think of himself as a Frenchman.

The drudgery of schoolteaching — it may have been in a lower grade — did not encourage Moritz into scholarly directions. Simon could not remember that his father ever expressed an intellectual conception or read a book.[9] However, Moritz did reveal in Louisville a firm conviction of the importance of education. His determination to support the authority of teachers over his own children might well indicate that the Jew from Bohemia had had searing problems in dealing with the children and parents of Herlisheim.

Simon's sister Mary remembered that it was dangerous to make in her father's presence any frivolous or critical remark about a teacher.[10] After Simon's brother Abraham had complained of what he considered an injustice done to him by a teacher, his father announced, "I will walk to school with you today." Abraham knew it would be useless to ask why, since the father never explained to his children.

Abraham followed Moritz into the office of the school principal. "I need only a few moments, Professor Hurt," the father said. "My son has complained to me of what he regards as the injustice of one of his teachers. I should like you and all his teachers to know that if any question arises between my son and his teachers, I shall always regard his teachers as being in the right."

"Not a word," Abraham remembered, "was said as to my complaint. My father arose, shook hands with Dr. Hurt, bade me goodbye and left." The matter was never referred to again.[11]

When in Louisville, Moritz was to mourn his having been taken away from his parents so soon.[12] However, he did not in Alsace build a family of his own. Perhaps it was dissatisfaction with his lot as a humble schoolteacher, a desire not to impede possible escape by tying himself down, that made him allow the years to climb, until he was past thirty, without marriage.

It took an exterior crisis to break him loose. His wife wrote that in the early 1850's, "when conditions in France were restless," Moritz became involved in political intrigues that forced him suddenly to leave France.[13]

He had not achieved even mild prosperity, as is revealed by his traveling steerage with the poorest emigrants on some hulk of a sailboat that took ninety days to reach America. Even at that, he arrived in New York "practically penniless."

Alone and without connections in the alien city, needing a "fellow countryman" whom he could tell of his plight, he looked not for a German but a Frenchman. He found one in a wine store. The proprietor immediately offered him a job which he gratefully accepted. But he had no gift for selling wine and "of his own accord [so he told Esther] gave up his position."

If the dates given are correct, Moritz struggled unsuccessfully in New York for some two years before he was informed by compatriots longer in the United States of a city called New Orleans, where, because the French community was much larger, "one could make a better living." Moritz, with five companions, sailed for New Orleans.

"But," so Esther continued, "it was the wrong time for foreigners ignorant of the country to settle there, as there was raging at that moment a yellow fever epidemic." In a very few days, all six came down with the disease.

Moritz was carried to the City Hospital, a charitable institution staffed by nuns, where "he lay unconscious, hovering between life and death. How long he lay in this condition he did not know and could never remember; neither did he know until he had been out of the hospital many weeks that four of his comrades had died. His own recovery he often recounted as a miracle."

All his life, Moritz was to remain grateful to the nuns who had nursed him. To Esther he told of a philanthropic Frenchman "who attended him night and day, never leaving his room. Stating that many who had suffered from yellow fever died during convalescence because, feeling hungry, they ate too soon," the Frenchman stood over him, allowing him for the most part to "eat only with his eyes. Thus his life was spared."

As soon as he could stand upright, Moritz was determined to leave the hospital. He knew that other refugees, who had fled Strasbourg at the same time as he and for the same reason, were now in Louisville. The Frenchman bought him a steamboat ticket and gave him several dollars.

"When he reached Louisville, he was so weak that he had to use crutches, but his friends at once took charge of him, nursed and sheltered him, notwithstanding the fact that they had hardly more than they themselves needed. And with them he stayed until he was completely recovered."

Who these samaritans from Strasbourg were is lost to history. Although Esther "came to know these good people," they were not part of the Louisville world in which Moritz raised his family, which was made up completely of German-speaking Jews. By the time Simon became truly conscious of his surroundings, hardly a trace remained to indicate that the father had lived from his early adolescence into his thirties on French soil. There had been, of course, much that was Germanic in Moritz's Strasbourg environment. What was truly French seems not to have penetrated to the roots of his psychology and character. Thus, when he shed his European past, the French experience peeled easily away, leaving behind the fundamental German base.

With the approach of spring, Moritz's strength returned. He threw away his cane. After the roads opened, he fastened to his back a pack (containing what merchandise we know not) and joined up with a group of peddlers — German Jews all — who, "for safety as well as companionship," set out from Louisville in a group, fanning out at last individually into the countryside. The former schoolteacher made the happy discovery that he had gifts as a salesman. Esther Flexner told their son Simon, expressing some surprise, that her husband had looked back on his pack-carrying days not as a time of hardship but as a happy time. In Europe, restrained formality had been forced on the Jewish schoolmaster. Beyond American thresholds, Morris Flexner (as he now called himself) could relax. He became jovial; he discovered a gift for telling anecdotes, for repeating the gossip and news that was so delightful to the ears of isolated farm families. His new friends purchased his wares with gratitude and begged him to spend the night.

Soon, Flexner's growing earnings enabled him to set up with a fellow peddler a small store in a rural village. Although he now had a stationary base from which to serve not only the immediate countryside but also lesser peddlers, he did not abandon the road. Able now to hitch an able-bodied horse to a neat wagon, he called with increasing infrequency at farmhouses, more and more at other little retail stores. He sold at wholesale the goods he had purchased in Louisville.

This required frequent trips to the city. He bought primarily from the leading establishment, Bamburger, Bloom and Company. The partners spread the word that he was a coming man. He made many friends, principally business friends, and it was communicated to him that his partner "was not the best company for him." However, he did nothing sudden. He worked harder until he could buy the partner out. This was observed with satisfaction.

In the German-Jewish community on Market Street, every merchant's family "lived where the store was, and the families exchanged visits." Morris got on well with the women: he was invited to stay overnight on feast days.

Morris had been in Kentucky for from three to five years when exciting arrivals appeared in the home of the wholesale and retail china merchant, Godshaw. Two nieces, young, diminutive, and pretty, electrified the community with their stylish clothes: like Morris they had had French experiences, having been seamstresses in Paris. But they came from solid German-Jewish stock in the Ruhr Valley. Morris was particularly taken with the younger of the pair, Esther Abraham.

2

Germany — Paris — Kentucky

SIMON Flexner's mother, Esther Abraham, was born on December 14, 1834, at Roden, in the Rhineland, a short distance over the German border from France.[1] Her birthplace was tiny and agricultural. Being only two miles from the larger local community of Saarlouis, the village contained hardly any shops, but there was a Catholic church and beside it a little public square. German-speaking Jews, the Abrahams had inhabited Roden at least since the time of Esther's grandparents.

When Simon visited his mother's ancestral village in 1895, he located and had photographed the house in which she had spent her childhood. It combines architectural decoration with agricultural utility. The tall two-story building — the residential ceilings must have been high — has a line of dentils all the way across under the roofline. Behind the plain, whitewashed facade family living quarters were to the left, and to the right, quarters for cattle. The family section is neat and airy-looking, and three windows high. The tall narrow doorway boasts simple carvings and a pediment. Although the facade of the barn section is hardly broken with windows, the utilitarian door, which is large enough to accommodate wagons, boasts verticals on both sides which imply columns, and a keystone decorates the arch.[2] (PLATE 1)

Knowledge of Esther's early years comes from a manuscript, titled "Memoirs of My Youth," which she wrote with a fine pen in German script when she was old. The text ends with her marriage. When asked why she did not carry her account into her later years, she confided to Simon that whenever she made the attempt, her eyes were blinded with tears: her life had been so hard.[3]

* * *

"My youth and childhood years," Esther wrote, "were as happy as those of most children whose parents had modest means. My father worked hard so as to maintain respectably his family, which consisted of six children, three sons and three daughters. He was a cattle dealer and oftentimes the opportunity came to him of acting as agent for people who wished to sell houses and other property, for which he received from both parties a certain percent, and this made many friends, all of whom admired and respected him." He had in his younger days been a schoolmaster.[4]

Esther wrote that her mother was regarded as the wisest woman by her neighbors, both Christians and Jews. She had proverbs suited to every occasion which her daughter was to repeat to the Flexner children. To urge moderation: "As my mother used to say, *'Zu scharf schneidet nicht; zu spitzig stecht nicht'* " (too sharp will not cut; too pointed will not stick). Against making enemies: *"Der Hund im Weg kann uns Wohl oder Weh thun"* (the dog in our path can do us good or ill). Don't leap to hasty conclusions: *"So schnell schiessen die Preisen nicht"* (the Prussians do not shoot so hastily). Also: *"Unkraut verderbt nicht"* (ill weeds grow apace). When, in his later years, bothered with advice he did not relish, her son Abraham remembered his mother's saying, "It is very easy to get a rabbi but very difficult to get rid of him." As misfortunes piled upon her, Esther would repeat as a litany, *"Der Starke kommt mit der Notwendigkeit"* (strength comes with necessity). It was basically with such folk-wisdom that Esther guided her children.[5]

Esther's own mother could read only a little Hebrew needed for religious purposes. She resented her general illiteracy as a great handicap. Seconded by her onetime schoolmaster husband, she resolved that her children "should receive as thoroughgoing a training as was possible to persons in their circumstances." This did not mean, as it did in Helen Thomas's family, a bachelor's degree from a leading college and perhaps a Ph.D.; it meant attendance at a good elementary school.

Probably because of their position as Jews in Germany near the French border, languages were the Abrahams' primary concern. They were dissatisfied with the school at Roden, which taught only German. They sent their oldest children — Aaron, Caroline, and Esther — to a school in Saarlouis that also taught Hebrew and French. The children pursued, despite an age span of three years, the same studies.

The three little Abrahams walked the two to three miles to Saarlouis every school day. In warm weather they came home to lunch: an hour of trudging back and forth, a half hour for eating. In the winter, the Abrahams carried their lunch with them. But, so Esther wrote, their mother would not think of letting them eat cold food in that season. They went to the home of some family friends, "who kindly heated [our food] for us and often insisted upon our sharing their food, as they knew how deeply concerned our mother was about our health.

"We competed continually with our schoolmates and most of the time brought home the best reports, which gave joy to our parents and often made our classmates envious." The Abrahams could only afford two textbooks for the three children: Esther, as the youngest, shared with the others. When the teacher discovered that she had no book of her own, "he did not say a word, but the next day when he came to school he handed me a book with these words inscribed therein: 'From Mr. Levy. For industry and good behavior, I present this book to Esther Abraham.'

"The whole school was excited over it, and when we reached the marketplace the boys almost murdered me, crying out through the marketplace, 'Mr. Levy is Esther's sweetheart!' This annoyed me very much. Naturally, the school heard about it and the following day everyone was punished, and I was consequently more thought of than before. This was a source of great satisfaction to our parents."

After supper, the father, using his ancient skills as schoolmaster, supervised the children's lessons. Then, until bedtime, he read aloud in German to the special pleasure of the mother, who could not read to herself. The oldest son, Aaron, developed a passion for literature which so impressed the Abraham family that they supported him for the rest of his life as a poet. Esther was to help. If only because the name Aaron Abraham is so common, his work cannot now be traced. But whether he wrote well or badly, in German or Yiddish, the sacrifice to such a career made by an obscure and only modestly prosperous family speaks volumes.[6]

When she was thirteen, Esther's schooling ended. Her mother, who had always been sickly, had taken a turn for the worse, and her older sister Caroline had been from infancy considered frail. Esther on the other hand was robust. She relished the nickname of "Fatty" (she had slimmed down considerably by Simon's time) and enjoyed the perpetual cry around the house of "Let Fatty do it." "Mother knew that whatever I did was well done. She was very particular, always extraordinarily neat and tidy, and during her illness she became even more so, and it brought me the greatest happiness to do for her everything she wished."

Esther was "in charge of the house" for two years or more, until she was fifteen. Then her mother was stronger, her sister less frail, and loud and clear calls were coming in from Paris.[7]

A niece of Esther's mother operated with her husband a lingerie shop and could use accomplished seamstresses. Arguing that in Paris she could offer them "a more interesting life than was possible in Roden," the niece urged that the two eldest Abraham girls be sent to live and work with her. Caroline at eighteen, Esther at sixteen, were sent off. They stayed in Paris for five years, having, Esther wrote, "interesting experiences."

In an account that was usually not devoid of detail, Esther gives no hint of what these experiences were. However, we may assume they were not lurid since respectability was always Esther's watchword. Living with the relatives for whom they worked, the sisters had no need to roam the streets among the midinettes who at noon crowded out of their sweatshops to catch eyes and have adventures. Esther undoubtedly was so vague about her experiences because nothing specific had happened that would justify her lifelong sense of superiority because she had lived for five years in Paris.

Letters were coming in to the Abrahams from Uncle Godshaw in Louisville who "wanted to have the two eldest daughters." Then Godshaw appeared in person to argue that America, "as a new world," offered greater opportunities than even Paris. He was eager to take Esther and Caroline back with him at once, but the Parisian cousins had to be consulted. Since their own children were growing up, they were not displeased. Godshaw sent steamboat tickets. However, the elder Abraham, certain that such a newfangled contraption would blow up, changed the tickets to passage on a sailing ship.

That the two girls should set out thus by themselves started rumors in Roden. "Everyone wanted to know why we were obliged to leave for America, and this made the leave-taking harder for us all." It was agreed that the girls would either return in five years or send for their parents.[8]

As the train taking them to the ocean departed, the girls looked backwards until "we lost sight of the station and could not see even the shadow" of their family and friends. "Then the two of us wept until we could weep no more." On the ship, they examined the passengers who were traveling steerage as Moritz Flexner had done. "We decided we need not have anything to do with them, since we are second cabin passengers."

However, there was no second-class dining room. The Abrahams had brought food with them to last out the scheduled three weeks. At the end of the three weeks, the ship was still tacking laboriously in mid-ocean. "I would have starved had not the second officer taken pity on me, sending daily food down from the cabin since I could not eat the ship's food, which was all cooked in one pot, from which everyone was supposed to help themselves." The girls concluded that their parents, particularly their sickly mother, could not stand the strain of coming to America. For the daughters the strain went on and on.[9]

After "nine awful weeks," Esther and Caroline landed at New York on September 5, 1855. A distant cousin, who met them at the shipside with a note from Uncle Godshaw, took them home to his wife. He urged them to postpone their trip to Louisville as the weather was too hot. A tailor with a good business, his intention was to intercept the two expert seamstresses. "He promised us a good salary if we remained with him." But Esther and her sister wrote to their uncle for help. He replied that he would locate a Louisville merchant trading in New York who would take them along when he returned to Kentucky.

As they were waiting, they met a neighbor from the Saar. Joseph Hannau "could scarcely believe his eyes when he saw us. He put his arms around us, saying, 'What do you want to do in America?' We told him our plan, to which he replied, 'For pity's sake, go to your uncle if he wants you, but I will give you my address, since in America relatives do not all get along happily together. I employ one hundred workers and I can give you employment, and you can make your home with us.' "[10]

When the girls reached Louisville, "our uncle received us with tears in his eyes and introduced us to our aunt, who said she would take our mother's place. We, however, had lived in Paris for five years and saw that our aunt was a businesswoman who wished neither to take advantage of us nor lose anything on us. She allowed us time to recover from our voyage, and told us that in this country everyone must help himself, or, in other words, each one for himself."

Godshaw had a wholesale and retail china store. His wife helped in the store when necessary; otherwise she worked as a seamstress, which she had been in the old country. Her mother lived with the Godshaws, managing the housekeeping with the assistance of a slave she owned. The result was slovenly.

"It did not take us long to realize that the household was not conducted according to our system, and we at once confided in our uncle, saying to him that we were not content to live under these conditions.

He knew our mother and how we had been brought up, and it was therefore easy for him to understand us, and he promised to speak about it to our aunt, which he did."

The mother-in-law became ill, and Esther took over the housekeeping. "It was not long before one could see a difference everywhere. Our aunt even noticed the change, and our slave had a hard time of it." Caroline was doing needlework. When the older woman died, seeming to leave Esther in the permanent role of housekeeping martinet, Mrs. Godshaw decided that it would be better for the girls to get employment outside and earn wages. They would then be able to pay for their board and other expenses, and might have something left over to send to their parents.

The Abraham girls agreed immediately. "We had come to America to earn money," and it was their fondest wish to return home with enough to make their parents independent. "Naturally, we had no idea how this could be done, but it was our purpose in coming." The girls were invited to work with a Mrs. Fox who supervised the making of cloaks for her husband's large dry goods store. In a few days Esther "saw that we were giving satisfaction as we were asked to finish the finest clothes. We took our midday meal with the family which tasted very good to us. In the evening Mr. Fox sent his nephew from the store to see us home."

To how great an extent the little German-Jewish community felt itself a separate entity within Louisville is demonstrated by Esther's statement that "the whole city knew already that two of the Godshaws' nieces had arrived from Paris, and that they could do everything . . . because at that time the city was a small place, and everybody knew everybody else. We therefore had many callers, for many young people came and went in our uncle's business and [our aunt] took great pride in introducing her nieces to them, for everyone said to her we were not 'green' which gave her great pleasure, and to which she replied, 'Why should they be green? They come from Paris.'

"Soon we received invitations and thus became acquainted with the best people. I went to the New Year's ball with Mr. A. Rosenbaum, and created quite a sensation as we had brought stylish clothes with us and were much admired in consequence, for Louisville in those days did not keep up with Paris fashion."

As the celebration of Passover approached (in her old age Esther referred to the time as "Easter"), Aunt Godshaw "insisted that we have silk dresses, for without them we could not be called Americans." The girls had saved enough to buy silk, which they could then fashion into elegant dresses, but their intention was to send the first money they earned to their parents. Promising to send an equivalent sum to the Abrahams in Roden, Uncle Godshaw backed his wife. The girls agreed, "knowing well what was in our aunt's mind, namely, to marry us as soon as possible. . . . We heard day in and day out that this was a country where one must marry young."[11]

Among the many bachelors who came to call at the parlor behind the china shop was Morris Flexner. Godshaw had from the first "taken a fancy to him, as he had heard from his business acquaintances, his neighbors, how he had worked up, and how highly esteemed he was."

Esther's account of their courtship makes no mention of the twelve-year difference in their ages: he was thirty-four; she, twenty-two. She notes that he had "not yet acquired riches." However, in that society it was understood that everyone was on the way up; if a man "was industrious and respectable, he could marry well." Esther's worry after he had proposed concerned the traditional taboo against a younger sister's marrying before the elder, and Caroline was not yet engaged. Uncle Godshaw's and her suitor's insistence that this rule did not apply in Kentucky almost boomeranged. She feared lest she "did not know enough of the American way of living to marry." And if she did marry, how could she return to her parents in five years as she had promised, or even send them her earnings?

Into Esther's reminiscence there now intrudes an equivocal sentence, perhaps reflecting later disappointments: "He soon had the courage to ask me to marry him, as he thought I was the person who would be satisfied with what he had to offer me, and in this he was right." Esther asked for time to think the matter out. Morris assured her that "he did not wish to hasten our marriage, only to have my promise, leaving me to set the day, and so I promised him to have my answer ready the next time he came to the city, and with this he was satisfied."

When salesmen met on the roads, messages were sent back to Louisville and usually scrupulously delivered. But Morris chose a messenger whose response was to propose to Esther himself. Paradoxically, this hastened Morris's suit. In turning the interloper down, Esther made up her own mind. "And so we celebrated our engagement on Easter Day, when many of his friends and acquaintances were in town, as they always spent their holidays there. They were all invited to the party, and some envied him while others congratulated him. . . . Of one thing I am sure," Esther wrote in her memoir intended for his children, "that Father felt as if he had suddenly become a wealthy man."

The wedding date was set for September 15, 1856, almost exactly a year after Esther reached America. During the intervening summer, as Esther noted with admiration, Morris "worked hard ... and saved so much that we were able to start a nice household without the help of anyone, for in those days wedding presents were unheard of." Esther, for her part, was busy sewing, "as whatever one wanted, one must make for oneself, even all of one's linen."

The married couple "started a little home and thought ourselves very fortunate." In her old age, Esther still possessed "several pieces of furniture and some vases which adorned our first home, and we are proud of them, since in my opinion they are still in fashion."[12]

Morris Flexner was about five feet eight inches tall, his wife about five feet four. Photographs taken at the time of the marriage (PLATE 1)[13] show that they resembled each other only in having dark hair. Morris is lank with narrowish sloping shoulders. His long head seems longer because of the height of his forehead under a receding hairline and because his features are enclosed by black sideburns. He has narrow eyebrows, deeply sunken eyes, a strongly jutting aquiline nose, and a full mouth. His carefully trimmed black beard, which continues from his sideburns, adds to the verticality of the image. Although Morris looks gravely into the camera, his mouth carries a little smile, and his pose, as he leans on his right arm, is jaunty. The total impression is of a handsome head, both shrewd and innocent, a lack of true aggressiveness tempering the self-confidence of a man whose fortunes seem to be swelling on a high tide.

Esther is as petite as her husband is lanky. Her head, shaped oppositely from his, is short and round, the applelike appearance fortunately dispelled by high cheekbones. She wears her dark hair parted in the middle and falling in ringlets behind her shoulders. The features are grave and firm, the mouth turned down over a strong chin. Her expression is intense and determined. But she is an extremely pretty girl, her face made the more striking by a dramatic contrast between her raven hair and bright, very light-colored gray eyes.

Esther leans forward intensely in the black silk dress which her aunt and uncle had insisted she make for Easter. The dress is topped with an extensive white collar edged with a wide band of lace and held together at the neck with a horseshoe-shaped brooch studded with stones. The dress comes in tightly at the waist and then bells out into a tremendous skirt. Most remarkable are the sleeves, which explode from just above the elbows into yards and yards of pleated black silk that hang down from her forearms far below the bands that attach them to her wrists.

After the Flexners had been married only ten months, Jacob was born. Now that they were starting a family, they decided to follow the custom of Market Street and live over or near their store, but this they could not yet afford in Louisville. Morris sold the rural shop, which had kept him so much away from home, and combined the proceeds with his earnings to procure a larger establishment in a larger community. Joining in a partnership with a son of Esther's Uncle Godshaw, he selected Lawrenceburg, which was in the bluegrass region of Kentucky, closer to Lexington than Louisville.

Perhaps Morris, whose most prosperous memories were associated with brewing, fancied Lawrenceburg because it was a center for the manufacture of whiskey. In any case, the choice was an excellent one. The community was attractive, with broad, tree-shaded streets. Distilling what might almost have been liquid gold, the leading citizens bought whatever appealed to them and paid little attention to price. They did, it is true, prefer to pay not in cash but with kegs of whiskey. However, the liquor was easily salable, and capital could be comfortably laid away by stockpiling kegs in the cellar, a method of accumulation that had a particular satisfaction to Morris. He was never at a loss where to find a dram.

In rapid succession, Esther had three more sons: Henry, Isadore, and then one named in gratitude for American bounty: Washington. The American dream, however, was collapsing into its worst nightmare.

During the Civil War, in the border state of Kentucky, the inhabitants of the Bluegrass were almost all romantic and passionate supporters of the Southern cause. Morris, who had been forced to flee Strasbourg because of his radical ideas, could not help being opposed to slavery. The impression got out that the shopkeeper was not a loyal Confederate.

The Flexners went through a period of intense anxiety when Morgan's raiders, the Confederate cavalrymen who were enabled by southern sympathizers to dodge through Kentucky while avoiding stronger northern forces, appeared in Lawrenceburg. They arrived there one evening, encamped on a nearby hill, and were off with the dawn. Their mission always was to destroy the property of Union sympathizers. Family memory reported that the Flexners' store and storehouse were raided, but it is clear that — perhaps because Morris's partner was considered less suspect — the business was not destroyed. Having tried for some months to brave the situation out, Morris decided again on political flight. He sold his share of the business to his partner and returned to Louisville. The trip was somewhat encumbered because Esther was again pregnant. On March 25, 1863, in Louisville, Simon Flexner was born.[14]

3

~⟨∞⟩~

Simon Flexner, Delinquent

WHEN Simon was about ten years old, he received a peremptory command to join his father on the street. Without further words, the tall bearded man set out with long strides as the undersized boy trotted after him. Simon knew that it was useless to ask where they were going, and in his habitual vague, indeterminate melancholy, he did not really care. His father turned into a dooryard and knocked on a door from which there emerged a "big, fat German with a limp." Simon's attention, which had been wandering, was caught by the sight of the German holding in a fleshy hand a wide ring from which dangled tremendous keys. The keys clanged in rhythm with the German's limp as they all proceeded down the street.

Simon recognized the building before which they halted. It was the county jail. As Simon watched with real interest, the German fitted one of the huge keys into a huge lock. They were soon in a long corridor between two rows of tall cages. In each cage was a man. Simon noticed particularly that outside the door of each cage there lay an empty tin plate.

In his thick accent, the German identified the prisoners. Simon's gaze fastened on two moonshiners — spare, middle-aged men, tall and with beards. There was, even here in captivity, a wild free look about them which made them seem to the boy admirable, a different order of creation from the city shopkeepers Simon had always known.

The demonstration over, the father, without any comment, ordered the boy to go home. As he walked along, Simon was unconscious of the familiar scenes around him. He had been carried into another world by excitement over what he had just experienced. After his arrival home, Simon found his older brothers awaiting him full of glee and triumph. They hoped he felt properly punished and depressed at having been shown where he would end up if he did not change his ways and behave like a responsible human being. Simon looked at them in amazement. "I had had a swell time."[1]

During the years following World War I, Simon Flexner liked to assert that he had been in arms during three wars. When asked how this was possible for an American born in 1863, he replied that he had been in the army during the Philippine Insurrection (that outgrowth of the Spanish-American War), and also during the recent world war. That was only two, his friends objected. Ah! said Simon. He had been a babe in arms during the Civil War. It may indeed have been in this earliest capacity that he was in the greatest danger.

After their retreat from Lawrenceburg during the Civil War, the Flexners had taken refuge in "a shabby part of town," their house so cramped that the front door opened directly into the living room. On a hot day, Esther, holding baby Simon in her arms, sat in the draft she had achieved by leaving the front door open. A shadow fell upon her, and she saw that a drunken soldier had staggered up the two or three steps from the street. He pulled the child out of her arms. Esther, always brave and efficient, snatched the child back, screaming the while. The soldier shambled indignantly away.[2]

The house on East Street did not hold the Flexners for long. Already an exciting business opportunity had opened up to Morris. Emanuel Hirsch's brothers-in-law, Bloom and Ullman, were willing to set Hirsch up in the hat business, but although a competent businessman, he had no gifts as a salesman. A venture of the size contemplated needed to take advantage of Louisville's commanding position as supplier to all the southern states west of the Mississippi. Although Morris could offer little capital, he was, because of his skill as "a traveler," made a full partner in the new firm of Hirsch and Flexner.[3]

This change in the Flexner fortunes dictated a change in their dwelling. They were, down the years, always on the move, to larger houses in better locations with prosperity, down the ladder again with hard times. Simon was to write his fiancée, Helen Thomas, "You are entirely right in your view of the restlessness of American life, and particularly of my family. In a country as young as ours, and among people who are the architects of their own fortunes, there is no hope or possibility of fixity where ambition reigns."[4]

Simon's earliest memories were of the next house. On Center Street, it was three stories high and made of brick. Although the Flexners had not yet advanced to a central hall, they did have a hallway — it ran along one of the inner walls, preventing the parlor from being the center of domestic traffic and opening onto the street.

Behind the back door, between the Flexner house and its neighbor, was a narrow yard down the middle of which was an open gutter carrying the waste water of both households to the gutter in the street. Here stood outside privies and also a hydrant offering yellowish muddy water from the Ohio River. This water was carried into the kitchen in an iron bucket for general household purposes. It was heated on the stove once a week, when the whole family bathed. Little Simon often carried a smaller bucket, this one of tin, to the corner pump for drinking water. This "surface water" was clear, but, as Simon later speculated, more contaminated than the river water because of the privies behind every house.

The widow Oberdorfer, who lived on the other side of the backyard, often invaded the Flexner kitchen: "a dreary person wearing a shawl over her shoulders." She had a six-year-old daughter, some two years older than Simon. One day, she rushed in angrily to announce that her daughter had "again wet her bed." This statement so shocked Simon that it became his earliest memory.[5]

After two years, the family moved "up" to a larger house in a better part of town. Sixth Street was broad: Jews lived on one side of it, Gentiles on the other. They never mingled. The children played separately. Even if the men had business connections during the day, their families never visited across the street.[6]

Simon brought home a dead sparrow and cut it open to determine what went on inside. It smelled and his father made him throw out the subject of his first autopsy.[7]

A dramatic break in the family routine was the appearance of a doctor to vaccinate the children for smallpox. Having removed a suitable "crust" from someone who had the disease, the doctor had brought it along in his pocket. He scratched each child's arm with a lancet, and then rubbed in a little of the crust that had been mixed with water. It was a long process since Simon now had four younger siblings: Bernard, born February 19, 1865; Abraham, born November 13, 1866; and then the only girls in the big family — Mary and Gertrude.

Discovering that a neighboring Jewish family named Small had not been vaccinated, Simon decided to "remedy the lack." Jake Small, who was Simon's age, was glad to assist in the vaccination of his younger brother, Morris. Simon scratched the little boy's arm with a jagged piece of tin that had been discarded by the local tinsmith, and rubbed in some chalk that he had filched from school and mixed with water. When an abscess resulted, Simon looked as oracular as the doctor had done: "Yes, that's a good vaccination."[8]

There was the time when a doctor prescribed quinine pills. "Long before the days of sugar and gelatine pills," the bitter quinine was covered with powdered starch and then with jelly, the result to be swallowed whole. "By some wretched contrivance, I managed to swallow the jelly but not the pill." When he was reduced to tears by the bitterness in his mouth, his mother scolded him for being a "doppus," so stupid.[9]

The firm of Hirsch and Flexner was doing brilliantly. When Morris came back from a business trip to New York, he brought brown velveteen suits for Simon and Bernard, then about eight and six. The father walked with the children up Broadway, proud to show off this elegance. Soon Simon and Bernard strutted out by themselves. They came upon two Irish urchins standing in front of a grocery store. One picked up an egg, took Simon aside, and whispered that he had bet his friend that he could hide the egg where his friend could not find it. It would never be found if hidden on Simon. The friend covered his eyes; the egg was put under Simon's hat; the friend uncovered his eyes and instantly smashed his fist down on the hat. Egg yolk and white streaming over Simon's face and onto his velveteen suit, he ran home in tears. Again no sympathy. His mother washed him off under the hydrant, "telling me quite frankly what she thought of me."[10]

According to Kentucky usage, children started in the public schools either on the day they turned six or at the beginning of the following term. The eager Flexners chose for Simon the earlier alternative. He was to remember his insertion into a crowd of strange boys as his next major "shock" after the bed-wetting incident. In his fright he wept so hard that the teacher had to sit him on the platform beside her.

"School," Simon remembered, "did not interest me in any way." Never once was he "aroused" by anything he was taught, "either the substance or the method of teaching." Considering himself trapped, year after year, in "a dreary, uninteresting place," he engaged in mischief and paid as little attention as he could. "Punishment . . . became a commonplace of my days."[11]

Simon never forgot Miss Johnston: "I see every line and coloring.

Blond, corn-colored hair, sharp features, slender, of middle height, slight, a virago! She used the strap daily, hourly almost, with a frenzy of pleasure. Her method was to sit the victim in a chair and lash him "over the knees. I was often the victim."[12]

Miss Belle Kirby ("I thought her very good-looking ... medium height, dark, trim figure, in her twenties") treated Simon "for the first time with a certain amount of sensitivity. ... In one contest she put me first. How she did this I cannot imagine." Simon was awarded a hexagonal ruler which he cherished "with unbelievable joy."

To prepare the shy and unsure boy for a recitation at some school program, Miss Kirby invited him to her house. But all her coaxing encouragement could not enable him to get his tongue around the somewhat complicated passage she had chosen for him. She finally settled for an eight-line jingle:

> *There was a man in our town*
> *And he was wondrous wise.*
> *He jumped into a mulberry bush*
> *And scratched out both his eyes.*
>
> *And when he saw his eyes were out*
> *With all his might and main*
> *He jumped into the mulberry bush*
> *And scratched them in again.*

This Simon, when the time came, was able to deliver without a flaw to his great satisfaction.[13]

As Miss Kirby may well have surmised, there were problems at home linked with Simon's backwardness. The ever-mounting prosperity of his parents, which had begun almost simultaneously with his birth, was starting to come apart.

When Simon was still small, his parents were confident that the pot of gold which the United States was said to offer immigrants was waiting for them. They were entranced with the financial rise, year after year, of Hirsch and Flexner. Twice they moved up to better and larger houses. Esther felt she could afford both the materials and the time to create with her own expert needle a masterpiece of complicated dressmaking in which she had her picture taken, surrounded by the photographer's classic urns and in front of a backdrop featuring columns.

Morris spent months every year away from home, first buying whole-sale in New York, then traveling with his trunks of samples through the Southwest: Tennessee, Alabama, Georgia, Texas. According to Esther, this was "one of the trials of his life" since he was "naturally a home-loving, domestic person." There is better reason to believe that the once-cramped schoolteacher relished the movement through spacious America, the random conviviality, and his impressive successes as a salesman. He collected adventures with which to bolster on his return his reputation among his fellow German-Jewish merchants as a story-teller. Simon remembered some of the anecdotes he told in the home circle.

Morris was staying, as he often did in small towns, with a customer. The door of his room was one of several leading off a long porch. Setting out in the morning, he failed to memorize the exact location, and on his return he opened a door that revealed his host's wife in the middle of a bath. He withdrew with all speed. Knowing how sensitive Southern men were about their wives' honor, he was a good deal perturbed. He hurried to his host and explained everything. There was an ominous si-lence, and then his host laughed. "It's probably not the first time you have seen a naked woman."

On another occasion, Morris stopped at a "hotel" in Texas: a bar-room, with a few bedrooms attached. He was writing a letter when a man entered the barroom and announced that he would stand every-body a drink. Not thinking that the invitation referred to him, Morris kept on writing. At this, the stranger turned to him and preemptively repeated his invitation. Morris thanked him and continued his writing. But the bartender hurried over to whisper, "You'd better accept. He's been known to shoot a man for less." The invitation was warmly ac-cepted.[14]

When in Louisville, Morris ate lunch at a "kind of restaurant" where one Fuerst served a hot midday meal with beer and other drinks. The Jewish merchants played cards there and gossiped in German. Sunday, being "family time," the merchants lunched at home, but in the after-noon they took their middle-sized sons to Fuerst's. Simon remembered these excursions with great pleasure. Although he had to hang around for a long time while his father played cards, the moment came when he got a slice of cheesecake.[15]

There seemed no limit to the height that Hirsch and Flexner would attain, when forces far out of the Flexners' view came into malign conjunction. Railroad construction in Russia had been excessive. The opening of the Suez Canal had interrupted established commercial patterns. France had lost a devastating war with Prussia. In the United States there had been destructive fires in Boston and Chicago, and the wave of prosperity that had followed the end of the Civil War had begun to sink into a deep trough. In the optimism of his high spirits, Morris had given his customers extensive credit and now, all over the highways and byways of the South, his customers were unable to pay.

A relatively new firm, with almost no capital reserve, Hirsch and Flexner responded in 1872 to what became known in history as the Panic of 1873. It was one of the first Market Street houses to go under.

Esther's sister Caroline had married a better businessman than Morris, and the Jews, having been forced in Europe down the generations to stick together if they were to survive, were bred to a deep sense of family solidarity. The brother-in-law, Edward Klauber — he was no relation of the Bavarian Hop King — owned a very successful photographic studio. Coming to the rescue, he decided that Morris should not be encouraged again to travel resplendently around the country. He would set the Flexners up in a retail hat store. Klauber further demonstrated his lack of faith in Morris by traveling to New York himself to select, although his experience was in photographs not hats, the stock he was paying for but which Morris would have to sell.[16]

The Flexners moved to a small three-story house on Market Street. The street-level front was occupied by the store. Behind was the "dining room," where the members of the family, when not otherwise engaged, sat at the long table or played beneath it. A door opening into the store contained a glass window through which a watch was kept for customers. Upstairs, the children were packed together. Simon, sharing a bed with Bernard, was one of four sons in one small room. There was hardly any space between the beds and, of course, no hope of privacy.

It was Simon's duty to sweep the store and dust the counters before he went off to school. When he came back, he would find his father eagerly awaiting him: Morris could then dash off to join his former companions at Fuerst's. Seated at the table behind the windowed door, Simon was supposed to do his homework while keeping a lookout for customers. However, he did not find himself overly occupied. His schoolbooks rarely caught his attention; there were few customers.

It was surely not Morris's fault. The depression was deepening all over the land, but that did not make what happened less agonizing.

There was a longer-established, larger hat store a few blocks away. When the Flexner store was empty on Saturday nights, Simon was sent to see whether there were any customers at the competitor's. Peering through the window, he usually saw a good many.[17]

A strong Jewish tradition urged that every family educate its oldest son for a profession, and Morris seemed blessed with the ideal eldest son: Jacob was precocity incarnate. Morris had happily destined him for medicine. The necessity to abandon this hope, as now too expensive, was for Morris perhaps the most crushing of all his blows. Jacob was apprenticed to a pharmacist, but even at that he would earn nothing during the two years of his indentures. The next three brothers, Henry, Isadore, and Washington, were put to work at whatever jobs they could secure, but being all in their teens and utterly unskilled, they brought home very little. Simon, the next in line, was still at grade school along with the four younger children.

When hats failed to sell, there was almost no money, and bills piled up. It followed that if a hat did sell, what was received was used not for replacing stock but for satisfying some importunate creditor. Simon remembered that boxes on the shelves proved increasingly, when there was a reason for looking into them, empty. In his innocence, he believed that this was an indication that the business was doing well; he did not realize that the business was bleeding to death. Fewer and fewer of the fewer and fewer customers who came in could be fitted. The store staggered along, always more haltingly, for almost two years, and then no one could doubt any longer that the family would have to set their sights lower.[18]

It was decided to move the store and the remaining stock more than a half mile further down Market Street to a poor district where the demands of the customers would presumably be less specialized. The particular spot was chosen because in the middle of the street there was a public market, a frame building to which farmers brought their produce and housewives came to buy. Surely they would find a hat store a convenience! They did not.[19]

Simon's self-identification with the family plight was revealed by a continuing nightmare. He was borrowing money and then more money, making promise after promise until the total "became so colossal a figure that it was unpayable. Just when the terror disappeared," Flexner wrote in 1934, "I cannot recall."[20]

Once more, a new family location sent Simon into a new school in the middle of the year, but this time with tougher classmates from a rougher neighborhood. On his first day, a piece of paper moved to him from hand to hand across the classroom. He found scribbled on it a challenge to fight as soon as school was over. Looking around, he saw, waving at him mockingly, a boy considerably bigger than he.

The final bell rang and the boys swarmed out. Hanging behind, Simon saw the challenger leaning with nonchalant defiance against the door through which he would have to pass. As he continued to hesitate, wondering how to escape, he observed that the bully's books were encumbering his arms. Dropping his own books, Simon dashed to the attack. His opponent was bewildered and getting the worst of it when the watching circle of boys joined in. They knocked Simon down and pinned him to the floor. Then, amazingly, Simon was released. Frank Adams, the biggest boy in the class, came to his rescue.

Whether or not the challenge had been inspired by anti-Semitism, the rescue brought Simon his first Gentile friend, who was to prove the only friend he made during his entire school career. Frank Adams's home seemed to Simon "palatial" because, no store being included, all the rooms were devoted to living. (The elder Adams was a bookbinder.) A head taller than Simon and much more heavily built, Frank became the unquestioned leader of the twosome that excluded from their intimacy all others. Frank undoubtedly had strangeness in him: he became an alcoholic, and after marrying and adopting a daughter, he walked out of his home one day and disappeared.*

While the two boys were together, Frank fascinated Simon with his ingenuity. Best remembered was his invention of a private postal system. They mailed each other letters in a hollow tree or pulled them back and forth with strings. Their intimacy, which lasted for more than a year, faded when Simon fell behind in school.[21]

Since the school was in a poor district, boys were often withdrawn as soon as they were old enough to earn anything. The administration handled the shrinkage by combining, in the next to last elementary school year, boys and girls in the same classroom. The boys sat on one side of the aisle, the girls on the other. Although Simon's attention was not attracted particularly to any girl, their presence made him "self-conscious." It did not take much in his scholarly situation to tip the scale. He was sentenced to repeating the fifth grade.

That a child would have to repeat a grade was unheard of in the Flexner family. There was much "shaking of heads" among his elders,

* When, years later, Simon's name was much in the newspapers, he received a note from Frank that surprised him by being almost illiterate. Adams was living in Minneapolis and seemed to have married again. Simon's reply disappeared into renewed silence.[22]

Simon remembered, but he did not himself take the setback seriously. "It seemed a natural development."[23]

Small of stature and weak of muscle, shy, never temperamentally attuned to physical exercise, Simon was from the start a failure at the games which gave boys prestige among their companions. Most often played was "townball," a version of baseball adapted to city streets. Simon languished in the outfield where balls rarely penetrated. He was used to hearing groans from his teammates when it was his turn to bat.

Sometimes he got to professional baseball games. Instead of being further depressed by the stupendous contrast between what he saw and his own incompetence, he was exhilarated and encouraged. This was a world completely outside his experience, a world which he could enter in dreams. In dreams he was a great pitcher, summoned from the bench when the score was close, the bases full of enemy runners, and three outs to go. How nonchalantly, in that crowded stadium, he stood on the mound. To the raging excitement of thousands, in nine pitches he struck out three enemy pinch hitters. As an old man, Simon commented that he had never again experienced visions so vivid, or in real life enjoyed so great a public success.[24]

One afternoon, Simon was as usual standing with his glove on his hand at the outskirts of the townball game, a seemingly pitiful figure on a slum street, but listening in silence to thunderous cheers, when a voice cut in from the real world, "Where's Mary?" He had been entrusted with taking care of his little sister! He looked around but could not see her. He had not the slightest idea where she was.

Esther's screams were loud in the street. Other housewives came running, and a hysterical search got under way. That the little girl was soon discovered in a backyard, unharmed and playing happily by herself, in no way mitigated Simon's guilt.[25]

It was at this point that his father escorted Simon to the county jail. The object lesson having misfired, Simon's mischief and muddles went on. When that family paragon, his eldest brother Jake, bothered him by snoring during a noonday nap, Simon put under his nose an open ammonia bottle. It rapidly became expedient for him to lock himself up in the bathroom. He enjoyed repeating this anecdote to his sons, but would never answer our questions on how he safely got out of that bathroom.[26]

Our mother, who had heard our father's stories so often, did not get the amusement from them that his sons did, but one story never failed to bring sentimental tears to her eyes. Simon's only pair of shoes being completely worn out, Esther reached into her little cache of money and sent him to the neighborhood shoe store. He saw on a shelf shoes with red tops, and he lusted for them. They were much too small but Simon rammed them on anyway, and despite the expostulations of the proprietor, limped triumphantly home. One look was enough to fill Esther with outrage. Having given Simon a round scolding, she led him back to the store, waving the red shoes angrily in her hand, and gave the proprietor the piece of her mind which experience with her had led him to foresee. And Simon was sentenced to plodding around for another year in hateful, hideous, heavy black shoes.[27]

On returning to school for a second try at the fifth grade, Simon found that the girls were again off in a separate class. This time he got through his studies and was promoted. One year more and he would have completed elementary school! However, he started the sixth grade with "no enthusiasm," and during the Christmas holidays resolved that he had had enough of school. His parents made no objections: Simon did not seem to be learning anything, and what wages he could earn, however tiny, would help with the family expenses.[28]

But one school activity Simon was unwilling to leave behind: a projected concert at the Masonic Hall. While he was still a student, the singing teacher had called for alto voices, and "I volunteered without any particular notion of whether or not I could sing alto." Simon was kept away from the rehearsals by his first job. But on the night of the performance, there he was among the altos. The concert had hardly started when the teacher appeared at Simon's side to command that, while going through the motions with his lips, he should utter no sound.[29]

Thus, moving his lips in dumb show, Simon Flexner ended forever his academic schooling. He never did finish elementary school, and never went to high school or college.

4

⸺⸻◈⸻⸺

Hard Times

A s good luck would have it, an effective artist moved in Esther's and Morris's world. Although Joseph Krementz's reputation as a painter of landscapes and likeness extended well beyond Louisville, he earned much of his living by resurrecting the dead in Uncle Klauber's photographic studio. The largest possible enlargement having been made and lightly printed from a photograph of someone deceased, Krementz would draw over the form to make a lifelike rendition in pastel.[1] His portraits of Esther and Morris were in oil and have been translated the other way around: the originals, which have vanished, survive only in large photographs. We see moving renditions of persons whose history and personalities Krementz must have known reasonably well. The likenesses clearly indicate that they were painted when the Flexners had passed their euphoria and were on the way down.[2] (PLATES 2 AND 3)

Krementz's portrait of Morris is a sympathetic rendering of a sorrowful, elderly man. The smoothness of the cocky face seen in the bridegroom's photograph of some twenty years before has disappeared, exposing powerful plastic forms: the high cheekbones, the jutting nose with its broad nostrils, the full mouth of a strongly molded, handsome face. But in the set of Morris's head and features there is no force, only the laxness of discouragement: the head a little bowed, the dark eyes shrewd, apprehensive, defensive, withdrawn.

Morris's had indeed been a tragic fate. The early fall from opulence, the long stint as a minor schoolmaster in a considerably alien environment, the enforced flight, and then a new phoenixlike rise. On the upward projectory, he had undertaken the family life he had so long delayed. This involved grave responsibilities since the Flexner household was set up on German lines, the father being cast as arbiter and provider.

For ten years it had seemed as if he had forever left trouble behind him. And then he found himself, when he was more than fifty years old, responsible for a wife and an augmenting band of children, but deprived of the business that had been his means of support. He borrowed from his bossy brother-in-law, engaged in mean shopkeeping, struggled and struggled, but the road was always down.

Esther was too well trained as a housewife in the German tradition ever to upbraid her husband in Simon's hearing. Perhaps she never gave him a real dressing down. But her irritability must sometimes have flashed out, and in any case, there was no need to say anything: they both knew he was not living up to his duty as head of the house.

Esther felt no humility towards her husband's background; indeed, she could remember little of it in her later years. He may have come from a rabbinical family and have lived once in affluence, and her family may have been small traders, but they had been the more financially stable and had been longer rooted in Louisville. It had been her brother-in-law, not a Flexner, who had come to the rescue when Hirsch and Flexner had failed. She could not resist referring often to what was a considerable matter in a society made up entirely of immigrants: Morris Flexner had crossed the ocean in steerage and she had come over in a refined manner in second class.[3]

His life as a salesman had habituated Morris to drinking — every deal, even if it took place in the morning, was facilitated and celebrated with a dram. With failure, he drank more heavily. This Simon was conscious of, although Morris had too great a sense of his appointed role as master at the house ever to appear visibly intoxicated before his children.

Five feet eight, broad but not fat, Morris towered over his family, who were mostly short and delicately boned like Esther. In contrast to her quickness, he moved slowly. Simon remembered that in his boyhood he was too young to "feel much" of his father's "tragedy." He saw Morris as an awesome figure whom there was no possibility of approaching. "He was my father. I obeyed him." Although Morris never resorted to the corporal punishment to which Simon had become habituated in school, "my principal memory of my father is that I was afraid of him."[4]

As an older man trying to account for what had taken place, Simon was puzzled and disturbed by the picture given in Abraham's autobiography of their father as a man of dignity, wisdom, and intellectual concerns, whose inspiration had been responsible for the Flexner family's rise. Simon queried his other siblings, who agreed that, although Morris was in the established Jewish tradition ambitious for his oldest son, he had no concern with the education of his other children, and was himself never seen to read a book. Yet surely Morris Flexner's influence, worldly within its limits and deeply dissatisfied, had its effect on the boy who, after he became a man, felt for his father deep pity.[5]

Krementz's portrait of Esther reveals that, although only about forty years old, she had abandoned all efforts to be a pretty woman. True, her hair is still black and her light gray eyes startle in her brunette face, but there remains nothing outgoing in her posture or her look. Compared to her photograph as a bride, her almost circular head seems flatter, the chin under her very short lower lip withdrawn and thus less pronounced. The firm line of a mouth in essence gentle, the joyless intensity of her eyes, connote both resolution and sadness. Although she dangles large and elaborate earrings, her dress is simple — black under a narrow white ruching at her throat — and decorated only with a miniature of her husband when he was a younger man and his beard was still black.

Simon's early memories of his mother were, he confessed, "ordinary." It was only after the trouble struck that his "understanding and appreciation" began. "My mother was the steady force around which the family life revolved."[6] Years later, in generalizing about slums to his fiancée, Helen Thomas, Simon wrote: "Poverty is a small part of the problem compared with the pernicious habits of generations, or squalid living and ignorance. What can you do? You can expect no help from the mother."[7]

Simon remembered that his own mother was "acute and quick. All her reactions were fast ones. Her mind worked quickly and so did her fingers. Nothing said escaped her; her retorts were prompt and apt. . . . She could do anything domestic with her hands. And, with so large a family, her hands were never idle. She made clothes, mended them, kept the household articles, linen, etc., mended. . . . She was famous as a cook and her homemade bread was famous among her acquaintances. She nursed the sick and was, of course, skillful at it." But Esther never undertook the more menial tasks of housekeeping: however impoverished, the Flexners always had a servant. Lizzie Kallan, of Swiss extraction, lived with the family until she died.

Esther deeply impressed her slovenly middle son with such neatness as he was himself to make a fetish of during most of his career. Despite the poverty that kept her from buying new clothes, "I do not remember that she ever let herself become careless in dress, and she was the cleanest person ever. Her hands were always clean, including the fingernails so easily neglected. Possibly her fingernails had the conformation of mine that need not be scrubbed to be kept clean. Her voice was low and modulated. I do not recall a harsh use of her voice, but she could be definite and final in a restrained way. . . . There was no hardness in her makeup, but there was a firmness and decision."[8]

Esther's great contribution was to keep high, along the years of deepening adversity, the self-respect of the Flexner family, and its respectability within whatever community poverty tossed them. The more squalid the surroundings, indeed, the more her little domain stood out for being spick-and-span. She handled whatever household money became available to her with efficiency and effect. The local tradesmen admired and trusted her for the impressive frugality of her purchases and because, even if she did not pay at once, there was never any doubt — the rarer that situation the poorer the neighborhood — that as soon as it was possible for her and at not too distant a time what she owed would be paid.

Although there existed little opportunity to be finicky about the probity of her small sons' employers, the sons were not allowed to range through the streets. She would not let them broadcast the family poverty by peddling newspapers or becoming bootblacks. Each was to move in a straight line home from the store where he was employed.[9]

Simon's growing realization of his mother's key position in holding his world together made more disturbing her lack of any particular sympathetic concern with him. A corollary to her "quickness of action and decision" was irritation with incompetence that added to her trials. "So unpromising a boy," a "liability to the family" and yet not actively bad, Simon captured his mother's attention only to receive scoldings for clumsiness or minor mischief. Looking back, Dr. Flexner could summon up no conception of what were "her thoughts about me before I began to emerge from a kind of shadow under which I moved." The reminiscing Flexner passed quickly on from this painful realization. For a lonely boy, wandering bewilderedly in a world he found alien to him, his mother's seeming lack of concern must have been both frightening and deeply discouraging.[10]

At a depressed moment in his courting correspondence with Helen Thomas, he wrote, "I feel like a child always dependent upon its mother" but separated from her. "As the mind passes from subject to subject, it is continually alert to a presence that is felt but not seen, and in being searched for is found absent."[11]

The father being dethroned and the mother not presuming to expand from her role of housewife, a power vacuum developed in the eleven-member Flexner family. Into it there stepped, with the utmost self-confidence, the eldest son, Jacob Aaron Flexner.

From the moment in 1857 when he had been born, Jacob had been a live wire; from the moment he could talk, he had been voluble; from the moment he could read he was an infant prodigy, impressive not only to his parents but to outsiders, and even, we are told, to "Christians."

Morris's sense of personal guilt because Jacob was not being trained as a doctor made it all the easier for the son to usurp his father's role. At seventeen or eighteen, Jacob took over the control of the family with results of the greatest importance to Simon, who was six years his junior. So much so that the question of whether he should be more grateful to Jacob than resentful of him, to what extent his continuing hatred of his once so dominating brother should in all justice be tempered by admiration, remained a reiterated quandary in Dr. Flexner's autobiographical jottings.[12]

He admitted that the active intellectual life in the Louisville household began with Jake's hegemony. Jake avidly read the most serious books, had perfect retention of what he had read, and used it as ammunition in gleeful cutthroat arguments aimed less at settling matters than annihilating his opponent. He was determined to mold all his brothers still young enough to be malleable into his own image. This provoked a head-on conflict with Simon.

Contemporary photographs reveal the combatants.[13] Jacob at about twenty is instinct with aggressive vitality, and conspicuously handsome in a mode that must either attract or repel. His copious black hair grows energetically from his scalp. His head is long like his father's, and his mother's light eyes are protrusive under heavy lids. His expression is serious, intelligent, facile, combative, challenging, and, if uneasily, self-assured.

Where Jacob is natty, Simon's clothes are amorphous, hanging messily down. His dark hair, clumsily cut by a domestic hand, has resisted combing. The thirteen-year-old face is set in no characteristic pattern, but he carries his head to one side. His intent eyes give life to the image: they are sad and wary, as if he expects someone to put something over on him from which he will be unable to protect himself. (PLATES 4 AND 5)

At meals, the conversation was dominated by Jake, who held forth on the books he had read and the conclusions he had drawn. From the head of the table, Morris listened with perpetual admiration. Jacob pounced on any of the younger children who disagreed with him, easily routing them all, except, as time passed, the youngest son: Abraham was as voluble as Jacob, thought more or less on similar lines, and was equally argumentative. Once Isadore, battered beyond bearing, threw a fork at Jake. Striking a wall, prongs first, the fork penetrated far enough to be caught there, quivering, a sight Simon never forgot. Everyone was shocked, although Simon also felt exhilarated. It was with boredom and resentment that year after year he listened to Jake's philosophical and scientific theorizing. Throughout his long life, the future experimental scientist's mind was not attuned to what he called "philosophies and speculations" that were separated from facts.[14] As a boy, he was too retiring to expose to what would certainly be Jake's ridicule the different kinds of thoughts, so different from Jake's, that naturally entered his mind.

Towards the end of his time in school, Simon had begun to read in a desultory manner. He stayed home from a family Sunday outing, although these were very rare, because he could not bear to abandon some book. Boys' novels by Oliver Optic were in much currency with his schoolmates and passed from hand to hand. He borrowed a copy of *Pickwick Papers*. When he won in a raffle at the temple — a child's publication, *The Annual Chatterbox* — "I was greatly excited . . . and carried it home in triumph." To own a publication was a double delight because he had almost no other possessions except the unattractive clothes his family supplied.*[15]

A single sheet of cheap paper, folded into fours and headed *Frank Leslie's Boys and Girls Weekly*, supplied Simon, until a cataclysm intervened, with his major excitement. There was the recurring effort to procure somehow the necessary five cents; there were first the days and then the hours of expectation before the new issue was scheduled to appear at the newsstand around the corner from the Flexner house. When the delivery truck arrived, Simon would be waiting. He would eagerly

---

* As a distinguished elderly scientist, Simon was fascinated by five-and-ten-cent stores, where so many objects he would have loved to have owned were purchasable for a few pennies. He would lose himself among the aisles, and eventually reappear bearing trinkets he had been unable to resist.

watch the little pile of sheets being unloaded and unwrapped. As soon as he had secured his copy, he was "captivated" by a sensory pleasure: the smell of fresh printer's ink. He could hardly wait to peruse the new installment of "Custer's Last Rally," but he knew that caution was now necessary. Jacob would rule the story and the publication "trash," and the older brother felt no hesitation about enforcing his rulings. Simon carried the magazine home under his coat and kept it hidden until Jake was theoretically tied down outside the house by his job at the drugstore. Theoretically! One afternoon, Jacob came home ahead of schedule and caught Simon red-handed.

"What's that you're reading?" Jacob snatched the sheet out of Simon's hand, took one scornful look at it and tore it up. "Have you got other copies?" Simon was too afraid of his brother to refuse to show him where his precious pile was hidden. All were destroyed.

No more point now in earning pennies! No more "Custer's Last Rally"! Simon passed the magazine store on the other side of the street, mourning for the smell of fresh printer's ink.

"I wasn't a difficult person," Dr. Flexner commented in January, 1936. "I wasn't awfully good at school, and I wasn't awfully happy. Why not let me have something steadying?" Then he added: "To this day, sixty-three years later, I have not forgiven Jake."[16]

5

‒‒‒‒⚬‒‒‒‒

Simon Flexner, Unemployable

AFTER his retirement from school, Simon was added to the group of Uncle Klauber's relations who worked at his photographic studio. Here was an excellent opportunity if Simon could take advantage of it.

Klauber had the most flourishing business of any member of the family. He was a large, handsome man, very rigorous and domineering, who "was not supposed to treat Aunt Caroline too well." But Klauber had an inquiring mind. He enjoyed making his own experiments with the new photographic processes he read about in professional journals. The curiosity of the future medical investigator was aroused, but his uncle would not even let him watch. Simon had been employed to begin at the bottom of the ladder. He was "stuck away in dark, disorderly quarters where the printing was done." Under the direction of his slightly older brother Isadore, he was supposed to keep his eye on the negatives in the developer. He paid little attention. "It was a humdrum business, the same day after day."

One afternoon he was trusted with watching a large "silvertone print" which was ripening in the sunlight in preparation for being worked up by Krementz into a pastel or even an oil portrait. Simon's duty was to open the frame periodically, peer in, and notify Isadore when the print was dark enough but not too dark. But Simon had procured a jigsaw, which absorbed his interest as passionately as he was absorbed years later by the microscope. Having procured a wooden cigar-box top, he had outlined a fascinating design at which he was sawing away with all his being. When Isadore finally called him back to reality, the silvertone print was ruined. On top of Simon's other incompetences, this was the last straw: Simon was fired.[1]

The debacle extended much beyond the loss of a job: Simon had stepped off the family's normal ladder of progression. The dominant Klauber turned his back on his godson and nephew, even stopping the small presents Simon had been receiving on his birthday. (Klauber was to continue to ignore Simon until he learned that the scapegrace had become director of the Rockefeller Institute for Medical Research.) And Simon's parents concluded that their worst fears had been corroborated: the boy was either incurably stupid or incurably lazy. All they could hope for was to find some way to keep Simon from being a dead weight on the family pocketbook.

Simon received a curt command to follow his father and was led into a plumber's shop. Morris pushed the boy forward and offered him to the plumber as an apprentice. The plumber said he did not need an apprentice. Morris went out and walked off, leaving the boy standing on the street.[2]

However, an employer was eventually found for the unlikely lad: Lemuel Hecht, whom Dr. Flexner was to characterize as "a crook with a crookeder brother." Hecht operated a cutrate dry goods store dedicated to passing off lower-grade goods for better. He would buy at auction the cheapest possible cottons. Simon, having distributed handbills announcing a fire sale, was instructed to cut off all the labels, soak the bolt ends "just enough" in a tub of water, and then pull them back and forth over the dirty floor until the soaked-in grime could be mistaken for smoke damage. The final doctoring was done on Saturday nights and Sundays, behind closed blinds, when the store was closed. His brother Bernard was sometimes called in to help. On Mondays, people jostled outside before the store opened, eager for a first chance at the "bargains." Simon felt neither dishonor nor amusement at thus fooling the public. It was just another aspect of an unpleasant job that included sweeping floors, dusting counters, putting stock back after it had been shown, wrapping parcels, delivering.

Although Simon remembered that he had liked Hecht's "fat, mild, German wife" who was "good-natured and cordial," concerning Hecht he exclaimed, "God, how I hated him!" The boy despised "the flat-footed, splay-footed" way he walked. Wearing reddish side-whiskers and gold-rimmed glasses, decked out impressively in a Prince Albert coat, Hecht would walk up and down the store "as if he were God Almighty."

One morning, Simon arrived to find the store locked. Hecht had skipped town, leaving debts behind him.[3]

Dobbin's drugstore came next. Although Simon was to find himself as a druggist, this was not the place. No effort was made to teach him anything and he learned almost nothing. "If you start work at seven in the morning and continue to ten at night, I tell you, you have quite a different outlook. You live like a vegetable. You have your breakfast; you rush away. You come home to lunch; you rush away. You come home to dinner; you rush away. You don't have any fun. Come home at ten; you're dead tired. You drop into bed. Nothing!"

Leonard (Len) Dobbin ran so modest a store that he could not afford a licensed clerk, which meant that he could legally leave the premises — drugstores were then available to customers twenty-four hours a day — only on rare occasions when he hired an accredited pharmacist by the hour. He lived over the store with his wife, a tall rawboned woman. At breakfast time, he would shuffle downstairs to pour some "spirit simplex" (a sweetener for bitter medicine) into a cup for griddle cakes. Simon assumed that his wife, being "rooster-pecked," never got any.

Simon had been instructed by his parents to ask for $2.50 a week. Dobbin replied that if he were not worth that, he was worth nothing. But, after two weeks of observing Simon's services, the druggist told him he could either go or stay for $1.50 a week. Simon returned to his parents indignant and determined to leave. After a family conference, they told him to accept the $1.50. As he walked his unhappy way back to the store, Simon for the first time "had a real sense of defeat and discouragement."

Dobbin's joy was to sit in the evening by the tall iron stove with his cronies, talking politics, chewing tobacco, and spitting into a sandbox conveniently placed. So as not to be interrupted, he did teach Simon how to roll pills (which did not in those days come ready-made from a manufacturer).[4]

One evening a little girl came in to get some quinine pills for her mother, a Mrs. Levy. Simon weighed out the quinine, prepared the "mass" with glycerine, rolled the result to the proper length, cut the required number of pills, and rounded them with his fingers.

After the child was gone, Simon noticed that the morphine bottle, also containing white powder, was standing beside the quinine bottle. Could he have made a mistake? He tasted in a most gingerly manner what was left on the pill slab. It was bitter. As he left the store for the night, he asked Dobbin how morphine tasted. "Bitter."

Simon did not really believe that he had substituted morphine, but he spent a night of horror. He was up early. Mrs. Levy, as he knew, also rose early. She toddled with her basket over her arm to the market, passing Dobbin's store before it opened. Over his mother's protests, Simon, gulping a cup of coffee, ate no breakfast. Almost instantly, he was at the steps of the store, watching. One minute, five minutes, ten minutes, fifteen — and there was Mrs. Levy coming along as usual with her market basket. Simon hurried home and clamored for the breakfast he had missed.[5]

Simon's passion for the jigsaw was no more. Now he wished to be a published writer. His first opening seemed to come when he had a backache. He took home a box of Alcott's Porous Sticking Plasters, used them, and the pain disappeared. In the box there were printed testimonials. He composed a glowing one. "Some glint of caution," Dr. Flexner remembered in 1936, "at the last moment said, 'Don't send it.'" The distinguished scientist "often thought" of how embarrassing it would have been if such a testimonial had been unearthed in later years and printed over his name.[6]

He soon found an inspiration closer to home. He had only to respond to the sound of a bell rung in the street to see Rufus Childers come along in his little one-horse cart that contained two large cans with spigots. Housewives emerged from their doors carrying pitchers that Childers filled with milk. "The Milkman Poet" had a local reputation for his verses that were published in the *Louisville Weekly Sun*. Simon read them and was sure he could do as well. One verse that he composed remained in his memory:

> *What makes the people fume and fret?*
> *What makes the people burst with sweat?*
> *What makes the people wringing wet?*
> *The heat.*

Simon was too shy to send the editor his effusion, but his muse would not lie still. He penned on Dobbin's wrapping paper an epic entitled "A Dying Arab to His Steed." Inspiration came so fast that the stingy pharmacist, who put out only a few sheets at a time, began asking Simon accusingly what was happening to the wrapping paper. When in a good storytelling mood, Simon liked to say that he was fired because of his poetic prolixity, which used up so much wrapping paper. But the fact seems to have been that Dobbin concocted a special face powder, had handbills printed, and sent out Simon, seconded by Bernard, to distribute them on the streets. The brothers became bored after a week or so, and were caught throwing the handbills into the sewer. Simon had held this job for an unusual length of time, almost a year.[7]

New jobs came and went, and then, when he had been working for some two years and was almost sixteen, Simon was hired as an errand boy at David Sternberg's dry goods store. His bad reputation having not gone before him, he was given "enormous pay": three dollars a week. The store did a brisk local trade in a cheap part of town where many of the customers were black. The dominant figure was Sternberg's sister Bertha, who was vividly recalled to Dr. Flexner's memory when decades later he met the poet Amy Lowell, the only other woman he had ever seen who smoked a large, black cigar.

One evening, just at closing time, two black women entered the store and started to sit down on the small stools before the ribbon case. "An imp took charge of me. I slipped the stool out from under one of the women. As she fell, she put her arm through a glass showcase. No blood spurted, but the broken glass had to be replaced." It is probably indicative of the attitude towards blacks in Louisville that, although the cost of the glass was deducted from Simon's pay, his outrageous act did not result in his being fired.[8]

6

---···◦∞◦···---

New Departures

A T about the time that Simon dropped out of school, the Flexner family moved to a larger house in a newly opened part of town. Paradoxically, the family finances had been improved by the final failure of the final hat store. All of Morris's business efforts since the collapse of Hirsch and Flexner had lost money, but now he took a job that brought money in. Back among the business community, he found some compensations — he heard the gossip and could go to Fuerst's for lunch when he did not feel too ashamed to do so. The onetime successful merchant felt degraded by serving as a salesman for a triumphant rival of his own departed business. Simon had become old enough to be conscious of his father's humiliation.

Not only was Morris supplying earnings, but the various sons, being older, were bringing home more cash. Even Simon contributed his pittance. Feeding and clothing the large family was easier, but their moving to a better address brought its own strains. The family only partially occupied their new house and they could not be easy there until they claimed it all. The master bedroom was rented to an itinerant photographer, and the washhouse provided the humblest of lodgings for the almost-destitute: first an unmarried pregnant woman (Esther was outraged when a doctor charged the unfortunate twenty-five dollars for delivering her child), and then a black woman with a little daughter.[1]

The house was directly behind the newly built Temple Adas Israel, described by the *Memorial History of Louisville* as "one of the handsomest church edifices in the city ... an oriental structure in the Byzantine style of architecture, having domed turrets at the angles which impart a very bold and striking effect." Across a narrow alley from the Flexner house was the part of the structure inhabited by the sexton. Jacob married his "buxom" daughter, Rosie Maas. At the wedding, a pretty Maas niece kissed fourteen-year-old Simon. "I was astonished, amazed, quite agitated."[2]

When Simon was eight or nine, he had happened into his parents' bedroom and surprised his father, who had a leather tape, on which were imprinted Hebrew characters, wound about his forehead and his body. The parent was mumbling something to himself. Simon thought it very funny. That the boy received neither a scolding nor an explanation indicates that the father was embarrassed at being thus discovered.[3]

If Simon's parents and their many brothers and sisters who followed them to Kentucky had left Europe as orthodox Jews, none of them remained so for any length of time after their transplantation. By the time Simon was growing up, his parents had become communicants of the Reformed temple, beside which they later established themselves.

Simon's early memories included elongated metal containers for scrolls that were fastened to the front doors and other doors of his successive homes. At first, when the family moved, the scrolls had moved with them, but the time came when they disappeared. However, the Flexners continued to have two sets of dishes as required by the dietary laws, and special dishes for Passover. Simon prayed, at least until he was thirteen. He had no recollection why he stopped praying.

Never were the Flexners so poor that Esther failed on Friday nights to put on the supper table a spotless white cloth with candles in candlesticks. "It was a beautiful sight to see her, as I sometimes did by accident, in a fresh neat dress, just before supper was served (which she more often than not had prepared with her own hands), burning the candles. She said a prayer silently, while making movements with her hands. Just what the custom signified was never explained to me."

Her children played with the candles for secular ends. During the Franco-Prussian War, each child dedicated a candle to the combatant he preferred, eventual victory to be prophesied by which candle burned the longest. Simon remembered that he had supported the French.[4]

Reliance for the children's religious education was put on the temple. Morris and Esther went on Friday nights and Saturday mornings, the children on Saturdays. Simon was bored at the services. They were conducted in German, which he was unable to follow. He was sent on Sundays to the temple school, his teacher being his older cousin "Painy"

Godshaw. He paid as little attention as he did in grade school. Perhaps because he had failed to learn enough to pass the examination, Simon was the only one of the nine Flexner children who was not, as he put it, "confirmed."

The proximity of the Flexners' new house to the Reformed synagogue brought into Simon's life two successive rabbis who were the first mature individuals of ability and intellectual achievement he got to know. However, their influence on his attitude towards Judaism was the opposite of what would today be expected.

Dr. Flexner remembered that the earliest to appear, Dr. Emil Hirsch, was "a striking figure, young and modern, an excellent preacher [he spoke English]." He had been born in Luxembourg, where his father was chief rabbi, but had been brought to America when he was fifteen. He was graduated from the University of Pennsylvania, and then undertook deep theological studies in Germany. After his two years in Louisville (1877–1879), he settled in Chicago. There, according to the *Dictionary of American Biography*, he became nationally famous as "the Jewish apostle to the non-Jewish world." He denied that the Jews were a "chosen people." The Jewish mission was not to stand apart, but to gather in all others, uniting "mankind in righteousness and peace."

Hirsch came to the Flexner household because he enjoyed arguing with Jacob. The first person to catch a gleam of Simon's potentialities, he offered to teach the boy Greek. But Simon was too submerged to try.[5]

Hirsch's successor at Temple Adas Israel, Rabbi Adolf Moses, was called to Louisville after Simon had begun to get hold of himself. Born in Prussian Poland, educated at Breslau, Moses had fought as a revolutionary with Garibaldi before coming to America at the age of thirty. He remained in Louisville until he died, a friend of the Flexner family. He became one of Simon's earliest admirers.

Rabbi Moses' religious ideas carried to a greater extreme the contentions of Rabbi Hirsch. His major work, entitled (with a regrettable pun) *The Religion of Moses*, was published in 1891 by an ill-fated venture of Washington's and Bernard's, named the Press of the Flexner Brothers. The rabbi divided historical Judaism into two parts. The first, as described in the early books of the Old Testament, was the advance from a family religion to a tribal one. The second was yet another advance — to a world religion as enunciated by the prophet Moses: "revealed religion . . . intended to embrace all mankind." The rabbi was so eager to cast off all tribal implications that he wished to abolish the name "Judaism" and substitute "Jehovaism."[6]

Abraham was to attribute his own early departure from Judaism to the doubt cast on all religious faith by the doctrines of Herbert Spencer and his ilk that were so profusely repeated by Jacob.[7] Simon's boredom and irritation with these arguments stemmed from an innate set of mind still more damaging to religious conviction. The future scientist was psychologically immune to undemonstrable philosophical or religious considerations.

The new Judaism, which swept the Flexner household with those two able rabbis, Hirsch and Moses, contended that a person from whatever background was a Jew if he believed. Since the rabbis denied the Jews were a separate people, it followed that a person, whatever his background, who did not believe was not a Jew.* Simon and Abraham were thus, as they grew older, encouraged to consider themselves not in any true sense Jews. That they were nonetheless sometimes discriminated against by Gentile prejudice seemed to them, throughout their lives, irrelevancies that they should do their best to ignore and, as far as possible, eliminate.

Simon was never fired from Sternberg's dry goods store. One morning — he had now become sixteen — he was unable to eat his breakfast. He went to work anyway. He was not very long in the store before he was overcome with severe illness, suffering with a chill. He was rushed home and the doctor was sent for. He was now bleeding alarmingly from his nose. Esther, remembering a traditional Jewish remedy for nosebleeds, rushed to the synagogue and came back with the sexton, who was carrying the keys to the various parts of the temple. The sacred keys were suspended from Simon's neck down his back. Soon Dr. Goodman appeared to make the diagnosis: typhoid fever.

Simon's case was so severe that Dr. Goodman called in for consultation a distinguished physician, Dr. Hewitt. After examining the youth, Hewitt told the Flexner family that there was no point in his coming again. Simon would die. But Simon did not die. He was to be, although not in a religious sense, born again.[8]

Dr. Flexner always believed that the change was the most important and remarkable event of his life. Finding himself unable to explain, he

---

* This doctrine was far from untypical of the Reformed synagogues among German-speaking Jews in Europe as well as America.

occasionally played with the theory that the disease had created some physiological alteration in his brain. But it is possible to come to more searching if less dramatic conclusions.

Simon had been on the verge of death. Early in his recovery, when "not well enough," he was taken to visit a slightly younger playmate, Bella Hess, who had come down with typhoid somewhat later than he. It was hoped that seeing Simon not dead would encourage Bella to believe that she could recover. Simon was horrified with what he saw. "My childhood sweetheart" seemed a still-breathing corpse. So this was how he himself had been only a few weeks before! The vision, which hounded him for a long time, "increased the shock that changed my life."[9]

To feel that you have risen from the grave is to be encouraged to a new beginning. And the illness shattered what had seemed the inevitable and inescapable progression of his life. The period between the first blow of his illness and his being enough recovered to go back to work included months of convalescence during which, for the first time in his sixteen years, he was allowed to contemplate in tranquillity himself and his world.

Simon's environments outside the home had always been dominated by personalities he found repellent. His school teachers were as a group ordinary women, some of them sadistic, with no interest in their duties. Despite his inattention, Simon was ten times the brighter and, as he was to tell Helen Thomas, even then he possessed "a strong tendency for formulation my own way." However, he did not argue, as his brother Jacob would have done, thus attracting the attention of his teachers even if he annoyed them. His "rebellious spirit" expressed itself in "determined, obstinate reserve." He receded so deeply into withdrawal that, although he was grateful for them all his life, the efforts of Belle Kirby did not suffice to draw him out. At his various schools, he was made to feel, sometimes more and sometimes less, excluded as a Jew. "I was aware of it, but accepted it."[10]

Simon's lamentable school record, followed by his debacle at Uncle Klauber's photographic studio, made his parents conclude that he would be employable only on the lowest level. Except for the incompetent druggist Dobbin, his employers had all been, within the German-Jewish community, those who had least effectively adapted to the American environment: shopkeepers driven by lack of success to shabby and even dishonest tricks. Simon resented them all the more because, despite the contrast between their sluttishness and Esther Flexner's determined respectability, the Flexners were, in the eyes of the world, linked with them by their common Jewishness.

At home, Simon had never enjoyed privacy. The Flexner houses, always small, had teemed with the family's eleven members, often augmented by relatives just arrived from Europe who would stay until they could find their own way in Louisville. And in the coming and going, Simon had been ignored except when he was scorned. But a dying family member, resurrected to become an invalid slowly gaining in strength, was an object not only of attention but of solicitude. His weaknesses, the incompetencies that had once enlisted jeers, were now blamed on the disease. Above all, Simon had become an object of his mother's passionate attention. During the considerable period when his life was in danger, she had slept with him in the same bed, and during his long convalescence, she had added perpetual care of the invalid to her multitudinous tasks.[11]

Simon was thus for the first time enabled to get to know the mother whom he had long recognized as the stronghold of the family battle against circumstance. Although there was little that she could contribute to his as yet undeveloped intellectual side, close association enabled him to understand her gallantry, her determination that did overcome obstacles, her ability to earn respect despite the handicaps her situation forced upon her. Admiring her, he imbibed "a sense of struggle, of the value of money, and the difficulties of making ends meet." This influence towards probity and hard work within the lot assigned you, he was to comment, "perhaps took the place of the temple."[12]

By now the family had achieved complete occupancy of their property. The indigents who had lived in the washhouse being gone, there was a little garden where Simon sat in the sunlight. Rarely before had he experienced the quiet of being home during the daytime when most of the family were off on their various tasks. He was uninterrupted. Since Louisville had no free library, he was unable to procure such books as he would have enjoyed reading. Probably this was just as well. Other men's thoughts might have interfered with the voyage of exploration he was undertaking within himself. Every day, as he felt his body becoming stronger, he penetrated further beneath the discouragement and chagrin that had held him back so long. He found within himself a surprising mental strength, increasing self-confidence, a growing conviction of inner potentialities to be realized.

Towards defining those potentialities, deciding where he wished his efforts to lead him, he received almost no hints from his parents' backgrounds in Europe. How completely Morris and Esther had played down before their children all their imported attitudes and skills is revealed in the matter of languages. Although Esther wrote her parents in Yiddish, she never spoke it in Louisville. Both parents possessed, in addition to what Hebrew was needed for ritual purposes, French and German.[13] When, as a famous man, Simon was invited to read the lesson at the temple, he was unable, to his mother's great disappointment, even to attempt the Hebrew. The parents spoke French only when they wished to convey to each other something they did not want the children to understand. Although Morris and particularly Esther (she never lost her German accent and could never write easily in English) often spoke to the children in German, the children replied in English. When Simon came to need German for his professional studies, he found what skills he had brought with him from his childhood utterly inadequate. During his extensive studies in German universities, he failed to experience any special identification with that nation. During World War I he was passionately anti-German.[14]

Simon felt himself no more European than he felt himself a Jew in any sense that divided him from the major tides that surged through the United States. It was now, as it was to be during his entire career, his temperament and his gift to bring directly to the solution of a specific problem, whether scientific or environmental, the deepest and most imaginative insight. He was a visionary realist. He wished to apply the energy and ambition he now felt beating through his veins to knowing and becoming part of the best that America had to offer. But how was this ambition to be attained? Where were the paths that would lead him to favorable American climes? He had never had more than a superficial association with any able or admirable native-born citizen of the United States. Between him and the Elysium he yearned for there intervened, as was the case with many other immigrants' sons, a maze towards the traversing of which he knew no way.

As he grew stronger, Simon sometimes wandered into the older sections of the city. Here was serenity, a sense of the dignity of life, an escape from the hectic pulsing of Market Street. He regarded the "style of building homes" as "generous," since it permitted "a free look into the grass-covered plots and yards in which old-fashioned and stalwart trees still flourish." But he could not penetrate into those yards, or imagine with any hope of accuracy such a life as was the birthright of his future wife, Helen Thomas.[15]

II

Old Americans

7

---···◦◇◦···---

Puritan to Quaker

As immigrants to America arriving in the 1850's, the Flexners wished to start out altogether anew in a new world. As far as they could, they drowned their heritage and their past in the Atlantic Ocean. However, the Thomas clan into which Simon was to marry, and which had been on the North American continent for more than two centuries, felt no such need to discard what had gone before, either in the New World or in the Old. They regarded themselves as exemplars and continuers of traditions of which they were proud.

The Thomases boasted two talismans, which were believed to have come to Maryland with their first American ancestor: a silver-headed cane and a ponderous silver service. In Helen's lifetime, the cane was said to be in the possession of an unidentified relative. The service was said to have been melted down, at the command of a pre–Civil War Thomas bride, and recast into what she considered more fashionable. A skeptic may wonder whether the objects existed, or if they did, whether they were actually brought to the wilderness on the banks of the Chesapeake by the Thomas immigrant some two hundred years before. No matter! Since the family fully believed in them, they were part of the psychological heritage Helen Thomas brought to her marriage with Simon Flexner.

Every member of the family could describe the coat of arms engraved on the cane and on each piece of the silver service: a shield bearing a chevron and three ravens; on top a fourth raven flapped its wings. The motto greatly amused Helen: "God feeds the Ravens." Most delightfully, the arms were those of Rhys ap Thomas (1449–1525), who could therefore be claimed as an ancestor.[1]

Behind Rhys ap Thomas a web of Welsh myth carries the family genealogy back to the court of King Arthur — not to the heroic knights but to the villains. Helen's innumerable-times-great-grandmother would undoubtedly have been at least a match for the powerful mother and aunt and older sister by whom Helen was brought up. She was Morgan le Fay, the wicked enchantress who plotted the death of King Arthur with another reputed Thomas ancestor, Arthur's treasonous brother-in-law, Mordred. As a result, Arthur was killed in battle.[2]

To connect King Arthur's court and Rhys ap Thomas, legend and history supply a mixed bag of Welsh kings and heroes who expressed their Gaelic patriotism by plundering the Anglo-Saxon lowlands. Bardish literature tells how Gruffydd ap Nicholas, learning that the English Crown was sending commissioners to arrest him, met them as they entered his hills. He was attended by only four or five men as ragged and as miserably mounted as was he. To the astonishment of the commissioners, he offered to guide them on the difficult road to his castle. They had not gone very far when they were led through a gate to see drawn up a hundred horsemen clothed handsomely and gallantly mounted. Behind was Castle Alberlais, at which the lowlanders were graciously received. With the hundred horsemen in attendance, the party advanced until they came to the ancient fortress of Dinevawr, where they were greeted by Gruffydd's son, Owen, at the head of two hundred horsemen. On to the little village of Aberqwili, where stood five hundred "tall men" on foot, well armed and well accoutered. Thus magnificently attended, the commissioners entered Caermarthen, the capital of South Wales. Escorted to a banquet, they were seated on the dais "splendidly hung with cloth of gold." Galleries on the sides were crowded with the "bards of that land of minstrelsy," and the commissioners were plied with ypocras, garbhiofilac, and other "delicate and precious drinks." Feeling himself getting tipsy, Lord Whitney, the principal commissioner, stored his royal order in the long sleeve of his coat. It was easily abstracted.

The next morning, Gruffydd ap Nicholas received the commissioners in great pomp with his private army around him and meekly asked what was the King's will? The commissioners replied that they had come to arrest him. Where, asked Gruffydd, was the royal warrant? When the commissioners could not produce it, Gruffydd dropped his assumed reverence: "What? Have we cozeners and cheaters come here to abuse the King's Majesty's power and disquiet his true-hearted subjects? By the Mass, I will hang up all your bodies for traitors and imposters!"

Finally, Gruffydd relented on condition that Lord Whitney wear the "livery of Gruffydd's servants at the Royal Court and justify the Welshman's proceedings."[3]

Who could fail to be fascinated with such legends, particularly when they seemed to relate to oneself?

There was nothing legendary about Rhys ap Thomas. At the head of several thousand Welshmen, he contributed much to the defeat of King Richard III at Bosworth Field, which established the Earl of Richmond as King Henry VII. Family historians insist that Rhys killed Richard in personal combat. Rhys served Henry as a statesman and military commander, and accompanied Henry VIII to the Field of the Cloth of Gold.[4]

Beloved of the Baltimore Thomases was the fact that Rhys's seat in Pembrokeshire, Carew Castle, had not altogether disappeared, but stood, a turreted pile of ruins, highly visible in illustrations. When outdressed at school by children who were unhampered by Quaker taboos, the little Thomases would ask pointedly whether their rivals also had a castle in Wales?[5]

It is a very obscure path, most dimly lighted with genealogical speculations, that leads downwards from Rhys ap Thomas to the Philip Thomas who inaugurated the line in Maryland. Yet Helen's parents considered calling their country house Carew and they did push Quaker principles aside to display, in their Baltimore residence, the talismanic coat of arms. I was trained to believe — a partial misconception encouraged by the red hair I had inherited from my mother, who had inherited it from her father — that my mother's background was almost altogether Welsh. Helen's aunt, M. Carey Thomas, felt it particularly suitable that the college she presided over was located in, and named after, a community with a Welsh name, Bryn Mawr.[6]

The Thomas immigrant, Philip, was a Welshman who had been a merchant in Bristol, England, before he found it necessary to flee persecution as a Puritan. A new opportunity had just been opened in America by the failure of Lord Baltimore's attempts to establish a Catholic colony in his proprietorship of Maryland. Catholics, happy in England, proved unwilling to emigrate. His Lordship tried to lure Puritans from recently settled New England, but they were happy in their New Zion. Finally, Lord Baltimore bagged some three hundred Puritan families who were being persecuted in Virginia.[7] Reaching Maryland in 1649, they established on the west shore of Chesapeake Bay, across the

Severn River from the present site of Annapolis, a settlement they called Providence.

The first record of Philip's presence in America was a grant of five hundred acres "in consideration that he hath in the year 1651 transported himself, Sarah his wife, Philip, Sarah, and Elizabeth, his children, into this province." Settling with the other Puritans, Philip was soon amassing the asset that was easiest to come by: land. It was an almost worthless commodity until the primeval trees were killed one way or another so that sunlight could reach the ground, rich loam from which crops would rise as if summoned by an enchanter's wand. The crop was that southern staple, tobacco. Finding a market was no problem: British ships traded up the Chesapeake. Philip made at least one return trip to Bristol to attend to the property he had left there, which included two houses.[8]

Less than four years after his arrival, he helped fire the first, distant gun of the American Revolution. The Battle of the Severn, preceding Bacon's Rebellion by more than ten years, was the first bloody conflict between two sets of British Americans. Although the primary concern was religious, also much involved was the basic issue that sparked the American Revolution: self-determination versus domination from overseas.

When the Cromwellian Revolution broke out in England, Philip Thomas and his coreligionists announced a revolt against Catholicism and Lord Baltimore's proprietary government. Settlement in Maryland was then a long, narrow, irregular ribbon along the west bank of the Chesapeake. Gathered around the proprietary capital of St. Marys, the original Catholic settlers were some fifty miles down the bay from the newly arrived Puritans. From among them Lord Baltimore's governor, William Stone, organized a mighty army of between one hundred and fifty and two hundred men. The Puritans, including Thomas as a lieutenant, could muster only about a hundred. The Catholic Cavaliers advanced up the Chesapeake during March, 1654–5, expecting to be met with abject submission by the little settlement of ragtag immigrants. However, the Puritans attacked, their religious passion overwhelming the surprised and relaxed Cavaliers. The Puritan casualties were reported at six; the Catholics lost some fifty killed or wounded. The rest surrendered, foreseeing good treatment. However, a council of war, of which according to some records Thomas was a member, condemned ten to death. They actually shot four.

The wave of ferocity having passed, everyone realized that final decisions would have to be made by the authorities in London. The truly effective cannonballs would be contradictory dispatches fired across the ocean at London, and also polemical pamphlets published there. In the meantime, six Puritan high commissioners — Thomas was one — announced themselves rulers of Maryland. They passed strong laws, such as the confiscation of all Catholic and proprietary property, but dared not try to enforce them. The Jesuits, it is true, considered it wise to hide in the woods where, so a Catholic propagandist shouted in outrage, they huddled "in a mean hut . . . much like a cistern," deprived of servants to wait on them and of wine with which to administer the sacrament.[9]

In London, Lord Baltimore got on the right side of Cromwell. After the resulting orders had reached Maryland, Philip Thomas was one of the commissioners who formally returned the rule of the colony to Governor Strong. This brought to an end his political as well as his military career.

He then occupied himself with patenting more and more of the wild land which, although then of little value, was to establish a firm foundation for the prosperity of his descendants. However, his "soul," like the souls of his Calvinist neighbors, was — so a religious observer wrote — becoming "sore and tender." The little Puritan colony, out of the way on the Chesapeake, was being ignored by fellow sectarians in both New and Old England. No Congregational ministers journeyed there to revive faith, and the few dozen families produced no religious leaders of their own.

As the Maryland Puritans sank painfully into increasing religious stagnation, a new group of passionate sectarians sifted in between the plantations of the former warriors of the Severn.

During the 1640's, a cobbler's apprentice named George Fox had founded in England a religious sect disruptive of established institutions. In the temporal sphere, the Quakers — or more correctly, the Society of Friends — threatened national security and denied the basic value of male populations by being doctrinally opposed to war and refusing to bear arms. They sabotaged legal proceedings by regarding the taking of oaths as blasphemy. They disturbed the relationship of the sexes by contradicting the Puritan conception stated by Milton — "He for God, and she for God in him." Women, they believed, being just as likely to hear the word of God as men, could expound that word even as men could. To these abominations the Quakers added irritants that mocked the pretensions of the mighty. It was common for gentlemen to address their inferiors not as "you" but as "thee." The Quakers called everybody "thee." Refusing to uncover except in the presence of the Heavenly Lord, they insulted their temporal superiors by wearing their hats in the presence of kings.

On the religious side, they denied the legitimacy of ministers and priests, mocking paid ecclesiastics as the "hireling clergy." The Friends, inspired, as they believed, by the Lord, preached to each other. They upset tax collectors and further menaced the paid clergy by refusing to pay tithes. At the heart of Quaker belief lay a doctrine pernicious to established religions: the priesthood of all believers.

Himself in and out of jail, Fox attracted among his tens of thousands of followers men and women with a taste for martyrdom. Their inner voices gave seeming sanction to the most perfervid compulsions, and the unorganized, exploding movement possessed no way to renounce or control anyone. By warning Quakers away, communities attracted zealots. The theocracy of Massachusetts Bay enacted that on first appearance a Quaker should have one ear cut off, on a second appearance the other ear, and on a third have a hole bored in his tongue. All this failing, Quakers would be hanged. Several were hanged. The persecution of early Friends was a source of pride to their prosperous descendants. *Fox's Martyrs*, a long book retelling a succession of bloody episodes, was a staple in every household. It fascinated Helen Flexner during her childhood.

In the early years, it was hard for those Quakers who were not inspired to martyrdom to find places where they could live in peace. Eventually, the rich convert William Penn was to establish Quaker colonies, first in West Jersey and then in Pennsylvania. Before he did so, Quakers found succor through the religious freedom that Lord Baltimore, in his desperation for settlers, had promulgated in Maryland.

Philip Thomas's new Quaker neighbors did not lack for attention from the leaders of their religious Society. The voice of God, speaking in susceptible breasts, again and again commanded Friends to undertake religious journeys. During 1672, a missionary on his way back from Maryland to England called a farewell meeting close to the Thomas homestead at the town of West River. In the light of subsequent events, we may be sure that Philip and his family were among the crowd of "seekers" who attended.

The meeting was already in progress when something took place as might have been described in the Gospels. A boat unknown in the neighborhood came up the West River and out of it stepped a man of whom William Penn wrote, "God has visibly clothed him with divine preference and authority, and indeed his very presence expressed religious majesty." To the wonder and exhilaration of the inhabitants of that obscure place, they welcomed into their midst the founder of the Society of Friends, George Fox.[10]

Fox in no way resembled an inducted Calvinist minister. His long, straight hair hung down "like rats' tails" around a homely and massive face. His preaching was not erudite or finished. "Abruptly and brokenly... his sentences would fall from him about divine things." God, so Penn believed, had chosen "to be the first messenger in our age of his blessed truth... one that was not of high degree or elegant speech or learned in the ways of the world [so] that His message ... might come with less suspicion and jealousy of human wisdom and interest, and with more force and clearness upon the consciousnesses of those that sincerely sought the way of truth in the love of it. . . .

"Above all he excelled in prayer. . . . The most awful living frame I ever felt or beheld ... was his in prayer. And truly it was a testimony that he knew and lived nearer to the Lord than other men, for they that know Him well will see most reason to approach Him with reverence and fear."

While Fox presided over the four-day meeting, Jesus manifested Himself in breast after breast. Then Fox's inner voice called him on to New England. He promised to return.[11]

Fox was again in Maryland during 1663. He traveled widely, staying in the homes of Friends, addressing the local inhabitants. He finally called a general meeting that became Maryland's most exciting event since the Battle of the Severn. As the time approached, so Fox noted in his journal, the Chesapeake "was almost like the Thames. The people said there was never so many boats seen there before. . . .

"It was a heavenly meeting, wherein the presence of the Lord was gloriously manifested, and the Friends thereby sweetly refreshed, and the people generally satisfied, and many convinced, for the blessed power of the Lord was over all: everlasting praise to His Holy Name forever!" Many of the grim warriors of the Severn adopted with equal fervor religious beliefs that included pacifism. Philip Thomas, or at least his wife and children, joined the new faith.[12]

Their conversion by the founder of the Society of Friends was the most determining event in the entire history of Helen Thomas's family, and through her, profoundly influential on Simon Flexner.

8

———•⚬—•———

Manumission and Aftermath

Philip Thomas's grandson, also named Philip, who was born in 1694, sat grandly on the governor's council, supporting the proprietary government his grandfather had so bloodily fought.[1] This reflected a change in station. The original settlers had patented the best land. Buoyed up by the land-hungry immigrants that flooded in beneath them, the radicals of the Battle of the Severn became an aristocracy, watching from mansion-house windows slaves cultivating extensive plantations. Staying within their class, they intermarried. It is startling how many of Helen Thomas's bloodlines stem, often interweaving several times to the same progenitor, from the veterans of the Severn.

The family annals reveal little beyond prosperity and local power until the appearance of Helen's great-grandfather, John Chew Thomas (1764–1826), who married his first cousin Mary Snowden (1770–1844). She had been brought up in one of the most sophisticated social environments in all North America: Montpelier, the house of her uncle, Major Thomas Snowden.[2] (PLATES 8 AND 11)

Montpelier was on the main road from Virginia and further South to Philadelphia and the whole Northeast. The taverns along the way were not suited to the comforts of well-bred humans or well-bred horses. Since Major Snowden carried to its apex the tradition of southern hospitality, every evening a succession of elegant equipages turned in at the decorative gates. Invitations were not necessary. If, as was unlikely, an unsuitable person dared to appear, his lack of position would be recognized at a glance by the black servants and he would be sent away. Within, courtesy abounded. If not themselves friends or acquaintances, the self-invited guests were sure to be related or connected with people who were. Political intelligence was exchanged along with the personal gossip so delightful in closed societies; toasts were drunk; the men stumbled congenially to bed in the small hours. Mary Snowden grew up in a continual house party frequented by almost everyone who was considered worth knowing in her world.

When southern delegates traveled to Philadelphia for the Constitutional Convention, the parlors and bedrooms at Montpelier were full to overflowing. Towards nightfall on May 19, 1787, there appeared in the doorway an unusually elegant coach of somewhat old-fashioned design, with paintings of the four seasons on the four doors. From it alighted a large man topped by a massive face. The seventeen-year-old Mary Snowden curtsied to General Washington.

The General, although as always affable, was in a dark mood. He had left Mount Vernon that morning a little after sunrise to attend a convention which, although it was to be venerated, was then regarded as another in the series of efforts, all so far unsuccessful, to unite the thirteen colonies into a single nation. Whether the meeting turned out well or badly Washington saw himself a loser. Should it fail, the reputation he had so arduously won during the Revolution would be tarnished. Should it succeed, he would surely be dragged by the demands for leadership of the newly united nation from "under the shadow of my own vine and fig tree" where he had hoped to live out the rest of his life in "philosophic retirement." Frightened and disapproving, Martha had refused to accompany him. "Mrs. Washington," he wrote testily, "has become too domestic and too attentive to two little grandchildren to leave home."

At the Snowdens' the hero's nerves were on edge. "Feeling very severely a violent headache and a sick stomach," he wrote in his diary, "I went to bed early."

The Snowden household had been alerted that the General would set out, as he always had in wartime, at dawn. Less exalted early travelers were allowed to get themselves off with the help of the slaves, but surely Mary, in her most becoming dress, was present at the breakfast served by candlelight. The candles burned on and on, since daylight was held back by clouds and, Washington wrote, "a little rain falling." The General said he was "well recovered," but hesitated to set out in a storm. By 8 A.M. the sky somewhat lightened. The great coach appeared at the door, one of the decorated doors shut noiselessly behind the tall soldier-statesman, and the equipage rumbled off towards destiny.[3]

* * *

After their marriage in 1788, Mary Snowden and John Chew Thomas reopened the bride's mansion house, Fairland, in Prince George's County, where they lived grandly, entertained and visited extensively. One of their grandsons wrote with a combination of pride and Quaker disapproval that they "surrounded themselves with pleasant things, and became, in a refined way, worldly people."[4] In 1799, John was elected by the Federalists to the House of Representatives from a district that included Annapolis. Towards the end of a term as an undistinguished supporter of President John Adams,[5] he intended to run again, but when the upcoming presidential campaign, which pitted Adams against Thomas Jefferson, degenerated into the most violent vituperation, he decided to retire into the peace of his plantation. However, he was picked up and thrown into the very vortex of the most dangerous constitutional crisis the United States has ever faced.

As every schoolchild should know, but many adult readers may have forgotten, in 1800 each member of the electoral college cast two undifferentiated ballots, one for president and one for vice-president. The Republican electors, who were the majority, all voted for Jefferson to be president and Aaron Burr vice-president, but as the ballots were undifferentiated, the result was legally a tie. The Constitution provided that, in case of a tie, the president would be chosen by the retiring House of Representatives, each state delegation casting a single vote. Thomas was a member of the retiring House.

The Federalists decided to take the opportunity for sidetracking Jefferson, whom they regarded as a Jacobin and an atheist, by elevating Burr. Since there were then sixteen states, to accept what was clearly the popular will would require nine votes for Jefferson.

When the balloting began on February 11, 1801, Jefferson secured only eight: New York, New Jersey, Pennsylvania, Virginia, North Carolina, Georgia, Kentucky, Tennessee. Burr had six: New Hampshire, Massachusetts, Rhode Island, Connecticut, Delaware, South Carolina. Two states could not be counted since their delegations broke in half: Vermont with two members, and Maryland with six. Thomas contributed to the Maryland tie by voting for Burr.

Day after day the representatives met from morning to evening; oratory was punctuated with votes that came out always the same. The possibility loomed that the deadlocked House would be forced to abandon both Jefferson and Burr, between whom the people had chosen, and designate some individual more satisfactory than either of the defeated Federalists.

Such a situation would be dangerous today: it was much more dangerous in 1801. The national union was only fourteen years old, and it was common for political theorists to prophecy that America's republican experiment would founder on succession. One reason Washington had stepped down after his second term was his desire that the precedent for a nonviolent change of presidents be established during his lifetime. But his successor, Adams, would have, as vice-president, automatically succeeded if Washington had died in office, and he kept on all of Washington's cabinet. This, then, was the first presidential election that was a real conflict, and it looked as if the will of the people might be thwarted.

The responsibility on Thomas, who had so wanted to avoid the whole fracas, was tremendous. By changing his vote in any of the ballots, by merely casting a blank, he could throw Maryland into the Jeffersonian column, and the crisis would vanish like a bad dream.* But the orders from the Federalist leadership were to stand firm. Across the nation anger and menace rose. Warnings came in from various pro-Jefferson states of potential insurrections should the rightfully elected idol be pushed aside. The governor of Pennsylvania even alerted his militia. But the orders from the Federalist leaders were to stand firm.

Finally, John Chew Thomas took part in a compromise. It was agreed that Delaware would abstain, that the South Carolina delegation would stay away, and that the Maryland Federalists would cast blank ballots. Thomas cast his blank ballot and Jefferson was elected president of the United States by ten states to four.[6]

Although Thomas tried to assuage the wrath of his constituents by asserting that he had not been elected as a puppet but to use his own judgment, he was hung in effigy at the gates of Fairland. Remaining popular in his own social circle, he passed his days in comfortable elegance. With almost annual births, his wife was approaching her total of fifteen children. His oldest surviving daughter, Eliza, became what the family regarded as a "remarkable musician"; she sang and played classical songs "with the greatest sweetness." During winter evenings John Chew read the most recent books aloud to the family, gathered around

---

* There were four other representatives who could single-handedly have elected Jefferson: the one pro-Burr member from Vermont, the two others from Maryland, and little Rhod) Island's single member.

the fire. A younger daughter remembered the excitement that greeted the appearance of a new novel by Scott.[7] So everything went on tranquilly until there appeared in the neighborhood a Quaker evangelist considered the most effective since George Fox.

Stephen Grellet (Etienne de Grellet du Mobillier) had belonged to a Royalist family. His parents were imprisoned during the French Revolution. He had fought vainly for the restoration of the Crown, wandered in exile, and been converted to Quakerism.[8] It was during February, 1809, that he preached at the meetinghouse nearest to Fairland, at Indian River. As he spoke, his eye was caught by an attractive woman who was conspicuous because of her fashionable clothes. Recognizing her when they actually met several years later, he told Mary Snowden Thomas that he had watched on her face the impact of his preaching. "I thought there was something good in thee, that day."[9]

In slave states, Grellet preached primarily against slavery, nailing home his points with moving anecdotes. He told how a physician, called to visit a sick slave, was led by the owner into "a miserable cabin," where he saw "the poor slave stretched on a little straw." The owner addressed the slave "with very coarse epithets," shouting: "By pretending to be religious and going to your meetings, you have got this sickness, but, as soon as you are better, I will cure you with a thousand lashes!" The physician, Grellet continued, "told the owner that from all appearances the poor man had only a few moments to live — upon which the slave suddenly raised himself, lifted up his eyes, and, stretching forth both hands, said in an audible voice, 'I thank Thee, Lord Jesus, my blessed Redeemer, for all Thy mercies to Thy poor servant; now receive my spirit into Thy Kingdom' — and then expired. The slaveholder stood speechless and amazed; amidst his threats and reproaches, the poor slave was taken out of his power. His spirit had triumphantly quitted its afflicted tenement. The slaveholder and the physician both remained silent for about ten minutes, and, without uttering a word, the latter mounted his horse, and left the place with impressions that continued deep upon him, as he related the circumstance to me."[10]

Mary Thomas returned home with the impression of Grellet's sermon deep upon her. What about the slaves at Fairland? They were treated well, but the basic abomination of bondage remained. Although most were part of her inheritance, according to the laws of the time they were the property of her husband. He too became deeply troubled. The ultimate conclusion to free the slaves — they numbered nearly a hundred and were unusually valuable because they were well trained — was reached by the Thomases after almost a year of soul searching.

"As soon as his intention was known," so a grandson was told by his Aunt Henrietta (1799–1874), "every possible pressure was brought on him by his friends to dissuade him: the serious loss of money involved; the loss of caste; the difficulty of procuring free labor; the supposed result of turning loose so many vagabonds on the community; and the danger of causing dissatisfaction on the part of slaves of other families — even the risk of producing that abiding dread of all slave-holding communities, a slave rebellion."[11] And surely further resentment was stirred up by the unpleasant appeal to the neighbors' consciences: the morality of slavery was an issue not discussed in such polite southern circles as those to which the Thomases belonged.

Furthermore, freeing slaves was not the uncomplicated act of humanity envisioned by modern hindsight. It could be shirking responsibility or actual cruelty. A slave serving a just planter could count on support for life: he was fed, clothed, and housed; nurtured when too young to work; nursed in sickness; supported until death in invalidism or old age. A slave freed because he was not worth his keep could die by the roadside. And able-bodied free blacks were in danger of being kidnapped and resold to infinitely worse bondage on the steaming plantations of the Deep South. Benevolence required great care in freeing slaves. Schools for freed Negroes were set up by the Quakers, but they were badly attended.

John Chew Thomas's deed of manumission (dated April 23, 1810), which has through the mazes of family inheritance come into my possession, is not the major deed, but deals only with twenty young slaves all of whom had been hired out to work for others. Three males and one female, Flora, were freed at once, but Flora's three children would not be free until her sons were twenty-eight, her daughter twenty-five. Various younger slaves were to be freed at various dates: two girls, Phoebe and Mary, not until 1820, which implies that they were in their early teens. None of the six younger girls had borne children: any they might have while still slaves would be held until the males were twenty-five or twenty-eight, the females until they were eighteen, twenty-one, or twenty-five. There is no explanation for the difference in the specified ages. An interesting aspect of this document is that there is no recognition of marriage or the identity of fathers.[12]

Henrietta, who eventually brought up Helen Flexner's father, was then eleven. She remembered how heartily she wept when the slaves departed, "for she loved some of them, and they were not, she said, desirous to go, although they were glad of freedom." According to Henrietta, the slaves too young to be released were hired out and their

wages laid aside so that they would have nest eggs when their time finally came. Arranging that the slaves freed at once should go to the free
state of Pennsylvania, the Thomases "took pains to see that they were
properly started in life. . . . None of them became vagabonds, and we
were able to trace them for years, and all did well."[13]

Henrietta insisted that the manumission had bred no discontent
among slaves in the neighboring plantations. However, the slaveholders
remained indignant. Although their relations stood by them, the Thomases were generally snubbed or insulted in the circles in which they
had formerly moved. They sold Fairland for $50,000 and moved to the
city of Baltimore.

The $50,000 received for Fairland was in those years a large sum but
nothing in the Thomases' experience had taught them how to make
money breed money, or even how to hold on to capital not in tangibles.
The eldest son, Thomas Snowden Thomas, found an alluring business
opportunity — it probably involved the "road stock" which John Chew
tried for the rest of his life vainly to turn into cash — and, having been
backed by his father, not only lost the whole fortune but threw the family, to their amazement, into debt. They left Baltimore, first for the corner of Maryland that was furthest from the slave fields, and then for the
west bank of the Delaware in free Pennsylvania. "The cup . . ." daughter Henrietta remembered, ". . . seemed very bitter."[14]

In various ways the Thomas fall was more grievous and damaging
than that suffered by the Flexners decades later, after the collapse of
Hirsch and Flexner. The Louisville family had for some years climbed
up one side of a low economic hill and had then slipped down the other.
The Thomases had tossed themselves over a precipice. At the bottom,
they still had greater assets than the Flexners ever had, but the descent
had been a hundred times greater.

The Flexners' decline engendered no controversy or hatred in their
neighbors. Their difficulties were indeed commonplace among the immigrant merchants who, as they tried to rise quickly, often fell back
again. And the Flexner nemesis, the Panic of 1873, toppled many a
business.

No society in the United States was more stable, less responsive to
outside economic shifts, than the aristocratic plantation world of the
pre–Civil War South. The Thomases had not been pushed around by
exterior economic forces. Their phenomenal decline resulted from an act
of the parents' own will, consciously and prayerfully undertaken, in

obedience to the noblest principles. How far did this make the result easier to bear? Does a man who has lost his eyesight during a heroic rescue not sometimes curse the dark and his own high motives that had brought his loss upon him? And what of the children who had been separated from their birthright, subjected to economic imperatives which they had in their natural environment been taught to despise?

Under Esther's efficient leadership, the Flexners had, as their fortunes declined, shrunk their expenses to suit their income. Henrietta came to realize that the Thomas family should have practiced, consistently with the act that had created their situation, "the simplicity and plainness of Quakers," rather than "indulging in many expenses and bad habits, striving to equal their neighbors."[15] But the Thomases could not bear to drown themselves in strange and, it seemed to them, degrading waters. Henrietta's letters, which were crowded with news of relatives, reveal with what passion the exiles tried to hold on to old associations. Yet, actually seeing their relatives opened wounds. On a trip to Montpelier, "Mother was much affected but bore the reminiscences better than I expected."[16] When Henrietta, visiting in her old world, witnessed the whipping of some slaves, she felt cowardly because she did not intervene. She dared do no more than slip out into the night, after her hosts slept, to comfort and feed the victims.[17] Hospitality was, of course, essential to all southern relationships, but after the Thomases had been reduced to employing, as the Flexners did in Kentucky, only a single "maid of housework," they dreaded visits that would reveal their shame.

The daughters were helpless. Julia married at the age of thirty-seven Bond Valentine, an elderly Quaker preacher, who soon died, leaving her a childless widow.[18] Henrietta, plain and unable to afford ameliorating finery, steeled herself to being an old maid. "Riches," she wrote, ". . . are the one thing that is needful according to the present code of laws. With them, you are amiable, attractive, and desirable; without them, insignificant and worthless."[19]

Of the four sons, only the third, Richard Henry (Helen's grandfather), had the determination and vitality to operate successfully in the new environment they all faced. He secured an M.D. from the University of Pennsylvania and gradually built up a practice in Baltimore. His purposeful, hard work annoyed his siblings. Henrietta addressed him as "most potent, grave, and reverend signor . . . feeling pulses, blistering, etc., with imperturbable gravity." Brother Samuel sneered: "Our Sir Dick will be a rich man one of these days. I always thought he knew how to calculate well."[20] (PLATE 9)

Richard's three brothers, Thomas, Samuel, and John Chew, Jr., could not really get their teeth into anything. John also procured a medical degree, but he made no serious effort to practice. "We all want energy," Henrietta wrote Richard. "Sometimes I despair."

The family set up a quarry, but "nothing is done in quarrying stone. There is some difficulty in procuring men to work, and you know some of us are not of a disposition to overcome difficulties." She mourned the contrast with their brother-in-law, George Gray Leiper, who was "always in high spirits and uses the greatest exertion. The most indefatigable man I ever saw."[21]

The Leipers, who had been brought into the Thomas family when the musical Eliza married George, stood for the new world into which the Thomases had thrown themselves. George's father, Thomas Leiper, had built mills to manufacture tobacco products. When he located an outcropping of stone that would support a profitable quarry, he was not stopped because the stone was back from the navigable Delaware and somewhat above it. He built America's first permanent tramway, which can be ruled, by using favorable definitions, the first railroad in the United States. After grading the hillside, he laid two lines of oak scantling four feet apart. These supported the flanged cast-iron wheels of a long, thin wagon which, when empty, was light enough to be drawn uphill by a single horse. Loaded with stone, it was pulled by gravity to Leiper's wharf beside the Delaware. Leiper did not call the mansion he built near his mills and quarry an impersonal name like Montpelier or Fairland. He named it after himself: Lapidea.[22]

We can visualize John Chew Thomas, before his plunge in fortune, deploring the go-getter family into which his eldest daughter had married. But after "poverty" had come upon him, he found Lapidea a welcome haven, and longed to have his sons catch some of the Leipers' money-making magic. The drooping Thomases proved immune, but in 1830, when the Leipers procured a tremendous contract for stone to build the Delaware breakwater, they hired John Chew, Jr., and Samuel. The father heaved a sigh of relief that "two of my sons now have means afforded for profitable employment."[23]

John Chew, Sr., became obsessed with what he had never before had to worry about: money. His letters mention almost nothing else. Since there always seemed to be better opportunities in another place than where he was, he was always on the go. He dreamed of big achievements that would at one stroke raise his family to "comfort." Perhaps he could sell the old, disastrous "road stock" for fifty dollars a share; perhaps Charles Calvert, to whom he owed £7,211, would see reason and forgive what Thomas regarded as an unfair debt — or at least forget the interest. Perhaps he could organize a company "to turnpike" the "great post road" from Chester to Philadelphia, the shareholders collecting tolls.

In the meanwhile, he bought anything he thought he could sell at a profit; borrowed from banks and paid back in belated installments. He got into the business of manufacturing whetstones, sending them by the hundreds to Baltimore for his efficient son Richard to sell.

As one reads the frenzied correspondence of the former plantation aristocrat so reduced to scrounging, there emerges, combined with self-pity and chagrin, an overtone of excitement, of pleasure in the wild dance into which the aging man had been driven. It had been a standard occupation among his former companions to fill idle hours with gambling, often for stakes that were high but not really crucial for a man of means. Now he was gambling for his livelihood, without the monotony of one card laid upon another in duplicating game rooms among his social peers.[24]

Despite all difficulties, John Chew and Mary Snowden Thomas continued to express pride at what they had done. Had they not given "close attention to the leading of Truth"? But the father suffered from perpetual guilt in relation to his children. A southern gentleman with many generations behind him, John felt it the duty of an aristocrat to nurture his descendants, to perpetuate family position. Having abdicated this function, for however noble a reason, was a dreadful thing, all the more because almost all of his offspring had been so dreadfully wounded.

John Chew was even uneasy at not supporting Richard, who could so well support himself. When the Baltimore doctor married the daughter of a wealthy banker, the self-exiled plantation owner felt deep humiliation that he could not match the largesse of the rich businessman father-in-law, could not indeed help endow the marriage with any gift at all.

9

The Midnight Cry

DURING 1830, at the age of twenty-two, Richard Henry Thomas was confronted in the most poignant form with the choice of whether or not to follow "the leadings of Truth," which his parents had dramatically followed. He had been so in love with a young lady in Baltimore (her name is never mentioned in the Thomas papers) that he had hesitated to go away to the University of Pennsylvania to secure his medical diploma lest her favor turn elsewhere. On his return, he proposed and was accepted. But Henrietta was soon writing her brother that he should be grateful to "that merciful Being" who withdrew the veil and revealed "the cold and flinty rock which would inevitably have shipwrecked your happiness."[1]

His fiancée's father, identified as one of the richest men in Baltimore, was a slaveholder, but this seemed to present no problem as the girl professed to be a Quaker. What was Richard's "surprise and sorrow" when the fiancée casually stated that she intended to bring along some house slaves her father had given her. To Richard's protests she replied that she had no objection to his keeping his own scruples, but she had no intention of appearing before her friends as a self-righteous prude. When Richard told her she would have to choose between him and the slaves, she chose the slaves.[2]

Richard was so upset that for a while he feared for his sanity, but within a year and a half he fell in love with the exact opposite of the pert and sprightly girl who had preferred her slaves to him. He was attracted by the "unobtrusive modesty and sweetness of manner," by the "timidity and diffidence," of Martha, the daughter of James Carey.[3] Their son

James Carey Thomas attributed his own "over-acuteness of sensibility" to his inheritance from his mother, and it may well have been passed on to Martha's granddaughter, Helen Thomas Flexner, and even to the author of this volume, her great-grandson, whose full name is James Carey Thomas Flexner. But Martha's diffidence entirely skipped over the granddaughter most exactly named after her: the determined Martha Carey Thomas, who became president of Bryn Mawr.

Although the Careys have become an important family in Baltimore, the snobbish Thomas genealogist preferred to whisk James Carey on the scene from nowhere, allowing him no forebears. All we know is that James Carey Thomas pointed out to his daughter M. Carey a mean cabin by a stream in the wrong part of Baltimore as the first Maryland home of the Carey family.[4]

James Carey raised himself, as Simon Flexner was to do, by his own bootstraps. He secured "a considerable fortune" in shipping and importing and became president of the Bank of Maryland. He married into the Ellicott family, who applied various mechanical inventions of their own to their tremendously prosperous flour mills in what is still called Ellicott City, near Baltimore. On the matter of slavery Richard had nothing to fear: a dozen years before John Chew Thomas had taken his decisive step, James Carey had helped organize the Maryland Society for the Abolition of Slavery and the Relief of Free Negroes.[5]

Shortly after marrying Martha in 1830, Richard wrote that it was entrancing to see how "the new train of affections" dispelled Martha's gloom. But her first child died in infancy. She had two more sons: James Carey Thomas and John Chew Thomas. Then her father died and her cough came on.[6]

Richard was, after his wife's death, to publish *Memoir of Martha C. Thomas, Late of Baltimore, Md.* (1841), which went through many editions and remained in print for several generations. The appeal of this little volume was as a religious tract. It told how a woman afflicted with morbid melancholia sought throughout a long illness and found on her deathbed surcease by abandoning herself to God. The evangelical purpose was strengthened by the objectivity of a doctor's scientific report, although he suppressed the nature of her illness, undoubtedly to avoid the then-dreaded word "tuberculosis."

When an ocean voyage was prescribed, Martha expressed fear, but was finally persuaded. She and Richard "traveled leisurely through England, France, and Ireland." Quaker meetings were always on their stopping list, but "she was never once tempted to visit any place of

public amusement, however attractive, on the pretext of its being innocent." She did allow herself to be "shown many castles, palaces, and
princely domains of noblemen and kings. Though their splendor and
magnificence struck her with surprise, the prevailing sentiment in her
mind was 'all is vanity.' " However, her husband was exhilarated by
everything he saw.[7]

As postage was charged according to the number of sheets of paper,
Richard used for each letter home a single sheet measuring a foot and a
quarter by almost two. Folded, it provided four large pages. These being
inadequate to express his enthusiasms, he employed a method cursed by
scholars who have to read such manuscripts: in a loose hand through
which the sentences underneath were supposed to be legible, he wrote
up and down across pages already written on horizontally. His ecstasies
started in New York: "I have seen nothing to compare with it. So vast,
so grand, so rich, so thronged, such forests of masts, such bustle of business!"[8] From abroad, he tried to describe everything: architecture; the
paintings he saw on the walls of great houses; the animals in the zoos;
the carts on the roads. In Paris the Thomases stayed at the Meurice, opposite "the garden of the Tuileries. . . . Thousands of well-dressed people throng the avenues or plant themselves on chairs placed alongside. A
band of music is added, children flock about, all seemed gay and light-
hearted, delighted to see and be seen. What a world of levity, irreligion,
corruption, and depravity Paris is, is shocking to think of."

The sudden change of tone was undoubtedly because Martha had
looked over his shoulder. She added a postscript: she and a female companion had had "a hearty cry" over the immorality of the French.[9]

When the Thomases got back to America, they learned that their
younger son had died. Martha's worsening condition called for a southern climate. They went to St. Augustine, Florida. The climate proved
"raw and damp . . . and the town was threatened with an attack by Indians, who approached within a few miles, burning houses and killing
inhabitants." But they dared not return north "at imminent risk of ag-
gravating her symptoms." Finally, a column of smoke rising from the
water heralded a steamboat which came into St. Augustine harbor in
search of wood to feed its furnaces. The captain agreed to drop the
Thomases off at Key West. During the six-day voyage, Martha "suffered much from high fever and exhaustion." Her condition was not
helped when, on waking one morning, they discovered that the boat was
burning merrily, having caught fire during the night while the crew
slept. The fire was conquered, but at Key West, where they landed, the

weather was unusually cold and their accommodations, although "the best in the place," had no chimney. As in an Indian wigwam, the fire burned on the open floor, while the smoke, supposed to exit from a hatch in the roof, hovered below in an acrid haze. Hardly the place for a tuberculosis sufferer! After almost two months, the Thomases managed "to get across to Cuba." Here they found "congenial temperature and a balmy atmosphere," plus "comparative comfort." Martha spent her time reading the Bible in "striving for the blessings she so earnestly desired."[10]

As it became increasingly certain that Martha was on the road to death, she sought assurance that she would be gathered into the Kingdom of Heaven. "She felt herself a sinner, the subject of condemnation and wrath," in need of "the interposition of a Saviour." She yearned for mystical experiences of "the acceptance in the Beloved. The want of these blessings occasioned her to mourn as one who will not be comforted. She bewailed herself as a reprobate. . . . Earnestly as she sought the blessing, it nonetheless pleased the Father of Mercies to withhold from her, for a season, the consolations of the Gospel."[11]

On May 1, with the oncome of spring and clement weather, the Thomases sailed for home. Martha's state of mind, so her physician-husband wrote, "was a very interesting one. Earnestly engaged in seeking the pearl which she prized above all price, at times she believed herself almost in possession of it, then a sense of her unworthiness would press heavily on her spirits and lead her to doubt whether it could be."[12]

At about the end of August, the break came. Returning from attending to his practice, Richard mounted to his wife's room, where he found her as usual reading her Bible. But she was unusually excited. "Doctor," she said, "I have been looking for something I had no right to expect; some supernatural intimation of my acceptance, a light from heaven as in the case of the Apostle Paul. . . . I find now that I have only to believe, and leave the rest to my Saviour, and he will in his own time grant me the assurance and pardon which I have so long sought in vain, because I looked for it in my own time and way."

"Her path was now comparatively plain, and her progress in the best things proportionally great."[13] Her need was to lay herself at the foot of the cross and have no further desire than to serve and have complete faith in Him. One morning, when her sister asked her if she felt firm, she replied, " 'Oh yes!' and hearing her little son's voice [James was then four] asked to see him, saying, 'I have given him up. It was a hard struggle, but I have given him up entirely.'

" 'An evidence,' said her sister, 'of the powerful effect of grace on the heart.'

" 'Yes,' said she, 'I hardly thought it possible at one time.' "[14]

Now she lived from day to day, regarding each one as her last. "It would be impossible to convey in words an adequate idea of the holy tranquillity which prevailed in her apartment: Death, so completely robbed of its terrors through the power of the crucified Redeemer." Not that she did not have terrible moments of doubt. On November 14, she said, "Satan has buffeted me today very sorely. Thou hast no idea how hard I have had to hold on. Sometimes he seems almost ready to snatch me away, but my Saviour holds me."[15]

On the fifteenth, Richard was awakened at an early hour by her voice repeating Scripture. Then she exclaimed, "Lord, now lettest thou thy servant depart in peace!" Finding her husband awake, she said, "Oh husband, I have had such a peaceful happy night. . . . How wonderful to think that so poor, unworthy, and miserable a creature as I am should go to heaven to be so happy." But then she confessed that she was worried because the Lord was waiting so long to take her to him. Although she was not in pain, she was afraid that her faith would not hold out and that "I should be lost at last. I desire to have my lamp full of oil and trimmed, my lamp burning ready to enter with the Bridegroom when He cometh, and to have the door barred after me." She wished to be prepared to answer instantly "the midnight cry."

When the final hour came, she turned to her husband, "Doctor, I am dying, am I not?"

"My dear, I believe thou art."

She cried out, "Oh, I am happy now — glory-glory-glory — precious Jesus; blessed be the Lord God — hallelujah — hallelujah — hallelujah! — pray! pray to Jesus; I feel his presence in this very room — Lord Jesus be with me. . . . Come, Lord Jesus." These were her last words.[16]

Richard lived for the rest of his life in the elegant town house James Carey had built for them when he had married Martha. There were stables and carriage houses, and gardens for little James to play in. After two and a half years, Richard married another banker's daughter, this one from New York. Phoebe Clapp Thomas produced six children in fourteen years.[17]

As a result of his two rich marriages, Richard was in a position to be as much a man of leisure as his plantation forebears. However, that was not the atmosphere of the urban world into which manumission had thrown him. He pursued the practice of medicine, taking advantage of his financial position to devote much time to the poor. He became a professor of obstetrics at the University of Maryland. He was the first of the Thomas line to make major use of the right of every Friend to preach. Deeply concerned with Quaker doctrine and politics, he led the Baltimore orthodox meeting in fighting various schismatics: the Hicksites on the radical side, the Wilburites on the conservative.[18] The iron in his makeup, which had enabled him to escape the repinings of his brothers and sisters, made him always determined to have his own way.

In ill health during his fifties but eager to attend a yearly meeting in England, Richard consulted the Lord and received assurances that he would be protected. What then his amazement to see his ship being driven by waves against cliffs on the coast of Wales. Even as he asked himself, " 'How can this be?' . . . her mizzen sails began to fill with wind. . . . The captain," Richard continued, "said he had never seen or heard of such a deliverance."[19]

After his second wife died of Bright's disease, Richard proposed to Deborah Hinsdale, a Quaker preacher in New York much younger than he. She was tall and blond, but gushy and encumbered with an invalid mother.* Richard agreed to take in the mother, but Deborah was worried by the fact that her suitor seemed to be dying. His friends asked him why he was preparing for marriage when he ought to be "preparing for the grave." But Richard had no intention of preparing for the grave. Using all the power that made him an effective preacher, he persuaded Deborah that he had received assurances from above that his illness was only temporary.

Resolutely, he set out with his bride on his wedding journey to Nova Scotia, but he had to send for his oldest son James to bring him home. "Wait until I am well," he said to his bride, "and I will show thee how I love thee." According to a stepson, she "marveled at his pain and patience" while "longing for the promised revival of his strength."

One evening, Richard said, "I believe I shall live to preach the gospel in California yet." The next morning he was dead. The stepson believed

---

* The mother remains anathema to atheists. As Mary Roscoe, she had lived in the house of Stephen Grellet, the very evangelist who had convinced Mary Snowden that slaveholding was evil. With Grellet, Roscoe had visited Thomas Paine during his last illness. She gave public testimony that, feeling death upon him, he had renounced his free thinking. Crying that he wished every copy of *The Age of Reason* burned, Thomas Paine had called on the name of Jesus. Needless to say, Paine's disciples regard this as a preposterous lie.[20]

that she was more upset by this denial of a promise given by God than by the actual death of her husband.[21]

Although Deborah had been married less than a year, she decided not to return to her family and friends in New York. She remained with her stepchildren and became the "Mother Thomas" whose emotional sermons at meeting so irritated the future Helen Flexner.

10

Testimony Against War

A DEVOTED feminist, who had adored her mother, Helen Thomas Flexner signed her personal letters Helen Whitall Flexner, preferring to use her mother's family name. "Even as a child," she wrote, "I felt closer to my Whitall relations than to my father's people, whom I saw so much more often."[1] Whether in fact her character was shaped more powerfully by the Whitalls with their extremism, their more impassioned religion, their literary achievements, and their tradition of dominant women than by the less flamboyant, quietly effective, aristocratic Thomases, the Whitall strain appealed strongly to the romantically emotional side of Helen Flexner's nature.

Certainly one of the most determining acts of Helen's life — her violation of convention by writing a man what was in effect a proposal of marriage — had a clear Whitall precedent. The story of Elizabeth Haddon and John Estaugh was familiar in Helen's time to most literate Americans since it had been, along with "Paul Revere's Ride," told in Longfellow's immensely popular book *Tales of a Wayside Inn*.

The daughter of rich English Quakers who owned land in West Jersey, Elizabeth Haddon had been considered remarkable for her unusual rapport with the Deity. While still in her teens, she announced to her parents that she had been commanded to cross the ocean alone and found on the family land a holy colony of Friends. Such behavior was unheard of for a young lady in those days. Yet, as Helen's Aunt Hannah wrote, "Not the most tyrannical male Friend, even if he wanted to, would ever curtail the liberty of his womankind if they could maintain that their course of action was attributable to the will of God." Sailing for America in 1702, Elizabeth Haddon established the community that included the villages (now suburban to Philadelphia) of Haddonfield and Haddon Heights. She imported from England into wooded America not only the bricks but also the boards with which she built an elegant mansion. However, she was lonely.

It was an established practice for Quaker itinerants to ask and receive lodgings from Friends wherever found. A knock on Elizabeth Haddon's door, and there stood John Estaugh, a preacher whose eloquence she had admired in England. Elizabeth soon informed her visitor that the Lord had ordered her to marry him.

Estaugh, who also held communication with the Lord, had received no matching command. Since he was middle-aged and poor, while she was young, rich, and handsome, he feared that the thoughts raised by her declaration would interfere with the religious purposes that had brought him across the ocean. He promised that he would question the Lord concerning Elizabeth. If the answer was favorable, he would be delighted to marry her. He had received no such orders when the divine voice called him back to England. He assured Elizabeth that he would continue his questioning.

God finally spoke. Estaugh reappeared in West Jersey, and the two were married. However, the divine will did not extend to their being blessed with children. Elizabeth's heir was a nephew from England, Benjamin Hopkins, who became an ancestor of Helen Flexner's.[2]

New Jersey was in effect two disparate colonies: it had two capitals. The eastern part, settled by proprietors primarily interested in financial gain, fitted comfortably with the ideas and economy of New York directly across the Hudson River. West Jersey, settled by Quaker proprietors including William Penn, was linked to the Quaker colony of Pennsylvania directly across the Delaware. Penn had at the start considered building his metropolis on the Jersey side of the river.

James, the Whitall progenitor, emigrated to the eastern shore of the Delaware in 1688, presumably from Wales.[3] The family remained in that part of West Jersey for generation after generation — prosperous Quaker farmers who intermarried with their neighbors.[4]

It was 1739 when another James Whitall married Ann Cooper. He must soon have concluded that he had used extremely bad judgment. However, down the generations, a procession of powerful "Whitall Women" (considered by a male descendant, Logan Pearsall Smith, to have been "Ogresses" all) have regarded Ann Cooper as their tutelary spirit, being the prouder of the "Cooper Snap" because its gleeful energy so often transcended common sense.[5]

The diary Ann Cooper handed on to her descendants shows her as a Quaker Jeremiah: "Oh, the fashions and the running into them! The young men wearing their hats set up behind, and it's likely will be a ribbon to tie their hair behind. The girls in Pennsylvania have their necks set off with a black ribbon: a sorrowful sight indeed.... Oh, I think could my eyes run down with tears for the abomination of the times. So much excess of tobacco. The tea is as bad and so much of it. ... And there is the calico. Oh, the calico!"

Her husband would go fox hunting on the Sabbath. Ann dreaded "fishing time" — her children fished — and thought the harvest evil because it kept the men from prayer. Her suspicion that her family was not "preserved out of wickedness" as a punishment to her for her own sins made her desire never "to laugh or say one word but what would be of service, but to grieve and mourn always for myself and my children and this wicked world." If only she could change her home from "a house of feasting" to "a house of mourning."[6]

The American Revolution had the audacity to violate Ann Cooper's principles against war with a battle fought on the Whitall farm and named after it: the Battle of Red Bank. In 1777, a British expeditionary force from New York had sailed up Chesapeake Bay, marched overland, brushed Washington aside at the Battle of Brandywine, and captured Philadelphia. They now controlled the rebel capital, but if their army were not to wither for lack of supplies, their navy would have to open the Delaware to British shipping.

The patriots had built up from the bottom of the river chevaux-defrise to rake out the bottoms of enemy ships, and at the spot where the ships would be forced to stop, or at least pause, they had placed forts on both banks of the river. Fort Mercer was raised on the wreck of the Whitall apple orchard. Patriots, whose property was thus damaged, were paid at least with certificates, but Quakers, as noncombatants, were considered Tories. The Whitalls' religion was not only outraged but they were offered no recompense.

Enter Du Plessis de Manduit, a French military engineer who was serving as a volunteer in Washington's army. He found that Fort Mercer, although garrisoned by only a few hundred militiamen, was an oblong of ditch and mud large enough to hold fifteen hundred men. Manduit cursed the Americans' inability to realize that in forts bigger was not better: since every foot of rampart had to be defended, compactness brought strength. Ordering that most of the interior be abandoned as indefensible, he cut off a corner with a wall of double boards, filled the space with the Whitalls' hay and lumber, and crowned it with a screen of branches on which the leaves still hung. Behind this, the fort's fourteen guns were mounted.

On October 22, 1777, there came marching down from Philadelphia twelve hundred Hessians in their brass helmets. Up from the ocean sailed His Majesty's *Augusta*, man-of-war, 64 guns; the *Roebuck*, man-of-war, 44 guns; a frigate, 32 guns; the *Merlin*, sloop, 18 guns; and a cloud of British row galleys, each with several cannon. As these converged on the Whitall farm the three-hundred-man garrison joined their cannon in the prepared corner of Fort Mercer, while in the river above the chevaux-de-frise the Pennsylvania navy of tiny row galleys splashed nervously. James Whitall retired to his cellar, but his wife exclaimed, "God's arm is strong and will protect me, and I may do good by staying." She sat down to her spinning, conspicuously in front of a window on the second floor of the farmhouse.

The Hessian commander, Carl Emil Kurt, Count von Donop, was aide-de-camp to the landgrave of Hesse; he scorned to attack the unprofessional mud ramparts and their handful of amateur defenders with anything more lethal than a drummer. To his own martial racket, the drummer strutted up to Fort Mercer and then intoned, "The King of England orders his rebellious subjects to lay down their arms. If they stand battle, no quarter whatsoever will be given."

Colonel Christopher Greene replied, "We ask no quarter nor will we give any." The Hessians planted their cannon; the British fleet moved into range, and the prophetess twisted flax on her spindle.

In midafternoon, the naval and Hessian artillery shouted together, but Fort Mercer did not answer with even the weakest whisper of musket fire. The sprawling dirt enclosure continued silent as a storming party dashed for it, and leaped with shouts over the walls. Inside the fort the Hessians found only an empty mud floor. Obviously, the American yokels had taken to their heels, as was to be expected!

The drummer was again called forward. Beating out a tattoo of victory, he led the jubilant troops towards a foliage-topped wooden wall which they carelessly assumed was the far rampart. Donop, who was in the shadow of the Whitall house holding in preparation a second wave of attackers, heard the beat and the cheers. Assuming victory, he advanced his column in parade formation towards the little fort-within-a-fort where the Americans waited motionless, guns cocked and matches flickering in artillerymen's hands.

The patriots finally fired at such short range that not only lead but gunwadding inflicted mortal wounds. Hessian officers could not believe their eyes and ears; and when they did believe, they could not bring themselves to order retreat from an enemy they considered so contemptible. As long as they had sword arms to move and nerves with which to move them, the officers beat at their men, keeping them lined up without cover under the fire of a foe shielded by curtains of wilted leaves. When, after fifteen or twenty minutes, the Germans finally broke, they left behind 87 dead, 101 seriously wounded.

Not to be outdone in boneheadedness by the military, the British navy ran two of its major ships, *Augusta* and *Merlin*, aground in the mud flats below Red Bank. In its agony, one of the ships sent a cannonball through the window behind which Ann was spinning. Its force being almost spent, it settled docilely at the prophetess's feet. But her iron visitant might soon be followed by another. Remembering that she suffered from the sin of pride, Ann concluded that further challenges to gunpowder in God's name might be considered by the Almighty ostentatious. She joined her husband in the cellar.

After every Hessian who could move had disappeared towards Philadelphia, Manduit, as he was to tell Lafayette, sallied forth. He was addressed from a pile of bodies by a voice that remarked in Germanic English that it had offered no quarter and expected none. When Manduit replied in his French accent that prisoners would not be harmed, a tall, bemedaled, and bloodstained body rose up on one elbow: "You appear to be a foreigner, sir. Who are you?"

"A French officer."

"Je suis content," replied Count von Donop. "Je meurs entre les mains de l'honneur même." But almost instantly the Hessian commander was in the hands not of European honor but of a New Jersey Quaker prophetess.

As the wounded were carried into her house, covering the floor in room after room, Ann Whitall took charge in an overpowering rush of energy. Her medical resource is attested to in an earlier passage of her diary: "John fell into boiling water and scalded himself so badly I thought he would go into fits. If we had put Indian meal and cold water on it, it might not have been so bad; or molasses and salt to get the fire out; or Irish potatoes, or spirits of turpentine, or sweet oil and white of egg beaten together, or oil that they paint with, linseed oil, or rattlesnake root boiled in hog's fat. Now we have got sumac root — the inside bark — boiled in hog's fat to bathe it three or four times a day, and it does a great deal of good."

As Ann attended strenuously to the wounded, she did not shirk her duty to scold each sufferer for having engaged in warfare. One of her lectures undoubtedly touched off Count von Donop's cry: "See in me the vanity of human pride! I have shone in all the courts of Europe, and I am now dying here on the banks of the Delaware in the house of an obscure Quaker." Finally, the American officers ejected, to her loud protests, the prophetess.[7]

The British did finally open the Delaware and captured the Whitall farmhouse. The owners fled. After six months, the British retreated and the Whitalls returned, to find all their movable property stolen. Another two years passed as the war flamed on elsewhere, and then James Whitall was interrupted as he sat cleaning herbs by his kitchen fire.

Across the threshold came Manduit, ushering in two more Frenchmen, one in the uniform of a French general and the other in that of an American general. They were, he explained, visiting military sites along the Delaware. They were in need of the refreshment which Mr. Whitall would no doubt be eager to afford them when he realized how greatly he was being honored. Manduit introduced the general in the French uniform as the nobly born author the Chevalier de Chastellux, and the general in the American uniform as the Marquis de Lafayette.

Chastellux noted the upshot in his diary: "The old farmer did not deign to lift his eyes nor to reply to our introducer's remarks, which were at first complimentary and then sarcastic. Except for the silence of Dido, I can think of nothing more forbidding."[8] The Frenchmen had no choice but to retreat from the room and the house. As they walked back to their boat, half annoyed and half amused, they could not have realized how fortunate they had been to have encountered in that farmhouse kitchen the male and not the female Quaker.

Ann Cooper Whitall would surely not have been satisfied to repel the military intruders with Dido's silence. On another occasion she had looked up from her sewing to see disappear up the stairs a pair of strange male legs. She followed immediately, frightened the burglar into refuge under a bed, ordered him forth, led him by the collar down to the door and out of it, slapped his face, and "bid him begone." The chance that placed Ann elsewhere saved American history from what could have been one of its most embarrassing moments. Supposing she had pulled the Marquis de Lafayette out of her house by his collar and slapped his face?

*   *   *

Any family saga is spiced by a haunted house, and when was there a better candidate than the Whitall homestead at Red Bank? More than 150 Hessian bodies, grotesque with their waxed pigtails, had been dumped from carts into shallow ditches. In military grandeur, Count von Donop was laid near the house under a crudely lettered stone. None would stay still. As pelting thunderstorms eroded the ground, thin arms emerged to sun their finger bones in the lightning, and with ponderous jocoseness whole skeletons went swimming during spring freshets. Although Louis Whitall, then inhabiting the farmhouse, refused to have any monument glorifying the battle raised on his land, he could not resist, when Donop's skull kept popping up, keeping as a souvenir this relic of the royal aide-de-camp who had so mourned dying in the house of an obscure Quaker.

The floors of the Whitall homestead continued to reveal traces of the blood that had fountained during mass amputations. Naturally, ghosts walked, or so Helen as a girl believed. On the stairway and down the halls there was a courtly bowing of dead officers. Restless militiamen crashed, again and again, invisible loads of stone on the lawn; and "a rushing sound," a "door burst violently open," preluded the Hessians' tattoo of false victory drummed out on the washbasin in the northwest upstairs bedroom.

As for Manduit, he could not resist revisiting the scene of his triumph. Who else could the French officer have been who stepped in at the window of the second floor guest chamber, pulling by the hand an attractive ghostess in the rich décolleté of eighteenth-century Paris? Too intent to note that the room was occupied, the Frenchman turned and pointed proudly to where the triumphant fort had been. But when the occupant of the bed screamed, the officer leaped with terror into thin air, pulling his companion after him.[9]

Manduit's shade need not have been frightened: Ann never rose from her grave to scold away the ghosts who haunted her old home. But she was followed, in other places, by Whitall Women even more formidable, who personally influenced the lives of Helen and Simon Flexner.

11

Private Intercourse with God

HELEN Flexner's great-grandfather John S. Whitall (1757–1843), being the youngest son, did not inherit the haunted farmhouse, but he did, through marriage, bring into the family the Haddon-Hopkins inheritance. He inhabited a large brick residence "with a pent roof over the door," in Woodbury, New Jersey; read early romantic works like Young's *Night Thoughts,* associated with the local fox-hunting squires of family and fashion, set up as a merchant, went bankrupt, and moved his family to a dirt farm.[1] In this crisis, the Cooper Snap arose in two of his daughters. Determining to found a school, they spurned the small local scene. Hannah and Sarah invaded Philadelphia in 1823. They intended, they announced, to pay off their father's debts. As a starter, they would accept creditors' daughters at half price. The "universal esteem" thus inspired among Quaker merchants set their school on a flying start to success.[2]

Their younger brother, John Mickle Whitall (1800–1877), was by no means born for farmwork. When not yet seventeen, he shipped as an apprentice on the *William Savery* for a voyage to Calcutta and Liverpool. Although he neither smoked nor drank, and resisted "the worst temptations" of a sailor's life ashore, he lived, so he later testified, "a heedless, careless life ... delighting in foolish talking, jesting, and such like ... joining my shipmates in their folly, telling long yarns and so forth ... without a God in the world." It was winning a Bible from a shipmate through the toss of a coin, and his decision "that it would be a nice thing to tell at home that I had read the Bible through," that made him "see my undone condition. ... Almost the horrors of death and hell seized me, and I feared being forever lost. Oh, the desperate sorrow and grief that possessed me! . . . However, after this deep baptism of the Spirit had reduced me and brought me low, it pleased my Heavenly Father to lift up the light of his countenance upon me, and give me a sense of forgiveness. And then the joy and peace that was my portion no tongue can describe."[3] Whitall abandoned foolish idleness. At the voyage's end, the captain gave him a testimonial: "I do not hesitate to pronounce him one of the smartest young men that ever came within my observation in the whole course of my life."[4] (PLATE 9)

The next determining event took place when Whitall was at Trenton, New Jersey, on some business for his father. After drinking tea he went to his room, and the question arose in his mind "whether the Lord did really care for His people in all the little details of their lives, and took the management of them on Himself." Being unable to reason out the matter, he prayed for some sign, and "in a little while his heart was made glad by a manifestation of the divine presence assuring him of the Lord's intervention in all our affairs." This laid the foundation, his daughter Hannah wrote, "of that singular simplicity and directness in his dealings with his Heavenly Father." He now consulted the Lord about everything.[5]

Having risen to second mate, and being back in Philadelphia, Whitall learned that the berth of first mate on the ship *America* was being filled. He was just setting out to apply when the Lord stopped him with a command that he wear Quaker plain clothes. Whitall expressed concern lest being thus accoutered would prevent his getting the job. The Lord replied that Whitall was to leave the matter to Him. Having never before worn plain clothes, the sailor had to borrow the pleated silk bonnet and the coat with a standing collar and long swallowtails which he wore to his interview. He informed the captain of the *America* that, as a Quaker, "I could not 'mister' and 'sir' him as was common." The Lord did not let him down. He got the job.[6]

Whitall was only twenty-four when he was offered the "summit of my ambition as a sailor": to superintend the building and serve as the captain of the *New Jersey*, which was to be the largest ship out of Philadelphia. She was to trade to Canton, skirting innumerable hostile shores where pirates lurked. As a matter of course, East Indiamen were armed. But a delegation of elders called on Whitall to point out that Quakerism forbid the carrying of arms.

Here was a poser to put in silent contemplation to the Lord! Whitall was assured that he could satisfy the owners by loading arms since it would be seen to that no need would arise for their use. Whitall reported this to the elders but they were not convinced. In great distress, he again "brought the matter before the Lord. He, in His mercy, as in the case of Gideon of old, gave me a second time an assurance." With no further hesitation, Whitall accepted the command. So great was his jubilation "when we were fairly at sea and I found myself truly master of the ship," that the Lord impressed upon him "a caution not to feel as Nebuchadnezzar did, and say, 'Is this not great Babylon that I have builded?' "[7]

We can visualize the majestic vessel, its square sails towering from three masts, sailing the pirate-infested China Seas, protected only by the captain who, as he stood on the quarterdeck in his Quaker plain clothes, turned his thoughts to heaven. The guns lay unshipped below. Captain Whitall was careful to radiate self-confidence, but his heart almost failed him when it was necessary to navigate the *New Jersey* close to unexplored shores. At any instant pirate sails might emerge, or fleets of rowboats filled with savage marauders.

Had the voice that months before had given his assurance truly been the Lord's? Did not the Devil have wiles? If the Lord had truly spoken, were not Whitall's very doubts indications of a lack of faith that would make the Lord desert him? He had forbidden profanity, but blaspheming sounds arose from the decks below. When he had himself been in a rage, he had been horrified to hear blasphemy issuing from his own lips. Perhaps the Lord had withdrawn his shielding arm! Was that the reason that during the months of sailing the Lord had never repeated his assurances? He was risking the valuable ship and cargo, perhaps condemning himself and his crew to death or lifelong slavery. Captain Whitall pleaded for a new reassuring word!

"Oh for the wisdom to act in this affair according to the divine will, be the consequence whatever it may! I believe the Lord's power is over all. . . . But what he requires me to do if we should be attacked by pirates I know not. Oh, for the right direction, and help to be resigned to the Lord's will!" On his knees in his cabin, he continued to beg for specific instructions — but on that subject the inner voice remained silent.[8]

The Lord did, however, impart "wisdom and judgement in conducting the ship." At night, the *New Jersey* passed nearly halfway through the pirate-haunted, narrow strait of Banca, moving without lights, "running by the lead." After dawn brightened, they got through the other half too. "Oh, how thankful I desire to be for the Lord's goodness and mercy to one who am so unworthy!"[9]

Off Java Head on the way back to Philadelphia, Captain Whitall expressed gratitude to his merciful Creator for helping him "thus far [to] preserve my faith in His power over all creatures, to prevent me from making any preparation for defense against pirates." But he dreaded the reaction of the owners on learning what he had done. "If it is the Lord's requiring . . . I desire to be willing to lose my situation for His sake. . . . I know the Lord is able to provide for my parents and sisters even in a way that seems impossible to me."[10]

But the *New Jersey* remained under Captain Whitall's command, and the question of weapons never arose again in his diary. We can only assume that the Lord accepted the expedient that enabled the Quaker-dominated legislature of Pennsylvania to protect the frontier against Indians: they voted an appropriation for the governor to spend according to his secret desire. Probably, authority for defending the *New Jersey* was assigned to some other officer than Captain Whitall.

The assurances the Quaker received from the Lord often served the owners' advantage. Vessels leaving Philadelphia before June greatly reduced their time to Canton by sailing through Sunda Strait and on through the China Sea. Departures after that date took a long way around because of the danger of running into monsoons. In 1826, the *New Jersey* did not get off until mid-July, but she made a quick passage to the strait, and the wind was fair. Captain Whitall chafed at taking the extensive detour through the Pacific. The Lord approving, he turned into the shortcut. But not with an easy heart. On November 26, near the change in the moon, he was in the China Sea, and the gale seemed to be mounting into a cyclone. He tried to comfort himself with scripture: "Can a mother forget her suckling child? Yea, she may forget, but I will not forget thee. Behold, I have graven thee upon the palms of my hands." But he remained anxious.[11] That Captain Whitall found himself thus disturbed during every crisis was doubly painful because his nerves were questioning his basic faith. At such times, he resolved never to go to sea again.

Without mishap, the *New Jersey* reached Canton in advance of a ship that had left Philadelphia three weeks earlier, but had prudently taken the eastern passage. Both vessels were loaded with ginseng. "In consequence of our early arrival, we were enabled to sell the whole of our cargo . . . before the other ship arrived." When, two months later, the *New Jersey* sailed for Philadelphia, "with a full return cargo of silk, teas, etc.," they left behind the other ship "with her cargo of ginseng still aboard and unsold."[12]

The Lord egging him on, Captain Whitall carried exaggerated

amounts of sail, defied storms, sailed full speed through perilous waters, and moved so expeditiously that with his slower craft of a previous generation he made the trip from Canton to Philadelphia in 101 days, only two days less than the all-time record for that later invention, the clipper ship.[13]

Returning in the spring of 1829 from his fourth voyage to Canton, Whitall found that the *New Jersey* had been sold. The new owner, Benjamin Wilcocks, was eager to have the triumphant captain stay on, but Whitall soon discovered that the intention was to engage in the contraband opium trade, by which the noxious drug was procured in Smyrna and smuggled into Canton in violation of Chinese law. When Wilcocks was informed of the moral stance taken by the captain, he wrote that it "lessened him in my opinion. I hope I have due and proper respect for the prejudices of my fellow man, but when a captain stipulates for the particular articles which he will take on my ship, why, let him go *you know where* for a cargo. I am done with him forever."[14]

At the age of twenty-eight, Whitall allowed this to end his seafaring career. However, for all his life he liked to be called Captain Whitall, and he enjoyed telling his adventures on wild seas and off savage coasts to his grandchildren, including Helen.

Having married and begun a family, the captain established a dry goods store on Market Street in Philadelphia. Finding retailing, as Morris Flexner was to do, "a slim affair," he moved on to wholesale operations. He was wiped out by a financial panic in 1837 as Morris was to be in 1873.

Whitall owed what would have seemed to the Flexners an unbelievably large sum: $105,000. His creditors proved to be willing to settle for seventy-five percent. Yet the Quaker bankrupt felt morally committed for the other twenty-five percent. To pay that off took years,[15] forcing on his family economy, although by no means the poverty of the Flexners. Helen was amused by a story of her mother's sassiness. When Mary spread her butter too thick, the captain reminded her that butter was expensive. "Worth every cent of it," said Mary, spreading it thicker.[16] Such behavior would have been unthinkable among the truly poor Flexners.

However, Whitall suffered from a potentially shattering quandary to which the Flexners were immune. Why had the Lord approved the disastrous involvement in the dry goods business that had cost him all his savings and eight years of unrewarded labor? Rehearsing in memory his

conferences with the inner voice, he concluded that he had misunderstood: the assent had not been as clear as he had taken it to be. And
surely the Lord's advice had helped him through the bankruptcy proceedings.[17]

During 1838, a brother-in-law and another Quaker asked Whitall to
join them in manufacturing glass. "Heavenly Father" not only approved
but, as Whitall later explained, "gave us wisdom and discretion in managing the business; gave us favor with our customers, and a quick perception of the state of things in competing for the market."[18]

Captain Whitall's conviction that the Lord directed him in his business affairs raises such questions as were eventually to induce Helen
painfully to abandon the faith in which she had been brought up. When
one businessman triumphs, another loses, and many of Whitall's competitors were good Christians, often Quakers. Why then should Heavenly Father take the captain's side?

The answer may well lie in the captain's favorite text from the Bible:
"Draw nigh unto God and he will draw nigh to you."[19] Whitall could
assume that none of his competitors were as devoted as he to personal
association with God. The captain may well have spent more time conferring with God than anyone ever has with a Freudian therapist: at
least a full hour seven days a week for more than fifty years. Being unable to bear setting out or going to bed until he had felt again the personal presence of the Lord, he held two daily sessions, morning and
night. Sometimes he had a long wait, which may have been an explanation for the tears that sometimes drenched the handkerchief he laid over
his eyes. At other times, the Lord came quickly, full of admonitions
concerning his personal and business life. Hannah wrote that her father
"made the Lord literally his partner and did nothing without consulting
him."[20]

Helen Flexner remembered: "He was a Quaker mystic, my mother
said, which meant, she explained to me, that he lived in close communion with God. . . . It was in these quiet hours that he heard God's voice.
So when I came suddenly upon my grandfather one day seated motionless in his armchair with closed eyes, I knew he was not asleep. He was
talking with God. I stopped short where I was and stood very still. Perhaps if I listened intently enough I might hear God's voice. . . . But the
room remained quiet. After a long time my grandfather opened his eyes,
saw me, and smiled at me gently. These moments of intense listening for
God's voice in the room with my grandfather are among the most vivid
memories of my early childhood. He died when I was six years old."[21]

The glassworks were at Millville in the old Whitall territory on the west bank of the Delaware. That part of New Jersey had the basic raw materials: sand in abundance and of excellent quality, and wood for fuel. The Maurice River bore into the Delaware and thus to the outside world the little fleet — at one time two sloops, two schooners, and a steamboat — that the former sea captain had collected to distribute his wares. Whiskey bottles, of course, were banned, but Whitall, Tatum and Company supplied containers for many a patent medicine that fought "female weakness" or other disorders with healthy doses of alcohol. The specialty of the company was serving doctors and apothecaries. An 1880 catalogue recently reproduced in facsimile for glass collectors runs to seventy-two pages, featuring along with more ordinary ware, cologne bottles, flat cups to hold leeches, "breast pumps" resembling old-fashioned automobile horns, brightly colored globes for drugstore windows. The enthusiastic author of a collectors' manual engages in the wildest praises — Whitall, Tatum and Company's pomade jars have the "blue-green cast of Colombian emeralds," et cetera.

The company established in 1865 the first chemical laboratory in the American glass industry.[22] It earned for the senior partner floods of gold that washed his descendants sometimes in strange directions. The Thomases were well off; the Whitalls were rich.

The captain's wife, Mary Tatum, came, as he did, from old Quaker stock in the neighborhood of Woodbury, New Jersey. A life written of her by a granddaughter — the Whitalls spawn family biographies as naturally as guinea pigs produce piglets — states that "humility [was] a striking feature of her character." From the first, "her correspondence shows how weak and faulty she felt herself to be, and how ready she was to admire and appreciate others."[23] By no means herself a Whitall Woman and utterly devoid of the Cooper Snap, she became dominated by her daughters, including Helen's mother, who were Whitall Women indeed.

The wooing by Captain Whitall had frightened Mary Tatum. She feared that she could not be a suitable companion for so religious a man. But he swept her into marriage on December 5, 1830. Although she regretted the simplicity he had insisted on for their wedding,[24] she soon reached out for orthodoxy as a solid rock to cling to. She considered music irreligious. When, during Helen's childhood, a visit from her was expected in Baltimore, it was necessary to "hide" the piano. This was done by pushing the instrument into a corner of the living room and covering it with a rug. Serious-minded little Helen noted sententiously the hypocrisy behind this subterfuge.[25] The child could not know how consistently her mother and her aunts disguised their religious radicalism from her grandmother.

Mary Tatum's true concern was with domesticity, and in this she was increasingly seconded by her husband. After the glassworks were a self-perpetuating success, he retired from active leadership. He had then little to draw him out in the world. Although before the Civil War he had set up a mission to receive runaway slaves and help establish them in freedom, after the war was over he laid to one side the crusading, reforming spirit of his ancestors. Now concerned primarily with his personal relationship to the Lord, he became one of those "Inner Light Quakers," who were taking over the Philadelphia Meeting, but were to become a target for the Cooper Snap of his daughters.

From the time when his children were in their teens to his death when grandchildren abounded, Captain Whitall addressed his intelligence, power, and charm to the enhancement of opulent family living. Rich in the double sense of having a large capital and new money that came pouring in, he did not seek the grandeur of which the Friends disapproved, but wallowed in solid comfort: a city house as large but not as conspicuous as a mansion; country residences by the seashore or on broad acres with monumental trees; furniture, not elegant but upholstered to lull the body; and, of course, *food*. Eschewing alcohol and also sex indulged in for enjoyment, the Quakers reveled in what a weight-conscious generation would call gluttony. The Whitall board groaned (to use an old, happy phrase) under the richest soups, the best meat and vegetables, and sweets in redundance: pies and cakes and candies, and, as a standard treat for adults as well as children, ice cream. In Helen's childhood it was a much-enjoyed ritual during Sunday dinner for all the grandchildren — sometimes as many as a dozen — hilariously to run around the table shaking down the food they had eaten to make room for more.[26] (PLATE 12)

John and Mary Whitall established a tradition of family solidarity that was very different from the Flexners' compulsive alliance against penury. The Whitalls joined together to enjoy the good things of life in mutual love — or at least affection.

Buoyed up by their father's benignant energy and their mother's sheltering tenderness, the four children became, according to conventional canons, dreadfully spoiled, but they thrived on it. The one son, James

Whitall, carrying on profitably at Whitall, Tatum and Company, was a solid Quaker citizen who cooperated with his eventual brother-in-law James Carey Thomas on many educational and philanthropic ventures. There were three daughters: Hannah (born in 1832), Sarah (born in 1833), and Mary (born in 1836), who was Helen Flexner's mother. In their household, where the aging captain was the undoubted patriarch, the girls cemented a friendship of such remarkable intimacy that it overshadowed, after all three married, their relationships with their husbands. It was the Cooper Snap multiplied by three, devoted to extremities of religious seeking, a love of their own children that greatly favored their daughters, and a growing disdain for the male sex.

12

―――――-･-◦❦◦-･--―――――

A Young Marriage

WHEN Richard Henry Thomas — he of the three wives and the lu-
crative medical practice — married for the second time, his new
wife did not take on the care of her stepson, James Carey Thomas.
James remained in the charge of his maiden aunt, Henrietta, who had
been his surrogate mother ever since his own mother lay dying. Because
of Henrietta's influence, the boy who was to be the father of the future
Helen Flexner took a partial step backwards through time to the Thomases' plantation days.

His childhood home was, of course, a contemporary city home. Richard Henry's wives were all city women. But Henrietta, who was considerably older than Richard, had been eleven when the slaves were freed,
and a young woman when penury overwhelmed the graces to which she
had been reared. Prosperous again in the house of the brother she most
loved, Henrietta blossomed (despite her continued hatred for slavery)
into so much an epitome of the old South that she was alien and annoying to James's eventual wife, Mary Whitall, who stemmed from rural
New Jersey and middle-class Philadelphia.

It had been required of Richard Henry, if he were not to join his
brothers in crippling regrets, to break sharply with the plantation life
that had been pulled out from beneath him. There was no such stress to
prevent James from mingling naturally Henrietta's teachings with his
urban experience.

Thus he was more susceptible than his father had been to such advice
as this from Henrietta: "All kinds of knowledge is useful to a man of the
world, and none more than that of human nature. History and belles-

lettres expand the mind, and remove the professionalism in those who
have chosen a particular branch of science. I would have you be a
polished gentleman as well as a skillful practitioner."[1] How proud
Henrietta would have been to know that her pupil would be praised
by the "Zeus-like philologist" B. L. Gildersleeve, for "a rounded and
triumphant career worthy of the envy of any man of good will."[2]

One of James's half brothers remembered that Henrietta had "a mind
cultivated rather than soundly educated according to modern standards. . . . She was a great lover of poetry, and her mind was well stored
with poets held in the greatest honor at the beginning of this century,
and her conversation sparkled with quotations from Dryden, Pope,
Cowper, and Shakespeare, and not a few Latin proverbs, learned from
her father."[3] From Henrietta, James imbibed a deep love of literature
which inspired even more deeply his daughter Helen.

But there was nothing in Henrietta's attitudes to prepare James for
the resolute feminism in which he was to become immersed when he
married a Whitall Woman. "I never felt interested in having the equality
of the sexes established . . . ," Henrietta wrote. "Woman's influence is
and certainly ought to be great, but I would like it to be like the gentle
dew, felt not seen."[4]

In due course, James attended the Quaker college at Haverford, near
Philadelphia, where he roomed with his future wife's brother, James
Whitall. Becoming an intimate of the Whitall household, he flirted with
Sarah, who was the right age. But following them around, and having to
be avoided when a sentimental passage was toward, was little Mary, at
first a nuisance and then, as time passed, a revelation. James had finished
at Haverford, received a medical degree from the University of Maryland, and was assisting in his father's practice when he acknowledged
that he had been overwhelmed by the beauty of the younger sister.

The vision that entranced him returned to haunt their grandson when
I came upon the little daguerreotypes that James and Mary exchanged
after they became engaged.[5] She was eighteen, he twenty-one. A long
neck carries Mary's head high over extremely sloping shoulders. The copious hair is (as revealed by a swatch that lies before me) golden brown.
Parted with simplicity in the middle, the hair, gathered behind, billows
in natural waves. The broad, noble, tranquil forehead, so often described by her admirers, is terminated by long and level eyebrows that
impart an openness to the lower part of the face. Brown eyes — gentle,
confiding, firm — are generously spaced beside a nose short but jutting

strongly outward. The mouth, not full but wide, is curved in a composed smile over a chin that implies the firmness of later years.

The focus, more than a century ago, of the daguerreotypist's camera caught an expression that adds fascination to an appealing vision. We see charm enhancing beauty, gentleness that does not exclude resolution, control implying darker forces that need control, an adolescent melancholy signaling temperamental depths. This is a face to be loved, to be cherished, and perhaps to be feared. Is it altogether an illusion based on other knowledge that makes her grandson, as he stares at the image less than four inches high, conscious of hypnotic power drawing him in? For Mary's beauty, which took on an increasingly spiritual cast, enabled her to dominate her environment, her husband, and her daughters, including, to a frightening degree, Helen. (PLATE 10)

Her fiancé's daguerreotype, which he called, in sending it to her, "the sun's impression of me," reveals an altogether different physique.[6] James Carey Thomas is short, stocky, broad of shoulder, heavy of limb. His hair (a dark, powerful red, as we know from other sources) rises from his scalp in the same strong, tight curls that were to make my own red hair almost impossible to comb. His forehead, although high, is broader than its height, creating, I am sure, my own problem of finding ready-made hats that are large enough. The strong brows have at their extremities downward curves. The brown eyes, close in color to his hair, are so large and widely spaced as not to be overweighted by a broad nose expanding into full nostrils. Below the ears the powerful cheekbones curve inward, giving his face, as it descends to a long, strong chin, the shape of an heraldic shield. The expression is a vulnerable eagerness, a romantic sensibility touching on such large, heavy features. (PLATE 10)

When he was visiting the Whitalls over the Fourth of July in 1854, James proposed marriage. Mary was surprised to find herself acknowledging "feelings and affections that lurked in my heart, where they would have remained in their safe hiding place unknown even to myself had they not been called forth." Her parents were more than surprised, they were displeased. They considered her too young. The "ease and indulgence" of her parents' opulent domesticity had, indeed, so enveloped her that at eighteen she still, as she acknowledged, thought of herself as "a girl." In her first letter to her fiancé she wrote: "Thy fancyings concerning my employment of time in the past are quite correct. My days flow on uniformly, with very little excitement and a great deal of private enjoyment." She contrasted her life "with the anxieties of thine." He, indeed, was finding his introduction to medical practice so harrowing that he wondered if he were not too sensitive for the profession he had inherited.[7]

Her reluctant parents would agree only to a long engagement, during which the lovers were to be much separated. Many letters passed between them. Hers are so carefully inscribed, as to indicate conscious repression, the lines straight and even, the margins perfect perpendiculars. No clumsy sentences, misspellings, or scratch-outs. No girlish giggling, or high spirits. No rages or jealousies or doubts. The tone is cheerfully positive, but never ecstatic. When her lover complained that she seemed too contented with their separation, she replied, "I am sure thee would not think so if thee could see me at present. I am in the depths." But she could not resist adding, "I look forward to being as gay as ever this evening."[8]

Occasionally her control broke. The death of James's stepmother inspired her to passionate sympathy, and her disappointment when he was held back from an expected visit elicited an unabashed love letter. Very prophetic of her future troubled and triumphant religious course were her reactions when led by curiosity to attend a Methodist service, where she heard religious music — it was banned from meeting — for the first time. They chanted "several psalms beautifully and in the end they sang a hymn which was the most exquisite touching thing I ever heard. The deep tones of the organ mingling with the full, clear voices of the singers seemed to fill the whole church and make most exquisite harmony that it seemed unearthly. . . . I do not think I should like to go often as I can easily believe I could soon become fascinated with the music and the air of holiness and devotion which pervades the whole place." But she made herself conclude that the "service" only incited a "romantic kind of religious emotion" which could not be really effective or lasting.[9]

James's letters mingled religion with expressions of love which he had to keep from becoming too ardent lest she tease him for writing "gush." "Oh, Mary, is it not strange that two beings till a few days ago comparatively little known to each other, should now feel so absorbing an interest, a tie stronger than life, which binds their two souls together, no matter how far separated in body; and yet how beneficent the designs of our Heavenly Father for our happiness — who thus affords the scope for the development of those happy sentiments which unite them forever and make love's fetters, though apparently but roses, no less strong by reason of their beauty and sweetness."[10]

The bent that made the physician, when a trustee of Johns Hopkins

University, greatly concerned with the departments of language and literature, is copiously signaled. He was in danger, he wrote, of turning his head into the tower of Babel, because he was endeavoring to add German and French to his "some Latin, less Greek . . . a little Italian, to say nothing of English and doctors' gibberish." In another letter, he described how at night he prowled the streets because in the dark people unconsciously dropped the defensive mask they wore in the daytime, thereby revealing "the workings of passion and the play of feelings. . . . Often I have been struck when the gleam of a chance lamp has happened to fall on the countenance of some passer-by to see how plainly could be read in its master-feeling: joy or despair or avarice."[11] To these sallies Mary attempts no reply, although she asks him to tell her what he is reading so that she can feel close to him, by reading it too. Preferably by moonlight. Mary had a passion for moonlight.

So the months pass until finally it is agreed that the couple may marry at the end of November, 1854. As the date approaches, the regularity of Mary's written pages shatters: ragged lines now and scratch-outs. She expresses lack of faith in her adequacy to meet the responsibilities of marriage. She expresses in highly emotional terms her unhappiness at the "thought of leaving my dear father and mother."[12]

It is traditional for brides to expatiate on the glories of the married state, but this was not the style of Mary Whitall Thomas. Her first existing letter as a wife, addressed to her sister Sarah, begins, "I have just finished sewing buttons on the Doctor's [she was always so to refer to her husband] shirts, keeping time to the needle with "The Child's Grave at Florence" drawled out as you and I used to do up at our own room at Germantown. It reminded me of thee so much, and of the dear old times — for dear they were and no mistake, even if these are dearer. But, alas, what it is to be a bride!" She was interrupted by call after call of compliment from her husband's friends and connections. She had been "trying to persuade the Dr. to give up his cigar for today," when yet another caller was announced.

"It seems a perfect age," since, when departing from her wedding, she had "beheld the light of thy tear-stained countenance." How soon could Sarah come to visit? "Don't be the least concerned by our wanting to try how it feels to be alone. I have not the slightest desire to experience the delights of entire solitude except when my good husband chances to come in."[13]

Alive with historical irony was Mary's resentment of a reception given partly in her honor by her husband's kinsman Johns Hopkins. The munificent bequests Hopkins left behind him were to revolutionize American higher education and medicine. They were to play a major role in the careers of her husband and her daughter Carey, of her daughter Helen's husband Simon Flexner and brother-in-law Abraham Flexner. But Mary found Johns Hopkins's party "a species of torture." She felt slighted and was surrounded by strangers. "Two other brides there and who knows what else!"[14]

Already at heart a primadonna, the beautiful Mary was unwilling to be absorbed into her husband's environment.

Captain Whitall had built, as a wedding present for his daughter Mary, a small but elegant house on a Baltimore block originally purchased by James Carey's grandfather for his married daughters. The larger of the two resulting houses now belonged to James's uncle, Galloway Cheston, and the other to Richard Henry Thomas. Mary had been married for two years when her father-in-law moved to the country, and she was urged to move from the house her father had built for her to her husband's "gloomy" childhood home. Responding with hysteria, she begged her parents to rush from Philadelphia and intervene.[15] Nonetheless, the move was made, it being argued that the more conspicuous location would increase her husband's practice by a thousand a year.

Although her father-in-law became important to her as a religious teacher, Mary never got on well with her husband's relatives or with Baltimorean society, which, in writing her parents, she referred to scornfully as "the natives."[16] It may well be that Mary, who defined her own greatest sin as "pride," resented coming into that tight, dynastic world as an outsider. In any case, she continued to regard her parents and two sisters as the "home ones," and longed, when in Baltimore, for visits from "homebodies." Taking her children as they accreted, she made long stays with her parents in town or country, often joining there her sisters with their broods.

The Civil War increased Mary's strain with her Baltimore environment, where the traditional society identified with the South. The issue was close to home. Union troops were fired on as they passed through the streets between railroad stations. The city, subsequently occupied by a Union garrison, was several times in danger of being besieged by southern troops. Mary and James, of course, were both abolitionists, but beyond that their attitudes veered. James, whose forebears had of their own volition freed their slaves, believed that the South, if left alone, would have itself solved the problem. He blamed the war on northern firebrands, and found himself unable to vote for Lincoln because of his backers. But Mary made no secret of her strong Union sentiments. When Lincoln, whose moderation had won James over, was assassinated, both Thomases wept, but Mary saw a bright side: Lincoln would have been "reluctant to administer justice to the Rebels. They will not fail to get it now — and they know it!"[17]

Fifteen months after her marriage, Mary gave birth to her first child. The emergence of Martha Carey Thomas, the future president of Bryn Mawr, utterly shattered Mary's cherished coolness and self-control. Despite her dislike of the sentimental passages in her husband's letters, which she described as "gush," surely no woman in the history of procreation ever "gushed" more about her baby, whose every pose and action seemed to her "cute" beyond belief. The word "sweet," which was surely never applied to M. Carey Thomas after she grew to her full, dominant stature as dictator of Bryn Mawr College, sounds down the mother's ecstatic pages like a reiterating gong.[18]

When Carey was four, her mother enthusiastically reported to a sister how the child had run amuck "throwing things about everywhere, breaking windows, pulling beds to pieces, taking the clothes from the washtub and hiding them in the parlor. . . . The Doctor was in despair." Her own reaction was that Carey "demonstrated her capacity to do thoroughly whatever she undertakes."[19]

All three of the Whitall sisters were fecund, but Mary the most of all. Over a period of twenty years she bore ten children (eight grew to maturity). Her pregnancies were on the whole not difficult. After the second birth, she asked rhetorically concerning babies, "Are they not the sweetest things in nature?" When her fifth child, succeeding three boys, proved to be another girl: "To have two daughters seems too lovely to be possible." Concerning her eighth child, she informed her sister Sarah that the newborn baby was "sleeping quietly upstairs. She certainly makes my hands full. But little Helen pays. She is quite the essence of sweetness, looks up into my eyes so steadily and so lovingly and so appreciatively, and answers a bright look with a smile. She is as good as gold."[20]

Born on August 14, 1871, Helen Whitall Thomas was eight and a half years younger than her future husband, Simon Flexner.

III

The Long Road Upward

13

The Gate Opens

IN remembering his long voyage "in and out of wretched jobs leading nowhere," Dr. Flexner commented, "To what a vast number of men and women does this aimless thing happen?" But his narrow escape from death made his family, when he was again well enough to work, "view me more considerably." Instead of sentencing him to "any kind of job," they considered his future "seriously." The decision, probably arranged by his brother Jacob, that he should become an apprentice in Dr. Vincent Davis's drugstore, was, he remembered, "one of the most important events in my life."[1]

"It was a most fortunate accident that brought me into a gentle atmosphere under a very nice, kind man, and in a business patronized by people with good manners." What a contrast to the squalor of Dobbin's drugstore, where he had fled into writing his epic, "*A Dying Arab to His Steed*"! "There was something about Dr. Davis's store that made me feel that pharmacy could be made into a profession."

It is touching to perceive the veneration with which the future leader of medical science viewed the obscure druggist. "He was the first gentleman I had ever worked for. All the others were cheap in some way. He was really a wonderful person to be with, and I learned a lot of good manners from him." That Dr. Davis was a Christian, a devout church member, added to the wonder and interest. There was at the drugstore no hint of discrimination, no implication that Simon was not welcome.

The greatly admired pharmacist was far from dynamic. Sandy-haired and very tall, he was a silent man who only waited on customers when there was a rush. He sat in a corner by the barrier to the prescription counter, reading a newspaper, or occasionally some pharmaceutical publication. But his courtesy was of the old southern school, and to his apprentice he was "just." There were, of course, bottles to wash, customers to serve, deliveries to make, but Simon was encouraged without words to undertake tasks from which something could be learned. Under the eye of the chief clerk, "also a neat man but no student," Simon quickly mastered the filling of simple prescriptions. Efficiency and cooperation came to him naturally now.

Everything was spotless to a point that even Esther could not have improved. "Everyone was polite and gentle and I cannot recall one moment of unhappiness" during his two years at Davis's drugstore. It was the crowning pleasure when he realized that he was "obviously liked."[2]

Dr. Davis was, of course, meticulous in honoring the provision of Simon's indenture that he be sent to the Louisville College of Pharmacy. For three months during each of the two years of his apprenticeship, Simon attended lectures three nights a week from eight to ten, and also a laboratory course one afternoon at four. The instruction was aimed at broadening and deepening what students learned as apprentices from their preceptors, who were usually their employers, and from practical work in a functioning drugstore. The college instruction was identical for both years, the theory being that the student's understanding would be deeper the second time around.

Simon found none of the wobbly amorphousness that had put him off in elementary school. This was a trade school aimed at imparting specific knowledge, and doing its job well. Only three subjects were taught: materia medica (remedial substances), pharmacology (the functions of the pharmacist), and inorganic chemistry. The methods were German, brought over by refugees from the Revolution of 1848. The most distinguished professor, Emil Scheffer, who had in his youth studied with leading chemists in his homeland, came to feel so strongly about Simon that he fought over him — details lost — with another member of the faculty.[3]

Remembering his previous mishaps with education, Simon approached the college with trepidation. Once there, he was caught up in an emotional transformation so great that he seemed to feel it inside his body. "I appear to have become wide awake almost at once." The lectures "roused my faculties in full force." He had feared that he was incapable of learning, but now he shot ahead of the other students as if his brain had been attached to a rocket. The only negative aspect was that the more he acquired specific skills at the college, the more he realized the inadequacy of his general education.[4]

A special excitement came in the summers when, weekly for five weeks, Dr. Scheffer took his class "botanizing" in the woods around Louisville. Each student carried a box and collected plants that he was later to classify, by consulting Gray's *Botany*, "in the old-fashioned systematic form." Simon felt "elated" to get out of the city — "this was my first acquaintance with woods."

Proud of the contents of his boxes, Simon resolved to create his own herbarium by extending his collection through personal botanizing expeditions, and then drying, classifying, and mounting his plants in scientific sequence. This was the first serious effort the eighteen-year-old had ever undertaken on his own. As long as he worked under the gas lamp at the dining room table, as he had done with his jigsaw, he encountered no problems. But he found it almost impossible to gather further specimens. As soon as he penetrated deeply enough in the woods, the city youth lost all sense of direction and had the greatest difficulty extricating himself.[5]

At the college, Simon came and went inconspicuously. He never took part in any of the official functions or was active in student affairs. Most remarkably, he made not a single friend. He practiced a similar reticence in the intimacy of his own family circle. "I was not a very communicative person, and said nothing at home of my class work or ambitions."[6]

Simon's family, of course, observed and were relieved by the conspicuous change in their backward son. Even though he was as silent as ever around the house, he had lost his hangdog look, and he set off for work cheerfully rather than with lagging steps. But this improvement seemed no more than an advance from abnormal to normal — and there was no telling how long it would last.[7]

When Jacob had preceded Simon at the College of Pharmacy, his conspicuous assumption of intellectual superiority, backed up annoyingly by his quick brain, had made him far from popular. However, he may well have been, as he was convinced, scholastically at the head of his class. He did not doubt that on his graduation he would be awarded the annual gold medal. The disappointed Flexner family blamed his being ranked only in second place on anti-Semitism. Simon remembered, "I never let myself consciously think of winning the prize."[8]

Past history being what it was, Esther undoubtedly felt concern when Simon's employer, Dr. Davis, appeared at the door in the middle of the afternoon and asked to speak to Simon's father. That perpetual if unobtrusive drinker was in bed upstairs, very sick with dropsy induced by cirrhosis of the liver. Surely Dr. Davis knew that the father was so ill he should not be disturbed except for some very important reason. What had Simon done now?

In fact, realization that Morris was dying made Davis hurry from a faculty meeting at the College of Pharmacy. He wanted the father to know before it was too late that Simon had just been voted the gold medal.

When Simon arrived home for supper, he was surprised to find his family buzzing with excitement. Morris had been brought downstairs, and was in a state of tears which, when he was told the news, Simon found himself joining.

The family's jubilation was tinged with astonishment. The gold medal, which Jacob, the acknowledged family genius, had failed to win, had been won by the recently reformed family liability! Proud and happy as the parents were, they could not keep feeling a little aggrieved. Why, the dying Morris asked querulously, had Simon not confided to them that he was doing so well at the college?[9]

But all negative considerations were soon washed under by the basic significance of the fact. The ugly duckling had been proved a swan.

Down the long years, Dr. Simon Flexner was to be given high honors by major governments in Europe and the Orient, and by the greatest universities in the world. Yet the gold medal from the Louisville College of Pharmacy was the family's most precious icon. It is, by some happy chance, a minor masterpiece of Victorian goldsmithing. The anonymous artist, who lavished loving care on even the tiniest detail, must have thought the design out anew: the name "Simon Flexner" is an integral part of it. Projections of filigree work extend from the top and bottom of the circle, and the delicately chased borders around the edges are different on the front and the back. The obverse bears a simple image: three books indicated in depth and labeled respectively "PHARMACY, CHEMISTRY, MATERIA MEDICA." The front mingles many varieties and sizes of lettering, all based on typefaces, into a dense, coherent pattern, fundamentally horizontal, although writing near the top and bottom repeats the curve of the circle. Spaces that would otherwise be empty contain delicate unrepresentational shapes. The legend reads, "Presented by the ALUMNIA of the L.C. of Pharmacy to SIMON FLEXNER of the Class 1881 & 82 for best average." (PLATE 12)

Above the top extends a loop of gold so that the medal could be hung from a watch chain. Simon had neither watch nor chain. His mother supplied a black silk ribbon, and he found objects with which to weigh down the ends in opposite pockets, while the medal dangled in front. One afternoon, on his way home from the drugstore for lunch, Simon wore the medal. "I can still see in my mind's eye that yellow light that flashed from the polished circle." But "something happened inside me. I never wore the medal again." He gave it to his mother, who stored it away among her treasures.[10]

Shortly after Simon had informed Esther of his engagement, Helen Thomas received in the mail the small cardboard box, embellished with blue tape, which had originally been made to hold the medal. Inside, next to the shining disk, there was (and still is) a small oblong of heavy paper, folded in the middle, and inscribed in a slightly shaky hand with overtones of German script:

Dearest Helen,

   I send you this Medal with much love and I know you will treasure it the same as I did when Simon got it.

As ever,
Mother[11]

14

Jacob's Drugstore

So strong was the Flexner family's conviction of unity that Simon's receipt of the gold medal which Jacob had been denied was considered, even by Jacob himself, an achievement of which they all could be equally proud. The same cohesion left Simon no possibility of choice after he had passed his state pharmaceutical examinations. Jacob, with the financial backing of his wife's family, had acquired his own drugstore. Simon would, of course, come in as his brother's registered clerk. This arrangement held fast until Simon, eight years later, left Louisville forever.

Despite strong differences of temperament and mental outlook, the brothers worked together without serious conflict year after year, further demonstrating how compelling was the family solidarity. After Simon and Abraham became famous, and Bernard widely respected and very prosperous, Jacob, seconded by his children, complained that, although he was in fact the ablest of them all, he had been sacrificed to the advancement of his younger brothers. But such resentments were far in the future. The younger brothers were still under Jacob's sway, and thus he felt that by encouraging them he was not only serving the team but proving the effectiveness of his leadership.

Simon could not help cherishing secretly the contrast between Jacob's losing and his winning the gold medal. The demonstration that he was at least as able as the former tyrant made it easier for him to pursue, year after year, what he acknowledged was his family duty of serving, under the command of his brother, the most profitable of the family endeavors. Thus, his annoyance because Jacob, preferring to talk, left most of the prescription work to him, was tempered by the realization of how much more quickly and efficiently he could put up a prescription than Jacob could.

"From the moment I was entrusted with personal responsibility at Jake's drugstore," Dr. Flexner wrote in 1926, "certain salient characteristics emerged which have remained essentially until today. I became punctilious to a degree. . . . The work — prescriptions, preparation, even parcels — must be done in an exact and neat manner." He expressed irritation if the apprentices under him failed to demonstrate "quickness of response." These characteristics, he believed, came from his mother.[1]

The Flexner drugstore was in effect open twenty-four hours every day, there being a bell that could be rung at night by any finger that pressed. To obey the law, one of the two registered Flexner pharmacists had to be present at all times. Simon slept over the store. The store opened at 7 A.M. and the doors were shut at 11 P.M. Simon went home for breakfast, lunch, and dinner. He calculated that, apart from answering the night bell, he was usually on duty for thirteen hours. He did have one evening off, from suppertime to closing, and one afternoon off, from lunchtime to after supper. He was also free part of every other Sunday. There was no summer holiday. "One's health seemed to stand it. What was more astonishing was that one's spirit should have done so."[2]

The drugstore was in the business section, strategically placed between the wholesale district to the north and the retail area to the south. Since adjacent to the store a number of faro banks flourished, the daytime bustle was followed by a subdued but active night life which went on until the small hours.[3]

Jacob featured toilet articles; "soda water and its appurtenances"; shelves of standard drugs that the Flexner brothers had made up in quantity and bottled; local remedies, which had often been mixed in the drugstore, bearing the names of the quacks who promoted them. Behind the counter were blankly labeled nostrums for venereal diseases and male impotence. However, the heart of the business was filling prescriptions drawn up by physicians whom Jacob encouraged to frequent the store.

Jacob's overaggressiveness had been somewhat tamed by the years, and thus his conversational gifts, his passion for reading and retaining what he read, enabled him to preside over a kind of medical salon. Practitioners would drop in at the store during their round of house calls, find colleagues there, exchange gossip, and talk over their problems. When not otherwise engaged, Simon sat in on the discussions, and when Jacob was absent, he took over as best he could his brother's role. He found he could do so with increasing effect.[4]

Learning through endless conversations the methods and results of the leading doctors — no others were welcomed into the informal fraternity — the Flexner brothers became a clearinghouse for such information. Furthermore, by subscribing to several periodicals, the brothers kept up "in a small way" with German and American medical literature. They published some numbers of a pamphlet called *New Remedies*, compiled for the most part by Simon, but the object being "mere business," the project was abandoned when it proved not adequately profitable. However, the time came when doctors with especially knotty problems would ask to speak not to Jacob but Simon.[5]

The night bell was the rogue force in Simon's drugstore experience. It usually tinkled at least once a night. Alone in the dark store, Simon would get out of bed, put on his dressing gown and slippers, turn up the gaslight, and open the door — to what? What awaited him out there in the black or under the dim glow of dawn? Imagine the stories O. Henry could have woven around the night bell! Simon remembered poisonings and fight wounds.

Most of the tinklings were inconsequential: someone was "taken bad" and needed a pill. Beyond that, Simon's recourse was first aid: bandages, a hypodermic injection to calm hysteria, an emetic to void poison. If these did not suffice and an immobilized sufferer had not brought a companion who could be sent for help, there was the police whistle. We can see Simon, forbidden by law to leave the store, standing on the threshold and shattering with his whistle the nocturnal silence. How long before he heard a patrolman's running footsteps? Could he corral a passerby sober enough and willing to carry a message?[6]

Dr. Flexner's overall comment on his early years at Jacob's drugstore was that they "taught me something of the real world, and it made for independence. I had to become self-reliant and able to handle all kinds of situations by day or night. In other words, I had to grow up."[7]

Since winning the gold medal, Simon had become a person of much more consequence in his own home. His mother, whom he had as an unhappy boy been forced to view almost as if he were an outsider from afar, was interested now that Simon was amounting to something. And, as Jacob had his own family to support, the $100 a week Simon earned became the mainstay of the household. Simon was so pleased and proud that he carried his sense of responsibility to extremes. Eating at home, spending as little on his clothes as decency allowed, he gave his mother almost everything he earned. His only splurges on amusement were occasionally to go by himself to the theater, paying twenty-five cents for a balcony seat. (He was so moved by *Camille* that he saw it twice in one week.) He never bought anything for his own pleasure, a fact made more remarkable by the passion he manifested for possessions whenever he got any.[8]

Rabbi Moses had given him, on his graduation from the College of Pharmacy, a copy of Bryce's *Commonwealth*. The "marvelous book," which he judged must have cost at least five dollars, was "the grandest thing I ever had. . . . Nobody can imagine what that meant to me." But, Moses borrowed the book back to read. Months passed. "I could not stop thinking of it." Finally, he wrote Moses asking whether he had not finished the book. It came right back. Then Simon was so overcome with shame that he put the volume out of sight and could not bring himself to read it.[9]

Although "crazy about books," he could not buy for himself any to speak of. He cherished until he died a copy of John Locke's *Conduct of the Understanding*, a slim paperback miserably printed with tiny, crowded type, which he bought for ten cents the year after his graduation in pharmacy.

Simon's younger brothers Bernard and Abraham, who were studying at the Male High School, had access to books they could bring home. Macaulay's biographical essays exhilarated Simon. As he tried to memorize paragraphs on moral philosophy by Noah Porter during hurried breakfasts, he could make out little, although he was so delighted to learn what "syllogism" meant that as an old man he could still quote the definition. More useful were general textbooks: Brooks's *Literature*, Jervis's *Logic* — "the rules of logic caught my fancy" — Wentworth's *Algebra* and *Geometry*, elementary works on ethics, physics, and organic chemistry. These he studied in the evenings when the drugstore, although open, was unfrequented. He worked out systematically what exercises the textbooks offered, buying sets of answers in order to check his results.[10]

On winter nights, with the windows closed and the oxygen depleted by the iron stove, the air in the drugstore became stuffy. Simon would find himself going to sleep. Dashes out into the fresh air on the streets had to be made rarely and quickly lest the store be found empty. Simon would take down from the shelves drugs to keep him awake, including a fluid extract of cocaine that no one then knew was habit-forming. Fortunately, he resorted to it rarely.[11]

During his early years in Jacob's drugstore, Simon still had no friends. Girls hardly entered his life at all. Jacob's wife did have two flirtatious nieces, one of whom had to his surprise kissed Simon at the family wedding. He was somewhat taken with her, but he did not think about her when she was not pirouetting around the drugstore.

For a while, Simon was a regular at the craziest weekly dances in Louisville — at the insane asylum. The superintendent had two daughters "just grown." Simon used to go to the Pusey home for Saturday night dinner, and afterwards to the dances. One of the Pusey girls would pull him around for a while, and then he would be "let loose" on the female patients, "with whom I managed somehow. . . . I cannot dance to this day," Dr. Flexner mourned in 1937, "although I would have loved to."[12]

It may well have been a sense of rebellion that inspired Simon with a passion for firearms. Having abstracted a dollar from the money he usually gave his mother, he bought a loaded revolver from a pawnshop. He secreted the weapon in his room at the drugstore and longed to fire it. One lonely night, he did fire it, out of a window overlooking Market Street. The satisfactory bang was followed by unexpected answering sounds, multiple groanings which Simon recognized as the scratching of chairs moved back on the bare wooden floors of the many gambling houses on Fifth Street. Closing the window, Simon hurried to another that looked out over Fifth Street. It was alive with men running in the direction from which they had heard the shot. Presently, they returned, "talking eagerly to one another, mystified of course."[13]

The pawnshop pistol now fades from history to be replaced by a .22-caliber rifle Simon bought at a reduced price after a fire sale. He would shoot from an upstairs drugstore window at the tin-covered cornice on an adjoining house. The sound of the bullet hitting the metal meant a hit, no sound a miss.

The rifle carried seventeen cartridges. To eject an empty shell and reload Simon used a lever. On one occasion, as he was going through this process, the gun went off prematurely, the bullet passing through the kitchen window of a pawnbroker named Flynn. Simon instantly remembered with horror that he had just seen Mrs. Flynn's bulky figure passing and repassing the window. There was now no movement there. Was Mrs. Flynn lying dead on the floor? How long would it take for the body to be discovered?

When there was no sign of any disaster at the Flynns, Simon's anxiety lessened. After a few days, "my desire to renew the target practice got the better of my discretion so that I began to pop again at the cornice."

A ring on the bell beside the dumbwaiter that communicated between the store and the prescription department; Jacob shouted up through the aperture that the Flynns were objecting because Mrs. Flynn had almost been killed several days before. As he sadly carried the gun home — to be "quietly spirited away" by his mother — Simon wondered why the Flynns had waited for a repetition before they complained. Firearms were an integral part of Kentucky life.[14]

15

---···⦿···---

Microscope with Wings

"My good luck came with the microscope."

THE specific microscope was made by Zenmeyer of Philadelphia and had lenses of low and moderately high power. It was used in Jacob's drugstore for urinalyses. Although superficially not as dramatic as the firearms Simon acquired, its possibilities were less restricted. "Never a card player and very poor at games," Simon used the instrument, as long before he had used his jigsaw, to relieve hours of boredom. Microscopy of this sort was a hobby all over the land. One procured some object that would look well when greatly enlarged; acquired a simple device for cutting sections with a razor; learned to preserve the specimen with various colored resins — for instance, red for arteries, blue for veins — and, then, to complete the effect, used a turntable to ring the slide with colored shellacs. Simon worked with the microscope both in the store and at home, where he impressed his siblings with his brightly colored display pieces. But he had no memory of inducing his mother to look through the microscope: "She would have thought such exhibits too remote from her knowledge and experience."[1]

The hobby soon gave way to a passionate desire for knowledge, and, most significantly, Simon was not drawn to the kind of knowledge that would help him along as a pharmacist. The microscopic structure of inorganic matter did not attract him at all. His first major study was the microscopic anatomy of small animals, mostly the cat. By now he had elicited the attention of the doctors who congregated at the drugstore. They brought him specimens of human tissue removed at autopsies or during operations. He taught himself histology (the microscopic study of normal organs and tissues) and moved on to pathology (the study of structures distorted by disease).

Simon's approach was exactly opposite to that of a student in a well-organized class. The student is introduced to a general principle, which is subsequently illustrated by specific examples. Simon, starting with some specific specimen that had happened his way, had to determine what general phenomenon it exemplified. This was the direction he would pursue when his researches had passed beyond the boundaries of the known. His task, although complicated, now was easier. The information could usually be found by searching through some book which he could procure by borrowing, or by gift, or even by purchase. If a doctor identified the tissue he was giving to Simon, this could cause anguished puzzlement until he finally accepted the conclusion that his professional patrons could be mistaken. He found himself turning ever more devotedly to Francis Delafield and T. Mitchell Prudden's *Handbook of Pathological Anatomy and Histology.*

When Flexner got hold of John Tyndall's book *Floating Matter in the Air*, and first came upon the name of Pasteur. Hardly had the principles of bacteriology become clear to Simon before he wanted to engage in research on the subject. Reading in medical journals that F. A. J. Löffler had isolated the diphtheria bacillus, he procured from Dr. William Cheatham some diphtheria membrane, which he sectioned and stained for bacteria. "I did not succeed. At least I tried."[2]

To what extent did Flexner realize, as he stared into his microscope amid hubbub at the communal family table, that he was taking part in one of mankind's great bursts of discovery? Had he been attending a leading medical school he would have seen how original he was, not because what he was interested in was of concern at his university, but because it was not. The professors, if they mentioned it at all, usually laughed. He would have to learn outside the curriculum from books.

Flexner had no curriculum except studying books, and most of what he found on their pages was new to him whether it had long been known or had just been discovered. What particularly caught his attention was, it is true, unknown to the medical profession in Louisville, but the doctors recognized that they were far fron the center of things. The synod that met at Jake's drugstore, although by no means apologetic for medicine as they practiced it, observed Flexner's activities with interest, and in one case even with awe. The youth did not meet in Louisville such opposition as he was to face when full professor of pathology at the University of Pennsylvania Medical School.

Simon's reading revealed how recent were the basic discoveries in the sciences he was pursuing: the 1850's for histology, the 1870's for bacteriology. Yet the Flexners' own historical span was short, not carrying their view back beyond the parents' arrival in Louisville. The youthful Simon could have no conception of how in older societies the newfangledness of scientific medicine was impeding its acceptance, thus keeping it possible for him to play a leading part in the revolution that was to sweep irresistibly across the United States and over the world.

Simon came into contact with a pair of doctors who were also microscope buffs; they induced him to attend the annual meeting of the American Microscopical Club in Columbus, Ohio. Although his older self remembered the proceedings, which were conducted mostly by amateurs, as dull, young Simon had never before been part of a group all similarly concerned. He was so enchanted that as soon as he got home he organized the Louisville Microscopical Club.

There were half a dozen members, including C. J. K. Jones, a Unitarian minister; a German doctor named Lieber; Henry Cottrell, editor of the local medical journal, *American Practitioner and News;* and the professor of chemistry at the Medical School. Exhilarated by having companions who shared his interests, Simon visualized the club as a mighty force, and suggested that they ask the American Microscopical Society to hold its next annual convention in Louisville. He later reasoned that his elders had agreed only because they were sure the invitation would be turned down. But competition for the honor seems to have been minimal. The invitation was accepted.

Now, Simon's fellow club members reacted with consternation, all the more because the letter of acceptance included a request for information concerning meeting halls, entertainments to be given, hotels, and so on. Simon refused to be cowed. The Louisville drug manufacturers would obviously be proud to honor the city by footing the bills. He rushed off to enlist Carey Peter of Arthur Peter and Company, whom he visualized as the bellwether for the industry. Peter said he was too busy to consider the matter now. Simon could try again later if he wished.

At this news, the Reverend Mr. Jones regretfully announced that he would have to attend to his orange grove in Florida at the scheduled time. Cottrell was equally regretful: he could not put off to any other period an already too-long-delayed visit. Simon was in despair, hardly daring to look at his mail, which brought increasingly shrill queries from the national president. Finally, a blessed event took place. Louisville was struck by a tornado, not a very damaging tornado, but it cut quite a swath in the newspapers. Simon rushed off a telegram stating his regret that, under such desperate circumstances, the convention would have to be canceled.[3]

Dr. Cheatham cut a small tumor the size of a pea from the lip of the august federal judge John W. Barr, and sent what he had excised to Simon for examination. Being familiar with the illustrations in books, Simon recognized the tumor as cancerous. The specimen included a bit of the bedding tissue, and the microscope showed that the small round cells in the tumor had invaded the tissue up to the edges of Simon's specimen. Simon "prognosticated a speedy return." When the tumor did return, this prophecy, achieved through techniques unknown in Louisville, seemed miraculous. The judge asked Simon to call on him.

Since Barr lived in a good part of town, Simon went with some trepidation. The judge received him enthusiastically. He was going to New York, Barr explained, for a new operation that would be executed by a distinguished surgeon, John Wyeth. He wanted Simon to come along, attend the operation, "and if you are not satisfied that they got enough out," Barr would demand a further operation. He offered a fee in addition to all expenses.

"Fortunately," Dr. Flexner wrote, "my better angel got me to decline." He replied that there were in New York so many abler pathologists that his intervention would be ridiculous. When Barr asked for a name, Simon recommended the author of the book he consulted, Dr. T. Mitchell Prudden. Barr agreed, but gave Simon twenty-five dollars and said that he would have some tissue sent to Simon so that he could check Dr. Prudden's conclusion.

Prudden ruled that the operation had been sufficient, but Simon, after he had received the promised specimen, was disturbed to trace in the "healthy" tissue little round cells. He found the courage to question Prudden — fortunately it was only by mail. The reply came that the round cells Simon saw were not extensions of the tumor but "inflammatory reaction." And Prudden was proved right when the tumor failed to return.

After Flexner and Prudden became close colleagues, Flexner, remembering with pride "the firmness with which I declined to go to New

York," tried to remind Prudden of the incident. But it had meant nothing to Prudden: he had no memory of it.[4]

On an afternoon when Jacob was away, there appeared in the drugstore a youngish stranger who, Simon noticed at once, was "very well dressed" and spoke with a cultivated accent. He introduced himself as Samuel Fairchild, senior member of the New York City drug firm of Fairchild Brothers and Foster.[5] The firm, he announced, was introducing a superior preparation of pepsin, and wished a leading drugstore in each city to make tests to demonstrate that the claims being put forward for its strength were not exaggerated. Simon made the tests and endorsed the product.

Fairchild reappeared in Louisville from time to time. On every visit, he sought out Simon for conversation. After the intermittent talks had gone on for two or three years, Fairchild said, "I am an officer of the New York College of Pharmacy. What do you know of the college?"

Simon replied, as he remembered, "It seems to me that the professor of pharmacy is Dr. Bedford."

"It is about Professor Bedford that I want to talk to you." Bedford was about to retire and the college was seeking a successor. "Would you consider coming to New York as professor of pharmacy?"

Simon knew that the New York College was second only to the Philadelphia college. He expressed amazement.

"Would you consider it?" Fairchild insisted.

"I haven't got a good enough education."

"I think you could do it. Would you at least consider coming to New York and talking it over?"

Simon asked for time to think the offer over, but when the day came for Fairchild to leave for New York, he still had not made up his mind. He would write a letter. The letter was a refusal: the college could surely find a person much better qualified than he.[6]

Simon had gone to no one for advice, not even one of his professors at the Louisville college. He had told no one, not even his mother. Perhaps he was afraid of being persuaded to overrule his instincts.

In explaining his refusal years later, Dr. Flexner stated that he considered among his most valuable traits the ability to know what he was capable of doing and his unwillingness to try more. Thus he avoided "mental confusion" that was worse than "ordinary ignorance." In the present situation, he did not really doubt his ability to learn quickly the pharmaceutical aspects of the professorship. His concern was lest, in the metropolis of New York, his lack of general education, his unfamiliarity with the ways of the world, would make him ridiculous. Although by now twenty-three or twenty-four, he had never been more than a few miles from Louisville. New York was as far away as another planet.[7]

We may add, although this was not included in Dr. Flexner's later self-analysis, that he had not yet prepared his mind to break out of the tight family circle, with its dominant mother, that had always circumscribed his life. One of the elder brothers had, it is true, aimlessly drifted away, but all the other eight children, including the ablest, were still held.

Yet Simon had kept his inner independence by refusing to confide in his family either his thoughts or his experiences. Hugging to his breast the great compliment Fairchild had paid him, he was keeping inviolate what was for him the true significance of what had occurred. Since he was not really interested in pharmacy, the offer had not truly been a call to immediate action. But it had demonstrated that action far beyond his present range was possible. He could achieve almost anything if he could secure the necessary education and then "use the wits I had!"

Someone had brought to the drugstore a brown, granular substance found in a beehive. Suspecting it to be a form of sugar, Simon applied to it Fehling's solution, which showed that sugar was present. Regarding this simple observation as worthy of publication, Simon sent a report to *Science*. Jacob subscribed to *Science* and there was excitement in the drugstore when Simon's note appeared. The local literary light, Mrs. Bowser, said, "Simon has hitched his wagon to a star." Simon had never before heard the phrase. It appealed to him.[8]

16

---❦---

An Unprepared Student
and a New University

Simon and Abraham Flexner, whose careers overlapped within the same institutional world, who were both creators of the medical environment in which we still live today, and who were both known as "Dr. Flexner," have become in many minds so entangled that they are thought of as a single individual. Yet the two brothers could hardly have been more different in temperament.

The differences are reflected in the records they left behind. The Simon Flexner Papers could easily fill a medium-sized room: what Abraham preserved hardly fills a library shelf. There are in Abraham's papers no parallels to the innumerable autobiographical jottings that appear in so many guises in Simon's papers. Yet Simon's efforts at a formal autobiography were in vain. He found himself unable to synthesize his various memories in a manner he considered frank, profound, and accurate. For his part, Abraham found writing his autobiography an agreeable act of fluent self-expression: in 1940 he published *I Remember*. (PLATE 13)

Simon characterized his brother as "a strong person, very generous, intensely egotistical, with a great capacity for self-deception. My belief is that he readily translates events into harmony with his own point of view and his own cogitations. He hardly ever admits mistakes or failure on his own part, although finding many faults in others." Abraham, Simon concluded, avoided self-analysis lest by weakening his self-assurance, it made him distrustful of himself. The introspective Simon ruled that Abraham was completely incapable of a detached pont of view about himself.[1]

How Abraham shifted his memories to suit the point he wished to make is amusingly exemplified by two passages concerning his father. In his autobiography, he stated that Morris had been a distant figure, who spoke of ambitions for his children "only, and then not often, to our mother." Writing his daughter Eleanor on her sixteenth birthday, Abraham mourned that when he himself had been sixteen, his father had died.

"From then on we got on as best we could without a father's advice. We suffered as the years went on because we had no older and wiser man to council us.

"I have never forgotten his injunctions: after forty years or more they are as vivid in my memory as yesterday, and, as best I could, I have tried to live up to them." Then, Abraham drew the moral: Eleanor and her sister Jean should obey the "injunctions" of *their* father, Abraham himself.[2]

Although Abraham and Simon were eventually to collaborate in important ways, they apparently were not close in their early years — Simon's jottings concerning that time rarely mention Abraham. When *I Remember* was published, Simon was annoyed by the sugary descriptions, so different from his own memories, of their common family life in Louisville: "Although the houses in which we lived became smaller and smaller," Abraham wrote, "and our way of living simpler and simpler, there was nothing either in the atmosphere or appearance of the home to suggest the poverty and hardship in which we grew up. I am still at a loss to understand the courage and confidence with which my parents contemplated the future of their large family. I do not recall a single word of complaint. . . . It made no difference to them that others were more fortunate and successful. They had pitched their own ideals incredibly high, and no pressure of external circumstance, no temporary expedient to which they had to resort, such as putting the older boys to work to help support the family, ever lowered their aims, even for the time being."[3]

Anyone who knew Abraham in his later years can only chuckle at his describing himself in *I Remember* as a youth so earnest, noble, and considerate that he comes out almost as a prig. It is impossible to believe that when young as well as when old he did not engage in high jinks and tease with practical jokes. Indeed, his younger sister Mary liked to attest to the longevity of his prankishness by telling of a trick he played on her when she was a small child. A neighboring housewife used to make her presents of cream puffs, which she ate in the presence of her siblings with ostentatious enjoyment. Too much for Abe! He intercepted a cream puff and doctored it with foul-tasting tooth powder, thereby reducing Mary to tears.[4]

Abraham attributes to himself none of the tribulations that darkened Simon's early experiences, and there is good reason to believe that his path was in fact much smoother. Three and a half years younger than Simon, Abraham did not occupy Simon's inconspicuous position in the middle of the family: he was the youngest of the eight brothers. Most importantly, Abraham appealed particularly to Jacob. Although he had by far the more original mind, his mental bent was close enough to his all-powerful elder brother's to make them relish each other's company. Abraham, too, admired Jacob's inspiration, Herbert Spencer, to whom he was to attribute his own early loss of religion. He stated, in *I Remember*, that no children's books or "trash" ever entered the Flexner household. Would he in truth have cheered when Jacob burned poor Simon's "Custer's Last Rally?"

Since Abraham was normally optimistic and outgoing, we can believe that he had none of Simon's difficulty with street games. "The reader," he wrote, "must not infer that the life of a poor boy growing up in the Louisville of the seventies and eighties was dreary or unhappy. We had our neighborhood playmates no better off than we, and we played in back yards and in congested streets, careful only to avoid an occasional one-horse vehicle or mule-drawn horse-car."[5]

In this modern era of elaborate education, it is difficult to believe what tremendous advantage accrued to Simon's younger brothers, first Bernard and then Abraham, because they went to high school. Since the so-called University of Louisville had never been able to get its academic department afloat, the high school was the most advanced liberal arts institution in the city. Its top teachers were entitled "professor," and its graduates were proud. The students were the only undergraduates resident in the community. Thus, the Athenaeum Society, a debating club of the ablest students, held a place in Louisville's intellectual life. Abraham tells us that he was president for several terms, empowered to levy fines for levity, as the group discussed such questions as "Was the execution of Mary Queen of Scots justifiable?" or "Was the Commonwealth of Cromwell a useful or harmful episode in English history?"

"The high tone of the society was surely in part due to the frequency with which former students used to attend," Abraham wrote. "I remember with especial pleasure and gratitude Shackelford Miller, a loyal graduate, at that time a rising lawyer, destined finally to become chief justice of the state. For some reason, 'Shack' Miller was especially kind to me. I sometimes walked home with him . . . and was always welcome at his office."[6]

First Bernard and then Abraham were employed, after their high school classes were over, at the Louisville Library, assisting from two-thirty in the afternoon until ten at night. Their tasks were intermittent, and they were surrounded, as no Louisville Flexner had been before, with a wealth of books to read. The library being open only to paying subscribers, it was frequented by what Simon called the "cultivated people" of Louisville. Becoming "favorites," Bernard and Abraham became acquainted with leaders of Louisville society, both Gentile and Jewish. Among them were the Brandeises, whose economic and social position in Germany and Kentucky put them many cuts above the Flexners. Bernard brought Simon into the circle. "There was quite a little literary set at the edge of which I stood and looked in. . . . I tried to peep over the walls made by my very slight schooling." Simon remembered the librarian, Mrs. Atwood, wellborn and still lovely, who had had a tragic marriage. Mrs. John W. Bowser was "the shining literary light, not only an authoress but a well-read critic and connoisseur." Simon fought his way out of the drugstore to attend a class on art, given by an elderly lady who had traveled in Europe. She spoke of the "great masters" and showed photographs. The *Mona Lisa* was already known to Simon as he had read Walter Pater's *Renaissance*. For the rest, "I learned little beyond a few names and the existence of a world" into which he had never had a glimpse.[7]

Concerning his own hours at the library, Abraham wrote, "I was continually in the company of mature persons who were infinitely my superiors . . . men and women who would even today be considered very unusual in point of scholarship and culture. The room was so small that I could easily hear what was said, and the conversation that took place dealt with politics, religion, and to some extent, with music and art."[8]

Of all the subjects discussed, Abraham was most interested in politics. Even before his experiences in the library, he had loafed around the polls on election day. Discovering that his library connections regarded the *Nation* as their bible on political affairs, the high school student considered it only natural that he should submit to the *Nation* brief communications on southern politics. In *I Remember*, he commented that

he "must have possessed a degree of self-assurance at which I myself
marvel, but which, if truth be told, has since that day often stood me in
good stead."[9] His communications were published, first sounding the
name of Flexner in that intellectual air where it was to resound so
mightily.

On Abraham's graduation from high school, Jacob made a decision
that would have been routine in many environments but was sensational
in the tight family battling for survival. He would raise the money to
send the boy to college. More important still to Abraham's future — and
also Simon's — was to determine what college. On the advice of a friend
with Maryland connections, the boy was pointed at the Johns Hopkins.[10]

The establishment of the Hopkins ten years before Abraham arrived
was, he contended after he became a famous educational leader, "the
starting point of higher education in the modern sense in the United
States." He acknowledged that his entire career had been devoted to extending the revolutionary ideas the Hopkins inaugurated. Almost the
same could be said of Simon Flexner.

When in *I Remember* Abe expressed amazement that so beneficent an
explosion in American culture could have taken place in a "provincial
town" like Baltimore, the sneer may well have irritated Simon since the
Hopkins had been a fruit of his own wife's background, and indeed, to a
considerable extent of her immediate household.

Samuel Hopkins, the father of the Johns Hopkins who founded the
university, was a first cousin of John Chew Thomas, Helen's great-
grandfather. Like John Chew, Samuel destroyed the worldly position of
his family by freeing, as a matter of Quaker conscience, all his plantation
slaves. Johns himself, a member of the same generation as Richard
Henry Thomas, did even better than his cousin in the urban Baltimore
world into which they were both thrown. Hopkins was propelled into
great wealth along the twin bands of iron that nurtured Maryland's
greatest fortunes: he became the largest stockholder in the Baltimore and
Ohio Railroad.[11] When he died in 1873, he left seven million dollars to
be equally divided between a university and a hospital. For each foundation he appointed, although with some overlapping, a different board
of trustees.

The bequest to the university was remarkable in three ways: it was
the largest donation for such a purpose in American history; it was not
tied to any existing institution; and the founder, since he left behind no

instructions, gave the trustees a free hand to create as they saw best. To be chairman of the board given this responsibility and opportunity, Hopkins had designated Helen's granduncle Galloway Cheston. Also on the board was Helen's cousin Francis King, who doubled as chairman of the hospital board, and her father, who was to succeed to the position of chairman of the university executive committee.[12]

The jubilant inhabitants of Maryland assumed that the university bequest would be primarily dedicated to educating their sons. This would have followed an established pattern. But the trustees somehow — no one knows exactly how — collected what was for America an altogether revolutionary vision.

Daniel Colt Gilman, who became the first president of the university, was to explain that the trustees "soon perceived there was no obvious call for another college. . . . There was no call for another technological or scientific school. . . . On the other hand, there seemed to be a demand for scientific laboratories and professorships, the directors of which should be free to pursue their own researches, stimulating their students to prosecute study with a truly scientific spirit and aim. . . . A continuance of their inquiries led the trustees to believe that there was a strong demand, among the young men of this country, for opportunities to study beyond the ordinary courses of a college or scientific school. . . . The strongest evidence of this demand was afforded by the increased attendance of American students upon the lectures of the German universities." The trustees decided to seek the best professors wherever they could be found, and "hoped that the students who had already been *taught* in other colleges would be drawn by the eminence of the professors and excellent opportunities for advanced study."[13]

Concerning Helen Thomas's father, Gilman said, "He believed that Baltimore had then an opportunity such as had never before occurred in this country to establish a university of the highest character, which would be of service to the state, the country, and the world. He thoroughly understood the university spirit, and every endeavor to secure the advancement of higher education of men and women, the improvement of scholarship, the promotion of research, or the calling and retention of qualified professors was sure to have his approbation and aid."[14]

Realizing that they were venturing on ground unexplored in America, the trustees called in for advice the nation's three most distinguished college presidents: Charles W. Eliot of Harvard; James Burrill Angell of Yale; and Andrew D. White of Cornell. Each was asked whether the

new Johns Hopkins should attempt to give "a higher degree of education than has heretofore been done" or "should give education for a
larger number." All three insisted that the second alternative would
serve the greater need. In any case, the more radical alternative was not
practical. Where would the trustees find adequate professors? A university had to be a gradual growth, nurturing its own faculty. "It is impossible," said President Eliot, "that it should spring up fully armed from
anyone's brain.

"I should doubt very much," he continued, "whether any institution,
old or young, could cut loose from the educational foundations in which
it is placed. . . . We are as well off at Harvard as any place in the country
for carrying on education of a high order, but we could not deliberately
undertake to give only a high degree of education for a few. . . . We get a
very considerable bulk of moderately well trained youth. We teach them
for a year all together. Then they begin to branch out into separate subjects. As the four years go by we carry those who have special ability in
certain subjects far above the line of average attainment."[15]

But the little junto of Baltimore laymen were not dissuaded by the
three august presidents. When their determination became clear, all
three advisors recommended the same man for president of the Hopkins. Gilman was an educational visionary seeking an opportunity. He
was having a hard time as president of the new University of California.
As soon as he heard what the Baltimore trustees wanted, he resigned the
California presidency. So completely did his ideas jibe with those of the
trustees that he was offered the post as the result of a single meeting.
Never has an appointment been more happy.[16]

Gilman's most intimate friend and coadjutor in Baltimore was to be,
as long as both were alive, Helen's father, Dr. James Carey Thomas.
When Dr. Thomas died, Gilman is reported to have said that he did not
know where to turn.[17]

The university did not long continue to restrict itself to graduate
studies. Pressure from the community became so great that in 1879 an
undergraduate college was added. But the influence of the university remained dominant. At the Hopkins, the university was not an outgrowth
of the college — the college was an undergrowth of the university.
Abraham, who reached the college in September, 1884, remembered
that, although instruction was geared to undergraduates, "research was
the air we breathed."[18]

When Abraham arrived in Baltimore, he found there were entrance examinations to take. However, the Hopkins faculty, unimpressed with American secondary education, were less concerned with what knowledge an applicant brought with him than with indications of an ability to learn. Abraham, who radiated intelligence, was in a stronger position than he realized when he entered a classroom to take the entrance examination in Greek. Although he intended to specialize in Greek, he realized, as soon as the questions were passed around, that they were "absolutely out of my reach."

He was, he tells us, so shy he was ready to flee. He did not flee. Sitting on the platform was Professor Charles d'Urban Morris. Abraham threaded his way through the other students and up to the professor. He could not, he explained, answer the questions.

"You are frightened?" asked Professor Morris.

"No, I have studied very little Greek."

Morris looked Abraham over and then picked up a small copy of Xenophon's *Anabasis.* "All I have to do is satisfy my conscience. Suppose you translate this passage for me." When Abraham proved unable to do so, Morris turned to an easier passage. Abraham could understand only a few words.

"Well, you don't know very much. How old are you?"

"Seventeen."

"Where are you from?"

"Kentucky."

"I have a class from twelve to one every day. You seem to be in earnest. Come to me promptly at one o'clock daily, and I will tell you what to study."

Abraham was there regularly. On each occasion, the professor would ask a few questions and favor the eager boy with another assignment.

Abraham tells us that he devised a system for learning declensions, conjugations, irregular verbs, and the like. Having done his best to memorize the conjugation of a particular verb, for instance, he would cut a sheet of paper into slips, writing on each a different form — "aorist indicative," "second person singular," "present tense," "perfect infinitive." After shuffling the slips in a hat, he would then bring them out one after another. Unless he could give the correct answer, he would return the slip to the hat. Thus, without the assistance of a teacher, he drilled himself and became rapid and accurate. About Thanksgiving time, Dr. Morris told him he knew enough to take a course. At first the studies were over his head, but he soon learned to keep up with and even surpass the other pupils.

His readers, Abraham commented in *I Remember*, might be surprised that he, "always an advocate of high academic standards," was proud of his self-education. Yet, "a half-taught boy, bitterly aware of the fact, who can keep quiet, learn, and constantly — without an inferiority complex — compare himself with his superiors," had a rosier future than someone who was "too acutely conscious" that he was well educated.

The Hopkins had no dormitories and offered no extracurricular activities. Abraham boarded in the town with a Jewish family called Kaiser. A Jewish classmate, Julius Friedenwald (who was to become a distinguished specialist in diseases of the stomach) invited him to the home of his father, a prominent oculist. Abraham, normally so outgoing, made no other friends. He worked without ceasing, partly because when he was idle he was overcome with homesickness. As he walked down the street he would stop, pull a postcard out of his pocket, and holding it on his knee, write to his mother. He communicated with her at least once a day in German.

In contrast to Simon, who as a student was a loner given to working solutions out for himself, Abraham indicated his later concern with formal education by emphasizing the relationship between master and pupil. He stated that his attitude towards the faculty at the Hopkins — he listed ten names — "was one of reverence." Whatever they said to him he took with the greatest seriousness; whatever they advised him, he tried to do. This attitude on the part of a prodigy so obviously brilliant was most gratifying to his teachers.

Abraham (so he remembered) spent during his entire stay in Baltimore only fifty cents on amusements: twenty-five-cent seats to see Edwin Booth in *Hamlet* and *King Lear*. Yet it soon became clear to him that the money he had brought would not last more than two years. To earn his degree in that time he would have to do four years' work in two. Every conceivable shortcut was called for. Some came easily. On being shown his contributions to the *Nation*, his professor of English excused him from writing themes. He persuaded his professor of physics to give him credit for an elementary course because he had already learned enough when in high school. However, as he majored in the classics, he was forced to enroll in two courses that unfortunately met at the same hour. He did all the homework, attended lectures and recitations in turn. Everything was going well when he realized that the examinations he would have to pass for the overlapping courses also overlapped.

Abraham appealed to Gilman. The president replied, "Very well, if you know the subjects that is all we require. Take such examinations as you please among those that conflict and I will arrange to have you examined separately in the other courses." At the end of two years, Abraham Flexner received his degree.

In the summation of his career at the end of his autobiography, Abraham wrote, "Little that was said to me in those two years faded from my consciousness." They "gave in a general way point and direction to the rest of my life." It was, indeed, ideas then and subsequently imbibed at the Hopkins which he applied to the reform of medical education, to his conceptions concerning schools and colleges and universities, and to his own creation, the Institute for Advanced Study at Princeton.

Back in Louisville during June, 1886, the nineteen-year-old was not sure what he wanted to do. Although Abraham could now read Latin and Greek with great facility (this remained for years his principal "intellectual pleasure"), he did not yearn to make classics his profession. "Somehow I came to feel that I was not meant to be a college professor — and thirty years of subsequent experience with professors has convinced me that I was not designed to be one of them. With all my reverence for learning — and this can hardly be exaggerated — I came to know that my interests were too broad to be satisfied with what is now called 'a field of concentration.' "[19]

When considering the practice of law, Abraham read Blackstone but was not intrigued. Political economy he found more interesting but he could foresee no future in it. His duty to help support the family spoke loud, and he secured an "assistantship" at a thousand dollars a year in the high school from which he had graduated only two years before. It was this opening, not any premeditation, "that made a teacher of me," he wrote, although he had found the direction that, on a much grander scale, was to come naturally to him.

All the recessiveness, the eagerness to take advice, he had felt at the Hopkins, vanished in his home environment. Disapproving of the prevailing system, in which every teacher taught many subjects, as in an elementary school, he offered to work out a system that would permit specialization. This the principal permitted him to do. He assigned himself all four Greek classes and one in Latin. At the end of his first term, at the age of twenty, Abraham was promoted to what was called locally a "full professorship," at the highest salary the school paid.[20]

The "exuberance of my spirits," he wrote, enabled him to inspire his pupils with enthusiasm for Greek. But when one of his classes did not develop the necessary enthusiasm, Abraham took the drastic step of failing the entire class of fifteen or so. His draconian act created a furor in the newspapers and produced an investigation by the school board. The principal, Abraham tells us, offered to resign if the board reversed his action. He was supported.[21]

Abraham was now well known in Louisville. Prosperous parents, whose sons were having difficulty getting into college, hired him to tutor the delinquents after school hours. This soon became a second and considerable source of the income Abraham added to the family resources. His growing prosperity was, although this could not be foreseen, preparing escape for Simon.

17

---◦⟨∞⟩◦---

Pathways for Escape

D URING Abraham's two years at the Hopkins, Simon was becoming more and more restive under his "dog's life at the drugstore." The disciple of the microscope was yearning to pursue medicine as a science. However, this did not involve any conscious intention of breaking permanently out of the family web. Simon's dream was to serve the family by setting up in Louisville his own pathological laboratory.

"I had never heard of any such a private laboratory anywhere in the country," but he felt his could succeed. He would assist the practitioners by making blood counts, analyzing urine and gastric solutions, and the like. He would examine surgical specimens. And then there was the new science of bacteriology. Since neither pathology nor bacteriology was taught at the Medical Institute, he could hope for a small appointment there, with the privilege of conducting classes and receiving from his pupils a small personal fee. He would also have a chance to use his microscope for research.

To achieve this, he knew that, like Abraham, he would have to go away for a period of study. Since a dream needs no restrictions, he visualized himself as escaping to Germany, where, so his reading taught him, modern pathology and bacteriology were advancing fastest.[1]

Abraham brought medical news back from the Hopkins. True, the hospital which had been provided for in the original bequest was still under construction. The medical school, planned under the aegis of the university (where Dr. Thomas was the medical trustee), was still no more than an intention. But President Gilman had added to the faculty, as professor of pathology, Dr. William Henry Welch.

During Abraham's second year at college, Welch, having returned from German studies, had delivered six lectures on pathology. Abraham attended several. The classics major, who had no inkling that his career would ever involve him in any way with medicine, was impressed not for himself but for his brother. Dr. Welch was obviously a leader of men and a brilliant scientist whose interests comprised those which Simon had developed for himself by reading and staring into a microscope.

A freestanding building on the Hopkins campus, which had been erected as a morgue, was being refitted into a pathological laboratory, and there Welch was planning to begin, during the year after Abraham's return to Louisville, instruction to graduate doctors.[2] The immediate import of this news to Simon was that, in order to be eligible for the studies required for his ambitions, he would have to secure an M.D. degree. Of all the problems that lay before him, this turned out to be the easiest to surmount.

Biographical compendia concerning Simon Flexner state that he received an M.D. degree from the University of Louisville in 1889. This is factually correct, but highly misleading if interpreted to mean that Simon's formal education had begun.

Although the charter of the University of Louisville had been on the books for decades, all efforts to establish an "academic department" had failed, since no way had been found to pay teachers. The university, therefore, consisted of two professional schools — law and medicine — staffed on a part-time basis by practitioners and managed by them for their own emolument. In medicine, such schools existed across the nation by the hundreds, established by practitioners who wanted to be professors — there were usually a half dozen or so schools in Louisville alone. The title of "professor" attracted and reassured patients; each teacher got his share of the students' fees; and the graduates, when they felt the need for consultation, brought the business to their teachers. Between the different teams of practitioners competition for students was cutthroat, and hardly anyone who could pay the fees would fail to graduate somewhere — and usually a degree was the equivalent of a practicing license. This was the system that Abraham was to mow down, killing off hundreds of schools, with his famous "Flexner Report" of 1910.

The Medical Institute of the University of Louisville, the best of the local schools, was staffed by the leading practitioners, the doctors who frequented the informal club in the Flexner drugstore. They were sympathetic to Simon's desire to bring pathology and even bacteriology to Louisville, and had it within their power to make what concessions were necessary to supply him with the degree he needed.

The continuing financial situation of the Flexner family tied Simon to the drugstore where his tasks left almost no time for medical studies. However, he stated that he had no intention of practicing medicine. Why should he then, the doctors asked themselves, be required to go beyond satisfying formal requirements? Of course, once he was an accredited physician, his determination never to practice might change — but then no one could deny that Simon was a mighty able fellow![3]

The scheme of the Medical Institute resembled that of the College of Pharmacy. The instruction was almost altogether by lectures that were duplicated during the two years of study. It was the plan that the instruction at the institute, which occupied only four winter months, be supplemented by advice gained and experience received during the apprenticeship of the pupil to a practicing physician.

The dean of the institute, Dr. James M. Bodine, agreed to reduce Simon's fees from $150 to $75 a year, due "when and if convenient." Furthermore, Bodine would write himself down as Simon's preceptor. Both men regarded this as no more than a formality to meet a requirement. "I never made a physical examination," Dr. Flexner remembered. "I never heard a heart or lung sound."[4]

Simon could most easily get away from the drugstore from nine to ten in the morning. This enabled him to hear Dr. Bodine on anatomy. He recalled one lecture on surgery, one on gynecology, one on obstetrics, a few on practice and materia media. Simon attended some demonstrations of medical chemistry, and dissected during a few evenings. On one of these, he took along Sandy Lieberman, "a curious jeweler," who was horrified the following morning to find a human ear in his coat pocket. "It was the gift of a wag among the students."[5]

Simon kept abreast as best he could by reading what paralleled the content of the missed lectures, this being the more effective if he could identify the book on which the professor based his orations. And, during his second year, Simon presented a course of his own: histology and pathology. He carried the drugstore microscope to the institute and for a small fee gave demonstrations of sections to four or five, "perhaps fewer," students. One was Rabbi Moses.[6]

While he was studying, this peculiar pupil read a paper before the Kentucky Medical Society at Danville. Entitled "A Report on Pathological Histology and Urinalysis," it was a statistical report on the analyses made for the Louisville physicians at the Flexner drugstore. It was printed in the local *American Practitioner and News,* and reprinted in the *Memphis Medical Monthly.* Before he left Louisville, Simon was to publish two more articles in the local journal: "Chemical Aids to the Diagnosis of Diseases of the Stomach" and "Remarks on the Histology of the Blood Corpuscles."[7]

The examinations required for graduation from the Medical Institute were all oral. Most of the professors were so familiar with Simon that they saw no need to question him. He did, when laid up with an attack of quinsy, prepare himself for his test in obstetrics by memorizing a "quiz compound" by Dr. Craigen (who was eventually, in another era of Simon's life, to deliver the author of this volume). However, the professor of obstetrics, Dr. Anderson, took a dim view of delinquent students. "What are you doing here? You have never been to my lectures."

"Yes, I have," said Simon (he had been to one). "You didn't see me, but I was there."

Anderson then thought up some tough questions. Simon was able to answer them all correctly, even when he did not know the meaning of the technical terms he used. Finally, Dr. Anderson gave up. "Simon, I've got to pass you. According to the rules, I've got to pass you. But God help you if you're ever called to treat a pregnant woman!"

"I'd know what to do."

"You would? What would you do?"

"I'd send for you."

"Passed!"

And so, with no objections raised, Simon Flexner became Simon Flexner, M.D.[8]

His medical degree clinking (so to speak) in his pocket, the new doctor could not resist a call to cure an ailing cousin, Zerlina Frank, "a dark, attractive child of about ten or eleven." Simon diagnosed malaria and prescribed quinine. Her condition worsened. Simon called in an "old practitioner," who pointed to some rose-colored spots on the girl's body and gave the correct diagnosis: typhoid. Simon was disgusted with himself. Never again in his whole life did he attempt to practice medicine.[9]

At the ceremony held in Macauley's Theatre accompanying his graduation from the Medical Institute, Simon ushered in a rented suit. He was told by one of his professors that he looked "handsome" which, for the first time, "called to my attention" that his appearance could be an asset. He was thus encouraged to be more particular about his clothes. Up until then, being eager to give every possible penny he had earned to his mother, he had welcomed hand-me-downs or, when he bought something, selected the cheapest. Now he sometimes chose nicer things, even if they cost a little more — but not without a sense of guilt. His realization that the family finances were gradually loosening up did not keep him from looking at the floor when he handed to Esther a smaller sum than she had come to expect. She never commented, but he knew that she was disappointed.[10]

Surprisingly for so young a man, Simon's hair had receded beyond his forehead some distance across the top of his head. This caused him so much regret that when I, in my twenties, began showing a similar symptom, my father used his medical leverage to send me to several skin specialists.* However, Simon's semibaldness did make his forehead look impressively high and deep. A very strong nose continued the forehead's downward line. It was flanked with gray-green eyes that burned with intelligence and intensity. The mouth and chin were also strong, although his features in no way were heavy: he was delicately made. Few would have joined with Simon's professor in calling him handsome, yet his was a face that was not easily overlooked.[11]

Simon's first close companion since his boyhood friend Frank Adams was an easterner who worked in a Louisville hardware concern. Frank Cooley was very tall and thin, with a prominent Adam's apple. "It was a sight to watch the larynx bob up and down as it did when he laughed. He had an odd laugh, not outright, but rather spasmodic with gurgling sounds" made in rhythm with his larynx and a movement of his shoulders.

Frank's attraction for Simon was that, in addition to supplying companionship long lacked, he knew his way around in a fascinating but strange world to which he introduced Simon. He lodged with a genteel but financially reduced family named Miller. The "lovely Mrs. Miller," who was part of "the high-brow set," particularly impressed Simon with her mild and gentle manners.

Simon occasionally spent Saturday nights at the Millers'. On Sunday mornings, "it was customary to sing hymns after breakfast and before church time. Cooley played on the piano at least sufficiently to provide accompaniment for the singing. I look back with amused amazement to my singing of the hymns. I have neither voice nor ear, and it must have

---

* I still have, some fifty years later, hair enough between my forehead and my bald spot to accumulate into a satisfactory hedge.

jarred on all their sensibilities to listen to my blundering efforts, and possibly to reflect on the anomaly of my taking part in so Christian a practice. I did not, of course, attend church with them. I suppose I made my way to the drugstore."[12]

However, Simon got some of his own back when he and Cooley spent two nights in a Trappist monastery at Gethsemane, Kentucky. "We ate in the hall with the monks and attended services at all hours" in "perpetual silence except for the chanting at services." As the friends were leaving, a monk who was permitted to talk asked them their religious faith. Cooley (who was to become a minister) replied, "Episcopalian." Flexner said "Jew." The monk pointed at Flexner and said, "You are nearer."

To pay New Year's calls, Simon and Cooley hired a carriage with two horses and a driver in uniform. Simon, considering it more discreet not to stir up his family, carried his rented clothes to Cooley's rooms. There the friends decked themselves out in Prince Albert coats, top hats, and gloves. It was fun to pull up in style before elegant doorways, but in the drawing rooms, shaking hands with the ladies, Simon felt strange and ill at ease.

As time passed, he became more acclimated. Since he could not always be renting, he finally decided to buy an evening dress suit. Feeling in imagination his mother's reproachful eyes upon him, Simon entered the tailor's shop of Samuel Slaughter. He agreed to pay the sum, frightening even though it could be met in installments, of fifty-seven dollars.

After the final fitting, Simon steeled himself to carry his purchase home. The big, flat box attracted attention, and when it was opened the contents inspired amazement and disapproval. Nothing like this had ever been seen in the Flexner household before! Simon took the suit upstairs to his bedroom and put it on. As he was admiring the effect in his mirror, the door opened and his mother came in to stand silently behind him. In a surge of rebellion, he turned to her and said, "Mother, tonight you lose your son."

Esther did not say a word.[13]

During the three years between Abraham's return from Baltimore and Simon's graduation from the Medical Institute, the medical scene at the Hopkins had expanded. Although the establishment of the medical school was blocked by lack of funds, the hospital had just opened. The principal physicians and surgeons were appointed professors in the university: William S. Halsted, William Osler, Howard A. Kelly (with Welch the famous "Four Doctors" of the Sargent portrait — see

PLATE 20), and Henry M. Hurd. Welch's instruction in pathology was ready to enter its third year. A fellowship was open for competition — and in Louisville Simon now had his qualifying M.D.

With Abraham's encouragement, Simon applied for the fellowship, sending his paper on urinalysis with the microscopic slides that supported his findings. This was an exercise in naiveté. How the slides were viewed at the Hopkins Simon learned when he and Welch were colleagues. "Popsy," as the great teacher came to be called, "loved to tell stories that would put his friends agreeably in the wrong. Thus he insisted all his life that . . . I submitted as examples of my work in pathology slides of insects' eyes and butterfly wings which young ladies make in finishing school." Simon never got over being slightly annoyed at this travesty against his youthful self.[14]

At the drugstore, Simon had encouraged Jacob to go into manufacturing. All drugstores were in those days little factories, putting up the pills and fluid extracts they sold. As the big drug manufacturers had not yet got into the specialty business, it was natural for druggists, who developed specific remedies successful in their neighborhoods, to move on to other neighborhoods.

Simon conceived the idea of merchandizing albuminate of iron: simple solutions in syrup and mixtures with quinine and other substances. After he and Isadore had made promising sales trips to central Kentucky, Cincinnati, and even Chicago, professional drummers from New York were employed and the country generally canvased. The sales grew very much larger, but Simon became worried. Was overexpansion, which had ruined Hirsch and Flexner, to destroy the drugstore that was the most successful enterprise of the next generation? There were disturbing signs. Jacob dunned for a small debt an influential physician who had sent many patients to the drugstore. The doctor paid at once but no more of his patients appeared.[15]

Simon, having failed to secure the Hopkins fellowship, made, during the summer of 1889, an extensive trip which (quite coincidentally) crossed his path with the two sides of his future wife's family, the Whitalls and the Thomases. The drugstore bought its glass from the New York branch of Whitall, Tatum and Company. On what was his first trip to New York, Simon called at the salesrooms and was taken to lunch at the Astor House. Then came the nerve-racking part of the trip: a visit to Baltimore, the Hopkins, and especially the Pathological, as the reconditioned morgue was called. (PLATE 18)

The Pathological proved to be an ugly building of stone, two stories high with a six-window front, made both hideous and grotesque by square chimneys at both ends which were as tall as the building below them, and heavily decorated at the top with courses of brick. It being vacation time, no one was there but the janitor, Shutz. He led Simon into the large room where classes were held. On the walls cases with sliding glass doors held the sections, ranged on shelves. Simon explained to Shutz his eagerness for knowledge and his need for any materials he might take home with him for study. Shutz, who doubled as laboratory assistant, showed Simon some refinements in methods of staining, and also gave him sections left over from classroom teaching. "I did not exactly buy them, but gave him a present."

With what excitement Simon carried the slides home to Louisville and laid them out on the family dining room table where he had so often worked under the familiar gas jet. His anticipations were great: he would teach himself — as he had always taught himself — what he would have learned at the Hopkins had his fellowship application been accepted. But alas! Consulting passionately what books he could get together, straining his intellect to the sticking point, he could make no sense out of the slides.[16]

This was clearly the end of the road: Simon had gone as far as he could by working in isolation altogether on his own. Observing his brother's quandary and despair, Abraham came to the rescue. He would extract, from what he was earning as a teacher and had been handing on to his mother, the necessary funds to pay for a year's study in Baltimore or, if Simon preferred, Philadelphia.

When this offer became known in the Flexner household, it by no means received universal support. That this deviation from the Flexner system should be arranged without any consultation with him was a major blow at Jacob's long-held family hegemony — and by threatening to remove Simon, it struck at his drugstore. Jacob offered to make Simon his partner if only he would stay. Simon's reply could only have deepened Jacob's chagrin: he doubted that the drugstore was making enough money to support them both.

Esther expressed worry at the effect on the family finances of the disappearance of Simon's earnings and also of the money Abraham would advance him. Her concern may have had a deeper emotional base. Did she foresee the actual loss of her son, then twenty-six, to a world she could not penetrate and hardly even imagine?[17]

Simon assured his mother that nothing in his plans indicated a permanent or even an extended absence from home. He would stay in the outside world only long enough to procure the knowledge that would enable him to set in motion what he had long intended: a personal laboratory, serving the medical profession in Louisville. How strongly he himself believed this is revealed by his amazement at what Dr. Bodine said when he called to say goodbye. Down the years, he would again and again repeat the physician's statement as a remarkable example of prophecy. "Simon," Bodine said, "you will never again return to Louisville."[18]

IV

Privileges and Traumas

18

Helen's Childhood

FROM the summary of the year 1871 in Mary Thomas's journal: "In the eighth month a little girl was born and named Helen Whitall Thomas. A black-eyed, red-headed little puss, the merriest, smartest baby that ever was seen. Nellie's nursery was the great point of attraction in the house, and she soon got to know all her sisters and brothers and love them very much."

The sisters and brothers, whom the mother stated that the newborn infant almost instantly loved, were to look down on Helen year after year from the higher rungs of a ladder that increased in height as Helen grew, so that the distances remained always the same: Carey (sixteen years her senior), John (twelve), Harry (ten), Bond (eight), Grace (five), and Margaret (two). Events in the lives of her elder siblings, even if they took place before the younger child was born, foreshadowed Helen's existence. As for Helen's personal experiences, however important they were to her, they seemed to the others trivial happenings after the parade had passed. Helen in her book of reminiscences, *A Quaker Childhood,* was to reconstruct the lives of her elders, her siblings as well as her parents, as part of her own life, to dwell again and again on the burden and loneliness of being so far down in so large and energetic a family.

When she was eighteen months old, a little brother, Frank, was born. "A great pleasure to Nell, who did not know," Mary commented, "that her privileges were somewhat curtailed by 'the cry baby' as she called him at first. Afterwards, she called him 'little felly,' until it became almost his name." She was pleased that Frank could not come down to breakfast: she could now have the nurse all to herself. The little tot was bossy. "Come my shilions, come to bed," Nellie ordered the children directly above her in age, "or I'll tell Moze." She called herself "Molia's Nella." She was "the most daring talker, she attempts everything she hears." When eight years old, she wrote her sister Carey a self-proving sentence, "Iccuze the spelling." She never could spell, a characteristic she handed on to the author of this volume.

In her own account of her earliest years, Heien equated the nurse with peace, her father with reassurance, her mother with love, fascination, and fear. The memoir opens with a scene: Helen stands above a stairwell she is too young to descend, staring down at the front door of the house beyond which a thunderstorm rages. Her mother is out in the storm. A terrific flash and crash! Nellie screams. Her father appears, gathers her up in his arms, and calms her sobs with assurances that God is watching over her mother.

"Moments of complete peace when I was a tiny child I also remember. My mother's soft embrace enfolding me, my father's voice singing of trust in God, his figure looming opposite. . . . My mother has lulled me into a state of enchanted oblivion."

Then come two memories of terror. Her mother urges her to control her temper by repeating, "Get thee behind me Satan!" Helen takes the phrase literally; she dares not turn her head lest she see Satan's face. The entire house, even the sunny nursery, even her mother's room when empty, is haunted by Satan. God, to whom she prays every morning and night, was said to control Satan. But, God is far away, and Satan is there, ever lurking behind her. However, her mother can control Satan.

When Helen was six, Dora, the last child, died, becoming a wept-over doll in her mother's lap. Then a strange man brought through a side door a narrow white wooden box. "My baby sister was to be shut up in that shining white box, and this was what it meant to be dead! Horror seized me."

With Dora dead and no more children expected, the nurse departed and the nursery environment collapsed. Now was the time when most younger children would secure protection through alliance with an elder. Not Helen: she assumed the care of Frank, now four years old. The two children became so inseparable that they were known in the family as "us." One of Helen's bitterest memories was the hooting reaction of her elder brothers when she walked over to her mother and said, "Will thee please take care of Frankie for me while I go into the house? I won't be long." The incident was kept alive with jeers: "Since Nellie won't be here to manage, I suppose we shall have to ask Mother to do the best she can." To the end of her life, Helen was outraged by such unfairness. She was not trying to take over from her mother but to help her — a mother who was weighed down by so many tasks. (PLATE 14)

Another early memory. It was Christmas and the big folding doors between the front and back parlors had been closed all day. "When at last the doors were thrown open, there at the foot of the glistening tree stood Santa Claus himself. Thrilled that we should be so honored, I gazed with deep excitement at the great Christmas fairy" and saw, between the cap and the beard, "the brows and eyes of my father. 'It isn't Santa Claus at all,' I cried out. 'It's Father, it's Father!' One of my elder sisters tried to quiet me, to stop the scene, but I would not be still. 'Take off thy beard, Father; take it off please.' Jumping up and down in excitement, I began to sob and stopped only when my father, wig and beard discarded, took me up in his arms."

Frank, who had been looking on disapprovingly, took to urging Nellie not to ask about the Easter bunny; she might find out that rabbits did not lay eggs. For her part, Helen stayed upset: her mother had taught her that deception was wicked, and her father had pretended to be someone he was not. Then she overheard a conversation that brought her relief: her mother said she had never approved of the Santa Claus charade. This and other crises persuaded Dr. Thomas that Helen was so "easily excited and stimulated" that her mind should be given a rest. She was held back to go to school with Frank. However, the delay did not serve to perpetuate "us." A growing boy will not put up forever with being governessed by an elder sister, and Frank enjoyed the privilege of being his father's favorite. Finding herself moving alone through a large house inhabited by a large family, Helen turned to an ever more vehement worship of her mother.

Her mother was amused when little Helen stated, after attending a religious meeting for small children, that from now on she would live a more holy life. Mary could not visualize how her daughter could be more devoted to God. But, as Helen remembered in her later years, her thoughts never rose to God. "My imagination never traveled further than my mother." Her mother was the beneficent spirit who presided over her life, whose principles (consistent, so she believed, and infallible) the child labored to observe and serve.[1]

Helen was eight when she heard what was for her the most terrifying possible news: her parents were planning to go by themselves on a trip to Europe. She would be left behind! Her mother would disappear!

It was explained to her that this vacation would be the first extended period in more than twenty-five years that her parents would be together alone, without any children. But, Helen would not accept separation from her mother. "I neither ate nor slept." Expressing fear that Helen's health would be permanently damaged, Mary insisted on taking her along, a decision that involved also taking Frank. "The theft of my mother's holiday," the mature Helen Flexner wrote, "seems to me by all odds the worst piracy I ever committed." But perhaps the piracy was not against her mother but against her father. A few years before, Mary had written: "The Doctor and I came home without any children. . . . The feeling was perfectly desolate. Seems too lonely to be possible. I could not sleep and tossed and turned."[2]

In England, where their parents attended the London Yearly Meeting, Helen and Frank were assigned to a governess. But, when Mary and James made a quick trip to Italy, the children were left for a few weeks at Leipzig with their sister Carey.

Carey was, like Jacob Flexner in Simon's family, the oldest sibling and the most powerful and effective. For the dominant role to be played by a girl well suited Whitall predilections. That Carey was less a force than Jacob in managing the household was only because no power vacuum existed. Over the long run, Carey exerted a much greater influence on Helen's personality and behavior than Jacob did on Simon's. Carey's influence was one of the things Simon had to fight to win his bride.

In 1865, when eight years old, Carey had set herself on fire fooling around the family kitchen. Mary put out the flames by wrapping her in a rug, but Carey was so seriously burned that she seemed about to die. Once recovered, she returned to venting her tremendous energies as a tomboy. One of her happy memories as an old lady was how she and another girl, scornful of the boys who cowered timorously on the shore, skated on ice "that cracked like all creation. . . . My, but it was dangerous! The ice just waved up and down and heaved in great billows while we passed over it. It was perfectly elegant fun." She earned by the unladylike act of dissecting a dead mouse notoriety so extreme that it made trouble for her years later when she labored to found in Baltimore the Bryn Mawr School.[3]

Having returned from a public lecture, Carey wrote as a girl of fifteen: "One thing I am determined on, and that is by the time I die *my* brain will weigh as much as any *man's* if I study and learning can make it so. Then I'll leave it in the hands of some physiologist so that after that no miserable man can stand up on a miserable platform and tell" that it was a "FEW — this is eight ounces — less than any other man's." (The slip that made her write "any other man's" need not be overlooked.)[4]

Her parents sent her to an excellent Quaker boarding school, the Howland Institute. The choice of this school came naturally, but the educational steps that were to follow involved marching in the very front line with those who insisted on violating established sex lines. Carey refused to go to Vassar, which she considered a polite female seminary, but was bent on attending the great roaring, democratic college of Cornell, which was about to open its doors to a few women.

Concerning family objections to Cornell, Carey fabricated a story, expressive of hatred for her father, that was to influence considerably the attitudes of her youngest sister, and since the false story is much cited in feminist literature, it has also affected the attitudes towards men of many other women. According to the story, which is repeated with complete belief in Helen's book, James had been dead against Carey's receiving such a serious education as Cornell offered, but Mary had passionately supported her daughter. Finally, the mother said to Carey: "Nothing is left us except tears. I have used every argument I can think of in talking to thy father. Reason will not move him. Now we will see whether he can stand out against our weeping. We shall both have to cry day and night." So they cried and cried until "worried and distressed beyond endurance by their wet eyes and wet faces, my father surrendered at last."

Helen went on to state that her mother's being "forced to employ a method so alien to her noble courage was dreadfully painful to me. Without suffering that indignity she should have been able to give her talented daughter, on whose career her heart was set, the education she herself had longed for and been denied by destiny.... I remember too well the expression of composed sadness that habitually settled on her face when she ceased to smile or speak. Although she was always cheerful in action, I knew even as a small girl that my mother was fundamentally sad at heart. This profoundly intuitive knowledge aroused my passionate devotion."[5]

What had really happened? The crying episode is completely disproved by Carey's own diary. Furthermore, Carey knew perfectly well that her father was not opposed to educating women since he had spoken thus at her own graduation from the Howland Institute: "Surely the woman is most fitted to be useful who had most highly developed her intellect.... The power to gain such culture constitutes the undoubted right to its attainment. . . . Surely, in this day we need trained and cultivated women, we need their aid in the vast struggles that are today arranging the good and evil forces of society. . . . Nowhere does the need for the purifying and ennobling influence of culture and refinement more prominently appear than in the present home and social life of the country."[6]

This last sentence undoubtedly outraged Carey, but her mother did not disagree. Mary was to tell Carey's intellectual female companions that not one of them was as happy as she was herself "whose concern lies in temperance work and reformations, and preaching, and housekeeping."[7]

The actual family objection to Cornell was thus expressed to Carey in a letter from her mother, which quoted President Eliot of Harvard. Eliot, who was in Baltimore consulting with Carey's father concerning plans for the Hopkins, had said that "coeducation does very well in communities where persons were more on an equality, but where persons of all classes are thrown together it works badly: unpleasant associations are formed and disastrous marriages often result."

"I should be unwilling," Mary continued in her own voice, "to place thee at a mixed college so do not set thy ideas that way." After Carey had beaten down her parents' objections and was off to Cornell, her mother continued to express disapproval: "What earthly good will a wretched degree from that wretched university do thee? Absolutely none" beyond "a little satisfaction for thy pride and ambition."[8]

Carey had overcome the objections of her indulgent and not-altogether-unsympathetic parents by the indomitable force of her own will. The traditional resource for rebellious Quaker women of claiming a command from the Lord was here inapplicable since Cornell (this was one of her parents' objections) was not likely to do a Quaker's soul much good. That it had not became manifest when, after her graduation, Carey came back to Baltimore.

During Carey's absence at Cornell, her father had voted as a trustee of the Hopkins that the emerging university be coeducational. He had been voted down, yet Carey returned to Baltimore convinced that at no other university in the United States could she secure the further education she desired. She tried to get around the ban with unofficial studies. Despite her father's backing, the result was two years of frustration, which made her far from pleasant in her parents' household.

"Our household is not constructed right," she wrote in her diary. "I do not think there is enough ceremony observed. Everything goes at loose ends. . . . I am *sure* there is a possibility of everything about a house being managed; things cooked properly and dusted and proper behavior at table, without precluding all outside interest. If people realized that to have more children than they can afford to train and support properly was a greater crime than anything else I am sure it would be better."[9]

It was during Carey's stay at home, from Helen's seventh to her ninth year, that the child first got to know her older sister. Carey encouraged reading, was dictatorial, sometimes indulgent, often difficult, and not above raising storms.

In her book, Helen recalled with amusement the drama that ensued when Carey told her that she had personally named her after "the most famous woman that ever lived. . . . Thee ought to be thankful to me for being named after Helen of Troy." As Carey expatiated on the choice, it became clear that the namesake had run away from her husband with another man and had caused a terrible war. Helen threw herself on the floor wailing that since she had been named after so wicked a woman she would have to be wicked too.

"Nonsense!" replied Carey. "Thee needn't worry. Thee'll never be like Helen of Troy."

Helen hesitated to bother her mother, but on this occasion she raced. Mary Thomas calmly dried the child's tears, saying that Helen of Troy had nothing to do with it. She herself had made the choice because "Helen Whitall Thomas" would sound so well when read aloud before that great occasion for Quakers, the London Yearly Meeting, when Helen was old enough to be sent there as a delegate. "Everything was all right. My mother never failed to make things right for me."[10]

Eventually, Mary had it out with her oldest daughter. Carey noted in her diary, "I have just had a talk with Mother and I do believe I will shoot myself. I almost think I will. . . . She says I outrage her every feeling, that it is the greatest living grief to have me in the house. A denier and defamer of Christ whom she loves more than she loves me. That I am a finder of fault in the house . . . that I make the other children unbelieving, that I barely tolerate Father. . . . Oh, heavens, what a religion that makes a mother cast off her daughter!"[11]

With four other Baltimore women in their early twenties, Carey set up what they called "The Group." It was what today would be called a "consciousness-raising session," but in those days the women needed to sail much more perilous seas. When the Doctor was out of town, Carey collected a pile of his medical books: they made a thorough anatomical investigation of sex, in the process becoming nauseated and filled with revulsion at the bestiality of men who would wish to inflict such things on women.[12] The young women wondered whether marriage would be possible — they doubted it — without such barbarous practices, and considered the superiority of love between women whose "warm kisses" did not imply bestialities. Malthus's newly published theories about eventual overpopulation were cited as relieving women of the duty of having children. There were also less emotionally harrowing discussions on how women could achieve an education and become less enslaved to fathers and husbands.

The fact that one member of "The Group" was M. Carey Thomas, and another Mary Garrett, who was to achieve great power as an heiress, made these obscure discussions in Baltimore parlors lead to events of national moment.

A fissure in the ice pack opened in Germany. Andrew D. White, president of Cornell and now American ambassador in Berlin, was a friend of James Carey Thomas. He reported that a few women students were to be allowed at the University of Leipzig.

This erupted a family crisis, the issue now being, even in Carey's telling, not female education but a duty to protect the safety of a daughter. For an unmarried and handsome woman in her mid twenties, accompanied only by a similar companion, to go abroad and become one of the very few female students in a large, traditionally male foreign university was a prospect that would have daunted even the most sympathetic of nineteenth-century fathers. James said no. But Mary was more daring than he and, being a woman, more dedicated to feminine issues. She was willing, however regretfully, to take the risk. The matter was solved through the traditional Quaker expedient of delegating a required decision to someone else. James abdicated his traditional male responsibility. "Mother," Carey wrote, "took the whole responsibility of my going, and afterwards Father was lovely. It made me see even with Father's liberality how tremendous a sacrifice it was for him . . . of parental responsibility, authority, traditional feeling about women, etc." But this flash of understanding did not prevent Carey from adding that such male prejudices called for "invectives like those of the French Revolution."[13]

Although Mary had accepted the responsibility, she wrote, "I can't help pitying her. It seems dreadful to me."[14]

* * *

Carey's companion was another member of "The Group," Mamie Gwinn. The lives they felt required to lead in Leipzig seem today to belong on another planet. The preconception was that unchaperoned single women being presented with so many opportunities as they moved freely among hoards of young men would practice sexual immorality damaging to the honor of a university and disgraceful to the practice of education. During Carey's stay she was in danger of being expelled because the behavior of some Russian women in Berlin threatened to close all German universities to women. Denouncing the Russians as traitors to their sex, Carey and Mamie moved through the streets and the lecture halls with their eyes fixed on the ground, speaking to no male, not seeming to notice the male students around them. They never went out after dark. They saw to it that conferences with professors were rigorously chaperoned.[15] And now they had two small children foisted upon them!

Helen remembered: "Frank and I created a sensation, as Carey put it, when we first appeared on the streets with her and Miss Gwinn. Several of the young men stopped short on the pavement to watch us all go by together — university students, my sister said they were. She denounced their rudeness, but somehow seemed more amused than annoyed by their staring. 'It's a good thing the children are no younger,' I heard her say to Miss Gwinn with a laugh." Helen puzzled over why her age and Frank's made any difference.

On the first Sunday after Helen's arrival, Carey casually told her to get ready to go to a concert in the public gardens. Carey must have forgotten, Helen replied, that it was Sunday.

"Of course, it is Sunday," the answer came. "Does thee think I have time to go to concerts on weekdays?"

The fact remained, Helen pointed out, that going to a concert on Sunday was a sin of which their mother would not approve. To all of Carey's growingly irritated expostulations, the child had only one answer: her mother would not approve. Finally, Carey and Miss Gwinn went by themselves under the disapproving stare of the nine-year-old, who was confident that she was standing up for an inviolable moral principle.

The next crisis. Frank needed a bath. There were only public baths. The public baths were segregated by sexes. Carey and Mamie having eschewed all male acquaintance, the only solution was to get Frank in during women's hours by dressing him in Helen's clothes. No sexual considerations bothered Helen — she had long shared a bedroom with Frank — but she knew that it was a sin to act out a lie. Her mother would not approve. Her loyalty to her mother made her upbraid Carey, who this time angrily overruled her. As for Frank, he was delighted by the lark, giving a comic imitation of Helen after he was dressed in her clothes.

Carey, of course, would complain to their mother when the family reconvened, but Helen felt no qualms. Principles were principles, and she had behaved as her mother's faithful representative. She would receive from her ideal the praise she deserved.

Shortly after the family came together, Carey told the story of Frank and the public bath. Helen was outraged to hear her sister make a joke of it, and flabbergasted when her mother laughed. After a stunned moment, Helen broke in: "Please, Mother, listen to me. Carey hasn't told thee about wanting us to go to concerts with her on Sunday afternoon."

"My mother's face," so Helen Flexner's memoir continues, "lost its smile. . . . 'Thee must not forget that taking care of Frank and thee was very hard for Carey. She had to do what she could in the circumstances. Thy duty was to obey her, and not make things more difficult by objecting. It was not thy business to judge.'

"I stood by my mother's chair speechless with amazement. Never could any human being have been less prepared for disaster." Having kissed Helen, her mother let her run off alone to hide her tears.

Even that was not the end. The whole party, which included Mamie Gwinn, now traveled together. As they advanced through Switzerland in a carriage, it was fun for Nellie and Frank to throw to the begging children who followed them the religious tracts their parents had brought along for that purpose, even when the children, after they had struggled with each other for a piece of paper and then discovered what it was, shook their fists at the retreating vehicle. But disaster lurked in a hotel at Geneva where a dark bottle stood upon the dinner table.

Informed that the bottle contained wine, Frank said he would like to discover what wine tasted like. Beverages containing "the creature" were for Quakers anathema. The answer was a firm no. But Frank pleaded and he was his father's favorite. Finally, James decided that it would be educational for Frank to learn that wine was not sweet like sarsaparilla. He poured a spoonful in Frank's glass.

Could Helen's parents have forgotten, could Frank himself have forgotten, how, in the basement room of the Baltimore Meeting House, she and Frank had, by pledging never as long as they lived to touch liquor, become members of the Infant Band of Hope? Had they not on innumerable afternoons marched around the room singing temperance songs? And now Frank was actually lifting the glass to his lips! At the horrifying sight, Helen burst into tears.

"My father turned to my mother, and said in a tone of utter exasperation, 'Do quiet the child, Mary. The children are a dreadful nuisance. . . . I begged thee to leave them at home where they belong.' "

Unable to quiet Helen's sobbing, Mary led her upstairs to her bedroom. Then "she talked to me very severely, blaming me for lack of self-control, big girl that I was. The public exhibition I had made of myself had disgraced my father and her. She had expected better behavior from me.

" 'I will try to be better, Mother,' I promised, struggling to control my sobs. 'I'm terribly sorry. But what will happen to Frank? He has broken his pledge.' At the thought of my little brother's deadly sin, my tears gushed out again."

Taking no notice of the question, her mother put Helen to bed, told her to stay there until she returned, and departed.

Helen stared into the dark, trying to puzzle out why her mother had not defended her own principles, why she had punished her daughter for trying to defend them. Eventually, Helen fell asleep. She woke up to see her mother standing tranquilly by her bed. But Mary never explained.

As the party traveled on, Helen, too puzzled and unhappy to join the others, wandered in perplexity through the large public rooms of alien hotels. Why? Yes, she had disgraced herself by making a public scene. "But I was right about the temperance pledge. I was right about Sunday too and acting a lie." Why had her mother laughed at her and scolded her? Always, so it seemed, occupied with Carey and Miss Gwinn, the mother seemed utterly indifferent to her younger daughter's unhappiness and confusion; and Helen lacked the courage to ask questions of her idol, all the more because the answers would be to her of such transcendent importance. A terrible thought haunted her: "Was it possible that my mother did not mean what she said to be taken seriously?"

Time passed, there was a diverting trip through Switzerland, an ocean crossing, and Helen was back again in her usual world with her usual occupations. "Whatever the deeper psychological effects," she was, so she remembered, "superficially" the same little girl. Yet, "I now know" that her experiences abroad "affected me profoundly." Her object in life, to please her mother, had enabled her to follow comfortably the main drive of that religiously oriented household, since her mother was for her the surrogate of the Lord. But now she no longer knew how to please her mother. "I became anxious and uncertain. I could no longer automatically apply the rules I had lived by before. . . . The joy had gone out of being good."

Her idol had become capricious, strange, implacable. The door was opened to fear.

Most fortunately, the stay at Leipzig had also opened for Helen an escape. "For the first time I got a sense of interests that were not inspired by religious motives." Carey's passion to make herself a signal fire of female learning communicated itself to Helen, although the results were delayed. Mamie's love of poetry offered a more immediate and, in the long run, a deeper resource.

Mamie's "appearance fascinated me. Tall and exceedingly slender with crinkly black hair and pale skin, she was quite different from anyone I knew. The Thomas family all had hair that gleamed in the light. We were inclined to be short and sturdy and were energetic and quick in our movements, not languid like Miss Gwinn. . . . The slow smile that often curved her lips puzzled and fascinated me. I did not quite know what it expressed. Since she attended few lectures, she spent her days in her room. Always when I got a glimpse of her she was curled up on the sofa there, absorbed in a book that somehow seemed too heavy for her thin white hands to hold." Sometimes, Helen continued, "she read poetry aloud to me, Swinburne's poetry only, as I remember." Helen joined in by learning "The Garden of Proserpine" by heart.

Her love for poetry filled "the void left by a gradual fading away of religious emotion. . . . Uncertain and given to brooding by temperament from earliest childhood, I had relied on hypnotic effects of half-understood Biblical phrases to help me through my inner difficulties. . . . I now slid easily into repeating a line of poetry for purposes of incantation." Swinburne's poem "gave me comfort when I most needed it. Almost any of the verses could be crooned until I was at peace."

What Helen remembered as the greatest emancipation of her life emerged when she achieved the ability to read fluently to herself. No longer was she impelled to wander the house seeking some elder who would read to her or at least allow her to hang around. Now she had a resource ever at hand. She read mostly sentimental novels aimed at growing girls. However, she never forgot her excitement when she found on an older sister's bookcase a volume of Shelley's poems which she appropriated. Now she had another magical voice to add to Swinburne's. However, the final verse of "The Garden of Proserpine" continued to suit her melancholy spirit best of all:

> *Then sun nor star shall waken*
> *Nor any change of light;*
> *Nor sound of water shaken*
> *Nor any sound or sight;*
> *Nor wintry leaves nor vernal*
> *Nor days nor things diurnal;*
> *Only the sleep eternal*
> *In an internal night.*

19

Evangelists

THE immigrant Flexners, wishing to start their children in America with a clean slate, underemphasized their ancient religious tradition, all the more because it would set them apart. The religious tradition of Helen's parents also (although to a lesser degree) set them apart in American life, but was so cherished and stressed that Helen summarized her early years as a "Quaker childhood."

After Carey's recovery from her almost mortal burn, Mary wrote her sister Sarah that she had experienced how "utterly vain it was to depend on man in any way, but that our dependence must be on the Lord. . . . How is it that I can have passed through what I have, should have cried out unto the Lord in my trouble, should have been heard, and been conscious that he had intervened in our behalf — and yet I do not find my heart filled with love and gratitude as I ought." She begged Sarah to "write something to strengthen me."[1] She depended on "the sympathy and fellowship" of her sisters. Her husband was less sympathetic. "The Doctor says I must be darkening council with an excess of words."[2]

When the Thomas-dominated Baltimore Quakers built a new meeting house, Mary was not inspired by the colorless cushions on walnut benches chosen "to give an example of simplicity." The worshippers, she commented, looked as if they were sitting on a rail fence. "There is not one extraneous or objectionable thing in it, yet is it calculated to impress people with its superiority to the meeting houses of other denominations?" The drabness, Mary could not resist adding, suited her husband's preaching.[3]

James's preaching was downright, rough and ready. Eager to take any opportunity to spread God's word, he went to the docks at noonday to preach to the sailors. His favorite congregation was composed of young men, whom (as it was common to comment praisingly) he "loved" and wished to help start out in the world on paths that would lead to noble and successful lives. He established a Sunday mission school for boys in the poorer district of Baltimore — he would get his daughters, including Helen when she was older, to teach Bible classes there — and was active in the Young Men's Christian Association at the Hopkins and elsewhere; he was concerned with boys in reform schools, and with protecting youth from temptation to vice. Helen thus described his oratorical style: "His broad figure occupied a raised platform powerfully; his arms moved in swift, emphatic gestures; his sonorous voice, rolling out his sentences, came to a pause always on the right word. Practical and direct as my father's preaching to the boys was, the voice and gestures produced a kind of exultation."[4]

Mary found her husband's attitude towards religion stodgy, too directly practical, and worst of all, impersonal. Following in her father's footsteps, Mary saw religion as a quest for personal communion with the Savior. She was, she wrote one of her sisters, "mercifully preserved in much quietness of spirit but I long for joy." The reading of scripture she took with great seriousness, but she also needed "experimental knowledge." By this she meant consciously altering your attitudes and behavior, and then discovering through introspection whether this brought you closer to the Lord. Much could be gained by comparing methods and results with those other seekers. Furthermore, shared emotion could carry you over hurdles which you by yourself could not transcend.

The three Whitall sisters exchanged experiences and reactions in thousands and thousands of words. Quaker meetings could be inspiring and informative: there would be, for instance, "a good outpouring about not loving God enough." However, there often were dull meetings from which Mary came away depressed. Putting on her Quaker bonnet (whether as protection or a statement of principle) she attended Methodist services, in which exhortation was passionate and religious emotion was inspired by the singing of hymns. "I am not going forward," she explained, "and I cannot stand still."

Very valuable were prayer meetings at which pious women from different denominations got together, often in the Thomas parlor, to seek "outpourings of the spirit." At these meetings, Mary began collecting the constituency of female followers that was to augment during the rest of her career.

Although revivals were anathema to Quakers, Mary began envisioning a revival to stir up Baltimore.[5]

In the history of ideas, as in physics, every thrust produces a counterthrust. The era which fostered the scientific theorizing of men like Herbert Spencer that undermined religion in Simon's childhood home was also, as reflected in Helen's world, an era of passionate religious revival.

When it was possible to communicate over thousands of miles by telegraph to people you could not see, why could you not communicate with the dead? When you could speed over the ground by power drawn from minerals, why could you not levitate through the air by power drawn from faith? Individualism, working hand in hand with democratic thinking, made multitudes of all ranks and preconceptions want to know God as a personal experience. Improved transportation enabled crowds to gather where the word of God was conspicuously spoken, and romanticism encouraged roaring surges of emotion.

Hannah exulted to her sister Mary when Helen was still helpless in her cradle: "The age is too far advanced and the mantle of Christian charity is too widely spread over the church of the present to make the narrow judging limitations of the past at all tenable now. I am far more concerned with the wonderful revival of spiritual holiness that is spreading everywhere. I believe a flood is soon going to sweep over the church," washing away all small doctrinal issues. "It seems to me like the bride making herself ready for the Bridegroom; like the five wise virgins filling their lamps with oil in preparation for the midnight cry."[6] (PLATE 16)

Hannah had married Robert Pearsall Smith, scion of an old and distinguished Philadelphia family and, when Hannah got to know him, a most persuasive salesman for Whitall, Tatum and Company. Both he and Hannah were religious seekers: they tried to revolutionize the Philadelphia Yearly Meeting, and subsequently joined successively the Methodists, the Plymouth Brethren, and the Baptists. Robert suffered from a period of mental illness, attributed to a fall from a horse, and then became associated with William Boardman, an itinerant evangelist who argued that it was not enough to have Christ, when you were "born again," take your sins upon himself. You must be enabled to walk this earth with Christ. "Forgiveness does not satisfy me. I want the dominion of sin destroyed. Purification no less than pardon!" Boardman's

Higher Life Movement, of which Robert became the outstanding expo-
nent, demanded a second conversion, being reborn a second time.

Robert typically converted himself. He was preaching at a camp
meeting when the second blessing he was urging on the others broke
upon him like a thunderclap. As the burden of sin lifted from him, he
heard a call to spread everywhere the divine and purifying word.

On a missionary trip to England, the Smiths preached at Broadlands, the mansion of the Honorable William Cowper Temple, where
more than one hundred rooms filled up periodically with evangelically
minded aristocrats. Robert was a sensation. Extremely handsome and
well-mannered, unlike other evangelists a gentleman, he poured out in a
red-hot stream untrammeled emotions. "Emotions," his wife was to
comment, "are more contagious than the most contagious disease in the
universe." Hannah gave Bible readings that included saner comments.

The Smiths' ministry made the "Broadlands Conference" so "fruitful" that Robert was called to organize a greater meeting at the Oxford
Union, where for ten days thousands of rich and blue-blooded Britons
fell on their knees to their own great satisfaction. Then they returned in
elevated moods to their denominational churches.

Most amazing was Robert's success in Germany. He knew no German and thus had to talk through an interpreter, but crowds, gathering
in a church personally supplied by Kaiser William I, were swept into
jubilation by the aura that glowed and radiated from his appearance, and
by his manner of speaking, described as "wholly different from what
men were accustomed to hear." He spoke urgently, "grasping out to
gather in at once each individual hearer." As Christ's apostles had been
baptized by the Holy Spirit ten days after the Ascension, he assured his
audiences that they would receive such a baptism in ten days. There
was no lack of German listeners who regarded him as an embodiment of
God in human form and spoke of a Second Coming.

The next great explosion was back in England, at Brighton, where the
Royal Pavilion, despite its tremendous area, could not begin to hold
the crowds. Hannah was again at Robert's side, and had it been possible,
the Smiths were even more successful than before. But a few weeks after
the Brighton meeting, the noble patrons and the cooperating evangelists
and ministers deserted the Higher Life Movement in a body. Further
meetings were canceled, and Robert was publicly denounced for "un-
scriptural and dangerous . . . teaching and conduct." Robert had exulted,
as his disciples roamed widely, that "all Europe is at my feet"; now the
Smiths fled back to America in disgrace.

Robert had been accused by a female disciple. From the speed with which the whole movement collapsed, it may be assumed that there had been charges (like those against the "house parties" of a later "Oxford Movement") of general debauchery.[7]

Even before the debacle, Hannah had been fascinated by the relationship between religion and sex. Eventually, she wrote a detailed examination of "religious fanaticism" which proved to be unpublishable until years after she died. Her theme was that "the strongest emotions are passions," and that "religious emotions are close to and linked with sexual emotions." Preachers who "became slaves to their emotional nature . . . end in giving their carnal passions the place of authority they meant to give God." Hannah fortified her contentions with example after example. To cite one: after a minister and a female disciple stripped together as a religious observance, the minister's erection was regarded as a manifestation of the indwelling spirit. Hannah's curiosity had made her, although this she did not record in her manuscript, investigate for herself the borderline between religion and sex. She was thus able to come up with sound advice to evangelists: they should recognize that God spoke in many voices in addition to that of passion: "the voice of circumstance; the voice of the Bible; the voice of higher reason; the voice of one's own impressions." Before one might act, all the voices had to agree.[8]

Others of Hannah's writings were very much part of Helen's childhood experiences. Her book, with the perfect selling title *The Christian's Secret of a Happy Life,* incorporated the message of the Higher Life Movement in clear, simple prose anyone could follow: "All that we claim then, in this life of sanctification, is that, by an act of faith, we put ourselves in the hands of the Lord, for Him to work in us all the good pleasure of His will, and then, by continuous exercise of faith, keep ourselves there. . . . Just as you believed at first that He delivered you from sin because He said it, so now believe that He delivers you from the power of sin because He says it. . . . You have trusted Him as your dying Savior. Now trust Him as your living Savior."[9]

Today, more than a hundred years after its first publication, *The Christian's Secret of a Happy Life* is offered on the American book market in five different editions. The signature, H.W.S., attached to tract after tract, was in Hannah's own lifetime known not only throughout the European world but wherever there were missionaries capable of translating her works into native languages. Her Bible readings were in perpetual demand, whether she was in England or America, and she received thousands of letters clamoring for spiritual and temporal advice. It did not surprise her that so many of them were from women who blamed their troubles on their husbands. Years later, Bertrand Russell wrote that she hated men. "Her treatment of her husband, whom she despised, was humiliating in the highest degree."[10]

Helen was a small child when the Higher Life Movement collapsed, but throughout her upbringing, Aunt Hannah was a major power in the Thomas household: Mary considered her sister's advice vastly superior to her husband's. When Hannah moved to England — Helen was then fourteen — Mary wrote despairingly, "I am constantly feeling I must ask someone who knows . . . and then I remember I have no one to appeal to who knows better than myself, and I feel ever so flat."[11] Helen's sister, Carey, was more congenial with Hannah than with her own mother.

Helen's father had always felt that, because of his extreme sensitivity, medicine was not for him the right calling. He had increasingly yearned to abandon his practice and devote all his time and energies to the service of God. The call came to James so powerfully and perpetually that it sometimes seemed to him a "leading" from the Heavenly Father. This was a matter he could not mention to his wife since the Quaker ministry was not paid, and she believed it was a man's first duty to support his family. She was so infuriated when Robert, at the height of his greatness, wished to fly free, allowing his family to be supported by his admirers, that she accused him of having no pride, and wrote him an angry letter that James would not let her send.

James wrote Hannah, at the high point of the Higher Life Movement, a letter he asked her to destroy. In her reply she stated that the Lord had undoubtedly given James his medical gift for a purpose, and "there are the absolute necessary responsibilities of which no one can relieve thee." However, if God called him *"beyond a shadow of a doubt,"* James should let "nothing hinder thee from answering the call." Others had done so, and God had provided for their temporal wants, "but I almost tremble when I think of what will be involved in this. It does not seem possible."

Then Hannah for once admitted that there was some advantage in a woman's lot. Were she a man she would face a similar quandary. "But as a woman it is easy for me to do both."*[12]

As little Helen sat on her father's knee, playing with his watch chain,

---

* Hannah later had a terrible thought. Although doing God's work made her neglect her children, she feared that, if she preferred her children to the Lord, He would clear her path by killing her children.[13]

she could not guess that he was asking, worrying, listening for an inner voice to give the ultimate command to abandon all and follow Him. Nor did Mary guess, as she blithely gave most of her own energy to her religious concerns and took for granted her husband's role as protector and provider.

Having reached the age of seven, Helen was well aware of the great evangelical excitement of her mother's career. While the personable Smiths were converting the British upper classes, the rough son of a Massachusetts bricklayer was taking by storm the British industrial cities. Dwight Lyman Moody has been ruled the most effective evangelist in the English-speaking world after John Wesley, the founder of Methodism. In 1878, he decided to carry his mission to Baltimore.[14]

Appointing a local committee to guide him, he placed at its head James Carey Thomas, but Mary was to play in the revival the much greater role. James, whose preaching and temperament were not ebullient, could not rival Moody, but the evangelist had no effective female counterpart. Hannah was soon writing her sister that she had heard in Philadelphia that "thy gift is wonderful." Hannah had been warned, she said, that "if I don't look out, you will get ahead of *me.*"[15]

Moody was such a man as Mary had never known before. Short, almost as broad as he was high, wearing a heavy black beard, he had cyclonic energy, inexhaustible cheerfulness and good will. Blunt and uneducated, he spurned all refinement as an impediment to his gifts. He would stop a stranger in the street and ask, "Are you a Christian?" His intentions were so plain, pure, and hearty, that most strangers found the intrusion not impertinent but attractive.

The man and his mission were epitomized by his activities in Chicago one New Year's Day. He set out at "an early hour" with a group of followers in an omnibus, carrying a carefully prepared list of families mostly "living in garrets and the upper stories of high tenements. On reaching the home of a family belonging to his congregation he would spring out of the bus, leap up the stairway, rush into the room, and pay his respects as follows:

" 'I am Moody; this is Deacon De Golyer; this is Deacon Thane; this is Brother Hitchcock. Are you well? Do you all come to church and Sunday-school? Have you all the coal you need for the winter? Let us pray.' And down we would all go upon our knees, while Mr. Moody offered from fifteen to twenty words of earnest, tender, sympathetic supplication.

"Then springing to his feet, he would dash on his hat, dart through the doorway and down the stairs, throwing a hearty 'good-bye' behind him, leap into the 'bus, and off to the next place on his list; the entire exercise occupying about one minute and a half.

"Before long the horses were tired out, for Mr. Moody insisted on their going on a run from one house to another; so the omnibus was abandoned, and the party proceeded on foot. One after another of his companions became exhausted. . . . The tireless pastor was left to make the last of the two hundred calls alone. He returned home in the highest spirits to laugh at his exhausted companions for deserting him."[16]

In Baltimore, at the largest meetings, Mary sat on the dais as a fascinated spectator: "Thousands there. The speaking is done by men altogether. Moody has some splendid redeemed drunkards, opium eaters, and prize fighters."[17]

But at the meetings held for women, Mary was both the organizer and the principal speaker. She had the pleasure as she preached of seeing women rise like rockets all over the floor shouting that they were saved. She organized temperance meetings, commenting, "Moody is, of course, a great help." She particularly remembered a very large room which "opens right out of a business street close by a grand drinking saloon. . . . The people poured in until they filled our two hundred chairs and stood in *crowds:* ladies and gentlemen, carters, Christians and sinners all together. Moody spoke admirably, and Bliss and Mrs. Riley and I, and then we had a grand after meeting in which we talked with lots of the men and much good was done. It was a *grand success*. Men came in who never went into a church. One came up where I was talking and said, 'Is this where you are getting introduced to the Lord?' So I grappled with him."

At the "after meetings," sinners who had at large revival meetings emotionally declared themselves, were individually "grappled with." To staff these one-to-one confrontations, Mary expanded her phalanx of woman followers. The women were at first shy, Mary noted, but quickly learned to speak out boldly. She herself was delighted, having for so long been concerned only with the souls of her fellow women, to have "such a good chance at getting at men."[18]

She dealt with two Jews who, she wrote, did not believe in anything, but for whose salvation she had high hopes. Episcopalians became her particular abomination: their church was "a place for them to sit down with their sin." A tailor freely admitted that he had been a drinking and gambling man and his eloquent jubilations at his reformation so enchanted the beautiful Mrs. Thomas that less favored converts spied spitefully on him and reported that he had been currently seen at one of the hotels "drinking wildly." Mary flamed with indignation.[19]

Then there was the woman who confided that she was being driven to the brink of suicide by the drunkenness of her husband. Mary lost not a minute gathering up the female delegation who followed the wife home. The husband proved to be a lawyer possessed of so great a flow of words that he was able to talk the women down, insisting that it was his wife who drank. Mary, in her high spirits, was amused at how she and her companions had been discomfited, but she refused to believe anything against the wife. They would find a way to grapple into submission the loquacious husband![20]

As the revival progressed from month to month, Mary again and again wrote her sisters that she had never had so much fun. When Moody thanked her for her self-sacrifice, she had to hide a smile. But Moody had more to say: he hoped she would lead the women's activities at his future revivals. "I *wonder*," Hannah was to write, "thee don't enter more willingly the open doors Moody gives thee. It is a *grand* chance. I think thee ought to take it."[21]

By going through those doors, Mary could have the joy of concentrating on the activities that gave her the greatest pleasure: religious organization, preaching to audiences she deeply inspired, rearranging to their heavenly profit the lives of her converts. Indeed, she might achieve international fame. Moody's musician, Ira D. Sankey, became so associated in the common mind with the evangelist that the team was known everywhere as Moody and Sankey. Moody, Sankey, and Thomas?

Yet Mary did sincerely love her children, particularly the daughters, and not being a battler like Hannah, she was dependent on the security of home and husband. She was careful not to undermine in the household and with their children James's role as the man of the house: protector, disciplinarian, and provider. Her charm and her methods always remained conventionally feminine. She admonished her contentious sister Hannah to pursue "the Christ-like way of bearing testimony *for* truth rather than *against* error." She told her daughter Carey, who was growing from a tomboy to one of the most determined women of her generation, to remember that reverence to elders "puts ideas across. . . . Thee wants to be a refined and cultivated woman."[22]

The result of her experience with Moody was that she ceased to be a religious seeker. You do not seek after you have found, and her great public triumph, the invitation that would, had it not been for family obligations, have carried her so far, persuaded her that she was so blessed because she was acting entirely according to God's will. Except for occasional doubts in occasional moods, the old painful introspection disappeared from her intimate letters to her sisters. She was blithe and sure, efficient in doing God's work, wasting no time and energy on doubts.

Mary had come to feel herself closer to God than her mystical father had ever been. He had consulted the Lord every day as a distant advisor and had believed that the Lord answered him. By the time Helen was twelve, Mary was conscious of no separation between herself and the Lord. "God is so vivid to me that it is such an entire oneness I cannot seem to know any difference."[23]

20

———— ··◦≈◦·· ————

Helen Growing

THE Thomases moved from house to house, although less often than the Flexners, and not up or down as financial fortunes changed. The Thomases moved always to larger, more comfortable quarters, where they lived on a scale that would have been for Simon, during his Louisville years, almost unimaginable. Helen grew up in the third Thomas house at 1228 Madison Avenue.

Her memory loved to dwell on the garden beside the house, there in the middle of Baltimore: "a fascinating place for children. A wooden grape arbor arched up to the second story over a brick wall that bordered the grass where a magnolia tree grew with flowering shrubs — *Hyrus japonica*, syringa, and forsythia. Along the fence bloomed a row of flowers, my father's special delight." The Thomases had a stable and carriage house with a big hayloft above.

Across a narrow alley was the garden of a wealthy lawyer. Looking out of an upstairs window, Helen often watched "a fair-haired little girl play in her garden, sometimes alone and sometimes with her brothers. I watched her with such close attention that before we ever spoke a word to each other, I felt that Peggy White and I were friends.

"In the wall of the alleyway that separated Peggy's domain and mine there was a big iron hook to which my father's coachman, old black Horace, used to tie up the horses, one after the other, when he washed and curried them. Frank and I enjoyed standing in this alley to watch him at work, and one day our neighbor and her brother joined us there. . . . From that moment the doors which had been shut between our two families stood open. Peggy and I played together at home, but Frank ran out on the streets with the White boys."[1]

As Simon and Frank Adams had done, the children established a private postal system, pulling around boxes on strings. But their principal excitement was one that would never have occurred to Simon. Mary's correspondence reveals that when Helen as a small child was given a present of money, she spent it on a silk wedding dress for her doll. Now, she and Peggy sneaked into churches, attending the weddings of strangers. Ostensibly, the girls wished critically to compare, from wedding to wedding, the gowns, the flowers, the composure or lack of it of the brides and grooms. "Secretly, I, at least, was intoxicated by the suspense of waiting for the bride's coming, the thrill of the organ's deep voice announcing her presence, the slow procession up the aisle, and the final release of the blessing with the gay march out to the carriages."[2]

Like Simon's Jewishness, Helen's Quakerism intensified her isolation. Prevented by her mother's principles from taking part in amateur theatricals, she was separated from her school friends. Add her father's social conservatism. He made her return with a stiff note, written at his dictation, a penknife given to her, by a boy she had ice-skated with but whose family the Thomases did not know. This discouraged the naturally retiring girl from seeking further acquaintances with boys.[3]

When the Thomases decided they needed even more room, the garden disappeared, making way for an extensive new wing. This enlargement gave Helen, then in her early teens, for the first time in her life a private sanctuary. Before, she had shared her bedroom with her next older sister, Margaret. Now she had a narrow room all of her own, where she could hide away, weep if necessary (she no longer wept in the presence of others), read her books, and try to puzzle out the meanings of what she saw when she opened the door and ventured beyond her threshold.

The large Thomas family was perpetually augmented by a flood of visitors. Mary attracted waves of female constituents. Furthermore, southern hospitality was southern hospitality, and Quakers traditionally boarded visiting Quakers: there were always strange adults in the drawing rooms. At the time of the Baltimore Yearly Meeting, the huge house was so stocked with overnight guests that someone was sleeping in almost every cranny.

The adolescent Helen no longer tried, as she had when younger, to make her presence felt by intervening with pert comments on what went on around her. "My attention was solicited by too many people and things." As her shyness increased, so did her "critical faculties." She passed through the halls and sitting rooms, "noting, comparing, pronouncing judgement . . . in the quiet of my mind."[4] She felt a deep need not only to understand what was going on around her, but to evaluate what she understood.

It was basically, Helen remembered, her six older brothers and sisters who drove her into shy seclusion. "None cared to hear the opinions of the smallest girl in the family; still less would they tolerate criticism from me. The affection they showed me I could return in kind, love for love, only not criticism for criticism, though I was often subject to remarks that pierced my heart like a dagger."

Her brother Harry, ten years her senior, was, except for her father, the only male important in the life of young Helen. For an introspective and unsure growing girl, his companionship was far from an unmixed blessing. Although Harry petted her and encouraged her to tag after him, he used the insights supplied by his own sensitivity to grievously wound hers. She was particularly ashamed of her thick legs, to which he often called attention, commenting on how proud she must be of them enlarged by the gaiters her mother made her wear, despite her protests, in snowy weather.[5]

In 1883, when Helen was twelve, Carey returned from her four years in Europe with a doctorate in philosophy summa cum laude from the University of Zurich. Her presence reinforced the atmosphere of optimistic reform, of belief that the world and the people in it could be perfected by a specific panacea, which was to dominate Helen's entire life. Where her parents saw the reform as religious, and Helen's future husband was to view it as scientific, Carey's interest was educational and feminist. Her immediate objective was to demonstrate that women, given the opportunity, could prove they were as intelligent as men by profiting from the same education. (PLATE 21)

A Quaker college for women was in the process of being established at Bryn Mawr, Pennsylvania, with three of her relatives on the board of trustees: her father, her uncle James Whitall, and her cousin Francis King. Carey had written frankly from Germany that she herself would make the ideal president.

The board would have been glad to appoint her father — he refused out of hand — but those not related to Carey were far from enthusiastic about the daughter. She was still in her twenties and considered a wild woman. An elderly philanthropic Quaker physician, Dr. James Roads, became the first president of Bryn Mawr College.

Now Carey wished to be dean. Despite her hostility to her father (a resentment that may have been increased by the necessity she felt for appealing to him), Carey made maximum use of his influence, which, with that of her other relatives, did secure her the deanship.[6]

Persuaded that few Baltimore girls were well enough educated to pass the entrance examinations she had devised, Carey mobilized the former members of "The Group" to establish an advanced institution, the Bryn Mawr School. Her mother had a dozen years before undertaken a similar task, but her "Friends School" had quickly died, partly because one of the Thomas half brothers perfidiously married the headmistress, and partly due to lack of funds. In sending Mary the five hundred dollars needed to meet the defunct school's debts, John Whitall had scolded his daughter for trying to step out of the "province of women."[7] No one would have dared thus to admonish Carey.

When the president of the Baltimore and Ohio Railroad died during 1884, it was discovered that he had, in a manner then revolutionary, made his unmarried only daughter, Carey's intimate, an equal inheritor with his sons. As Mary Thomas jubilated, Mary Garrett became in one leap the richest unmarried woman in the United States. Carey dashed to her friend's side.[8] The establishment of the Bryn Mawr School was now certain.

In the fall of 1885, Helen became a student in the Bryn Mawr School, where her sister was a major power. A disadvantage soon became clear. In protest against an unpopular rule, the girls made a tremendous racket for five minutes by slamming the tops of their desks. Because Helen had been present, Carey attacked her in a fury. When the younger sister stated that she herself had not slammed a desk, Carey was in no way placated: Helen had known in advance of the protest and should have warned the authorities. Helen had humiliated Carey and disgraced the family through disloyalty. Her mother backed Carey. "So henceforth I devoted myself wholly to my studies in which there was no catch that I could see. . . . I did manage to stand well in my classes and instead of blame to win occasional praise from Carey."[9]

In sharp contrast to Helen's sister Carey was her sister Grace, not fifteen but five years Helen's senior. Grace had insisted upon being sent to a fashionable school so that she could reestablish for herself the family's traditional southern connections which her mother had pushed away. To the pleasure of her father, she expressed pride in the Thomas ancestry.

After the Baltimore house was enlarged, the Thomas crest, done in stained glass, glowed in one of the windows. The motto *Deus pascit corvos* — God feeds the ravens — seemed to Helen apposite to her parents' happy-go-lucky finances. Although Helen's eye for hypocrisy made her rule the crest unsuited to Quakers, throughout her childhood she imbibed a southern aristocrat's belief in family caste, a belief resembling the Jewish reliance on family solidarity that Simon Flexner inherited.

Grace seemed to Helen "the young lady triumphant, skilled in all the arts of elegance. . . . Her umbrella was famous for being faultlessly rolled, slender and smooth as a walking stick. . . . When bustles were being worn, young girls affected the 'Grecian bend,' leaning forward at a fascinating angle as they walked." At this gait Grace was acclaimed the height of perfection.

That Grace was encouraged not squelched reveals that the Thomases were not as unworldly as the faith they professed. In confidence that she would not outrage Quaker canons of behavior — during dances she stood beside the piano, gaining from her quaint, virtuous obedience admiration as the men gathered around her — Grace was assigned in the Thomas home a special sitting room where she could fly in her own atmosphere. Helen was welcome there when Grace entertained her circle of male followers who crowded her parlor, playing the piano, singing songs from Gilbert and Sullivan, flirting with Grace. Admiring with neither jealousy nor disapproval the way her sister used charm to direct and control the young men, Helen set up her sister in her mind as a "heroine."[10]

Many a southern belle was already exercising her charm in her early teens, a "little lady" catching the attention of the older men. But, Helen seemed still a child. She did not carry her head high as her grandaunt Henrietta would have made her do, even if it proved necessary to strap her forehead to a board. Raising only her eyes, she looked upward from a downward-tilting oval face. The eyes, under straight, slightly lifting brows, were a dark hazel, their gaze intense, serious, questioning, both frank and timid. Her chin was firm but not prominent, her cheeks full, her nose straight with wide nostrils, the bridge only slightly indented from the line of her forehead. The forehead was high, and over it, parted in the middle and pulled unceremoniously back over her ears, was her copious, delicately stranded, wavy golden-red hair. This "crowning glory," this duplication of sunlight, which was to prove so important in her life, was not yet appreciated in a family naturally given to redheads. Helen was short — she never grew to more than five feet four — and sturdily built in the manner of the Thomas inheritance.

* * *

While Esther Flexner, both apprehensive and unhappy when the family owed money, struggled to preserve the family respectability by paying bills as quickly as possible, Mary Thomas kept her family continually in debt. If she worried about money, she wrote, "I would lose the happiness out of my heart and a fortune would not pay me for that." Helen remembered that her mother loaded some of the children into her carriage, stopped at several stores, summoned the proprietors, stated that she could not pay, and informed them of what date she would pay. Tradesmen, she explained to her daughters, should be enabled to plan ahead. Such was the social atmosphere that Helen, while pitying and admiring her mother for thus demeaning herself, was untroubled by any thought that it might have been nobler to meet the bills when they were due.[11]

Because James Carey Thomas had adhered to the family profession of medicine, refusing to join Whitall, Tatum and Company, Mary was poorer than her brother, James Whitall, and her two sisters, whose husbands had gone into the firm. Her husband had a good medical practice and some private income — he was the breadwinner — but he could not supply the cake. While her parents were alive, Mary received gifts that encouraged extravagance by being irregular. After her parents died, Mary enjoyed a considerable inheritance, but it never seemed enough. Periodically, her brother, who was high up in the glassworks, baled her out.

Mary hoped, so she explained, to "bring things down to the lowest notch of very comfortable living."[12] According to her definition of "very comfortable living," this was usually more than she could from day to day afford.

Mary got as much pleasure out of treats as if she were a child. Eating herring with tea was delightful because she felt she had been extravagant to buy the herring. A flight of ecstatic letters was inspired by Hannah's unexpected gift of five hundred dollars to Grace. Everyone, including Grace, understood that this was a maneuver for sending the money to the family in a way that barred it from being applied to ordinary expenses. In unison, the family bought a dogcart, a light, open pleasure carriage with two traverse seats set back to back. The search for the right horse resulted in the purchase of a fast mare which Grace named La Reine. When the horse and dogcart were first brought together, all the Thomases took rides in rotation. Mary was enchanted.

From Helen's view, the most favorable aspect of the increased entertaining was that the more visitors the more various and delicious the food. The dinners routinely staged during Yearly Meeting would today make legend. However, not only at these special times was the Quakers' one acceptable indulgence duly honored. Helen's father, short but weighing almost two hundred pounds, could not in his later years see his feet when standing. The once lissome Mary had put on weight without anyone's commenting that it reduced her beauty.

The Thomas women shuddered away from jewels, bare flesh, and ostentatiously worldly clothes. Yet it was inconceivable that they should be dowdy. Mary, as she walked the streets from one religious assignment to another, kept a sharp enough eye on the fashionable ladies so that she could dress her daughters, if simply, in the latest mode. Although she no longer found the pleasure in fine sewing she had as a young woman, she enjoyed trimming her daughters' hats with just the right combination of style and restraint. For herself, she developed a uniform: simple, expensive, distinctive, becoming. Except for one white dress she had bought in London at her husband's pleading, she wore only black. Her clothes, Helen remembered, were "always cut according to the same pattern: a long princess overdress was buttoned close from the throat almost to the knees, then flared to reveal the skirt. They were made of excellent stuff, of the softest cashmere, of the heaviest silk, of fine velvet for ceremonious occasions. Her street mantles were of black silk," doubled in winter with a lining of gray squirrel skin. "At her throat, she wore a small, white ruching of a bit of folded net, fastened by a shining black brooch in the very center of which was a tiny pearl. This was absolutely the only jewel my mother possessed. . . . The bonnet I knew was small and made of black silk, with strings but no trimming. You did not really notice it since it left visible the hair above her smooth forehead and her level eyebrows. The gaze of all beholders was attracted to my mother's face. Its harmonious proportions and quiet coloring, soft golden-brown hair, gray eyes not conspicuously large, and faintly red, composed lips, seemed somehow to have a spiritual quality."[13] (PLATE 15)

Always worried about what she considered her mother's worries, Helen was much concerned over the family's debts. She spent her allowance carefully so that she would not need extra sums. It was a family tradition that the boys at twenty-one and the girls at sixteen were given gold watches as tokens that they had reached maturity. As Helen's sixteenth birthday approached, there was so much talk about the need to save money that she expected her gift would be postponed. The family was in the country: she found at her breakfast place a full-blown rose and a poem her father had composed for the occasion and left before he had set out on the train to his medical practice in Baltimore. In the evening, after James had returned, everyone gathered in the living room for a ceremony that led up to giving Helen a little box. Even then, she did not believe. But, "there it was, shining and beautiful, with a little gold chain ending in a ball attached to its ring. I was overcome by astonishment as much as by joy.

"My mother smiled at me, understanding my feelings: 'Don't worry, child. My last check was larger than I expected.'

"I valued my watch enormously. . . but for a long time I worried as to how the bill was to be paid."[14]

After Helen had received her gold watch and was officially a young lady, Harry took her to a laboratory at the University of Maryland Medical School where he was studying. Two young men jumped up and greeted her with gallantry. One encouraged her to look into a microscope. She actually saw something, "and I managed to ask a shy question or two about it. . . . I was greatly pleased with the visit and the two handsome young men who had been so charming to me."

Back home, Harry fixed on her angry eyes. "I cannot imagine what made thee speak in such an affected tone of voice and stand with thy shoulders raised up almost to the level of thine ears." If she thought she was being fascinating, she was wrong.

Poor Helen! "I realized that in my shyness and desire to make a good impression I had a made a fool of myself. I had been really interested and it had not entered my head consciously that I could 'fascinate' the young men as Harry said. My humiliation was intense. From that moment, I avoided young men, telling myself they were no concern of mine and never would be. Thus I constructed a suspension bridge of indifference to walk on over the turmoils of humiliation."[15]

21

———··◦∞◦··———

Sexual Divisions

THE battle between the women and the men, so conspicuous in the twentieth century, was mightily presaged in the Thomas family, but existed among the Flexners not at all. The Flexners could not afford it. As a German-trained housewife, Esther had been glad, when her husband fumbled the traditional male role, to have her eldest son take over. However, her labors "in the female sphere" kept the family afloat, and were so visibly important and even heroic that most of her six boys fell automatically under her sway. The embattled housewife exerted a much greater influence on the Flexner sons than the charismatic, affluent Mary Thomas did on the Thomas boys.

The eight Thomas children were equally divided between the sexes. None of the four boys, as he grew past childhood, continued under Mary's sway. All the four girls, including the also-dominant Carey, continued to adore their mother. Carey spoke for both the Whitall tradition and for her side of the Thomas household when she stated that no intelligent woman should have anything but daughters. Girls reinforced the household team.

Although Quaker meeting was a beacon light of religious equality between the sexes, the females sat on one side of the floor and the platform, the males on the other. There were two annual meetings, one for each sex, at which doctrine, policy, and finances were discussed. In the absence of a "hireling clergy," the two secretaries were the top administrators. (During most of Helen's childhood, Mary was secretary of the women's meeting, James of the men's.)

Throughout the nineteenth century, in middle-class America, separation between the sexes was basic to the social structure. Men went outside the home to make the family living, enjoy the company of their male friends, follow their own interests. If a man were seen in more than casual association with a woman not a relation, "the worst was feared." Women functioned in the home and, except in special circumstances, could pursue their interests abroad only in the company of other women. Except among the Quakers, women were usually not permitted to preach, although they could, as Hannah so perpetually did, conduct "Bible readings" which included their own interpretations. Men might attend if they pleased.

During the Moody revival, Mary had first tasted the heady excitement of passing beyond her labors with women actually to "wrestle" with men. The transformation had been achieved by supplementing the saving of souls with attacks on drunkenness, considered almost exclusively a male failing.

The "Temperance Crusade," led by the Woman's Christian Temperance Union, which achieved its fruition in 1919 with the disastrous prohibition amendment, was during the late nineteenth century the means across the nation of bringing female reformers out of their parlors and churches into the streets and the political process, thus sowing the seeds for the woman suffrage movement. Hannah helped lead in this direction, becoming a close friend and coadjutor of Frances Willard. Mary became president of the Maryland Woman's Christian Temperance Union — the Baltimore headquarters was to be named after her — but she was never, as was Hannah, interested in the political process. She was opposed to "votes for women," contending that they could be more effective in their traditional role of inspirers and persuaders. One of her inspirations was to have "ladies in their carriages" sit beside the polls, handing out leaflets that would awe lower-class voters into voting away their right to drink. Mary's basic method was to have the ladies seek out and reform individual tipplers. She herself was so active that, one of her husband's half brothers commented, if she was seen talking to a man in the street, *his* reputation was endangered, it being assumed that he must be a drunkard.[1]

Mary's daughters boasted that she was simultaneously president of many religious, charitable, and reform organizations. These were all female organizations. Mary managed them from a command post in her own home, a broad hallway between the two main living rooms through which much of the family life passed. To achieve her multiple tasks, she cut every corner she could. She never walked when she could ride, nor did she do anything that someone else could do for her. Her servants and the workers in her many organizations were trained to come to her only when crises arose that they could not themselves control. The same went for her children, to whom, under normal circumstances, she paid almost no attention. James was made nervous by their offspring's being permitted so great a freedom from supervision, but he had to be satisfied with a general understanding that he would be, as far as possible, kept in ignorance of their escapades and narrow escapes.[2]

Confident of their position in the world and not tied down by gainful employment, the Thomas boys ranged Baltimore much more freely than the Flexners ranged Louisville. In unhappy moods, Helen walked the back streets, between the melancholy lines of cheap houses.

To some extent, Mary's lack of attention boomeranged. The boys were too soundly trained (and too well placed in the community) to get into any trouble with the police, but in their deeds of derring-do they were prone to accidents which, after they got home, created a drain on their mother's freedom. Although she paid little attention to her children's psyches, she acknowledged that her role as mother required her full attention at any sickbed.

Helen was too timid to get physically injured — she never could bring herself to carry through the standard family adventure of climbing up and around and down the three roofs, each a different height, that covered the large family house. But she was sometimes taken ill, and then she was accorded what should have been the delight of receiving the full attention of her mother. However, she was perturbed by guilt at thus taking her mother's time away from more important things. She may have sensed Mary's own resentment, which was made the more troublesome to her mother because of her own sense of guilt at being annoyed by the only repeated sacrifice she made for her children.

Sometimes Mary did take Helen shopping, but efficiency reigned to such an extent that Helen dreaded the trips. "Before I realized which one of the hats I tried on pleased my mother, off she had gone down the aisle and between the heaped-up counters and out the shop door. I was forced to run as quickly as I could to catch sight of her before she disappeared between the swinging doors of our next shop." When she lost her mother entirely, Helen "felt the disgrace of my incompetence," which had made her mother waste time by turning back to find her.[3]

According to the mores of the time, the family home was the mother's preserve. Mary had accentuated this hegemony by refusing adequate courtesy to any members of the aristocratic Maryland circles into which her husband had been born, except Quakers whom she could meet on religious grounds. For the rest, she received primarily her followers. "Everyone who came to the house," Helen wrote, "paid tribute to her, and the admiration of which she was the object separated her [in Helen's mind] from ordinary people." Clearly, "the small categories of ordinary human judgment did not apply to her."[4]

Being slighted in his own home was made easier for her husband because he presided, without feminine opposition, over another household: the home of his stepmother, two elderly maiden aunts (Henrietta was one), and his much younger half brothers and sister. The women there were not sympathetic with Mary, whom they considered religiously flighty and neglectful, as she pursued her interests, of the upbringing and welfare of her children. Mary's family team retaliated by regarding James's female relations as stupid, stodgy, and old-fashioned.

"My father's commanding position in his own family," Helen wrote, "could not escape my observation even as a small child."[5] This wording speaks volumes. Helen "could not escape" noticing. And the other household she describes as "his own family," in contradistinction to the family she was a part of, the one presided over by her mother.

James remained always very much in love with his wife. She overwhelmed what Helen called "my father's beauty-loving temperament."[6] And there was nothing boring about her: she was a fascinating woman.

So great indeed was his admiration for the wife whom he called "the beloved one" that Mary's daughters wondered how their father could be so unreasonable as not to lie down flat before her. When the parents disagreed, the daughters automatically sided with their mother, all the more fervently if feminist principles were involved. Helen remembered, with "passionate indignation" against her father, a conversation she happened to overhear. James insisted that Mary might not bring a divorced woman into the house. Mary replied that the divorce had been caused by flagrant misconduct on the part of the husband. James's answer was that women by their behavior "often drive their husbands into temptation." Mary began to weep. "Men are very cruel to women. I cannot understand how thee can be so unjust."

"Father, look!" exclaimed the little girl. "Mother is crying! Thee has made Mother cry!" James responded by putting his daughter out of the room.[7]

Although James would stand by what he considered moral principles, there can be no doubt that he loved his wife more than she loved him. She admitted to finding reassurance in his presence, her "material na-

ture" indeed made her anxious when he was late in coming home.[8]
However, in her frank correspondence with her sisters, she almost always referred to him slightingly, an attitude that was subtly communicated to her daughters. Helen never saw the terrifying father figure
defined by Sigmund Freud.

Adding the comment that "distance creates reverence," Helen remembered that she could count on having more time with her father
than her mother. When she was small, he would take her along. Rolling
behind his fast mare Annie in the light carriage he always drove himself,
he made early morning medical calls in the country. "My father points
out to me the different trees, names of birds singing their morning songs.
Together we enjoy the flickering of light and shade, the flash of dew-
drops in the thick grass. When we reach our destination, I am left to run
under the trees by myself for a long time. . . . As I'm becoming tired and
a little lonely he appears. When I get back home again my brother is just
eating his breakfast."[9] (PLATE 15)

The Doctor managed to find time for his hobbies, one of which was
"exercising his well-known skill at choosing delicacies for his family" at
the open-air market where the farmers came on Saturdays. When Helen
was older she often accompanied him. It was usually dark when they
arrived. "The flares were already blazing. Black Horace [the family
coachman], short and broad, a huge basket over his arm, followed my
father. The lights, flickering in the wind that blew through the unwalled
shed, cast strange shadows. As he passed along my father was solicited
from every side by his name. 'I have a fine fat pair of ducks for you this
week, Dr. Thomas. I have been saving them for you,' or 'Dr. Thomas,
the asparagus is just as you like it today, green and tender,' or 'Our sau-
sage meat has turned out wonderful, Doctor. Just you try it!' While he
felt the breast of a chicken or admired the tender green row of peas in an
opened pea pod, my father asked after the families of the stallkeepers.
Sometimes he knew the names of the children. He had visited the farm
perhaps to prescribe for one of them in a crisis of illness. Often he was
forced to pause and give a bit of advice even when he purchased nothing,
but his progress seemed very rapid to me, trying not to lose him. The
movement of people, the strange flickering lights under the high market
roof delighted and confused me. I wanted to linger and look, but on
went my father, and Horace's basket filled up as by magic. All too soon
we were outside again at the place where we had left the carriage. The
basket, flowering on top with fresh lettuces, with cauliflowers, with

boxes of strawberries, with cherries tumbling out of a paper bag, was stowed away in the front beside Horace. I sank back on the cushion close to my father, leaning against his shoulder in happy exhaustion."[10]

When he was at home, Helen found her father "easy to approach. He seemed almost on a level with me. When I annoyed him he showed his annoyance frankly. He scolded me with the irritation of an equal so that I felt free to answer him back. I liked to do little services for him. When he settled down on his bed to rest after midday dinner, I used to tuck the warm cover-lid under his shoulders and give him a little pat before I left him. Then, if I were going out with him, I came in an hour to wake him and put the cuff links in his fresh shirt. We were such good friends that he even permitted me to tease him, seeming to enjoy his own follies, but my mother did not approve of this. Taking me aside, she reproved me gravely for impertinence to my father. . . . She spoke so seriously that I tried not to displease her again in this way. However, my father was well able to hold me in check whenever he desired. 'Wisdom will die with thee, my dear child,' he sometimes assured me in a suspiciously flattering voice." Quoting to his redheaded daughter from *Macbeth*, he would say, 'Shake not thy gory locks at me.'

"Every now and then one of his children would annoy him beyond endurance and then he said the most devastating things, but if we reproached him with them when he was no longer angry, he more often than not repudiated his own words.

" 'I never said that, child. How can thee imagine that I would say such a thing?' he asked, shaking his gray head from side to side.

" 'But, Father, thee did say it,' we insisted and called a witness, when one existed, to support the accusation.

" 'Well, perhaps I did,' my father sometimes conceded. 'I cannot remember every word I may let fall when you are making such a racket.' "[11]

Helen was fourteen when Mary wrote Hannah, "Sisters are certainly the most satisfactory relations. They are your own age which your children are not, and they are your own sex which your husbands are not, and they are your blood relations which your friends are not. No one else can fill the gap. As for me, I have a general love for humanity — to some degree a Christlike love — but when it comes to being very intimate with people or loving them very much, I can tell you there are mighty few who have the power to move my innermost being."[12]

Helen, of course, could not know that her mother had (or, indeed, could) write a passage that excluded all the Thomas family — her husband and her children including Helen — from her deepest emotions. Yet, down all the years, Helen felt insecure in her relationship with her mother. Mary's letters to her sisters demonstrate that she had become, by the time Helen was a little girl, one of the most cheerfully self-confident of mortals. Yet Helen persuaded herself that her mother walked the world in basic sadness. This "intuition" may well have grown from Helen's own need to find in her idol a vulnerability that would open to her the possibility of serving and propitiating the deeply loved but awesome central figure in her existence.

22

———⋯⟨∞⟩⋯———

Sexual Revulsion

THE Bible, of course, was for the Thomas household standard reading, and, as Helen's curiosity in such matters developed, she had
been struck by the story of Lot and his daughters. It was stated without
equivocation that the daughters lay with their father to produce children. The Bible could not conceivably be wrong, but no mention was
made of a doctor bringing a baby in his black bag — or of a stork. Helen
asked her immediately older sister, Margaret, who communicated the
fundamental facts, which she had been told by her own older sister
Grace. Grace, informed by a schoolmate, had rushed for a denial to her
mother. Although outraged at girls discussing such things and "terribly
embarrassed," Mary had confirmed the information. "My mother's attitude," Helen remembered, "had stamped the whole subject of the birth
of children as not to be spoken about, as somehow shameful." However,
Helen observed phenomena that fell into line, such as the amazing fact
that unmarried couples could have children. "In time, the information
Margaret had given me ceased to haunt me."[1]

But the issue was to reemerge.

Mary had long been concerned with the plight of "fallen women."
When she and her ladies invaded saloons to kneel on the floor and pray,
the girls who served the men usually wept. At first Mary had regarded
this as the entrance of a glimmer of light into souls inherently bad, but
as time passed she adopted a feminist reversal of the accepted theory
that fallen women were to blame for their heinous sins and consequently
were the lowest of God's creatures.

Mary's logic ran as follows: in their natural state, women were pure, without sexual desire, lust being an obscenity limited to the male sex. Women could not be betrayed by evil appetites unnatural to them: they were corrupted by lustful men. It followed that fallen women, far from being the lowest order of creation, were pitiful victims of male bestiality. The cure for the situation was not to ostracize or imprison female unfortunates but to reform the male sex.

Mary Thomas argued with male legislators against laws cruel to prostitutes, and appeared at courts where women were tried for sexual crimes. Not permitted actually to intervene, she sat there, so clearly a lady, so beautiful in her black dress, a silent call to the male conscience. But that was at best a palliative. As president of the Baltimore Woman's Christian Temperance Union, she sponsored an organization for men, the White Cross Knights.

"These knights," she stated in a presidential address, "wearing the white flower of a blameless life, have pledged themselves to purity, chivalry, and self-restraint. They hold the divine truth that men ought to be as pure as women, and they believe that what a man *ought* to be that he can be, and they *mean* to be. Nothing could be more fitting than that this association, which represents the motherhood and sisterhood of our country, should take hold of this work and adopt the White Cross as a pendant to the white ribbon" of temperance.[2] But, alas, few men could be persuaded by their motherhood and sisterhood publicly to set for themselves the goal of being as pure as the temperance ladies considered all women naturally to be.

In 1885, when Helen was fourteen, Hannah sent a bombshell from England to Coombe Edge. It was an insignificant-looking pamphlet: *The Maiden Tribute to Modern Babylon: The Report of the Pall Mall Gazette's Secret Committee*, endorsed by the Archbishop of Canterbury and other religious leaders. The subject was the flourishing traffic in young virgins made legal and profitable in England by three phenomena: First, although women were not considered ready to hold property until they were eighteen, the "age of consent" was set at thirteen, which meant that their "priceless jewel . . . what a woman ought to value more than life" was then available for the taking. Second, there were men eager to pay twenty pounds or more for taking that priceless jewel. Third, a young girl who had been lured to London by respectable pretenses and then raped, "frightened and friendless, her head aching with the effect of the drowse [drug to make her passive] and full of pain and horror, gives up all hope and within a week she is one of the attractions of the house." She was too ashamed, even if a possibility existed, to get in touch with her family.

The report was full of horrifying details. As pig-tailed schoolgirls danced gaily home from school, procurers peered from behind bushes to assess the best merchandise to be tricked away from their parents. Each girl had to be delivered to the purchaser with a doctor's certificate testifying to her virginity. Girls were locked in bedrooms not knowing why, and in many cases the drowse was omitted as the victims' pleas, struggles, and screams heightened the fun.

Mary wrote Hannah that the *Pall Mall Gazette* revelations made her physically sick, filled her "with burning indignation and a perfect scorn against men." Grace and Carey, she reported, were practicing with revolvers to protect themselves against men, and Carey was taking her revolver out driving. Men, Mary continued, deserved to be shot, "a million or two of them."[3]

There is no mention in *A Quaker Childhood* of the *Pall Mall Gazette* revelations or the pistols, but Helen Flexner did write that her mother had filled her with horror by dilating to her about "a half-witted girl no older than I who had been attacked by a brutal man as she returned across an empty lot to her own home. This poor creature was too stupid to defend herself," and was now with child.[4]

Such causes for indignation and wrath were out in a world which the Thomas women viewed only as reformers, not as possible participants. Whether or not they carried pistols, they and their daughters were not menaced by rapists or the "White Slave Traffic." However, sex within respectable marriage raised for the Whitall sisters, as for all women of their time and persuasion, issues as paradoxical as they were physically and psychologically profound. The difficulties became more severe as the years of marriage moved along — the wives becoming less enchanted with their husbands, less bemused by the "secret mystery" of marriage and procreation — and as nurseries became well populated.

The conviction that a good woman could get no pleasure out of sex dictated that a husband who tried to arouse his wife would be degrading her in her own estimation and also in his. However, her husband's desire for what was legally decreed his "conjugal rights," had to be accorded serious consideration by a wife who wished peace in the home and to keep her man from straying elsewhere. A very troublesome dimension was added by the moral impossibility of a nice woman's interfering with the Lord's will by using any type of birth control. Thus, engaging in what could be simultaneously considered marital duty and degrading submission to male bestiality, often resulted in another unpleasant pregnancy and the appearance of another child to be taken care of. Nature usually dictated that the mother love the child, but the resentment could remain.

Of marital sex, Hannah was particularly resentful. During her second pregnancy she wrote in her diary blistering attacks on her husband which (although the result had been her daughter Mary, whom she adored) she encouraged her niece Carey to copy into her own diary. Carey had long been on a rampage concerning this matter, finding in it a reason for hating her father.[5]

Mary had been by far the most fecund of the Whitall sisters. Although only eight grew to maturity, she bore ten children over a period of more than twenty years: from when she was twenty-one to forty-four. Carey had, as the first, and then again during her long recovery from the burn, been the center of her mother's attention. But as soon as she recovered, Mary's attention was divided among her augmenting brood. Carey's resentment inspired a lifelong series of diatribes against large families. She refused to believe that her mother had willingly cooperated. The reminiscences she wrote in her old age contain a conversation she claimed to have overheard at the age of twelve, some years before Helen was born.

Carey's mother had exclaimed to one of her father's elderly female relations: "I will not have any more children than we can take care of and bring up properly. I cannot bear it any longer! I will tell the Doctor it must stop." The reply was that unless Mary wanted the Doctor to have recourse to another woman, "you must go on bearing it and bearing as many childrern as the Lord sends."

"I was," so Carey's reminiscences continue, "overcome with horror as I realized that, if he chose, there was something my father could do," and that he refused to do it. "I used to look at him and wonder how he could seem to love my mother and be so unkind to her. . . .

"When I used to come home after a few months' absence at school or college I would give my mother a frightened glance. If she wore the short velvet jacket she wore before her babies were born, I would rush away to my room and sob there until my mother would come to find me and join her tears to mine."[6]

Carey easily altered her memories to fit her preconceptions. The Thomas children were so spaced — about two years apart — that there seems to have been an agreed-to plan. In Mary's voluminous and uninhibited correspondence with her sisters, she criticized her husband in many directions, but never on the matter of childbirth. Nor did she express resentment during her many pregnancies. Babies, she wrote, "are the sweetest things in nature." She did complain that so many children, with their multiple sicknesses and accidents, tied her down. However, her most energetic protest was: "There must be a screw loose somewhere, or it would not be so."[7]

Yet Carey communciated to Helen that she had been guilty of cruelty to her mother by being born. Furthermore, Helen's existence, so Carey continued, was a block to their mother's achieving what it should have been her destiny to achieve. Helen was only too willing to agree that there was no greatness Mary could not have reached had she not been hindered by the size of her family.*[8] Thus, every time Helen in her personal need could not resist calling to her mother, she was, she felt, compounding her sin of being born. The resulting anxiety may well have contributed to her resentment against her father, despite her love for him, and to her obsessive desire to support and please (to placate?) her mother. The psychic stress, heightened with tragedy as time passed, was to open a wound that almost destroyed the woman Simon Flexner was to marry.

When, during Helen's mid-adolescence, the Thomases spent the summer at Coombe Edge, their country house in the Blue Ridge Mountains, parents and children would relax on the lawn in the cool of the evenings. Often they would recite poetry, each in turn. One evening, Helen quoted from Shelley:

> *I arise from dreams of thee*
> *In the first sweet sleep of night,*
> *When the winds are breathing low,*
> *And the stars are shining bright.*
> *I arise from dreams of thee,*
> *And a spirit in my feet*
> *Hath led me — who knows how?*
> *To thy chamber window, Sweet.*

As Helen paused in preparation for the second verse, "my mother interrupted. It was late, she said, and getting up from her chair she led the

---

* It never occurred to Helen or any of the other daughters that James was also tied down by his responsibility for supporting so large a family.

way into the house. Puzzled by her interruption and even more by the tone of her voice, I went slowly up to my room, and without lighting my lamp undressed slowly, thinking this over. For some reason my mother did not like love poems."[9]

The reason comes clear in Mary's correspondence with Hannah. Although their own childbearing period was long past, sex was menacing the sisters' lives in a new form. Their children were growing up. It was not the sons, who in any case were rarely mentioned in the correspondence, whom the sisters were worried about. Nor did they suspect the daughters of engaging in illicit affairs — that was inconceivable. The menace was that the daughters might want to get married.

Carey seemed immune: she was continuing on the path, then conventional for career women, of emotional friendships with other women. The first casualty was Hannah's attractive and scintillating oldest daughter Mary (known as Mariechen). She became engaged to Frank Costelloe, a politically minded, intellectual Irishman who was resident in London. Erupting like a volcano, Hannah threw off hundreds of red-hot letters.[10] The ostensible objection was that Costelloe was a Catholic and that Mariechen intended to adopt his faith. This was indeed for Quakers an abomination, but the deeper emotional issue was the breaking up of that triumvirate: Hannah and her two daughters. (The son, Logan, did not count.) Hannah's inability to prevent the marriage resulted in her moving the entire Smith family to London. She would not be separated from her daughter.

Mary was horrified to see her own daughter Grace manifestly falling in love with a cousin, Tom Worthington. Although Grace was twenty-one (three years older than Mary was when she married), Mary insisted that her daughter was too young; the marriage would have to be indefinitely postponed. Marriage was such a gamble. How sad "to break up a bright and happy family." They had all had "such fun" at Coombe Edge. Surely Grace would look back longingly if she went off "with one dull man." But there was more to it than dullness.[11]

After what she had learned and concluded concerning the violation, prostitution and persecution of "fallen" women, Mary was so "utterly indignant" that men had permitted "such unrighteous laws on the women question to be made all these centuries . . . that it was impossible to prevent an indecribable revulsion of feeling against the whole sex which made marriage an impossibility."

Mary wrote Hannah that when she had so expressed herself to a Mr.

Bragg, he had replied that if noble women refused to marry, the men would marry ignoble women. Mary was unshaken. "Men must make themselves worthy," she repeated, "if noble women are to consent to marry them." Men should suffer the inevitable result of their evil deeds, and she would not relieve them.

Her son Bond was courting a neurotic and literary-minded friend of Mariechen's named Edith Carpenter. "I suppose," Mary wrote Hannah, "I must let Bond suffer and encourage Edith to be firm!" Then she added, "My own marriage has been exceptionally happy so I can speak to other women without embarrassment."[12]

Allowing the obligation of motherhood to overcome principle, Mary did not intervene in Bond's marriage, but she did wrestle with Grace. Surely her pure daughter could not subject herself to the bestial desires of a male! The result of all this was to be a disastrous marriage, but the marriage itself was not prevented. Mary commented to Hannah that what was even more "cruel than for mothers to give up their daughters was having the daughters want to go." Mary was able to report that on the night before Grace was to be married, the bride "cried herself to sleep. I believe at leaving me." But the news was, twenty-four hours later, "Poor Grace is married."[13]

During the courtship, as Helen passed through the front hall, she had caught sight of Grace and Tom. "Her side was strained against his side and her face lifted up to his face bending down to meet it." She was amazed to recognize in her sister's posture and face passion that matched her lover's. Was it possible that Grace was seeking rather than dreading the extreme embraces required of a bride?[14]

However, Helen could not be unconscious of her mother's passionate revulsion. The girl who had once found happy adventures in attending the marriages of strangers, was now appalled at the thought of taking part in her sister's wedding. She pleaded that she was too young to serve as a bridesmaid but Grace insisted.

"The wedding day passed in a nightmarish haze." Helen saw her mother carry off the occasion "like a strong wind," giving the impression of "cheerful efficiency," but she also saw the terrible expression on her mother's face when the bride appeared in her traveling costume, ready to depart with a man.[15]

23

———— ⊷∞⊶ ————

Catastrophe

IT all started more or less as a lark. Mary was so intimate with her religion that she felt it would be fun to see if she could cure herself of a bad cold, eschewing all medicines, by faith alone. Her doctor husband admitted that faith could be an important part of a cure, but insisted that to ban medicines was "limiting the power of God, who worked through them as well as through belief."[1] Mary replied gaily, "I understand that the essential I has not got a sore throat, but I am so joined to this body that is, that I have to cough when it coughs, despite myself." Her difficulty was that she did not believe resolutely enough. "I am ashamed of myself that I am not well." What a triumph it would be when she could carry "only one clean handkerchief for looks and to wipe my weeping eyes at weddings!"[2]

When Helen came down with "material trouble" in the form of "stomachitis, terrible sore throat and mouth," Mary's usually docile disciple demanded material medicines: "gargles, pills, washes and ointments." After having hurt his leg, Frank also preferred his father's "carnal medicine." "They are all such unbelieving wretches" that "I have no one to practice on."[3]

In that time of belief in spiritualism, table rappings, and communication with the dead, Mary wrote, "There is no doubt about it, wonderful things are happening now. . . . I am sure there are heights and depths unknown to us. . . . I have had glimpses of what might be done in an atmosphere of faith, how *miracles* become *naturals* in such an atmosphere."[4] Mary consorted with other advocates of faith healing. "The Doctor," she wrote, "is good-natured I must say. He doesn't mind our vagaries a bit, I believe, although I wonder at it." However, the Doctor did put his foot down at her staging in their house a "parlor meeting" for a healer whom the medical profession considered "a faith tramp."[5]

Mary had had some victories in "dealing with the temptations of sickness" when at the end of May, 1887 (Helen was going on sixteen), she became possessed "with fear of a terrible disease of which I was absolutely sure I had the symptoms." She had found what she concluded was a cancerous lump in her breast. "I went to meeting on the 5th day in the depths, seeing nothing before me but succumbing to its inroads. I felt cold and dead spiritually. . . . But the life rose in the silences, and as the Doctor spoke and Mary S.T. prayed." She saw that it was God's will that she *"renounce* absolutely and utterly all part or lot in every false or usurping thing. We are to know that we are set free from all bondage, all servitude, all corruption. . . . My fear vanished. Faith in the Son of God dispelled it. I will not live or believe a lie, nor dwell upon it, nor talk about it."[6] Ignoring as best she could her symptoms, confident that the Lord would protect her essential self from her body, she told no one, not the Doctor, not Hannah.

Mary believed that Christ "waits for our faith to afford Him the opportunity of manifesting His power in the world." He had sent her cancer as a challenge to be met triumphantly in His name. Had there not been before "grand and noble exceptions," those "men and women who have stood out like mountain peaks" from "the low level of demi-semi spiritual life which passes for Christianity now throughout the length and breadth of Christiandom?"[7]

When the "material" symptoms could no longer be hidden, the Doctor, at last informed, reacted with terror and then with blessed relief; the tumor, although definitely cancerous, was still operable. His "beloved" would be saved! But no! Mary scorned to permit the intervention of "carnal medicine." This determination threw the Doctor into a horrible quandary. He could persuade her to an operation only by weakening her faith, but the faith cure would, according to the doctrine Mary followed, triumph only if faith were absolute. If he argued and his arguments failed, any doubts he had succeeded in raising might sentence his wife to death along the religious road she would not abandon. The poor Doctor was forced to support as enthusiastically as he could what he distrusted and greatly feared.[8]

Mary had written that one of James's prayers before meeting had helped prepare her mind, yet the decision she reached was completely outside the religious sphere of the Thomas clan. It was a return to the mystical directions of her father, but went far beyond what Captain Whitall had ever thought or attempted. He had asked God only for boons that could have come to him in the normal sequence of events: safety under specific circumstances from pirates or monsoons, business success. Mary asked for such a laying aside of natural law as could be considered a miracle.

How far was Mary's decision an act of aggression and scorn against the husband who adored her? Certainly she was striking the most violent and wounding blow conceivable against what he had achieved and stood for professionally: the medicine he practiced, the Johns Hopkins with its scientific courses and medical school. Her putting her body in jeopardy was for him a true source of horror.

That autumn was a dramatic time in the annals of the Society of Friends. At a general conference held in Richmond, Indiana, every orthodox meeting in the world was represented. Mary and James went as representatives from Baltimore. A declaration of belief was adopted in an effort to impede the perpetual splintering of doctrine. After that, came the Yearly Meeting in Baltimore, which most of the foreign delegates attended. The Thomases, as "clerks" respectively of the men's and the women's meetings, were in the center of everything, and Mary closed the occasion with a prayer that seemed then (and even more so afterwards) a masterpiece of "power and tenderness." Only once again was she ever to enter the meeting house "where for a quarter of a century hers had been such a pervading influence."[9]

This was Helen's last year in school: she had been studying hard for the Bryn Mawr examinations, and enjoying autumn rides with her father. When Mary took to her bed, which had been moved into the front room, Helen was comforted by the statement that she was suffering, uncomfortably but not dangerously, from lumbago. But the time was at hand when Mary's situation and her religious fight would have to be announced to the world.

The mother did not choose to break the news gently to her worshipping daughter. One afternoon when Helen came home from school she sat the girl down beside her. "I have something to tell thee," Mary said, and then "she opened the front of her gown, uncovering her left breast, and pointed with her hand to an angry redness spread out there. Then she took my hand and laid it on her breast. Very hard and rough, the lump was under my fingers. 'What can it be mother? It feels dreadfully hard.'

" 'It is a cancer. But God can cure even a cancer. Thee must have faith.' "

Helen was engulfed in tears. "Dearest, why can't I have the pain instead of thee?"[10]

The whole family was now told. So that Mary would be sustained by having all her daughters around her, Grace was called back from Europe, thereby cutting short her husband's studies. Mary protested but not strongly enough to prevent the call. Tom could, her family ruled, study as well in Baltimore. No one bothered to dread any ill effect on Grace's marriage.

Carey raged against her father. Although she had habitually been furious if James dared in the smallest way to oppose her mother, she now blamed the catastrophe on his weakness of character: he should have forced Mary to accept an operation. She said to Helen, "We must say nothing about it. It is too dreadful to speak about."[11] Carey herself was not to be gainsaid. She rushed her mother off to New York and a medical specialist. To the despair of everyone, the specialist said that it was too late to operate. Mary had about six months to live.

But the verdict applied only to that illusion, her body: Mary still refused to be untrue to her faith in Christ. As word of her challenge of material illness spread in the religious community across the United States, the death sentence provided by the doctors doubled the urgency and glory. What a marvelous "testimony" it would be when she stepped from her bed completely cured! Surely, if anyone was ever chosen to demonstrate Jesus' role in the world it was Mary Whitall! A disciple saw "thee whole in Christ as I speak to thee." Her "strength and her beauty and many gifts" had "always been gloriously triumphant over everything." She was "as true a saint as any in this world."[12]

Prayers were synchronized "as far away as Cincinnati" so that a united voice of faith would rise to Christ.[13] Faith healers flocked to wrestle with the Lord at her bedside. "Nature healers" were summoned from afar, bringing remedies acceptable because they were based on Biblical texts. What Mary called her "train" of Baltimore ladies were perpetually appearing and falling on their knees. And also present, trying to stem the flood, to drive the zealots away when her mother was collapsing with exhaustion, was Helen, aged sixteen.

The other members of the family were out of the house on weekdays. On weekdays, Helen should have been at school, preparing for her college entrance examinations, but this was not considered of primary importance — and Helen had a passion to be with her mother. She cut her classes until the school authorities intervened: she would have to attend or drop out. To let her drop out was more than the family could accept, but the only result of her staying in school was that she was more strained, dashing home for a few minutes, trying to do her homework while paying attention to her mother. The management of the large and populous house devolved on Helen, a task she was able to carry through only because the servants were experienced. Hour after hour she read to her mother from texts that revolted her: the faith healer's tracts that had brought the person she most adored to this tragic pass. At night Helen could not sleep for fear that her mother was not sleeping; she tiptoed perpetually through the dark into her mother's room.[14]

Mary accepted the services, but could not hide her resentment at being dependent on her younger daughter, whom she referred to in letters to Hannah as "my little boss." She tried to put on her stockings and slippers when Helen was not looking, and was annoyed when she had to call for help with the slippers.[15]

Helen's faithfulness did not rank high in the opinion of her siblings. Grace, having outraged her husband and endangered her marriage, felt she was the heroine. Carey was the oldest and in any case never allowed anyone else precedence. The two women squabbled, in the presence of their dying mother, to Helen's horror. As for Helen, she accepted that, as the youngest daughter, "I did not count."[16]

One afternoon, as her mother lay half invisible in the twilight, she said to Helen that she was worried about the Doctor: he would be so lonely. She asked the youngest daughter to promise that she would put off going to Bryn Mawr for at least a year. After the year had passed, "things will not be so difficult for him." Helen could then decide for herself whether or not it would be best for her to give up college entirely.

"I will try very hard to do what I think thee would want. Thee may be sure of that, Mother. I give thee my promise."

"Now we might turn out the light," said Mary. And she closed her eyes.[17]

When the cancer was not deflected from its inexorable advance, Mary's religious rivals asserted that her saintliness was proved deficient. Not at all, said Mary's supporters: it was because of her very saintliness that she was not being cured. Her work on this earth having been done, the Lord was calling her to Him. He had "prepared her crown." But

Mary, dismayed to find herself failing, would not let herself off so easily.

One evening Helen was attempting to read her to sleep "when I saw her eyes wide open and fixed on me in a kind of desperation. . . . My mother spoke in a low inward voice, 'God has cast me out like a branch that is withered. I have rebelled against His will. I have been selfish and self-seeking.' "

To Helen's protestations that no one had ever lived more for others, she replied, "God sees our most secret thoughts. . . . He knows how often I felt dissatisfied and rebellious when my family duties prevented my working for Him, as I said to myself. Really, I enjoyed going off to meetings and conferences with thy father and Aunt Hannah, and was bitterly disappointed to be left behind. By taking me now when I have many fewer duties to keep me at home, He is showing me that I am not fit to do His work in the world."[18]

Mary could, indeed, have hardly hit on an explanation more wounding to the daughter to whom she confided it. By blaming her impending death on the conflict between her religious and family duties, she reinforced Helen's sense of guilt, long encouraged by Carey, at being one of the younger children who had prevented their all-beautiful mother from carrying out her glorious destiny. And Carey did not hesitate to be more specific. She "voiced" her conviction that "by suckling at her breast one after another, we [the younger children] had given my mother a mortal wound."[19] Although Helen was not the youngest — two births had followed hers — she took to herself the blame for Mary's cancer of the breast. She was killing the individual she most loved, the most "wonderful" person in the world.

Such thoughts gathered into a "tangle of inner torment" during sleepless nights. Helen felt it was useless to pray for her mother's recovery. If her mother's prayers were not heard, of what use could her prayers be? Nor could Helen call on God to help her in her personal anguish. "My thoughts sheered away from Him. To deny consciously the existence of the God of justice and mercy and love in whom my mother believed would have been to separate myself in spirit from her, but in my heart there was no God."[20]

Although Mary suffered from ever increasing weakness and discomfort, her dying was unaccompanied by acute pain. With the coming of summer, she was transferred in a private railroad car to Coombe Edge. Her entire immediate family (except for Harry who was under treatment for tuberculosis) was in attendance. Each one labored to make her last days and hours as easy as every attention could achieve. Carey prepared an hourly chronicle for Hannah: "Saturday night was terrible to Nellie [Helen] and me. We knelt on either side of the bed, rubbing her and giving her water, and changing her position. We called the boys twice to lift the mattress and change the slant of the pillows. Father was totally exhausted by three nights of watching and we woke him every hour to feel mother's pulse. At one o'clock, she became unable to swallow her gruel and at half past father gave her chloral in the hope that she would sleep. She still groaned but Nellie and I thought she was unconscious. At six Sunday morning she began to breathe quietly." She would say, "I want to get through, but I did not know it would take so long."[21]

Her brother, James Whitall, when fanning her face to keep away the flies, was deeply moved "with the beauty of her countenance, and what would be the glory of her angelic form. Her beautiful hair, in ringlets over her face and forehead, seemed all ready for the crown of victory."[22]

At six o'clock on the morning of August 2, 1888, Carey "was holding Mother's left hand and saw her eyes open for the first time in twenty-four hours." The daughter called out, and instantly the whole family, including Helen, were in the room. They saw her "gently cease to breathe without the slightest struggle or disturbance of any kind. At the last," so James Whitall continued to his children, "she opened her eyes wide and her spirit looked through them at Uncle Doctor with earnest gaze, and then it left the body and all was over. It seemed as if she had said, 'Let go, for the day breaketh.' "[23]

"After a little while," the four daughters sent everyone from the room. With her sisters, Helen undressed her dead mother. As the body, which in life had always been modestly covered, lay there limp and naked, the deformed left breast, the mortal wound for which Helen felt herself guilty, was horribly visible. The daughters carefully washed the body. They "dressed her all ourselves. We put a wire mattress on four chairs and laid Mother on a sheet with her head on a little 'pinky,' the down cushion she always used, and put tubs of ice under her and all around her. . . . When the undertaker came with the ice casket, he had nothing to do. Father and Bond lifted her in, so that no one except ourselves touched her."

The body, surrounded by Mary's immediate relatives, was taken in another private car to Baltimore, where it was laid in state in the big Thomas house. The daughters had dressed the corpse in "a white serge wrapper with a full front of white silk . . . with crepe lisse ruffling at her hands and throat . . . with red roses at the throat. . . . We uncovered the coffin entirely. Throngs of people came to look at her," exclaiming at Mary's unearthly beauty.

Above the crowd at the funeral rose "two great palms tied with a white ribbon" sent by the Woman's Christian Temperance Union of Maryland, and, at the foot of the coffin stood "a great wreath of heliotrope surrounded with palms" from the Temperance Section of the Young Women's Christian Association. There was a sea of other flowers. A cousin, Mary Snowden, prayed "a prayer of victory which broke down the self-control of almost everyone in the room: 'Oh, Lord, we thank Thee for the glory and joy of Thy servant. Thou livest with her here in her house and now she has gone to live with Thee in Thy house.' "[24]

James's half brother John wrote his wife that the family, with representatives of the Baltimore meeting and some of her "temperance ladies," proceeded in thirteen carriages to the cemetery. "The day was immensely hot, and an awning was spread over the grave. A large mattress of smilax and fern, bright green, was thrown over the pile of earth, and the grave was lined with some of the same, looking very pretty. Dr. Rhoads said a few words, Annie Stabler prayed, and after the coffin was lowered, Brother James said, 'A perfect life, perfect trust, perfect love,' and then prayed that when they should meet around the throne, it might be with rejoicing."[25]

A resolution adopted by the Young Women's Christian Association read: "She has shown us what it is like to be Christ."[26]

Although Helen suffered from recurring nightmares, "all emotion seems to have gone out of the waking world. I reacted listlessly or not at all to things that would formerly have sent me into high excitement." None of her relatives paid attention to her because, as she wrote, "I no longer made the lively protests that used to burst from me under provocation. . . . In the family group," so Helen closed her account of her childhood, "I had become, as it were, anonymous."[27]

V

Miraculous Destiny

24

————··❦··————

A New Life Starts

E AGERNESS brought Simon Flexner to Baltimore — in late September, 1890 — while the summer doldrums still ruled at the Pathological. Since his "almost $500" might at best not suffice for the whole academic year, his premature arrival could prove a serious blunder. The wisest man in the world could not have foreseen that the financial shortage which did in fact develop would touch off a happy turning point in his career.

What fears Flexner harbored that his poor preparation would prevent his admission were dispelled as soon as he had walked up the steps of the administration building. He filled out a form, handed over his fifty dollars, and that was that. He did not even have to flourish his degree from the University of Louisville.*

Simon discovered that he was the only student who had arrived and that none of the faculty had yet come in. He did not know a living soul in Baltimore. Taking a room at the Albion Hotel — he soon moved to a cheaper boardinghouse — he haunted the office of the registrar, hoping that Welch, the first professor expected, would appear. Finally, Flexner was told that Welch was there, closeted with President Gilman.[1]

The eager student fidgeted on the edge of his chair until a door opened and out came the registrar accompanied by a short, stocky man in his mid-forties. Welch — for it must be he — wore a black mustache that merged with a black spade beard parted in the middle to create curls under his chops. His dark hair had receded as far as had Flexner's;

---

* There were too few American doctors who desired this newfangled course of study for anyone to be excluded.

he had bright-blue eyes and was a handsome man. Against the trousers of his meticulously pressed dark suit he dangled "a conventional derby hat." Simon noticed — or perhaps this was later when he was less nervous — that Welch's feet were very small for the bulk they carried.[2]

When Simon was introduced, Welch's "manner was very quiet and comforting. Perhaps this impressed me in contrast with my own agitation." The professor made an appointment to meet the student at the Pathological at two.

The resulting interview was for Flexner a great disappointment. "He did not seem particularly interested in my desire to study pathology. What was the culmination of adventure for me was routine for him." Although this Flexner did not so guess, Welch may have been somewhat annoyed: surely a professor should have been given a few hours after he got back from Germany before being pestered by an overeager student. Welch may indeed have identified this slight young man dressed in a cheap, provincial suit, as the applicant for the fellowship who had submitted amateurish slides that had made the judges smile. The newcomer's most conspicuous feature, his intense gray eyes, stared with passionate anticipation at the easygoing older man who did not like to be hustled.

When Simon asked when the course in pathology would start, Welch replied that there might be no class — perhaps not enough students would show up. Flexner, who had trusted so much on this spin of the wheel, expressed concern that Welch ignored. Shutz, the laboratory assistant, would assign the young man a seat and supply a microscope. Having to think up some kind of a project to keep Simon busy, Welch remembered some tubercular glands, fixed in Müller's fluid, which he had brought from New York when he had come to the Hopkins five years before. Flexner should embed and section the glands, stain them, and examine them under the microscope for tubercle bacilli.[3]

The technique was new to Simon but Welch gave no advice and paid no further attention. Flexner got what advice he could from Shutz and struggled ahead. He examined hundreds of sections, hour after hour, for many days, but could find nothing. Eventually, a large ruddy man, with short walrus mustaches, walked energetically into the room, beckoned Flexner to get off the seat, sat on it himself, and looked into the microscope. He then asked Flexner "what in the blazes" he was doing. When the student explained, he laughed heartily and asked, "Who the devil put you to work on such a fool job?" Tubercle bacilli could not be preserved in Müller's fluid.

When Flexner replied that he had got the assignment from Welch, he was told to tell Welch he could find nothing and ask for another assignment. The bluff newcomer seemed to regard the whole thing as a joke. Flexner had met the assistant professor of pathology, William T. Councilman, just back from Germany.[4]

After enough students had gathered, the formal class in pathology began, meeting three times a week from two to five. There were some fifteen students, all medical school graduates. Despite his recognition of his own lack of education and manners, Simon assessed his fellow pupils as a pretty stupid lot. For one thing, they neglected to supplement the classes with reading, which had been Simon's only school and remained for him a principal one.[5]

Each session began with a twenty-to-thirty-minute talk on the subject of the day, often given by Welch. Welch's "talks were such a marvel of lucidity that I never tired of hearing them through all the years I spent in Baltimore. He never used notes, nor did he look up the subject beforehand, for his constant and wide reading kept him always up-to-date. Indeed, as I was to discover later, he very often did not know what topic was to be discussed until he entered the classroom. Yet it was always a delight to watch his mind attack the problem under consideration; after a few preliminary words, he would swing into the heart of the matter, and each year the inevitable logic of his thought produced again the same technically perfect structure as in the preceding year; identical words and phrases fell into the same perfect order, but he himself, so he said, was unconscious of the repetition. It was as if the machinery of his intellectual processes could not run otherwise than true.

"During my first year of study with him, as always, he began each lecture with a discussion of the normal organ; a few words of description, possibly a hasty sketch on the blackboard, and the class had the necessary background for the pathological description to follow. This he developed clearly, simply, and adequately, with something of the special history of the subject, so that a close student might evaluate present views in relation to the past. The demonstration at the microscope was as illuminating as the lecture. With a few quick shifts of the slide he would bring out the important points, showing detail under high power and relations under low. The whole proceeding, from the introductory talk to the last field under the microscope, was a fascinating demonstration of Welch's ability.

"Attendance at autopsies, of course, was regarded as an important part of the work in pathology. They usually took place in the forenoon in the presence of the chiefs — Osler always, Halsted less often, and

Kelly rarely — and the house officers and graduate students. After Councilman's return, Welch seldom did autopsies, but when he did, he studied the frozen sections and made bacteriological examinations until late in the afternoon or even into the night."[6]

Whenever Councilman undertook an autopsy, including unscheduled ones called for by the clinicians after patients had died, Flexner was sure to be there. Soon he was allowed to help by keeping the "log" and doing other routine jobs. Around the autopsy table, Councilman and the student, only nine years his junior, became close friends.

An accurate observer, Councilman was an expert pathological anatomist. He excelled as a teacher, and in Flexner's case, he carried this gift over to helping the arrival from a much simpler and less cultivated world to learn and practice, as he passionately wished to do, the ways of the environment in which he now found himself. "Counc" would humorously correct Simon's pronunciations, affectionately improve his manners. Perhaps he was not the perfect social mentor. While scrupulously courteous to the ladies, he was primarily a man's man, a perpetual cigar smoker, his favorite drink beer, his pleasure raucous good humor and practical joking. His enthusiasm "was rather of an exaggerated, vocal kind. I easily acquired it, and added to my naturally quick responses, must have been at times rather tumultuous." In a little while, however, as Simon looked around him more, his behavior moved in the opposite direction. When not sure of himself in a social situation — which was often — he remained silent, an observer and a listener.

Flexner was never such an "intense microscopist" as Councilman, "who could spend hours over the microscope without fatigue, picking out fields to be studied" and drawing what he saw. "Perhaps it was the long-stemmed porcelain pipe which Councilman could puff at without getting the smoke in his eyes that kept his mind composed during these long vigils." To encourage Simon, "Counc" gave him such a pipe, but although Simon became a good microscopist and learned enough pathological anatomy to serve his purposes, he developed almost from the start a greater interest in the experimental aspect of pathology, more concerned with "the nature and causes of disease than in the pathological changes" resulting from disease. "Bacteriology provided me with a set of such causes of which many examples were brought to me at the autopsy table."[7]

Although Flexner believed that Welch was hardly conscious of his existence, he was being watched. Much of the limited space in the Pathological was occupied by the two-story amphitheater for autopsies. Several railed-off tiers provided standing room for some thirty men. Beside it on the ground floor was the pathological laboratory, a long, narrow room along one side of which a counter ran under small glass cupboards in which the students kept their cultures. The width of the cupboard assigned to him showed the student how much of the counter he could use. On the floor above was the almost identical bacteriological laboratory. Welch preferred to work at the counter beside his students, and the very smallness of the total space enabled him to observe in a variety of contexts the young Kentuckian as he ranged around, seeking things to do.[8]

Welch was fascinated to see how much more "usable" were Flexner's drugstore-acquired skills than what the other students had been taught in medical schools. The more formally educated men, when not given assignments, were usually at a loss, but Flexner would always find a task. He was quick and handy; he focused his attention; he could do several things simultaneously without getting confused; he did not shy away from unconventional means or conclusions; and he would undertake "anything and everything that came along." If the janitor was too drunk to appear, Flexner would sew up the cadaver, clean the autopsy table, and then dust and sweep the room. "Luckily," Flexner remembered, "I could do chores without repulsion."[9]

Had not Simon come from a background that placed him in a lower social rank than that of his companions? Was he not liable to be downgraded because he was a Jew? Under the circumstances, should he not have been oversensitive and resentful of doing menial tasks? He had certainly been resentful of the meanness of his environment during the first sixteen years of his life. But now ambition had been born and a strong sense of direction. As he put it, "deep interest in the work and a sense of getting forward made all this [whether or not the task was considered menial] a matter of little importance."

Throughout his long life, Simon cherished the memory of his drugstore experience. As children, my brother and I used to pretend to beat our family automobile, as if it were a horse, to get it past a drugstore. Indeed, a horse would automatically have stopped since Father almost always wanted to go in, look around, and purchase something. When he was able to find in his study some unusual book, he would appear with it happily and ask, "What kind of a drugstore do you think this is anyway?"[10]

Early in his stay in Baltimore, Simon's unconventionality of approach created results that both amused and impressed everyone. A specimen of urine, presumably passed by a young woman, had been sent to Welch because it contained a baffling sediment. Had there been in the bladder a parasite yielding those curious bodies? Himself puzzled, Welch showed around the slides he had prepared, and the bottle with its red-yellow sediment. The Hopkins faculty was stumped. But Flexner, who had often seen his mother can tomatoes, exclaimed, "Why, they are tomato seeds." Welch sent to the hospital kitchen for a tomato, squeezed it, and sure enough! The conclusion: "It must have been a case of malingering."[11]

What most impressed Welch was that the somewhat uncouth young man, who had on his arrival from Kentucky been almost completely self-educated, gave every indication of being able to proceed in this new sophisticated environment primarily on his own. Welch's seeming indifference to his pupils, the laxness of the routine at the Pathological, was based on the conception that advanced students should not require waterwings to keep them afloat. Welch did give assignments for research when they were asked for, but he did not follow up to see if they were carried out, and was more pleased if the student deviated into something effective of his own.

The first fruit of Welch's judgment of Flexner was for the young man frightening. Welch advised him not to enroll in the course offered in bacteriology; it would take too much time away from his pathological studies. Respectfully, Simon explained that his plan for making a living in Louisville combined bacteriological with pathological services, and he was more ignorant of bacteriology because the equipment had been too expensive for him to procure for personal study. Welch replied that Flexner now had access to the equipment, and that he could teach himself more quickly than if he took the course. Consulting the students who did enroll, doing the assigned reading, carrying through the experiments on his own, Flexner fulfilled Welch's prophecy.

When Flexner failed to show up at the clinic conducted at the hospital by William Osler, the kindhearted physician expressed worry lest the idealistic young man, who clearly had the least financial assets of all the pupils, could not make his living purely from laboratory work. He should join the other students in preparing for practice. Flexner was relieved to have Welch say no. He had no intention of practicing, and he was afraid that, in the give and take of the clinic, his ignorance would become embarrassingly manifest. He was, indeed, glad not to have closer contact with Welch. He believed that Welch believed he knew more than he did.[12]

There was no need to prod Flexner to undertake his original studies: he had, indeed, brought a problem with him from Louisville. Dr. Cheatham had given him a small bottle containing an eye preserved in alcohol. It had been removed from a child because of a tumor of the retina, which had appeared soon after birth. Flexner now made sections through the eye and the tumor, and examined them under the microscope.

Eye tumors were then recognized as sarcoma (a fleshy excrescence) or glioma (consisting largely of cells from the central nervous system). Flexner was familiar enough with sarcoma to rule that out. He went to available books to study glioma but could find no resemblance. The tumor, he tells us, was "in fact, a remarkable structure," being made of regular whorls (he dubbed them "rosettes") of cells. The inner ones were spindle-shaped and elongated, and came together in such a way as to surround a little cavity. The outer ones were small and round with little or no protoplasm. Staining darkly in hematoxylin, these seemed to consist of round nuclei. The whorls, staining pink in eosin, seemed to be made up of protoplasm. Fine projections or droplets of the pink substance could be detected in the cavities.

Councilman had seen nothing like it. Welch, "who was always intrigued by odd tumors and was famous for working out problems," had no suggestions. Councilman finally put Flexner on the right track by suggesting that the tumor was composed of retinal rods and cones that had got misplaced during the formation of the eye.

To follow this lead, Flexner had to study the embryology of the eye. The Hopkins library being inadequate, he had the excitement of his first visit to the great Surgeon General's Library in Washington, where he found atlases depicting in each successive stage the formation of the retina. From these, he worked out in detail "a possible and plausible scheme of development of such a tumor from embryonic odds and ends." He named the phenomenon — Councilman undoubtedly helped out with the Latin — "neuroepithelioma retinae."[13]

After he had been at the Pathological only about five months, Flexner presented his discovery to the Johns Hopkins Hospital Medical Society. This society, with its voice piece, the *Johns Hopkins Hospital Bulletin*, played a major role in teaching and research. The weekly meetings on Monday evenings were attended by the professors, the postgraduate students, and the clinical staffs, up to a total of thirty or forty. Interesting cases were presented, work in progress discussed, and papers read. "Hardly a subject could be mentioned at one of these gatherings that did not lead to further work in view of the free and suggestive exchange of ideas," so wrote Harvey Cushing in his life of Osler. "In the history of medicine there never was anything quite like it."

The valuable contributions were quickly brought out in the *Bulletin*, as was Flexner's paper, for which he made his own clumsy drawings. Since such tumors, although their nature had not previously been recognized, were not rare, the young man had the honor of having his work, complete with the term he had invented, plagiarized by an Austrian textbook writer. He had made the first of many discoveries that were to find a place in medical literature.[14]

During the early months of every year, Welch gave a series of weekly lectures in the hospital auditorium. His subject in 1891 was diphtheria. While discussing how the disease manifested itself in inoculated guinea pigs, Welch stated that Löffler, the discoverer of the diphtheria bacillus, had strangely been unable to confirm Oertel's report of diphtheria lesions in the lymphatic glands. The body of an infected guinea pig was handed around the class. On leaving, Flexner found it lying beside the incinerator. It occurred to him to secure the guinea pig and make his own examination of the lymphatic glands.

Although the body was about to be thrown out, Flexner felt he could not appropriate it without Welch's permission. "At that period, I was very much in awe of Dr. Welch." He was "a good deal agitated" when he made the request. Without comment Welch granted the petition.

What Flexner found when he began his research was amazing. The lesions that the great Löffler had failed to see were conspicuously there. How could this be explained? Perhaps what Flexner was identifying as diphtheria lesions were a normal part of the anatomy of the animal. He studied uninfected glands without finding any lesions. Another theory was necessary. Perhaps the infected specimen he had originally examined was a rare exception. But the lymphatic glands of another infected guinea pig revealed the same lesions. The time had come to lay the matter before Dr. Welch.

He had observed Welch's schedule. Having one morning given the professor time to open his mail, Flexner found the courage to knock on his door. After as quick an explanation as he could manage, he handed Welch slides of the lesions. Welch put one slide under his own microscope, took one look, and asked, "Has Councilman seen this?"

"No, sir."

Welch rapidly passed the other slides under his lenses. Then he spoke. "The lesions are essentially those described by Oertel." He rose to indicate that the interview was over.

In writing up the discovery for the *Bulletin*, Flexner signed it with Welch's name ahead of his own. On seeing the manuscript, Welch asked, "Why did you put in my name? I had nothing to do with it." Flexner explained that no one would take an unknown's word against Löffler's, but if Welch's name was there ... "All right. Do what you please."[15]

The discovery was important because many physicians were still skeptical concerning the bacillus Löffler had discovered eight years before and announced as the cause of diphtheria. Naturally Löffler's failure to find the characteristic lesion in guinea pigs infected with his bacillus strengthened the doubts. Not only did Flexner's finding back the validity of the bacillus, but since his guinea pigs had been infected with poisons secreted by the germs, he had further demonstrated what was also a subject of controversy: that the effects of a disease could be induced by soluble toxic agents.[16]

Everything was going well except for the state of Flexner's finances. His money would clearly not hold out until the end of the term. This would have been no problem if he had been willing to continue accepting Abraham's generosity. His brother had written him, "I want you to do the things that are best for yourself, for I realize that when you are again at work [in Louisville] you can hardly hope for any opportunity for further study except, perhaps, such as would come with a vacation trip abroad." Abraham hoped himself to make another foray from Louisville to increase his own education, but "I will shape my course," he wrote in accord with the way that Welch or Councilman advised Simon "to shape yours." Abe would even send Simon abroad. Family loyalty dictated that they could not both be away from Louisville at the same time, but if Simon needed another year, Abe "would wait my turn just as you have had to await yours." His own "objective is at best too vague to be taken into account."[17]

Early in May, 1891, although the term of instruction ran for almost another month, Flexner informed Councilman that he was going home. Councilman expressed dismay. After Flexner had "told him a little of my situation, not much," Councilman became all smiles. If the trouble was no more than that, the matter could easily be managed. Councilman would himself take care of the expense. Thanking him, Flexner said he was already too much in debt. "I could not see my way to repaying him." Councilman argued, but not to the extent of creating embarrassment. Then he said that Flexner would of course be back for the following year. Simon said he would be tied down in trying to make his living in Louisville.

Councilman inquired whether Flexner had told Welch. Flexner replied that he had not thought Welch would be interested. Might Councilman tell Welch? Of course.

Two or three days later, Councilman brought the matter up again. Would Flexner accept the fellowship in pathology for the following year?[18]

The offer was financially modest — Abe would still have to fill in for some living expenses — yet it cast a mighty shadow before. Although in modern times almost every student is supported by some kind of fellowship, during the 1890's fellowships were extremely rare and difficult to secure. The whole Hopkins pathological laboratory had only this one, and during the previous year (when Flexner's amateurish application had been turned down) no adequate applicant had been found. The fellowship was an honor of which the Flexner family could be proud.

Yet Simon's family reacted nervously, with a foreboding all the more remarkable because he had, with their acquiescence, applied for the very same fellowship the year before. Then it had seemed that he was asking for temporary assistance towards a project that was part of the family plan. Now the fellowship pulled at Simon from the outside: strangers were intervening to keep Simon away. Could not one intervention be followed by another, permanently alienating Simon? And if one sibling broke the circle, might not the circle itself, on which the family rise seemed to continue to depend, fly apart?

Jacob sent Simon a letter full of financial arguments for his immediate return to Louisville. Abraham made alternate suggestions which, while involving more self-sacrifice on his part, would keep Simon dependent on family funds. Was the Hopkins the best place for Simon to spend another year of study — perhaps he should attend another medical school, to which Abraham would send him, perhaps take a brief trip abroad? Whatever his misgivings, Abraham assumed that Simon would return to Louisville after his second educational year, and according to the old plan set up a private laboratory from which Abraham naively believed, Simon could make contributions to all mankind.

Concerning his eventual return, Simon kept his mouth shut, but after what he had learned about the necessary equipment and resources, he could no longer accept the feasibility of the Louisville plan. The best aspect of the fellowship to his mind was that it strengthened his ties to Baltimore. With delight, he accepted the fellowship. A firm road seemed, for the first time in his life, to be opening before him.

25

Settling In at the Hopkins

S IMON did, of course, return for the time being to Louisville. There
was no question of his filling in at the drugstore. Not since he con-
valesced from typhoid fever had he had leisure to spend with his
mother, and she now had more leisure to spend with him since the rising
family prosperity had reduced her household tasks. She enjoyed taking
him visiting, introducing him proudly as her son from the Johns Hopkins University. However, a disappointment arose when the elders at
the temple invited the prodigal to read the lesson. Simon had to admit
his utter ignorance of ritual Hebrew. His mother brightened up again
when someone offered to read the Hebrew if Simon would read the
English. He was embarrassed and read so fast that the service was said
to have been the shortest on record.

Worried by his ignorance of gross anatomy, Flexner bought for
twenty-five dollars from the Medical Institute a cadaver that had been
preserved in brine. An outhouse on the college grounds was made available, and the demonstrator in anatomy agreed to supervise Simon's
work for a small fee. As it was a hot summer, the task was very unpleasant and had to be carried through somewhat inaccurately.

Flexner was back at the Pathological early in the fall before any of the
faculty arrived.[1]

The Johns Hopkins Medical School, which was to rise beside the hospital, had remained an unfulfilled plan because a catastrophic fall in the
value of Baltimore and Ohio stock had left the university without the
necessary funds. Members of Helen Thomas's family now came to the
rescue.

An opening gun had been fired during July, 1889, when Helen's father wrote President Gilman, "I think our lady friends might be good for $200,000 ... provided we give women entrance."[2] The Baltimore daughters who had, under the leadership of Carey, founded "The Group" to discuss feminist problems, now saw in the lack of funds for the medical school an opportunity to be seized.

President Gilman was firmly opposed to coeducation, as were the majority of the trustees. In response to the suggestion Dr. Thomas had forwarded to them, they merely expressed doubt that the women could even raise $100,000. At this, Carey and Mary Garrett, who began the subscription with a large gift, organized the Women's Fund for the Higher Education of Women. They were soon able to face Gilman and the trustees with a hard offer of $100,000. According to Carey, this would have been refused out of hand "had it not been that two of our fathers, mine and Mamie Gwinn's, were on the [university] board, and another father, Francis T. King, was president of the hospital board."[3] As controversy boiled around Flexner (who was, of course, too lowly to be consulted) three of the four medical school professors, Osler, Hurd, and Halsted, signed a letter urging acceptance, but Welch, who was embarrassed at the thought of having women present at autopsies, refused. Finally, a compromise was reached: women would be admitted if their backers could raise $500,000.[4]

As the funds remained lacking to get the medical school in motion, the environment Simon was coming so much to enjoy showed signs of falling apart. The hospital trustees threatened a step backwards: they would found their own medical school, which would be supported by student fees. Thus it would resemble more closely the Louisville Medical Institute than the endowed school the university trustees envisioned. And functioning medical schools were angling for the frustrated Hopkins professors. Welch and Osler turned down calls from Harvard, but Dr. Thomas was privately informed that Osler was considering returning to his alma mater, McGill.[5]

In December, 1892, Gilman received a letter from Mary Garrett. She was adding to what the Women's Fund had now collected her personal gift of $306,977, thereby filling out the required $500,000. But she added to coeducation further conditions that had been worked out with Carey: students would have to have a college degree before they would be admitted, and they also must have taken various premedical and language courses. These were objectives toward which the university intended gradually to move. However, the trustees feared that if put in force at once the requirements would be suicidal: students could become the graduates of other respectable medical schools at an age when they would still be preparing to enter the Hopkins.

In recalling the negotiations Carey wrote, "When it came to laying down requirements, our fathers deserted us." Her father, she stated, "almost wept, and told me it was incredible that two young women should take such a position. The trustees called on us separately and together (I was always present)." At last, the necessary concession was made, with Welch acting as mediator. Osler commented, "Welch, we are lucky to get in as professors, for I am sure neither you nor I could get in as students."[6]

Plans were now speeded for opening the Johns Hopkins Medical School in the autumn of 1893.

When Flexner had reappeared in Baltimore early in September, 1891, his shortage of money proved again to his advantage. For the nominal sum of ten dollars a week, Dr. Henry M. Hurd, the superintendent of the hospital, agreed to house him in a staff bedroom, with all expenses paid including laundry.

During the previous year, when Simon had lived on the other side of Baltimore in the boardinghouse, his contacts had been exclusively with his fellow workers at the Pathological. Now he was in daily and nightly proximity to a whole roster of young men, including most members of the clinical staff, who were enjoying, separately and together, high scientific adventure.

The newness of pathological and bacteriological techniques, combined with their limited acceptance elsewhere, opened innumerable opportunities for fruitful discoveries. The weekly meetings of the Johns Hopkins Hospital Society were electric as one speaker arose after another to announce exciting results. The monthly issues of the *Bulletin* were crammed. In this euphoric environment there were no elderly devotees of obsolete traditions. Dr. Hurd was forty-eight and the only married professor. At forty-two, Osler was next in age. He was then writing *The Principles and Practice of Medicine*, which was to light the spark that would kindle the Rockefeller Institute for Medical Research. Welch was forty-one.

Unlike other hospitals, which were staffed by local practitioners, the Hopkins sought the best clinicians wherever they could be found. Dr. Thomas was, in his guiding role as a trustee, the only Baltimore practitioner importantly linked to the Hopkins. None of the department heads was a Maryland man, and the interns and residents were almost all outlanders. (PLATE 17)

Perched on a hillside on the outskirts of the city, the Hopkins medical establishments were — despite Dr. Thomas's efforts to close all gaps — separated psychologically as well as physically from Baltimore.[7] Looking down on the distant streets, Flexner could not imagine that there walked there a little redheaded girl in pigtails who would one day be his wife.

Their semi-isolation urged the young scientists into tight cohesion. A professor visiting from Harvard compared the medical community on its hilltop to monks behind the walls of a medieval monastery. However, they did not live austerely. "Our rooms in the main building," Councilman remembered, "were capacious, comfortably furnished. . . . We breakfasted together. . . . The luncheon hour, at which most of those working at the hospital gathered, was the most delightful of the day."[8]

Simon had never before shared in any communal life beyond his own tight, nurturing and stifling family circle. One of his later notations ran: "A young institution, full of ambition, purpose, and energy, with a rare group of able, charming men at the head, not only attracted ambitious men but by taking them into the heart of the enterprise charged them with a sense of future importance and devotion. Everyone put forward his best efforts, and the spirit abroad was so generous that men easily warmed to each other."[9]

Although he was politely treated and "got what I was entitled to," Simon did not feel really at ease. Considering "my origin, very restricted upbringing, lack of conventional education, etc. . . . it was intensely lucky for me to have come in early in the Baltimore experiment, when it was forming." Even as it was, he was more accepted in "the small family group" by some colleagues than others. "I was a green person, had had few or no social opportunities. It was proper that I should [have to] prove myself."[10]

During his first year at the hospital, Simon made a particular friend of Walter Reed, whose role in stamping out yellow fever was in a few years to make him famous. But Simon's mainstay remained Councilman. They played poker together, drank beer together, and Councilman gave the city youth his first real contact with nature when he took him to his brother's farm.

During a duck-hunting expedition with Councilman, Flexner missed several birds and then finally hit one. Concerning what followed, he wrote, "I do not believe there was any possibility of my using the gun except as a gesture to recover the duck which the fisherman in a little sailboat was about to hook out of the water. Still, the guide was frightened, and I was too after the little incident was over. I was angry at the brazen behavior of the boatman, and an accident might have happened with consequences too serious and disagreeable to think about."[11]

In his official role as a Fellow, Flexner proceeded much as he had done the year before, except that instead of sitting with the class he helped with the teaching. There was no consistent routine. Welch did whatever he wished to do, Councilman did as much of the rest as interested him, and Flexner picked up the fragments. "Autopsies fell to me. I did them poorly and slowly at first. Although this must have been trying to Osler and the other clinicians who brought their staffs and graduate students, no one complained to Welch."[12]

As before, Flexner's main personal concern was his own research. He studied previously undescribed and unexplained pathological formations, which he identified as they appeared during autopsies. Most attention was attracted — his article was translated into Spanish — by his discovery of amoebas in an abscess of the jaw.[13]

Early in 1892, Welch informed Flexner that the Maryland State Board of Health was worried about an epidemic in the coal-mining district around Cumberland. The disease, which had been diagnosed as spotted fever, might well be cerebrospinal meningitis. Simon agreed to hurry there but was worried because he had never before attempted such a mission. Surely he would need a companion who was better than he at ingratiating himself with strangers! Welch acquiesced to his taking along his cosmopolitan young colleague Lewellys F. Barker.

At Lonaconing in Cumberland County, the miners' houses clung to the precipitous sides of the cut made by Bitter Creek. The snow was deep and the temperature often sank to zero. Flexner and Barker were put up by a doctor named Skillings, who was practicing with his father. The physicians stated that there had been no new cases for more than a week. However, at the house of a miner named Wilson, a girl about ten years old was "comatose and surely doomed." Flexner and Barker called at the Wilson house every day. It was essential to secure a cadaver for autopsy.

One evening after dinner, the elder Skillings hurried in to report that he had seen the undertaker walking in the direction of the Wilson house. "This caused me," Flexner remembered, "to spring up." Could they not by driving reach the cottage before the undertaker arrived there? Lanterns having been hung from a buggy, Flexner, Barker, and the older

Skillings set out at a trot and arrived to find the undertaker in conversation with the bereaved parents.

After expressing condolences, Flexner made a plea for an "examination" to determine beyond doubt the nature of the epidemic. The parents objected; the disease, they said, was known to be spotted fever. Flexner then explained that there were several kinds of spotted fever, and asked the elder Skillings whether he was certain which kind it was? After some hesitation the doctor acknowledged that he was not sure. The family then agreed to an autopsy but requested that nothing be carried away.

The autopsy was held in the front parlor in the presence, requested by Flexner, of the undertaker. The room could not be adequately lighted, and other conditions were poor: it was midnight before the corpse was again dressed. Doing what was necessary if a true scientific result were to be achieved, Barker had, when the undertaker's back was turned, put pieces of the brain and spinal cord in his pocket.

Back at the Skillings house, Flexner and Barker retired to the stable, made cultures "from the exudate of the meninges, and put the specimen in the preservative fluid." They then went to the parlor where they found the younger Skillings in a state of hysteria. Having learned from his father that the body had been "opened both front and back," he shouted that, when the miners found out, all four physicians would be roughly treated — perhaps hanged. He went on to say that "while hanging might well be enough for Barker and me," he had a wife and children to care for.

The scientists from Baltimore did not know how frightened they ought to be. Young Skillings may have lost control of himself, but he was familiar with "the attitudes of the miners." Upstairs in their bedroom, Flexner and Barker did not undress: it was a bitter-cold night and they did not want to be hanged in their pajamas. "We sat up smoking endless cigarettes until 2 A.M." But, on finally getting to bed, they slept soundly.

At breakfast, young Skillings, "looking gloomy enough . . . sat looking down the road." Suddenly, he sprang up and exclaimed, " 'Here they come!' And as we all looked out, sure enough a group of miners, led by Wilson, was headed for the doctors' house. As they reached the door, I asked to be permitted to receive them."

During the long night's vigil, Simon had been thinking out what, under these circumstances, he could most effectively say. Marshaling his thoughts, he opened the door to see Wilson respectfully taking off his cap. The other miners took off their caps. Flexner invited them in.

Wilson made a little speech, thanking "Barker and me for all the trouble we took to help his poor child. He had no money to pay us," but "he and his friends had come to invite us into the mines if we would care to see how coal mining was done." The invitation was enthusiastically accepted.

The pathological findings fully established that the epidemic was meningitis. The bacteriological studies, undertaken after the return to Baltimore, were inconclusive, since the cultures seemed to have been contaminated by stable dust. The smears showed practically no bacteria, although after much searching and staining in various ways a few rod-shaped bodies were found. It then being the direction of research at the Hopkins to link meningitis with pneumonia, "my notion was that" what he had found were "degraded pneumococci." That was wrong — but Flexner was by no means done with his work on meningitis.[14]

In Simon's perpetual correspondence with Abraham concerning his plans and possibilities for the following year, the idea that he would eventually return to Louisville, although still basic to the family preconceptions, was little mentioned. Opportunities were opening because of the growing gulf between the interest in modern pathology and the lack of scientists competently trained. Simon was tentatively approached by the Rush Medical College in Chicago and by the University of Minnesota. Councilman was being angled for by Montreal. If he went, he wanted Simon to go with him. But Flexner, feeling a need for more and more education as a scientist and as a citizen of the larger world, believed it would be almost suicidal for him to leave the Hopkins. Lest they block his road to promotion, he eyed with concern two young men — Barker, Thayer — who had appeared at the Pathological from more sophisticated backgrounds with better training.[15]

Flexner's future was still undecided when Councilman agreed to go to Harvard. This created an instantaneous crisis. Welch could not be left without assistance in pathology and Flexner felt he was not ready to be put on the faculty. Councilman, it is true, pooh-poohed such fears: Flexner, he insisted, would get the job and be a professor in three years. But Simon knew the warmth of his friend's partiality, and was deeply disturbed by the rumor that, there being no adequately prepared candidate in America, a young pathologist would be imported from Germany.

As he was returning to his seat after delivering one of his many reports to the Medical Society, Flexner overheard Welch say to Halsted, "I think he will do." And sure enough, he was appointed assistant in pathology. This made Flexner, not yet two years out of Louisville, a member of the greatest medical faculty in the United States. Furthermore, he was to succeed Councilman as resident pathologist at the hospital. He would join the "privileged inner group" who sat during meals at the high table in a bay window overlooking the hospital grounds. The chiefs, Osler, Welch, and Halsted, were often there.[16]

This time around, there were no hesitations and objections in the Flexner circle. They welcomed Simon's achievement as "the highest distinction that has come our way." Abraham hailed the news with "inexpressible joy. . . . It is perfectly evident that promotion along this line awaits you in due season. I cannot see what more any human being could desire."[17]

Welch had "chanced it," Dr. Flexner came to conclude, because he felt that a German-trained pathological anatomist would be limited to that specialty. Welch's own interests were shifting from straight pathology to a combination of pathology, bacteriology, and experimental research. Despite his lack of conventional training or perhaps partly because of it — Flexner himself wrote "by chance or good luck" — the primitive from Kentucky had shown interest and skill in all the linked directions.[18]

An aspect of the situation which Flexner could not possibly have understood and which Welch himself undoubtedly did not recognize was that Welch had come to the end of his own original laboratory work. An open road lay ahead of the recent arrival from the back streets of Louisville.

26

---·⟨∞⟩·---

Breaking Trail

A s resident in pathology, Flexner was held at the hospital doing autopsies during most of the summer of 1892. When the fall semester opened, he was flooded with official work. The autopsies were now held in the amphitheater with students observing. Instruction in the form of interpolations was given by the clinicians, usually Osler, who was very careful never to seem to push the younger man aside. Flexner developed a somewhat histrionic technique for "gross dissection." "With a few precise incisions, I could expose at autopsy this or that structure with clarity. I was always, I remember, pleased when before the class a deft incision exposed the thoracic tract as it ran along the bodies of the vertebrae, and I do not recall injuring the duct itself. However, my stunts never took in [Franklin Paine] Mall when he came to the medical school in 1893. He would show with the grin on his face that I was skating on thin ice." Welch was impressed into fearing that his disciple would desert pathology for surgery.[1]

An autopsy consumed a morning from ten to lunchtime. Samples from the most damaged organs were removed and frozen to make immediate sectioning possible. Simon wrote out the report in the autopsy records, including the microscopical appearance of the sections. If there were evidences of infection, cultures were taken and bacteriological tests added to the record. Finally, blocks of the tissue were hardened for later sectioning and added to the reservoir of such materials for class use.

Flexner went back for lunch to the hospital. He sat at the high table, where the group often included Welch, Osler, Halsted, Mall, and "the usual visiting stranger." The conversation, so remembered Simon's predecessor Councilman, "was always lively and interesting; everyone sought to bring something to the feast. There was talk about work; jokes, and laughter. A favorite game in which Osler rather excelled — his early experience with . . . the Caughnawauga Indians having given him previous practice — was to relate the impossible and to lead up to this so skillfully that the line between fact and fiction was obscured. It was very well for us who knew the game, but occasionally it would be played when the serious visitor was present and he often carried away with him striking information on new facts in medical science. The exchanges between Osler and Halsted were always a delight, and we all sought to get something on the other.

"I remember once that I had gone to Philadelphia to read a paper on a subject in which we were all interested, but unfortunately I had mistaken the date by a week. . . . I was naturally somewhat fearful of the fact being ascertained, and the first thing, the next day, Osler asked me about the paper, how it had been accepted, what was the discussion, etc. I rather welcomed the opportunity to get the matter over with and spoke of the enthusiastic reception accorded the paper and gave at some length the discussion upon it. 'What did Wilson say?' asked Osler, and I thought it well to put Wilson in oposition and gave as well as I could his opposing argument. 'Yes,' said Osler, 'Jim Wilson spent last night with me and said he immensely enjoyed your paper but he could not quite agree with you.' "[2]

After lunch, three times a week there were the laboratory sessions, from two to five. They opened with a lecture that Welch was supposed to give, but he often did not appear, either having warned Flexner or not having warned him. If he was not there within fifteen minutes of the hour, Flexner would start. Sometimes he would then hear Welch's short, quick steps ascending the stairs. Flexner would step aside and Welch would begin the topic all over again.

Having always to be prepared, Flexner kept a step ahead of the class by studying texts, usually on the previous evening. Sometimes he was so pressed that he could not stay after he had finished his lunch "to enjoy the friendly and often interesting talks either at the table or at the staff room, with its easy chairs."

The lecture over, sections were distributed for individual examination under the students' microscopes. Now the instruction was one to one. When present, Welch would start from one end of the room, and Flexner from the other. When Welch was not present, Flexner had to hurry through the whole class — some twenty-seven students. Each one would rise from his stool to make way for the teacher; the teacher would look through the microscope, manipulate the slide, and explain.*[3]

There was often a public lecture in the evening which Simon felt it would help his general education to attend.

All this left little time for original scientific work, but Flexner was indefatigable, and he had the great advantage of not having to seek for problems: these were turned up by the autopsy routine. He chose those morbid specimens that seemed to offer possibilities for bacteriological studies. During 1893, he made fourteen presentations to the Hospital Medical Society, sometimes more than one a session; all were subsequently published in the *Bulletin.* His most important work was on lymphosarcoma (a malignant tumor of the lymph glands). As he proceeded, he added another case and cited previous studies. The result was voluminous enough for a reprint: "my first monograph!" In his elation, he sent several copies to Leipzig for sale. His mind was turning to Germany.[4]

It is axiomatic in American cultural history that the Hopkins brought European — particularly German — expertise and educational standards to America. However, the Hopkins was by no means an extension of European culture. It transplanted Old World seeds into the New World soil, where it was hoped that they would nurture richer fruits. When President Gilman took a sabbatical abroad in 1889, Dr. Thomas, then chairman of the university trustees' executive committee, expressed his hope that "a nearer view of the fading glories of the older civilizations will send you back to us . . . with your confidence increased in the grand possibilities of your own country."[5]

When scouting abroad for the Hopkins in 1881, Thomas showed none of the anglophilia of his wife's Smith relations. He reported to his friend Gilman that, despite the beauty of the buildings, Oxford was too moss-backed for anything to be hoped for from there. Cambridge was more in the spirit of the Hopkins, and its history faculty was so dissatisfied that any one of its professors would be glad to come to Baltimore. (None was appointed.) As for Germany, "the great attention to specialties seems to me to dwarf all originality."[6]

The founding faculty of the Hopkins — professors and associate professors appointed between 1883 and 1889 — numbered thirty-nine. The

* Dr. Flexner remembered with amusement that he once had Gertrude Stein in his class. Too fat to rise without great effort, she merely moved over, leaving a corner of the stool for Simon, a cozy arrangement.[7]

origins of six, all with Anglo-American names, I was unable to identify. Three came from England and Scotland and one from Germany. Twenty-nine — 87 percent of those identified — were Americans.[8] Gilman preferred to look around his own continent, selecting young men of some achievement and great promise. Every one of Simon's superiors at the hospital and the Pathological were American-born, but all had received education in Germany. Although the necessity for German training had been greatly reduced by the Hopkins itself, it was standard for the younger men to have a period of German study. Simon sailed at the end of the first semester in 1893 and returned in time for the inauguration of the medical school the following fall.

Crossing for the first time three thousand miles of ocean was for Simon Flexner less of an adventure than had been his first trip from Louisville to the Hopkins. The European environments he now encountered were exotic, but so had been the Hopkins environment, which concerned him a thousand times more. And he did not feel, as had earlier Americans seeking professional knowledge, that he was reaching a treasure house of otherwise unreachable wonders. He was familiar with even the latest European discoveries through reading scientific journals, and he had made his own contributions, if small, to the world flow. Furthermore, the great German centers of pathology were less suited to his own temperament, training, and gifts than what he had experienced in Baltimore.

The Hopkins was an American phenomenon, based on the conceptions of equality of opportunity, individual freedom, and self-reliance. This created the perfect environment for the ingenious former druggist from Louisville, who abounded with ideas and could be confident that, when he got far enough on a project to deserve it, he could secure his teacher's advice. But, as Welch himself realized, his methods were only applicable in very special situations. It would be good for Simon to learn the rigid and effective routine of German teaching laboratories.

However, this opportunity was not what Welch emphasized in discussing the trip with his disciple. He offered to supply letters of introduction that would enable Flexner to meet the great founders of modern pathology. By getting to know them personally, Flexner would be better able to understand their methods and the bent of their scientific achievements. In addition to traveling, Flexner should spend some months with Friedrich Daniel von Recklinghausen, Dr. Welch's own teacher, whose specialty was bones. "He is a great master of pathology," Welch explained, "and I believe it is worth more to you to come in contact with his clear profound thought than with many of the younger men whose views are more modern." Furthermore, Recklinghausen had a tremendous collection of abnormal bones. Modern pathology being new to America, the reservoir of preserved pathological materials there was pitifully low. Wherever Flexner went, he should examine the invaluable German archives of specimens, and beg for duplicates to carry back to the Hopkins.[9]

Flexner sailed late in March, 1893, for Rotterdam. Some medical visits were paid in Holland, where Simon "got my initiation into pictures . . . especially at Amsterdam and the Hague. But it was not until many years later, after my marriage, that I paid a more intelligent interest to the galleries of art."[10]

On to Recklinghausen and Strasbourg. Although Simon had been told that his father had taught school there, he could trace nothing.* The cathedral had often been described to him in his childhood, and he admired it. With a fellow member of the Hopkins group he lived at Frau Zimmerman's, at Breiterestin 1, beside the river. They had two small bedrooms and a common study of good size. Their landlady gave them coffee and rolls for breakfast, and dinner when requested. Unless asked for something else, she served them squabs "which she prepared extremely well." The young men wandered the city, and Simon, when left alone by his companion, instantly got lost.

In his first interview with Recklinghausen, Simon ignorantly addressed him with the intimate *du*, to the horror of his companion. But this was not what caused trouble. Though he pleased the professor by choosing to study the softening of bones, he disobeyed when commanded to cut sections by hand in the old-fashioned manner, which he did not know how to do effectively. He made use of a microtome in another laboratory to cut his sections and kept a clumsily hand-cut slide on his table to substitute quickly when he heard Recklinghausen's footsteps come down the hall. One day, he was not quick enough. Recklinghausen stamped out of the small room Simon had been assigned — table, stove, old-fashioned microscope, and a few dishes — but in a little while he came back. Flexner now openly used the machine-cut slides.[11]

The Hopkins being what it was, Recklinghausen's lecture course was Flexner's first that systematically covered the whole field of pathology.

* It was on this trip that Simon made the visit to his mother's birthplace described in Ch. 2.

The lectures came just after lunch. Forever the eager student, Simon assigned himself a seat on the first bench immediately under the professor's eye, but his lunches were, in the best Germanic tradition, heavy, and the professor "was not a lively lecturer." Simon would fall asleep to be periodically wakened when Recklinghausen emphasized loudly the connective *"und es war* [and it was]." For some reason, the elderly Flexner loved to tell this story over and over with relish.[12]

Flexner was most impressed by the autopsies and gross pathology classes. After the specimens had been exhibited and explained, sections under a microscope moved on a track from student to student. Recklinghausen, who used no assistant, would advance with the display and continue into the evening if that was necessary to reach the last student. By then, all the others had left.

Welch had cautioned his disciple not to try to complete a piece of work — he could do that at home — and so Flexner did not finish out the semester. He wished to visit other universities before the teaching was over. He went to Freiburg; Heidelberg, where he was rebuffed; Tübingen, where he was assigned to two young students who saw that he had "a very good time"; and then to Berlin, where he met the great Virchow, then in his seventies. On his way to Vienna, "the marketplace, as it were, for the medical visitor," he was stopped at Prague by Councilman's teacher, Chiari, with whom he spent two profitable months, performing autopsies beside Chiari's assistants and studying the healing process in ulcer of the intestine. Then via Leipzig and the Hook of Holland to London, "where I spent some interesting days." He was back at Baltimore in good time for the opening of the first year of the Johns Hopkins Medical School.[13]

Flexner was impressed but not moved by the systematic organization of the German pathological institutes, which largely duplicated each other. "The professor was supreme in a way I had not seen in Baltimore," and was, unlike the relaxed Welch, present "all day long, often from 7 A.M. to 6 P.M." Lectures, laboratory courses, autopsies, "special studies, what we would call research," were all closely knit. One day repeated another. Everything was strictly departmentalized. The clinicians were almost never present at autopsies, which, Flexner commented, prevented the close relationship between them and the pathologists "through which one received impressions of disease as a whole." There was no give-and-take between the heads and their younger assistants, and the students were kept at a distance in a manner that would have utterly frustrated such an unconventional enthusiast as Flexner had been when he arrived at the Hopkins.

"There was an intensity in the institutes that could not be missed"; everyone worked seriously and hard; but there was none of the atmosphere of good-fellowship, of cooperation, of excitement and optimism, of springing achievement that made Flexner's heart expand as his thoughts ran back to the hillside overlooking Baltimore.

But he had "loved much of German life — its out-of-doors element, at a garden at supper with music, the long walks on Sundays, the amblings on holidays, the cheap theater and opera, the picture galleries. . . . To one whose education had been so defective as mine had been, it was no little thing to have had these enlarging experiences."[14]

27

---⸎---

Rising

O<small>N</small> his return from Europe during the autumn of 1893, Simon saw the Pathological, which had been the womb of his new career, standing higher. There were now not two but four stories, one additional floor for nonpathological anatomy, the other for pharmacology and physical chemistry. The atmosphere was alive with excitement over the opening, so long delayed, of the medical school.

First-year instruction was concentrated on the two upper floors. The difficult entrance requirements had indeed proved limiting. There were only fourteen men and three women. Even so, they doubled the population Simon had become habituated to in the Pathological. As the students traversed the stairs and lingered in the halls, the women's higher voices added to the familiar sounds.[1]

The hospital community was expanded by an influx of more staff (all male). Most important to Flexner was Mall, the new professor of anatomy. Burdened with less routine than a pathologist and undertaking only one experiment a day, Mall finished early in the morning. He would drop into Flexner's room and propose a walk. The invitation was hard to resist. Almost exactly Flexner's age, Mall had pointed his brilliant mind in directions which Flexner, whose thoughts had not passed beyond immediate scientific work, had never considered. Mall talked of medical education "in general and the abstract. . . . I learned something of the German university system from him."[2]

Abraham was to credit much of his pioneering in American medical education to the influence of Mall, whom he had not yet met. Simon, although much interested, found his scientific work so interrupted by the walks that it was agreed that he would lock his door when he was occupied. Mall would, if he found the door locked, go away. Hearing familiar footsteps and then the rattle of the door, Simon found it hard to adhere to his resolve. He and Mall became "fast friends."

Mall was to pry Flexner away from his laboratory one summer and take him to the U.S. Marine Biological Laboratory at Woods Hole, Massachusetts. Simon, who would not otherwise have allowed himself to do so, escaped from the heat of the Baltimore summer; his knowledge of biology, a subject rarely studied in those days by medical scientists, was enlarged; and — he considered this most important — he worked in the laboratory of Jacques Loeb, the great experimental biologist, whom he would later summon to the Rockefeller Institute for Medical Research. Flexner struck a widely variant note in his bibliography with an article entitled "The Regeneration of the Nervous System of *Planaria torva* and the Anatomy of the Nervous System of Double-headed Forms."[3]

Mall "fell from grace," to use Welch's phrase, by marrying one of the first three female medical students. Noting that another of the students was also marrying a professor, Welch commented that this boded well for coeducation. For Simon, Mall's marriage provided a warm domestic hearth where he was often invited for further talk about medical education.

Simon's closest friend was Lewellys F. Barker, who had gone with him to Lonaconing and with whom he shared his private laboratory room. They were so perpetually together that Osler referred to them as the pathological twins. But in appearance they were anything but twins. Barker was very much taller than Flexner. He was perpendicularly built, arms and legs seemingly interminable. Copious curly hair, parted in the middle, topped a long, handsome, quizzically self-confident face.

Barker's youthful experiences had been close enough to Simon's to form a bond. Although he was of old Canadian stock and the son of a Baptist minister, Barker's family had been low in cash. Like Simon, Barker had been apprenticed to a druggist. His medical education had also been financed with difficulty. He had done brilliantly, as he continued to do at the Hopkins. He was to become a successor to Osler as professor of medicine.[4] (PLATE 19)

During their friendship in Baltimore, Barker could be freer with his earnings than Simon because he had no need to send money home. On one occasion, he lured his friend to a gambling parlor. Simon put up five dollars and instantly lost. "My face must have shown consternation, as the croupier told me to go into the rear room and eat and drink champagne to make up for the loss, and not to play again."[5]

The ordinary drink of the hospital brotherhood was beer, often consumed across the street at a bar, humorously designated as "the church," where conversation ran to life, love, and the "cosmic problems of the hospital."[6] However, Simon and his friends did not forget the superior exhilarating powers of whiskey. Whenever his family sent him a bottle from Kentucky, Simon would give a party. And there was a notable Christmas Eve.

Having dined in the city, Flexner and Barker felt the need for "a nightcap or two. I still see us waiting for the Center Street horsecar . . . and while waiting throwing ice balls at the electric lamp in the street. So we were already pretty lively." Arriving at the hospital about midnight, they woke up Mall and "had drinks all around" until the supply gave out. The grave crisis was not beyond the skills of the Hopkins prodigies. They remembered that an absent doctor kept a jug in his room. "We broke into his room and the cupboard and filched it. . . .

"B. and I were desperately sick in the night. I had a study across the hall, and in the early morning made for it. B. had already appropriated it and the couch. Then, I got into a hot bath and, while there, Dr. Hurd came looking for me to do an autopsy in town." Flexner arranged for someone else to do the autopsy.[7]

Simon had previously known almost no food except what his mother had cooked, in German farmhouse style, to combine economy and nutrition. He was fascinated with the delicacies of the Chesapeake: "There were oysters and crabs, hard- and soft-shelled. . . . But, there were delicacies which were rarer, so much rarer. There were, for instance, diamond-backed terrapin and wild duck." Such delights Simon felt he could not, under normal circumstances, afford. However, after he had examined specimens sent to Welch by medical practitioners, Welch, although he wrote out the reports himself, sent Simon the checks. Each of these bonanzas "meant a feast."[8]

An important figure at the hospital was the "purveyor," Mr. Emory. Himself from the Eastern Shore, he procured delicacies in season especially for the high table. As an annual event, he staged a special dinner for the select few. Simon saw the most distinguished doctors, merry from cocktails drunk in Emory's room, file into the dining room in evening dress to be served a meal even the odors of which made Simon's senses faint. Then came the year when he too was invited! The initiates, he noted, were careful to eat little until "the terrapin came, a steaming dish dark with the meat and squares of liver, and variegated with yellow eggs floating in the delicious juice. The terrapin à la mode was always passed twice. Crisp celery was served with it, and, at precisely the right moment, the champagne!"[9]

Barker's ever-present charm helped open doors for Simon in Baltimore, but the major catalyst was Dr. Henry J. Berkly, a practitioner concerned with the anatomy of the nervous system, who had a working place at the Pathological. Through him Simon was elected to the Journal Club, where graduates of the University of Maryland Medical School met for scientific discussions. Habituated to the more exciting sessions of the Hopkins Hospital Club, Simon's principal interest was getting to know the Baltimoreans — and in the two annual sprees. For their summer outing, the club hired a small steamer, sailed down the bay, and landed for a picnic that was very "wet," but not with Chesapeake water. During a hilarious baseball game, Simon's lack of athletic gifts, which had so embarrassed him in his boyhood, induced genial mirth rising to cheers when he succeeded in catching a fly ball, as he was permitted to do, in his cap.

The winter banquet also had its liquid component, and one year Mrs. Berkly forbade her husband to go. She relented on condition that Simon keep a stern eye on his friend. It is indicative of how at home Simon had become that he considered his promise a joke. He was taken aback to be received by Mrs. Berkly, when they next met, with indignant coldness. It developed that instead of being asleep when the doctor came home, she had been waiting to tell him that one of his horses had taken sick. Setting out for his stable across the snowy street while his wife watched from the window, Berkly pitched as if he were on the deck of a ship during a hurricane. How could Simon justify such neglect of her trust in him? Simon replied that Berkly was old enough to take care of himself and that "he surely drank no more than I did." This last remark was not well received, and it was some time before Mrs. Berkly would smile again on her husband's friend.[10]

Nurses, of course, presented a perpetual temptation to the doctors. In planning the hospital building, Dr. Billings had attempted to impede seduction by keeping all the closets shallow. The matron, Miss Bonner, warned Simon never to propose to a nurse until he had seen her in her street clothing.[11] Simon admitted to only one escapade with a nurse, which was obviously innocent because in his memoirs he identified the lady.

A "great belle" from South Carolina, with blue-black eyes, had appeared among the nurses. Simon asked Susie Reed, "How much of a sport are you?"

"I'm a sport."

"Are you enough of a sport to take a trip down the bay?"

Although it was against the rules for nurses and doctors to go out together, Susie agreed. But no sooner had the boat left the dock than they ran into Hurd, his wife, and two daughters. It is only necessary to add that Susie soon joined the hospital elite by marrying William H. Thayer, who was to be Osler's immediate successor.[12]

When Simon was sitting close to a pretty medical student, their heads almost touching as they examined a specimen of heart tissue under the microscope, Osler happened along, and whistled the tune of "Two Hearts That Beat as One." Flexner was much irritated: Osler knew very well that the rising, impecunious scientist had "put his heart on ice."[13]

Helen Thomas's brother Harry was in charge of the neurological clinic. During the bicycle craze, he joined Barker and Flexner in executing a "century" — riding a consecutive hundred miles — a feat that required spending a night on the road. One Sunday, Harry invited Flexner and Barker for dinner at his family's house. Helen was away and Simon did not even know that Harry had a sister. He remembered only "the magnitude of the delicious meal" and that Harry's father, the important trustee, sat at the head of the table and carved. Barker was soon invited again (he got to know and admire Helen) but not Simon. Harry's wife, Zoe, who was much concerned with family backgrounds, seems not to have approved of Simon's.[14]

It was some years later, after James Carey Thomas had died, that Simon ingratiated himself with Zoe by introducing her to the novels of Sudermann, which he was reading over and over. Again with Barker, he was invited to a dinner and theater party at the Thomases'. He first met Helen, then visiting from Bryn Mawr. "I never forgot Helen's voice and her marvelous deep bronze hair," he wrote later, but at the time the two did not get together. Simon was shy with women, and Helen seemed to him worldly and out of his range. He made so little impression on her that she was never able to remember this first meeting.[15]

A letter from M. Carey Thomas to Mary Garrett records that on the afternoon of February 28, 1898, "Harry and Dr. Flexner" arrived at her Bryn Mawr house to spend the night. "We walked about and visited

Helen, and talked." Neither Helen nor Simon recalled this second meeting.[16]

Flexner's relationship with Dr. Welch had been at first distant. Indeed, that the professor was often not present at the Pathological, Flexner wrote, increased his "majestic aloofness." By breaking down academic routine, Welch made room for his own personality to expand. He led "by example and pressure." As had been endlessly valuable to Flexner, Welch never favored older scientists over newcomers in giving credit for achievement or making recommendations for promotion.

Attended by an elderly housekeeper, Welch kept comfortable bachelor quarters in town. His personal library being the best in Baltimore for scientific periodicals, Welch arranged that Flexner should be let in early in the mornings, before he himself was awake. Savoring the pleasure of being where he was, Flexner would work happily, hear Welch get up, take his bath, and then set out to the Maryland Club for breakfast. Only rarely would Welch look in to bid Simon good morning.[17]

When posters were "all the rage," Flexner borrowed a collection, hung it in a hospital corridor, and gave a party. Osler, as usual, was the life of the occasion. Finally, he asked, "Where is Welch?" It had not occurred to Simon to ask so august a figure, and now, since the party was a great success, he was sorry.[18]

It was part of Welch's pedagogical technique to invite his juniors periodically to dinner at the Maryland Club, where he spent most of his relaxed time. These occasions were, Flexner wrote, "among the rosiest memories of the young men who worked under him." The food was "a conglomeration of almost unbelievable delights.... But strong as were the material attractions, a stronger magnet was Welch himself. To the young men the talk of their master, whom they so rarely saw outside the lecture room or laboratory, was a delight and a fascination. It seemed that his fund of knowledge on every topic was inexhaustible. He could be a good listener, too, but his disciples usually preferred to draw him out. Although he never raised his voice or spoke with vehemence, he often became so absorbed that the ash from his perpetual cigar dropped unnoticed onto his swelling waistcoat to join the thick gray powder that was already there. A spell fell over the room as the quiet voice talked on, and the young men, some of them already a little round-shouldered from too much peering into the microscope, felt the richness of the world and resolved not to be dry-as-dust scientists concerned only with the ramifications of one tributary of knowledge. They resolved to go to art galleries, to hear music, to read the masterpieces of literature about which Welch discoursed so excitingly."[19] (PLATE 18)

Welch's favorite companions, whom he called the Old Gang, included Mall, Halsted, and Osler, and, among native Baltimoreans, the distinguished bachelor-lawyer Major Richard M. Venable.

As time passed, Flexner was occasionally included in their convivial sessions. Much of the diffidence, which he had by now sloughed off in ordinary intercourse, returned. He felt deeply humiliated when Venable made fun of him for telling the company an ancient and trite anecdote.

The Old Gang were inveterate practical jokers. Simon was entangled when Welch took him along uninvited to a dinner at Venable's. "Who's this?" asked the host, as if he had never seen Simon before.

Welch explained they had been working late together, and so . . .

"That's all right, I suppose," said Venable. "I suppose you want him to stay to dinner."

"Yes."

"I suppose it's all right. I suppose there's enough to eat." In the dining room, Venable rang for the maid. "I suppose there's going to be enough soup for one extra. If not, don't give any to Flexner."

There was plenty of food, but at the beginning of each course, the major said, "Serve the rest of us first, and if there's any left, give it to Flexner."

Simon was relieved when the dinner was over and Venable had to drop his joke.[20]

It would be possible to interpret this episode as anti-Semitic brutality, aimed at making Simon realize he was only marginally acceptable. But the correct interpretation must be exactly opposite. Neither Welch nor Mall — indeed, none of those present — would for an instant have countenanced such an act. The caper was only conceivable because Flexner was *not* regarded as an outsider. Conceivably Venable was trying to help Flexner by reducing to absurdity any idea that he did not belong.

When, during his later years at the Hopkins, Flexner was encouraged into personal friendship with Welch, this involved no intimate confidences: both men shied away from personal revelations. In temperament they were otherwise far from alike. Welch, indeed, resembled much more closely Helen Thomas's father, even to their both being unusually fat. Welch and Thomas knew and respected each other. One of Thomas's greatest disappointments, so Helen remembered, was a weekend visit by Welch and Gilman to Coombe Edge during which a continuous rain prevented the enthusiastic gardener and nature lover from showing around the men he so admired.

Although one had sprung from Connecticut and the other from Maryland, Welch and Thomas had both been by birthright leaders in the communities where they had formed their points of view. As men, they both exerted charisma with a relaxed benevolence based on a fundamental conviction of their power and right to lead. Both took it for granted that little they wished to know, appreciate, or achieve, would be, if they really cared, beyond their potential grasp. The resulting easygoingness was greatly admired by Simon. He never got to know James Carey Thomas, yet the influence of the father on his daughter Helen surely created a strand in the net that eventually drew Simon to his bride.

As the Baltimore years passed, Welch mounted to that prominent position in Flexner's esteem that he was to hold for the rest of Flexner's life. Welch came to return his affection. Their congeniality was grounded on mutual admiration and shared scientific interests. In addition, Flexner relished their friendship for the opportunities it gave him to study more closely the qualities and behavior of his elder as a man. Flexner always said that he had consciously modeled himself on Welch. He admired Welch for his "strength of mind and memory, clear understanding, high ideals, knowledge of what can or cannot be known at a [specific] moment"; for "his ability to lead without any exertion of force, any display of wisdom, any self-seeking pettiness." Flexner was to summarize all this as the "quality of statesmanship."[21]

Did the young man, still almost exclusively a laboratory scientist, feel within himself a stirring towards the statesmanship that was to make him Welch's closest collaborator and eventual successor as the leader of scientific medicine in America?

Flexner was by no means as easygoing as Welch, and the result was that additional work was laid on his shoulders. Routine responsibilities at the Pathological, from keeping the halls clean to keeping the laboratory assistants sober, were sloppily attended to by Welch, if at all. Hurd asked Flexner to take over. Flexner was willing and Welch was delighted, all the more because he could indulge the softness of his heart by pleading for employees who needed to be fired in the comfortable assumption that Flexner would fire them anyway.

* * *

When the medical school entered its second year, the students' instruction in pathology began. Welch was inspired to be more attentive to lectures and demonstrations, but the impetus soon faded while each successive class became larger. Flexner and Barker, although helped by various new instructors, became busier and busier. It was part of the system that each student be given a research assignment. Flexner was meticulous in making assignments, conscientious in following up, and revealed irritation when tasks were poorly done. He himself realized his tendency to set overly difficult problems, but commented that the ablest students "always tried to do more than was required of them. Somewhere there was a balance struck between the excess of my demands and the advantages to be gained! [The exclamation point is his own.]"[22]

Autopsies had to be executed for the clinicians and for instruction, but also because they were the source from which Flexner extracted many of his research problems. From the beginning of 1893 to his departure from Baltimore in 1899, he published more than seventy papers in the *Johns Hopkins Hospital Bulletin; Johns Hopkins Hospital Repository; Medical News; Transactions of the Association of American Physicians; Maryland Medical Journal; Journal of Pathology and Bacteriology; American Journal of Medical Science; Biological Lectures Delivered at the Marine Biological Laboratory at Woods Hole; Philadelphia Medical Journal; Transactions of the Pathological Society of Philadelphia; Annals of Surgery; Journal of Morphology; Journal of Nervous and Medical Diseases;* and the *Journal of Experimental Medicine,* which was founded in 1896 under the editorship of Welch to contain longer articles than the *Johns Hopkins Hospital Bulletin* could handle and to gain a wider international circulation.[23]

During the academic year 1893–1894, Flexner launched an experimental study of the actions on tissues and organs exerted by toxalbumins (now simply called toxins). The discovery of the diphtheria bacillus had led to the isolation during 1888 by Pierre Roux and Alexandre Yersin, from cultures containing the bacillus, of an "amorphous substance" that could, when separated from the bacilli, nonetheless cause all the symptoms of diphtheria.* This led to the conclusion that the bacilli, being living organisms, discharged, as they sustained themselves on the materials in the hosts' bodies, poisonous "excrementitious substances . . . into the host." Scientists on various parts of the globe

---

* As we have seen, Flexner had, during his first year in Baltimore, made a contribution to the acceptance of this discovery, by finding tubercular lesions in injected guinea pigs.

soon identified additional toxalbumins, some secreted by germs, others present in poisonous plants and the venom of snakes.

The study took on tremendous importance for the cure of disease when, between 1890 and 1893, Emil von Behring at Koch's laboratory in Berlin worked out how the toxin of diphtheria, when inoculated into animals, could induce the production of antitoxins which, when subsequently injected into the human body, cured the disease by creating immunity to the diphtheria bacillus. Thus was inaugurated the science of immunology, in which Flexner, as he continued to move at the forefront of scientific medicine, quickly involved himself.

Needed, if immunologists were to foresee results, was an understanding of the extremely varied and complicated ways toxins act within the body and the body reacts to them. Communication being mostly by the printed page, Flexner undertook experiments as part of an international network. He drew conclusions from what other workers had found, and made findings of his own that strengthened the slowly spreading web of knowledge. However, in his later years, he remembered less the positive conclusions he reached at this time than a great opportunity he had missed.

It had already been discovered that the blood of some animals had a toxic effect on the blood corpuscles of other species: dogs' blood, for instance, destroyed rabbits' red blood cells. Flexner wondered what would happen if the corpuscles of an animal were permanently reduced by the injection of incompatible blood plasma. Would changes in the bone marrow and the liver simulate those of pernicious anemia?

He made careful blood counts of a small number of rabbits to determine normal variation. He then injected dog serum, and the rabbits' corpuscles were markedly diminished. A few weeks later he injected more dog serum. The rabbits quickly died!

Flexner had happened on an extremely important phenomenon, later named anaphylaxis, but he did not appreciate the significance of what he had found. This form of hypersensitivity was subsequently worked out in detail by Charles Richet. He thereby earned a Nobel Prize, an honor Flexner was never awarded.

Having routinely, as was his wont, published the lethal effect of a second injection, Simon allowed the observation — he had published so many — to vanish from his memory. After anaphylaxis had been dramatically defined, he was surprised to be reminded, in a history of the subject, of his prior observation which, so the account revealed, was the second to be found in all medical literature.[24]

In 1894, Flexner received an exciting but frightening invitation to address the Pathological Society of Philadelphia on the effects of toxalbumins. The society was a meeting place for a wide range of medical scientists, and this would be Simon's first major public address. When he walked out on the stage, he was further pleased and frightened to see the large hall crowded: the subject was new but not so new that curiosity had not been raised. His speech proved to be perfectly suited to the situation: he oriented his hearers with a historical summary, and then described his own discoveries in the context of international research.

In later years Simon identified that speech as one of the milestones of his career since it established his reputation in Philadelphia, then the accepted capital of American medicine. The speech eventuated in his being sought by the Jefferson Medical College, and then called to the University of Pennsylvania.[25]

Flexner's researches on toxalbumins did not prevent him from taking advantage of various opportunities presented to him by autopsies or even through conversation. An autopsy on a case of acute pancreatitis revealed that the fatty tissues of the entire abdomen had been decomposed. Having postulated that the causative ferment had been secreted by the pancreas, Flexner confirmed his hypothesis by producing such lesions experimentally in animals. Continuation of his experimental studies of the pancreas led, thirty years later, to the isolation of insulin.[26]

He identified a previously unrecognized bacillus that he called *Piogenes filiformis*.[27] He found a very rare condition resembling tuberculosis but caused by a different organism.[28] In collaboration with Welch, he continued and expanded Welch's research on the gas bacillus.[29] A chance remark of Osler's that sufferers from chronic illnesses, say of the kidney, usually did not die from the chronic illness itself but from an infection which their debilitation had made them susceptible to, resulted in his clinically important "A Statistical and Experimental Study of Terminal Infections."[30]

During 1895, Flexner was elected to the American College of Physicians, a "great honor" that enabled him "to appear regularly on the program of a national medical society."[31] In the same year, Councilman's prophecy was realized by Flexner's being raised to associate professor of pathology at the Hopkins. Welch's all-seeing eye reported that "Flexner is the coming man in pathology in this country."[32]

————⚬————

28

Danger at the Crossroads

When, early in Flexner's courtship of Helen Thomas, she was immured by illness in the Johns Hopkins Hospital, she wrote Simon, "I can quite understand how charming a place this must be for a doctor or scientist to live. The good companionship of it, the exchange of ideas with so many of one's own kind, the independency and sufficiency of it. You once told me that you spent the happiest years of your life here."[1]

Simon himself remembered that "everything there at the Pathological and the hospital, the friends I had made, the work I was doing, conspired to hold me while making a change seemed dangerous. And yet, I knew that a change had to be made." Welch was only in his early fifties and no room existed for two professors of pathology. Furthermore, the meagerness of Simon's salary as associate professor — $1,800 a year — limited his ability to get out in the world, and barred his sending adequate contributions to his family in Louisville. Nor could he rule out forever the possibility of marriage.[2]

The first offer of a full professorship came from the University of Buffalo. It was hardly worth considering, but Flexner did make an exploratory trip to Buffalo. Then, in the fall of 1895, came a call from Jefferson Medical College, one of the oldest schools in America (1825), with a good reputation, although entirely supported by student fees and second in Philadelphia to the University of Pennsylvania Medical School. The research possibilities were minimal and the teaching load heavy. However, the offer, which included a raise in salary, was respectable. Osler, who Simon felt had never really approved of him, was determined that he should accept because — or so Simon believed — his leaving would open advancement in pathology to Barker, whom Osler preferred. Welch wrote John Shaw Billings, the medical Nestor who had designed the Hopkins Hospital and was head of the Surgeon General's Library, to ask whether there might not soon be a vacancy at the University of Pennsylvania. The professor of pathology there, Dr. Juan Guiteras, was a Cuban patriot, who could at any moment feel himself called back to his homeland, which was struggling to throw off Spanish dominion.

Billings, so Welch reported to Flexner, was unsure about Guiteras but advised against the Jefferson Medical College. "As Dr. Billings said," Welch continued, "you are likely to be selected for any important chair in pathology in the country, and the chances are that something better than Jefferson will turn up in the course of three or four years. You are gaining a reputation so rapidly by your scientific work, it would be a pity for this work to suffer interruption just at present."[3]

Flexner gladly refused. He did not feel that his training was complete enough for him to leave the Hopkins. "I was in practical control of the teaching at the Pathological." Besides, his research was profiting from the development of the medical school and from his close association with other active men.[4]

Mall, by making Barker associate professor of anatomy, withdrew Simon's close friend from the succession in pathology. Yet Welch was training up Louis E. Livergood, who would soon be prepared to step into Flexner's shoes. Despite Welch's expansive mention of "three or four years," Flexner was becoming more and more anxious about his future.

The New York University Medical College, which had been in essence owned by its professors, in 1898 broke its slender ties with New York University to become an integral part of Cornell. A million and a half dollars was donated for a building which was to be designed by Stanford White.[5] During July, Flexner received what Welch described as "a brilliant offer in pathology at the Cornell University Medical School in New York [City]: salary $5,000 and other things in proportion."

Welch and Mall hoped Flexner would not go. As had been the situation at Jefferson Medical College, the professorship of pathology required teaching all subjects that involved the microscope, including bacteriology and clinical microscopy. And the "commercial" atmosphere of New York was considered hostile to research. However, the

Hopkins could not possibly equal the offered salary. Welch wrote Mall, "I suppose $2,800 would be as high as we could think of going. . . . After all, if one has enough to subsist, the environment is everything, and environment is our strong point." But Flexner had his family at home to help support. He had resolved to accept the New York offer when the unforeseeable intervened.[6]

The French Atlantic liner *Bourgogne* collided with another vessel, drowning Livergood. Welch reacted with a hysterical determination to hold on to Flexner. In a letter to his sister, he wrote that not only was Flexner "the best pathologist in the country of his age," but "if he goes, with the loss of Livergood, I shall have to start building the department over from the foundation again, and it takes years to get young men properly trained and with the necessary experience. I feel like the Spaniards, all my ships gone."*[7]

In the Blue Ridge Mountains on vacation with his mother, Flexner received an emotional letter from Welch: "I do not see how I can let you go to New York now. . . . However, you must do whatever seems best for your future."

Four days later: "Have you heard from the New York people? I am going to make a strong effort to keep you here and believe that a considerable increase in your salary can be secured."

Another nine days: Gilman had approved an increase in salary to $3,000. "I know how tempting the New York bait is, and how difficult it must be for you to come to a decision. I shall be delighted if you decide to remain with us, and so will everyone connected with the hospital and the medical school."

The instant Flexner was back in Baltimore, Welch urged him to come for dinner. Flexner was persuaded to stay at the Hopkins.[8]

Councilman sent Flexner his hearty congratulations. "There can be nothing more delightful for the rest of your days than such a position in Baltimore."[9] But despite the salary increase, Flexner's position at Baltimore was no securer than it had been. Welch was now training up a brace of able men — William G. MacCallum and Eugene L. Opie — and Flexner had been given no assurance of permanence at the Hopkins. Supposing no other advantageous offer came to him? Pathology was still no more than an emerging science in America.

"Suddenly, I developed a nervous crisis. . . . The immediate inciting cause was a prepossession that my opportunity had passed irrevocably."

* The reference is to Admiral Dewey's recent victory during the Spanish-American War.

The childhood home, in the German Saar Valley, of Simon Flexner's mother, Esther Abraham: partly a house, partly a barn

Simon Flexner's parents, Esther and Morris (Moritz) Flexner at the time of their marriage in Louisville, Kentucky, in 1856

PLATE I

*The sad faces of Simon's parents after misfortune struck them.
Photographs probably taken from oil portraits, now lost, by Joseph
Krementz*

PLATE 2

PLATE 3

Simon about 1870, a bewildered seven-year-old

PLATE 4

Simon's antagonist: Jacob Flexner, his oldest brother, also about 1870. Dominant in the family, he was determined to shape Simon in his own image.

PLATE 5

The Flexner family in Louisville. In front: Bernard. First row: Jacob,
Morris, Mary, Esther, Gertrude, Isadore. Back row: Washington, Henry,
Abraham, Simon

PLATE 6

*John Chew Thomas, Helen Thomas's great-grandfather, who
impoverished the Thomases and banished them from the plantation life of
Maryland by freeing all of his many slaves. Watercolor by B. J. F.
de Saint-Mémin*

PLATE 7

Richard Henry Thomas, Helen's grandfather. As a practicing physician and a husband of heiresses, he established the Thomases in Baltimore.

John M. Whitall, Helen's other grandfather. He captained ships in the China trade, communicated (he believed) daily with God, and established a vastly successful glass manufactory.

PLATE 8

*Helen's parents, Mary Whitall and James Carey Thomas, exchanged
these daguerreotypes during their courtship*

PLATE 9

Montpelier, in Prince George County, Maryland, the childhood home of Helen's great-grandmother Mary Snowden. The proprietor, Major Thomas Snowden, was famous for his hospitality. George Washington, on the way to the Constitutional Convention, spent his last night of freedom from governmental duties at Montpelier. He was ill during the night.

PLATE 10

John M. and Mary Tatum Whitall surrounded by their children and grandchildren during one of their innumerable family gatherings

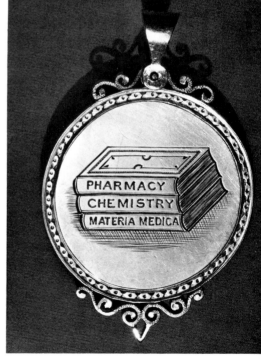

PRESENTED
By the ALUMNIA of the
L. C. of Pharmacy
TO
SIMON FLEXNER
of Class 1881 & 82
FOR
BEST AVERAGE

PHARMACY
CHEMISTRY
MATERIA MEDICA

The gold medal that was the first proof of Simon Flexner's emergence from incompetence. Simon's mother sent it to Helen as a symbol of relinquishing her son to his bride.

Abraham Flexner at twenty-one or twenty-two

PLATE 12

Helen Thomas and her brother Frank, who were so inseparable that they were known in the family as "us"

PLATE 13

*Mary Whitall Thomas and
James Carey Thomas in their
later years*

PLATE 14

Hannah Whitall Smith, Helen's redoubtable aunt, author of religious books and tracts, family historian, fighter against alcohol and for women's rights, mother of a remarkable brood

PLATE 15

The house in Baltimore where Helen passed most of her childhood. Her parents are in the doorway and the Doctor's buggy is to one side.

The Johns Hopkins Hospital, about 1890

PLATE 16

Some Welch rabbits

*Max Brödel's drawing, celebrated in medical history, of Dr. William
Henry Welch and most of the young Hopkins scientists who worked under
him*

PLATE 17

The Pathological, the hideous building on the Johns Hopkins grounds that was the incubator of Simon Flexner's scientific career

Lewellys Barker and Simon Flexner lunching at the Johns Hopkins Hospital. Drawing by Max Brödel

PLATE 18

"Four Doctors," the famous portrait by John Singer Sargent of the
original faculty of the Johns Hopkins Medical School. Left to right:
Welch, Halsted, Osler, Kelly

PLATE 19

*"M. Carey Thomas" by John Singer Sargent: Helen's oldest sister
when she was president of Bryn Mawr College*

PLATE 20

Helen Thomas when a senior at Bryn Mawr College

PLATE 21

Lucy Martin Donnelly, Helen's lifelong friend

PLATE 22

Friday's Hill, the Pearsall Smith country home in Sussex. In the foreground: Hannah, Robert, Alys (Mrs. Bertrand Russell), and Logan

PLATE 23

Bertrand Russell, Helen's close friend, and his wife, Alys,
Helen's cousin

PLATE 24

Logan Pearsall Smith, the author of Trivia *and Helen's literary mentor*

Mary (Mariechen) Pearsall Smith, who was a friend of Walt Whitman, and who subsequently married Bernard Berenson

PLATE 25

Abraham Flexner in the 1890's

Abraham's wife, Anne Crawford Flexner, who wrote the play Mrs. Wiggs of the Cabbage Patch, *one of the great successes in the history of the American theater*

PLATE 26

*John D. Rockefeller, Sr.,
and John D. Rockefeller,
Jr., at about the time
when Simon Flexner was
chosen to be the first
director of the Rockefeller
Institute for Medical
Research*

PLATE 27

Louis Schmidt's drawing for the menu of the farewell dinner given for Simon Flexner when he left the University of Pennsylvania for the Rockefeller Institute

PLATE 28

Helen Thomas Flexner. Pastel by Adele Herter

PLATE 29

Simon Flexner. Pastel by Adele Herter

PLATE 30

The board of directors of the Rockefeller Institute for Medical Research at the laying of the cornerstone of the first building. Left to right: unidentified, Drs. Holt, Prudden, Flexner and Biggs

The Rockefeller Institute shortly before Flexner's retirement in 1935

PLATE 31

His career, he feared, had come to an end. "No amount of reason could banish the obsession."

The deadly times were the nights. Flexner could not sleep, and as he lay wide awake, horror engulfed him. Reason could not dispel or even weaken the obsession because reason inhabited an altogether different area of his psyche. The rational judgment that his fears were madness merely made them more destructive because of the implication that he was going insane.[10]

All his life Simon had suffered from anxieties that could leap in a moment to painful heights. Long before the current crisis he had suffered, when overstrained, from what he came to call his "old enemy": an irregular heartbeat which, although it was never to prove really dangerous, sent him, even as an old man, into spasms of concern.

By the time of his semicollapse in 1898, Flexner had been overworking for years. He was surely balancing on the edge of a precipice when the toppling blow came. It was a shrewdly aimed blow. Ever since his late teens, he had been driven by twin desires: to educate himself and improve his position in the world. Until he was in his middle twenties, he had been held back by loyalty to his mother personally, and to his family. At last, he had escaped. But now new loyalties had clamped down: to Dr. Welch personally, and to the Johns Hopkins. Would there never be any escape!

His mother and Dr. Welch were the two persons who so far in his life had meant most to Simon. He refused to acknowledge any resentment against either, a repression that surely made his actual feelings harder to bear. It is impossible for the biographer to assess the effects of the denial, year after year, of emotional and sexual expression, which Simon had forced on himself in pursuit of his ambitions. Now he had been compelled to betray these ambitions. How long-lasting would be the punishments for this betrayal?

Barker and Frank Smith, an English doctor celebrated in the hospital group for his high spirits and practical jokes, took Simon along on a trip to Chester, Nova Scotia. But Simon could not be made to relax. He spent "sleepless nights and days of acute fear." He remembered "with horror" how "at dawn, I got out of bed and rushed into the woods feeling like a pursued animal. On the little boat between Yarmouth and Boston I drugged myself with potassium bromide — how much I took I do not know — to reduce a maddening nervousness which prevented my being quiet a moment. That night I slept soundly.

"The ensuing winter in Baltimore was a horror. I felt my teaching was bad." He resorted to other calming drugs, but the morning depression that followed was so painful that he tried to use the drugs as little as possible. A bottle was put in Barker's room, which was next to his. Often, in the small hours, in misery and guilt, Flexner would hunt it out.

Flexner said no more to Welch than that he felt his teaching was falling off. Welch replied only that he had heard no complaints. Habitually concerned with achievements not weaknesses, Welch seemed oblivious to Flexner's agonies, and, insofar as he did recognize them, he did not feel guilty. To Welch, the Hopkins was a holy cause, and surely he had done much to create Flexner as a scientist. Flexner, he believed, would soon receive a better offer. And Welch knew that he possessed the power to assure in the long run the young man's future.[11]

Mall, not Welch, took the lead in securing for Flexner at the start of the fall term, the title of professor of pathological anatomy. This full professorship, although off to one side of the normal progression, was intended to calm Flexner's fears by its implication (although "tenure" had not yet been invented) of permanence. But, Flexner's later memory was that he was less reassured than shamed by this sop thrown to his weakness. "I felt I had, in a manner, forced Dr. Welch's hand. I don't recall that the insomnia grew less. What worked the cure was time chiefly, combined with good friends."[12]

The speed with which MacCallum and Opie demonstrated their readiness to fill in enabled Flexner, early in the term of 1898–1899, to renew his negotiations with Cornell. Cornell eagerly raised its offer from $5,000 to $8,000. But a new outside happening intervened. The Spanish-American War was establishing the independence of Cuba, and Guiteras, eager to be on the scene, resigned the professorship of pathology at the University of Pennsylvania. The salary there was $3,000 less than Cornell's new offer, but the professorship was more prestigious and promised better possibilities for research.

Flexner's shyness concerning New York, which had years before figured in his refusal of the College of Pharmacy offer, had by no means vanished: would the bustling business capital of America permit an atmosphere conducive to science? The link of the medical school there with Cornell was newly forged and tenuous, all the more because the university was hundreds of miles away. The Philadelphia school had for generations been an integral part both administratively and geographically of its university. Furthermore, the Pennsylvania chair would be of pathology only. Alexander C. Abbott, who had been Welch's assistant in bacteriology when Flexner reached Baltimore, now taught that subject in Philadelphia. Clinical microscopy was taught by the clinicians, and there was at the college a premedical faculty.

The oldest of American medical schools and still the traditional leader among them, Pennsylvania regarded the Hopkins as a bumptious and interfering upstart. The revolutionary new school was, indeed, eager to convert the older schools, long staffed by local clinicians, to a major concern with up-to-date (and often still controversial) scientific discoveries, and with research. Fighting for Hopkins practices and ideals at Harvard, Councilman was finding life there "no bed of roses." Abbott was embattled in Philadelphia. It was he who passionately desired Flexner. Anxious to help win over the most sacrosanct of all American medical institutions, Mall was eager for Flexner to go there and perturbed when President Jacob Gould Schurman of Cornell made a special trip to Baltimore to persuade Flexner, and Flexner was seen "prancing around with him . . . a $7–8,000 smile on his face. . . . Schurman is a wide-awake man and . . . evidently knows what Flexner can do for them."[13]

The thirty-five-year-old who had so recently envisioned his career in ruins, now had alternative possibilities, both alluring. He concluded that despite the smaller salary, he wished to go to Philadelphia. But did Philadelphia want him? Would they make up their minds quickly? Could he put off responding to the New York offer until Philadelphia decided?

At the University of Pennsylvania, the situation was much more unpleasantly complicated than Flexner could, in his more anxious moments, foresee.

In following his Cuba enthusiasms, Guiteras had long neglected his department, allowing it to be run by Alfred Stengel, a clinical professor who was a son-in-law of the previous provost, William Pepper. Stengel had written the textbook in pathology used in the classes and was confident that he would succeed Guiteras. His textbook was behind the times and his scientific reputation was nil compared to Flexner's, but there were three strong objections to the outsider: first, Flexner would be, if elected, only the third professor in the one-hundred-and-fifty-year history of the medical school to have had no previous connection with the university; second, he was coming from the troublesome Hopkins, and with his conspicuous energy, who could foresee what he would perpetrate; and third, he was a Jew. In the entire university there was only one Jewish professor, Morris Jastrow, who taught Semitic languages and was also librarian.

Since Guiteras's place would be filled through election by the medical professors — the result to be routinely approved by the trustees — electioneering became the order of the day. Anti-Semitism arose as a much-agitated issue. Flexner, who had suffered so little on this score at the Hopkins, was "astonished" when Osler informed him of the prejudice and advised him not to accept even if he could be elected. "Tell them to go to hell!"

Years later Flexner sometimes stated that he would have withdrawn from the race could he have done so without letting his backers down. But at the time, he revealed his eagerness for the post by carefully avoiding any move that might supply his opponents with further issues. He made no stipulations, asked none of the obvious questions concerning staff, budget, and the like. He did not even find out that a new laboratory building, including improved facilities for pathology, was being planned. Osler might recommend grand gestures, but Flexner had no personal financial resources to fall back on and a lifetime career to think of.[14]

In Philadelphia, Abbott was dashing around, a determined campaigner, dwelling on Flexner's scientific eminence and the passion of the Cornell Medical College to get him. Provost Charles Curtis Harrison, the chief executive officer of the university, was on the fence: he wanted no more vexatious Hopkins men but wanted to upgrade the faculty. J. William White, professor of surgery and a member of the board of trustees, was the leader of the opposition, closely seconded by Horatio C. Wood, an eminent pharmacologist and longtime professor of general therapeutics. John Marshall, dean of the medical school and professor of chemistry, weighed in for Flexner. Most important was the support Abbott secured from S. Weir Mitchell, the leader of the Philadelphia medical profession, both clinician and scientist, a successful poet and novelist, "a patrician to his fingertips," chairman of the medical committee of the trustees. As it became clear that Flexner would be elected, Stengel withdrew, and White comforted himself with the thought that accepting the Jew as professor did not involve accepting him as a man.[15]

The faculty meeting was held on January 16, 1899, at Marshall's house. Stengel did not appear. White announced that were Flexner to become a member of the Medical Faculty Club, he would resign from the club. Abbott sprang to his feet and shouted that if Flexner were *not* elected to the club, *he* would resign. Marshall backed Abbott. Then, Harrison, as presiding officer, sidetracked this issue, which did not require immediate decision, and called for a vote. Result: nine for Flexner, two for J. Allen Smith (who was to succeed to the professorship when Flexner moved on to the Rockefeller Institute). In response to a motion by a Stengel supporter, the vote was made unanimous. However, it took the trustees two months to ratify the election.[16]

The post at the University of Pennsylvania was generally considered the highest in America available to a pathologist. Since Flexner envisioned staying in it for the rest of his career, what he had heard about anti-Semitism from Osler and subsequently from others could not help being disquieting. There was a poultice, however, in the regret expressed by his companions at his leaving the Hopkins. He received from Welch a letter which remained among his greatest treasures:

"I feel unhappy in rushing away just as you are about to depart, but I cannot get out of this trip to New York. I am sure that no words are needed between us to express our mutual feelings in severing relations over which has never come even the shadow of a cloud. These relations have been the closest and the pleasantest which have ever joined me to a colleague. I have no words to express my appreciation of your faithful services. My pride in your good work is so personal that it would be selfish to speak of it. But we will not call this goodbye, for when you return I shall claim an opportunity of a more festal way of bidding you Godspeed."[17]

29

Mission to the Philippines

For Simon Flexner, the symbol of the adventure was a bottle of sweet dessert wine. The wine was poured early in January, 1899. That was for him a time of exterior strain — the unpleasant controversy over the Philadelphia appointment was in full swing — but it was also a time of interior release: his psychological horrors had been evaporated by the excitement and the promise of his double negotiation with Cornell and the University of Pennsylvania.

At a Baltimore club, Barker was entertaining Flexner and Rupert Norton, a former Hopkins Hospital resident now in the army medical corps. After dinner the three men were lounging before a fire. The food had been excellent and the Château Yquem even more so. The friends discussed "past experiences, present occupations, and future prospects." Suddenly, Flexner heard himself proposing a visit to the Philippines to study tropical diseases. The idea was enthusiastically received and discussed. As Flexner and Barker saw Norton off on the train at midnight, it was determined that Flexner should, as the first step, beard the Surgeon General of the Army.[1]

Flexner's inspiration was in accord with the times. From various nations other than the United States investigators had visited the tropics and had discovered the bacterial causes of Asiatic cholera and bubonic plague. Furthermore, as a result of the Spanish-American War, the Philippines had just been annexed by the United States. An American army, in trying to put down an insurrection by Filipinos desiring independence, was riddled with diseases.

Flexner journeyed to Washington but the Surgeon General refused adequate cooperation. Flexner proceeded to Gerstenberg's, where "I lunched on Frankfurter sausages and beer, followed by camembert cheese, and more beer." Having the afternoon to kill, he sought out Walter Reed (who was about to make his yellow fever discovery) and carried him off to a matinée. Reed promised to push the expedition in army circles. But Norton was refused the orders he needed to take part in the expedition. Flexner and Barker decided to shift their point of attack from the army medical corps to the Hopkins.[2]

Barker, the silver-tongued, easily persuaded President Gilman. He then took on Osler, while Flexner took on Welch. Osler responded enthusiastically but Welch proved apprehensive (as he was to remain until Flexner had returned safely) lest his favorite disciple be killed by disease or bullets. Yet general enthusiasm mounted to where it could not be stopped. The Johns Hopkins University Special Commission, with Simon Flexner as chairman, was quickly born.

As Barker and Flexner collected sophisticated pathological, clinical, and bacteriological equipment, Gilman raised funds from friends of the university. Only enough was secured to support the two leaders. A pair of medical students who could pay their own expenses — Joseph M. Flint and Frederick P. Gay — were delighted to go along as assistants. The group was also joined by John W. Garrett, the rich nephew of Carey's friend Mary Garrett. The future diplomat wished to study the political situation.[3]

As preparations for the expedition proceeded, Flexner's appointment at the University of Pennsylvania was confirmed. He was thus placed in a situation that had once seemed beyond his fondest dreams. The longtime wanderer had found what could be a permanent and elevated professional home. This seemed the perfect moment to celebrate with an adventure so extensive that it could involve circumnavigating the globe, the Philippines being half a world away from Baltimore.

But Simon was of an apprehensive nature. In Louisville for his thirty-seventh birthday, he wondered to his brothers Abraham and Bernard whether it would not be better to relax into simple pleasures rather than "get an ambitious bee in your bonnet and go traipsing off to the Philippines." While traveling on the Canadian Pacific Railway to Vancouver, he was depressed by "the desolation of the prairies," and worried, as snow fell in the Rockies, lest his train be engulfed. On the *Empress of India*, bound for Yokohama, he felt during sleepless nights the approach of his nervous horrors. "I was quite surprised to find my

old enemy so near me in the seas." But once he found himself surrounded by such a civilization as he had never imagined, his anxieties
collapsed. "There is," he wrote, "no such thing as a Japanese without
love for the beautiful."[4]

The commission could have proceeded directly on, but decided to
spend ten days in Japan. Flexner's delights, as described in a voluminous
journal and equally voluminous letters home, were primarily visual:

"The love of bright colors of the women . . . the universal pigeon-toes
of the race; their wonderful kimonos and obis; their sandals and split
toes necessary to keep them on; the wonderful headdresses of the
women and the bare-headed men; the little almost toy-like shops, where
the whole staff sits on mats and cushions poetically in the street because
the whole front of the houses seem to have been removed in order that
wares may be displayed; and then — although by no means finally —
the endless procession of ginrickshaws with their bare-legged, thick-
calved draft men, the former containing every kind of person — old,
young, European, native, and often painted and bepowdered young
women, spotless and demure, looking wonders out of almond-eyed
spaces called eyes, and never chancing by any accident to display emotion — so that altogether you are compelled to attention, amusement,
and wonder with an intense pleasure that keeps you gurgling all the time
and saying to one another, 'How good this is!' Then one more pinch to
make sure it is not all a dream and you are really awake and in Japan."[5]

Flexner felt so exhilarated that he became worried lest the continuing
"round of pleasure and excitement" would make it very difficult for him
to settle down again. He was badly in need of the sobering efffect of systematic work.[6]

Tokyo was the site of the Imperial Institute of Infectious Diseases,
which was presided over by Shibasaburo Kitasato, a codiscoverer of the
diphtheria antitoxin. Kitasato sent an assistant to invite the commission
to his laboratory. Informed that the emissary was below, Flexner and
the others came downstairs to meet a short Japanese decked out in full
European morning dress. The exaggerated formality of his behavior was
belied by a boyish grin, and irrepressible ebullient gestures perilously
rocked his high hat. In hardly intelligible English he stated that he had
been chosen to deliver the invitation because of his fluent command of
English. He introduced himself as Hideyo Noguchi, and informed
Flexner that he wanted to come to America.

Gay remembered that Flexner replied casually, "Oh yes. That will be
fine."

Noguchi then stated that he would work in Flexner's laboratory at Baltimore. Flexner said that he was moving to Philadelphia. That was all right with Noguchi. He would work in Flexner's laboratory in Philadelphia. When Flexner asked if he had any publications to show, Noguchi replied that he had published in a hospital journal some observations on foot ulcers in children, and that he had once received twenty-five yen for translating an article into English.[7]

Flexner could not know that this young man was to play a major role in the history of science, in his own career, and in his affections. Yet he must have been somehow drawn to the half-comic stranger. He said he would ask Kitasato about him, and if the report was good and an opportunity should open there, he would call Noguchi to Philadelphia.

The Kitasato institute proved to have been modeled on Koch's institute in Berlin, "but is perhaps less tidy and certainly smaller." Kitasato's first assistant, Kiyoshi Shiga, "interested us most. He had isolated a bacillus from epidemic dysentery which he believed to be the specific organism from the fact of its agglutination with the blood of dysentery patients." He had prepared a serum of which he reported results. His work had been published only in Japanese but for the visitors he translated the main points into English. "Shiga is a polite and modest fellow of about thirty years," Flexner wrote. "He impressed one very favorably." As it turned out, Flexner was to become linked with Shiga, in the history of science and in friendship, by parallel discoveries.[8]

The six-day voyage from Japan to Hong Kong brought Flexner's commission into the geographic zone of the Philippine Islands. They now outfitted themselves for tropical living. And at the British hospitals they found "excellent opportunities" to start their personal acquaintance with tropical diseases.

"The plague," Simon wrote, "is still here and if anything slightly on the increase. We have been able to see it in several forms, both in the living and the dead, and the public mortuary has been open to us, so that we have been permitted to view and examine cases to our complete satisfaction. Besides this disease, we have seen other interesting and important ones, especially beri-beri."

Barker remembered that on their first visit to the morgue, they were careful not to come in contact with the bodies of plague victims, and even avoided drafts of air leading from the vicinity of the cadavers. On the second day, they cautiously examined the swollen lymph glands by touch. "And on the third day we found ourselves making postmortem examinations of the internal organs!"[9]

They were informed that the American army controlled hardly more of the Philippine Islands than the capital city. Even in Manila "conditions are very unfavorable; everything topsy-turvy, and a certain risk perhaps. The army is operating not very effectively." For the scientists, the one optimistic note was that there was a plethora of diseases for study.[10]

The commission reached Manila on May 4. During their stay of some two months, Flexner found himself, for the first time, part of a ruling establishment. The commission presented potent letters, and President Schurman of Cornell, whose offer to join his medical school Flexner had just turned down, was in Manila as president of the American governmental commission, and he was very courteous. The scientists were assigned a house in a suburb along the bay, just across the street from the governor general's palace. As a result of advice in Hong Kong, they had brought from there five Chinese servants.

So that they could go out at night after the military curfew, Flexner and Barker were commissioned first lieutenants. (His transformation into a presumed warrior for such a purpose was always a source of amusement to Flexner.) The two lieutenants were issued pistols. They regretfully concluded that military dignity prevented their using their weapons for target practice. Meeting no enemy, they fired only once: at a stray dog, which they both missed.[11]

Flexner wrote that the Filipinos, whose "lines are only a few miles from Manila," refused to fight. "They have no clothing or rations to carry and no wagon trains to wait for, and as they know the country perfectly, they have no difficulty getting away." The nature of the country through which the American troops had to pass made it "impossible for the column to unite before the enemy could escape.... The army marches in and out, extending American territory, losing a few men, killing perhaps more natives, and then because of the small force of men abandons the conquered territory.... The end is very, very far off."[12]

The scientists felt they could not settle down to work until they had visited the front. The army had just captured San Fernando, a city thirty-five miles northwest of Manila. Having collected a quantity of camping equipment, Flexner and his companions started out on a supply train that rocked over partially sabotaged tracks for some twenty miles to the Bayhag River, where the bridge was down. The army engineers were building a temporary replacement but so far it could be crossed only on foot. Having carried their baggage over, Simon and his companions realized that they had brought along so much gear they needed a wagon. Using telegraph wires strung by the signal corps, they appealed vainly to two bases for mounts and a wagon. Eventually, an artillery major, who had already given them coffee, lent them his "one-horse trap." Since the light wagon could carry, in addition to their equipment, only one man, the others, including Flexner, set out on foot for San Fernando, some ten miles distant.

Trudging along in the afternoon heat, they came to a native village that stretched for miles along the road. Because the village had not been burned, Flexner was able to admire the bamboo work on the rows of native huts, which he found "very pretty . . . intricate and regular. The town was deserted of human beings, except for an occasional straggler or family, and a few miserable starving cats and kittens, some hungry cows and swine. A few chickens usually too young and small to pay for the trouble of catching them, wandered around freely." The furniture which had been in the huts was to be seen in the tents of American soldiers. Bullet marks were everywhere, and there were "shell windows" in the stone walls of the convent.

"The next place of any size to which we came . . . was an ash heap, and a few natives were searching in the ruins, and an American soldier was in pursuit of a chicken for dinner. These were the only living objects."[13]

About nine o'clock in the evening the exhausted scientists neared San Fernando. Since Americans did not normally traverse the war zone on foot, the sentries were perturbed at the scientists' approach, but when they saw the uniforms and heard the American vernacular, they let the visitors through immediately. At General Arthur MacArthur's headquarters, the scientists were given a most satisfactory supper. They had expected to camp out, but were bedded down in a field hospital, which was just as well as their luggage had not arrived. The next day they visited the farthest American outpost. With the aid of binoculars, they had the pleasure of "distinctly" seeing a group of Filipino soldiers.[14]

That afternoon they walked around the charred ruins of the city of San Fernando. The few larger houses left now housed American officers and troops. The huts of the poorer natives had become barracks. No Filipinos could be seen. They were either dead — as the many new graves in the cemetery attested — or they had fled with the Filipino army. "It was a sad and desolate sight."[15]

Part of their way back to the railroad was eased for their legs but not their behinds by a lift in a springless bullock cart. They saw some Filipino soldiers at a distance, and were made fun of by a Major Rucker, who was unimpressed by Flexner's and Barker's shoulder straps: "I thought you were pretty new or you wouldn't be walking through this country." He gave them coffee and hardtack, and they gave him graham crackers.[16]

Flexner and his colleagues had not slaked their desire to be spectators at some fighting. For invaders in alien territory where native ears and eyes were hostile and success depended upon catching the enemy by surprise, the American command was amazingly careless concerning military secrecy. Twice the scientists were informed in time for them to journey (with who knows how many other sightseers) to a vantage point from which to watch the intended encirclement of an enemy force. Naturally, in both instances the enemy declined to be present. The only firing Flexner witnessed was from a gunboat attempting to halt a Filipino "caser," which proved, after it had been driven ashore, to contain no contraband.[17]

The commission's objective was to identify and study the diseases endemic in the Philippines, not according to clinical analysis but through the still-novel techniques of pathology and bacteriology. Their auspices were such that they were offered instantaneous cooperation in the military hospitals, which was soon seconded by the civilian hospitals. A few representatives of the Hopkins were already present: Hopkins-trained Lieutenant Richard B. Strong, who was to carry on some of the work of the commission after it had departed, and two former Hopkins nurses who presided over an operating room which Flexner insisted was "by far the best we have seen in the East, far surpassing the one in the civil hospital at Hong Kong."

The second floor of what had been the house of a prosperous Filipino was designated their laboratory and fitted up by the medical corps with tables and other equipment. It was close to the First Reserve Hospital, which was connected with all the other hospitals by the signal corps telegraphic system. It contained the morgue to which were carried all the army dead. Postmortems on native dead had to be performed at the hospitals in which the patients had died.

The prevailing diseases among the natives were different from those among the soldiers. The Spanish had allowed smallpox to be so prevalent that the natives had lost their fear of it. The Americans were stamping it out through vaccination. There was a considerable leper colony, some of whose inhabitants were discovered on autopsy to have suffered actually from tuberculosis. The commission diagnosed the causes of a prevailing itch as scabies or ringworm. Since native washerwomen rubbed the soldiers' clothes on stones in cold water, the itch was invading the army. Beriberi was by far the most destructive of native diseases.

The commission was unable to confirm previous claims that beriberi was caused by streptococci. They inoculated large quantities of blood into culture media; at autopsies they cut sections; but they could find nothing that suggested a bacterial cause. Frustrated, they carried materials back to America "for study and arrangement." They never found any bacteria because there were none. Not until the discovery of vitamins was it found that beriberi was a dietary affliction caused by the removal of the vitamin-rich husks from the rice that was the Orientals' staple food.

The diseases affecting Americans included typhoid fever, malarial fevers, tuberculosis, dengue fever, topical ulcers, and above all, dysentery, to which the Americans were very susceptible and which was much more destructive to the army than enemy action.

Making dysentery his personal problem, Flexner did bacterial studies of fresh stools passed by living sufferers, and of "intestinal contents, mesenteric [intestinal] glands, liver, etc.," from cases examined at autopsy. What he called the "intestinal flora," he examined by means of plate cultures. The first task was to distinguish between the different microorganisms. Those known to be present in cultures where dysentery was not involved were discarded. Also separated off were the amoebae that, although the distinction was often not made clinically, caused a different type of dysentery, usually less severe than the bacterial type.

Flexner finally came up with microorganisms "having affinities with a group of bacilli of which typhoid was the type." The group could be, he found, distinguished from true typhoid bacilli "by its action in litmus milk, its slight mobility, its tendency to become immobile in artificial culture, and its serum reaction." Its causative relationship to dysentery was indicated by the fact that the blood serums drawn from many patients suffering from the disease caused the dysentery bacilli to clump together (agglutinate).

Although he did not have time to complete his study — he would take the cultures back with him to the United States — Flexner concluded that "a bacillus of this group . . . would seem to agree" with the bacillus that Shiga had isolated.[18] The microorganism that became known as Flexner's bacillus was lurking in these cultures but Flexner was not to learn this until some years later.

*   *   *

Apart from the exciting scientific opportunities, Flexner found Manila depressing. The Filipinos were, as he saw them, pitiful: small in stature, dirty and raggedly clad, obsequious to the white men whom they would "treacherously" — Flexner borrowed the word from the military — kill if opportunity offered. All Flexner could see in their appearance to admire was the posture of the women which was fostered by their carrying pails and bundles on their heads; and also their shoulders, amazingly rounded over their underfed bodies. He and his colleagues allowed a dozen or more families to move into their cellar and were amazed to see how little space each family occupied and how little they ate.

"The days," Simon wrote home, "now are not different from each other." He rose early, had breakfast, smoked a Filipino cigarette, wrote of read a bit, worked in a hospital or the laboratory until noon, went home to tiffin, gave in to the climate with a siesta, had a second session of work until about five. Then he took a cold shower, dressed in spotless white, and in a hired carriage joined the daily social ceremony. The top-ranking Americans and Englishmen, with what ladies they had or could collect, drove around and around the roads that flanked the bay, bowing to each other as military bands played. After an hour and half of this, Flexner "turned up" at the Club Inglese or the Army and Navy Club for a scotch and soda. Between eight and eight-thirty, everyone went back to their quarters. In the daytime it was dangerous to walk on the streets (Flexner complained of lack of exercise) and there was no way to make riding in carriages safe after dark. Flexner went out in the evening only two or three times during his entire stay. The scientists had dinner, chatted for a while, read or scribbled, and went to bed about ten. Awake in the dark, Flexner heard only the cries of frogs and insects, the heavy tread of sentries, and occasionally the shout, "Halt, who goes there?"

By mid-June, it rained every evening and often poured during the night. Simon was told that when the rainy season really arrived there would be no intermission for days. "This is not a cheerful prospect, but I hope we may be accorded the experience before we depart." However, the tropical climate, to which they had not learned to accommodate themselves, "began to tell upon us all. We were not doing well physically and had not for a month past been up to par." Believing that he would need all his strength to deal with the problems at the University of Pennsylvania, Simon agreed with the others to leave Manila ten days before they had intended.[19]

Having returned to Hong Kong, the group separated. Flexner, accompanied by Gay, decided to take the long ocean voyage that would enable him actually to have circumnavigated the globe. He was to boast to his mother that he had sailed "through the following bodies of water: China Sea, Strait of Malacca, Bay of Bengal, Indian Ocean, Arabian Sea, Gulf of Aden, Strait of Bab el Mandeb, Red Sea, Suez Canal, Strait of Messina, Tyrrhenian Sea, Strait of [illegible]." There had been twenty-four-hour stopovers at Saigon, Singapore, and Colombo. He had "put his feet" on Cochin China, the Malay Peninsula, Ceylon, Egypt, and "other eastern places, and have gotten glimpses from the ship of Sumatra, Arabia, Crete, Sicily, Italy, Corsica, Sardinia."[20]

Flexner disembarked at Marseilles and then set out across the Atlantic. After a brief visit to his family, he reached Philadelphia in plenty of time to start his new post.

30

---·· ∞ ··---

The Further Adventures of Abraham

DURING the autumn of 1890, as Simon was first setting out for Baltimore, his brother Abraham also took a decisive step. He procured from five fathers, all of whose sons were having difficulty with their schooling, the promise of five hundred dollars apiece if he would tutor them so that they could get into the colleges their fathers preferred. The total being the equivalent of his salary as "professor," Abraham resigned from the Male High School. His venture was to grow into "Mr. Flexner's School," where eventually six teachers were employed, including the two Flexner sisters, Gertrude and Mary. It was to be the center of Abraham's professional career for fifteen long years.

At the outset of his independent effort, Abraham "dealt only with boys who had had a disastrous career at school," so much so that any "good boy who was brought to me" was assumed to have faults which the community had not previously perceived.

"The school," Abraham wrote in *I Remember*, "was operated without rules, without examinations, without reports. I relied upon other things: first, enthusiasm; second, cleverness in outwitting my students as they tried to dodge their responsibilities; third, good humor; and finally [by encouraging the good pupils in the presence of the bad] emulation and competition."[1]

Although this activity gave him ample opportunity for exercising his gifts at manipulation and persuasion, although it taught him much about secondary education that he later found very valuable, in essence, the operation was distasteful to him. His idealism involved not giving crutches to mediocrity but encouraging and achieving excellence. This passion fired his great generosity to Simon whom he tried to insulate from the family problems — at least until the home situation became really desperate. It also inspired him with a continuing desire to escape from the drudgery of his classes for an extended period of study at some intellectual center. "I am dried up and worn out with the few husks of learning that have already lasted so long," he complained to Simon in 1893. "I fear that unless I make a change in another year I will begin to lose a capacity for profiting by it."[2]

Abraham was not then held at Louisville for practical considerations. Although his contributions to the Flexner family support were very welcome, they were not absolutely necessary, and had he held on to his earnings, he could quickly have saved enough to get away. But he was not sure in what direction to apply his hunger for learning. He had never profited from such a guide as the winged microscope which had led Simon out of Jacob's drugstore and was continuing to guide him on a consistent path. Abraham's imagination did not extend beyond returning to his educational wellspring, the Hopkins; rooming with Simon; and studying he was not sure what — perhaps political economy, perhaps something else. He was to describe the career he eventually worked out for himself as "educational administration and management,"[3] but there was no specific way to study for that. University presidents worked up through the ranks by being what Abraham considered too confining — professors of a single discipline — and even when a professor got to the top, his originality was curbed by his trustees.* Abe was preparing for what he could not then imagine and did not then exist: the career of a foundation executive who is supplied with the millions he needs to realize the reforms he envisions.

The Flexner system of family cooperation, although still very compelling, was no longer dictated by necessity. The objective had shifted from meeting essential needs to achieving and maintaining what Abraham defined as "a position . . . in the community." Jacob had presided over the building of twin houses in a good neighborhood: one for Esther and the unmarried children, the other for his own growing family. Abraham, whose earnings helped fuel the enterprise, boasted that the houses were "as handsome as any in town."[4]

Although Simon had to a considerable extent broken away from the family system, his closest human ties were still his relatives, whom he

---

* Significantly, in his biography of Gilman, Abraham invested the man he idolized with solitary stature. He did not take into account, despite evidence to be found in his own book, the creative role of the trustees.

addresssed in his letters as "my dear ones." Returning to Louisville for
vacations, he was worried since he suspected that the houses had been
built on borrowed money. His concern turned to active disapproval
when he observed the effect on the "dear one" who was by far the
dearest to him, his mother. Separated from her old neighbors, from the
local shopkeepers who had cooperated and sympathized with her longtime efforts to keep the impoverished family afloat, Esther walked in
loneliness the quieter and cleaner streets. Time lay heavy on her hands
which had once been so quick and efficient in achieving necessities. She
tried to fill in with reading, although she had never been a fluent reader.
Her pleasure was in her grandchildren next door but, so Simon concluded, "on the whole, it was for her an artificial life."[5]

Simon was not reassured by the rising self-importance with which his
brothers bustled out of the new houses. Jacob's business stationery now
declared him a "manufacturing pharmacist." He had branched out far
beyond the national distribution of albuminate of iron that Simon had
initiated. Jacob had even bought a machine to bottle soda water on a
large scale. Washington and Bernard felt confined by the quiet operation
of a bookstore: they ventured into publishing and door-to-door selling,
and were beginning to switch into the much larger field of lithographic
printing.

The year 1893 marked the twentieth anniversary of the Panic of 1873
that had bankrupted Morris Flexner, but his children saw in this no
warning. As a new set of storm clouds began to cover the economic
skies, they borrowed more and more money, not only to remedy the
damage caused by the approaching storm, but to plunge onwards.

The management of the large family had for some years now been divided between the oldest and the youngest sons. Jake, the traditional
leader, considered himself, and was considered, a financial wizard — he
was a director of the German Bank and advisor to the president of the
Bank of Kentucky. His domain was the new family houses he had financed, the care of his mother, and his own wife and children. Abraham's domain was the younger half of the family: his three immediately
older brothers — Washington about five years his senior; Simon, three;
Bernard, one — and his two younger sisters. As staunch an advocate of
female education as any Thomas, he was supporting Mary at Bryn
Mawr. He helped Simon with loans. But he was most involved with the
affairs of Wash and Ben, whom he called "the Boys" and fathered even
though he was their junior. Consulting with them daily, he financed the

purchase of a newly invented press which they believed, although it was too advanced to function more than spasmodically, would, when the kinks were ironed out, enable them to monopolize the lithography business in Louisville. And beyond!

When the Panic of 1893 mounted into the catastrophe of 1894, Abraham felt the exhilaration of a champion put on his mettle. "We have had our share of trouble in money matters this winter," he wrote Simon in March, "not more than most people, I think, but still enough and to spare. . . . The whole business community seems to be in one boat, but we have had all along so many evidences of confidence on the part of bankers, merchants, etc., that I cannot but view it as one of my highest duties" not to damage, by failing to forge ahead, the position which the family "have been working for and have partly obtained in the community. Now that we have brought matters so far, it does not seem unreasonable to hope that a short period, after the revival of trade, will put things where we can rest confident as to their [the family's] future."[6]

But Jacob began to show distressing symptoms. He smoked cigar after cigar in a frenzy; he drank heavily. The family came to suspect that he was helping himself to the narcotics on his drugstore shelves. And then the awful truth came out. He was heavily in debt and had reached the end of his ability to borrow. The drugstore was on the edge of bankruptcy. Forced, for the first time in his life, to doubt his own powers, Jacob sank into a nervous collapse. He had to be sent off on trips lest his visible condition terrify his creditors into making immediate demands.

If the drugstore went down, the Boys' business, which was also overextended, might well follow. Mr. Flexner's School, not encumbered with debt or dependent on capital, was the rock on which salvation of the family would now have to be grounded. Thus, Abraham became the undisputed leader and chief reliance of the family coalition which had been the center of all their lives from as far back as he could remember. A heady role, not easily relinquished, for the youngest of seven sons.

The five years of his life, from the ages of twenty-seven to thirty-two, which Abraham devoted almost exclusively to extricating the family finances, is no more than glancingly referred to in his autobiography. The only remaining record — and it is a voluminous one — is contained in his correspondence with Simon, which Simon preserved among his papers.

The correspondence reveals as Abraham's salient characteristics during those years, a determination and an ability to lead; a disdain for moving cautiously; glee (which comes out boastfully in the letters) at carrying off complicated and sometimes secret manipulations; a gift for accommodation to sooth the impact of his drives; and boundless energy, which enabled him to remain optimistic in almost any situation.

With perspicacity as well as loving-kindness, Abraham attended to the psychological needs of his battered dependents. Although he did not share Simon's preoccupation with their mother, he saw to it that the feeble old lady was treated with consideration. He crooned over his former mentor and patron Jake with touching solicitude. He was much concerned when Ben's long-damaged eyesight was worsened by strain, planning, although this he could not achieve, to give his brother a vacation in Europe. He continued to pay Mary's expenses at Bryn Mawr.

Abraham's ability to charm the well-to-do into parting with money, so essential to the achievements of his later years, was already present. We learn from his letters how elaborately and invisibly he entwined what he called "confidential money" — funds secured from the personal confidence he inspired in rich men (an ability he was not to lose) — and the more impersonal "bank money." The Flexners, he admitted, had formerly failed to recognize that borrowed money was not their money, to be regarded as permanent capital. If the family had recognized this a few years before, they would have spared themselves a great deal of trouble.[7]

Abraham labored to postpone paying interest and particularly repaying capital while he raised additional loans to support the family, meet pressing indebtedness, and finance new ventures that he believed would increase earnings. The method was to expand the guaranteeable earnings of Mr. Flexner's School in a manner only possible if Abraham preserved the confidence of banks and rich men in his own abilities and in the probity of the family as a whole. Although there is no reason to believe that laws were actually broken, it was important that none of the creditors be cognizant of how, in juggling funds, Abraham played them one against the other. The more desperate the situation, the more important to keep expedients hidden.

Abraham's often boastful letters to Simon leave no doubt of the satisfaction he found in the hazardous game that so stretched his ingenuity and wits. But Simon's bent was very different.

One morning at the hospital, as Simon was on his way to have breakfast with Dr. Hurd, he received a telegram from his brother Washington "stating that he had drawn on me for three hundred dollars," and enclosing a check for that amount. Noticing that Simon was distraught and ate almost nothing, Hurd asked him if something was wrong. Thus encouraged, Simon showed him Wash's letter and asked him how to proceed. He was told to deposit the check and when the draft came, pay with his own check. But when Simon reached the bank, he found that the draft had already arrived. The cashier, ascertaining that the draft and check were both from the same person and for an identical amount, suspected some shenanigans, and frowning disapprovingly at Simon, he refused to accept Wash's check. "In terrible stress," Simon returned to Hurd who asked no questions but drew his own check for three hundred dollars. Simon saw to it that Hurd was quickly repaid but this did not heal his humiliation at having been driven to involve his friend and benefactor in an underground operation he did not understand. "I saw to it . . . that I was never again involved in the Louisville crises."[8]

Increasingly needled by Abraham as the situation darkened, Simon did send home as much as he felt he could. But he did not hide his belief that his gifted brother should let the Flexner finances take their normal course of bankruptcy (which in those dark times was too common to be a disgrace) and should turn his attention to his own future career. Himself pursuing wholeheartedly directions to which he was wholeheartedly dedicated, he considered Abraham's maneuverings "quixotic," all the more because they were "of doubtful advantage to anyone."[9]

In the fall of 1896, "salvation" seemed on the way for Jacob's drugstore, the heart of the problem. Despite all Abraham's assistance, the store was in debt for $40,000 and, "even worse," it was still losing money. But possible purchasers named Bushmeyer had appeared. With what they paid, Jake could perhaps buy a smaller store that he could handle economically and at the same time pay his debts.

The bluebird! But the Bushmeyers proved to be vultures. Realizing that they could get the store for less if Jacob were forced into bankruptcy, they spread rumors that he was planning to sell out secretly and skip from Louisville with the proceeds. "In these times," Abraham wrote Simon, "men will believe anything, but imagine *our* having to refute such calumny. The world will not easily let men do right! Assuredly we have our cross to bear."

Jacob's creditors, whom Abraham had been staving off this way or that way, now descended on the drugstore in a body. The bankruptcy that Abe had labored to prevent in the cause of the family's respectability came on in a "most painful and humiliating manner." Jacob's condition, "physical and financial," became common gossip. And the extent of the bankruptcy was "as bad or worse" as it would have been had not Abraham poured in, as he estimated to Simon, "up to $40,000, certainly $30,000. It is not nice to see this amount swept away, as it might have established us in comparative affluence. . . . Still, we were right to make the fight and I for one have no regrets."[10]

It would be prudent, Abraham realized, to let the Boys go through bankruptcy also, but he would not give up, thereby adding to the family disgrace. He helped pay their debts by selling off their stock and equipment (which brought less than he had hoped), but was left with the empty store that no one would buy. He did succeed in selling the two family houses. They brought only enough to pay off the mortgages, yet Abe had kept the mortgages from being foreclosed. Mary's Bryn Mawr degree paid off: she became a teacher in Mr. Flexner's School. Wash was able to get employment in the printing business. But Jake and Ben had to be given opportunities for new careers.

Jacob revived his early ambition of becoming a physician. Even more lenient than they had been to Simon, the doctors who owned the University of Louisville school had, without requiring any study, given Jake an honorary medical degree. Abraham now sent him to the Hopkins as a presumptive graduate student for a quick polishing.[11]

Simon felt called on to ask his brother to lunch as his guest at the hospital high table. Welch and the other chiefs happened to be present. Their presence made Jake the more eager to show off. As he had done among the local practitioners in Louisville, he dominated the conversation, "asserting his ideas and giving others no chance." In the Baltimore world where Simon was now at home, his brother's ideas were crude, his voice loud, his manners reprehensible. The occasion remained one of Simon's bitterest memories.[12]

Jake's determination to assert himself as top dog came between him and the studies he was supposed to be undertaking. Simon gave him a lecture, which induced him to complain to Abe. Abe in turn sent a remonstrance to Simon that he would have found very embarrassing had it become known at the time he was destroying unscientific medical schools with his "Flexner Report" (1910) and using Rockefeller funds to enforce the ideas of the Johns Hopkins Medical School across the United States.

Abraham reminded Simon that it was hard on Jacob to have himself and his family, after all his work, dependent on others. He must be encouraged, not discouraged. Of course, a few months could not make Jake a doctor in the Hopkins manner, but there was no need to admit this to the world. Simon should remember that the issue was not scientific but economic. It was essential that Jake should make his living, and he would be competing not with Hopkins graduates but with Louisville practitioners. Obviously, he could not start as an experienced physician. However, the ability to present an impressive front was almost as important as knowledge, and Jake had gifts in that direction. Abraham then pointed to his own situation. As a scholar, he would be laughed at by university professors, yet "tact and management" had carried him ahead. Jake would have to get his knowledge in the way Simon had got much of his: through experience rather than prior instruction.[13]

Abraham was putting squibs in the newspaper about Jacob's being at the Hopkins. "We must get a little newspaper talk of him from time to time as a business move. I don't like it but it is necessary." Simon must see that Jake gives up cigars as well as liquor. To have his breath be a denial of the rumors circulating about him "is the important matter beyond any amount of skill in medicine. . . . So it goes!"[14]

After his few months at the Hopkins, Jacob moved on to another few months at the Mother's and Baby's Hospital in New York City, and then he set up as a practitioner in Louisville. "The struggle," Simon remembered, "was sharp and strong. . . . Mother and Rosa [Jake's wife] held together like twins." In the end, Jacob won out, becoming one of the most trusted physicians in the city.[15]

In long hindsight, Simon viewed the collapse of the family system, which had dominated the Flexner siblings ever since Morris's failure in 1874, as a great liberation. They continued to feel emotionally close and to feel responsibility for each other, but no one — except Abraham until all the debts were paid — was tied by the leg anymore. Separate careers were developed. Only Jacob spent his life in Louisville, and he had returned successfully to an earlier dream.

Washington became president of a short-lived newspaper, the Louisville *Herald*. Seeking larger fields, he dared mightily, suffering some bad financial falls and having to be bailed out by his siblings, who were to be paid many times over by his eventual triumphant venture. During 1915, in Chicago, he established the Lincoln Printing Company, which with a New York branch became, before the 1929 crash, the largest printer in the United States of the stock certificates that poured out in those days as copiously as if they were really showers of gold. He died a moderately rich man.[16]

Bernard was released by the general family collapse into the study of law, becoming the third distinguished Flexner brother. He was much concerned with reforming juvenile courts and saw to it that the complete transcript of the Sacco-Vanzetti trial was published and distributed to libraries throughout the world. Having, as a corporation lawyer, accumulated considerable wealth, he endowed at Bryn Mawr the Mary Flexner Lectureship and at Vanderbilt University the Abraham Flexner Lectureship. When Bernard felt left out during World War I, Simon secured for him an appointment to the American Red Cross Commission to Rumania. Horrified by the plight of the central European Jews, he became, unlike Simon and Abraham, a Zionist. He was counsel to the Zionist delegation to the Paris Peace Conference, and played a major role through the Palestine Economic Corporation in economic support for the settlers of Palestine. He was active during World War II in organizing succor for refugees from Hitlerism. His sister Mary lived with him for many years.[17]

VI

Chiaroscuro

31

⎯⎯⎯··⟨∞⟩··⎯⎯⎯

Seesaw

Had it not been for the deathbed promise Mary had exacted, Helen would have escaped to college some two months after her mother died. But now she was trapped for a minimum of fourteen months in the domestic environment where her mother had been the dominant spirit; where her mother had crumbled away because of a wound Helen felt she had herself inflicted; where the beautiful inanimate body had been washed and laid in state. Unable to disentangle herself from guilt and painful memories, the girl who had for the first sixteen years of her life been healthy, became sickly and morbid.

Her basic function proved not to be supplying companionship for her father, who was often away from home and in any case closer to Frank with whom Helen quarreled. She was sentenced to be housekeeper and executive-of-all-work for the large establishments, in city and country, that remained the base of the expanding family. Directing the servants, doing herself what they would not or could not do, she arranged the long or short stays of her seven siblings, along with their friends, fiancés, wives, newborn babies. Her relatives felt pangs of guilt at pouring so much on Helen's "seventeen-year-old shoulders," but they had their own affairs to attend to. Carey wrote in the same sentence that she was "dreadfully sorry" and that she found Helen's activities "a great comfort."[1]

Helen diagnosed in herself some female ailment and wrote Carey about it. The Dean was instantly up in arms. Helen would have to tell her father. He could not, Carey supposed, refuse to let her have treatment, but if he did —! Although Carey had recommended a female doctor, Helen's father called in the famous Hopkins surgeon Dr. Kelly. Kelly handled the problem with perfect success. Much more menacing to Helen's future were "excruciating" earaches.[2]

Carey's panacea for Helen was that she "be sure to sleep late and go to bed early." Helen replied, "I try to go to bed at the proper times, and do everything I ought to do. But it takes all the irregularity out of life and leaves that dreary sameness that it is impossible to endure. However, if you say so, I suppose I must."[3]

Housekeeping, Helen wrote, "is the most villainous thing I ever tried to do. I don't think I was intended for it either. However, my hand says that I am going to get married." She had bought a book on palmistry.[4]

Helen tried to prepare for an examination in geometry which she would have to pass if she was ever to get to Bryn Mawr, but she could not keep her mind on it. She realized that a young man Harry brought for the weekend was very conversable, but announced that Margaret would have to entertain him.[5]

The summer months at Coombe Edge were no better. Helen was plagued by headaches, nausea, and vomiting: "I was wretched in every way." Others in the family only made a cheerless situation worse. Grace, for one, appeared with a new baby, the second in two years of marriage. She had suffered a very difficult pregnancy, towards the end being unable to stand, and now both she and the baby were ailing. "Grace is an object lesson to me," Helen wrote. "I feel glad for my experience for, as Margaret the nurse says, I shall know all about it when I get married." This pessimism was reinforced by Zoe, Harry's fiancée. She was still unmarried because of Harry's tuberculosis. One day, after being lost in "deep thought, she suddenly announced that she thinks it nicer to be engaged than be married."[6]

Even Helen's birthday, though a relatively bright spot, could not dispel her depression. Her father tried to make the occasion as happy for her as he could. "I got many more presents than I expected," Helen wrote Carey. "Father wrote a very pretty little poem to go with the rose he left by my plate at breakfast. Besides that, he gave me four little pins, two gold and two enamel, and some money to buy books with." She would get a "nice set of Shakespeare." But she could not resist adding, "When one feels fifty, the change from seventeen to eighteen does not disturb one at all."[7]

The plan, as Mary had worked out on her deathbed, finally released Helen: Margaret, graduated from Bryn Mawr and not averse to housekeeping, took over. On September 30, 1889, Helen set out for the family college. This was the eighteen-year-old girl's very first departure from home.

Although within easy walking distance of the railroad station and only twenty minutes from Philadelphia, the college was embedded in a landscape almost totally rural. The environs had not changed greatly since they were described in 1688: gently rolling ground, "some springs and running streams of as good water as any I ever saw. Good, stately oaks . . . and many kinds of trees grow plentifully. English hay does very kindly and especially white honeysuckle." Hardly distinguishable from the land around it, the campus, an old farm with its orchards still standing, was extensive in relation to the buildings so far erected. Taylor Hall, a Victorian structure with a tower, contained the library, administration offices, and classrooms. There were also two dormitories known as "cottages" — they were kept small to establish a homelike atmosphere — and a gymnasium. Antiquity as America knew it was all around. Gulf Road still had milestones bearing the Penn coat of arms. Once a main highway, it had seen Revolutionary fighting, and there were soldiers' graves at the bottom of the college hill. The name Bryn Mawr, taken from the nearby village, was suitably Welsh for the Thomas inheritance, the whole area having been granted by William Penn to Welsh Quakers.[8]

Although the campus was physically so much part of the country, the college itself was isolated, a female enclave. The male president was a pale figure beside Carey, the Dean. Gardeners, janitors, a few male professors moved as exceptions through a world of women. All the students were normally present twenty-four hours a day. They were in revolt against the attitudes towards female intellect rife in the world around them. Many had been forced to fight hard in order to come through the gates. They all realized that courtship and marriage, even if they were to succumb to or eventually welcome them, would now exile them from the intellectual world they inhabited. There was little of that yearning for the companionship of young men that was to characterize later college girls: no male callers other than fathers and brothers; no dates; no mixed dances. Indeed, a puritanical austerity in relation to the opposite sex was as essential as it had been to Carey and Mamie Gwinn at Leipzig. The most damaging charge that could be made against higher education for women was that it encouraged immorality.

It would have taken a "depraved" mind to suspect any immorality in the close friendships that grew up between the girls. That the association of women with each other was "pure" was a rock on which the whole structure of nineteenth-century society was built. Indeed, in the world surrounding the campus, women, even in marriage (as with the Thomases), associated primarily with each other. Thus, the girls' all-female social life was bothersome to parents only because it kept them from meeting possible husbands. More worrying were the intellectual preoccupations the college fostered which might make the girls less attractive to the men they did meet, or — perish the thought! — make them resolve never to marry.

For the girls themselves, passing beyond the physical relationships with each other that were not only accepted but encouraged by society — holding hands, stroking hair, kisses, warm embraces that did not involve nudity — would have been as great a violation of taboo as that against incest, which also regulated the sexual behavior of persons living intimately together. Lesbianism, as we know it today, would have created in its practitioners a sense of heinous self-besmirchment or a dedication to sexual revolt that would have utterly violated the tone and direction of an institution like Bryn Mawr, where not only the students but the faculty, from Dean Thomas down, visibly found their close companions among other women. Lesbianism would, indeed, have been shattering high treason against the struggle for female emancipation to which Bryn Mawr was dedicated: emancipation of the female mind through learning.

The lives the women lived with each other were far from drab. Regarding housework as degrading for an intellectual female, Carey had seen to it that the "cottages" were well staffed with maids. The students loved to dress up and attend the parties they gave for each other, and it was easier to admire without envy the prettier girls when no competition for male attention, for agreeable marriages, was impinged upon. Attractive classmates were, furthermore, an answer to the male charge that women cultivated their minds only if they were too ugly to cultivate anything else. Although her best friend was far more beautiful, Helen, who had so cherished the beauty of her mother, all her life long admired beautiful women. One of her favorite memories was of how handsome Blanche Oelrichs had looked as she led on a white horse the first woman suffrage parade in New York City.[9]

Helen expressed to her father delight at the number of tea parties to which she was invited. Caught up in such a social whirl as she had never known, she was no longer a shy observer — very much the opposite.

What was to be the glorious banner that set her off from almost all other women was suddenly unfurled. In a family of redheads, her own red-gold thatch had gone unnoticed. But now her hair was doubly appreciated because it fell in so perfectly with the latest esthetic taste. For generations, red hair had been considered an ugly blemish, but the pre-Raphaelites, led by Dante Gabriel Rossetti, were painting with worship redheaded women, a predilection seconded by Jean Jacques Henner, the greatly admired French figure painter.

Each Bryn Mawr class staged a pageant for the others. "Never did I see anything so provoking!" Helen wrote her father. "The Sophs. have the gym and it is our time for rehearsing our march, and we have to hang around until they see fit to go. The worst of it is that all the town girls have stayed out on purpose to practice, and this is almost the only chance. . . .

"Although we had to give up our general practicing, yet some things were tried, and, of course, I was in them. I don't think I have told thee yet what our entertainment is to be and what part I am to take in it, but if thee will solemnly promise not to tell the Sophs., I will recite it now. Besides thee must promise not to laugh when thee hears my part, and thee must remember that I accepted it under protest. . . . Thee knows the Pallas Athena in the form of one of the Sophs. gave us our lanterns while the rest of the class chanted a Latin song. We are going to return this by a Greek* entertainment, and the opening is to be the consecration of our lanterns around the altar of Pallas Athena. We will all march in in Greek dress swinging our lanterns and singing a Greek song. . . .

"The rest is to be a series of tableaux from the Iliad and the Odyssey primarily, a dramatization of Shelley's Ode of Mercury, and a simple Greek dance. One of the tableaux is to be The Judgement of Paris and I am to be *Aphrodite*. Isn't it astounding how greatly a want of Greek features red hair atones for! I am also going to take part in a dance which is nothing more than a game of ball played by twelve Greek girls, and it will be most effective, I think.

"Thee can imagine that we are busy. In fact, we have no time to do any studying, and the whole class is seriously thinking of taking an impromptu holiday next week, for Friday is the fatal day. We are awfully anxious for it to succeed for if it does it will be really lovely. I wish thee would come on for it, but unfortunately men are not admitted."[10]

Helen's freshman pageant succeeded so well that it gave birth to one

* Greek outclassed Latin because it was more difficult and was normally taught only to men. Mary Whitall Thomas, when first married, had tried to learn Greek from her husband.

of Bryn Mawr's favorite traditions, described at the college's fiftieth anniversary as the "lovely ceremony of Lantern Night." The Greek song written by Helen's roommate and another girl, "was sung in the moonlight or under the stars" in the library cloister.[11]

For the first time in her life, Helen is euphoric. She is intensely happy in a social world altogether her own, where everyone is absorbed in what she is absorbed in, where she shines. The absence of young men is to her advantage since she has not yet learned to get on with males outside her family. She finds it soothing to be in an environment that does not perpetually bring to her mind the death of her mother. Her letters to her classmates are full of affectionate insults and intimate jokes, abounding in high spirits. She works hard and does well, so much so that she is embarrassed at getting a higher grade than Lucy.

Lucy Martin Donnelly was taller than Helen, not buxom but gaunt and bony. Her black hair contrasted with Helen's red; her eyes were dark. Her appealing, sensitive, and emotional young face was strangely dominated, despite the intensity of her gaze, by rimless, almost invisible eyeglasses. It was as if she had psychologically withdrawn behind the thin but protective panes of glass. (PLATES 22 and 23)

"I am getting very fond of her," Helen wrote her father. "She's very clever and looks it too. In fact, she is one of the most interesting girls I ever saw, although not pretty.... We like the same things and books.... I expect we shall see a great deal of each other." Almost simultaneously with her arrival at Bryn Mawr, Helen had found a friend with whom she was to be intimate for more than forty years, as long as they were both alive.[12]

Helen had hardly returned to Bryn Mawr after Christmas vacation when the "excruciating" earache she had suffered during her imprisonment as family housekeeper returned with violence. "I feel rather worried," she wrote her father, "as I am sufficiently deaf already, and so do not wish to get any deafer, which I seem to be doing."

Ten days later: "I am not quite ready to return home for good ... but my ear has bothered me considerably. The gathering or whatever it is at the opening has grown worser and worser. I could not stand the syringe."[13]

During mid-March, Carey took her to a specialist in Philadelphia. He said that if she wanted her ear to get well she would have to build up her strength in other ways. At Carey's insistence, she dropped all work except nine hours of study a week. "I can't imagine how I shall occupy myself." But the nine hours themselves became frightening — her "power of studying and understanding ... seems to be disappearing with terrible rapidity. . . . My own darling father, don't forget your little daughter."[14]

Helen had been shuttling back and forth between Baltimore and Bryn Mawr, retreating with a relapse, returning to college as soon as she felt better. But on March 19, 1890, there seemed no point in returning.

In long retrospect, Helen attributed the illnesses that haunted her young womanhood to the strain and anguish she had suffered during her mother's last illness and the psychic wounds inflicted by her mother's death. Now trapped again in the old environment — she could not foresee for how long — she found what solace she could in visiting her mother's grave.[15]

Helen's ear hurt her so much that she expressed a wish to find some simple way to end her life and the pain together, but the pain was not the most threatening part: the final result could be utter deafness, a life into which no human voice ever again sounded. And her physique seemed to be breaking down in many ways. "How," she asked in a letter to Lucy, "do people who are always sick stand it? I don't think we give them half credit enough for their heroism."[16]

Had Helen been willing to settle for that heroism she might have become one of those women with whom nineteenth-century affluent life abounded, who lived out their lives reclining in half-darkened rooms. The pressure was on her not only from her own body but from outside: from her medical advisors and from her family, who loved her and wished her well. Helen had on her hands a hard fight. Psychically it was at least as difficult as her future husband's struggle to escape from poverty and obscurity on self-made wings.

Her father was no help. He treated her "as if I were made of glass." When she returned at night from a brief visit to Bryn Mawr — of which he had disapproved — he insisted on unpacking her bag, "looking like a preternaturally solemn and very much overgrown housemaid. . . . I silently looked on as he hung my very bestest hat on a sharp and very ragged nail."[17] All her father's precautions did not prevent her from periodically losing control of herself. She would call him, so she reported to Lucy, "Jimmie" and sometimes "boy." She gleefully described how "I sat upon his bed and tormented him until he did not know whether he was on his head or on his heels. . . . These moods of wild hilariousness which sometimes come upon me alarm him excessively."

This same letter to Lucy goes on for page after page after page, the characters becoming long and spindly and cramped together, while the gaps between the words disappear until the writing completely fills the sheet of paper, a solid illegible mass. "My writing today," she finally recognizes, "looks as if lightning had struck it, and exactly expresses my mood. I feel just as up and down, just as scratchy and scrawly and incomprehensible. I wonder if we would be happier if we really understood ourselves and each other."[18]

Her physicians concluded that nervous excitement underlay all her ills. The remedy was to isolate her from nervous strain, which they primarily defined as intellectual effort. This meant no continuation at home of her work at Bryn Mawr; indeed, no studying at all. She did, by hard begging, get permission to read German, but only on condition that she look up no words in the dictionary.

Although Carey was one of the strongest advocates of this regimen — we shall see how Helen, after she got back to Bryn Mawr, was forced to fight "the Dean" on this matter — one cannot help wondering whether this interference with what was conventionally considered outside the female sphere was not a hangover from old prejudices. When Grace, Margaret, and Zoe had been studying hard for their entrance examination to Bryn Mawr, Mary had expressed worry lest they damage their health. If it had been her sons rather than her daughters who had been doing the studying, surely she would not have been similarly worried about them. Victorian households were not haunted by men lying on sofas with vials of smelling salts in their hands.

Helen was not yet truly rebellious since she had been told that her obedience to instructions would give her the strength needed to return to Bryn Mawr for the next academic year. To keep up her own morale and to persuade the doctors, she ended all acknowledgments of suffering by stating that nonetheless she was as "gay as a lark" or "as jolly as a sandboy."

With Margaret continuing her efficient services, Helen was entirely freed of housekeeping. Around her the family eddied, as it had ever since she could remember. As before, Helen was an observer, acutely aware of foibles and inconsistencies, but she was not given to the righteous censoriousness of her younger days. After the certainties inculcated in her by her upbringing had been torn into shreds by her mother's tragedy, she had lost forever her belief that there could be only one right and one wrong. This emancipation, abetted by the distant overview she had achieved at Bryn Mawr, was bringing out an appreciation of the comedy of life, the humorous tolerance that was down the years to be one of her most endearing gifts. After her father, "with his usual impetuosity," had got himself cheated in the purchase of a horse, she wrote, "Dear Dad! He looks so persistently on the bright side of things that everything he possesses is the best of its kind because it is his" so "he is perfectly contented. Strange as it sounds, I am dreadfully fond of him for getting cheated and taking it so sweetly and not objecting to our discouraging comments. The worst of it is that he will never get a good horse, and that is rather trying for those who have to use them. High ho ho! . . . How we all deceive ourselves into thinking that what we have is the best, or, if we are inclined to pessimism, that our things are the worst, our lot the hardest."[19]

Her apologies could be humorously equivocal. To Lucy: "When I laugh at you for eccentricity it simply means that I can see what is amusing in cleverness because I am not clever enough myself to have any inclination towards eccentricity."[20]

Helen was not forbidden to read as long as it was for pleasure. That she was permitted to write and receive letters enabled her to hold onto her Bryn Mawr world. Each of her letters to Lucy — three or four a week — usually ran to twelve or more pages.

After returning from a drive with her father, she wrote, "The country seemed more beautiful than ever today, and the trees and grass under the sky all breathed of peace and rest. . . . Nature always has something for us, I think, and the mission of the poets is to . . . enable us to see her gifts in all their power and beauty. . . . Every day I am more thankful for the knowledge I have of poetry. I sometimes feel lifted out of my usual commonplace self and for a short delirious moment I forget the limitations of my nature. Alas, how bitter it is to return to earth. Oh, that we all could be poets! Do you never feel when you see something beautiful how much of its perfection you miss because your appreciation, your power of feeling, is so faulty? Perhaps you have no need to feel this, but I am haunted by it nearly every day. The spirit of the thing I want to get at, yet it is always hidden."[21]

It becomes amply clear that what she described as her loss of belief in God, which accompanied her mother's death, had not prevented her from seeking with the passage of the years a more personal and broader faith. As she "watched the fading light, a voice seemed to say distinctly

in my heart, 'Be still, and know that I am God.' And when in the evening I knelt down at my window, as I have done every night for many
summers, and looked at the stars shining so brightly over the mountains,
it seemed to me that was to be my work for the summer. Just to be still."

"God is a spirit and in truth we worship Him not only in our outward
lives but by that inner, more subtle existence. And this, it seems to me,
is prayer. The daily communion ... of our spirit with God, and that
which is infinite within us with that which is infinite in all things, is true
religion. Thus we go to nature, we go to art, we go to literature, and in
them all see the power and love of God, and through these our souls
hasten to Him who alone can satisfy us."[22]

Helen prays that her love for Lucy will get "stronger and purer every
day." She believes that their friendship "is deep and true and good for
us both." More emotional passages open and close many letters: avowals
of how deeply she loves Lucy, how she misses her, how her heart fails
her when the post brings no letter, how her heart leaps when one comes.
This endless reiteration, almost the same phrases used over and over,
seems, as one reads on and on, to be primarily a litany against darkness.
"My love for you," Helen writes, "keeps me from being bored or lonely.
I have always something to think about." She carries Lucy's letters
around with her everywhere, comforted even just to be able to touch
them with her hand. "I love and admire and respect you so much. You
are so truly the best friend I ever had."[23]

In mid-June, Helen wrote Lucy, "Last night I had a most curious
dream. What do you suppose? It was about the conquering hero. He had
come, but alas, he was very poor, and in my devotion I was willing to
marry him on an income of eight hundred a year. I was more than willing: I was eager. Yet in my dream I remember thinking, 'How shall I tell
Lucy?' When I woke up I was so glad to find it all untrue, and to know
that nothing had come between us. May the Gods keep that horrible
dream from coming true, yet there is another one which might be even
worse."[24]

What Helen considered a worse alternative it is impossible to determine, but what is clearly stated is highly revealing. Lucy's objection to
Helen's marrying, which was to make so much trouble in the future, is
presaged. Very intriguing is the metaphor, obviously already understood between them, of the "coming" of the "conquering hero." The
meeting of Brunhilde and Siegfried is so apt an analogy that it is hard to
believe that the girls did not have it in mind. As pioneers at Bryn Mawr,
Helen and her group might well think of themselves as female warriors.

They would not stoop to entice or accept ordinary men. They would have to be conquered, if at all, by heroes who could penetrate unscathed through encircling rings of fire.

Helen might have seen her conquering hero pass by on a Baltimore street: Simon Flexner had just arrived from the slums of Louisville to the Pathological at the Hopkins. She would not have been impressed, despite his remarkably intelligent face, by the little man of meager physique, who was far from conventionally handsome as he moved energetically in badly cut provincial clothes.

32

Entrapments and Escapes

CONSIDERED well enough to return to Bryn Mawr for the opening of her sophomore year in September, 1890, Helen instantly regained her previous pleasure. "Every Friday," she exulted to her father, "we have some entertainment." She attended a ball "with great success as Juliet in a white cheesecloth dress made for the purpose."[1]

All her life Helen needed to view the world through her imaginative sympathy with another person: first her mother, now Lucy, and eventually Simon Flexner. Lucy was a much more benign spirit than Mary Thomas had been. There was no need to fear or revere her. They shared a passion for English literature; they educated each other. Lucy infected Helen with an admiration for Browning which stayed with her all her life as a happy memory.

Although Lucy had no specific ailments, she was a neurasthenic, always threatened, so Helen believed, with a "breakdown." Helen blamed herself for encouraging Lucy to come with her to Quaker meeting, although this involved walking some miles in the blazing sun. Just as the meeting was breaking up, Lucy fainted, and "we had to lay her out flat on the porch. I was never so frightened in my life, but she soon came to, and Dr. Rhoads took her home in his carriage."[2]

She lectured Lucy against doing too much. Herself under strict doctor's orders, she wrote her father, "I am going to be a model of sense and laziness." But she could not resist expressing pleasure when she had worked hard and successfully for an examination. "I am rapidly developing into an infant Hercules."[3]

That she was under the surveillance of the Dean made her situation easier from a practical point of view, but psychologically more difficult. Carey saw to it that she got passing grades with little work, but she felt that she was losing the respect of all her professors. When she justified to Carey studying harder on the grounds that she was feeling better, her sister replied, "Very well! I won't pity thee as thee spends the rest of thy life in a hospital."[4] Helen responded with a fury which, she complained to her father, made her head ache more than study did.

She visited an ear specialist twice a week in Philadelphia. Dr. Theobald "is doing his best to make the obstinate hole heal up, but he hardly thinks it will. . . . He is trying a fake drum and doing what he can. . . . My hearing in that ear is no duller, but the other ear seems to be falling off." She "foolishly" told Carey. The older sister instantly insisted that she would take Helen to a different doctor. Helen refused to go, and agreed to let Carey come with her to Dr. Theobald only on condition that the voluble Dean let her do all the talking. "Carey is exaggerating, as usual. I am gay as a lark and in fine health."[5]

But Helen was finding it all the harder to study. Unable to hear the lectures, she had to copy other girls' notes.

The contrast between the pleasures she was freely allowed in her social life with the opposition and frustrations attendant on her studies finally induced Helen to consider extreme acceptance of the advice that she work only little. "To grow wise and strong and happy together" while reducing their work load, she and Lucy dreamed of extending their undergraduate Elysium. Instead of finishing in two more years, they would finish in three.[6]

Shortly before the start of her junior year, Helen informed her father that she had been thinking seriously all summer about her studies, "and what I shall do after college, and how I can earn my own living. As I have not the slightest intention of getting married — seriously, Father, this is the truth — I must provide for myself in some way. . . . The first and most important thing at present seems to be my health, and I am determined at all costs to get really well." She had been planning her courses, "and there seem to be only two alternatives, either to work hard, fifteen solid hours a week, or a fifth year. What would thee say to that, dearest Father? Thee can't possibly hate the thought more than I can." She wished to discuss it with him but not with Carey or anyone else. "Only I want thee to be serious about it, for it is a serious matter, just as if one of thy sons wanted to decide his profession or business. Dearest Dad, how I do miss thee and long to see thy dear face again.

Thee is so good and lovely and sweet that the very thought of thee and thy love is a great inspiration in my life. I long to be worthy of thee and of mother, but the standard seems to be a hopelessly high one."[7]

The letter fails to mention that Lucy was involved in the plan. The statement that Helen would never marry was obviously new to her father and is, indeed, the first found in her papers, although the decision was undoubtedly a long-pondered result of pressures exerted on her from childhood. Delaying her graduation would, of course, postpone the day when she could become self-supporting, but if she did not delay and disobeyed the orders of the authorities she might become an invalid forced into permanent dependence. Or her hearing might completely close down.

There is no inkling of how Helen intended eventually to make her living. The options open to her as a woman were few. She lacked the physical stamina or the aggressive temperament to try to storm a male bastion like law or medicine. Women who went into business for themselves were limited to small operations and, in any case, business was not in the Thomas blood. Helen would not wish to be a schoolteacher or a companion to a rich old lady — or an immoral woman. Her ambition was to create literature, but that would help little since she considered writing to make money "a kind of prostitution." Her best hope was teaching in a woman's college. However, the kind of scholarship Carey promoted and desired did not appeal to her artistic interests and ambitions.

The interpolated avowal of love for "dearest Dad" again reveals (as do her reiterated transports to Lucy) the belief inculcated in her from childhood that she would receive attention not because of her own qualities, but only in return for love.

She was indeed on the horns of a dilemma. Undertaking the harder work required by the results of her previous invalidism might bring on disaster. But if she accepted three years of semi-indolence, she might permanently relax her ability to stand up in the world. The only favorable alternative was to go bravely ahead without destroying her health, but it was far from clear that this play was on the board.

The decision was soon determined by a happening exterior to the problem: Margaret became engaged to a cousin, Morris Carey. Her marriage would leave the post of family housekeeper dangerously vacant. Although it was understood that Helen should continue without interruption her orderly progression to a degree, this was certainly not the moment to consider relaxation of studies.

Helen began the letter in which she informed Lucy of the abandonment of the plan for an extra year with one of her most high-flown panegyrics: "Dearest, there is nothing under heaven to which I do not compare you. Sometimes it is a flower, sometimes a star, and again the great glowing sun." After this preamble, she broke the news, going on to sketch a schedule of courses that would enable them both — she assumed Lucy would stay on if she did — to finish in two years without damaging their healths or "self-sacrifice in relation to society." Having assured Lucy that her heart was broken, she expressed eagerness to show her family that "in spite of everything" she "had some brains. I feel alive with energy," although "distracted with disappointment."[8]

Her ear infections spluttered along without materially increasing her deafness. She inaugurated the series of violent "colds" (as they were then called without differentiation) which were to trouble her winters for the rest of her life. But the gods, although holding invisibly in reserve a devastating thunderbolt, were on the whole kind to Helen during her remaining two years at Bryn Mawr. Like Lucy, she carried to the end, without any major relapse, the work necessary to her graduation. And there were many cheerful times.

At a pageant, some of the girls, masquerading as male undergraduates, confronted the others. The marching songs which Helen and Lucy wrote pleased Helen so much that she preserved them. Helen's was the men's song:

> *We, the undergraduates, will have none of this:*
> *Women are usurping man, and the work of his.*
> > Chorus:
> *Women should be modest, ornaments of home:*
> *Man is what the beer is, woman is the foam.* . . .
>
> *Nature never meant them like us to think and toil*
> *They must soothe the tired ones, pour on balm and oil.*
> > Chorus:
> *Women should be modest, ornaments of home:*
> *Man is what the beer is, woman is the foam.* . . .
>
> *Sitting by the cradle, pouring out the tea,*
> *Smiling at me coyly, that's the wife for me.*
> > All:
> *And me! And me! And me!*

The tone of Lucy's reply for the women is angrier:

> *All you undergraduates, you had better go;*
> *If you claim obedience, we must answer "NO."*
>   Chorus:
> *Mortify them daily, keep a stern control;*
> *Man is but the body, woman is the soul. . . .*
>
> *As a beast of burden, he can have his use;*
> *Ours to polish manners, his to polish shoes.*
>   Chorus:
> *Mortify them daily, keep a stern control;*
> *Man is but the body, woman is the soul. . . .*
>
> *Man is only brutal, quite unfit to rule;*
> *Woman is the driver, man is but the mule.*[9]

Helen's chef d'oeuvre, on which she worked much of one summer vacation, was published in the college magazine: a mild and gracious essay on Fanny Burney, primarily biographical, more literary than scholarly. She particularly adored the writings of Walter Pater (a taste she tried to hand on to me with no success), wishing in his phrase "to burn with a hard, gemlike flame." However, her own flame was not hard and gemlike but blown by the winds of youthful emotion: "I can hardly sufficiently command myself to write, for I have just finished the last pages of *Pericles and Aspasia,* and my brain is still vibrating with its marvelous sentences. . . . It is for his intellectuality," she added defensively, that she "loves" the work of Walter Savage Landor. "He seems to live in a fine, clear atmosphere apart from the world."[10]

Her own separation from the world, her blissful studies and friendships, were menaced by the turning pages on the calendar. Graduation was ever closer. Lucy, whose lawyer father possessed ample funds and whose mother was alive to keep house, was preparing to take the correct next step: a trip abroad to extend her experience and begin studies for a Ph.D. Lucy's companion was not to be Helen, but Lucy's roommate, Laurette Pease. Helen was to return to her father, the family homesteads, and the tasks of a housekeeper.

In some ways, things were easier than when last she had been immured at home. Her mother's ghost no longer walked so actively: Grace, Margaret, and Zoe, all living nearby with their husbands, helped with the housekeeping. But Helen found time hanging very heavily on her hands, and the atmosphere of the Thomas house, which had been electric (if sometimes unpleasantly so) during her childhood, was now depressing.

There was an acute shortage of money. The Thomases had always lived above their income, but this was not in the old days a serious matter since Mary's parents had always come to the rescue. When her parents died, Mary inherited an income derived from Whitall, Tatum and Company. When she died, part of this was divided among the children — Helen got a small stipend — who had their own expenses. And now, although the glassworks were flourishing, the share that came to the Whitall side was reduced as the more aggressive Tatums took over. They discharged Helen's brothers John and Bond. To cap the difficulties, the Doctor was no longer energetic enough to pay much attention to his practice, while his physician son, Harry, preferred to set up his own office.

The lack of money not only made Helen unable to join Lucy in Europe, but forced on her personal economies she found frustrating. Although far from an elaborate dresser, she felt it her duty to herself and her family and Bryn Mawr to look well. She found herself making over some clothes that one of Miss Garrett's friends, on going into mourning, had discarded. "To me," she wrote, "dressmaking is the most uninteresting thing in the world."[11]

Helen's fellow permanent inhabitants of the big house, her father and Frank, were, like her, unhappy. To James's sorrow, his most beloved son, now aged twenty, wanted to go off on his own. Aged sixty and extremely overweight, James found it hard to get around in Baltimore. He felt unloved and neglected. After he had been unwell when the Hopkins was in a financial jam, Harry wrote him, "Dr. Welch came to me and said that everyone was saying that thee was the one member of the Board of Trustees who would have been active and effective in the crisis, and spoke enthusiastically of thy interest in the university. So thee sees thee is appreciated, even if thee doesn't think so." But Dr. Thomas would not be comforted.[12]

Helen diagnosed her father's fundamental trouble as a need for a companion of his own age. At the time of her mother's death, the thought that James might marry again had filled Helen with horror, as treason to the most beautiful of spirits. Now, eager to act as matchmaker, she regretted that she could not find James a suitable second wife.

Helen herself felt no temptation to abandon celibacy. Having resolved that she would be interested only in a conquering hero, she had established for males a much higher standard than that for females. Only with difficulty could she conceal her boredom with the young men who were attracted to her by her gentle charm and redheaded beauty. Taught to regard male attraction as a snare in the path of intelligent women towards self-fulfillment, she did not repine.

A road to continuing emotional companionship that banned all impropriety and bypassed the social and sexual impediments of marriage had been part of Helen's experience ever since she had, as a small child, stayed in Leipzig with Carey and Mamie Gwinn. Lucy Donnelly had been Helen's closest companion during her happiest years. She loved Lucy, she wrote, even more than she loved her father. Lucy's letters, coming erratically now from Europe, were her talisman during her exile at home as they had for so long been.

On the last day of 1893, Helen wrote Lucy, "I have been thinking of how we can arrange to be together for the future, and what will be best for us both, and fair for the rest concerned. Of one thing I am sure: we must have it understood in our families that we are necessary to each other for happiness, aye, and usefulness too. My family are learning this lesson very thoroughly, and I lose no opportunity to impress to everyone of them that you are the dearest thing in the world to me."

Not having the Dean as a "notable precedent," Lucy would have a harder time making her family "understand . . . the idea of such a devotion between two women." However, "we cannot leave things to chance, for if we do we shall be separate and unhappy all our lives. Whoever lives with us or wherever we live, we must be together."[13]

As the months passed, Helen was so plainly "ill and unhappy and discontented" that Carey finally advanced her the money to join Lucy in European study. She was doing this, Carey explained, on the assumption that Helen would become "an advanced woman of the period and help the cause." Helen replied, "Anyone who really cares for women's education and who really understands about it, can't help considering thee its good angel." As for the cause of "higher work" for women, Helen asserted that she was "unfeignedly devoted to it."[14]

In July, 1894, little more than a year after her exile from Bryn Mawr, Helen joined Lucy in Leipzig. She anticipated six months abroad, during which she was supposed to lay the groundwork for a Ph.D. in English. However, although she expressed a desire to do whatever

Carey wished, she found the German professors dull and could not thrill to a pedantic study of Anglo-Saxon and *The Nibelungenlied.* She longed for studies more literary. Perhaps scholarship and literature could be combined. In the meanwhile, she and Lucy were imbibing "point of view and outlook." Helen postulated that "point of view is the important thing," even if only as a framework that had to be filled in.

Lucy, having been happy in Europe while Helen had been crying out in frustration from Baltimore, had felt no need to face down her mother concerning their relationship. Helen found with Lucy not only Laurette, but Lucy's younger sister Emyly. Mrs. Donnelly was expected and soon arrived. This in no way blocked Helen's pleasure. "I should be happy with Lucy on a desert island, and here in the midst of such lovely things, my joy knows no bounds." She and Lucy were "far happier than anything that ever was, I believe." Helen did feel a little guilt in relation to Carey because she was not being more serious. She would, she promised, live up to expectations soon.[15]

The little party traveled down the Rhine via Nuremberg and Bayreuth to Munich; then to northern Italy and Rome; then to Paris for the winter. Helen developed a passion for Wagner's operas, probably in part because the tumultuous sounds so triumphantly overwhelmed her deafness. At Bayreuth, she was untrue to her mother's temperance principles. Having eaten some plums that disagreed with her, Helen was "obliged to support myself through the opera with brandy."[16]

When they reached Paris in November, Helen met a man who had all the makings of a "conquering hero." His name was Bertrand Russell.

33

Exploding Horizons

HER Pearsall Smith cousins had been too old, when she was growing up, to be Helen's playmates: Mary, known to her family as Mariechen and to history as Mary Berenson, was eight years Helen's senior; the future writer Logan, seven years; Alys, who was to marry Bertrand Russell, five years. Helen's first signal of what lay ahead for her when she was older appeared dramatically in Baltimore when she was thirteen.

Mariechen was as self-willed and powerful as her senior Thomas counterpart Carey, but they were altogether differently aimed. Although basically handsome, Carey made no effort in that direction to flash. Statuesque, with golden hair and dark eyes, Mariechen made sexual flashing a specialty. She persuaded all comers that she was much more of a beauty than her heavy-faced photographs corroborate. Unconcerned with Carey's desire to demonstrate that women's minds were "at least" equal to men's, Mariechen's concern was with surging emotional self-expression. She surrounded herself with disciples of her own age, including her Thomas cousins Grace and Bond, both of whom married other members of the coterie, with eventually disastrous results.

At twenty-one, when a student at Radcliffe, Mariechen took to lecturing on her philosophy, which she called (as a paraphrase of her parents' Higher Life Movement): Higher Selfishness. At Hannah's urging, Mary Thomas, in all innocence of what would be said, gathered a large number of her own disciples together in her Baltimore living room to hear her niece and namesake speak. Helen, being present, was much impressed with Mariechen's appearance and panache. (PLATE 26)

But what Mariechen advocated had a strange sound in Mary Thomas's sanctuary. The "higher duty," the speaker argued, is to develop your own gifts. Since the pleasure taken in an activity is the measure of your power to carry it through effectively, duty consists in discarding what you find disagreeable and pursuing wholeheartedly what gives you pleasure. Mary Thomas's disciples listened with rapt attention but manifest disapproval. When Mariechen had finished, Mary Whitall rose from her chair. It was, she agreed, our duty to cultivate the talents God had given us, but the fact remained that some of our impulses could be evil and that some duties had to be carried through however unpleasant they seemed. Having thus spoken in a low but distinct voice, Mary quietly left the room "nodding" to Helen "to follow her."[1]

Mariechen had always been a law unto herself. At the age of eighteen, while a student at Smith College, at a time when Walt Whitman's poetry was generally considered crude, barbaric, and indecent, she had resolved that she would personally carry her homage to this poet at his house in Camden, New Jersey, across the Delaware from her home in Germantown. So she wrote her father. Viewing her proposal with alarm but knowing how difficult his daughter was to stop, Robert decided to spy the situation out. Appearing at the humble brick house on one of Camden's back streets, he sent up his name. Whitman was about to have the stranger sent away when he looked out the window and saw drawn up outside an elegant carriage behind two beautiful blooded horses. Whitman decided to go downstairs.

The once-flamboyant evangelist and the now-flamboyant poet hit it off at once. Robert invited Whitman to spend Christmas at Germantown when his daughter would be home. The poet stayed for three days and was back for New Year's. As the Germantown neighbors expressed shock and outrage, the disheveled "poet of the people" was soon making himself at home whenever it suited him in the elegant Smith residence, enjoying having "the servants at my beck," relishing "the over-flowing table," and sneaking around the corner to get the "tipple" his temperance-minded hosts barred. He called Mariechen his "bright, particular star," his "staunchest woman friend," and after she went to live in England, he wrote her thirty-five letters in four years. Alys was so shocked by some of his poems that she cut passages out of the book, but she smiled at him so sweetly that Whitman hailed her as "the most American, the most democratic, best calculated to measure *Leaves of Grass*. ... Oh, she is handsome too — the finest specimen of womanhood I know, almost." Although Logan was to enjoy telling the admirers of his exquisite prose that he had been deeply influenced by close friendship with Whitman, the poet dismissed the future esthete as a "nice boy."

Whitman disliked Hannah, who made no effort to hide her disapproval of *Leaves of Grass,* which she insisted encouraged "the overpowering passions" already too rampant in the male sex. However, she did not interfere with his lolling around her house and holding forth day after day.[2] She was practicing the dialectic that was to enable her in England to accept and enjoy her children's strange friends and unconventional behavior. She complimented herself on demonstrating the ultimate mother love by accepting for her children's sake persons and behavior which she pleased herself by denouncing. She was always drawn by her curiosity to eccentrics, in whose vagaries she insisted she never participated.

Mariechen's marriage drew Hannah towards England. After fluttering back and forth across the ocean and turning around on various perches, the Smiths finally, during 1889, settled there. To the dismay of Mariechen's husband, Frank Costelloe, they bought a London house within two doors of his house. Costelloe was among the intellectual founders of the Fabian Society, which by expounding evolutionary, not revolutionary, socialism, engendered the establishment of the Labour Party. He contributed to literature by defeating Bernard Shaw in a primary, and helped govern the city through his election to the London County Council. Mariechen had two daughters — the second unintentionally — named Ray and Karin,* and for the time being worked beside her husband in the political vineyard.[3]

Hannah, having picked up again with her old aristocratic evangelical friends, continued writing the religious international best-sellers and answering the flood of correspondence they stirred up among troubled women around the world. She achieved in the British temperance movement the prominent place she had occupied in the American. Alys became a traveling speaker for temperance. Logan had been miserable filling his profitable hereditary place in the glass company and, on the

---

* Ray, a feminist leader and prolific author of overserious books, was to carry the family's female primogeniture on to the next generation. Both Ray and Karin married into the Bloomsbury group. Karin became Virginia Woolf's sister-in-law, and Ray the sister-in-law of Lytton Strachey. Ray's daughter, Barbara Strachey, formerly a power in the BBC, has become the chronicler of the English family. In America, Carey's successor as the oldest female of the following generation was Margaret's daughter Millicent Carey McIntosh, who became president of Barnard College.

advice of Carey, had broken away. He grounded a new life in Balliol College, Oxford, whence he launched his efforts to fashion an immaculate prose style.

The Smiths procured, in a part of Sussex already inhabited by eccentrics and intellectuals, Friday's Hill, a large house featuring ivy and a hideous central gable. There were bedrooms for nine or ten guests, parlors, a smoking room to which the men could retire, and a picture gallery eventually filled with sixty or so canvases resulting from Logan's insistence that every guest, whatever his calling, create a contribution. There were also a billiard room, two cottages, two coach houses, a tennis court, ten acres of ground, and two hundred of woodland. Soon Friday's Hill was awash with young people talking.[4] (PLATE 24)

The group had started with Costelloe's Fabian friends, including Bernard Shaw and the Webbs, who were reinforced by Logan's esthetic friends from Oxford. Soon Friday's Hill secured a wide reputation as a pleasure ground for the gifted, where all night until after dawn anything might be said as vociferously as anyone pleased. This freedom from restraint was made possible for Englishmen because the Smiths were American. Outside established categories, with no social position the British could define, sprung from a culture notoriously free and easy, they served as catalysts who broke down taboos that normally separated Englishmen from each other. To the horror of the Spanish-born philosopher George Santayana, the Smiths called the Earl Russell "Frank," which no one else presumed to do, and the earl relished a familiarity he would have resented elsewhere. Frank's younger brother Bertrand wrote that in getting to know the Smiths "above all I enjoyed their emancipation from good taste."[5]

Two of the young men who frequented Friday's Hill eventually became members of the Smith and, by extension, the Thomas families. They were Bernhard (as he then spelt his first name) Berenson and Bertrand Russell.

Berenson appeared in 1890 as a twenty-five-year-old Bostonian of Lithuanian-Jewish origin who had achieved at Harvard such a reputation for brilliance that Mrs. Jack Gardner and other rich Bostonians were financing his trip abroad so that he might cultivate his extraordinary talents. Hannah boasted that their guest was "considered by those who know him one of the most rising young men of the world. He has devoted himself especially to pictures, and seems to know *everything* about *every* picture that has ever been painted. And the way he demolished the idols of the young people was perfectly delicious. He *proved* by the most masterly criticism that most of the old pictures they admired were either bad originals or bad copies. . . . You are sure to hear of him some day."[6]

There was no "some day" in Mariechen's reaction. She was bored with her husband and her children and the Fabian do-gooders. "When this beautiful, mysterious youth appeared, for whom nothing in the world existed except a few lines of poetry which he held to be perfect, and the pictures and music which he held to be beautiful, I felt like a dry sponge that is put in water. Instinctively I recognized that those were the real values for me, however wicked and self-indugent they might be." The call of Higher Selfishness was too strong to be denied.[7]

In the sharpest contrast with Berenson, Bertrand Russell appeared at Friday's Hill in the wake of his Uncle Rollo. A shy stripling of seventeen, he was gawky, with a conspicuous lack of chin. Yet he represented one of England's most elevated and powerful families, and would inherit a great earldom should his brother die without an heir.

Orphaned when young, Bertrand had been brought up by his grandmother. The relict of one of Queen Victoria's prime ministers, the first Earl Russell, she was reputed to have steered the British Empire by means of nocturnal scoldings. She and Bertrand's aunt, Lady Agatha, lived so altogether in the past that they did not even notice that the garden in which the boy played was sinking into ruin. "Big trees," he remembered, "lay where they fell and slowly decayed; the bushes choked the paths, and where the flowers should have been there was nothing but overgrown box hedges," His grandmother would "call me by mistake the names of people long dead." The conversation at the dinner table was of the long dead, and Bertrand was perpetually reminded of the role of his own ancestors in steering history.

His older brother Frank, when permitted to go off to school, had become reckless and disobedient. Lady Russell concluded, in the words of Santayana, that "Bertie at least must be preserved pure, religious, and affectionate. He must be fitted to take his grandfather's place as Prime Minister." Kept at home, taught by a succession of tutors too stupid to interest his brilliant intelligence, Bertrand brooded and lost his faith in the Christian religion. This heresy made him the more lonely because it precluded any confidential relationship with the elders who were his only company. "I was a solitary, shy, priggish youth. I had no experience of the social pleasures of boyhood and did not miss them."[8]

Down the years to his old age, Russell ruminated on what he considered his underprivileged upbringing. He was twenty-five when he wrote out and sent to Helen Thomas childhood recollections aimed at inciting her pity. But she chose to tease him. The "reminiscences," she began, were "awfully jolly and filled me, I must confess, with envy. Such a distinguished childhood seems thrown away on a mere mathematician! The atmosphere of sorrow in which you lived, the brooding sense of past tragedies that had so marked your grandmother's face which you loved to muse upon, ought, I feel, to have made a man of letters of you. And the neglected garden and the old oak tree were — I must not say thrown away since you were evidently keenly susceptible to their influence, but — they would look uncommonly well in the first chapter of the life of a poet.

"I find myself furthermore quite unable to pity you for the trials you suffered under. They seem to me all entirely delightful. The world in which there was nothing to prevent a lion's taking tea in the drawing room, even if on one occasion he did make you shed some tears by failing to do so,* was surely an enchanting world. And to help you to endure the misunderstanding and arbitrariness of those about you, you had your sense of their injustice; and, in spite of the cruel old gentleman, you must have felt that when you grew up, you would be free and happy, and powerful. No, I do not pity you."[9]

The seventeen-year-old Bertie found Friday's Hill, with its informality and energy and freedom for intelligent argument, a revelation. To complete the wonder, he "fell in love at first sight" with Alys: "She was at the time [he remembered] one of the most beautiful women it is possible to imagine, and gifted with a sort of imperial stateliness, for all her Quaker stock."

Alys's beauty, based on a fine complexion, blue eyes, and curly blond hair, was in no way frightening. She was not a flirt, but drew the youth gently to her side. Yet, "she was more emancipated than any young women I had ever known," having traveled across the Atlantic by herself, lecturing resolutely at temperance meetings. She was five years older than her mercurial and often morbid admirer. That she was in their relationship the leader, always competent, calm, and cheerful, would probably have annoyed the young nobleman had it been possible for him, as a Russell, ever to feel in an inferior position. And he was clearly many more times intelligent than she. When she expressed con-

---

* Bertie understood that a lion was coming to tea but the guest proved to be a Mr. Lyon.

cern about the contrast, he replied that he had plenty of brains for them both.[10]

In writing about Russell's marriage, his biographer, Ronald W. Clark, accused the Smiths of being unspeakable Americans who trapped the innocent future earl to serve their despicable social climbing. Of course, the Smiths were (as would be any English family, however high in social class) gratified by the exalted position of their daughter's suitor, yet the courtship was far from a reach-out-and-grab operation.[11] Hannah was to some extent opposed to the match, partly because she did not wish to lose her daughter and partly because she found distasteful the toploftiness of English aristocrats. Before Bertie had appeared on the scene, she had written Alys, "I am glad thee doesn't like Englishmen. . . . They have no manners for one thing, and they are arbitrary."[12] As it turned out, Bertie's close relatives became as rudely condescending (from Hannah's point of view, as insolent) to the Smith family as it was possible to be.

Alys proved to be as cautious and straitlaced about sex as Bertie then was himself. Their courtship could hardly have been more inhibited and hesitant. According to Russell, he fell in love with Alys during 1889. Although he was a continual visitor at Friday's Hill, the couple did not get to know each other well until June, 1893, when Alys visited Cambridge. Russell had by then been exposed for three years to the social and intellectual currents of the great world. Yet he and Alys did not exchange their first kisses until January, 1894. At that point, Russell was eager for marriage, but Alys refused to acknowledge that she loved him for another period of time.[13]

When told of their engagement Lady Russell and Lady Agatha insisted to Bertrand that Alys was "no lady, a baby-snatcher [he was now twenty-two], a low-class adventuress, a person incapable of all finer feelings, a woman whose vulgarity would perpetually put [him] to shame."[14] But surely an aspect of Russell's motivation was revolt. He defied the relatives who had so confined his boyhood.

The Russell family doctor was then induced to inform Bertrand that the long record of insanity in his family would, when combined with the insanity which it was assumed must be in Alys's family (she did have an Uncle Horace who suffered from melancholia), make all their children stark, raving mad. Alys and Bertie took this very seriously. After long and anguished discussions they came up with the idea that they would not have children. To that the family doctor replied in horror that using "checks" (as birth control was then called) would drive both Alys and

Bertie mad. As for Russell's waiving his conjugal rights, that was too dreadful to contemplate.[15]

It was finally decided, Hannah for once agreeing with Lady Russell, that Alys and Bertrand should be completely separated for three months. After that, if they still so desired, they might get married at once. The British ambassador to France obliged with an invitation for Russell to stay at the Paris embassy as an honorary attaché. He crossed the channel during September, 1894.[16] In early November, he received a letter:

> *Dear Mr. Russell,*
> *Ever since I first heard of Alys' engagement to you, I have been wanting to write you a letter of congratulations, since my great admiration for her almost seemed to warrant it, even though we were still strangers. But out of deference to the ordinary way of doing things I refrained, and now I write only to tell you that Miss Donnelly and I arrived in Paris yesterday, and are staying at the Pension de l'Etoile, 26 Avenue de Friedland, for the present. We shall be at home almost any day after five o'clock and shall be most pleased to see you and very grateful for any information you can give us with regard to lodgings, since you were so kind as to offer your services through Alys.*
> *Very sincerely yours,*
> *Helen W. Thomas*[17]

Alys and Helen had got to know each other well at Bryn Mawr, when she was a senior and Helen a freshman. Now Alys was banned from Paris, since, if she as much as shook hands with her fiancé, the three month's period of separation would start anew. However, as Helen was gathered into the family group, Mariechen was very much in evidence.

For some three years now, Mariechen had been making trips through Italy with Berenson, as his pupil and disciple. Together they explored obscure churches in search of exciting Renaissance paintings. They always stayed at different hotels. Costelloe, who also admired Berenson, preferred at first not to suspect the realities of the situation. Eventually, there was a showdown, but the pretense had to continue. Mariechen scorned the idea of returning home as a faithful wife — she sometimes added other lovers to Berenson and made him put up with it — and Costelloe as a Catholic could not agree to a divorce, nor could he, as a rising politician, afford a scandal. Hannah, leaping into the vacuum, took over the children and fought off, with all her passionate resolution, the efforts of their Catholic father to influence their upbringing.[18]

Alys and Mariechen — one an actual but tranquil beauty, the other only incandescent; one a serious moralist, the other a serious hedonist — disliked each other. Neither Berenson nor Alys being present in Paris, Mariechen took the opportunity for a violent flirtation with the fiancé of her exiled sister. Using the license allowed a future sister-in-law, she stayed in the same hotel with Bertrand, encouraging him sentimentally to let down her hair and to kiss her in a presumably brotherly manner. Writing two daily letters to Alys, Bertie not only described these scenes but repeated with approval, as suggestions towards reformation, Marie-chen's criticisms of her sister. When Alys responded with tearful anger, Bertie's apologies were "copious and graceful."[19]

Helen had sharp eyes, and ears that understood all that penetrated her deafness. How much she deduced we do not know, but it is clear that she took a dislike to Mariechen. After Mariechen had taken Helen and Lucy on a tour of the Italian paintings in the Louvre, Helen reported, "She has studied the subject thoroughly, and no doubt knows a great deal about it. I hardly believe that she has much originality [a reference to Berenson's influence?], but have no very definite reason for saying so, except perhaps the impression her general appearance and way of talk-ing makes." A few months later, Helen was to add, "There is a certain fatuousness about her, a desire to be always interesting, that takes the charm from her conversation."

Helen's earliest reactions to Bertrand Russell were even less enthusi-astic than her earliest reactions to Simon Flexner were to be. She found in the young man, who was several months her junior, "much conceit, much youthful eagerness in expressing opinions, and a propensity to generalize. But, of course," she added with a typical modest effort to be fair, "I am more than likely to do him an injustice, for I have had very little opportunity to judge." Still: "He and Alys seem a strange combi-nation. I wonder how she can do it!"[20] (PLATE 25)

Three weeks later, Russell wrote Alys: "I felt very bored all morning and disappointed at not seeing Mariechen" who had telegraphed post-poning an arrival. "I was wondering how on earth I should kill these last two days, when at luncheon I hit on the beautiful idea of taking Helen Thomas for another walk, by which I could combine kindness and plea-sure, and at the same time get some exercise." He got rid of a friend who "wanted to accompany me on my walk, fetched Helen and went to Co-lombin's with her, which, I think, amused her and refreshed me. Then I walked her back, and reflecting that I am going and M[ariechen] does not like her, I took her to see Edith and Bryson." Helen found Edith "perfectly delightful, and reproached me for not having spoken of her looks in describing her beforehand. . . .

"I enjoyed talking to Helen too, though I had to do most of the talk. As far as I could judge, she was pleased with me, and thought me kind though my motives were selfish. I like her better and better — there are great possibilities latent in her, of humor and shrewd observation and taste — but at present she is quite undeveloped. Being deaf and diffident, she is a little hard to draw out, but I have succeeded now and then to some extent. However, she seems to prefer the irresponsibility of listening — she doesn't like to hazard statements on her own account, except, like most of her countrywomen, to abuse the atrocious twang of the Americans she has been thrown with, and yet object to English people saying she talks almost like an English person, which I have never said to her."[21]

As the time for the wedding approached, Helen — with some heartburning because this, by depleting her funds, might shorten her period of European escape — went to the Paris shops and bought a dress. She felt it "necessary, she explained . . . to appear well-dressed for the good of the college." Carey had just been elevated from dean to president at Bryn Mawr. Furthermore, Alys's team needed all the shoring up it could get.[22]

The wedding was held in the Smith manner at a Quaker meeting, with Alys's family there in force. Bertrand's closest relatives were conspicuous by their absence. His aunt, Lady Stanley, did appear, but (so Hannah wrote) she "employed" the Quaker silences, "in dropping her stick, and shawl, and various belongings which someone had to rush forward and pick up."[23] The couple then took off for Holland and Germany.

Five or six weeks had passed since Helen first met Bertie. She thus summarized her present view of him: "His is pretty ugly to begin with, is he not? But very, very nice, I think, and very, very clever, I suppose."[24]

34

---◆⟨∞⟩◆---

Friday's Hill

CAREY again came to Helen's rescue, promising to see that she would have funds to stay in Europe until she returned to America with Lucy in August, 1895. She should pursue her studies, "have a good time, and don't grudge the theatre and opera." However, if Lucy were called home sooner, Helen should not endanger her reputation — Carey repeated the admonition twice — by staying on unchaperoned.[1]

In thanking Carey, Helen wrote that she and Lucy had celebrated by seeing Bernhardt in ten-franc seats where Helen could hear, and she added a question: was there any way she could make her living at Bryn Mawr?[2]

Fortunately for Helen, Bryn Mawr was still a Thomas preserve, even more so now that Carey was the president. Her appointment had taken Herculean efforts. A majority of the trustees were apprehensive about her. Although her achievement as dean was acknowledged to be outstanding, she was for those days an extreme feminist and they feared that she would (as she did) cut the leading strings that attached the college to the Society of Friends. But, of the ten trustees, four were still Carey's close relatives: her father, her uncle, and the two cousins. With some difficulty they won over two more trustees, achieving a majority.[3] The new president instantly appointed her dear friend Mamie to the professorship of English that Carey had held along with the deanship. Carey and Mamie were highly sympathetic to Helen's and Lucy's desire to stay together. Mamie appointed them both instructors in the "essay course [composition]." The appointments, which were to begin with the next academic year, were, Helen wrote, "like a gift from heaven."[4]

A clear road seemed to have opened ahead of Helen — but there remained her deafness. She went to a specialist in Leipzig, where she and Lucy were now studying. "He blew up my ears with some sort of a queer instrument that went up through my nose," and at once, to her delight and amazement, "I seemed to hear better." The doctor said that in a short time he could permanently improve her hearing, possibly very much. "I was delighted, of course, but upset. No one who is not deaf can know what a trial it is, what a daily hindrance and annoyance. The hope of getting rid of the trouble was almost too much for me. I was afraid of another disappointment. And yesterday already it seemed to have come. When he took the cotton and things . . . out of my ear, it had discharged a great deal, and it was terribly sensitive so that in merely wiping it out he hurt me more than I like to remember. The doctor himself looked discouraged, was unable to repeat the nose machine process, and told me to come back today."

Helen left the office with an excruciating headache and the conviction that total deafness was inevitable. "I did not sleep very much," she wrote Carey, "but this morning not all my low spirits could keep me from realizing that I felt better. My ear had stopped aching and beating, and when I went to see the doctor he was entranced." Saying that "it was getting used to the treatment . . . he repeated the blowing up, told me to continue with my gargle, and come back tomorrow. So thee sees," Helen continued to Carey, "I am in for it. My good ear is full of cotton, yet I hear quite as well as usual. Lucy says even better."

Continuing the treatment involved more money than they had — they took a third girl into the room in order to save rent — and Helen sent an anguished appeal to her father, stating that if this opportunity to avoid "such a burden through life" were lost, she would never be "happy again." The money was forthcoming. In order to complete the treatment, she had, despite warnings concerning chaperonage, to stay in Leipzig after Lucy had to leave.[5]

Her deafness, she assured Carey, was the most effective of chaperones. She now realized painfully how much the absent Lucy "stands between me and the world. . . . When I am with her, I hardly realize I am deaf, but without her I am helpless." However, in the same letter she wrote, "I am strong and healthy and twenty-four years of age. . . . I am perfectly able to take care of myself." She was, as protection against the hot weather, "growing to be a terrible toper of beer. It is the only cold thing we have to drink, and I am drinking it with rejoicing, much to my surprise."[6]

When the doctor finally dismissed her and she sailed for home, her hearing was only a little improved. "I dare say that after all it is my fate to be deaf, and I must put up with it, and it has certain advantages too, eliminates much of the commonplace and the tiresome in life, as well as much joy."[7]

Living again in a college dormitory, sharing a suite with Lucy, looking out the windows as she worked at the beloved rural landscape of Bryn Mawr, Helen felt she had regained the closest approach to paradise she had ever known. She became so infused with the college spirit that she shared the general "state of excitement" at the college basketball games. "My own interest in them surprises me. I am always first among the spectators and last to leave the field. . . . It is great fun and a complete intellectual rest. The girls do look so pretty on the field and funnily different from their usual demure selves." She hoped the President would not object to her playing on the graduate basketball team.[8]

Trying to drum a literary style into her students was arduous but for the time being amusing. "The last one I interviewed was so affected by my admonitions that she gave way to tears and ended by asking me in a tragically serious voice, 'Do you think I *think*, Miss Thomas? Do you think I think?' I assured her that I did — may I be forgiven."[9]

Both Lucy and Helen had resolved to make their contribution to the demonstration of female potentiality by becoming distinguished writers of literary prose. During the summer vacation of 1896, Helen proclaimed, "My ambition and determination to succeed grows daily greater." However, as she stayed with Grace at Cape May, she could not get started on serious writing, partly because of an intangible but rending uneasiness in the air, partly because she was taunted for her high literary ideals by Bond's wife, who under her maiden name, Edith Carpenter, had published a "historical portrait" of Lorenzo de Medici, and was currently having a novel brought out in England and America. Both books were competently written, but Helen regarded them as commercial trash.

Before the college year had opened, Helen was brought to another halt by an ailment much more menacing to her future than anyone could realize: sciatica. Although the attack passed rapidly Carey used it as a basis for urging that Helen not attempt anything beyond her work in the essay course. "I am sure thee will amount to a great deal, whatever the direction the amounting takes, and even the enjoyment of things worth caring for seems to me in itself a good deal."[10] This was hardly comforting to someone who wanted to be "a great writer."

Helen was hardly back at Bryn Mawr when Grace's letters to various members of her family revealed what had been the hidden troubles of the summer. She had assisted her husband in divorcing her. They remained close friends, Grace wrote, and she implored her family not to intervene in any way, particularly not to harass Tom.[11]

It soon became clear that Bond and Edith had testified against their sister. The grounds were denial of conjugal rights, a refusal to have sexual relations with her husband, which was legally classified as desertion. Grace, by admitting the charge, had taken what a lawyer in Hagerstown, Maryland, where the case was tried, denounced as "a very absurd, semi-crazy and hurtful position." What the lawyer defined as "a doctrine of degradation" seemed to Grace a crusade for purity.[12]

Old chickens had come home to roost. At the time of Grace's marriage, her mother, on the rampage against the "bestiality" of men, had argued that good women should refuse to marry all but the few men who, swearing to be as "pure" as women, would become "White Cross Knights." Mary had tried to prevent Grace's marriage, and had felt guilty at not having tried to persuade Edith not to marry Bond.[13]

Grace had suffered much during her pregnancies. After she had borne three children, she decided to "convert" her husband by using her strong "influence over him for the good" into becoming the equivalent of a White Cross Knight. She induced him to sign an agreement that they would for three years live "as brother and sister." When he found this more than he could accept, she had agreed, with the encouragement of Bond and Edith, to the divorce on the conviction that he would return chastened and purified.[14]

The divorce had been granted before the Thomas family was informed, but it included a thirty-day delay during which the decision could be challenged. Carey relayed to Mary Garrett news Helen had brought from Baltimore. Frank had gone to Tom "and told him he was a liar and a scoundrel who would be kicked out of gentlemen's society . . . and that if he found there was another woman in the case . . . he would kill him instantly. They have kept Frank with difficulty from executing his threat at once." James Carey Thomas's "eyes are full of tears all the time," while "Harry is ill and falls to sleep, whenever he is not talking, from exhaustion. . . . His pride had suffered a death blow, and his tender-heartedness and sympathy with Grace have completely prostrated him. . . . Even Bond has come to his senses and says he shall feel like killing himself if Tom has been deceiving Grace." Helen herself "is full of Grace and says she is hopelessly deceived; says if Tom has been in love with another woman he is an inconceivable villain and she cannot well believe it. Tom writes her [Grace] three letters a day and often telegraphs between."[15]

Grace's plea that Carey keep her hands off was of course utterly without avail. Carey sent a Garrett retainer off snooping to Hagerstown. It was suspected that Tom was living there with a Miss Higby who had nursed him through scarlet fever four years before and with whom he had often been seen. Helen became convinced of it, but Grace "disbelieves it utterly."

Grace was infuriated when Tom got word of the Garrett snooper. Bond and Edith were treated as pariahs by the other members of the family. Carey was put on the defensive when the Thomas family lawyer accused her of unwarranted interference.

Carey was, of course, not permanently squelched. She continued to inspire covert surveyance and in less than a year was able triumphantly to report that Tom had married Miss Higby and a child had appeared with unconventional speed. Helen, although she believed Carey had been right in ascertaining the facts, was frightened by the "shock" the news would bring Grace. But after Grace had been informed, Helen expressed astonishment.[16]

Carey's interference, in a manner far from her intention, had done Grace a tremendous service. It enabled her to believe that her crusade had failed not because the effort was in vain, not because Tom was weak, not because her own influence over him had not proved strong enough, but because her high-minded effort had been degraded and sullied by Carey's spying. For the rest of her life Grace hated Carey and continued to believe in the fundamental purity of her brutally severed relationship with Tom. Grace never married again. When I knew her in her later years, she was serene, sunny, and altogether charming, my favorite of my many aunts.

In England, the Russells were the Russells, but at Bryn Mawr and Johns Hopkins, the Thomases were the Thomases. Alys and Bertie were planning, for the autumn of 1896, a trip to America, primarily to meet her relatives. Russell, who had secured no invitations to lecture in his native land, hoped that while overseas he would be allowed to deliver six lectures on non-Euclidean geometry. They would be an enlargement of the dissertation that had made him a Fellow at Trinity College, Cambridge.

Russell's marriage made an invitation to speak at Bryn Mawr automatic: President Thomas gave the order. And James Carey Thomas wrote President Gilman of the Hopkins. Putting forward Bertie's most conspicuous attribute to date, that he was related to the Earl Russell, James carelessly got the relationship wrong, stating that the earl was Bertie's uncle rather than his older brother. Russell, Dr. Thomas continued, was "a rising man and said to be quite remarkable. . . . So far as I can learn, they are expecting much of him in university circles." The candidate was married to his niece. Suppressing an equivocal letter from the Master of Trinity — could Russell lecture? — James enclosed panegyrics by two of Bertie's professors.[17]

Gilman asked the advice of three distinguished American mathematicians. They were all opposed: the subject would be over the heads of the Hopkins students, and in any case Russell had no professional reputation. However, the Thomas influence prevailed.[18]

The Russells spent three months in America. They stayed with James Carey Thomas in Baltimore and M. Carey Thomas at Bryn Mawr, which Russell considered "immeasurably superior to Girton and Newnham," the women's colleges of Cambridge. It was at Bryn Mawr, so Bertie remembered, that he became really interested in Helen Thomas. "She was gentle and kind, and had very lovely red hair. I was very fond of her for a number of years."[19]

During the following summer, Helen got to know the Pearsall Smith clan in depth. With Lucy she secured lodging at a farmhouse within easy bicycle ride of Friday's Hill. Alys and Bertie, also nearby, invited them to dine every day, but Helen thought three times a week was enough.[20]

"I enjoy immensely seeing the way these people live . . . their utter lack of ceremony and their passion for croquet. Women have no rights on the croquet field, wherever else they may rule, and if you happen to be Logan's partner or Bertie's, you must do as he directs. But, I noticed the other day that poor Mr. Cobden-Sanderson, the pre-Raphaelite book-binder and Bertie's guardian, was tyrannied over in just the same way." The forty-nine-year-old creator of the famous *Kelmscott Chaucer* "arrived on his bicycle, clad in a shirt of the most wonderful blue, a white jacket and knickerbockers, carrying as his luggage, strapped on his machine, a cloth of the same blue in which was wrapped a large, lightly-tied-up sponge bag. Not a vestige of anything else. . . . He speaks wonderfully cultured English in the gentlest and most musical of voices."[21]

"Such an absurd crowd of people they are," Helen wrote, later changing the phrase to "dear, strange oddities." At Friday's Hill "there was always so much going on . . . so many people to see and talk to that it was really exhausting. Personally, I cannot understand how they endure the life they lead — for a permanency, that is. Rush, rush, rush; talk, talk, talk, with hundreds of people always around. . . . And the people do not seem to me of any interest or charm, many of them, though some, of course, are."[22]

"Bertie came out a half hour ago — I am sitting on a garden bench in the midst of flowers — and induced me to smoke a cigarette, which I rashly attempted to inhale. As a result I feel extremely dizzy and vague and am able to continue writing only by a determined effort."[23]

"Bertie I like immensely, but he is really not much better than a spoiled baby. He scolds his partners at croquet and whist, so that everyone hates to play with him, and he has to be arranged for and pampered every hour of the day. He has just taken his revenge on me for making a display as his partner, and I am inclined to scold in return."[24]

"I had an exciting talk with Bertie last evening, and as a result saw the dawn break. The consequent languor has kept me from working this morning."[25]

Although Bertie (who was a good despiser) despised Logan as an enervated poseur and esthetic snob, Helen described her devoted literary cousin as "my favorite." Logan lived on a hill above their farmhouse in what he called High Buildings, and spent the mornings and afternoons with Helen and Lucy, whom he often saw again with his family during the evenings. He escorted Helen and Lucy to London for the prowls he enjoyed through antique shops, and gave Helen some old vellum which was bound around the elegant notebooks that were later to contain her cries of pain. He seemed, Helen felt, "definitely older" than when she had seen him two years before. She recognized that the almost frenetically energetic environment of Friday's Hill was not conducive to his talent, but found him "very delightful, jolly, and heart-whole and absolutely self-expressive." She and Lucy were enchanted to have "many a literary chat with him. He shows himself quite inclined to take us into his school": his group of disciples.[26] (PLATE 26)

Logan's greatest literary admiration was also Helen's: Walter Pater of the "hard, gemlike flame." Helen could thrill to Logan's statement that all he asked for was to be remembered for "one perfect phrase." This ambition did not lead to literary creations even as sustained as short stories. His recently published first book, *A Youth of Parnassus*, an imitation of Maupassant, had died at birth of anemia.

Logan gave Helen a handmade pamphlet: three sheets of expensively heavy paper folded and sewn together to make twelve pages on which seven of his poems were written out in his autograph.[27] Many passages were provided with alternative wordings. The poems lack the springing emotion required (at least in those days) of such lyrics, and the rhythms are prose rhythms.

Although he did publish some verse, Logan realized that his calling was not to be a poet. As Helen sat at his feet, he was perfecting the specialty that would carve for him a small but lasting niche in English literature. A few years later, he had privately printed three hundred copies of a little book he called *Trivia*. It consisted of very short essays or rather impressions, the prose refined and polished to the ultimate degree. They are urbane in the exact dictionary sense: "having the manners and refinement characteristic of a town."

Helen's natural literary tendency was, in the romantic manner, to write ecstatically of nature — the sights and sensations of the countryside. Thus, a year or so before her stay near Friday's Hill, she had written Carey, "In the afternoons I take my boots and wander far up the beach at low tide to where it turns and the waves break many yards out over a sandbank, and rush foaming shoreward. Then I read and muse and even write, conscious all the while of the changing light and shade on the water and the incoming tide. I return home late, fairly drunk with the blueness of the air."[28]

Logan could find pleasure in nature only if it called things to mind other than itself: "Cricketers on village greens, haymakers in the evening sunshine, small boats sailing before the wind — all these create in me the illusion of happiness, as if a land of cloudless pleasure, a piece of the old Golden World, were hidden not in far seas, as poets have imagined, but here, close at hand, if I could find it, in some English valley. Certain grassy roads seem to lead through the forest thither: the wild pigeons talk of it behind the woods."[29]

After the gems Logan was preparing for *Trivia* had been laboriously worked out on paper, he would carry the little sheets downhill to the farmhouse where Helen and Lucy resided. In discussion with the two sympathetic young women, he decided what to preserve, what to polish further, what to discard. After the book was published, Logan wrote his two friends that he considered them the "godmothers" of *Trivia*.[30]

Gently encouraged by Logan, his disciples showed him, for criticism, their own literary efforts. Helen was enchanted to have such a guide. Although the middle-aged, distant, ironic observer was basically unlike the young woman who was trying to break down the barriers that separated her from the common experiences of mankind, Helen and Logan did share a delighted appreciation of the human comedy. And Logan, as an utterly self-conscious writer, was able to describe exactly how he achieved his effects. Helen found herself falling under his literary spell.

After some six weeks at Friday's Hill, Helen and Lucy went on to Winchester. Alys gave them a letter to the scatterbrained wife of the vice-principal of the "college," a famous boy's school. No more than glancing at the letter, Mrs. Richardson decided that Helen and Lucy must be friends of Bertie's older brother, Lord Russell. She would bring them instantly together.

Lord Russell was known as "the wicked earl" because, unlike other aristocrats, he flaunted his sexual affairs in the face of the public, so much so that he came to be tried for bigamy in the House of Lords, the only tribunal commensurate with his rank. Helen had undoubtedly met some of the dried-out drunkards and reformed pickpockets who were part of her mother's temperance troupe, but she had never associated with an acknowledged and unrepentant villain. Always seeking "copy" to write about, she was full of eagerness to examine the wicked earl.

Bemused "at first" by Lord Russell's "handsome face, his soft voice and charming enunciation," finding him "irreproachable in words and action," Helen concluded that, "wrapped up in himself and his own affairs, blind to everything else," he surrounded himself with such an "impenetrable atmosphere" that she was not even sure that she could diagnose in him "lack of moral sense."

That Sunday the lascivious earl escorted the American redhead and her friend "up the hill behind the town to a beautiful old church." Having seated the ladies, he vanished and reappeared to Helen's "amusement" in a surplice. She was fascinated to see the aristocratic villain, his position in the community in no way undermined by his evil reputation, sit "up with the vicar in the chair of holiness." He "actually read the lesson." Afterwards, while pointing out to Helen and Lucy the antiquities in the church, he "showed himself in every way polite."

But, so Helen continued to her father, "Lord Russell was not the greatest swell we saw at Mrs. Richardson's." The little Duke of Albany and Prince Alex of Battenberg were visiting in preparation for attending the college. Helen and Lucy joined the group that went with King Edward's sons to a special concert given for them by the boys' choir. "It was fine to hear the boys shout as our party headed by the Royal Highnesses came in. How charmingly the boys did sing! I enjoyed hearing them as much as I enjoyed having my chair kicked throughout the evening by Prince Alexander — he sat immediately behind me. The princes were seven and nine years old, very small for their ages, and, especially Battenberg, dull-looking. But they behaved so simply and sweetly, seemed to take such genuine pleasure at the singing that my heart went out to them."[31]

Before she sailed home in mid-August, Helen undertook a brief farewell visit to Friday's Hill, "whether," she wrote, "for good or evil who can tell." Why did she see possibilities of evil?[32]

Before that summer, Helen had always dismissed the male sex as of secondary importance for her life. But at Friday's Hill she had become fascinated by two extremely able men. Very different, each spoke powerfuly to a different part of her nature.

In no way physically disturbing, Logan appealed to the esthete, the bluestocking. Unattracted by women, he seemed superior to sex, like the White Cross Knights her mother had envisioned. But his literary influence was seductive, and his dicta, being contrary to her natural interests and talents, must have been disturbing.

While Logan was withdrawing from the world, Bertie was always reaching out. During nighttime conversations with Helen that lasted until dawn, his mind would kindle again and again with brilliant, voluble, and eloquently expressed conceptions and generalizations concerning any aspect that happened to occur to him of human thought or behavior. As Helen listened and threw in her own comments, it was impossible for her not to recognize that his interest in her was sexual as well as — perhaps more than — intellectual. And what of her interest in him? Since he was the husband of her close friend and near relative, how could Bertrand Russell conceivably be her "conquering hero"?

35

·⋅◦∞◦⋅·

Death of a Father

O N the morning of November 10, 1897, less than three months after Helen had returned from Friday's Hill, President Thomas's usually languorous friend, Mamie Gwinn, was seen hurrying across the Bryn Mawr campus. Having entered Denbeigh Hall, she knocked on the door of a faculty suite and had a few words with Lucy Donnelly. A minute or two later, Helen was awakened "to see Lucy's white face above me, and hear from her lips that Father was dead."[1]

She rushed to join Carey in catching the train. When they reached Baltimore they were "really surprised" to discover that what they had considered a private errand of mourning was part of a city-wide lamentation. The three major Baltimore newspapers, in front-page stories and in editorials, were describing James Carey Thomas as "one of the best-known men in Baltimore." "Dr. Thomas was a kindly man and a courteous gentleman of the old school. His mission in life was to aid others, and he never wavered in what he considered his duty." "He was an earnest advocate of the best education for both sexes." "All who came in contact with him recognized that he was in every way a good, a noble, and a manly man." His contributions to the public weal, dilated on in paragraph after paragraph, amazed his daughters, who had been hardly conscious of his accomplishments.[2]

As soon as Helen reached the house, "I went up to his room and found there a quietness his voice would not break, his closed eyes, his folded hands. And we stood there in silence, his children, and Harry stood at a distance, the light from the window coming in on his bright hair. And suddenly he bent his head and wept, and we all wept together."[3]

James's love for flowers being widely known in Baltimore, hundreds of people had the same inspiration: florists' delivery boys lined up at the door. (Two wagons had to be hired to carry the blooms to the cemetery.) A stream of solemn individuals appeared carrying resolutions. It became a problem to find time for all the memorial meetings at the many institutions James had led. Helen heard that when James's death was announced to the pastoral committee gathered at the Quaker Meeting House, "Mrs. Watkins fainted away and many people fell back in their chairs sobbing."[4]

Helen was particularly impressed at "the love and grief and respect shown for him on every side by people of all classes." The boys from the poorer part of town that he had befriended and advised were now men and had not forgotten. "The very barber who shaved Mr. Williams said that Father's death was felt by him as a personal grief."[5]

Dr. Welch was quoted to Helen as having said, "the medical school had lost its best and most efficient friend. . . . President Gilman mourns as much for the university as for us." Dr. Osler, so Carey recorded, "dismissed his class . . . telling them that the man they were indebted to for the medical school had died."[6]

Carey was, as always, eager to run things, but the arrangement of the father's obsequies was firmly assumed by the sons — Harry with the help of Bond. Carey was chagrined by the obvious contrast with public reactions to her mother's death. There was no possibility of holding James's funeral where Mary's had taken place: the two linked parlors in the Thomas home. The Quaker Meeting House had to be requisitioned, and it proved hardly able to contain the crowd. Carey admitted that she "could not help caring" about "the love shown by everyone. I know how much it would have pleased him. He lived so much for people and among them."[7]

At the Hopkins, there was a memorial meeting at which Dr. Welch spoke on the "services of Dr. Thomas to medical education."*[8] At the funeral, Drs. Welch and Osler were pallbearers. The trustees and professors from the Hopkins marched in a body to the Quaker Meeting House.[9] Flexner, now an associate professor, saw among the chief mourners his companion Harry.

Helen sat there "absolutely stone deaf" from emotion and fatigue.

---

* Dr. Welch probably spoke extemporaneously since no manuscript survives.

But it was clear that the proceedings moved at a much more measured, less frenzied pace than they had at her mother's funeral. Helen could not know what it portended when there was a stirring among her sisters and the other women sitting around her, and a sudden burst of tears. As Carey put it, Rufus Jones, the speaker, "completely upset us all by speaking of Father's reunion with Mother after a nine-year separation, and of her work in Baltimore, etc. . . . I know it is foolish and unreasonable, but it was a solid comfort to me that, if the resurrection angel should sound his trumpet, Father would rise out of the grave with *one* wife not *two*. Mother so cared about his not marrying again."[10]

After the funeral, Helen "stayed for a long time in his room, trying to gather strength to look at the world as it is without him. . . . I fear I did not know how much I loved him."[11]

What Helen had learned about her father's achievements and the widespread love he had inspired did not in any way lessen her idolatry for her mother. Mary remained in her memory the romance, the inspiration, and the excitement of her upbringing. She believed always, and perhaps with reason, that had her mother received a man's education, had she not been tied down by so many children, she would have sailed as an iridescent trajectory across skies wider than had ever opened out to her father.

However, it was now altogether clear that James had been unfairly belittled in his own household, particularly on the women's side, and that Helen's own childhood had been impoverished by a lack of realization of what a noble and effective man her father was. This recognition of injustice, and the sense of personal loss, heightened surely by her recent awakening at Friday's Hill to the power and abilities of other males, she never stated in words, but it worked itself out in her subsequent career. During Helen's own marriage, the achievements of her husband were made the keystone of the domestic arch. Her sons were brought up with an overwhelming sense of the importance and nobility of their father's career, which, so she taught them, it was the basic function of the household to facilitate.

36

———— ·•◦∞◦•· ————

The Vellum Sanctuary

J AMES Carey Thomas, who undoubtedly had drawn his will before
Grace's debacle, left twice as much to his sickly and unmarried
daughter Helen as to his other children.[1] With what she had already inherited from her mother, this made her financially independent within
the way of life she preferred. She found it a release not only to be free of
monetary dependence on Carey, but gradually to pay back what she had
already received. Thus she removed her sister from any further implication of being her surrogate mother.

The family homestead in Baltimore had now become the private, if
hospitable, residence of Harry and Zoe. Helen was glad to spend the
summer vacation in England with Lucy and her Smith cousins. Joining
the Russells in Cambridge, she had "a most enchanting time. A dinner
party every evening, and on most days a luncheon and a tea. Alys and
Bertie are great swells. We dined with the Vice-Chancellor and a number of professors, and when Beatrice Creighton was staying with Alys,
she gave a most smart dinner. I saw a lot of amusing types, heard lots of
stories, and was thoroughly well entertained. In my black evening dress
I was supposed, I believe, to uphold the reputation of the family for
good looks. I remembered that I had a sister [Carey] painted by Sargent, and did my best. Alys and Bertie were, I think, sweeter than ever
before. We had endless discussions, and I feel quite stirred up intellec-
tually. Bertie is always an inspiring talker."[2]

Bertie's most intimate friend and collaborator was the great mathematician Alfred North Whitehead. The Russells and the Whiteheads, deciding on a junket to Paris, invited Helen and Lucy to come along. But

Lucy did not feel strong enough to endure "all the fatigue incident on being one of so energetic a party." Helen took her for a few weeks' rest in a small French town, and then they joined the Smith circle that clustered around Friday's Hill.

Logan had founded "The Hermits," a secret society devoted to esthetic and anticlerical whimsy. He invited Helen to a "Dionite Service," in which he played the part of the high priest. Helen reported to Carey that he "read passages from Pater and Don Quixote, and we read responses from the pastoral parts of Shakespeare. It was sufficiently ridiculous, priest, audience, and all. Two young Cambridge men and Mariechen's Mr. Blades [Wilfred Blaydes] assisted. I wonder what they thought."

Although Mariechen was still Mrs. Costelloe and primarily living with Berenson, she sought further variety. "She looked lovely, being dressed with great care for this same Mr. Blades, and poses beautifully with his immense great dane dog. Stretched flat on her back, she smoked cigarettes and repeats poetry, the dog stretched beside her, or she runs with him across the lawn. It sounds unbecoming to her figure [Mariechen was tall and heavy], I acknowledge, but somehow it really isn't. Mr. Blades seems harmless enough, wears an eyeglass [monocle] and sits with his mouth open, has languishing dark eyes, and lisps. Grace is shocked by his attentions to Mariechen, but if you are going to accept Mariechen at all, you must accept her ways, charming no doubt but not exactly conventional. As for me, being perfectly independent of her and undisapproving, [I] rejoice in the spectacle of her love of life. She has a fortunate temperament but, I think, no intelligence."[3]

"I must confess," Helen continued, "that I am getting terribly tired of conversation, especially the same conversation every day. . . . My deafness grows worse with too much exercise." She was sick of laughing because other people laughed, of smiling assent although she could not hear what someone was saying to her. Professor Whitehead, she complained, was capable of holding forth for two hours without stopping — and she could not hear a word.

Near one extremity of the Bryn Mawr campus, hammering presaged what was to be Helen's home until she married. At Low Buildings (named after Logan's High Buildings?), Helen and Lucy rented a top-floor flat with a porch that looked out over the kind of bucolic landscape Helen most loved.

That they had to move in before the plaster dried was the one drawback. Helen immediately started a series of severe colds. When she blamed them on the dampness, Carey was furious at her for maligning the first faculty residence built at Bryn Mawr. Helen, Carey insisted, was suffering for not having taken care of her health. Lest she die of consumption, she should wear nothing but high-necked gowns and never work more than five hours a day. Since this advice was not accompanied by any curtailing of her teaching duties, the implication was that she should abandon her independent writing.[4]

Helen was also furious on another account. Logan had given her and Lucy advice on how to teach composition, but Mamie Gwinn, doubly powerful as Carey's intimate and professor of English, scorned Logan's advice. She insisted that composition be taught her own way. Helen offered to resign. Carey appealed to Logan to persuade her sister to stay on, describing "in glowing terms [so Logan reported to Helen] thy influence and success." But it was Logan's conviction that Helen should have "lots of leisure to meditate and write." It was decided that she would take "a free year" in which to cultivate her muse.[5]

The influence of Logan was manifest in Helen's decision that the most salubrious environment for the creation of literature was isolation. "Oh," he wrote Helen, "the problems that will meet thee on the way, the chasm that will yawn, the ghost that will mock thee! All the strong phrases — and, alas, there are none too strong — refer to the question of form. The novel — well, there's something wrong about the novel, something off color and cheap. Writing short stories is like firing pistols. The prose poem is an affectation, and a real poet — one has to be born a poet." Polishing one's own memories and sentiments was "the best thing for people merely of temperament and talent. But, as long as one can enjoy the chance [that] things in life could mature, one is really all right, and if a gracious heaven gives in addition the chance, sometimes, of producing something however slight than can live — well, the adventure is a noble one and the reward great."[6]

Helen was to remain in her flat at Low Buildings as the campus emptied out for the summer. Two years before, she had procured in London with Logan's encouragement a pair of small, thick volumes of blank paper bound in vellum. This was to be the "sanctuary" into which she would copy her best literary flights. The soft, handmade pages remained untouched until July 15, 1890, when she could begin by recording the departure of Lucy.

"Dark, slim, exquisite, impossible to understand," Lucy was off to join on the seashore "another slender, dark-haired person as finely organized as she. What place have I with them? And yet there must be something in the mere coarseness of my vitality that attracts. . . ."

Red-haired Helen was anything but dark and her Thomas figure could never seem exquisite or slim. Far from wishing to be enigmatic, she prided herself on frank, level-eyed vision. Even as she began her experiment, she suspected that Logan's advice did not really apply to her: "For me the sun, the visiting moon, the [illegible] earth. For me the peerless strong beat, the swift coursing of the blood, the sound of rhythmical words."[7]

In mid-August, Helen wrote, "Out comes the sun and in comes Helen to sing her little noiseless paean of delight in the visible beauty of things. What a world of busy life down among the hydrangea blossoms. Bees pushing their heads deep into the honey-sweet fragrance, wasps with brown wings crawling over the flowers, and light-hovering butterflies making a bright patch against the whiteness."

On September 1: "Well, well, here I am into September with little accomplished. . . . I have been mourning that more than anything else in the world I care for external nature. A tree, a bit of sky and grass, a brook to reflect the clouds during daytime and dim the stars at night, these make up a heaven for me. And with contentment comes lassitude, and I have my work to do."

Early in October: "I have been reading, in my little old leather-bound book on the coarse lined paper in the scrawling handwriting, the records of my old passionate moments, and so deeply has the memory of these affected me — poor little wretched passionate girl crying out in the past! — that my hand trembles at this moment as I write. I am calmer now that I have moved into this leather-bound sanctuary, but the fire within me burns still."

In early November: "I have rebelled against the idleness and the pain, have lost my poise, have descended into that chamber of the mind into which the whirlwind blows. Why is it, I wonder, that one's peace is so difficult of attainment, so hard to be kept when attained? I stumble and fall and rise up and walk on, only to stumble again, and my face and hands are bruised, and almost, almost, my resolution falters. Why was I born so unlike the rest of the world, and why has this new pain been given me to bear? I must cast off reflection and go to work. Work, work, work: in that there is quietness, in that there is peace, and calmness, and rest."

A few days later: "My back is free of pain and my rebellious thoughts and desires, my wayward passions, closed tight in their cave. My will that has forced them back sits like King Aeolis but with sterner features.

He is too precariously lord to hold his scepter with anything gentler than a clutch."

She "rested upon nature," Helen wrote, because "in my conception," its beauty was without "imperfection . . . no restlessness, no pain. But in human relations, the most beautiful, what straining, what striving, what misunderstanding, what ruthlessness, what anguish! . . . And the heart of a woman, when laid bare, what a terrible thing it is! . . .

"No worse, of course, than the heart of man, but to a woman men are alien creatures, at least so tradition says, and the knowledge of the hidden depths of their natures comes with less of a shock, though to a philosopher human nature is one, and man and woman essentially alike in motive and desire. That is my creed, at least. I believe that if we know more we should discover more the oneness. And yet I am very ignorant."

During Christmas vacation in Baltimore, Helen attended an evening party at Harry's. "It is strange to think," she wrote years later, "that I first saw my future husband with a teacup in his hand, making himself agreeable to my sister-in-law. And it is disconcerting to remember that my inner comment was 'How did Zoe make such friends with so clever-looking a man?' "

Helen discovered that Dr. Flexner lived near Bryn Mawr, having been for four months at the University of Pennsylvania. He said that he had heard of the beauties of the Bryn Mawr campus and would like to see them. Helen offered to give him tea. He answered laughingly that he preferred beer. To this Helen replied that it might not be ladylike to serve beer, but beer he should have. Obviously, they discussed other subjects. He promised to get in touch with her when they were both back in Pennsylvania.[8]

In the meantime, Helen confided to her vellum-bound book: "Here I am back at my desk in [illegible] at my own idleness and impotence. Am heartily sick of that confounded story I am writing of Michael Farnell and Faust and Marguerite, drat them — that I can hardly bear to come near my table where they are entombed — poor pale corpses that won't be galvanized into life! I dare say, I stain this fair white handmade paper to no purpose. It speaks to me clearly of Logan, and reproaches me for my coarse realistic tendency, my slapdash diction, the discord and jerk — one can't call it rhythm — which is not rhythmical in my sentences. And *Bah*, I say, 'What does it matter?' "

Consider "the mass of people in the world: sufferers from the Boer

War, engine drivers, miners, capitalists, messenger boys, mothers nursing babies, beauties before their mirrors — all the striving and struggling, laughter, tears, kisses, scorn, and despair, and over all the quiet golden sunlight." And she was disquieted "because a morning of mine may be wasted! Because in the great shout that goes up from mankind my weak protesting voice is silenced. But I feel my voice alive (like a bird with struggling wings) in my throat, and I must, if I have strength, loosen that bird."[9]

She had admonished herself: "I must practice my hand at the depiction of people. I have done so little of it and do it so badly. Perhaps a trial or two would make it go better." She had a particular need to describe men. Simon Flexner, as an exotic in her world, would make fine "copy" — and he was coming to tea that Saturday.[10]

I was already at work on this book when I discovered, hidden away in a dark corner of a closet, my mother's vellum-bound notebooks. They had obviously once been in a humbler hiding place: the tops of the pages were crumbling with mildew, and the bindings seemed to have been gnawed by rats. Opening a volume at random, I found facing me, to my amazement, a character sketch of my father, written by my mother within a few hours of their first private meeting.

"After he had left," so the text ran, "I sat and thought about the little man with whom I had been laughing and talking for nearly two hours, and I found myself admiring and pitying him at the same time. Admiring the courage and determination with which he was carving out for himself success in his own special line, and pitying him for what seemed the dreariness of his existence and for the lack of really great powers of intelligence or of really fine perceptions [he knew almost nothing about literature] which would always prevent his attaining true distinction. He could only be a skilled intellectual machine, a builder after designs of others, never in any, even the smallest, sense an artist, a creator.

"Two things I seemed to see at war in him: a downright self-assertiveness and belief in his own way of doing things, which produces the effect of impulsiveness, is perhaps accompanied by it, and over against this, intellectual quickness to perceive where he has made a mistake and an intense realization of the necessity for being politic. Add to these things a keen sense of right and wrong, a deep moral seriousness, a feeling of moral responsibility. One can easily fancy what fits of despondency he must have to live through, how he must grit his teeth and curse his fate, and finally resign himself.

"Already he has greatly advanced his fortunes, but the time when he can afford to behave frankly, regardless of consequences, is yet at a distance. He has not an assured position. Moreover, he is less well bred than the people about him; whether he is aware of it or not — as of course he is not — the fact adds to the friction of his existence."[11]

Two days later, and continuing the same page, Helen wrote: "The only way to keep calm is to keep occupied, and when I have sworn for three hours each day to write or do nothing, how can I when the ideas won't come, when I can't go on with my twaddling story, how can I, I ask, help thinking? How can I help musing upon my own incapacity for living, my own aching difference from other people in the world, upon Lucy's own unhappiness. If I were a man, I should take to drinking. I wonder why I don't throw the whole thing up, why I don't once and for all cast ambition from me? The answer is simple enough. I suppose I can't change my nature. Ambition is in my blood, and seriousness of purpose. . . .

"I can almost feel it in my heart to wish I were the veriest empty head with a simple, loving nature and soft blue eyes to make myself beloved, a gentle hand and a gentle voice. Then at least I should know the ordinary joys. Mine would be the sorrows with which the world sympathizes, and I could fall back upon the common consolations as upon a soft couch. But who pities Caliban roaring out under the pinches of the fairies?"[12]

VII

Approaching Lives

37

<hr>

Settling In at Philadelphia

S IMON Flexner had arrived at Philadelphia early in September, 1899, some four months before he came to know Helen Thomas. An invader, so he had been given cause to fear, in hostile territory, he sought reassurance by reminding himself that he was no longer the "provincial" who had first appeared at Baltimore. At the Hopkins, he had spent years "among a superior group of people, who gave me every opportunity and treated me with consideration. I also got to Europe a number of times, except for the first time as summer vacation. It was a good thing to have seen something of the Old World, and a good thing . . . to have had a glimpse of the East. . . . I could indulge the hope that, transplanted to Philadelphia, I should not be too strange."[1]

He had, while absent in the Philippines, been elected to the University Club, one of the city's major clubs, and also to the Medical Faculty Club. He was not informed that admission to the Faculty Club, usually automatic, had been secured for him only through a threat of all the laboratory men that otherwise they would resign. However, the leading anti-Semite, Dr. White, was discourteous towards him almost to the point of insult, and, despite Flexner's desire to ignore such considerations, he sensed resentment elsewhere.

To his family Simon wrote, "Perhaps it is better that this is so. I cannot complain of much hindrance before in my laboratory and professional career, which probably accounts for an abnormal softness of the sensitive muscle."[2] He decided to move with care, particularly at faculty meetings. He had never attended such meetings before — Welch had represented pathology at the Hopkins — and found it easy to keep his mouth shut.

But basically he could not walk with care because what he believed it his duty to achieve was for the University of Pennsylvania revolutionary. The very building opposed his intentions: it was replete with large auditoria for lectures, but offered only cramped space for laboratories. "My quarters for pathology consisted of one large, well-lighted room which was the professor's room. I made it also the room for experiments. . . . There was a much smaller room for the assistants, and a class room for the microscopical course capable of seating about one half of the class, so that the exercises had to be repeated."[3]

During Flexner's absence in the Philippines, a major impediment was raised against his methods of teaching and research. The university had the traditional right to appoint a pathologist at Blockley, the municipal hospital and almshouse that was close to the campus. It offered, in Flexner's opinion, "the most valuable pathological material in the city." But Flexner's predecessors had made little use of the opportunities presented by autopsies at Blockley to renew their stock of specimens for teaching, or to raise questions for research. When the post of pathologist became vacant, they did not hold it open for the new professor of pathology, but appointed a holdover from the old regime. Welch called it "a shame that the university faculty let [Henry W.] Cattell slip in during your absence. . . . It would seem they ought to have prevented it, even if politics were controlling."[4]

Simon wrote bravely to his family, "I am not downcast." He would find a way around "either by compelling part of this material or finding other sources that can be developed." He called on Dr. de Costa, a university trustee who was "a reigning medical influence." De Costa was chilly and sent him on to Cattell. Cattell was frosty. He eventually "sent a few fragments, quite useless for demonstration."[5]

Flexner wrote passionately to Welch asking if he could borrow duplicate specimens from the Hopkins. Welch, not realizing the extremity of Flexner's eagerness, answered with a joke that did not go down well. He quickly picked up the mistake, writing that he had not supposed Flexner "needed assurance," that he should "feel at liberty to help yourself to what you want." Welch added reassuringly, although Flexner had not been at the university for more than a month, "I hear the best accounts from various sources of your success in Philadelphia, of which indeed I never had doubt."[6]

To his family, Flexner wrote that Provost Harrison and Dean Marshall were "cordial. . . . They are not far behind in filling my simple requests." However, "there are things they will have to learn before I can get everything I want or think I should have."[7]

Flexner regretted that he had not returned from Manila in time "to look around" for assistants, but it may have been just as well that he was thus prevented from outraging at the very start the medical school's tradition of employing only its own. He wrote unenthusiastically, "There are a few good men here, more or less interested in pathology." He employed part time two clinicians, one being David Reisman, who was to become a well-known Philadelphia practitioner.[8]

Flexner's class was vastly larger than any he had known at the Hopkins — some one hundred and fifty. They gave him a warm welcome when he first appeared on the platform, clapping and stamping. Some even whistled. He lectured three mornings a week and on Saturday mornings held a "quiz" at which attendance was voluntary. His objective in asking questions was not to stump the students but to make sure that everything was understood. At first, only a few appeared, but when his intentions became clear, almost the whole class attended.[9]

The professors traditionally assigned the textbooks, often written by themselves. Over Flexner hung the formerly used and inadequate text by Stengel, who, whenever they met, eyed him with hostility. Flexner got out of the quandary by handing around several textbooks, including Stengel's, and asking the students themselves to choose.

At the university library, there was a complete lack of medical works. Morris Jastrow, the librarian as well as the professor of Semitic languages, explained that there had been no demand. The medical professors used the library of the College of Physicians and the students were not encouraged to go beyond their textbooks. Jastrow believed that there were some medical volumes in the cellar. Exhumed, they proved to be out of date and worthless.

Jastrow said that he would gladly assign to medicine an alcove like those allotted to the other disciplines — that is, if Flexner could find money to buy the books. The newcomer decided it would be more tactful to wait for his second year. When finally approached, Provost Harrison replied that there was no appropriation. However, if Flexner would tell him what was needed, he would raise the money privately. Flexner suspected that Harrison gave the one thousand dollars himself. The alcove was soon established. As time went on, more and more students were attracted until they often overflowed the alcove into the general reading room.[10]

Flexner gladly accepted living quarters in a conveniently located dormitory. He was not charged for his bedroom, living room, and bath since he consented to act as a proctor. His principal duty was to approve or disapprove requests from students to entertain young ladies in their rooms, usually on Sundays or holidays. Having earned the reputation of being "easy," he was appealed to by students from distant entries. No complaints concerning misbehavior ever came to him.

Flexner had been at the university less than two months, when one day, as he was relaxing in his quarters, a knock sounded on his door. To his amazement, he saw standing in the hall, somewhat the worse for travel, bowing formally and grinning with anticipatory pleasure of a warm welcome, the diminutive Japanese bacteriologist he had met briefly in Tokyo. Invited in, Hideyo Noguchi unpacked from his scanty luggage present after present, each of which he handed to Flexner with much gesticulation. It finally developed that he had set off too quickly to receive a letter Flexner had written, telling him not to come as there was no opening in Philadelphia. This made no difference, Noguchi commented, beaming, since here he was.

When Flexner asked what he intended to do, Noguchi asked whether this was not America, the land of opportunity? And was he not with Flexner? To questions concerning money, Noguchi replied that he had none with him: he had entrusted his money to a secretary at the Japanese legation whom he had met on the ship. Where was his overcoat? — it was cold outside. With a cheerful grin, Noguchi confided that he had not expected America to be cold.

Flexner bought his uninvited guest an overcoat, found him cheap lodgings, and got in touch with the Japanese legation. Noguchi's money proved to be less than twenty dollars.

Putting Noguchi temporarily on an allowance of twenty-five dollars a month, Flexner spoke to Provost Harrison, who responded that there was no place for Noguchi at the university. Flexner then wrote to the Japanese consul general in New York, who replied that he could do nothing. The consul general in Philadelphia did come up with a suggestion: if Noguchi could hold out till summer began, he could become a waiter at a Japanese garden that was to open outside Philadelphia.[11]

There was nothing to do but take Noguchi into Flexner's laboratory and give him a bacteriological problem to solve. Noguchi ended up with tangled results because he had got his cultures contaminated at the start. "I was pretty severe with him and things improved."[12] There was something about this indomitable yet gentle, boyish man that soon induced Flexner to risk his own most important personal connection in Philadelphia, Dr. Weir Mitchell.

*   *   *

"Everyone in medicine in that day," Flexner wrote, "knew of Dr. Mitchell's distinction in medicine, neurology, and even as a novelist." At the University of Pennsylvania he was very powerful. Flexner had been led to believe (incorrectly) that Mitchell had opposed his appointment. He was thus surprised when Mitchell had dropped in at his laboratory. "He was a highly courteous person and welcomed me to the university."

Mitchell periodically called on Flexner. Many years before, he had made a study of the effects of snake venom on human tissues, which he had had elaborately published. Finding that Flexner's recent discoveries concerning bacterial poisons provided a base on which to proceed, Mitchell suggested that further research "along the lines of the new experimental immunology" would be fruitful. Mitchell offered to put up the money, and Flexner promised to keep an eye out for an able assistant who would carry through the day-to-day labor.[13]

Here was a chance to employ Noguchi. Mitchell was taken with the young Japanese (he was to regard Noguchi as his own discovery), and arranged that a "splendid lot of rattlesnakes" be shipped from Florida. This was January or February, 1900. The snakes arrived frozen stiff. But soon another lot arrived in good condition.

Being untrained in immunology, Noguchi needed daily supervison. In his perpetual enthusiasm, he combined carelessness with brilliant technique. He showed himself to be the most rapid of learners and possessed that imaginative insight which is the invaluable but unpredictable element in scientific discovery. He and Flexner cooperated amicably and easily.[14]

When Flexner moved on to the Rockefeller Institute, the only member of his Philadelphia group he took with him was Noguchi. The Japanese scientist became a leading bacteriologist, famous for his discoveries concerning syphilis and yellow fever. Although Noguchi was only thirteen years younger, Flexner came to feel for him a paternal affection and solicitude that continued until Noguchi's death in 1928, which Flexner deeply mourned. His departed friend and disciple, Flexner wrote in *Science*, was characterized by "a noble simplicity and dignity of personality." Noguchi was "gifted with a clear, apprehensive mind; his technical skill was phenomenal; his industry was extraordinary. His perspicacious intellect enabled him to state a problem sharply; his resourcefulness in devising means to ends prevented him from being blocked by methodical obstacles; his inexhaustible industry and physical prowess, which made virtually two days of one, immensely extended his range of activities." Since "his mind was many-tracked," he could keep several problems going at one time.[15]

Flexner was thrown naturally with his colleagues at the Medical Faculty Club, to which he had been so perilously admitted. They lunched together every day, and dinners were given by members in succession, according to rules aimed at keeping the prosperous from making displays unattainable by those less so. "Shop was not talked at these dinners which cultivated the lighter side of companionship." As a veteran of the inveterate drinking occasions in Baltimore, Flexner noted that the "gaiety" was "without hilariousness."

Flexner soon concluded that Philadelphia deserved its reputation "as perhaps the pleasantest city from the medical or professional standpoint." Among "the delights of the place were the medical societies and, notably, the College of Physicians and the Pathological Society." In both, Flexner was immediately active, being called on to deliver scientific papers, and getting to know the cream of the Philadelphia profession.

Much more than in Baltimore, Flexner's "life was diversified" by connections outside the medical community. During the evenings he spent at the University Club he got to know intellectual leaders of the city. A more choice selection was offered him by Morris Jastrow, considered the most influential religious scholar in America, and his literary-minded wife, "a rare and cultivated person." Although Jews like Simon, they were favorite figures in Philadelphia's cultural life. Equally important to expanding Flexner's horizons was his association, fueled by snake venom, with Weir Mitchell. At his Saturday evening "at homes," Mitchell introduced Simon to "the best talk in Philadelphia."[16]

Simon's activities during the week after he first had tea with Helen Thomas were detailed in a letter to his mother. He was out every evening. Monday night he attended a faculty meeting. On Tuesday he had dinner with the Jastrows, who took him to the Contemporary Club to hear a "woefully tiresome address by an Edinburgh sociologist." After the lecture cocoa and light refreshments were offered but Simon joined a group who repaired to a rathskeller for beer and cheese. He reached home after midnight.

On Wednesday, Flexner was sent to Boston — a sign of how well he was becoming accepted — to represent the medical school at a meeting of University of Pennsylvania alumni. Naturally, he found time to revive the old conviviality with Councilman at Harvard. A hurried train trip then carried him to Baltimore, where he stayed with the Harry Thomases and attended a belated farewell dinner given for him by Welch. The food and decoration were such as, in his opinion, only Welch could supply, and all his former colleagues were there. The eulogy Welch delivered "nearly sent me into solution.... Some of the things he said must have kept the blood in my head until I was in danger of apoplexy." When Simon tried to reply, his "voice was too uncertain and wet [with tears?] to be intelligible."

On Friday, he returned to Philadelphia for a lecture by Osler and a reception that followed. Saturday evening he spent with Weir Mitchell, "mixing whiskey and water, listening to good conversation, and seeing rare curios. Several unusual men were there including [the novelist] Owen Wister and [the journalist] Talcott Williams."

He confided to his mother that the next week promised to be equally busy.[17]

Flexner was to look back on his years in Philadelphia as the most socially active of his lifetime. That he was not altogether at ease is revealed by an anecdote he periodically told to his sons.

He had taken some special young lady to an elegant restaurant out of his usual range and she had ordered the most expensive things on the menu. As the figures queasily agglutinated in his brain, he realized that he had not brought along enough cash. A member of Helen Thomas's clan would have regarded the situation as irksome, but would not have doubted that he could carry through on a high plane. But Simon was upset. What should he do? It was his pride at the coolness with which he met this crisis that made him so often tell the story.

Nonchalantly, he rose and told the lady he would be back in a moment; with carefully measured steps he walked to the head waiter; he led the waiter to one side. Having explained his delinquency, he proferred his card, explained that he was a professor at the University of Pennsylvania, and a member of the University Club. Expecting to be asked to leave his watch behind as a hostage, he was not only relieved but complimented when the head waiter asked only that he should write his address on the back of the card.[18]

38

---·····‹∞›····---

Helen Thomas and Bertrand Russell

CONSIDERING Helen's usual diffidence with men, her friendship
with Simon grew surprisingly quickly. Twelve days after she had
first served him tea at Bryn Mawr — he had politely abjured beer —
Helen reminded him that he had agreed to dine with her and Lucy to
help them entertain the daughter of the Bishop of London. "To confess
the truth, I'm frightened by the thought of a bishop's daughter, but
hope you are not!"[1]

She was soon arranging to meet him at the railroad station in Philadelphia by "the gate where the train from Bryn Mawr comes in. Should I
by any chance miss you there, I will take my seat facing the long windows near the place where the man calls out the trains. I've a talent for
missing people so I rely entirely on your finding me." At a subsequent
rendezvous they walked together through the countryside near Bryn
Mawr. Simon confessed feeling shy about a social occasion he was to attend in Philadelphia. After it was over, Helen asked, "Did you make
yourself charming to the ladies on Saturday, and was not my method a
success?"[2]

Late in February, 1900, Helen sailed for England: Simon saw her off,
bringing books and flowers.[3] Shortly after her arrival, she went to stay
with the Russells in Cambridge. On March 21 she confided to her vellum-bound notebook: "The person who is now filling my mind is Bertrand with his face pale and dark hair and bright dark eyes.... He
looked like an inventor of something, the creator of a philosophical system, the discoverer of an unknown planet."[4]

On April 7, Lucy wrote in reply to information lost with the letter that had contained it, "My own Helen, . . . my whole heart goes out to you. It is a hard world, and since you went to England, it seems you have had many things to bear. . . . I think you have been wonderful about Bertie. I am sure you are quite right about men — to get to know all about them." Lucy did think Mariechen had "behaved badly about it."[5]

Helen's intention to use Russell for experiments to increase, avowedly for literary purposes, her understanding of men was surely foolhardy, but not as clearly so as it would have been after Russell launched on his crusade for sexual liberation. He was still in need of liberation himself. He had, by then, fallen out of love with Alys. Yet his road to sexual release was to be long. Not for another decade, so he tells us, did he achieve, with Lady Ottoline Morrell, the wife of Logan's best friend, "complete relations with any woman except Alys."[6]

Russell remembered that Helen had been "gentle, deaf, and rather timid with very lovely red hair." When he had first met her during his American trip, "Helen attracted me at once by her hair and her gentleness. In subsequent years, they [Helen and Lucy] often spent the summers at Friday's Hill. I fell more or less in love with her." He was "very fond of her for a number of years, culminating in 1900. Once or twice I asked her to kiss me, but she refused."[7]

During the same American trip, Russell's eye had also been caught by a Bostonian, Sally Fairchild, the only woman in addition to Helen whom he remembered as interesting him romantically between his consummations with Alys and Lady Ottoline. Sally, Russell wrote, "made a deep impression on me." However, "we were restrained by the strict code of those days. . . . I never so much as kissed her hand." A year after his fleeting romance with Sally, Bertie, in trying to kiss Helen, tried to induce her to break that "strict code."[8]

For Helen to have accepted and returned amorous embraces with a man to whom she was neither engaged nor married would have been, according to ideas that she and Bertie himself then harbored, a leap, perhaps irrevocable and uncontrollable, into an illicit relationship. Helen's repudiation of the temptation was not lightly or easily achieved. This is revealed by the fact that her adventure with Bertie became the only aspect of her past which Helen felt it necessary to confess to Simon before she married him. When, after long hesitation, she did so, it was verbally. But, fortunately for the record, on thinking over what she had said, she concluded that she ought to elucidate further. On April 27, 1903, she wrote her fiancé:

"You could not have been more understanding about Bertie or more sympathetic. It was hard for me to tell you because I felt that the whole story must prejudice you against him and Alys, and I was afraid I should fail to make it clear wherein I myself felt myself to blame. With the beginning I had nothing to do, but I feel that a certain intellectual pride, a determination not to let a thing I cared for very much be spoiled by a thing that seemed to me in its essence sordid and trivial — for Bertie's feelings were both, I thought — led me to behave in a way that was not irreproachable. I took serious risks, and it was perhaps my good fortune rather than my desert that I came out unscathed.

"That Bertie was much hurt I do not, and never did, believe, but I know that I contributed, though it was only temporarily, to both his and Alys' pain and perplexity, and I hate to think that I did so. With their fine and admirable and beautiful qualities are mingled others that thwart and debase them, and out of the struggle has come physical wreck for Alys and bitterness of soul for Bertie. . . . Do you think it strange that my affection for them should be unchanged by their behavior to me? I seem made to see people's faults and not to be much affected by them."[9]

Under the date of March 31, 1900, Helen penned into her vellum notebook a confused and hysterical passage that begins with her blaming herself because "I did not have my wits about me sufficiently to tell a lie" to her aunt Hannah. Alys's mother was sure to make a scene. Then Helen angrily blamed her troubles on the Smith environment, "a queer, strange, complicated world in which you cannot, indeed, let your left hand know what your right is doing. . . . These people seem to me to lead the most ignoble lives": deceptions, self-deceiving, triviality, gossiping, "and no seriousness."

"How earnestly one wishes to have everything in one's life open and visible! . . . As it is, one has to hide many things for the sake of other people. . . . Where mistakes affect other people beside oneself, one does not feel one can stand up to the consequences. Lack of malice, lack of intention of wrongdoing do not make the spectacle of the havoc one has wrought easier to bear. Harder, rather," because you must convict yourself of "folly and thoughtlessness."

"I wish not to get myself personally into any complications, for complications bring so much ugliness, so much sordidness with them, and though they add to one's experience, they seem to me not to pay. But who can tell? I write this in the greatest humiliation of spirit. . . .

"I have had sure warning against future transgressions, and I know my own weaknesses better."[10]

Whether or not Aunt Hannah, whose denunciations were a common-place aspect of the Smith scene, publicly excoriated her indiscreet niece, it is clear that neither the Russells nor any of their circle propelled Helen into the outer darkness. Gossip rather than outrage was the Smith way. A trip to the island of Sark had been planned by the Russells with Helen and "a small party of people, for a glimpse of the spring." Helen went along as scheduled. Alys was hurt and unfriendly, and Bertie placated his wife by being disagreeable. Having, after whatever vacillations, resisted Bertie, Helen considered herself more sinned against than sinful. She felt badly treated.[11]

But, the bitterness soon passed, or at least was buried to such an extent that, after Helen had returned to America, Alys wrote her in the old chatty cousinly vein.[12]

Bertie remembered the events of that summer of 1900 as the "culmination of his love" for Helen. "I remained good friends with her, although in the last years of her life I saw her seldom."

Seven months after the crisis, Russell carried off what he considered a dramatic feat. He had been slaving on the manuscript that was to become famous as *Principia Mathematica*. With a flourish he completed the draft — two hundred thousand words — on the last day of the nineteenth century, which he calculated as December 31, 1900. He wished to boast of the conjunction of the century change with his achievement, but to whom? Certainly not to his wife, with whom he was getting on badly. He had not written to Helen since they parted, but now he did so.

At the end of his life the Earl Russell, remembering this letter as a milestone in his career, wrote my brother and me (our mother had died) for a copy to include in his autobiography. Unfortunately, we could not then locate the letter in Helen's papers. When eventually sorted out, they were found to contain some sixty letters from Bertrand Russell.[13]

When Helen in due course married Simon Flexner, Bertie was not pleased. He insisted on still calling her Helen Thomas and decided that he disliked her. He considered it was "too complicated" to see her now that she was a bride, and repeated Lucy's jealous reports that the marriage was starting out unhappily.

When Bertie finally did get together with the married couple, he carried to the point of comedy the conventional reactions of a jealous admirer: the faithless woman had deteriorated, the husband is a brute, and it is impossible that his former love could take such a man seriously.

Helen, Bertie wrote, "put away romance when she married and has found it hard. She has become rather disappointed and puritanical. . . . Her mouth has often a pathetic droop, indicating much pain with much self-pity. Rather weak and defeated. It is sad. Her life has not enough color to keep her soul alive." Her husband seems "to have genius" in his work, "but he has no care for poetry or beauty or anything of that kind, no passion apart from his own work, and his work doesn't interest her. I dimly feel another person, very interesting and rather sinister, who would cut you up in the interests of science, a fanatic, removed from all love and hate. But I don't think she takes him seriously enough to have noticed this person."[14]

After his breakthrough to full infidelity with Lady Ottoline, Russell boasted to her about this prior relationship with Helen and sent his paramour a selection of Helen's letters. He was complimented when she found them attractive. "They are," he agreed, "good letters. It was only through her letters that I got to know what she was like. When I used to see her, I always talked myself."[15]

Eighteen years after he had first met Helen, Russell stayed with the Flexners in New York. His distaste for the American civilization around him made him, so he reported to Lady Ottoline, "more affectionate to Helen Flexner than I would have been in England. However, she was glad to find me so, and no harm was done."[16]

Helen's happy memories of her years with her English cousins, particularly Logan and Bertie, were among the agreeable family reminiscences to which I was brought up. Her affection for Bertie remained strong, and she thoroughly relished his becoming so famous and the Earl Russell. When, in trying to persuade Flexner that he should come to England and establish an institute for medical research, Lloyd George, as Prime Minister, promised to give Simon a knighthood, Helen amused us all by repeating the Russell snobbery about knights. If Simon allied himself with middle-class upstarts by agreeing to become Sir Simon, she would divorce him! Of course, Simon himself was too much of an American product to be in any way lured.[17]

Helen found it fun to tell a story on herself. She had been freezing beside a messy pond in Central Park in New York, watching her grubby sons ice-skate, when one of her married friends came sweeping triumphantly along on the arm of a lover. Helen thought to herself, "At least I could have eloped with Bertrand Russell."[18]

39

A Lion in Philadelphia

H ALF a world away when preparations should have been made, Flexner had been forced to meet the problems of his initial academic year in Philadelphia by operating hand to mouth. It was during his second year, 1900–1901, that he began to demonstrate the gifts at administering and fostering advanced medical research that were, with the passage of time, to overshadow his personal experimentation and discovery. Not that he had any premonition of what lay before him. His whole desire was still to be "a competent, respected pathologist" pursuing an "academic career."[1]

At the time Flexner regarded as a handicap the deep-seated indifference or opposition to what he wished to achieve. He wondered to Barker whether it was possible to move so large and deeply inert a mass. Only in looking back did he realize that it had been to his advantage that the facilities automatically offered to him were "meager," and that "no one was doing original work." Those "tepid surroundings," he wrote, had enabled him to rise quickly. It was his fortunate lot to hurry the august and obsolete Philadelphia medical institutions along what was a predestined road to modern science.[2]

The barricade at Blockley, the municipal hospital and almshouse, came down during the summer of 1900 with such a crash that Flexner, no longer deprived of pathological material, was almost inundated. His appointment to the position he wanted as one of the hospital pathologists coincided with a ruling by the new president of the city Department of Charities and Corrections that the staff of the hospital was empowered to order autopsies on any deceased patient "for examination of disease or teaching purposes." This meant that no permission had to be secured from the families of the deceased. Since the other medical schools were far from Blockley, they handed over many of their rights to autopsies to Flexner's department. If Flexner's small staff was hard put to it to keep up — in 1900 there were 608 postmortem examinations — the result was a pathologist's bonanza. Flexner's knowledge, which had previously been limited by access chiefly to acute illness, was, because of the almshouse, enlarged to include the study of chronic and degenerative ailments.[3]

From all directions rare conditions appeared, and the "gross" specimens of diseased organs could not be effectively preserved for any length of time. The wealth of material would not have been wasted in a German university inhabited by a flock of graduate students, but only a few specimens could be displayed in the courses Flexner and his staff gave as part of a general medical education. This situation made Flexner listen with more enthusiasm to the urging of Lippincott that he prepare a textbook on pathology (which he never finished). The Philadelphia publishers agreed to hire an artist, Louis Schmitt, who would preserve in pictures the gross specimens that would otherwise be lost. For companion drawings made through the microscope, Miss Montague was hired.

Miss Montague was very pretty. Simon particularly admired the way she did her hair. She was much younger than the professor and very flirtatious with him. He took her out on various occasions, remembering particularly how, as they were dining at a garden restaurant outside Philadelphia, they were interrupted by a tremendous downpour from which there was no method of escape but standing, it seemed endlessly, in the middle of a drenched crowd waiting for a streetcar.

Abbott became worried enough to tell his friend that, if he married Miss Montague, he would only regret it once, and that would be for the rest of his life.[4]

While Flexner was still in Baltimore, funds had been given to the Pennsylvania Hospital to establish the Ayer Clinical Laboratory. By the time Flexner had arrived in Philadelphia, the laboratory had opened under the direction of the same Dr. Cattell who had barred him from the Blockley. Cattell again disappeared, and on January 28, 1901, Flexner was appointed director and empowered to make arrangements with the president of the board* for necessary assistants. The total annual expenditure for salaries was not to exceed $1,625.

---

* The president, Benjamin H. Shoemaker, had originally joined the board to fill the vacancy left in 1867 by the death of Helen's grandfather John M. Whitall.

The specific purpose of the Ayer was similar to that of the private laboratory Simon had dreamed of when he was a drugstore clerk in Louisville: to serve as a scientific backing for practitioners. Flexner had then hoped to go beyond that, and now he saw for the Ayer much wider horizons, to be reached through original scientific research. He persuaded a leading member of the Pennsylvania Hospital board, the John W. Garrett who had accompanied him on the Philippines expedition, to state publicly: "The laboratory furnishes the link between distinctly scientific investigation and the practice of medical surgery. Much that formerly was indefinite and empirical in diagnosis and treatment has, through [such] means, been rendered definite and scientific. Already the service in the relief of suffering, the cure of disease, and the prolongation of life has been inestimable."[5]

Flexner made a daily visit to the Ayer after his work at the university was over, and he was available for consultations and important autopsies. As assistant he appointed Warfield Longcope, Baltimore-born (he was a distant relative of Helen Thomas's), and a Hopkins graduate who was eventually to succeed to Osler's post there as professor of medicine.

Flexner persuaded the hospital board, although they agreed somewhat reluctantly, that each intern should spend the first three months at the Ayer. This helped Longcope with routine examinations, and taught the young doctors valuable techniques. Interesting specimens resulting from the autopsies were shared with the university, but Flexner encouraged collection and study also at the Ayer. Thus he created a miniature Hopkins Pathological, which attracted ambitious medical school graduates who wished to prepare themselves in pathology before entering clinical work. In 1903, a new publication, *Bulletin of the Ayer Clinical Laboratory*, was added to medical literature.[6]

A senior physician at the Pennsylvania Hospital, a member of the medically entrenched Meigs family, shambled up to the new director of the Ayer Laboratory and said that he found ridiculous the notion that invisible bugs caused disease. However, he would not interfere with Flexner since doctors often disagreed and he believed that every man had a right to his own opinion. Flexner made courteous replies, but he was far from reassured. He could not foresee that Meigs's obscurantism was to do him a great favor.

The wife of Provost Harrison came down with diphtheria. Meigs, the family doctor, treated her in the traditional manner. As she approached nearer and nearer to death, Harrison called in an up-to-date doctor who treated her with diphtheria antitoxin. The seemingly miraculous cure utterly converted Harrison to the modern medicine Flexner preached. He began announcing, publicly as well as privately, that the traditional mission of the University of Pennsylvania — to prepare practitioners — was no longer enough. The university should also foster medical research.[7]

When Flexner had first been appointed, he had found that a new laboratory building was projected, and was shown the plans, but he had paid them little attention: he was off for Manila and had not yet reset his mind to include executive considerations. Back from the Philippines, he discovered that nothing had been done, and indeed the project languished until Mrs. Harrison's sensational recovery. Then the provost reanimated it on a much-expanded scale. He commissioned Flexner to work out with the architects provisions for pathology.

Flexner ran at once into a stone wall, or to be more exact, a whole construction of stone walls. The buildings on the campus that would surround the new laboratory were all English Gothic in appearance. English Gothic demanded heavily mullioned windows that did not allow in enough light for work with a microscope. To Flexner's urging that architectural unanimity be violated with large windows, the architects responded with as much horror as if he had asked them to dance around the campus naked. Flexner finally persuaded them to come with him to New York and examine Dr. Prudden's laboratory. While admitting the utility of plate glass, the architects remained adamant in refusing to desecrate the Gothic campus with anything so unesthetic. Finally, a way out was discovered. The building was to have an inner court, and there large windows could be hidden from outside view. The laboratory building, when completed after Flexner's departure from Philadelphia, was considered the most advanced in America.[8]

In organizing his department, Flexner wished to secure as first assistant Richard M. Pearce, who, as one of Councilman's pupils at Harvard, was a Hopkins man one step removed.* The provost, whose approval was required, asked why Flexner could not find a suitable man, as was the tradition, within the university itself? The university graduates, Flexner explained, were trained to be practitioners first and laboratory men second. Harrison then expressed doubt that any doctor worth his salt would spend his full time looking into test tubes for the inadequate salary offered: $1,500. However, he did not veto the choice put forward

* Pearce eventually became head of the medical division of the Rockefeller Foundation.

by his professor of pathology. Pearce accepted. The affluent Hopkins graduate, Gay, who had paid his own way to the Philippines, came into Flexner's laboratory as a volunteer. Another Hopkins man named Henrickson was slipped into the lowest rank. And there was Noguchi.[9]

All except Noguchi, who was protected by his bad English and specifically paid by Dr. Mitchell to do laboratory work, helped carry through the routine duties of teaching pathology to the successive large classes. As far as possible, they concentrated these tasks in the mornings. Then they were free to work at scientific problems, all crowded together into the little space available for laboratory work in a building designed for other purposes.

Welch's relaxed methods of teaching and administration, the outgrowth of his own expansive, self-confident and relaxed personality, were not suited to the disciple with hair-trigger nerves who had been born to a different rank in the world. "My natural inclination was towards order, and this I introduced at once at the University of Pennsylvania. I planned not for myself but for the young men around me. . . . These men were little trained in the experimental side of pathology which was where my research lay. Hence I took them with me, as it were. . . . Every man had his duties understood. With that, I left him much alone. Just because we worked in such close contact with one another, we got on as associates rather than professor and assistants. . . .

"In the main, the character of the work at the University of Pennsylvania differs from that at the Hopkins. I ventured into the opening subject of immunology which was not cultivated at the Hopkins. And this stamps, as it were, my Pennsylvania period as distinct from the Hopkins period."[10]

It seemed actually to have been more a change of emphasis than a new departure. He had in Baltimore studied the effect of injecting the blood serum of dogs into rabbits. Now he moved in a direction which international research was just entering, and to which he was being led in part by his and Noguchi's studies concerning snake venom. His new experiments examined the effects of toxins on the "systems" through which lymph and blood were formed in lymph glands and bone marrow. By injecting ground-up lymph glands and bone marrow into the goose, he "brought out," as he remembered, "interesting new facts" on the mechanisms by which "all mutiplication and growth are set in motion."

40

---·❦·---

The Black Death

As 1900 merged into 1901, Flexner received an imperative call from the federal government. Although it was a compliment to his skill both as a scientist and a negotiator, he found his appointment as chairman of the Plague Commission "not too welcome."[1] He knew that it would interrupt the cresting flow of his affairs in Philadelphia. But he did not foresee that it would place his life in danger.

The question to be determined was whether the Black Death of horrible memory was menacing California and by extension the entire United States. The specific assignment was to find out whether bubonic plague was building up in the Chinatown section of San Francisco. The very gravity of the potential danger had engendered in California a hysterical controversy concerning the presence or absence of the disease. The state government was embroiled with the city board of health, physicians of different ages and training were shouting insults at each other, and the business interests were divided: some were more afraid of a possible epidemic, others of the financial effect on California of a plague-scare.

Watching from Washington, Dr. Walter Wyman, surgeon general of the Marine Hospital Service, had become increasingly worried for the national safety. The Black Death had changed the history of Europe in the fourteenth century by killing three quarters of the population, and it had been scientifically determined that an irresistible epidemic could be set off by such small beginnings as had supposedly been diagnosed in Chinatown. Wyman persuaded his superior, the Secretary of the Treasury, to appoint a commission that would cut through local controversy with an impartial scientific investigation. On Welch's advice, Flexner was appointed head of the commission. The other members were Barker, now at the University of Chicago, and F. G. Novy, from the University of Michigan. All had seen plague in the Orient, although only Flexner (at Hong Kong) had done actual autopsies.[2]

The commission was ordered to set out for California with all speed. They were to "pay their respects to the Governor and Mayor," to get in touch with everyone who could give them information, and to keep regular office hours at the Oriental Hotel. But their principal function was to explore Chinatown, locating everyone who was sick and all cadavers of those recently deceased in order to determine whether any were suffering from or had died of the plague.[3]

As it turned out, there was no controversy about the existence of glandular swellings in Chinatown. The doctors who had long practiced there insisted that these swellings were benign and of common occurrence among Chinese. The city board of health and the more recently trained physicians pointed with dismay at what they considered symptoms of plague. Governor Gates had put the power of the state behind the determination that there was no plague. He ordered that Chinatown be closed to the "conspirators and ignoramuses" who were "for personal and sinister reasons" trying to upset the tranquillity of the state.[4]

Reaching San Francisco on January 17, Flexner and his fellow federal commissioners were welcomed by the municipal authorities. But the governor refused any communication with the commission, while making it clear that the order closing Chinatown applied to them.

Here was a clear collision between state and federal authority. Welch wrote Flexner, "What a hornet's nest you are in! In case you incite civil war you can doubtless rely on the cannon of the general government to protect you. What an ass the governor of the state must be! His pronouncements read like opéra bouffe. Your course is clear, if you can only get a case to examine."[5]

Although the commission was open to all comers, it was naturally more given to seeking cooperation from those who understood and sympathized with its mission than those who adhered to a different medical era and were opposed. This was not lost on the editors of the San Francisco *Chronicle*. On February 2, three days after Flexner's arrival, their lead editorial stated that the city was clearly not suffering from an epidemic and that it was "morally certain" that what had been found in Chinatown was "a disease that has been with us for many years. . . .

"A commission coming here in secret and sitting in secret, consulting only those interested in proving the existence [of the plague], will have no weight with the public, however eminent the members of which it may be composed. The public does not believe that bacterial evidence alone is sufficient to establish the presence of the plague."

Two days later, the commissioners got the *Chronicle* to publish, although inconspicuously, a list of their office hours, in which anyone would be received. "This," the reporter continued, gave "merchants and others" an opportunity to warn the commission against plotters.

However, the anti-plague faction was not satisfied at being merely listened to. In another lead editorial, on February 6, the *Chronicle* pointed out that not only were scientific reputations at stake, but that it was being charged that "the commercial bodies of San Francisco and the Governor of the state have deliberately set monetary considerations in balance against the possibility of spreading a dreadful infection across the land." It followed that all investigations should be conducted in the presence of the representatives of the public who were "as capable of judging the simple questions presented as a body of physicians." California was not inhabited by savages who gave witch doctors "blind belief."

The function of the commission being to use the new scientific techniques, which were being scoffed at, the commissioners could not allow themselves to become engaged in civil debates. Compromise was for them impossible. Still barred from Chinatown, Simon and his colleagues continued to await, without violating their impartial stance, some favorable break. It came in the most surprising guise. A delegation of hostile businessmen appeared and announced that on that very day, February 6, a bill was going to be passed by the state legislature making it a felony to say that plague was present in the state. "What," they asked, "would one do?"

The time seemed to be at hand for Flexner to point out that the state, if it arrested federal officials carrying through their orders, would create a constitutional crisis. But Flexner, as he remembered it, had "a flash of inspiration."

"One would," he stated, "pack one's bags and get out of California before one was held there by quarantines established by the surrounding states." The delegation was "thunderstruck." That the legislation would be interpreted as an admission and a menace had not occurred to them. They looked at their watches, discovered that there was a train they could catch which would get them to the capital in time to stop the vote. They vanished at a run.[6]

The next day, the *Chronicle* reported without comment that two bills before the state legislature creating felonies had been withdrawn before they were considered. One would have forbidden handling plague germs carelessly, and the other banned any public statement concerning plague in California which had not been approved by the state board of health.

The two proposed bills, one accepting the possibility of plague germs and the other aimed at prohibiting anyone from saying so, reflected the hysteria of those who wished to thwart the Plague Commission coming and going. But Flexner's comment brought them down to earth with a bump. They decided that they had no choice but to open Chinatown to the commission.

The *Chronicle*'s last editorial of the series — on February 17 — still insisted: "We all know that no trouble exists and the less said the better." However, "the physicians who have come unheralded from a far country upon their official quest are without doubt men of great learning, wide experience, high character, and upright intentions." The danger was that they were being misled "by the company they keep." Those who were convinced there was no plague were worried lest they be tried and condemned without having access to the evidence. The editorial closed with a statement implying that Flexner and his colleagues were subject to embarrassment, perhaps harassment: the commissioners, being "men of high character," deserved "all courtesy and respect."

The speed with which the commission got under way, once Chinatown was opened to them, reveals detailed preparation. They had secured from the city board of health a map on which was marked the locations of previously suspected cases. Although, local controversies being what they were, one of the commissioners had to be present at every examination, they were glad to have the physicians of the city health department organized to help. Most importantly, the true governing body of Chinatown, the central organization of the "Six Companies," had shuddery memories of plague in their homeland. They sent out to their members an order that all cases of sickness or death be reported to them. Wong Chung, the secretary of the Six Companies, led Barker to every case thus reported. If the illness was clearly not plague, no further attention was paid. But should plague be a possibility, Wong

Chung would act as an interpreter in gathering all relevant information, and the case was visited daily.

The dead were discovered in two ways, either through city inspections of the undertaking establishments or through reports from the Six Companies, which often informed the commission before the city authorities had been notified.[7]

Flexner and his colleagues considered it part of their function to examine the total environment. They explored the fourteen blocks of Chinatown, sometimes guided by city detectives, sometimes on their own. They found the poorer dwellings "shockingly unsanitary. . . . The rooms were overcrowded and small, often without light or means of ventilation, many filthy, those in basements damp and emitting a foul stench." These conditions were not limited to tenement houses. Some of the more pretentious buildings had behind them, in their basements and directly beneath their roofs, "sleeping and living quarters which are most objectionable from a sanitary point of view."

However, the Chinese were much better off than their countrymen Flexner had seen in Asia. There was almost no "utter destitution." In California, the Chinese were "on the whole very well fed, wages being high and food abundant and cheap." They were also well clothed. Since there existed a theory that plague infection was involved with bare legs and feet, the commission's report emphasized that the San Francisco Chinese wore shoes, stockings, and trousers. The commissions witnessed no opium smoking, although they were told it was common. They visited the quarters of prostitutes, which they found "more wholesome as regard to air space, light, ventilation, and cleanliness than those of other inhabitants of the district."[8]

The intensive study lasted eight days. Barker recorded case histories and made clinical examinations of the living (who often, during that short time, joined the dead). Flexner and Novy made pathological and bacteriological studies.

Flexner, to whom most of the autopsies were entrusted, was forced to conduct them under what the official report characterized discreetly as "disadvantageous circumstances." There being no mortuary in San Francisco, dissections had to be "conducted in the narrow limits of a dimly lighted alcove in an undertaker's shop, or in even worse habitations where the dead were found." It being not then known that the disease could not be contracted in that manner, Flexner was afraid that should his knife slip to give him the teeniest nick he would be infected.[9]

The true and deadly danger grew from the fact that there were in San Francisco no suitable scientific laboratories, except those at the University of California which, because it was a state institution, were kept closed to the scientists. The municipal authorities could do no more than provide a former licensing office in City Hall.

Injecting guinea pigs was an essential aspect of the bacteriological diagnosis, and in the cramped quarters there was no space for cages except beside the tables on which the scientists worked. Previous medical tragedies had revealed that breathing in dirt from the cages of infected animals caused pneumonial plague, the most dangerous form of the disease. Fortunately, the commission, as Flexner wrote, "got through without accident."[10]

During eight days of concentrated search, six cases were, by every scientific test then known, confirmed as bubonic plague.[11] This multiplied out to more than two hundred and fifty cases a year, plenty to start an epidemic. Why no epidemic had yet exploded was explained by an examination of the local rats, either those caught alive or those fished dead out of sewers. They were not spreading the infection because they had not themselves yet been infected.

Flexner's orders were to send the commission's report in a prearranged code to Surgeon General Wyman in Washington. Since the commission was being perpetually watched, the dispatch of the intentionally unintelligible telegram became instantly known. The fears of the anti-plague junta that they would be tried and convicted without access to the evidence seemed outrageously justified. The commissioners were besieged in their hotel rooms by angry protestors and stopped in the street. Governor Gates made his first appearance in a towering rage. Flexner could only say that he was obeying the orders he had been given. But he used the code to beseech Wyman to release the report.[12] When released, it revealed that there was evidence galore, but no one had been tried or convicted.

The report did not even mention that there had been any opposition. Only the names of those who had cooperated with the commission were cited. Detailed justifications for each of the six diagnoses of plague — clinical, pathological and bacteriological — made up the bulk of the report.[13] Since all methods had been employed, there was no basis for argument between the old medicine and the new. And every statement was so exclusively factual that there was no possibility of scenting the malign influence of trouble-making villains.

The report's extreme efficiency and its scientific impartiality made it not only acceptable but reassuring to all but the most extreme zealots. (Governor Gates still huffed and puffed and had to be silenced by a veiled threat from Washington of putting a boycott on California.) The general view was that great danger had been identified before it had become truly dangerous. And the tone of the report gave reassurance that what danger did exist would be, by similar scientific efforts, eliminated.[14]

"I am proud of the work which you and the others have done in the commission," Welch wrote Flexner. "Everything seems to have turned out most successfully, and you really have cleared the atmosphere by your tact and the scientific and practical results of the investigations."[15]

Welch was keeping a doubly sharp eye on his most effective pupil because of great events brewing in New York. The richest man in America was setting in motion a major effort to foster medical research. Plans were still nebulous, but the intention was to found an institution, probably like the Pasteur Institute in Paris or the Koch Institute in Berlin, but on a much larger scale. Welch had been made chairman of the board but had no intention of leaving Baltimore. Someone else would steer the great adventure. In the still youthful state of American science, the opportunity might come to a very promising man on the way up. During June, 1901, Simon Flexner received an invitation to join the board of directors of what had not yet been named the Rockefeller Institute for Medical Research.

4 1

The Valley of Despair

HELEN had envisioned her trip abroad in the summer of 1900 as the culmination of the free year she had taken from her duties at Bryn Mawr to launch herself as a writer. Her contretemps with the Russells behind her, she established herself in Grace's house overlooking the Thames. She intended to work in her bedroom for "a good six hours" every day.[1] An occasional brief essay turned out to be almost on a par with one of Logan's "Trivia." Concerning London — "Mentally, I had to square my shoulders and stand up to the pressure of so organized a vastness, so ancient an established order of things in which I have no part to play, in the midst of which I was the most unimportant of atoms. By comprehending it, by conceiving of it imaginatively — of all the many forms of life lived in its houses, of its power to command over the whole world — I tried to persuade myself that I was proving my right to be proud of it, to hold up my head and tread the pavements with the step of a queen, but I felt only a very small, weak woman and took myself home, glad indeed for the cup of tea that awaited my coming."[2]

Despite such effective flashes, Helen came increasingly to realize that her free year had been a failure. She did complete a first draft of a short story but on revision it refused to catch fire. As the time approached when Lucy, having finished her year at Bryn Mawr, would join her, Helen wrote: "Such terrible inquietness as there is in me I do not know how either to express it or control it. I feel like some strong man who has been touched by an enchanter's wand, and finds his muscles, once so vigorous, relaxed. . . . How can I face Lucy on the day of reckoning. All these months, and so little to show for them, and my own despair! Did I last year sympathize with her; was I kind when she went through the dark waters? . . . I told her to face failure, and now I am face to face with it myself. . . .

"And what you long for tonight, confess it, is for Lucy to put her arms about you, and soothe you as a mother soothes a sobbing child, to tell you how dear you are and how beautiful and how clever and how sure she is of your ultimate success, and to point out to you that your health is not good, and all the difficulties you have to overcome, and finally to say that whatever you do she will always adore you."[3]

This notation is quickly followed by another which, by implication, defines her relationship with Lucy as an escape from deep emotion. She accuses herself of being "a coward, shrinking first from knowledge and then from feeling. Dare to know? Yes, I do dare. Dare to feel? Ah, but I shrink from that. Feelings hurt one so dreadfully. . . . The only games that I can play are the games which I care not at all to win. . . . Suppose your vanity is wounded, suppose that your heart does ache? Who are you that you should be exempted from common woes? . . . Open your heart as you have opened your intelligence. . . . Your mental calm is not dependent on ignorance; let not your happiness be dependent on lack of feeling."[4]

In her letters to Helen written that summer from Bryn Mawr,* Lucy reiterates that her health and happiness are dependent on her longtime companion. "Help me! Help me! . . . Dearest creature, love me as well as you can, for I love you as I have no words to say." She longs "to kiss your shining hair and pretty hands." She will "try to be nicer to live with, more controlled and reasonable."[5]

The arrival of Lucy in England at the end of June, brought Helen's notation in her vellum-bound notebook to a close. It was a catastrophic arrival. Soon after her long-anticipated reunion with Helen, Lucy slipped over the edge into a nervous collapse.

As soon as they got back to America, Lucy was sent to her family in Brooklyn,[6] while Helen went to Baltimore for an operation that proved to be more serious than had been expected. Helen wrote Carey, "Thee cannot imagine how like life after death thoughts of Bryn Mawr seem in contrast to surgeon's knives and paralysis." Under the circumstances, Bryn Mawr seemed "the greatest institution in the country."

This backward compliment could hardly have pleased Carey, who

* Helen's letters to Lucy during this period are not preserved.

was surely further infuriated by what Helen wrote — it could well have been in defiance — after she had escaped from the hospital to family houses inhabited by her small nieces and nephews. "I adore children and believe from the bottom of my heart that I was meant by fate to have a large family of them."[7]

In her vellum-bound notebook, Helen asked herself what she knew "of man's love for women and women's answering love for men? . . . The joy of it and the pain of it; its power of exalting and degrading; the iron grip with which it takes hold of the human consciousness; the never-to-be relaxed bond that nonetheless relaxes — what can one say of it that is not both true and false? And human individuals, since the world began, have danced always to this tune as clouds of gnats dance in a sunbeam."[8]

Too upset to carry through her college duties, Lucy shuttled back and forth between Low Buildings and her home in Brooklyn. Wherever she was, Lucy was tempestuous.

And perpetually she demanded reassurance that she and Helen would spend the rest of their lives together.[9]

Early in January, 1901 (Flexner had not yet set out for San Francisco), Helen, whose correspondence with the Russells had always been with Alys, was surprised to receive a letter from Bertie telling her of his manuscript completed within "six hours" of the close of the nineteenth century. "I have been endeavoring to think of a good resolution to make, but my conscience is in so thoroughly comfortable a state that I have hitherto failed. In October, I invented a new subject, which turned out to be all mathematics, for the first time treated in its essence. Since then I have written two hundred thousand words, and I think they are all better than any I had written before. So I have no good resolutions to make, unless I could resolve that you should come over next summer. It will be very *sad* if you are unable to do so. I never pass Green Hill without wishing you were there, and I often make the same wish without passing Green Hill."

Concerning a copy of his biography of the philosopher Leibnitz he had sent Helen, Russell wrote, "I consider your government very benighted to charge duty on a work so admirably calculated to improve its citizens. You may tell it, if you meet it, that no amount of protection will enable America to produce its philosophy at home." He went on to say that "for filthy lucre" he was writing an article on the most recent mathematics for a "most contemptible" American periodical. He intended to point out that "all recent advances are due to Zeno, who was pre-Socratic. That ought to irritate your up-to-date compatriots!"[10]

In her reply, Helen ignored Bertie's anti-American sneers: "How charming of you to write me a letter, and on the last day of the century too! I feel very proud of it and only fear lest you may require an occasion like the end of an age to inspire you. And now that the Queen [Victoria] is dead . . . I cannot imagine to what future event I can appeal.

"I am very interested to hear of all the works you are doing. The thought of two hundred thousand words stirs my imagination. In my recent mood, I can no more conceive of writing them than I can conceive of creating a universe or ruling the British Empire; but I can fancy how happy you must have been under the impulse of such an inspiration. Was it very exciting, or did you take it calmly I wonder? I like to think of you seated day after day at your table driving your pen. For your publishing in the magazines, however, I rather despise you, especially as they are so lost to all grace as to refuse to accept me. My poor little story returned home accompanied, to be sure, by a very kind note from the editor of the *Atlantic*, but still rejected. I expect to send it off again before long, though. I have no smallest hope of its getting itself published. By the time I have tried every editor in the country I shall be able, I dare say, to declaim with some spirit against the bad taste of the new age. At present, I am merely a little dejected. . . .

"You must not . . . suppose that I despair, or that I am unhappy. Somehow, I still manage to walk erect rejoicing in life. It is sad, no doubt, to be nearly thirty years old and utterly undistinguished; but the sunlight is golden, the faded winter fields stretch in a harmony of color to the horizon, and I cannot take things too tragically.

"In a very few weeks — or days is it? — you will be going to Cambridge. I am glad you have taken the same house, for I shall be able to imagine you there, our long conversations in the study, and the more formal parties in the drawing room upstairs! Instead of talking to you, I shall have to read your *Leibnitz* — what comfort there is to be found in it! When I am toiling over its pages, I often wish you were here that I might abuse you first, and then demand explanations, but I know if you were, you would roundly advise me to give up the effort which I do not intend to do."

She and Lucy, Helen continued, had "finally decided, come what will," to leave Bryn Mawr so that they could devote all their time to literature. Helen was that very afternoon writing about a house in Concord, Massachusetts, where they could live cheaply. "This evening I am going down to break the news to Carey." Until they could sell some of their achievements, they would, of course, be strapped. The worst part, they would not be again able to get to England. But they might, "by chance, do something that may make you gladder to see us, even if gray-haired." Their plans were to be kept secret as they had still told no one.[11]

Whether Helen wrote to Concord and told Carey, whether the plan so dramatically announced to Bertie had been actually decided on, it is impossible to know. Lucy was in and out of the hospital. In March, Helen was told that she would have to send Lucy away next winter. "What this means, I realized yesterday, and in the evening was overwhelmed by it, shed tears I so rarely shed — three times a year at most — and this morning was forced to nurse my headache. All the ridiculousness of my taking things as hardly as I do is apparent to me, but I cannot change my disposition. I can and do control the expression of it [but] feeling is my master."[12]

In the fall of 1890, after Helen and Simon were both back from their summer occupations, the pull of their separate directions was so strong that two months passed before they got together. The preserved correspondence indicates that their friendship continued, but did not in any obvious manner ripen. When Helen writes, "Since you were here I have thought of you many times," it is a prelude to an apology: "Between doing my work at the college and nursing Miss Donnelly, I have not had a moment to write you."[13]

They did see each other from time to time and there passed between them what was to remain a talisman in the Flexner household. Simon sent Helen a copy of George Ade's *Fables in Slang*. Helen "laughed over them a great deal, but Miss Donnelly refused to laugh." Helen found "so much human nature in them as well as slang."[14]

Fables in Slang, by an American newspaper humorist, could be considered, in the context of Helen's experience, a counterpart to Logan's *Trivia*. Both were made up of unconnected short prose pieces which demonstrated what fools we mortals be. Beyond that, the books could hardly be more different. Logan's studied urbanity and exquisite prose beckoned to taste. Ade sought the salutary effect of a horselaugh. His readers are taken not to the drawing rooms and polite neighborhoods of Oxford or London, but to the small town parlors and farmhouses of the

American Middle West. Simple manners are admired, and all deviations from cheerful goodwill are regarded as affectations open to joshing. *Fables in Slang* would have made Walter Pater reach for his smelling salts; fill Logan with embarrassment over his American background; and seem to Russell perfect ammunition for his anti-American sneers. But Helen enjoyed her appreciation of the little volume as a bond, we must assume, with her friend from Kentucky.

On her way to Holland, Helen was seasick most of the time, forced, she wrote Simon, to leave "Miss Donnelly . . . unchaperoned on deck."[15] After they landed, Helen was struck with the excruciatingly painful and crippling sciatica which she always remembered as a catastrophe. In describing it to her sons, she linked it so closely with the traumatic effect of her mother's death that I always assumed the one followed directly on the other. That thirteen years of what Helen called "ill-health and despondency over my deafness" had intervened, surely made the sciatica for her even more frightening. Was it a further expression of an inescapable, lifelong curse?[16]

With Lucy, who was herself far from stable, Helen fled from Holland to England. After a brief rendezvous with Alys and Bertie, she was immured in two successive nursing homes.[17] In July, she received from Russell the self-pitying reminiscences of his childhood, to which she replied banteringly.* She wished she had "something amusing" to write him, "but when one lies in bed all day not much happens." Alys should be warned to expect a complaining letter. "I want to relieve my feelings, and she is the only person I know who won't take me too seriously. I am sorry for her, but I can't spare her."[18]

To Simon, Helen wrote that she was "a complete invalid, a cripple. Is it not bad luck? I have taken enough mercury and arsenic and other deadly poisons to kill any person of sense, and am now engaged in burning myself to a cinder every day."[19]

Lucy stayed near Helen much of the time. After one of her tantrums she wrote, "It breaks my heart to think of . . . being so cruel to you when you are ill." Without consulting Helen, she wrote Carey that Helen could not work the following winter: "I have planned for us both. Out of doors, bed, good food, milk, few people, *no visitors*, perfect contentment in our books and each other." If Helen's family insisted on disturbing her, Lucy would hide her away. "How I sympathize from my heart with my poor child!"[20]

* See page 289.

Logan wrote Hannah on September 13, "I think I will go down to Southampton tomorrow to see them off, as Helen is so crippled."[21]

After her return to America, Helen's ultimate ordeal began. Harry was "firm" about her going to the Johns Hopkins Hospital. The diagnosis there arrived at was that the hip and leg muscles were pressing on her "great sciatic nerve and its branches." The treatment decreed was to relax the muscles by placing her in as complete a state of hibernation as was possible for a human being. She was immured in her room twenty-four hours a day, allowed no books, no writing, no visitors. Into this white room there began appearing flowers. The cards were signed Simon Flexner.

On October 12, Helen wrote to thank him for roses and then violets. "Dr. McCray, the terrible, has forbidden my writing letters, but I am a very insubordinate patient.... Never during my whole life, I think, have I been bluer than I was the first of this week, so you may judge how much I needed cheering! I can't help regarding the hospital as a prison and when they refused to let me have even one visitor a day, I felt I had been put in solitary confinement! . . . However, I so worked on the head nurse's sympathy that she persuaded Dr. Osler to be more lenient, and I have decided to be cheerful again and I smile once a day, at least."[22]

A month later, she thanked Simon for more violets. "The flowers were no doubt an answer to my long epistle; a very deserved one but inarticulate. In other words, I should like to hear how you are." [23]

Lucy reported that Simon had called at Low Buildings to ask how Helen was: "Most nice and civil and paid me a long call. Too long." [24]

December 3 to Simon: "It is most charming of you not to forget me in my exile!" He had sent her chrysanthemums.

December 10, to Bertie: "I might repeat, what I still feel, that for a mathematician you are far too literary, and express a growing suspicion that after all you may not in the absolute essence be one. Suppose by chance that you are really a sort of twentieth century Plato, ruined — you see I am not by way of flattering; I must have my revenge for your book! — ruined, I repeat, by modern symbolic notation; and that, instead of setting awhirl the heads of bewildered pedants, you ought to be trailing after you along the pleasant paths between Cambridge and Granchester flocks of enthusiastic open-minded young men, bewildered perhaps, but alive. . . .

"After all these months of rest, the smallest exertion tires me so much as completely uses up my strength. And the worst of it is that all the while my mind is terribly active. I have to drug it with every possible drug. My favorite scheme is to conceive of myelf no longer as an individual but a part of an organized whole, an atom rising and falling, dashing up and lying at rest under the impulse of winds far beyond any control. In a word, I am taking a third of Goethe's advice — this is better than advice usually fares, you'll allow — and am living resolutely in the whole. Goodness and beauty have shrunk to be but parts. The whole in magnificence remains."[25]

When she had finally escaped from the hospital, Helen added to this doctrine in her vellum-bound notebook. Her death, when it came, could not truly "be called a death, since no thought or impulse of desire would perish with me. . . . What I call my personality, is but a variation in the light that shines on eternal substance." Should she nonetheless "grow passionate over this dream I am dreaming, over the *here* and *now* with its desires, satisfied or unsatisfied? Yes, even that, if I must. Let me be passionately glad and passionately sorry, and know that the living must live."[26]

Early in December, 1901, Helen wrote in her notebook, "Today I have walked without pain for the first time since the middle of May." She was told she would be out of the hospital by Christmas.

"With returning health must come the determination to take up the duties of life, and to put to some use for others the strength that may be vouchsafed to me. No one can descend as I have descended into the valley of despair, and have learned that the only light one can hold in one's hands undimmed for others and oneself is the willingness, nay the passion, to sacrifice everything for the person and the [torn]." She was tortured with a sense of guilt concerning Lucy. "To open one's eyes and find that through selfishness and blindness and levity one has terribly wounded the person one loved; that, while believing oneself to be a model of devotion to another, one has really preferred oneself is a terrible thing. And then when at last in scorn and hatred of oneself one looks at the ruin and would give one's life — and account it a small thing, as indeed it is — to help, to find it too late. . . . And finally to find the mere standing by as a spectator while the storm, which one has raised and cannot quell, rages in the mind and soul of one's friend, the mere offering of love is too much for one's strength, to sink under it and to fail is hardly to prize oneself.

"Now it seems to me that in the old days I did not even desire the right thing. I thought myself ill-used. . . . Now . . . I do desire to think of others before myself . . . at whatever sacrifice. . . . I do long in my own person to live the noblest life vouchsafed to man. . . . It is my duty as far as it is in my power to make the world a better and more beautiful, a kinder place for those about me. And having striven with a single heart to do my duty, I may leave the result in quietness to the great power which rules the causes and maintains the sum of results."[27]

In this heartfelt passage, Helen had returned to the conceptions of her parents but with a profound diminution. Separated by her loss of faith from religious utopianism, she could hope only for the narrow effect of her virtuous behavior on the few individuals around her. She served no cause that could revolutionize the world. However, in the great institution that she knew had nurtured Simon Flexner and where he had told her he had spent his happiest years, she was moved by the scientific utopianism of which he was now so vital and creative a disciple. As returning health gave her the "sense of vigorous upspringing of life that was an intoxication to me . . . this hospital, this great refuge for wounded human beings, which had seemed to me before so tragical a place," became "all alive and athrill with vital, healing forces — the powers of nature set at play by the skill of man. And the doctors assisting, directing, or merely observing with grave disinterest and impersonal devotion, seemed to me of all human beings the most beneficent."[28]

———— ··◅∞▻·· ————

42

Enter the Rockefeller Institute

WHEN Simon Flexner was living at the Johns Hopkins Hospital, Osler, usually the most gregarious of the older doctors, had retired daily for several hours behind the closed door of his study. Everyone knew that he was writing a textbook aimed at disseminating to practitioners the most up-to-date medical knowledge. He honored Flexner and others of the younger men by reporting in his pages discoveries they had submitted to the Hospital Medical Society.

Osler's *Principles and Practice of Medicine*, published in 1892, was an instantaneous success. It traveled all over the American continent and to England. During 1897, while Flexner was still at the Hopkins, the book spent day after day among the Catskill Mountains under the eyes of Frederick T. Gates, a former Baptist minister with a craggy face, a square jaw, and a full though short mustache. Gates was the most valued advisor of John D. Rockefeller, Sr.[1]

Rockefeller had accumulated infinitely more money than he could spend or bequeath to his heirs in its entirety without placing too heavy a burden upon them. Worried by the same problem, his friend Andrew Carnegie recommended that multimillionaires put the excess of their fortunes into the hands of trustees of their own choice to be used for philanthropic purposes. But what purposes? Rockefeller was making a gift here and a gift there, without any determining thrust worthy of his name and of the great assets he had it in his power to employ.

As a Baptist, Rockefeller's first really large gift had been to a Baptist university: $600,000 to the University of Chicago. During the negotiations, he had met Gates. The leader of the American Baptist Education Society, whom Rockefeller took into his own service, proved skillful in business and in philanthropy.[2]

Gates had at one time wanted to be a doctor, and his interest was revived when he went for walks with a young medical student whom he had known when a minister. Elon W. Huntington suggested that Gates read Osler's book. Its revelation "absolutely astounded and appalled me." Gates concluded that "the best medical practice did not pretend to and did not cure more than four or five diseases." With a few exceptions, "all that medicine could do . . . was to nurse the patients and alleviate in some degree the suffering. . . . A large number of the most common diseases were simply infectious or contagious . . . caused by infinitesimal germs. . . . I learned that of these germs only a very few had been identified and isolated."

Gates then meditated on how it was that the scientific study of medicine had been so woefully neglected. In the first place, he decided, the methods and instruments had been only recently discovered. And while chemistry and physics had been "endowed very generously in colleges and universities throughout the whole civilized world," medicine had been excluded "owing to the peculiar commercial organizations of medical colleges. . . . Research and instruction alike had been left to shift for themselves. . . .

"It became clear to me that medicine could hardly hope to become a science until medicine should be endowed and qualified men could give themselves to uninterrupted study and investigation . . . entirely independent of practice. To this end, it seemed to me, an institute of medical research ought to be established in the United States.

"Here was an opportunity . . . the greatest which the world could afford, for Mr. Rockefeller to become a pioneer! This idea took possession of me. The more I thought of it, the more enthusiastic I became. I knew nothing of the cost of research. I did not realize the enormous difficulties. The only thing I saw was the overwhelming need and the infinite promise, world-wide, universal, eternal."[3]

The state of medicine was, of course, by no means as abysmal as Gates described. Viewing in black and white, he missed the connecting grays, but he saw with the purity of naive vision the problem and the opportunity. The former minister's enthusiasm naturally took on a religious tone. After the great institute he then envisioned had become a reality, he described it "as a sort of theological seminary. . . . In these several rooms, He is whispering His secrets. To these men He is opening the mysterious depths of His being. . . . If God looks down on the world and has his favorites, it must be the men who are studying Him, who are working every day, with limited intelligence, and in the darkness — for clouds and darkness are around Him — and feeling their way to His heart." Would not the result be a greater understanding of God, the promulgation of higher moral laws?[4]

After securing Osler's cooperation, Gates dictated a memorandum to Rockefeller. Now he cited the Koch Institute in Berlin and the Pasteur Institute in Paris, cannily pointing out that the discoveries made in the latter "had saved for the French nation a sum far in excess of the cost of the Franco-German War." He added flatteringly that even if the institution Rockefeller founded should not in itself prove fruitful, the example given by so famous a man would induce others to back medical research. Gates emphasized the special possibilities opened by bacteriology for the cure of infectious diseases.

Gates's ideas did not instantly take root. Rockefeller himself and his other advisors had even less knowledge of medical science than Gates had had before he opened Osler's book. Furthermore, the headquarters of Rockefeller's huge business and fortune was a lush jungle of pressures. Rockefeller never even mentioned the memorandum to Gates, but Gates awaited another opportunity. It came when Rockefeller's favorite benefaction, the University of Chicago, planned to join up with Rush Medical College (where Flexner had refused an appointment as offering no real opportunities for research). With Rockefeller's approval, Gates dispatched protesting letters in which he included ideas from his memorandum. The merger would block the possibility of Rockefeller's establishing, in connection with the university, an institution following "a high ideal . . . magnificently endowed, devoted primarily to investigation, making practice itself an incident of investigation." When the university refused to listen to so wild an idea, one that practitioners opposed, the matter of a research institute sank back into the shadows.[5]

The situation was changed by the appearance on the scene of Rockefeller's son, twenty-four years old and just out of college. Much more accessible to Gates than the austere elder Rockefeller, John D., Jr., was soon indoctrinated with the glittering vision of a medical research institute. He made use of his opportunity to talk to his father at propitious moments: after dinner, or "when we were riding together." But even with this help, movement was not fast.[6] A problem was that the Rockefellers, being completely unfamiliar with the scientific world,* were unsure how to venture onto that strange ground. It seemed most prudent to entrust the preliminary investigations to a lawyer who was Gates's neighbor in Montclair, New Jersey: Starr J. Murphy. Murphy wrote some inquiring letters to established research institutions in Europe, but felt it most prudent at home to consult not scientists but the presidents of Harvard and Columbia universities. Seth Low of Columbia was entrusted with writing Drs. Welch and Prudden to ask whether American medical science was far enough along to support a research institution. (PLATE 28)

The university presidents, of course, regarded as close to blasphemy any idea that the institute should not be part of a university, and Welch and Prudden, one at the Hopkins and the other at the College of Physicians and Surgeons, which was affiliated with Columbia, agreed. But Gates believed that the chosen scientists should be enabled to engage in investigation "uninterrupted" by teaching. Furthermore, there was no American medical school except the Hopkins to which the institute could rationally be hitched. As Welch quickly discovered, it would be useless to suggest to the Rockefellers placing the institute anywhere but in New York City, where the medical schools were weak. And the Pasteur Institute, which the Rockefellers looked on as their model, was not connected with a university.[7]

Actual contact with the New York medical profession came about by chance. In November, 1900, John D., Jr., found himself on the same train with Dr. Luther Emmett Holt. Holt was the leading children's doctor in New York, head of the Babies Hospital, professor at the New York Polyclinic, author of both the leading textbooks on pediatrics and the leading manual for mothers. He was not altogether outside the Rockefellers' social circle since his practice had put him in touch with important families in New York.[8]

Rockefeller asked Holt whether medical research was "a promising field deserving generous support." Holt replied with a lecture on the diphtheria antitoxin as "not a chance discovery but the result of patient and laborious laboratory work in which fundamental biological principles had been applied." Holt added that the requirements "to solve many of the other great problems in medicine were men and resources which could be devoted solely to the work of research." [9]

* Senior's personal physician, to whom he clung while supporting an altogether different kind of medicine, was an elderly homeopath unconcerned with modern science.

Holt had several more talks with John D., Jr., on the subject during the winter. They were soon joined by Dr. Christian Herter, whose wife was a relative of Holt's wife, and who was a summertime neighbor of the elder Rockefeller.

The scientist's father, also Christian Herter, had been America's most accomplished and successful interior designer. He had created the mansions of America's post–Civil War millionaires, from Mark Hopkins in California to J. P. Morgan and the Vanderbilts in New York. His style, which brought together artistic inspiration from innumerable ages and civilizations, is today much admired. He sought to be the universal man in the arts, passing his culture and also the fortune he had made on to his scientific son.[10] The younger Christian, who became Simon Flexner's most intimate friend, married a lady of wealth and charm, built a mansion on Madison Avenue, and became so adept at finance that he was appointed treasurer of the Rockefeller Institute. He was also a neurologist of impressive achievement.[11]

The initial definitive step towards founding the Rockefeller Institute was taken when Holt, Herter, and the younger Rockefeller dined together during March, 1901. They discussed what scientists should serve on an administrative board, and concluded that Welch should be asked to head it. Rockefeller commented uneasily to his companions, "We don't know these other gentlemen, but we do know you, and you can serve as a medium of connection between our family and the medical men whom you have suggested as advisors." [12]

Probably because he had previously worked with Welch, Herter was entrusted with writing him a letter that outlined the plans as they then stood. A laboratory would be established in a small way, without endowment and hence no board of trustees. It was suggested that at the beginning it should be "given shelter" in the new laboratory building of the New York City Board of Health. There was to be an advisory board of which it was hoped Welch would become chairman. Herter presented for Welch's consideration a list of potential members that included Flexner.

The duties of the advisory board would be to set up plans, consult with the director from time to time, and keep the Rockefellers informed of progress. Obviously not empowered to specify any sum that would immediately be made available, Herter repeated assurances from John D., Jr., that support would be available at the request of the board and subsequently be augmented should that be justified by results.* "I have no doubt," Herter wrote Welch, "that the laboratory would be liberally endowed after having established its claim to support."

"The importance and difficulty of securing a suitable director is appreciated by Mr. Rockefeller [Junior], and he desired ample time be taken to secure the services of a man not only well equipped as regards scientific attainment, but also as regards common sense in dealing with his colleagues." Welch could be particularly helpful in selecting "a man who is not only an experienced bacteriologist and pathological histologist" with "some training on the chemical side," but also "a man who has shown distinct originality in some of his work, and who promises to do work of a very high quality under favorable conditions."

The director's salary should be comparable to a professor's in a well-endowed university, say $5,000, which might, Herter assumed, be increased if necessary. He should work with two or three assistants at about $2,000 a year "at the beginning."

Herter admitted that what was projected might seem too small to yield important results in a few years. However, there was a danger that too conspicuous a start might raise [in the minds of the donors] "unreasonable demands for results that would catch the public eye." Herter was inclined to think that the Rockefellers were right in contending "that better results might ultimately be obtained through gradual enlargement . . . than by attempting to start with a fully organized laboratory."[13]

Welch's reply expressed enthusiasm and an unwillingness to serve as chairman (which was, of course, ignored). His suggestion for board members omitted Flexner. He added to his own name Holt, Herter, Theobald Smith, Prudden, and Herman M. Biggs of the New York City Department of Health.[14]

On April 29, the younger Rockefeller finally wrote Holt: "I desire to put into concrete form the result of our various conversations. . . . My father is prepared to give for the purpose of medical research whatever amount may be required up to an average of twenty thousand ($20,000) dollars a year for ten years. This money will be given to a committee which shall be appointed which shall be empowered to formulate the policy and direct the organization of the result."[15]

---

* The Rockefeller setup was that Senior kept all the cards in his own hand, while relying on Junior to deal actively with situations and make recommendations to him. No commitment was final until Senior had sanctioned it himself in writing.

Taking advantage of the annual meeting of the Association of American Physicians, over which Welch was presiding in Washington, Herter, Holt, Biggs, Prudden, and Welch held a preliminary meeting on May 1, 1901. They empowered Welch to feel out Theobald Smith, a professor at Harvard, concerning the directorship.[16]

Having among other discoveries established the insect transmission of disease by demonstrating that Texas fever was carried between cattle by ticks, Smith was by far the most distinguished medical investigator in the United States. Welch wrote him, "We were unanimous in the opinion that you were the best man — it seemed to us the only man possibly able — to take charge."

The account Welch included of the development of the project reveals complete ignorance of the role played by Gates. He attributed much to the influence of Holt and Herter, who still constituted the closest contact with the Rockefellers. "It seems that Mr. Rockefeller is not prepared at present for a laboratory on such a scale as I inferred from President Low's letter of last summer." It was useless to consider any university connection or any site but New York City.

Although this could only be read between the lines, Welch obviously hoped that Smith's acceptance would act as a lever with which to open the Rockefeller pocketbook wider. He stated that the salary offered, $5,000, could be at least doubled for Smith. He dwelt heavily on future possibilities, and asked Smith to consider "under what conditions" he might be tempted.[17]

Smith seems to have regarded the whole matter as too tenuous to require a reply.

During the next meeting, on May 10, it was decided that for the time being the institute would not set up its own laboratory, but award fellowships to individual scientists who would carry on their research in existing American or European laboratories. This decision disgusted Gates (who was no longer active on the project) as ridiculous conservatism. However, it served a group of important ends: it enabled the board to move, before a director was secured and more funds allotted, in a manner too clearly temporary to establish precedents that might hinder future progress. The applications for fellowships would serve as a census to determine whether enough scientific work was being done in America to justify a major independent laboratory. The board's attention would be called to able and ambitious workers across the nation. And the fellowships would encourage widespread scientific activity.

George Washington Corner, the historian of the Rockefeller Institute, points out that what was a passing expedient for the institute pioneered a method for stimulating research in growing fields that was to have an important future in the development of American science.

At the May 10 meeting, the board added one more to their number: Simon Flexner.[18]

Flexner had undoubtedly heard of the intended Rockefeller benefaction. He was, he remembered, pleased to be asked to join the board, partly because it was his first such outside honor; partly because he enjoyed the idea of periodic trips to New York; and partly because he would have an inside track to the fellowships. And indeed, when he attended the third preliminary meeting (May 26) he was awarded one of the two grants that were voted at once because they had to be applied during the summer: $1,200 for work "upon the etiology of acute dysentery and summer diarrhea of children." At the first regular meeting, which followed a formal letter of gift from Rockefeller, Sr., Flexner presented rules he had drawn up for administering the grants.[19]

At the fall meeting on October 2 (Helen was now immured with her sciatica in the Johns Hopkins Hospital), Simon reported on the work done under his grant, and was voted another $600.[20]

On January 11, 1902, in anticipation of a meeting that evening of the institute board, Welch dined privately with Rockefeller, Jr. He subsequently reported to the board that the younger Rockefeller had stated his willingness to take up with his father any recommendation the board should care to make concerning the establishment of a laboratory, for the present in a rented building; and concerning the selection of a director, or any other plan the board should advise.[21]

The board concluded, so Welch reported back to Rockefeller, Jr., that the most important step towards establishing a laboratory was "to secure a man of first-rate scientific ability and administrative ability" to direct the work. Flexner voted with the others that Theobald Smith be requested "to let us know on what terms he would consider an offer of such a position." Smith, being present, "agreed to take the matter under consideration."

"I believe," so Welch continued to Rockefeller, "we would be most fortunate if we could secure him. He has, however, an exceptionally attractive position at Harvard. Still, I believe the head of our laboratory would have opportunities for investigation and a field of usefulness unsurpassed in this country. I do not consider that there is so much urgency in making a change in our present plans to prevent us from waiting until we have the right man."[22] Welch did not confide to Rockefeller that the board had agreed that Smith should make it a condition for acceptance that "some permanent endowment be forthcoming."[23]

On January 30, in response to urging from Herter that they should get moving, Welch wrote, "We cannot proceed until we get Theobald Smith's decision.... I think we should next learn whether Flexner would consider a proposal."[24]

Smith's reply dated February 11 was a refusal. He wrote that his obligations to Harvard were great; that he would lose several years of work making the change; that he was afraid that his deep concern with animal pathology might have an adverse effect on the institute. "I believe that my usefulness in the more restricted sphere I now occupy would be greater than the new and untried though very promising field opened by the founding of the Rockefeller Institute."[25]

The next board meeting was almost a month away (March 8), and Welch was in no hurry to inform his fellow board members of either Smith's refusal or his intention of appointing Flexner. On his own initiative, he consulted Flexner, taking it for granted that if he made the recommendation it would be approved. However, he held out no roseate visions. He was, indeed, surprised that an offer so financially modest and extending only for ten years should elicit such enthusiasm in a man from an impoverished background with no exterior financial resources. Welch may, furthermore, have been concerned lest Flexner's quick enthusiasm impede his using the possibility that Flexner might be persuaded to accept as a come-on for further Rockefeller support. Welch pointed out to Flexner that under present circumstances he would be abandoning a valuable lifetime appointment for a post that might prove no more than temporary. As Flexner remembered three months later, "I conceived that you did not think the directorship offered me inducements to leave Philadelphia where the field of pathology is undoubtedly widening."[26]

No such hesitation was felt by the Flexner family team in Louisville. "Your letter," Abraham wrote on February 26, "sent us to the highest pitch we have yet reached. Such an opportunity at the very moment you are ripe for it comes to few men in a generation; and that it should come to you, with Mother still here to witness and enjoy it, is almost too much for worldly happiness." In the family's view, the offer surpassed being elected President of the United States.

Abraham's letter goes on to reveal that Simon had, in informing his family, wondered whether he could be "useful" in the new position, and expressed apprehension as to the reaction at the University of Pennsylvania. On the question of usefulness, Abraham wrote that Simon should accept Welch's assurances. Concerning the university, "no institution will put forward any claim to a man thus 'divinely' called. . . . It looks to me like something more than human accident. . . . Your course is as clear as if you could see the finger of Providence beckoning you."[27]

As Simon considered what he should decide, he was haunted by memories of his nervous collapse of a few years before. Did he have the stability for so demanding and important a task? On the twenty-ninth he wrote Barker asking in confidence for "words of advice or caution" concerning a matter "about which I am pretty undecided, and of which I am not speaking outside. . . . It seems that Mr. Rockefeller is now ready to go forward." The plan was to start with at least one department and add others as the men could be obtained. The equipment would be "the very best obtainable," and the top staff would be paid large salaries equal to a professorship so that they would be permanently attached. "The proposition has been made to me tentatively to assume charge of the first department and become the central head. . . . This would give me more or less dictation of the first organization of the Institute, and of its policy, although all will be done under the direction of a board of directors. The Institute would come eventually to have chemical, zoological, and other departments as bearing on medical research. . . .

"Am I the man for the place, have I the originality to keep it going, and the physical strength and temperamental qualities? . . . The undertaking is so important for the future medical progress of the country, and so vast in itself that I cannot but view it with some misgiving. . . . If I should follow my inclinations, there is no doubt of my accepting. But is it best? . . .

"You know me better than any person, even perhaps than I do myself." Barker had seen him in many moods and psychologically "naked. . . . Tell me what your advice is, freely and 'from the heart.' Anything you say I will understand."[28]

In his reply, Barker ignored Flexner's concern about his psychological stamina. "The only three men who could be considered for the position are Theobald Smith, Herter, and yourself, and in my opinion you have more of the desirable qualities and clever minds will be attracted to you, will have confidence in you, and will work enthusiastically under you."[29]

Three days before the board meeting, Welch finally informed Prudden that Smith had refused. "As it seems to be the general opinion of the directors that we should aim to establish a laboratory, and as Mr. Rockefeller appears to be ready to consider any proposals to this end that we may offer, it seems desirable to continue our efforts to secure a director and working staff. . . . I think that Flexner is inclined to consider an offer such as we made to Smith, and if he could be secured I believe that we could not secure a better man. I have sounded him in this matter, and he seems to be more tempted than I thought that he would be." Welch favored making Flexner the same offer as was made to Smith, "but, of course, only in case the board is unanimous." Perhaps Prudden would sound out the other members of the board.[30]

In writing to the other members, Prudden stated that he was "a good deal puzzled" both concerning going ahead on a laboratory and wooing Flexner. Yet he was inclined to think that "if we could get Flexner and all the potential energy he represents, we would be very fortunate and our course in establishing a laboratory fully justified. If we cannot get him, I do not know anyone else,* and should think we had better be cautious about proceeding."[31]

March 8, 1902, was a banner day in Flexner's career. By unanimous vote of the board, he was asked "to consider under what circumstances he would be induced to take charge of the laboratory." He agreed to prepare for submission to the board a statement concerning the establishment and organization of such a permanent home for the institution as would lead him to consider favorably the post of director.[32]

---

* There had been talk among the New York board members of appointing William H. Park, the director of the laboratories of the New York City Board of Health, where it had once been thought the institute might be lodged. Park was a disciple of Biggs and a friend of Holt. He had made important discoveries concerning the dissemination of diphtheria and how it might, through public health methods, be curtailed. However, Park's achievements in basic scientific research could so little rival Flexner's that his candidacy never passed beyond informal discussion, which Flexner learned about at a later date.[33]

43

---·◦∞◦·---

An Offer and a Refusal

DURING the very week when Simon Flexner learned that he was to be offered the directorship of the Rockefeller Institute, Helen Thomas copied into her vellum-bound notebook a prayer which she seems herself to have written: "Oh, Almighty God, who in Thy irresistible providence hast brought Thy people to this moment of time in eternity, make us submissive to Thy unalterable will and obedient to the promptings of Thy holy spirit, teaching us and all nature to aspire to an ever nearer and nearer approach to Thy perfection. Thou hast commanded us neither unduly to desire nor unduly scorn peace and happiness in this world; vouchsafe to our weakness strength to accept without lamentation not only our own sorrow but also the sorrows of all mankind, and finally grant us faith to believe that if we live the brief days of our mortal life in serenity and love, we shall not have lived in vain."[1]

Helen was back at Bryn Mawr, her hospital imprisonment and her bout of sciatica behind her, living again with Lucy — but there was no serenity and only backbiting love. She had been, so we may assume, seeing enough of Simon Flexner to incite her longtime friend and roommate into passionate jealousy. "I must, I have learned to take upon me the complications of a morbid, abnormal mind, and help Lucy through with the situation that has developed [illegible] and desolating agonies, and yet one has no control over the third person, the determining cause of it all. I can help Lucy only by plunging in myself, by assisting and protecting her when I can.... It is useless to revolt against the task. It seems unnecessary, unreal, not sane, all this disturbance, but there it is, engulfing Lucy...

"I feel about these next few years as a general must feel when taking the field against an enemy stronger than he. There is a fighting chance of success, of victory, and if one fails and falls, honor demanded the attempt. [illegible], as though I could not endure the sadness of renouncing so much joy and peace as there is in the world. But renunciation is the first step to success, and where is there a joy to be found so pure, so unalloyed as the joy of doing one's duty? . . .

"Before I could reach this mood of calmness and resolution, I had to spend an hour out in the meadows."[2]

During the month from March 8 to April 8, 1902, Simon Flexner prepared the requested statement "bearing upon the future establishment of a permanent home for the Institute as well as containing a proposal of organization which, if found feasible, would lead to my considering favorable becoming one of the directors." Encouraged by the attitude of the board, he made no modest proposal, but he urged such expensive and extensive immediate steps as would lead to very much the kind of institution he was later to conduct to world fame. He was recessive only concerning his own role. Although he was to be called "Chief Director and Head of the Research Department," he recommended that the various departments, which would "cover the entire field of medical research in respect both to men and animals," should each be autonomous, although "when united [they] would still form a whole allowing for conjoint investigation of comprehensive problems."

Flexner outlined the staff needed for each department: the director; at least one highly trained assistant "so firmly attached to the institution that his permanent retention would be practically assured"; secondary assistants, well-trained fellows who were desirous of carrying on scientific work while completing their training; and workers not employed by the institute but capable of pursuing scientific problems at their own expense. All "should either be open to association with their seniors in conducting investigation, or permitted to pursue independent research. Their association with a senior should receive the recognition of a joint-worker." No one should be denied credit for his achievements.

"The service of the Institute should be of the most liberal kind, and should include janitors, cleaners, departmental servants independently of each other. There is no greater economy in laboratory organization than is to be derived from competent and well-trained servants." A liberal allowance should be made for equipment and running expenses. The directors and first assistants "must be offered in addition to excellent opportunities for undisturbed work, a compensation that will be a suitable reward for their services." Impressive salaries would enable the institute to secure the services of the scientists most desired. There should be ample provision for retirement and pensions.

"While the work of the Institute will, of necessity, be highly experimental, intimate relations with the problems of human diseases should not for a moment be lost sight of." Therefore, there should be attached to the institute a small hospital to enable clinical study of cases of selected diseases. Since "the work of the Institute cannot fail to be affected by the scientific atmosphere that surrounds and pervades it," there remained a question whether the institute would be more "favored by complete independence or some kind of an attachment to an institution of learning where study in collateral branches is carried on. . . .

"The Institute, as here contemplated, will come to possess considerable magnitude. While it would probably not be completely organized in the beginning, yet from the start its future policy should be reflected." Flexner's nervousness about New York led him to suggest that the availability of a large enough site at a reasonable cost "might determine somewhat" the location of the institute. Also, of "some importance" would be the living expenses at the place chosen.

"I feel it my duty to state that, although the position I now hold is highly agreeable to me, and, under any circumstances, I would leave it with reluctance, if it is the intention of the Founder and the board of directors to organize the Institute upon a liberal scale with the most advantageous opportunities for research in medical science, I should feel obliged to give favorable consideration to such a directorship, should the offer be formally presented to me."[3]

The next step was for the board to draw up for the Rockefellers their report concerning the activities of the institute during its first year, and their recommendations for the future. The document was written by Prudden and edited by Welch. It began by retailing the success of the fellowship program, and went on to state the board's convicton "that the conditions are now not only favorable but urgent for such expansion of the Institute as will enable it adequately to cover the field so full of promise of the highest usefulness. . . . With the view of giving precision to our conceptions" the document quoted Flexner's memorandum (without mentioning his name or his intended future post). They made only three considerable changes: his suggestion of a university connection was omitted; it was definitely stated that the laboratory should be in

New York City, and (at Welch's urging) the possibility was raised (this was never to be done) of educating the people in healthful living "by popular lectures, by hygienic museums, by the diffusion of suitable literature, etc." A budget was appended accounting for annual expenditures of $140,000. The director's salary was given as between $7,500 and $9,000. Any request for an endowment was tactfully omitted, but the implication was obvious.[4]

Herter and Holt carried this report to Rockefeller, Jr., and, as Herter wrote Flexner, read it to him out loud. They were pleased to see him "follow the report with evident interest." Herter, who himself combined scientific research with the practice of medicine, was particularly pleased that Rockefeller approved the hospital scheme.

When Holt and Herter pointed out that an endowment of five to six million dollars would be needed to get the entire venture started, Rockefeller "did not appear overcome." But he expressed doubt that his father would wish to provide any endowment whatsoever at that time. "He says his father's proposition would be something like this: to build and equip a laboratory equal to university requirements, perhaps also the hospital." To extend the yearly appropriation to "say twenty years" and increase it to between $40,000 and $60,000: "this sum to be used," so Herter continued to Flexner, "for your salary and that of five to ten associates and assistants. The plant and the yearly appropriation would be increased according to the increasing needs."

Herter "called to Mr. Rockefeller's attention rather persistently" that the permanency of the institution would be an important attraction to workers, urging that the salaries of the director and the heads of the departments should be enduringly assured. Rockefeller replied "that he considered the provision unnecessary because of the practical certainty that within five years there would be an endowment." His father's willingness to buy lands and erect a building "should be taken as an evidence of earnestness." It should also be taken into consideration that his father had never withdrawn help from any work in which he had become interested.

Herter had been pleased to hear that Carnegie, who was founding his own charitable institution, had promised Rockefeller to leave medicine entirely to him. "It seems clear that Mr. Rockefeller means to make our Institute national in significance." Herter was "a little disappointed that they are not prepared (probably) to make some endowment at once, but if one stops to look at the matter from their point of view, I cannot say the caution seems unreasonable."

Herter feared that Flexner would "look on the general proposition less favorably than I do." Accepting the directorship would obviously involve "a little risk as to the permanency of the undertaking, but I think it would be small and safely taken. . . . It is possible," Herter continued, "that we might secure some endowment now, but I doubt it and feel that we ought to show the same confidence in the Rockefellers' good faith that they show in us. It seems to me rather important that you should be at the June meeting."[5]

For Flexner, the issue of permanence was given a larger dimension by his growing love for Helen Thomas. He had always seen her as charming and admirable, but at first he had not thought of her as desirable because it was not in his makeup to yearn for what he considered impossible, far above his reach. But as time passed and he got to know her, sympathy grew up between them and he came to realize that on a personal level the possibility existed for their coming together. Simultaneously, the worldly gap between them shrank in his eyes. He became in Philadelphia more and more at home in a society where Helen Thomas would naturally be at home. He frequented her brother Harry's house and had become a particular favorite of her sister-in-law Zoe. Then came the Rockefeller Institute offer which, even if it presented financial dangers, would place him in a position worthy of the redheaded beauty's birthright.

For all his self-confidence when he felt his feet firmly on the ground, Simon was diffident if he feared he might be out of his depth. He could not visualize putting his fate in regard to Helen Thomas to the test. The climactic moment came on suddenly, in May, 1902.

In the earliest surviving letter from that month, Helen wrote to "Dr. Flexner," that "it was very charming of you to remember that I am starting out tomorrow, though the candies are rather against rules, do you not think? However, I shall not quarrel with you about them, as I am feeling very blue indeed and like being remembered. So occupied and successful a man as you are can never, I think, feel as despairing as I sometimes do." She hoped that he realized that he was much to be envied for his achievements. "I should like to tell you a few of the things I think about myself, but shall refrain, as lamentation . . . on the whole accomplishes nothing."[6]

In his reply, Simon thanked her for writing so warmly of his success in his work. "I should be ungrateful," he wrote in a style for him unusually stilted, "were I insensitive of a certain satisfaction and joy in it." But she did not need to be told that he had passed through many troubles and trials, "resistances that are overcome only to spring into fresh life. Still, there comes from all this a philosophic content not without real value. Sometimes to view one's discontents in the light of others, helps to minimize the pain of both. . . . For this reason if for no other, I shall hope that you may come to feel such confidence in me as will enable you to talk as freely as you will. I think I may say that your happiness means much to me."[7]

Helen replied, "Your understanding my feeling so well, even more than what you definitely told me, showed that my state of mind is not unknown to you from personal experience. . . . I think I once explained to you in part my difficulties. They are not in themselves great, but they seem great to me when I measure myself up to them. I often wonder what keeps us going, what it is we are all striving after. Surely it cannot be happiness, since the more hotly happiness is pursued, the faster it flies. . . . The question is a puzzling one, and I should like to know what you think about it.

"The children were as sweet and as gay as possible. My sister's house [where she had stayed during a visit to Baltimore] seemed to me the very home of contentment and peace, astir and amurmur all day long with happy life; for even the profound stillness that fell over it when the two youngest babies were taking their afternoon nap, was a breathing quietness."

Helen wondered what had happened during Simon's trip to New York (at which he had presented his plans for the future institute) and asked him for dinner.[8]

Simon reported that he had just missed her in Baltimore, where he had talked with Welch upon "the perennial New York" question. "The outlook for a suitable beginning is now excellent, and the attractions have become correspondingly more irresistible," yet he was still undecided.

Simon was much too astute to point out that Helen had described a road to happiness through domesticity. "I fear I only partially appreciate the specific doubts that assail your mind." To answer her question concerning "what keeps us going," he quoted Maeterlinck, "Mere rewards are the hope of every day, and yet one cannot live without greatness . . . the inextinguishable aspiration after the truly heroic."[9]

Helen replied, "I like what you say about the unquenchable desire of the human race for greatness. I believe you are right, and though it may be no more voluntary than a bee's turning to the light, our aspiration is somehow beautiful. You must talk to me more about it some day if you will." She remained anxious to hear the latest developments concerning the institute.[10]

On May 27, 1902, Lucy was away. Helen and Simon were alone in the flat at Low Buildings. Helen found herself telling Simon about her fear that she was trapped in a desperate situation. How was she to calm Lucy's mental storms, and if they could not be calmed, how escape the duty of remaining forever with her stricken friend, laboring unceasingly to keep her from toppling into visible insanity? Was this to be the content of all the rest of Helen's years?

As she described in words what she had never described so frankly before, as Simon listened with deep and sympathetic gravity, offering both reassurance and advice, Helen began to relax, feeling a burden lifting from her mind. Then the blow struck.

Simon was so exhilarated by Helen's confiding to him her inmost thoughts that, without any premeditation, he suddenly found himself declaring his love. He proposed marriage. The expression that appeared on Helen's face was devastating.

In her conscious mind, Helen had not foreseen any such outcome. How frightening that her search of comfort had opened in her path this other chasm! Even if the foundations had been weakening, her determination not to marry still stood as the citadel of her life. This man had taken advantage of her confidences. In embarrassment and indignation, she gave Simon a firm refusal.

Simon responded with apologies. He was to write her, when the catastrophe was well passed and the wounds healed, "When I found I had pained and perhaps surprised you, I suffered a double distress: from my failure to secure a promise that should show reciprocal affection in you, and the consciousness of adding to your trials at an inopportune and critical point in your life."[11]

The first shock over, Helen regretted the anger of her answer. She asked his forgiveness. He said there was nothing to forgive, and departed.[12]

Lying awake that night, Helen concluded that she had treated her suitor very unfairly. This did not mean that she had any intention of taking back her refusal. But surely her friend deserved an explanation and further apology. She wrote him the next day:

"Although I am half afraid I am being selfish again in writing you this letter, I cannot help hoping you may care to hear one or two things I very much want to say to you; and in any case, after all your generosity to me, I feel that I may venture to make one more claim on your forbearance, if it is a claim. I want you surely to know how great a help you have been to me during the past months. More than once I have felt myself quite without courage to face the knowledge of my weakness in circumstances that call particularly for strength, and the light of the wisdom and thought that enable you to do the things you do, and be the thing you are, have given me force to go on. Something you said yesterday made me think that you feared you had perhaps added to my burdens, but this is not the case. From time to time, I was indeed haunted by a sense that I had no right to accept the sympathy and friendship you offered me with such delicate generosity, for I was afraid you were caring for our friendship more than was consistent with your happiness, but it meant so much to me to talk out with you questions which were troubling me that I blinded my eyes, as I now see, to my own selfishness. You have paid the penalty that in an unjust world the strong so often pay to the weak. But, while I regret my behavior, I shall not grieve over it because you have been generous enough to say that you have nothing to forgive me, which I shall take to mean that you do forgive.

"You must not let what I told you yesterday about my sense of the dangers in the future bother you. It did me immense good to express to you my fears, for when they were put into words, I saw how largely nervous they are. I am really learning to take calmly things that have before deeply disturbed me, and I know how distorted one's vision becomes by turning things over day after day in one's mind. If you think for a moment you will see that it is impossible for me to express to any ordinary person, even to my friends, my fears for Miss Donnelly and myself, and if you have ever carried about you a haunting anxiety, though you may not have the weakness to disclose it, you will know how great a relief disclosure is, and so will perhaps understand my selfishness in bothering you, who have already quite enough to bear, with my troubles."

That morning she had received "the gayest possible letter" from Lucy. "Everything seems to be going well. I am sure that the worst is over and the future will simplify itself more and more. It is always, you know, darkest before the dawn.

"There remains only one thing to be said. I did not make clear to you yesterday, I am sure, my sense of the honor you have done me in caring for me as you do. You are entirely too modest, I am convinced, to fully realize how great the honor seems to me. That my feelings should remain what they are is one of those unaccountable facts it is useless to try to account for.

"I wish you every happiness and success in the future, and I thank you for what you have done for me in the past.

"Very sincerely. . .

"Please do not feel that you must answer this letter. It requires no answer. Of course, you will understand that should you ever care to write to me, I should be glad to hear from you."[13]

Although Simon's letter to Helen dated "Friday" has been much disfigured by dampness, enough can be deciphered. "Your kind note of Wednesday gives me the privilege of sending you a brief reply, I feel very keen [obliterated] of my action on Tuesday but the [obliterated] has under the influence of your generous note been much mitigated." He hoped he had not "caused you more than momentary pain and embarrassment by my ill-timed and ill-advised confession." She had not treated him "unfairly." He had "declined to see and believe the obvious. I wish therefore to assure you that whatever of friendly interest you permitted me to display in the past was [obliterated] misunderstood." She had given him "no grounds on which to base a hope I have already too plainly told you I cherished." He was "deeply flattered" by her "generous allusions" to his usefulness to her. "In return, you should know that you have helped to guide and sustain me [obliterated] of great uncertainty and perturbation.

"I congratulate you upon the favorable outlook for the next year, and that the sun of you and Miss Donnelly has broken through the clouds. Although I have never doubted, your success will ever be of the greatest moment to me." He would show his appreciation "of your goodness and generosity . . . by sending you a note when I have something to impart that I think you would like to hear."[14]

Although Helen's letter, particularly as expanded by the postscript, had in no way slammed the door, Simon took it as final. He did not beg her to reconsider, dilating, as so many lovers would have done, on his desolation. His only plea was that she forgive him for asking her to marry him. This was both pride and a deep lack of pride. Her refusal, as he wrote later, had seemed altogether natural to him considering "the great differences in our worlds."[15]

Helen had inherited as part of her very being the aspects of American life Simon most admired, that he had from his early years yearned and struggled to make his own. And she was a woman of beauty, intelligence, and charm.

To Helen's surprise, Simon utterly abandoned his courtship. But he had in effect left open a chance to inform her about what finally happened in relation to the Rockefeller Institute.

44

---···❦···---

Abraham and Anne

A BRAHAM had hardly got started with his independent school for boys when he was persuaded to tutor privately the girl, then sixteen, he was eventually to marry.[1]

Anne Laziere Crawford came from a Georgia family that had been impoverished by the Civil War. Her great-grandfather, William Harris Crawford, had in antebellum days been commonly described as the greatest man ever nurtured in Georgia. After holding a galaxy of high offices, he competed in 1824 for the presidency with Henry Clay, Andrew Jackson, and John Quincy Adams. Crawford instead of Adams might possibly have become President had he not been struck in mid-campaign with a paralytic stroke.[2]

His oldest son, Nathaniel Macon Crawford, Anne's grandfather, was a Methodist minister and the president of Mercer College. Nathaniel's oldest son and Anne's father, Louis G. Crawford, wanted to become a scholar, but his ambition was extinguished by the Civil War. He joined Lee's army, and his property was destroyed in Sherman's march to the sea. His proudest possession remained the sword he had carried when with Lee.[3]

On Anne's mother's side there was a mystery that intrigued Abraham: the wife of the president of Mercer College had arrived in Charleston as an infant. Her mother had died on the voyage from France. Nothing was known of the orphan's antecedents, but she was adopted by a well-to-do family. Abe liked to boast that her Gallic qualities — "gaiety, high spirits, intelligence, and charm" — reappeared in his wife, who was her namesake.[4]

Although born (on June 26, 1874) during a visit to Kentucky, Anne was reared in Georgia.[5] Since she was no more given to keeping records than her future husband, we know of her childhood from only two anecdotes. These she told, after she became a successful playwright, to a newspaper interviewer in order to demonstrate that she had always been interested in theatricals. Having cast herself as Mary Queen of Scots, she used pokeberry juice to circle her neck with a red line to indicate that she had been beheaded. On another occasion, when using a pantry shelf as a stage, she trudged along in the role of Bunyan's Pilgrim, so concentrating on her rendition that she walked off the end of the shelf and fell into the flour bin.[6]

Anne's parents faded from the record as she became the favoite niece of her uncle, John M. Atherton, a well-to-do Louisville businessman. It was his desire to send her to Vassar that brought in Abraham as her tutor. She proved to be vivacious and extremely bright. In less than a year she passed six examinations and was off to college.

Abraham remembered that he more or less lost track of Anne while she was at Vassar. But she resolved after her graduation to be no longer dependent on her uncle, and made her living as a teacher in Mr. Flexner's School. She and her employer were soon bicycling together.[7]

Anne was eight years younger than Abraham. She was physically much larger; in fact, she towered over most of the Flexner clan, who had difficulty attaining five feet six. They were delicately boned; she robust. Her moon-shaped face seemed almost flat because of the breadth of her cheeks. But she was a handsome, imposing young woman who made a strong impression on everyone she met.

As a girl, Anne had written poems in the manner of Kate Greenaway, and she continued to compose light verse. During her last two years at Vassar, she edited the college literary magazine. Back in Louisville, she published several stories — a typical title: "The Scale of Love" — in the Louisville-based *Southern Magazine*.[8] Her daughter Jean expressed surprise that her mother and Helen Thomas Flexner did not get together — they were both writers — but their sights were set in altogether different literary directions.

Furthermore, although the Thomas family had no Confederate sword and came from a border state, Helen's outlook remained, perhaps because no exterior force had blasted her family tradition, much more southern than Anne's. In New York, where Helen was to be drawn by Simon's career, she was always somewhat apart. Anne, it is true, remained proud of her descent from William Crawford, but as she pursued her own career in the professional New York theater, there was nothing in her manner to indicate her southern origin. Along with her early environment, she completely abandoned the Baptist religion. Abraham stated that this brought them closer together since he had also abandoned his ancestral faith. (PLATE 27)

In 1886, a year after her graduation from Vassar, Anne and Abraham became engaged, even though, so he wrote, "the financial situation of my [the Flexner] family required me to put off our marriage for more than two years. With the wisdom and generosity that have been characteristic of our entire life together, she at once consented, urging me first of all to do my duty by my family. Of course, delay tried our patience but we waited contentedly."[9] To her daughters, Anne described over and over her bitterness at having been pushed aside while Abraham struggled to shore up the tumbling-down finances of his brothers.

The delay may well have been a godsend for Anne as it enabled her to get going before her marriage on a career that rapidly yielded remarkable fruits. Abraham wrote in *I Remember*, "We agreed at the outset of our marriage that her interests and work were as sacred as mine; and for over forty years we have tried to respect each other's individuality, and that of our two daughters."[10] The first half of this statement is descriptive of what actually happened. The second half of the statement is pure moonshine. Abraham did his best to interfere with the individuality of their daughters.

Having saved three hundred dollars, Anne went to New York to become a professional short story writer. She visualized herself romantically as freezing and starving in a garret as part of a Knickerbocker *vie de bohème*. Instead, she roomed in a boardinghouse on Gramercy Park kept by a southern lady who spread a good table. She could only "boast," as she put it to the newspaper interviewer, of living in a small hall bedroom inadequately heated by a kerosene lamp.[11]

A very modern "Mimi," Anne enrolled in a course on short story writing at New York University. Her instructor told her that she could only handle dialogue. She was eking out her funds by sending theater news to the Louisville *Courier-Journal*, and the free admission to plays opened for her a "magic world." Switching to Frank Finley Mackay's National Conservatory of Dramatic Art,[12] she wrote the scenario for an original play, "A Man's Woman." Then she returned to Louisville where she married Abraham (June, 1898), with due rapidity gave birth to a daughter, Jean Atherton Flexner, and finished her play.

Anne sent the manuscript to Mackay, who showed it to Minnie Mad-

dern Fiske, the leading lady of the American theater. Mrs. Fiske was interested enough for Anne to be summoned. She arrived with her infant
daughter, "a baby bottle under one arm and a play under the other."
There was also a nurse.

The interview took place at the Murray Hill Hotel. Mrs. Fiske regretted that she could not use "A Man's Woman." She did not want a
"problem play." She was "tired of doing parts not moral: Becky, Tess,
Magda." Had Anne any other plays to offer? The reply that this was her
only one did not discourage Mrs. Fiske from suggesting a play in which
she might like to appear. Anne should dramatize A. E. W. Mason's
novel, *Miranda on the Balcony.* In this story, the heroine influences
men without ever getting into trouble by getting off her balcony.[13]

"A Man's Woman" found no producer, but Anne was not one to be
silenced. She had the play printed in Louisville. Thus we know that her
heroine is driven by passion and compassion to live immorally with a
married man, but is basically too noble and moral to be believable. The
writing has energy and bite, which reveals why Mrs. Fiske had been
impressed.

Abraham's brothers were now reestablished on their financial feet,
and Abraham had paid off the old debts. Mr. Flexner's School, having
changed from a facility of last resort to the most respected school in the
city, was demonstrating that the methods of teaching he had evolved for
the slow and unmotivated would accelerate the ambitious and intelligent. This was dramatically underlined when he received a brief note
from President Eliot of Harvard stating that his attention had been
called to the fact that boys from Mr. Flexner's School were coming to
Harvard younger than the other freshmen and were graduating in a
shorter period of time. "What are you doing?"

Abraham made this an occasion for calling on Eliot. "I told him it was
all very simple, that I treated these boys as individuals, and let each go at
his own pace. I took hold of pupils where they were strong, not where
they were weak, and having whetted their appetite by success in one
field, usually succeeded in interesting them in another. I did not insist in
attempting the impossible, and thus perhaps spoiling all." For gifted
pupils who were "morons" in some directions, he worked out purely
mechanical techniques for them to pass the necessary examinations, explaining "precisely what I was doing and why."[14]

At Eliot's suggestion, Abraham wrote an article which he titled "A
Freshman at Nineteen" and published in the November, 1899, issue of

the *Educational Review*. It presented as a national panacea the methods evolved at Mr. Flexner's School.

Under the accepted educational methods, he pointed out, students who needed professional training passed "their first manhood" before they could make a living. According to his system, the progression could be speeded up by enabling boys to enter college at seventeen so well trained that they could be graduated in three years.

The present trouble lay in the requirement that students in preparatory schools advance in a group from grade to grade, changing teachers at every step. By postulating "an average child who does not exist," this system held back the able and also left the slow starters forever at the bottom, unable to get going.

Flexner recommended that pupils be divided into groups of twelve. Each group would be assigned to teachers who would work from year to year with each student as an individual. It would not be necessary to give marks which, as things now stood, rewarded "small shrewdness, plausibility, and superficial readiness." The abler students, advancing at their own speed, would inspire the less able to emulation, and would themselves enter college at seventeen. In arguing for this emphasis on ability, Abraham wrote: "Educational inequality must be prized and sought if democracy is to be lifted over the dead-level of mediocrity."[15]

Flexner sent copies of his article to Gilman and Eliot. Gilman replied with a postcard saying the paper was "admirable. *Keep up the discussion.*" Eliot wrote, "It is much to be wished that your doctrine be brought home to every school committeeman and college trustee in the country." He would like forty copies for distribution to the governing boards of Harvard.

Abraham did not feel that such praise was enough. He wrote Simon, "The vested interest in the present school organization is so strong, for selfish and unconscious reasons, that I am but a voice crying in the wilderness. Hadn't I better do something that will tell?" He did not specify what.[16]

There was no question of Anne's being in a position to do something that would tell. The opportunity that had been opened to her by Mrs. Fiske would have made almost any veteran professional playwright leap with joy.

The famous actress and her rich husband, Harrison Gray Fiske, were opening a crusade against the "rapacious syndicate," which by bribing critics, blackmailing actors, and even burning down theaters, had gained control of almost all bookings in New York City and all bookings on the road. The syndicate had forced Sarah Bernhardt to appear in a circus tent, and had evicted Mrs. Fiske from the Fifth Avenue Theater at the height of her run in *Becky Sharp.*

Having bought the Manhattan Theatre, Mr. Fiske was pouring millions into rebuilding. No expense or fanfare was to be spared for the opening production which would throw the gauntlet to the syndicate.[17] In the competition for the play to be selected, the dramatization Mrs. Fiske had suggested of *Miranda* seemed to have a head start.

Anne was to boast that she wrote the play in eleven months. Early in January, 1901, she journeyed from Lousiville to New York and read Mr. Fiske the first two acts. He declared them excellent, Abe reported to Simon. After Fiske had read them to his wife, the word came that "her approval was as warm as his own."

Anne started on the third act with a bounce. Although a month later found her in New York still struggling, she heard that the other contenders for the opening had been shelved. "If so," exulted Abe, "millions!"[18]

Miranda was chosen. It opened in Montreal. Abe wrote Simon, "The play was well received. Mrs. Fiske's acting was good but not, I think, up to her or the play's capacity. But, of course, in New York she will look out for this. The general impression is that it will draw and please." Anne had gone along to New York to execute necessary changes — "not many to be sure but enough to make work and apprehension."[19]

The opening in New York was on September 24, 1901. "To the crowd that filled every seat," wrote Mrs. Fiske's biographer, "the most immediately striking thing was the theatre itself." Out of its "hideous" predecessor had been "created the most beautiful and comfortable theatre in New York, finished in restful dark green and bronze and gold, under soft lights, the chairs upholstered in dark red and spaced for comfort rather than maximum revenue." The five stage sets built at vast cost (over $60,000) "were each as beautiful and perfect as was ever seen on the New York stage." Matching them in elegance and expense were Mrs. Fiske's three gowns, one being the famous "wheat dress," which had won first prize at the Paris Exposition and was considered "the most beautiful gown in the world." With its overlay of pearls and gold it weighed about forty pounds. The audience was the best that New York could supply in wealth, elegance, and sophistication. There was only one sour note: the play.[20]

The New York *Tribune* was typical in finding the play amateurish and (although Mrs. Fiske had chosen the subject and herself revised the script during rehearsals) unsuited to her dramatic gifts. All the physical action showed the men in her life engaging before exotic scenery in der-ring-do, villainy, and heroism. Since she stayed at home, these events were "only relevant to her because her existence as a woman — her fas-cination, her social position, her mental and emotional states — affected the conduct of the men."[21]

Even if *Miranda* was ruled not up to its opportunity, the opening had been by far the most glamorous event in the history of the Flexner fam-ily. And the play did run for ten weeks in New York and was picked up by road companies. Anne's future as a playwright seemed rosy.

Abraham could not fail to feel the contrast between his wife's situa-tion and his own as he continued to plug away at preparing Louisville boys for college. His situation seemed all the less inspiring when his brother, who had once been his semi-dependent, was offered the direc-torship of the Rockefeller Institute. "I am," he wrote Simon, "patheti-cally anxious to do something, and [I] could were I in reach of publishers and periodicals. But I am fastened here like Prometheus on his rock with a grinding routine that is almost as hard on the liver as a vulture's beak."[22]

Having no better outlet, Abraham sent two letters to the New York *Post* that attacked the College Entrance Board examinations, which were interfering with his ideals as a teacher. He began by expressing a hope that "some day . . . a continuous organization will be substituted for the several abrupt and disjointed stages into which our educational system is now broken." Until then, some kind of formal test for college entrance had to be maintained. However, the tests as currently given "cut-off" nearly half the boys recommended by their teachers, depriv-ing from further educational opportunities "all who have not explicitly and minutely satisfied more or less arbitrary conditions." In their re-quirements for sterile fragments of knowledge, the examinations made "the teacher a machine and the pupils passive material." Such penaliz-ing of "seriousness and originality" was entirely out of tune with the rising movement in colleges towards an elective system that relied upon the student's "interest, purpose, and power."

The immediate remedy was for the entrance system to be revised so as not to encourage "forced and insincere scholarship." Questions should call for thoughtful answers, and the examination periods should be lengthened so that candidates would have a chance to express themselves. Furthermore, the results should be interpreted with some reliance on the scholastic history of each individual student.[23]

Abraham's letters were duly published, but this was hardly a forum suited to his desires. He wished that he could read a paper at a meeting of the Association of American Universities. "Thus I would leap into notice in taking, I believe, a new 'inward' and 'connected' view of the correct relationship between secondary schools and colleges." But perhaps it was just as well that he could not secure a chance "for I am ill-equipped in knowledge, training, and experience." He would have to see more and know more before he could "with confidence even outline what is vaguely buzzing in my brain."

He did begin a formal essay on preparatory schools "in which, in my familiar attitude as a kicker, I may do some knocking." In its finished form (it was not published until 1904), the essay continued Abraham's attack on college entrance examinations, and then went on to describe the ideal schools that could be developed were this block removed. These schools, by avoiding a sharp division between elementary and secondary education, would make "culture through use the foundation not the capstone of the educational structure. The child's school life will be co-extensive with his whole life, seeking to enlist his total physical, moral, and mental powers. . . . Subjectively, education will be genuinely individualistic, studying the individual bent, capacity, endowment; aiming to invoke the largest and freest individual response. Objectively, it will regard the actual context of our civilization, industrial, artistic, spiritual. . . . The school is thus no longer remote from life. It is no longer a clog on the child's eager spirit, but the congenial field in which all his attitudes can be naturally and productively utilized.

"The new school will from the first keep in touch with experience, but will in no point be meanly utilitarian. It will use the activities of daily life, but with ideal interpretation."*[24]

Such were Abraham's ideas when he was thirty-seven, before it had entered his consciousness that he would ever have anything to do with medical education.

Abraham was considering writing a series of magazine articles that he would subsequently combine into a book, but he continued to be

---

* Abraham's continuing interest in pre-college education resulted in the endowing, during 1915, of the Lincoln School of Columbia University Teachers College that was considered at the time very advanced. Subsequently, it was ruled obsolete on the grounds that its experimental methods were applicable only to children privileged by background or ability.

haunted by his strong suspicion, even conviction, that he was inadequately prepared. He had long realized that he had worked in isolation, removed from what was happening in other secondary schools both here and abroad. Would his ideas, evolved in lonely originality, stand up?

"Mr. Flexner's School" was so personal an operation that it required his continual presence. Far from being able to take a sabbatical, he even had difficulty getting off to attend the opening of his wife's play. The school promised to be highly successful as long as he continued its leadership, but it could not be sold to another schoolmaster. It would die if he departed. Killing off the source of prosperity for his family seemed improvident to the greatest degree. Yet this drastic step was essential to his attempting what his ambition and consciousness of his own abilities commanded him to do.

To Simon, Abraham wrote, "Having lost my faith in my avocation and being unable thus far to embrace another with confidence in *myself* and *it*, I have moments of greater depression than on those days when I had no choice and no prospect of one." He hoped to get his alternatives clearly in mind for a consultation with Simon.[25]

On August 21, 1903, Simon spent a day in consultation with Abraham and Anne. Having for so many years heard his brother expatiate, with no action ever resulting, on escaping from Louisville and his school, Simon was amazed to conclude that Abraham did actually regard himself "as the one member of the family without hopeful or congenial occupation."

Simon, who had for years urged Abraham to stop wasting his talents, decided that his brother's continuing "indecision" was due to his having reinforced his fear of failure with an "exaggerated" sense of duty; to give Anne and Jean "everything within reason." Abraham's resulting concern had "gone so far as to make him unsure that what he really wanted to do was really worth doing." Simon decided that he could not help Abe straighten the matter out unless the brother would come alone to Philadelphia while Anne and Jean were in New York where her new play was in rehearsal. He made Abe promise to give him this opportunity. Simon's objective was to persuade Abe to take an "unrestricted view" of "where his real, active interest lay." This determination would enable him to "detach himself from everything except what he wished and hoped to do."[26]

Whether or not Simon was given this chance the record does not reveal, but it does reveal that more than another year passed — Simon was

then in Europe as a married man — before Abraham and Anne decided
to abolish Mr. Flexner's School so that he could devote himself to the
study he needed before he could operate soundly as an educational re-
former.

The Abraham Flexners had been living in a quarter of Louisville that
was inhabited by "a considerable, mostly female, set of popular writers." Annie Fellows Johnston wrote the once-celebrated children's book
The Little Colonel. George Madden Martin wrote the "Emmy-Lou
Stories." Fannie C. Macaulay was responsible for *The Lady of the Decoration,* and the local poetess, Margaret Steele Anderson, came up with
A Flame in the Wind. Most important to the Flexners was Alice Hegan
Rice, the best-selling author of comic and sentimental fantasies about
the feckless inhabitants of back-country Kentucky towns.[27]

Anne decided to combine in a single dramatization two of Alice Rice's
stories: *Mrs. Wiggs of the Cabbage Patch,* a great best-seller, and a continuation not yet published, "Lovey Mary." To Mrs. Rice herself and
the rest of the Louisville literary set this seemed "absurd." They insisted that nothing like what Anne resolutely intended had ever been
seen on any stage. A critic was to specify "the incredible types, the almost incomprehensible dialect, the immense joy and zest with which
the Cabbage Patchers lived their sordid lives." Mrs. Wiggs was the ultimate slattern, endlessly ingenious and with a heart of gold. It was "her
little hobby of match-making" that made all the trouble.

The critic for the London *Daily News* thus related his favorite episode: "Mrs. Wiggs thinks Miss Hazy ought to get married. Well, Stubbins is willing. Stubbins is very tall, lank, desperately idle,
philosophical, but has an inveterate habit of thrusting his tongue in his
cheek after every remark. Miss Hazy is a timid spinster of forty with a
squeaky voice and an air of profound melancholy. Imagine the couple
making love! You can see Stubbins laboriously lifting the bridal veil —
fashioned by Mrs. Wiggs out of an old pair of lace curtains — before
implanting the first kiss. This scene alone would be enough to draw
lovers of clean, healthy laughter to Terry's Theatre."

Mrs. Wiggs had lured Stubbins into the match by passing off her expert cooking as Miss Hazy's. This raises much suspense: the audience
knows that Stubbins will eventually be faced with his wife's own cooking — and the scene, when finally reached, does not disappoint. Senti-
mentality is added by interweaving the plot of "Lovey Mary." Mary
rescues from an orphan asylum an infant who is being maltreated. Al-

though informed that the fugitives are being chased by the police, Mrs. Wiggs takes in the girl and baby and hides them in her shanty. Then Mrs. Wiggs's errant husband unexpectedly returns and is dramatically revealed as the father of the child. To the tears of the susceptible part of the audience, Mrs. Wiggs forgives and gathers all into her warm and ever-expandable family.[28]

Anne's dramatization required, as the action raced along, perpetual fine tuning since it was always in danger of slipping over one side or the other, either into unpleasant satire or bathos. *Mrs. Wiggs of the Cabbage Patch*, which opened in Louisville during Simon's final months in Philadelphia, did not reach New York until September 3, 1904. It was to run there for seven consecutive seasons, sometimes with three companies simultaneously on the road. It had two seasons in London, and was presented successfully in Australia, China, India, and Korea. Twice Hollywood made it into major motion pictures.

The success of *Mrs. Wiggs* had a determining effect on the futures of both Anne and Abraham Flexner. For her, it was a mixed blessing. It brought her quantities of money which, after Abraham had got his new career going, she kept as her own, establishing personal independence. But she was not immune to one of the most destructive maladies that afflicts writers: a sense of failure because a great success cannot be repeated. Although Anne became an accomplished theatrical technician, had other plays produced on Broadway, and was a force in the Dramatists Guild, she never again even approached the triumph achieved by *Mrs. Wiggs*.

The financial results of Anne's triumph so trivialized the economic worries that had tied Abraham to Louisville that, in June, 1905, he shut down Mr. Flexner's School. He took off for studies first at Harvard and then in Germany, mostly at the University of Berlin. His resulting publication, *The American College* (1908), in which he demanded that students engage in less extracurricular and more intellectual activity, attracted attention at the Carnegie Foundation for the Advancement of Teaching. He was entrusted with undertaking, for the purposes of reform, a study of American medical education. Visiting the one hundred and fifty-five medical schools in the United States and Canada, he examined each for its ability to teach modern medicine, and he published his specific findings. Without polemics and so factual that it engendered no successful suits for libel, the "Flexner Report" killed more than a hundred schools managed by local practitioners, abolishing the kind of haphazard medical education that Simon and Jacob had received at Louisville.

Having joined Simon in the Rockefeller philanthropies, Abraham was entrusted by the General Education Board with some fifty million dollars to carry into fruition his ideas for remodeling medical education. He selected in each geographic region a medical school which he built up as a major scientific center; and he pressed to have the clinical professors join their laboratory colleagues in giving "full time" — no private practice — to their teaching and research. He contended that he so helped the universities to raise further funds that he brought some six hundred million dollars in new resources to the medical schools.

As success and power came to Abraham, the lack of self-confidence that had held him back until he was almost forty was replaced by its opposite. When he could not persuade, he trampled down. To Simon's dismay, he scolded even Dr. Welch. Despite his brother's efforts to restrain him, in 1928 Abraham forced his alienation and subsequent resignation from the Rockefeller philanthropies.

In 1930, Abraham published his *Universities: American, English, and German,* in which he reiterated most effectively the advocacy of "conceptual" (as opposed to factual or practical) education — ideas he had imbibed in Baltimore and then in Germany. His final great coup was to found, himself raising the funds, the Institute for Advanced Study, where he brought into full realization the exclusively graduate university that President Gilman and the trustees of the Johns Hopkins, including James Carey Thomas, had envisioned but been unable to complete because of local pressures in Maryland.

Abraham Flexner wrote in *I Remember* that his gift was not original thinking but the ability to get things done. What he got done was of the greatest significance. When he died on September 21, 1959, the New York *Times* stated in an editorial: "No other American of his time contributed more to the welfare of his country and humanity in general."[29]

VIII

Joining Together

45

---·◦∞◦·---

Consummations

On the eve of the June 14 meeting of the institute board, Rockefeller, Jr., detailed for his father in a telegram the scheme "of which I spoke to you casually before your departure." It contemplated, eventually, for land, buildings, and endowment, about five million dollars. Present requirements involved land sufficient for the entire scheme and one building, the total cost to be between three and four hundred thousand dollars. Annual expenses from forty to fifty thousand dollars. "I strongly recommend a pledge of one million dollars to be drawn at the option of the Board during ten years" (not twenty as he had mentioned to Herter). This would be for the New York operation, while the original pledge of two hundred thousand during ten years would continue to support the fellowship program. "I feel confident this is conservative and wise. Have been considering the matter with individuals of the Board for some weeks."[1]

Senior replied with a much briefer telegram authorizing his son to pledge a million dollars, with the proviso that the expenditure be distributed across the ten years rather than expended at the opinion of the board, who might take a large portion at the start.* "We cannot say anything about five million now."

The board voted to express to Rockefeller their "appreciation ... of this generous gift," but Flexner was disappointed and perturbed. This was some two weeks after his break with Helen.[2]

From Philadelphia he wrote Welch, "I felt on Saturday [the day of

---

* At the University of Chicago, President William Rainey Harper had spent Rockefeller's benefaction quickly and then come back for more.[3]

the meeting] that you may have considered me lacking in enthusiasm regarding the directorship of the Institute. If I appeared at all indifferent either to the honor of the offer or the importance of the new gift of Rockefeller, it was due only to my embarrassment in the face of a great change in my future work and plans.

"You know so well every thought that I have had regarding the directorship and every doubt I have entertained that it is unnecessary for me to refer to them again. You also know how my inclinations have gradually increased until it seems to me that no one should ask for more ideal opportunities for scientific work." He had been greatly influenced by Welch's own change of attitude, from advising him to hold back to advising him to go ahead. It was true that "I have looked for a larger tenure of security . . . but in the face of your judgment and that of the other directors, and in view of the rapid expansion that has come within a year, I feel obliged to waive what doubts I had on the subject."

This hardly jubilant statement was taken by Welch as Flexner's acceptance of the directorship of the Rockefeller Institute. Flexner intended it to be so taken, but did not accord what was the most fateful decision of his life even the dignity of ending a paragraph. He continued without a break to reveal that he was being plagued by his old fear that the achievements he had built so rapidly from so unpropitious a beginning lacked foundations solid enough to withstand a major misadventure.

The illness which had been the most extreme expression of this fear had been caused on a previous occasion when he had followed Welch's wishes: his refusal of the professorship at the Cornell Medical College. However, that decision had, as he looked back on it, opened the possibilities for the present one. The limited professorship in New York City, where medical activity was so much more lively, would not have opened to him the opportunities supplied by sleepy Philadelphia to demonstrate his abilities not only as a scientific investigator but as an organizer able to create new facilities and effectively staff them with able young men whom he himself chose and inspired. Flexner also believed (or so he wrote in his later years) that had he been better known and more commonplace to the institute board they might have had more varied thoughts concerning his selection as director.

The fact that the most frightening of Welch's previous urgings had turned to his advantage should have encouraged Flexner again to follow Welch's lead. Furthermore, he was at thirty-nine the youngest, except for Herter, member of the Rockefeller board. Yet he continued the paragraph in which he had indicated his acceptance by describing his "consciousness . . . that another ten years may make no small difference in my working capacity especially in reference to academic work, and that having withdrawn from it and its associations for so long a time, I should probably not easily be able to return" should the "uncertain future of the Institute require it."

Having stated that he had brought this danger up merely to explain "any hesitation you may have discovered in my conduct," he brought up another problem. Welch knew that he would "go to New York without the comfort or assurance of any support except my salary." The proposed stipend was only slightly more than what he now received. In Philadelphia he had learned that the mere "exposure of being a professor" required considerable expenditure. Not only was New York more expensive than Philadelphia, but should the institute become a "signal success" he might have to meet demands similar to those on a university president. Although the subject was "very distasteful" to him, he would like to know whether it had been decided since the May meeting that "$7,500 should be regarded by me as sufficient?"[4]

On the very next day, Prudden wrote Welch that the board should guard against setting a precedent for salaries "disproportionately large. . . . The Institute is to be small at first, and, while I have the utmost confidence in the candidate [for director] whom we hope will accept, he is still young and in many fields has his mark yet to make. I should therefore think that seventy-five hundred or eight thousand dollars would be a fair salary. Whether, if the matter were crucial, more should be accorded might well be a subject for consideration."[5]

A letter from Welch quickly brought Prudden round. "I am delighted at the positive assurance of Flexner's acceptance. The matter of salary can, I think, be adjusted to his satisfaction."[6]

From Louisville, Abraham wrote, "I would rather far you had five million [for the institute] nailed down, but I cannot think you have done unwisely in accepting the assurances of those that know Mr. Rockefeller. So here are our congratulations on the greatest glory the name Flexner has yet won!"[7]

Welch lost little time in writing to Rockefeller, Jr. In a most statesmanlike manner he expressed personal appreciation of "the wisdom shown in the terms of the gift," adding that he and his colleagues on the board "have every reasonable confidence in the permanency of the Institute," which, they believed, would be secured by demonstration of the institute's usefulness. In the meanwhile, the board could use the money at their disposal without being carried in any direction "not sure to be to the best future interests of the Institute. You have wisely left open for future decision to be based upon larger experience a number of questions which would have to be decided if we were called upon to administer at once a large permanent endowment. . . .

"You will be pleased to know that Dr. Flexner has accepted the directorship of the new laboratory. . . . It is important that his decision should not become public at present, as otherwise his work for the coming year in Philadelphia would be embarrassed.

"In my opinion, we could not find a better man for this position than Dr. Flexner. He has demonstrated unusual capacity as an original investigator in the lines to be furthered by the Institute, has had experience in the organization and conduct of an important laboratory, is very attractive and stimulating to young men working under his direction, and has an established international reputation in his special field of research. They will do everything possible to keep him in Philadelphia, but he will not give them any encouragement, as my understanding is that he has definitely accepted our offer. His acceptance, I believe, insures the immediate success of the new laboratory. He will have no difficulty in getting a group of bright, young workers about him."[8]

Flexner's own memory was that he had made his acceptance conditional on consultation with Wier Mitchell and Provost Harrison, but Welch knew that for all Simon's success in Philadelphia, was not altogether happy there. He had written Welch, "I have the support of the provost and most of the faculty. Unfortunately, there is a small group of men to whom I have not been welcome. Those men you know and their attitude is about the same now as when I first came. There is no hostility. I have not taken the matter to heart."[9]

In general, Flexner complained to his former Hopkins colleagues, as he complained to Herter, of the opposition from closed minds that had to be overcome in "such conservative communities as Philadelphia."[10]

Abraham had been correct in foreseeing that neither Mitchell nor Provost Harrison would feel justified in trying to come between Flexner and so brilliant an appointment. The problem concerning Flexner's salary was informally settled to his satisfaction. However, no official action could be taken until the board met after the summer holidays. On October 25, 1902, Flexner was unanimously elected director of the Rockefeller Institute, his service to begin on July 1, 1903, after the academic year in Philadelphia had closed. He was granted a leave of absence, with a salary of $5,000, for one year, which he was to spend in Europe preparing for his new post. After entering active duty, his salary would be $10,000.[11]

Flexner's elevation, along with the whole institute project as it had then developed, would not be publicly announced for more than three months. However, a few days after his election, Simon broke a long silence by informing Helen Thomas.[12]

Helen had been complaining to Bertie of how her efforts to teach appreciation of literature at Bryn Mawr were being frustrated by demands that she teach pedantic scholarship. Shortly before her break with Flexner, his reply had come: "The American devotion to pedantry is very unfortunate. They have not realized that the ultimate aim of every dignified study is *emotion*. . . . They never inquire concerning *ends* but pursue *means* so completely as to insure non-attainance of the ends. . . . And this is what they (poor lost souls) consider their proof of intellectual superiority."[13]

"I am sorry you are having such a horrid time. Your 'theoretic life' in which you forget Lucy's existence, amuses me, but I don't wonder she finds it the very reverse of amusing."

Bertie went on to attack Helen's "conception of how to produce literature [which], like Logan's, seems to me mistaken. It is a far more difficult business than that. All great literature requires the rare and all but impossible combination of fiery emotion with an intellect capable of viewing it impersonally. Where the latter fails, you get mere Byron; where the former, mere precocity. It is, I am quite sure, a mistake to suppose that without an intensity of feeling which would wholly crush an ordinary mortal, it is possible to produce Shakespeare, Milton, Carlyle. But when the feeling has been got, it is necessary to have the strength of a giant to turn it into literature instead of mere lamentation. The intellectual emotion you speak of should be added to the other, not substituted in its place." If this put Helen and Logan completely out of the running, the fact remained that it was Bertie's opinion, and that he expressed it with awe-inspiring eloquence.

As for the arrival of spring in which Helen found surcease, "I find its frivolity offensive. The earth is too youthful, too ready to forget the storms and winter."[14]

Russell particularly liked to expatiate on "moral duties. . . . Cultivate honesty and conscience will soon grow up to it; no happiness results but exaltation, inspiration, the sense of fellowship with the heroic spirit of all ages, and finally a strange, almost mystical serenity when desire is dead and Destiny can no longer affect us with promises of good or threats of evil." And so forth.[15]

Helen replied that she had found Bertie's letter "full of hard sayings," and "I find it difficult to know what in the end to reply to it. The extraordinary vigor with which you think and feel and act and write makes my own personality seem to me pale and my thoughts not worth putting on paper. You recommend sincerity of self-analysis as a first step to right conduct, but I am by no means sure that for me self-knowledge is not among the virtues that oneself as an end ought to sacrifice to oneself as a means. I am by no means sure that I ought not to cultivate the virtues of vainglory and boasting." Had she not so just an estimate of herself he would hear in detail how she disagreed with various of his assertions. She would tell him for instance "just how impossible it seems to me that the best conduct should produce anything but the best person. Our perfections were never meant to hang on one's fingers like rings. I conceive of them rather as pickaxes and hammers and drills and saws, to be used though they harden one's hands."[16]

In the correspondence Helen received in that summer of 1902, another voice from England spoke in much gentler tones. Logan found relief in confiding to Helen one of the great blows of his life. His "old and intimate companion" Phillip Morrell had gotten married. He thus described the bride (who was to liberate Bertie's sex life and become his mother confessor): "Lady Ottoline is a stately, beautiful, shy, lost princess seeking for goodness, happiness, Salvation. Imagine taking into one's ordered, ironic life a noble, great-winged, grave-eyed bird like that! I grow giddy at the thought." Usually, Logan approved of marriages as providing "us spectators with human drama. . . . But when one's intimate friend marries, it is different; one is dragged into the play oneself and given a part that is melancholy, and ridiculous as well. When in *Trivia* I rashly asked the fates what part I was to play on this old stage of the world, I did not, I admit, expect so prompt an answer. Ask no questions of the fates!" These confidences were for Helen's and Lucy's ears alone.[17]

Logan had just brought out the privately printed first edition of what was to be his most famous book, *Trivia*, which he signed with a nom de plume, Anthony Woodhouse. Since Logan regarded Helen and Lucy "as the godmothers of Anthony Woodhouse," he was "glad that you approve of him, now that he is out in the world. . . .

"I have set up bee hives in my garden, and three of those marvelous republics fill the air with the murmur of their traffic. It is beautiful to see them towards evening falling down in golden showers out of the late sunshine. They ought to be an example to me — or rather, ought I not to be an example to them?"[18]

Bertie and Logan, the so disparate romances of her earlier years! At the far side of the ocean she had often crossed but was yet uncrossable: half reality and half dream! Closer tides were surging in her now. Wishing better to understand the scientific point of view she had, in her perpetual pursuit of some meaning in life, added to her perusal of classical and religious philosophy a careful examination of the works of the Darwinian Huxley.

Helen's literary efforts and hopes having not revived after the isolation and anguish of her sciatica, she had resolved to be practical. She would prepare for a lifetime career as a professor of English by undertaking what she had long skimped or avoided, serious studies towards achieving a Ph.D. During the summer of 1902, first in a New Hampshire inn and then at the Harvard Library, she tried to hold her attention on the "science of language and Anglo-Saxon literature." To Bertie she complained that "spending long hours over a thing one cannot take seriously is irrational and has a deteriorating effect, like all irrational action."

The autumn found her back at Low Buildings with Lucy. "Bryn Mawr has been worse than ever this autumn. All the troubles and anxieties it plunges one into have seemed more meaningless." Except for her sense of duty to her students, "desire seems dead in my heart." This to Bertie. In her vellum-bound notebook she wrote, "A divided self, unsatisfied yearnings, and deep sadness. God be my aid!"[19]

At the very end of October, Helen returned to Simon Flexner a book she had borrowed from him in the spring. She felt dashed when his response was no more than a stiff acknowledgment. But the next day another letter appeared. There had been, Simon now wrote, "one thing I might have said, but what had not lost by being deferred." He was to be the director of the Rockefeller Institute. His only excuse for sending her this news was that she had previously shown a "lively interest" and that he had gained insight from her advice. He hoped that her work was not making too great demands on her, "and that it is full of pleasure to you."[20]

Helen replied by return mail. It was "nice of you" to inform her of his final decision, "and I assure you I greatly appreciate it." She was "very glad" not only for his sake but for the institute's. "I shall read the announcement with the greatest interest. Indeed, since your janitor was bitten by your rattlesnake, I have begun to watch the papers for news of you." She was lecturing to 108 girls and Miss Donnelly "commented that it was clear I come from a family of preachers."

"If you cared for an afternoon in the country, I should be delighted to go for a walk with you — or not to go for a walk as you liked. But you are very busy, I know, so I can hardly expect you to come all the way to Bryn Mawr, and shall quite understand your not doing so."[21]

After five days, Simon replied, thanking her for her kind encouragement concerning the institute. "My present trust is entirely in the future, although I realize that it is a bank which infrequently makes good its promises.

"I know of nothing that could be more agreeable or certain to do me just the kind of good I need than an occasional afternoon in the country."[22]

Helen must have noticed that Simon had sidestepped any expression of pleasure at the thought of seeing her again after so long a separation. However, she looked forward to his visit with hopeful anticipation. When he arrived, she greeted him enthusiastically and indeed affectionately. He responded with restrained courtesy. As they walked side by side along roads bordered by gray trees from which the autumn leaves had fallen, Helen did her best to rouse him by expressing the interest she truly felt in his work and by the gently impertinent sallies that were her coquetry with men. He answered her questions politely but not fluently; hardly smiled at her sallies. As the embarrassing minutes passed, she tried to fathom what he was thinking, but failed.

After he had departed, still grave, polite, and withdrawn, she acknowledged to herself that the question of how to interpret his behavior was all important to her. To her amazement and dismay, she realized that she had fallen in love with him.[23]

If only he would accord her some hint of what his feelings were! But day after day, the little piles she found in her letter box did not reveal his handwriting. Surely he would not come to Bryn Mawr without first informing her, yet her heart jumped when a male figure emerged distantly on the walk that descended to Low Buildings, when a knock came on her door. Finally, the tension became unbearable. Perhaps she was encouraged to her unconventional act by memory of her ancestress, Elizabeth Haddon, who had, inspired as she believed by God, herself proposed to the man who became her husband.

Dear Dr. Flexner:

Since you were here two weeks ago I have thought over many things I should like to say to you until it has finally come to seem best to me to write to you about them! On that afternoon I quite failed to understand what you were thinking; I could not tell whether you had changed in the months since I had seen you before, or whether you still felt towards me as you did then. But you must, it seems to me, have seen that I had changed, and your not writing to me and not coming to see me since then have made me think that the change in me has come too late and is now indifferent to you. I can acquiesce in this, in its obvious justice; and be glad of it for your sake because I clearly see that the situation in which I am is highly complicated and must lead to complications for anyone who cares for me, and I also see that I am in myself a strange creature, too likely to prove unsatisfactory! Indeed, I have always doubted whether a better knowledge of what I am would not utterly disappoint you and change your opinion of me. I am writing to you now because I feel that the present understanding between us is a false one, and that its falseness must be a source of unhappiness to both of us.

I want you to know that I have found that I care far more for you than I had thought. If you have ceased to care for me it is better that we should not see each other. You must tell me the absolute truth and trust me to take my stand on it bravely. If you still feel that you do care, you would no doubt prefer to know how I feel, and to try to see whether a way can be found out of the complications, and whether I am really the sort of person you do in all seriousness like.

I do not want to cause you any more pain that I have already caused you. I want to feel that you are entering on your new life with its duties and responsibilities, unsaddened by me. And the best way to insure this seems to me to write you this letter. If I am mistaken, I can only ask your forgiveness. I can trust you, I know, to understand my unconventionality, and to answer my frankness with frankness.

Very sincerely,
Helen Thomas[24]

Simon received Helen's letter early the following morning. Before going to the university, he wrote:

Dear Miss Thomas:
  Would it be at all possible for you to see me this afternoon? . . .
Your letter has given me the greatest happiness and I want to thank you with all my heart. Thank you for entrusting it to me. I cannot express my admiration for its unselfishness and honesty.

Yours very sincerely,
Simon Flexner

That afternoon, he had again recourse to the mail: "I do not know whether this will reach you before I can see you. I am writing to say that I shall come out this evening after dinner."[25]

Concerning the meeting that evening, we know only its results. Simon got off too late to catch his train, "and thus had time to see something of the beautiful starry heavens and to reflect, in quiet, on my enviable state." So he reported in a very brief note, written early the following morning. He feared that she had had a "restless night," and hoped that her schedule that day was not too taxing. For the first time in their long correspondence, he addressed her not as "Miss Thomas" but as "Dearest Helen." They were engaged.[26]

46

Great Changes

SIMON quickly sent Helen an explanation of his withdrawn behavior, which had brought her to the unconventional extreme of declaring her love. He had, he admitted, been "obtuse" in not recognizing that her attitude towards him had changed, "but I am at best distrustful of myself in such matters." Interpreting Helen's cordiality as a desire to reestablish their former sympathetic friendship that ignored love, he had tried to accept "the old order of things," but emotion surged too strongly within him. Remembering how his previous impulsive avowal had given her pain and surely (although this he did not mention) had inflicted pain on him, he resolved not to open himself "to a similar, perhaps resistless, temptation." So, after being rigidly formal, he had departed as soon as politeness allowed.

Her letter of avowal — "an act of bravery that is almost heroic" — had "almost taken my breath away to think by what narrow a line I almost lost you." That she could love him seemed "one of the miraculous acts of good fortune" which experience had taught him to accept without asking questions. "If smaller favors can be thus accepted, I cannot be expected to ask for reasons for the conferring of the greatest that can come to any man. . . .

"You know something of the climbing, small as it is, that I have been able to do in the past few years. I could not say this was done alone for I have at all times had behind me a devoted family and loyal friends to cheer me over the difficult places and applaud me when a difficult step was made. To them I owe a deep debt of gratitude. But think how much greater incentive I have in the future, and much more may be accomplished with and for you. . . .

"For Miss Donnelly some way out does not seem too hopeless."[1]

Helen wanted to postpone any public announcement until after Bryn Mawr College had emptied out for the summer. Any earlier date would rock the feminine enclave. Was she not sister to President Thomas, who regarded marriage as a desertion of the feminist cause? Had she not resolutely dedicated herself to the cause and to celibacy? Furthermore, Lucy needed time to accommodate herself to the situation before it became public knowledge.

The spring college term had not yet even begun when Simon and Helen came together. Both had academic duties that had to be fulfilled. And Simon had obligations to the Rockefeller Institute and also to his research. His scientific duties would become even more compelling during the summer months, when hot weather brought on murderous epidemics of infantile intestinal disease which he was trying more certainly to identify and eradicate. But in the fall, the situation would be reversed. He was already committed to the long European trip during which he would further prepare for the directorship of the institute by acquiring the skills he lacked in biochemistry. The trip could double as a honeymoon. The wedding would take place in September, 1903.

Simon and Helen agreed that, while everyone else was kept in the dark concerning their engagement, they would in confidence inform their close relatives and a very few friends. Although she postponed writing Logan, since he was an incurable gossip, Helen felt free to inform Alys and Bertie: "All during my walk out over snowy fields and since I have been sitting by the fire drinking tea, I have wished that you were with me that I might tell you what I now must write. Already you have guessed it. I have made up my mind to get married. . . . The man is Simon Flexner, doctor of medicine and pathologist. It happened this way. He put the intelligence and imagination that have brought him distinction in his profession on the problem of understanding me, and while I still felt pretty secure of myself, free as air, I had in fact fallen in love with him and was in fact bound to him. The shock when I discovered the chain was severe. But I like it now, though in the course of events I made more than one rapid transition from heaven to hell."

"The tragical thing is Lucy's despair. . . . I have not as yet been able to feel my own happiness, her sense of grief has been so keen. For I love her no less than ever I did. You will understand as few others can. . . . Do write to Lucy both of you and make her feel your sympathy."

Helen counted on their liking Simon, "though his world is not the world of art but science. The pursuit of truth, of the little individual particular fact that throws such a light on the world of similar facts, that is his life. He is very like Pasteur, for it is the imaginative conclusion he leaps to that separates him off from mere investigators. He has a touch of genius, I think. . . .

"I feel I shall breathe with infinitely greater freedom when I am away from the stifling atmosphere of Bryn Mawr, where clothes count for so much and the undergraduate reigns. I want to be with people who think and have lived, not forever in contact with immature minds. I want to live myself with my whole nature, as now I shall do. Perhaps at last I may write. Already I have grown; you would like me better I think." [2]

Bertie replied that he had heard of Flexner, "and I admire very much the pursuit of science as he pursues it." He expressed himself as very glad she was getting married. She would have "the only experience where happiness has the intensity that is otherwise only found in pain. And marriage, though in the long run it usually brings many sorrows and difficulties to women, yet gives them a human life, a life full of ties and duties which, after all, constitutes the only serious reason for existing. And it takes away the feeling that the brief years are slipping by without our ever penetrating the inner sanctuary of the temple of life."

He would write to comfort Lucy. [3]

Logan's reply, after Helen had finally sent him the news, indicates that she had expressed trepidation: "I am grateful to thee for believing that I could understand and not be too thin and cynical to appreciate all the wonder of it. Everything in our mortal condition can be made fun of, but as one gets older, one believes that it is not the satirists who have the best of it in the long run, but those who hear [illegible] great music, to whom the [illegible] spring floods come, and who have the courage and richness of nature to accept the great gifts of life. I have my own little system of things, but it is only a personal one, suited to my own nature, and I confess I look over my ledge down on the stream of life with a certain envy of those in whose sails the great breeze of life is blowing, and who are sailing to new countries, while I grow middle-aged amid my pleasant but rather humdrum [illegible]."

Perhaps again responsive to what Helen had written, Logan assured her that she should not confuse "this wise adventure with a wise and noble companion . . . which those foolish chance-arranged expeditions of boys and girls we laugh at: from old custom the same music will be played and the same banners waved. I had already heard the name of Dr. Flexner as a man of great distinction. All Grace tells me sounds really splendid, and his photograph interested me immensely — one feels there is a man it would be a privilege to know — clever, strong, and kind. So if my sympathy and approval have any value be sure that thee has them in the fullest measure, and that my thoughts will follow thee in thy new life with unchanged pleasure. . . . I hope to hear from thee again."[4]

None of Helen's family could be notified earlier than the dominant Carey, who was temporarily in California. Visiting Baltimore at Christmastime, Helen hid her engagement ring under her dresses, and fought off Zoe, whose curiosity she had unintentionally aroused. But there was no reason why Simon should not tell his family during his visit to Louisville.

It could be postulated that a woman of Helen's background and social position, engaged to a Jew who had raised himself from a humble background, might take with light condescension what his family might think. Not so Helen. "Your family are, I know, immensely devoted and immensely proud of you, and are sure to think you are throwing yourself away, but in time I hope to make them like me." She was afraid they would consider her an alien (as she felt herself to be), and that this would have an unfortunate effect on Simon and their marriage.[5]

Simon was also worried about how his family would take the news. That Helen was a Gentile would present a stumbling block only insofar as it made her more of an outsider. Abe's Anne was also a Gentile. As a Louisville girl she had been known to the Flexners long before her engagement to Abe, but Helen belonged to an altogether strange environment. (Although Mary had been at Bryn Mawr when Helen and Carey were there, she had not been noticed by either.)

For the Flexner family the quandary was severe. It was natural that Simon, having penetrated to Helen's world, would fall in love with one of the inhabitants, but this emphasized that the member who had been most successful in carrying out the family ideals had, in the process, been drawn away from the family system. There was an evident danger that his engagement would deepen the alienation. The Flexner family, when threatened from without, had always drawn closer together. It was considered essential that Helen Thomas be welcomed into the family as far as it was possible to do so.

From Louisville, Simon wrote Helen: "Sunday in this household is not a day of rest. The relief from weekday occupations leaves the family free to seek each other's company." Yet he was being shielded from too much interruption "by a complaisant and nurturing mother." It was late in the afternoon before he could get his mother alone. Then, "supported" by Mary (who had by now met Helen), he gradually let her into the matter. "She was very sweet and very happy about the announcement. . . . You have been in our minds a great part of the time. . . . The happiness has visibly increased for my family, and you will have a most affectionate and cordial welcome to it. You will readily understand what this means to me."

Simon was being treated like a prodigal. All the old dishes he had loved "are gradually given to me, and I find some are obsolete in the family. Mother will look at me archly when I express particular pleasure over some forgotten concoction, and ask, 'Do you expect to get it in your own home?' "[6]

Replying that this "made me laugh," and commenting gaily that "I may have to take a course in a cooking school yet," Helen nonetheless expressed worry lest Simon be made unhappy by her own differences from his mother.[7]

Simon's Jewishness was never mentioned in the extensive correspondence during their engagement, yet she did not hide that she was worried by the cohesiveness of his family. What she said about their "devotion to each other" was, he wrote, "unfortunately true," but when she came to know them better she might be impressed by the quality of that devotion. Except for two brothers (Henry and Isadore) they were linked by "common interests and congeniality. So there is nothing peculiar in the devotion."[8]

Early in January, Helen wrote Simon, "By this morning's mail came the prettiest pearl pins to pin my collar from your mother and Mary. Quite lovely they are! And I don't see what I have done to deserve them. Your people ought, I think, to wait until I have shown what sort of person I am before spoiling me in this way."[9]

After Helen had met Bernard, Simon told Abraham that she had found Ben charming. Abe "became very jealous and determined to do his best when you meet." As it turned out, Abe did his best by showing off how clever he was. Helen reported to Simon in a combination of tact and annoyance, "He was very charming last evening, very amusing and

adroit at repartee — how well he does talk! — and very sweet and dear
to me. I tried once or twice to get behind his guard when we were 'answering back,' but he always turned my point against my shield and
pierced it. I may say more than once. I shall be put to it to get even with
him some day. His personality and his ideas interested me immensely.
You must tell me about him." She doubted that she "had been able to
please him *really*, though his affection for you will make him think himself pleased."[10]

Carey stood in Helen's and Simon's path. The older sister would
surely be outraged at Helen's desertion from the feminist cause, and as
Helen's employer, she could make serious trouble by insisting that
Helen abide by contractual arrangements with Bryn Mawr that would,
if enforced, block her going off with Simon.

"I shall have to have it out with Carey," Helen wrote Simon ruefully,
"as soon as she returns. We shall feel much more comfortable and *settled*, which you say is a good thing, when we make our plans without an
if." Helen wondered whether she could get away with writing a letter,
as Carey had "said things to me in the past that would make almost anyone dread a scene with her."[11]

Simon urged her to confront the Ogress face to face, but he regretted
this advice when the time came, fearing that Helen might be deeply
hurt. It did not make things easier for him to receive a letter telling him
that he might not back her up by coming to Bryn Mawr on the day of
the interview. "It would be very hard for Lucy to bear ... if I went right
from Carey to you," and because of her unstable nervous condition, "I
must think of Lucy first." Helen realized that the suspense would be
difficult for Simon, but she would write him instantly.[12]

Helen went to lunch with Carey and Mamie. She was surprised to
find herself eating a good lunch. Then she sprang the news. Carey,
"though I know she was completely surprised ... hardly showed surprise. I greatly admire her command of countenance." Mamie held
Helen's hand and "pressed it most affectionately," but Carey pretended
to be hardly interested. She did express pleasure that Flexner was an
eminent man, and seemed to know more about his reputation than
Helen did. "She said she approved of my marrying — may she be forgiven for it! — and that if I was going to do it, I might as well do it at
once." She offered to lend them the Deanery for the summer.[13]

Carey wrote her perpetual correspondent, Mary Garrett: "Helen
came to lunch and broke the fact after luncheon to Mamie and me that

she is engaged to Dr. Flexner. You know he was Welch's assistant and they thought clever[er] than Welch, much in orig[inal] work. . . . He is a Jew and utterly insignificant looking and of no social qualifications. He has been petted and lionized in Philadelphia and perhaps may have added some graces. Zoe is fond of him, but her and Harry's devotion has always amazed me. It is a blow I confess but I shall have to make the best of it for Helen's sake and at least he is very eminent and has the prize position in the country in pathology. Remember it is a dead secret."[14]

Simon expressed less concern about pleasing the Thomas family than Helen did about the Flexners. Perhaps this was due to his greater reticence; perhaps because the Thomas world was already known to him. Harry, he wrote, would have to be his sponsor, and perhaps Zoe would help, although she might not like him so well when she learned that he was "anchored" to her sister-in-law.[15] It was indeed fear concerning Zoe's discretion that made them decide to postpone revelation until midsummer, when Simon, on a visit to Coombe Edge, joined the family group.

That he was a Jew raised infinitely less fuss than Mariechen's engagement to a Catholic had done decades before. The Thomas clan was not immune to anti-Semitism, but their prejudice was endemic not epidemic: it struck here and there, called up by special persons or situations. The only documentary evidence, in addition to Carey's slighting description to Mary Garrett, is a communication that is particularly telling since it comprised four members of the family — in the United States, England, and Italy. Hannah wrote Mariechen, "Grace had a very nice letter from Bond this morning, saying that he had seen 'Simon' and was charmed with him. He said you might have a prejudice against Jews, but you could not possibly hold it against Simon for he was absolutely unexceptionable, and he thought Helen was very lucky."[16]

There was the impressive fact that Simon had just sprung into national fame.

Announcement of the Rockefeller Institute's greatly enlarged scope was being held back, as Welch put it, to suit the convenience of Flexner "or rather the University of Pennsylvania." But because of its real estate aspect, news began to leak. On February 9, 1903, the New York *Evening Post* reported: "The location of the new Rockefeller Laboratory, fragmentary accounts of which have appeared in the newspapers during the past year, will be three blocks from Sixty-fourth Street to Sixty-seventh Street, Avenue A [now York Avenue] to the East River." This part of the old Schermerhorn farm, comprising one hundred and ten building lots, was the only unimproved land of its dimensions still remaining south of the Harlem River. It stood majestically on a high cliff, "commanding a fine outlook up and down the river." The dimensions indicated "the magnitude of the enterprise."

The *Times*, having been scooped, sent out reporters the next morning but all the parties gave the same answer: "No deal has been consummated."

Another leak is revealed by an undated clipping from some Philadelphia newspaper: "DR. FLEXNER MAY LEAVE UNIVERSITY — Prominent Scientist Proffered Directorship of the Rockefeller Institute for His Remarkable Research in Pathology." The text reported that Flexner had "refused to state whether or not he had accepted the proffered leadership of what is one of the greatest institutes of modern science." Those close to university affairs believed Flexner would leave, while "university medical men" said that this loss would be "greatly deplored."

On February 21, the *Times*, without waiting for an announcement, ran on its front page: "THE ROCKEFELLER INSTITUTE — Dr. Simon Flexner, Eminent Pathologist, Chosen to be Chief of Staff." Flexner's career, from Louisville onward, was briefly and accurately summarized. His selection "assures that the Institute will from its very inception be in the forefront of medical research." With Dr. Welch also active as president of the board, "the new Institute will have the services of the leading pathologists of the United States."

Reading this story, Flexner must have been consumed with wonder and pleasure at being thus put on an equal plane with Welch.

An official release could clearly be no longer postponed. On the following morning, the *Times* devoted two columns on its front page to a statement by Holt, headlined, "ROCKEFELLER PLANS VAST INSTITUTE — Donations of $1,200,000 Merely a Beginning." The existing plans were accurately outlined: the immediate erection of a laboratory for investigations in all departments of medical research; a large resident staff and a coordinate staff of fellows; the building of a hospital in which special groups of patients would be treated in order to develop new methods for cure; and the establishment of a journal. Eventually, steps would be taken for the education of the public in hygiene. In confirming the appointment of Flexner, Holt stated, "Although a comparatively young man, he has already achieved an international reputation as a pathologist and investigator. . . . It can be authoritatively stated that he [Mr. Rockefeller] stands ready to contribute such additional amounts as the needs of the institution may demand."

Simon wrote Helen that his living room was crowded with members of the press. Most wanted to take his photograph, but he staved them off. (He always took a bad picture.)

Out of the welter of publicity there emerged one story, an anonymous interview published in the New York *World*, which topped all others, was widely reprinted, and passed from hand to hand among Simon's acquaintance.

Although the man "who is to head the greatest medical establishment in the country . . . the princeliest of all the benefactions of American millionaires" was "a figure of world interest," he was, the report began, "unknown to laymen. Who is this unknown who is to have the direction of fifteen million dollars* of Rockefeller money to be spent on medical experiment?

"Among the gruesome cans and jars of his work, busy as a hornet, the new celebrity was found yesterday in the big green stone laboratory of the University of Pennsylvania. . . . It was a great big room overlooking the campus and filled with tables heaped with apparatus. It was a hardworking scientist's laboratory. The tables represented a hundred experiments. A rolltop desk in the middle of the room had a neglected air. The jar-filled tables were the little man's desk.

"He had just dashed into the room from his luncheon. Off came the overcoat and short coat underneath. From the rack he took his white working jacket, and in a half minute's time he was plunged into his work. He was the cold, dry, precise, unenthusiastic scientist — the perfect ideal of such a man. His face was small and grayish, his head small and grayish, the thin hair sheered close to the skull, his deep, dark quick eyes shaded by glasses." At forty, he was "a young-old man. . . . Dr. Flexner might be thirty or fifty. Something about him suggested the fact, which he modestly admitted, that he was not married. His whole life has been given to scientific research. . . .

"How this quiet, single-hearted worker, who deprecates even the mention of his name outside the pages of a medical journal, came to be

---

* This sum was greatly exaggerated at that time, but it was only one fourteenth of the six hundred million dollars that the Rockefellers were progressively to entrust to the institute as, under Flexner's direction, it grew down the years.

selected by America's richest millionaire . . . is an interesting story. . . . Dr. Flexner is a Johns Hopkins man, a Southerner and a Jew, born in Louisville, Kentucky. His life had been spent in the quiet study, and for that reason he has become little known to the public.

"The little white-jacketed professor of pathology smiled when he was asked to tell the *World* of his plans for the Rockefeller Institute. 'It's pretty hard to tell eighteen months in advance,' he said cautiously. His eyes roved back to a jar filled with discolored tissues preserved in alcohol. . . . 'It is now an extensive scheme, embracing the whole field of study of the cause and prevention of disease.' " The whole world of medical discovery would be kept in view, and discoveries made elsewhere would be tested and applied to practical treatment.

That he was working on a project for the institute he admitted, but he would not say what. However, the reporter knew that "rattlesnakes of the most venomous kind fill the whole room adjoining Dr. Flexner's laboratory. These specimens have been gathered from various parts of the earth for his experiments." He was trying to develop an antitoxin for rattlesnake bite. A few months earlier, one of his rattlers got loose "and nibbled on the arm of Joe Corrigan, a hapless college employee who happened to be around." The antitoxin had been tried out on monkeys but never on humans. "In the dire extremity, he injected some of the serum into Corrigan's arm. The man got well."

The reporter commented again that Flexner was "unmarried, without any interest outside his beloved science."[17]

Looking ahead to the decades when Simon Flexner was to be first the coadjutor and then the successor of the cosmopolitan Welch as the major statesman of American scientific medicine, and when he was to deal "with level fronting eyebrows" (to use the old Quaker phrase) with millionaires, university presidents, civic leaders, heads of state, this picture of a small, grayish laboratory gnome is surprising. It seems belittling, almost insulting. But there was no such reaction among Flexner's associates. The article was published in the Louisville *Herald* over which brother Washington presided, and Welch made himself "very gay" about it. Helen wrote her fiancé, "I was much amused . . . and wonder how in so short a time you managed to touch the imagination of the reporter. He has given a most artistic account of you, has created you in fact." Then she added, "I fear my shadow in the background of the picture. Do you not feel a pang when you realize how much more complete you are without me?"[18]

But, of course, Simon needed Helen to become the man he was to be. Lewellys Barker had known Helen before Simon did. When informed of the engagement, he wrote Simon, his close friend, "I had great confidence in your future even if left to yourself, but with Miss Thomas beside you, there is no end to what you may do."[19]

47

·⟨∞⟩·

Lucy and Other Troubles

D URING the eleven months of their engagement, Helen and Simon exchanged hundreds of letters that have been preserved. Even before the end of their college terms, while they were still geographically separated only by the suburban train ride between Philadelphia and Bryn Mawr, they had the greatest difficulty getting together. Both were very busy with their professional duties, and Helen was afraid that if Simon were seen too often with her near the college, gossip would resound. Sometimes Simon would stay on the train, pretending not to notice Helen as she got on board at Bryn Mawr. They both got off at Rosemont and went for walks. But even this had its dangers. During a Philadelphia dinner party, a lady announced to the company that Simon had been seen in the countryside at Rosemont with a handsome redheaded woman. In later years, Dr. Flexner enjoyed boasting of his quickness of mind in remembering that a redheaded actress was appearing in Philadelphia. "Didn't you know," he asked nonchalantly, "that Cissy Loftus is in town?"[1]

For the couple to meet in Philadelphia was a scramble unless Helen broke chaperonage rules by sitting in the comfortable chair, which she later remembered with such pleasure, in Simon's rooms. Some busybody saw them entering the house together and complained to Carey. In her role as president of Bryn Mawr, Carey asked Lucy (of all people!) to warn Helen that she was compromising the reputation of the college.[2]

Lucy was, in fact, the overwhelming problem. Helen's close companion for more than ten years had been thrown into consternation by her friend's engagement. She seemed to be going over the edge into true insanity, which could not be hidden from the world. Helen insisted that she could not build her own happiness on her friend's destruction. Only by rescuing Lucy could she with undampened spirits and a clear conscience marry Simon.

The strategy for curing Lucy was laid down by Helen in consultation with their closest friends: unmarried bluestockings all. Helen was to concentrate what energies she had left over from her college duties on weaning Lucy from the extremity of her dependence and on procuring her acquiescence to the marriage. These objectives could only be achieved gradually, and it was essential that her upward path be assailed by the minimum of mental storms. Seeing Simon or knowing that Helen was with him inspired storms. This was the most determining reason why the couple had to depend on the exchange of letters.

There were times when Lucy seemed more reconciled, when she even expressed friendship for Simon. On one May afternoon the experiment was made of asking Simon to the flat at Low Buildings for tea. Helen reported to him that after he had left "we had a terrible scene. . . . It did not last very long, an hour and a half at most, for she ended by rather hurting my arm, and that sobered her at once. I was so completely exhausted that I slept soundly, and Lucy also slept under the effects of sulphonal. But, unfortunately, in the morning she insisted upon looking at my arm which was a little, though not badly, bruised. This threw her into utter despair as you can imagine." However, she pulled herself together and lectured at ten o'clock. But again, unfortunately, she was told that a professor's wife had said "that I was certainly engaged. And this was enough to loosen Lucy's hardly regained self-control, and the things began again, not violence but reproaches. At about four o'clock I completely broke down, and began to weep, and Lucy at once came to herself, and did everything to comfort me. But though I soon stopped weeping, I was utterly exhausted, and quite unable to go to town" for an appointment with Simon. "Therefore, Lucy herself took the telegram to the station. I wanted to send for you but feared the effect of your presence on Lucy, and her state of mind was not to be trifled with, even for the sake of sparing you pain which in the end would have been perhaps doubled."[3]

Simon could not help noticing that Lucy had quieted down after she had hurt Helen's arm, that she had successfully delivered her own ten o'clock lecture, and that it was she who had in the end felt equal to dispatching the telegram which communicated what she desired.

Lucy's parents, Simon knew, insisted on treating her as if she were completely normal, yet her visits home had not tossed her flaming into any abyss. But in his communications to Helen, Simon never went beyond an occasional hint that the dangers to Lucy's sanity were perhaps exaggerated. Such discretion was, he felt, called for because there were two actors in the drama, and his beloved Helen was one of them.

Surely Helen was holding on to Lucy as a life raft, even if not as convulsively as Lucy was holding on to her. Although marriage had been for Simon an ultimate objective, for Helen it would involve an almost irreversible veering onto an unexpected path. Lucy represented the continuity of Helen's old path. Violently to dislodge Lucy, if it could be done, might force a break too sudden for Helen's happiness, and conceivably induce her to refuse the marriage. How deep had been the change of heart that had made Helen, after she had dismissed Simon, call him back again?

It was basic in Simon's character to define directions and pursue what he sought without deviation. He had learned to wait out darkness in the confident hope of light. In the present situation, he remembered that it had been Helen's need for support in relation to her earlier, lesser problems with Lucy that had first made her confide in him. She still described the difficulties in a tone of sharing confidences and needing help. He recognized that she truly loved and felt responsible for her friend, and he truly loved and wanted to help Helen.

After Lucy had broken up a meeting with Helen, Simon wrote, "I left last night with regrets which I wished you to see and not to see, and I also left with a feeling that the mere accidents of life have treated you with scant kindness. I would not, of course, have you be less to Lucy than you are. . . . Remember when you are bluest that *I* am not to add a jot to your suffering, by which I mean consideration for me is not to weigh as a part of the causes or effects. Recall, dearest Helen, that I want and accept you as you are, with all real or fancied obligations, and all moods you have, and that I am regarding myself daily as more fortunate in having secured your love. . . .

"You will not wonder that I wish to take you out of conditions in which such states of unhappiness can exist. Not that I wish to withdraw you from Lucy, but only put you where you will be free of the contributing causes that precipitate the ills from which you both suffer.

"You must seek, dearest girl, some protection for yourself for the sake of her and yourself, and, if you will [this is as far as he ever went] for my sake."[4]

Simon wrote Helen that he often thought of Lucy with sympathy and affection. "We must be very kind and considerate of her — especially I must — for she gives up a great deal for me. . . . I can easily understand her deep sense of loss in thinking to lose you." She was "fighting an hereditary weakness of the nervous system with a strong and almost paralyzing force." His and Helen's responsibilities to carry Lucy through were "of a serious order," and he did not doubt they would succeed. "She must be made to feel . . . that she does not lose you and never can." Rather than intending to banish Lucy after his marriage, Simon promised that he would not interfere with "so firmly founded and rational a friendship." Lucy, he was sure, would, when she gained control of her faculties, acknowledge the primacy of marital love. "Only a monster would wish otherwise, and that surely and clearly she is not."[5]

Since marital love was considered to be a fulfillment beyond any other human relationship, Simon believed that he was leading Helen out of a backwater into the great ocean of living. Even Logan, that confirmed bachelor, had said as much in his half-rueful, half-envious letter. A letter from Mildred Minton expressed the attitude of Lucy's and Helen's circle of unmarried women. Despite expressing concern over the effect of the engagement on Lucy, Minton expressed herself as being "truly glad . . . that you are going to be happy in the simple, human way. I think most of us are happier in the end when we live in the world and feel the big emotions and know the sweep of things from our own personal experience. I am certain that it is a misfortune for almost any woman to have passed her days without a chance for one whole side of her faculties to get used at all." Miss Minton felt "quite shivery in my old-maidhood."[6]

That her entire environment, while offering her much sympathy gave Lucy no overt encouragement, did not, as the months went by, seem to alleviate the situation. Her cure was supposed to advance along a steady upward plane, but it was more like a wheel that never stopped turning. The original plan was that she would go to Europe with friends at the end of the college term. But no! She spent the summer vacation with a group of Bryn Mawr dons that included Helen, and still made trouble. It was only a month before the wedding when she finally left Helen's side. But she had made no better plan than to join her own family, who Helen believed were unkind to her. Helen wrote Simon that this made her unhappier than she had ever been before in her whole life.

By this time, it would seem that any man would wish Lucy in hell and resolve to get her out of his life the instant he successfully led her friend to the altar. But Flexner adhered to his promise that he would not separate Helen and Lucy. Perhaps it was faith that no one who was not fundamentally admirable could have been for so long so close to his beloved Helen; perhaps his own character study of Lucy had cut deep. In any case, his tolerance was amply justified as the years passed.

Lucy attended Helen at the wedding without any disruptive last-minute scenes. After the marriage, there was, it is true, a period of estrangement, of unslaked sorrow and bitterness in Lucy's heart, but by the time this writer was old enough to remember, "Aunt Lucy" was a recurring fixture in the Flexner home. She usually spent the summers there, tactfully and relaxedly, an agreeable extension of the small family circle. She had returned to the Bryn Mawr faculty, where for decades she was one of the most prominent figures on the campus. Eventually, she found a new house companion: a good-looking, wealthy, much younger instructor of English named Edith Finch. After Lucy died, Edith became the fourth and final wife of Bertrand Russell.

At the height of the Lucy difficulties, Helen took up passionately the cause of another suffering woman. While staying with her brother Bond in Brooklyn, she was appealed to by Ellen Giler, a former student at Bryn Mawr, who had been seduced, she claimed under promise of marriage, by Edward Hodder, a lecturer in English. Not only had Hodder cast Ellen aside, but he now refused to see her. She still loved Hodder with all her soul, so Ellen told Helen, and unless he would meet with her at least once more she would commit suicide. Helen, who had been brought up to a horror of the sexual exploitation of women, was deeply moved.

An intimate disciple of William James, Hodder had been appointed to Bryn Mawr at James's recommendation. He had brought with him a woman whom he introduced as his wife, while at the same time telling other women that they were not really married. Concerning Hodder, Bertrand Russell, wrote, "He had a very brilliant mind and in the absence of women could talk interestingly."[7]

A close Thomas connection had been created when Hodder seduced Carey's companion of more than twenty years, Mamie Gwinn. He expressed eagerness to marry her as soon as he could afford it — which meant when Mamie's rich mother would countenance the match. By the time Ellen collapsed on Helen's doorstep, Mamie had been Hodder's mistress for several years while still living with Carey, who perpetually upbraided her for immoral behavior.*[8]

In a series of interminable letters to Simon, Helen described Ellen's dreadful state of mind, and told how she was trying to keep Ellen from committing suicide by forcing Hodder to see her. Despite veiled threats that Helen would tell Mamie and Carey, who did not know of this other escapade, Hodder could not be budged. To nonetheless save Ellen, "I am," Helen wrote, "willing to make any sacrifice." She was considering bringing Ellen home to share her already tumultuous household with Lucy.[9]

This utterly unexpected development was too much for Simon. He matched Helen's hysteria with his own. To her, he wrote, "all manner of possibilities go through my mind. . . . I can only implore you to have a care of yourself, and in your endeavors to do all you can for Ellen not to fail in your duty to yourself and — may I say it? — to me. I cannot contemplate your present situation without anguish of soul. That your soul is tried every minute, I know, and how the drama is developing is wholly unknown to me, and fraught with so many serious possibilities that I shudder."[10]

Two days later, on the train to Chicago: "Since Sunday evening my thoughts about you and your serious involvement have tended to run riot. . . . The horrid ignorance of what is happening tears at the very foundations of my control."[11]

Helen finally followed Simon's advice about disentangling herself, and Ellen did not commit suicide.† The episode smoothed away like a

---

* In his autobiography, *Unforgotten Years*, Logan Pearsall Smith published a hearsay version casting Carey and Mamie as lesbian lovers and describing Carey's despair when she arrived home to find an utterly unforeseen note informing her that Mamie had eloped with a male. This anecdote so appealed to the acknowledged lesbian Gertrude Stein that she made it the subject of a short story, "Fernhurst." The story from so well-known a pen has branded Carey as the queen bee of academic lesbians. As a matter of fact, Carey's and Mamie's continuing to be house companions for several years while Mamie was to her friend's knowledge committing adultery with a man, argues against a lesbian relationship.

After Mrs. Gwinn finally loosened the purse strings, Mamie married Hodder in 1904. Living in New York City, he collaborated conspicuously in William Travers Jerome's fight against Tammany Hall. He published novels as well as polemical and philosophical works.[12] The presumptive wife he had brought with him to Bryn Mawr sued him for bigamy, but he died before the case could be brought to trial. As Jessie Donaldson Hodder, she became celebrated as a leader of reform in women's prisons.[13]

† It was probably just as well that Ellen never saw Hodder in the flesh again. She absorbed her love, her memories, and her admiration into her inner nature, carrying him always with her as her inspiration and reason for existence. After he died, Ellen wrote Helen Flexner that she had lost her reason for living: she could no longer assure herself that what she was achieving as a classical archaeologist would make Hodder proud of her.[14]

spent wave. Yet Simon had been given cause for real concern. Despite his still unwavering determination, he was beginning to wonder whether he could really be happy with Helen. He knew Helen had been for years in poor health and troubled. She had a way of warning him that he was involved with a fundamentally sad woman. Could he actually lift her into happiness? Would her depressions, her tendency to be overwhelmed by the pity and terror of the world, actually change with the changes brought about by her marriage to him?

She wrote him in mid-April, "I had a beautiful night after reading a few sonnets in the books you gave me and meditating a little on the tyrannous nature of happiness. One can no more help being happy with sufficient cause than being unhappy. Never until now have I experienced a joy that was *compelling* — though compelling sorrow I have known — and it frightens me a little, for under the strong impulse of such a feeling is one not in danger of forgetting one's duty? In grief, thought of others for the moment deadens the pain. In happiness, one has no desire to forget oneself."[15]

Simon replied, "Your state of last night was so greatly to my taste and stilled so completely all the fears I have had for you. . . that I could not get enough of dwelling in your image, your gay humor and your hopefulness. I was confirmed in a strong belief, namely that my Helen is naturally a cheerful, wholesome, and vividly interesting person. But like all sensitive persons, she runs the risk of losing her true temper and having it temporarily overlaid by unnatural and foreign counterfeits. Having won this conviction, I shall never doubt again in the future, or, at least, I shall try never to doubt again."[16]

Helen's fears concerning Simon took a very different course. Had it not been an axiom of her upbringing that women were normally so subordinated in marriage that any woman who wished to be herself and do anything on her own must not marry? Had she not herself resolved never to marry? Perhaps this determination had been strengthened by her inability to imagine as a husband a man whom a wife could reasonably hope to dominate. Bertrand Russell and Simon Flexner, the only two men other than her father who had in her entire existence stirred her emotionally, were among the most powerful of her generation.

It would be hard to demonstrate greater inner strength and control than Simon exhibited in his uncomplaining acceptance of the situation with Lucy. "Every day," Helen wrote him, "I admire you more for your determined optimism. How do you do it?" When he wrote her of the midnight horrors that sometimes overwhelmed him, she paid no attention, preferring to feel that she could confide to him her "state of mind with all its contradictions." "Your sanity of mind," she explained, "is such that I am not seriously afraid of disturbing you." Yet, if Simon's strength increased for her his fascination, did it not also increase her danger?[17]

Helen's principal self-criticism was an accusation — encouraged surely by contrast with the domineering Whitall Women who were her relations — of weakness of will. On this she blamed her lack of success as a literary writer. Sometimes she believed that the difficulty would be overcome through her marriage. Simon would, by putting his power behind her, dispel her crippling diffidence. But supposing he used his power in an opposite way? She did not doubt that he could overwhelm her. Her safety, the wisdom of her contemplated marriage, depended on how far she could trust Simon Flexner.

She had seen protection in the long engagement which should by all rights enable them, before irrevocably committed, really to know each other. During the months when they were frustrated by being kept so much apart, Helen wrote Simon more than once that he should not allow "male chivalry" to bar him from breaking off the engagement if he so wished. She herself never wrote any explicit threat, but surely she was too much of a feminist to forswear equal rights. She did intend to go ahead, yet wished to still her fears, and also to increase their mutual sympathies, by getting to know Simon better.

She was disturbed because, when they did succeed in meeting, Simon so often had other things on his mind than verbal communication. After a rendezvous which she seems to have ended with reproaches, Simon wrote, "It is easy for me to find nothing but faults in my conduct. When I am with you, I am lulled by your presence into a state of beatitude that to you must oftentimes appear as reserve or some worse fault. When I should be interesting you in my affairs or those of the world perhaps, assuming that I know enough of them to do that, I am allowing your dear head to rest on my shoulder, and I am perfectly contented to stroke your smooth face and rest my cheeks against yours. . . . And yet, my dearest, remember how very, very tired we both are and how necessary it is that our union shall be spiritual and our support both physical and spiritual. And one of the great comforts I bring away with me, after having you in my arms and by my side, is the feeling that you have rested there peacefully and happily, and for the time at least free from the disturbing thoughts of your routine life.

"You said last night that never before did you love me as then, and the words have rung all day in my ears, and they are ringing there now. Without them my concern would be far, far greater. . . . There have been times, yes many times, when I have distrusted my fitness for your love, but there has been no time when all the love I possessed was not centered upon you. What you have meant in deepening my nature you can never know for you have always estimated it as deeper than it was. But now you may sound as you please, for I am no longer ashamed of its superficiality."[18]

The delicacy of this wording did nonetheless convey its meaning: spiritual love was supported by the physical; physical expression did not convict his love of superficiality. She may herself have been at first carried away on the occasion referred to, since she had stated that she had never before loved him so much, but this did not quiet — it may indeed have encouraged — her anxiety. She had traveled too far from her upbringing to believe that physical love appealed only to bestial men, yet the repulsion that had been so indoctrinated in her during her adolescence undoubtedly had been involved in her long-adhered-to determination not to marry. She liked to remind Simon that he was marrying — she insisted on the phrase — "a logical woman." She was worried lest the physical play too great a role in their union.

In their correspondence, her red hair stood as the symbol of her physical attractiveness. If only she did not have red hair! Simon should remember that a head of hair did not make a marriage. When he could get away with it, he took all this lightly. He denied that he was marrying her for her gifts at logic. He asked her whether Helen of Troy had red hair, adding that he knew the question would not please her.

To more direct charges from Helen of an off-putting reserve, Simon replied, "You have, I must confess, made a capital discovery in respect to my temperament. I wish sometimes it were otherwise, and this is one of the times. I do not, of course, intend to be reserved with you, and you will very soon teach me not to be, but the habit must be deeply grounded in my nature. Twenty years ago, my family remarked on it."

He had made a number of friends since he had left Louisville, "and many of them are sincerely devoted to me and I to them." They had all "claimed sympathy in some form from me," but he wondered how many of them really knew him. He had given them little opportunity to see beyond "the apparent equanimity of my life." Helen possessed "the charm that must win the fullness of my reluctant nature . . . and I shall be able to offer no resistance to your sweetness and sympathy, nor shall I wish to." But there was so much to tell. "The flood of things that should get out are caught at the exit. This will all quickly change."[19]

But in fact, confidences continued to flow slowly and sparsely. Simon admitted to Helen that during long years of desiring not to have his discontents known, he had erected defenses that sometimes elicited accusations of "inhumanity."

Helen replied with a fascinating character study. "Your 'inhumanity' I can well understand. . . . You are one of those people whom Baudelaire called the *disinherited,* one of the people for whom the standards of the world and its preoccupations are insufficient, unsatisfying. I wonder if you have recognized how great your difference is? There is something in your force of energy, in your essential love of your work that might, I should think, have obscured the truth in a degree from you; moreover, you do not believe in repinings, and what is unformulated remains partially hidden from yourself. As I come to know you better, I come to see how strong a person you are; by that, I mean how strong are the elements that make up your nature, how compelling to action.

"And strangely enough, although this might make me in a sense afraid of you, it entirely fails to do so. I recognize my own weakness when compared to you, and I should hate, I suppose, to lose my personality under the overpowering influence of yours; but I shall love to have my nature deepened and enriched by living in sympathy with you, and I feel convinced that that is what will happen, since it has already begun to happen. We must never let ourselves be drawn into a struggle for temporary or unimportant things. You must not expect me to fit into the ordinary ideal of a wife. I shall try to be to you what you yourself wish, and I shall let you be judge of what that is, but you, on your side, must take care to clear your mind of ideas that rise purely from tradition and a worldly environment. . . .

"The sum of it is that I believe in you, and love you, and trust myself to you with perfect confidence, without *in fact a single reserve.*"[20]

48

A Hectic Departure

THE eight and a half months that intervened between the start of 1903 and the marriage seemed to Helen interminable. She had nothing rewarding with which to occupy herself. Finishing at Bryn Mawr tasks she found unpleasant; having, after the news of the engagement came out, to bear efforts she resented at prying into her emotions; struggling over and over with Lucy; going on vacation trips with her old associates whose way of life she was deserting, Helen found herself swirling around in anticipations and forebodings. To Simon, wishing to hide nothing, she confided her dark thoughts. Would she please him when he got to know her better? Would he suit her? Was he to be trusted after all not to carry out her subjugation? Would he encourage or squash her literary ambitions? Did he, despite denials, secretly dislike college women? And so on and so forth.

Simon was sometimes hurt, sometimes irritated as when Helen informed him of the maiden ladies' ruling that a successful marriage required the complete subjection of one partner. He would have been more deeply upset had not all Helen's worries spun like the blades of a fly wheel on the solid axis of her never-denied determination to go through with the marriage. And so much of Simon's attention had to be occupied with other problems concerning which he could confide to Helen as he could never before confide to anyone.

Until the end of the academic year, Simon was faced with the "heavy work" of carrying on his part of the medical school routine. To Herter he wrote, "I cannot express to you the quaint feeling I have when I reflect that this is the last year of my systematic teaching. Of teaching there will probably be no end while I remain active, but the teaching in the Institute [where the younger men would learn in their elders' laboratories] will be different and of a much more inspiring sort. Now a major part of one's energy is lost, and the return for a large part of the effort is deplorably small." Flexner had little interest in teaching ordinary practitioners.[1]

The waves which Flexner's departure were raising among the medical profession in Philadelphia were enlarged by the uniqueness of the situation. Such a professorship as he had held in America's most venerable medical school had always been considered so prestigious that no further advancement was possible. The faculty had reluctantly (and in some breasts resentfully) conferred this honor on a Jewish outsider from an upstart medical school. Had Flexner moved on to a job that could be considered inferior or possibly equivalent, that could have been accepted with a shrug of the shoulders and a pitying smile. But a new and higher opportunity had opened, such as America had never known before, and to this the newcomer had been called. To make matters worse, not only was the Rockefeller Institute an extension of the radical ideas of the Hopkins, but it was located in the ever-hustling city of New York, which Philadelphians both despised and envied. It was easy to conclude that Flexner, having been generously allowed in from the enemy lines, had used what Philadelphia offered to strengthen himself for a return to the enemy.

The medical school's official response was razing to the ground what Flexner had built. As his successor, the faculty and trustees appointed Allan Joshua Smith, a university graduate who was a brother of the vice-provost of the university, and, in Flexner's opinion, "the poorest choice who could have been made. . . . It is a great pity to block for another generation all progress in pathology, and with a $600,000 laboratory under construction!" But Smith's outstanding quality was pleasing in contrast to what had gone on under Flexner: he was famous for doing nothing.[2]

To complete the change, it was necessary to win back the Ayer Clinical Laboratory, which was just beginning to publish its own scientific bulletin. Flexner was urged to support Smith to be his successor there also. But Flexner helped persuade the hospital trustees to elevate his own assistant, Longcope. He then urged Provost Harrison to attach Longcope to the university with some nominal appointment through which they would get advantages at the Ayer.[3]

                              * * *

Medical school tradition dictated that a dinner be given for all retiring professors — and Simon could not be excluded. The occasion was duly staged at the University Club. The souvenir menu was decorated by Louis C. Schmidt, a Swiss medical illustrator whom Simon had imported to Philadelphia, and was to call to New York. On the front cover he showed Flexner vanquishing death, a skeleton dropping his scythe, by throwing a microscope and a test tube. Around the bony feet coiled Flexner's rattlesnakes. On the back cover, Schmidt attempted peacemaking. Flexner is shown as a forceps-waving baby being nurtured by two of the broad-rimmed figures in vaguely Quaker costume who were conventional symbols for Philadelphia. The implication was that the community should be proud of its native son. But all present knew that he was not a native son. (PLATE 29)

The menu was sumptuous: cocktails, three kinds of wine, and cordials; oysters, shad, roast beef, and sweetbread cutlets; salad, cheese, Montrose pudding, cakes.[4] Dr. H. A. Hare, a senior practitioner-scientist, read some presumably congratulatory verses that spoke for the Philadelphia medical establishment.

He imagined Flexner, while "busy" in New York, yearning for Philadelphia, and "all the ways of life that can be most dear." He would be welcomed back, Hare added piously, by "your good friends here." In another verse, he described Flexner "with his flow of words and soft inflection," lecturing his colleagues on "terminal infection." But, the gist of the poem accused Flexner of using scientific research to further his personal ambition:

> It matters little rattlesnake or adder,
> Kidney or spleen or well-infected bladder.
> Each helps him on to fame, renewed reward,
> Each adds a gilding to his two-edged sword.
> Each disease is yoked to aid his sway,
> And help him forward on his glorious way.[5]

However, reactions to the meteor who was passing out of Philadelphia skies were not altogether hostile. Simon wrote Helen that he and Provost Harrison parted "in the most cordial good humor with each other."[6] The most amazing convert was the anti-Semite White. He dropped in on Flexner to ask a favor and Simon said he would grant it if he could. White wanted to perpetuate Flexner's influence by establishing a committee on pathology with Flexner on it. Flexner replied that his successor would undoubtedly be unwilling to be put in such a position. He had thought Smith would consider it an honor, White said, but he agreed that it was probably a bad idea.[7]

The issues raised by Simon's career at the university did not disappear with his departure. A few years later, Harrison appeared at the Rockefeller Institute at the head of a Philadelphia group who wished to donate to the university Flexner's portrait. When they asked him to suggest the artist, he urged Christian Herter's sister-in-law Adele. The delegation objected to the idea of a woman. Simon, smiling inwardly, urged that they go to the studio and have a look. Himself far from immune to Adele's charms, he was sure she could "handle them," as indeed she did. Adele Herter was a pastelist who could create effectively what were for that medium gigantic pictures: her life-size, full-length portrait of Simon standing in his laboratory is an effective tour de force. It is reproduced here along with her bust-portrait of Helen, which is one of this writer's favorite possessions.[8] (PLATES 30 and 31)

Simon's portrait hung for years in a prominent position in the medical school library, but not until after their former professor had been showered with honorary degrees from other universities, including Harvard and Strasbourg, and Cambridge in England, did Pennsylvania join the procession.

Longcope's appointment at the Ayer Laboratory assured the immediate future of the young assistants there. But Simon's young men would no longer be wanted at the university. Since he was taking only Noguchi with him to the institute, he had to secure posts for the others, which he successfully did. (Each was to make his scientific mark.) It was also important for them as far as possible to complete, before the dislocation of moving, the work they had in hand.

The laboratory did not have to be vacated before the beginning of the new academic year, and in July, 1903, when Simon was deeply immersed in his grand project in relation to dysentery, he dropped in to find "a buzz of industry. Pearce, Bunting, Noguchi, and Yates were all there and working merrily. I caught the spirit and puttered among some embers of studies, and saw here and there a gleam I had not detected before." This, he continued to Helen, "is one of the mysteries that adds zest to investigation. Nature is a tantalizing mistress and gives her fruits only at particular seasons, when the spirit is on her — and you." He intended to look into "one of the gleams to determine whether the light was a true one or only a will-o'-the-wisp."[9]

The gleam he then saw was probably his inspiration concerning pneumonia. All doctors knew that sufferers' lungs filled with pus called out by the infection and inflammation. As the patients recovered, these pus cells were normally removed through coughing or self-digestion. However, in occasional cases, the clearing did not take place, some cells remaining to be converted into fibrous tissue that permanently damaged the lungs. Previous workers had identified enzymes in the pus cells. It occurred to Flexner that perhaps in the cells that were not removed the enzymes were absent or failed to act. He tested this supposition "in a rough and ready way" and the results supported his inspiration. For Flexner, to reach any results was to publish. He was pleased when the article attracted the attention of the celebrated Friedrich Müller in Munich.

Flexner had been at the time prevented from carrying the matter further because of his departure from Philadelphia. During the European years that followed on his marriage, he spent a semester in Berlin at the laboratory of Professor Salkooski, where the first studies of autolytic enzymes had been made. The knowledge he acquired of chemical methods for measuring enzyme activity was to be particularly valuable in helping make possible what was probably his greatest single scientific contribution: the "Flexner serum" effectively terminated the recurrent epidemics of cerebrospinal meningitis.[10]

An important and long-standing project in Flexner's Philadelphia laboratory was the work with Noguchi on snake venom.*[11] Their definitions of the toxins that made the venom so poisonous, and their discoveries concerning the destructive activity of the toxins in the body were creating excitement in the international scientific world. Simon was particularly delighted when, as he wrote Helen, a letter came from the laboratory of the celebrated Paul Ehrlich in Berlin, "which tells a further and very important confirmation of our venom work. We had distinguished between the principles in cobra venom acting upon the blood as a poison and upon the nervous system. The latter we called neurotoxin." Ehrlich and Keys had confirmed Flexner's and Noguchi's conclusions physiologically and determined the different chemical structures of the two poisons.[12]

* When Simon sailed for Europe in September, 1903, he turned the venom research altogether over to Noguchi, whose major publication in 1906 established Noguchi's reputation.

However, Flexner's major project during the summer of his engagement was a tremendous flowering of the work on dysentery he had begun in the Philippines four years before. We have seen how he brought home the cultures he had made there and had subsequently collected all the cultures he could procure that investigators had made throughout the United States and in various parts of the world. Undertaking his own tests, he concluded that, despite small variations, all the bacteria could be for practical purposes classified as examples of the Shiga bacillus.[13] He failed to recognize a significantly different strain which he himself had procured in the Philippines from a donor named Harris, and which has gone down in medical parlance as the Flexner-Harris bacillus, or more commonly, the Flexner bacillus.[14]

Meditating years later on his having left this discovery to the German bacteriologist Walther Kruse, he wrote, "I have never been educated in any branch of learning. There are great gaps in my knowledge, such as it is, of pathology. I am really a pathological Topsy. I often wonder what I have: I think a knowledge of what I do not know and perception of the value of problems — a value which helps me to choose, [illegible], direct, and determine when a piece of work is well done and the reverse. Technically, I am not well trained in the sense of meticulous and complete accuracy. I have rather used others to do finely detailed things — e.g. agglutination, etc. — than to do them myself. I should have discovered the agglutinative differences between the Shiga and my own variety of B Dysenteriae."*[15]

As soon as the Rockefeller Institute entered its first phase of giving grants, Flexner engineered support for studies of dysentery. In the summer of 1901, two young men, C. W. Duval and V. H. Bassett, one from Welch's laboratory and one from Flexner's, investigated several outbreaks of diarrheal disease among American adults and found the dysentery bacillus to be present. For the summer of 1902, attention was now turned to "summer diarrheas" — in their more severe aspect called "cholera morbus" — which were epidemic among children during hot weather and produced high mortality in infants. Duval and Bassett were again supported, and again identified dysentery bacilli. Welch wrote Rockefeller, Jr., that this finding, which opened the possibility of curing so great a scourge, by itself would have justified the activities of the Rockefeller Institute so far.[16]

---

* Flexner's public explanation ran as follows: "When it is recalled that the early tests of agglutination were made with human serum, and that the action of bacilli on sugars had been little studied, and further that in colony-form and usual cultural properties no differences are seen, it becomes evident why the bacilli should have been classed as identical."[17]

While still in Baltimore, Flexner had started efforts to find a serum that would cure dysentery. Now his work was spurred on by the findings of Duval and Bassett. With institute support he made an arrangement with H. K. Mulford Company to supply and stable horses in Philadelphia for use in the production of serum. There was to be no charge on condition that the Mulford Company keep possession of the treated horses, it being understood that they would market no serum without approval from the institute. Mulford was already producing a vaccine for smallpox.[18]

What Flexner intended was different. The smallpox vaccine gave the patient the disease in a mild form, signaling the body to create its own protective serum. Flexner intended to create a curative serum in the horse. This was to be done by injecting horses with the vaccine made from dead dysentery bacilli and then, when the animals had built up enough immunity, injecting them with live germs in such a way that the horses survived. Thus, the horses became a kind of antiserum factory, their bodies producing protective serum that could be drawn off in large quantities, the horse being a large animal. By repeated passage of infectious material through a series of horses, a serum, so it was hoped, would be produced that was safe for administering to humans.

As so described, the process sounds simple enough, but actually the complications were numerous. Quantitative determinations had to be made and then adjusted to specific needs. There were always possibilities of unrecognized adulterants that could confuse findings and create dangers. And then there were the multiplicity of organisms — Shiga's and Flexner's, and variants sometimes happened upon. The more general the application of the serum, the more useful it would be in the hands of practitioners who could not undertake elaborate diagnostic tests.

At its April meeting, the institute board adopted a plan already developed by Flexner. They resolved to "concentrate the work of the Institute during the summer upon the problems associated with dysentery and diarrhea." Sick children would be simultaneously studied by bacteriologists and clinicians in many institutions in Baltimore, Philadelphia, New York, and Boston. It was hoped to answer on a larger scale "the question of the local or general occurrence of the dysentery bacillus, and next [determine] the usefulness of the anti-dysenteric serum and its action upon a considerable number of patients." The entire effort was to be on such a scale as had never even been dreamed of for any medical project in the United States.[19]

To establish consistency of effort and to make sure that all workers understood the problems and methods, Flexner gave a short course in his Philadelphia laboratory for the twelve bacteriologists involved. But when the actual work was being done, he found that he had continually to visit one laboratory after another. The bacterial "flora" of the digestive tract was as various as the growth of a tropical jungle. To identify dysentery bacilli in this welter of microorganisms required under the best of circumstances the greatest attention and knowledge, and the circumstances were often far from the best. Differences in result were numerous. Thus, Duval and Shorer found dysentery bacilli in seventy-five cases, Lewis in eleven. Circumstances altered the effectiveness of the search. Cultures taken directly from the mucus in the intestine (always possible in autopsies, but rarely from living patients) was more likely to yield dysentery bacilli than cultures from "dejecta." The amount of time that elapsed between the making of a culture and its examinations was critical because some intestinal organisms multiplied so rapidly that they soon obliterated the dysentery bacilli. Poorer mothers, who would not let their infants out of tenements or their sight, created human problems often baffling to laboratory men. And so on. Flexner had plenty to attend to and advise about as he made his rounds.[20]

As the summer began, Simon wrote Helen that "the health of the children is exceptionally good." Although this was "a cause for rejoicing . . . it has nevertheless held up the current of the work." When the summer diarrheas did get going, Simon was soon convinced that the ubiquity of dysentery was being proved. Concerning his serum, he wrote his fiancée on July 6, "It is the crucial point of the work and I am very anxious it should be of benefit. To determine that will require the great part of the summer."[21]

Eight days later, he wrote from Baltimore that D. J. H. Knox, Jr., of the Wilson Sanitarium for Children, reported "banner results." He had used the serum more than anyone else, and most intelligently. "I saw a number of babies to whom it has been given, and they looked bright and cheerful and not ill *then.*" Knox was convinced that two or three lives of the very ill had been saved, and that the disease had been cut short for others. However, "I am not permitting myself to build castles which may be destined to fall upon me later." So much more had to be determined before anything could be considered settled that he was "putting away all temptations to draw conclusions."[22]

Although Flexner was "somewhat disappointed" at how cautiously the serum was being used in Boston, he received positive reports from

Dr. William H. Park in New York. "As far as I can judge," he wrote Helen as the autumn advanced, "the serum will be established as a remedy of promise. In another year, it will be further improved, made stronger, and that if used next summer it should be still more effective."[23]

The road proved to be long and dark. More than ten years later, in 1915, Flexner and Harold L. Amos announced a new serum. They were, of course, not the only workers in a crowded field. Serum after serum had been produced in one part of the world or another during the forty years before the development of chemotherapy.

Treatment by the "wonder drugs" has not been successful enough to elicit a stronger verdict than "there is a general consensus of opinion that it constitutes a valuable form of therapy."[24] There is still no sure cure for dysentery. Yet the scourge has been on the decline. In advanced countries this can be ascribed to improved hygiene and living conditions, particularly the purification of water supplies. But even where hygiene remains primitive, the disease has waned. There are many examples in the history of medicine of epidemic diseases receding as inexplicably as they rise.

Down the decades, more and more varieties of the dysentery bacillus have been isolated. However, they divide for the most part between the still-accepted major categories: the Shiga bacillus and the Flexner bacillus.

49

The Mildness of a Strong Love

CAREY had insisted that Helen's wedding, which was to take place on September 17, 1903, should be a formal occasion held in the elegant garden that Miss Garrett's money had created behind the Deanery. It was not to be a Quaker ceremony but more conservatively Episcopalian, the celebrant being Zoe's brother, Nielson Poe Carey.[1] Helen was annoyed by this plan. She did not want to enter the married state conventionally, as if hers were not a rare and personal adventure. More specific objections were exemplified by the two comic anecdotes through which she liked, in later years, to describe her wedding. She mocked the social pretension by stating that Carey, in a last-minute effort at perfection, had had the garden chairs repainted. But the paint had not dried and the chairs stuck to the guests.

Helen's second anecdote revealed her belief that Carey arranged so conservative a Christian occasion to gloss over the Jewishness of the groom. According to Helen, Noguchi, wandering around as he was inclined to do, appeared where the groom was supposed to appear, creating a flutter among the guests, who had heard that Helen was marrying something peculiar but had not heard he was Japanese.[2]

Whether or not Simon suspected — Helen, who always ignored the issue, would not have confided her suspicions to him — that an effort was being made to sanitize his Jewishness, he forced Helen's hand by welcoming the idea of a formal ceremony. Unlike Helen, who had moved with social position as her perpetual companion, Simon was pleased to be married in a most traditional manner.

Helen made fun of getting a suitable costume for her marriage. Her dressmaker, she wrote Simon, had made her buy a pair of stays "and insists on drawing them in." Perhaps Simon would "care less for the next beautiful figure" when she told him that "nine dollars and fifty cents and a little patience will produce a fair one. While with twenty-two dollars and a good deal of patience, a woman can be a sylph. She will probably die young, which is also an advantage, no doubt."[3]

To Simon, Helen philosophized: "Every woman thinks it her divine right to sit still in the shade while the man who is dubbed her lord and master toils for her in the sun, and, by receiving the fruits of his labor with a smile, she confers more than sufficient reward." If Simon wished her to have the feelings of an Indian squaw who carried the luggage for the tribe, *he* "must don the war paint. If I am to have the peacock clothes — emeralds and gold ornaments and rustling silk and waving feathers — you must be resigned to accept your inferiority."[4]

Helen denounced women's shopping: "Have we left the skin of the monkey for this? I give you two years, and then I shall surely adopt a uniform."[5]

Simon replied that he did not think she would wear a uniform when she saw how much her "simple finery" pleased him.[6]

Simon, the self-educated man who had a passion to learn, was eager to profit from Helen's knowledge of literature. After he had forgotten to bring a copy of *Trivia* along with him on a trip, Simon wrote, "you must really begin to take care of my education." Laughingly, she denied that his taste needed training, but offered to save him time by pointing out beautiful things she had read. "Do you, for instance, know Homer and the Greek dramatists?" On Sundays after they were married, "when you are not in the laboratory or sometimes in the evenings when you are not really tired, we might read together the best passages." Simon replied, "Thank you for your generous offer. . . . I shall be only too eager for it, and what you outline feels in the depth of my ignorance a field of pure joy."[7]

But Simon had his own eloquence as a writer. He thus described to her a daydream: "After spending the fleeting hours by your side in harmony and unison, without perhaps uttering a sound, I suddenly carry you off to the sea where we may listen to the breaking waves or together climb a hill or accessible mountain height where we own all that we can survey with our minds and eyes. Or again, we are sitting near each other and you are reading to me usually out of your favorite poets, or I am reading to you of the lives and thoughts of the men who have influenced my thoughts and actions. And we discuss on the beauties of the imagination enshrined in the one or the virility of action embodied in the other. And then we fall to discussing the relations of all this and all the unrecorded efforts of life to life, which leads us to the conclusion that a noble altruism is the leaven that makes mere living rise to a ponderable height. We never disagree — that is one of my fancies — although we sometimes differ in our views. But when the seance is over we have each been convinced by the other or by our own eloquence, and no sense of the ownership of a belief and acceptance of it remains — but merely the appreciation of harmony."[8]

There was no reason for Simon and Helen to dwell on their diversity of religious background, since neither was concerned with theology or dogma, and they shared as a fundamental conviction optimistic utopianism. Helen's upbringing had been dedicated to reforms which her elders regarded as reachable: greater holiness, achieved by throwing yourself at the foot of the cross; elevation of men through more profound education and of women by giving them the same education as men; sexual purity and the extirpation of the demon rum. In pursuing these ends, the Whitall Women were, although always in a Christian content, often violators of orthodoxy. And Helen's father had been concerned with the very scientific utopia, the denial of which had destroyed her mother, that Simon sought. When they were very newly betrothed, Helen wrote Simon, "What you say about the future touches me deeply. I am ambitious for you in this sense — that you use your powers to the utmost in the cause of science which is, in a way that no other cause can be, the cause of mankind."[9]

As for Simon, having imbibed no religious tradition, he made science his religion. His faith was not mystical like that of the Whitalls, but as direct and down to earth as anything possibly could be. Yet, by the most meticulous dealing with material things, the scientist penetrated philosophical mysteries, and the medical experimenter, although he could not create life, extended, within the bounds of time, the permanence of its creation. He quenched tears, relieved pain, bid the dying to rise and live. The question of what happened when (to use the Quaker phrase) you "stepped off the banks of time," did not bother Simon because he knew it was unanswerable.

Along with the religion of science of which her future husband was a high priest, Helen adhered to her esthetic religion. "I really believe that at the bottom of my heart I am unregenerate enough to think that beauty is as important as truth. It is not truth, alas! It transcends truth, how and why I wish that I knew. But truth after all is, I suppose, supreme, at least it is less subjective than beauty, and this fact must be one of the reasons that it appears more satisfactory to pursue."[10]

"What impresses me," Simon wrote, "when I can see you for more than a brief hour or two, and when the things which are uppermost in our minds have been disposed of, is the essential congeniality of our views and tastes. That you should have pursued literature and artistic things deeply and chiefly and I should have devoted myself almost wholly to science constitute no real difference in us. Our understandings are allied and our congeniality is assured by the constitution of our feelings."[11]

The differences between Helen's and Simon's worldly backgrounds proved a bond between them. Herself a child of privilege, Helen was deeply impressed by how far her man had traveled on his own. And Simon found no more reason to envy or resent (or even feel diminished by) her inherited knowledge than a pupil has to be anything but glad of the wisdom of his teacher. They had come together like two half circles joining to make a whole. Although in their thirties, neither had truly known love before. When their lives converged, each was, although in different ways, both knowing and naive. Helen had seen a landscape much wider than Simon's, but almost always from afar. She had been held back by deafness and shyness, sickness and mental turmoil. Simon had with unwavering determination followed a single trail that led upwards between narrow walls to exhilarating peaks. What Simon gave Helen was more of the earth, firmer ground beneath her feet, an acceptance of the ordinary realities of living. What Helen gave Simon was a true expansion of his personality.

Simon never lost to his dying day his sense of wonder that so resplendent a creature had come to dispel his loneliness. He had been very lonely. Except for his filial relationship with his mother, whose horizons had been too restricted for her to follow his growth even before he had left Louisville, Simon had never before allowed any human being to come close to him. She could not realize, he wrote Helen, how much she had changed him, "for you have not known and could not know my intimate life before we found ourselves intimately drawn together.... Your love has brought into my life an alteration so profound as to affect my most vital nature through which my actions and the currents of my thoughts are elevated."[12]

In the "revelation which your subtle feeling has brought distinctly before me, I see many things of which I am thankful. I see the deep currents of your nature towards which there is in me a corresponding flow. I see how essential we are to each other and only by being wholly each other's can we arrive at happiness, and that life for us cannot succeed on superficialities but that we shall demand to enter fully into each other's intellectual and emotional lives."[13]

"In feeling you are, as I have said to you before, more deeply and hence richly endowed than I am. And while this is in itself a gift, it is also, as you unfortunately have learned, not an unalloyed one. Unfortunately, deep feeling is susceptible of being aroused to pain as well as to pleasure, and where it exists the slighter and less profoundly expressive chords are very apt to be wanting.

"But, while being less deeply endowed, I am, I think, not insensitive. In fact, I have always been alive to an uncomfortable degree of over-sensitiveness that I do not cease to regard but which, in the light of yours, seems less significant. I am glad to appreciate this difference now and fully (as I seem to think) for it assures that I shall understand you in a way that the absence of this appreciation would make impossible."[14]

"The road that you and I are to travel together we must travel alone, guided by our sincere love and regard for each other, by our wish each to see the other as happy as a human relation can make a life, and by the employment of our intelligences in the ways that promise to make for sustained interest and usefulness. This no one can help us to do, no example or precept will illuminate a way that these desires do not render light. . . . While mere age is no security against failure and no insurer of success, there are conditions of knowledge and experience and values of personality for which prediction may be ventured. It is, of course, easy to delude oneself with the view that where others have stumbled and fallen, you can walk with security. But with tempered ambitions and simple intentions, and abiding faith in the mildness of a strong love, the road to happiness should not be too devious and too stormy for us to find our ways unaided."[15]

IX

Conclusion

50

---•◦◦◦•---

The Later Years

THIS narrative, like many a Victorian novel, has ended with the successfully achieved joining of two lovers. In such novels it was taken for granted that with marriage all problems ceased. "And," so goes the refrain, "they lived happily ever after." Did the Flexners live happily ever after?

The worst blow Helen received was out of human control. Her sister Carey liked to say that no intelligent woman would have anything but daughters. Helen's childhood home had been divided between the male team and her mother's team of daughters. Married to so powerful a man, Helen looked forward to female allies. When her first child was still unborn, Helen referred to it as "she." But the baby that appeared was suitably named William Welch Flexner.

After an interval that indicates family planning — almost three years — another child was on the way. I was supposed to be called Lucy. But I was named after my grandfather, James Carey Thomas Flexner.

Try again? Had not Helen's mother borne ten children? But it was an axiom of Helen's upbringing that Mary Whitall Thomas had been submerged and then killed by the size of her brood. Concerning the Flexners' intention, most unusual but altogether convincing evidence appeared from the family silver chest: a baby cup elaborately engraved LUCY, bearing a later inscription with my name. Had there been any hope of another Flexner child, Lucy undoubtedly would have reserved the cup.

Helen was sentenced to an all-male household, the only subsequent recruit having been an excessively male Irish terrier. But Helen had Lucy, who stayed with us for extended periods and with whom she exchanged several letters every week. Many years later, when she was a widow, it gave her great pleasure when my wife Beatrice and I had a daughter, who was named Helen after her.

During her marriage Helen's unique femininity brought strong compensations. Simon always regarded the woman he considered beautiful and who was the only love of his life, as a miraculous gift. His sons were trained to treat her with the utmost consideration, and Simon went to great lengths to serve her predilections. To give one example: he enjoyed liquor and remembered with pleasure tipsy occasions. However, he honored Helen's ancestral temperance principles by agreeing that no liquor should be allowed in his home until Helen came to her own conclusion that the failure of the Eighteenth Amendment had proved the unwisdom of prohibition. By that time I was at Harvard, where my innocence concerning the effects of alcohol had, at the start, almost got me into serious trouble.

Few men who operated so powerfully in the world could ever have been more dependent on their wives than was Simon Flexner. Having never been truly close to anyone else, he continued to make her the only sharer of what private confidences he could bring himself to reveal. To his sons he was loving and, although I was more afraid of him than I realized at the time, kind. At the age when Simon had been forced to repeat a grade in school, I became so nervously entangled that my teacher warned my parents that they had a subnormal child. They took no steps beyond trying in practical ways to make things easier for me. My school not being given to leaving children behind, I was promoted with the rest of the class, and as the years moved along I justified my parents' hands-off policy by changing from the class dunce and pariah to the exact opposite. My parents made no comment that I can remember on this ugly duckling rise. They communicated closely only to each other.

In the upbringing of their sons, Simon and Helen were in complete agreement on objective. That we should become businessmen was never an open option, and we were made to understand that what was considered reasonable achievement for others was, because of the privileges of our upbringing, not adequate achievement for us. A birthright member of the world into which we were to be thrown, Helen was the accepted mentor as to clothes and manners, although Simon sometimes feared that we were being made soft by being spared all the privations and hardships he had experienced. As he relied on her to bring the humanities and the arts to him, he relied on her to bring them to his sons. He did not press us to be scientists, fearing that if we followed too closely in his footsteps his reputation would keep us from achieving credit on our own.

The fears Simon felt during their engagement that Helen would be a sad and depressing wife proved largely unfounded. It is true that Helen procured more vellum-bound notebooks in which she wrote more despairing passages concerning her own lot and the miseries of the world; it is true that her health remained precarious, particularly during winters that were plagued with horrendous colds and infected sinuses; but she joined her menfolk in relishing jokes in the style of *Fables in Slang*. Our household was much given to laughter. Helen used her deafness (or so we suspected, although she never admitted it) to poke fun at the pretensions of the world. Thus she insisted on calling a little gamecock of a naval officer Captain Capon, being deaf to his protests that his name was Capron. And then there was Professor Tosser of Harvard, whose snobbishness seemed to be unsuitable for a scholar. She called him Professor Towser and when he objected, said, "I am so sorry that I did not hear your name correctly, but I have it right now, Professor Trouser." More in the Logan vein was her research, carried out with all the blandishments of a southern belle, to determine whether it was possible to flatter a man too much. Her conclusion stated at the end of her life: "Jimmie, it is impossible."

To what extent was Helen justified in her fear that the man she was to marry would use his power to overwhelm her? Even as she had dreaded that power, she had, when engaged, rested on it. There can be no doubt that Simon supplied the backbone of their life together. This again she relied on, but sometimes resented. The painful issue concerned her writing.

Helen had hoped that Simon's gifts for getting things done would help her overcome her writer's blocks. When her difficulties continued, she complained that the environment her marriage to him had created stifled female achievement. There were the chores involved in managing a considerable staff in a large house: at its maximum a governess, a cook, two maids, a part-time cleaning woman and a part-time janitor. She found almost unbearable having to start every morning by discussing menus with the cook. Simon tried to help by assigning her a room at the

Rockefeller Institute. However, she did not find the hours she could spend there the complete escape she needed.

Early in her marriage, Helen did complete a novel and send it to at least one publisher. She sought to deepen understated action taking place in polite drawing rooms with analyses in the manner of Henry James. But, hers was by far too straightforward an intelligence to weave complicated webs like those of the "Master."

In another of her writing activities, Simon literally marched with Helen. He was one of the little platoon of men who took part, to the jeers of spectators, in the first woman suffrage parade in New York City. Helen became a publicity director of the woman suffrage campaign in New York, her duty being to inspire and create propaganda publications. For this her logical turn and clear prose were admirably suited. Simon put his scientific reputation behind a pamphlet he wrote to demonstrate that women's intelligences were not inferior to men's.

It was a satisfaction for Helen to have trained up her younger son — she was by far my best literary teacher — to become an author widely published during her lifetime. Eventually, she followed Logan's advice that, for such writers as they, reminiscence was the most grateful literary form. *A Quaker Childhood* was brought out by the Yale University Press, and achieved such a *succès d'estime* as, despising "popular writing," she most desired. I have never come across anyone who had read her book who was not charmed by it.

Both Helen and Simon had been nervous about their impending move to "vulgar" New York with its noise and eternal rush. Before they were married they spent a night in the Herters' mansion on Madison Avenue. Helen had been distressed by the clamor that came in the windows, and Simon assured her that they would hide away in some quiet corner of the metropolis. In actuality, they were to live happily for some twenty years next door to the Herters, their most intimate friends.

Perhaps Simon, with his childhood memories of squalor, would have been dazzled by the opulence and display of the nouveau riche: the door was opened to him by his fame. But Helen drew a firm line against associating with millionaires who told her that the only way to judge a man's worth was by the money he made. This decision surely contributed to Simon's career, all the more because such New Yorkers as the Herters and the Rockefellers admired her taste. Helen was indeed in the eyes of the world the perfect wife for a serious scientist of position and power. No one could fault her family background, her instincts, education or behavior, yet she wore simple clothes and practiced simple manners. Her red hair glowed and even after it had faded her attractiveness was acknowledged.

Out of a British archive there has come to me a letter advising Sir Kenneth Clark about a trip he was planning in 1926 to the United States. He was urged to look up Mrs. Simon Flexner since Roger Fry, Bloomsbury's reigning art critic, had ruled her among all the women he had met in America the most charming.[1]

In congratulating Helen on her engagement to a distinguished scientist, Bertrand Russell warned her against allowing her admiration of her husband's career to turn with the passage of time into jealousy. I was never conscious of any such jealousy. Helen's eagerness to make furthering Simon's career the first priority of her household was facilitated by her playing in that career an interesting and important part.

Helen was undoubtedly enabled to follow her husband's scientific work more than might be expected: he had a gift for simple explanation and she was eager to understand. However, concerning research she could be no more than a sympathetic listener. Her role as an advisor was in the human sphere, and a large part of Simon's achievement was to rest on his ability to lead people.

On his election as director of the Rockefeller Institute, Flexner had been an accomplished rather than a towering figure. While the Pasteur and Koch institutes were built around a single scientist whose personal interests shaped the nature of the work undertaken, the Rockefeller, as Simon himself urged, was concerned with all promising branches of medical science. The organization, as far as it had been thought out in theory, would consist of several departments, each with its own director, with Flexner as the chief of these directors who was to be ruled by an executive committee of the board. That things did not work out that way was because of the way Flexner immediately took hold.[2]

Perhaps it was his drugstore experience, which had taught him to do many things at once; perhaps it was his self-education in Louisville, which had to be general because he lacked the facilities to specialize; but in any case, as Peyton Rous wrote, he had, as his career had developed, "continually scouted on the broad front of scientific medicine, never confining himself to a sector though that way led to academic security ... but winning himself an education unique in its comprehensiveness."[3] That he did not intend to accept any narrowness is revealed by the fact that a major professional purpose of the trip to Europe (which included his honeymoon) was to study, at the Pasteur Institute and in Germany, a specialty still outside his grasp: biochemistry.

If Flexner became, as many knowing observers came to record, in his own person the embodiment of the Rockefeller Institute, it was not because he was appointed to the post. His position was, indeed, not officially recognized until in 1920, after seventeen years, he was designated director of the entire institute.

Flexner had made his task more difficult for himself by resolving not to establish, as in a university, departments that added up to a comprehensive whole. When he secured a scientist of genius or great promise, he would build a department around him. Should a scientist drop out, the department would be eliminated. Should two men appear in the same field, if their labor could be separated in such a way as to prevent overlapping, there would be two departments. This made administration an aspect of personal relationship.

The senior scientists were called not professors but members. They did not, as in a university, occupy positions on a preestablished web, their connections with the administration determined by where they were placed. Each had his own fiefdom with his henchmen around him. To hold what Simon called his "prima donnas" together as part of a single enterprise covered by a single budget, working side by side cooperatively without feuding, was a task of legerdemain in which Simon called perpetually for advice from Helen.

Applying his encyclopedic knowledge, his "steely" foresight as to possibilities, and his insight into inherent pratfalls, Flexner tried to help workers at various levels to achieve fruitful ends. He believed that scientists who had a record of discoveries might be argued with, but would have to be backed, if they insisted, in projects of which he disapproved. But there were exceptions like Noguchi, who needed to be aimed and then kept on course. Less experienced workers needed guidance of many different kinds. Upon occasion Flexner would suggest projects even to the most distinguished members. The extent of his personal role in the multitudinous discoveries that poured out of the institute cannot of course be defined, but it is generally assumed that his influence on scientific results was considerable.

Interviews with the director could be rigorous. I was amazed, after I had grown older, to be told by extremely distinguished scientists that they were unable to sleep during the night before they had an appointment with Dr. Flexner. It could be expected that the often self-enchanted individualists would resent the interviews. It is therefore indicative that there never emerged among the staff even a suggestion of a revolt.

According to the historian of the institute, Dr. George Washington Corner, Flexner's "consideration and solicitude for the welfare of people dependent in one way or another upon his leadership extended from members to new employees in shops or animal house. He made himself acquainted with the families of staff and employees, gave sympathy and practical help in time of illness, and at times surprised them with special attention. . . . He kept a sharp eye on the operating personnel and when he spotted a bright ambitious youth marked him for promotion and sometimes arranged special training for him. The present superintendent of maintenance, Bernard Lupinek, related that Flexner, seeing him sketch a floor plan, promptly had him take a course in architectural drawing, and thereafter saw to his advance."[4] Lupinek paid the debt back by coming to the rescue of the Flexner Papers when they were being endangered by Detlev Bronk, the president of the newly dubbed Rockefeller University, who resented the idea that he had had a predecessor.

By 1953, eighteen years after Simon Flexner retired, the Rockefeller Institute for Medical Research was ruled so deficient in momentum and results that it was changed from a purely research institution dedicated to scientific medicine into the present Rockefeller University. A basic problem had been that the institute had lost its unique position: medical laboratories and research professorships had come to flourish all over the United States and in many parts of the world. Flexner's problem in getting the institute going had been the opposite: the project was then so novel that the attention it attracted also attracted doubts.

The conception of an institution devoted purely to research seemed crackbrained to "common sense." Did not discoveries and inventions appear in a flash of inspiration like (as popular legends taught) Fulton's flash when he saw a kettle boil or Newton's when an apple fell from a tree onto his head. For their part, academics were afraid that scientific inspiration would not come when called: if they abandoned the comforting routine of teaching, they might well find themselves flapping in a void. To make matters worse, the institute still lacked an endowment, and it was understood that so novel a conception would have to earn permanent support by results. Flexner, while expounding the value of basic research, felt pressed to find some important, highly visible discovery. And then, in 1906, New York was struck with a murderous epidemic of cerebrospinal meningitis.

The disease was a rare one, but as we have seen, Flexner had studied a small epidemic thirteen years before in the mining town of Lonaconing. Since then the diplococcus that caused the disease had been isolated. With cultures of that diplococcus made from patients in New York, Flexner produced meningitis in monkeys and showed that it closely resembled the human disease. The infected monkeys yielded materials with which he infected horses. From the horses he succeeded in producing an antiserum. Subsequent research revealed that the antiserum cured monkeys in the early stages of meningitis, but only if injected directly into the cerebrospinal fluid. Flexner was now prepared to treat humans. What came to be known, despite counterclaims by workers engaged in parallel research, as the Flexner serum, reduced fatalities from three in four to one in four. The Rockefeller Institute seemed vindicated, and in the eyes of the public Flexner became a wonder worker.[5]

In 1910, an epidemic of a disease new to America, infantile paralysis, swept the eastern seaboard, creating a wave of terror because it struck mostly children, and the children who did not die were often maimed for life. Public expectations turned to Flexner and the Rockefeller Institute. He got rapidly to work and discovered that the cause of the disease was a virus, and that the disease could be communicated to monkeys but not to other animals. His efforts to find an antiserum were frustrated by universal ignorance among scientists concerning viruses — thirty years were to pass before Jonas Salk and others developed antisera for infantile paralysis. Yet Flexner's work laid the basis for future research and "went far to tranquilize the public." The disease "no longer loomed mysterious, but was a material enemy to fight; something was being done."[6]

The popular interest in Simon Flexner reached such a height that when he was known to be sick, reporters were posted on the steps of his house in a "death watch," each newspaper trying to scoop the others with the first news if he died.

The institute being now solidly on its feet and suffering in fact from too much attention, Flexner resolved to take it and himself out of the public eye. When I became old enough to be conscious of the situation, he was keeping as low a profile as he could. Newspaper reporters talked with both admiration and irritation of the Rockefeller Institute's "antipublicity department." At social occasions, Simon preserved a modest mien, although he was conscious of his worth and did not enjoy being slighted. He found it annoying that handsome women, on being informed that he was a distinguished doctor, automatically assumed that he must be a surgeon.

Although Flexner continued his scientific researches and writing for the rest of his career, important results did not come to him. He was baffled by diseases like sleeping sickness (lethargic encephalitis) that were beyond the scope of medicine in his time; and other projects, like establishing a "mouse village" in which to study the laws by which epidemics spread, he had for lack of time to hand on to other workers. The institute was growing and outside activities of great moment also pressed upon him.

As Welch became older and then vanished from the scene, Flexner became the central figure in American scientific medicine. And his international reputation spread so mightily that he was elected to seven learned bodies in France; five in Germany; three in England; and one or more in Italy, Belgium, Holland, Sweden, Denmark, Venezuela, Argentina, Ecuador, Japan, and Russia. The Kaiser Wilhelm Institute in Berlin was directly modeled on Flexner's organization of the Rockefeller Institute. When a medical research council was forming in England, Prime Minister Lloyd George tried to persuade Flexner to take over. Subsequently, in the double role of Eastman Professor and a Fellow of Balliol, Flexner helped Oxford University organize more modern laboratories. He received, among other medals, Japan's highest award, the Order of the Rising Sun (which he refused to return during World War II because he considered science international) and became a commander of the Legion of Honor (which, we were told, would entitle him to a regiment at his funeral if he were buried in France).

Successive governors made Flexner chairman of the Public Health Council, which supervised health activities in New York State. To the great amusement of his sons, who did not know of their father's earlier alcoholic escapades, he was appointed by Governor Alfred E. Smith on the commission that decided how, after the repeal of prohibition, liquor could in New York State be bought and served. (They decided that women should be allowed in barrooms but prohibited them from standing or sitting at the bars.)

During World War I, Flexner organized a base hospital on the institute grounds to teach doctors in the army medical corps the most up-to-date techniques for treating wounds. He was ordered to France to inspect the army's medical laboratories. His rank as lieutenant colonel (he

rose to full colonel) was far less impressive than the ribbons he was persuaded to wear on his chest, which reflected the medals he had won as a
scientist. He considered the most embarrassing event of his life the occasion when at the Paris headquarters of the American army an elevator
operator, who had had an arm and leg shot off, said to him admiringly,
"Sir, you are very brave." Flexner saw no fighting, but being in Paris
when the armistice was announced, bravely stood his ground on the
Champs-Elysées as, in his role as a high American officer, he was kissed
by hundreds of pretty French girls.

Criticisms of how the Rockefeller fortune was amassed and of the
power of the resulting philanthropies were rife then as they are today,
but Simon Flexner was never bothered. It might be supposed that memories of his own tribulations caused by his father's bankruptcy would
have made him particularly disapproving of the way John D., Sr.,
crushed small competition. The effect was opposite. Had not the
Flexner family by hard work and probity overcome their misfortune?
Was Simon not where he was? He subscribed in the economic sphere
(as did many of his contemporaries) to the Darwinian doctrine of the
survival of the fittest. This could be defined as the doctrine of individualism, an interpretation more acceptable when there existed greater opportunity, than in more recent years, for self-advancement.

In Simon's generation, when government offered no equivalent support, philanthropies on a large scale were made possible only by large
fortunes. Even if in the business world "trusts" were menacing individualism, Simon felt that he was being enabled by the Rockefeller fortune
to liberate human beings through knocking off shackles of illness and
fostering institutions that gave the humbly born ladders which, if they
had ability, they could climb. Although deeply involved with health
measures that would help populations in the mass, he felt no special responsibility for the mediocre, the stupid, or the improvident. Self-made
Simon did not share the theoretical sympathy which delicately nurtured
Helen felt for liberal and even radical causes. But he found it much easier to make peace with the rough and tumble of the world. Thus, to
Helen's horrified outrage, he was amused to cultivate, for institute ends,
the crooked local Tammany district leader who came to be known, because of his grafting techniques, as "Tin-box" Tom Farley.

Flexner's influence came to circle the globe, yet he did not allow his
attention to wander. He focused directly on feasible prospects for
achieving the tasks to which he was devoting himself. To Carey's ex-

postulations that exporting modern medicine to "lesser breeds without the law" would destroy civilization by swamping the "Aryan race," he accorded the amused tolerance with which he normally took Carey's tirades. In response to my questions concerning possible overpopulation of the globe, my father replied that his duty was to those living. Limiting births would be handled by those whose competence it was to do so. When I teased him by asking whether, in curing weaklings, he was not undermining the survival of the fittest, he replied that the strongest were not necessarily the cleverest, and that the human race would be advanced by brain not brawn.

Much of Flexner's leverage in the world came from his power on Rockefeller boards. This grew as John D., Jr., took over from his father, although Simon had the unswerving support of Senior's grizzled advisor Gates, who stated that if the Rockefeller Foundation had any sense, it would turn all its money over to Simon Flexner to spend as he pleased.

In relation to the institute, Flexner's problem was not begging money but rather refusing, without hurting feelings, huge sums offered for projects which he felt would bring bureaucracy into the institute by expanding it in directions where he could not personally lead. His refusal of millions so added to his prestige that if he acknowledged a need for money the money was immediately forthcoming. Simon accepted, all from Rockefeller sources, sixty million dollars.

Corner, the institute historian, describes how at the time of Flexner's retirement there were on the York Avenue hillside "four chief buildings housing twenty-two active Members with twelve Associate Members, about thirty Associates and sixty Assistants and Fellows, a staff numbering more than a hundred and twenty which he had built up from the twelve who began with him in temporary laboratories at Lexington Avenue thirty-one years before." There were in Princeton, New Jersey, a division of animal pathology and a division of plant pathology, where the most basic discovery concerning viruses was made. (PLATE 32)

On the library shelves at the institute, so Corner continued, "were an even hundred of bound reprints, *Studies from the Rockefeller Institute.* . . . Scattered through the heavy volumes were records of achievement that placed the Rockefeller Institute in the front rank of the world's scientific institutions." Furthermore, "its influence as a training center for the universities had been incalculable. One hundred and fifty-two persons had gone from the Rockefeller Institute to become professors and associate professors in sixty-two American universities, colleges, and professional schools and twenty to equivalent positions in seventeen foreign countries."[7]

The Rockefeller Institute had been the first philanthropy to which the founders lent their name, and its great success encouraged aiming the Rockefeller benefactions at science and health. Partly due to Simon's urging, the Rockefeller Sanitary Commission undertook a successful campaign against hookworm infection in the American south. To further the development of nonmedical biology and chemistry (which he had refused to take into the institute) Flexner procured, with most gratifying effect, Rockefeller funds for research fellowships administered by the National Research Council. Supported with overpowering funds from the Rockefeller General Education Board, Simon's brother Abraham reshaped American medical education on the model of the Johns Hopkins Medical School. An original trustee of the Rockefeller Foundation who continued to serve there for seventeen years, Simon did much to steer the multiple projects, national and international, which that organization undertook. He played a major role in creating the Peking Union Medical College that brought modern medicine to China.

Raymond Fosdick, a former president of the Foundation, wrote in his biography of John D. Rockefeller, Jr.: "One of the puzzling aspects of the younger Rockefeller has been his extraordinary intellectual development. Coming from a restricted social and religious background, immersed in his early years in his father's office in a preoccupation with minute business detail, how did he develop the breadth, tolerance, and catholicity of understanding which characterized his middle and later years?" An obvious answer "is to be found in his intimate relationship with the men who, particularly in the early days, were called to positions of leadership in the foundations which his father created."

Fosdick specifies George E. Vincent, who was president of the foundation from 1917 to 1929, and Dr. Wickliffe Rose, who occupied a series of top positions; but he named first and particularly Simon Flexner: "His slight build, his soft voice, his gentle manner were all in striking contrast with the steely precision of his reasoning. His mind was like a searchlight that could be turned at will on any question that came before him. He was incisive, exact, cautious, and diffident, and his influence on John D. Rockefeller, Jr., was incalculable. For the first time in his life the younger Rockefeller was exposed to the severe logic and the disciplined vision of a scientific mind."[8] How strange that the poverty-bound, self-educated youth from back streets in Louisville, Kentucky, should come to have so determining an influence on the most powerful millionaire-philanthropist in the history of America and probably in the world!

At a memorial meeting, Rockefeller spoke thus of his advisor and friend: "The spirit of Simon Flexner . . . lives on in the lives of countless young men he has trained; in the work of many whom he had inspired; in the grateful remembrance of hundreds of thousands of human beings who bless him each day as the unknown cause of their being alive; in the ever-widening circle of his influence radiating from his myriad services to mankind; in the hearts of his countless friends and fellow workers in many lands, who join us in thanking God for the enrichment that has come into their lives and ours because Simon Flexner has lived among us."[9]

Dr. Peyton Rous, who was to win the Nobel Prize for his research on cancer, declared succinctly, "Perhaps no man save Welch has done so much for American medicine."[10]

Simon Flexner retired in 1935, at the age of seventy-two. He then undertook, with foundation support, a life of his beloved mentor, Dr. Welch. Too old to learn a complicated new technique, he finally called in this writer, who had by then published two books of biography, to help him get the manuscript into shape. The resulting work, *William Henry Welch and the Heroic Age of American Medicine*, was published under both our names in 1941. Simon, who was then seventy-eight, attempted, not more than half-heartedly, a task for which he was not temperamentally suited: preparing a formal autobiography. He was not bothered when the manuscript failed to flourish; the drive that had carried him so far had left him. He died on May 2, 1946.

Helen survived Simon for ten years, but her spirit died with him. She sank into a combination of ill-health and lethargy from which neither her sons nor anyone else could rouse her. She was finally released in April, 1956.

Acknowledgments

I have been greatly assisted in the preparation of this volume by a Guggenheim Fellowship, two annual grants from the Rockefeller Foundation, and a three-year grant for expenses from the Commonwealth Fund. The Rockefeller University helped out by administering the Commonwealth grant.

Graciously acceding to my request, Whitfield J. Bell, Jr., director of the American Philosophical Society, and Stephen Catlett, the manuscript librarian, agreed to send from Philadelphia to New York City those of the Flexner Papers I most needed. The documents were temporarily deposited at the New-York Historical Society. In accepting this responsibility, and in many other ways, the Historical Society has continued to extend to me the hospitality and assistance which it has been my good fortune to receive from them for many years. I have continued to profit from access to the Frederick Lewis Allen Room in the New York Public Library, where I am an honorary trustee. My wife and I were privileged to spend a month at the Rockefeller Foundation's Bellagio Study and Conference Center on Lake Como.

My cousin, Barbara Strachey, put up my wife and me in her house at Oxford and made available to me her beautifully catalogued holding of papers from the English side of my mother's family. Another cousin, Jean Flexner Lewinson, has been most helpful concerning her father and mother, Abraham and Anne Flexner.

Beatrice Hudson Flexner has suffered through my labors as an author's wife is fated to do, and has often proffered a helping hand.

Dr. E. H. Ahrens, Jr., of the Rockefeller Hospital, has done his best to lead me through the mazes of my father's scientific work. I am also grateful to Sonya Mirsky, librarian of Rockefeller University, and Caroline Kopp, archivist.

Extensive examination of the overwhelming mass of Flexner papers that remained in Philadelphia at the Philosophical Society was carried through with the greatest efficiency and goodwill by that queen of research workers, Dorothy B. Templeton. Lucy Fisher West, custodian of the M. Carey Thomas Papers at the Bryn Mawr College Library, has guided me through the archives she knows so well. I am grateful for similar assistance from Kenneth Blackwell of the Bertrand Russell Archives at McMaster University.

I have been greatly assisted by Nancy McCall, assistant archivist of the Alan Mason Chesney Medical Archives, the Johns Hopkins University, and, also in Baltimore, by Pamela Jane Gray. Everyone who has been on the staff of the New-York Historical Society Library during my three years of labor has helped me with my tasks. Particular mention should be made of the two successive directors, James J. Heslin and James Bell; the librarian, Larry E. Sullivan; and the associate librarian, Katherine H. Richards. The manuscript librarian, Thomas J. Dunnings, has, as has been the situation down the years, cooperated with great generosity and listened patiently to my typewriter.

My relationship with my publishers, Little, Brown and Company, goes back more than two decades. Arthur Thornhill, Jr., has long been my mainstay there and is now my editor. Chris Coffin has ably assisted him in dealing with me and my equally recalcitrant manuscript. As in the preparation of three of my previous books, I have profited from expert copyediting by Jean Whitnack. When Moses Carr agrees to design one of my books, I am filled with joy. In this case, I am also grateful for designer Dede Cummings's expertise.

This is the second of my books which Ruth Flaherty has typed without going blind or mad.

Acknowledgments
for the Use of Photographs

Plate 14: from the *Monograph Series*, No. 1, XVI, Plate XCVIII. Copyright © 1930 by Russell F. Whitehead.

Plates 15, 20, 22, 23: from the photograph album of Logan Pearsall Smith. Courtesy of John Russell.

Plates 18, 37: courtesy of Jean Flexner Lewinson.

Plates 24, 26, 27, 28: copyright © The Alan Mason Chesney Medical Archives, The Johns Hopkins University.

Plate 29: courtesy of Bryn Mawr College.

Plates 32, 33, 34, 35: courtesy of Barbara Strachey.

Plates 38, 39: courtesy of the Rockefeller Archive Center.

Plate 42: courtesy of the University of Pennsylvania.

Plates 43, 44: courtesy of the Rockefeller University Archives.

All other photographs are from the author's collection.

451

Cast of Family Characters

Only persons of some prominence in the text are here included. Roman numerals indicate the number of generations that intervened between the individual listed and the generation of Helen Thomas and Simon Flexner. Thus, "+III" would specify a great-grandparent, "−II," a grandchild.

FLEXNER

Philip, said to have been in the 1780's chief rabbi of Bohemia and Moravia. +III

Michael, son of Philip, 1789–1871; m. *Therese*, daugher of *Leopold Klauber*, d. 1885. +II

Moritz (Morris), son of Michael, father of Simon, 1819–1882; m. *Esther Abraham*, 1834–1905. +I.

Jacob A., son of Morris, brother of Simon, 1857–1934; m. *Rosa Maas.*

Isidore, brother of Simon.

Simon, 1863–1946; m. *Helen Thomas* (see *Thomas*).

Bernard, brother of Simon, 1865–1945.

Abraham, brother of Simon, 1866–1959; m. *Anne Crawford*, 1874–1955.

Washington, brother of Simon, 1869–1942; m. *Ida Barkhouse.*

Mary, sister of Simon, d. 1947.

William Welch, son of Simon, 1904–; m. *Elizabeth Wray.* −I

James [Carey] Thomas, son of Simon, 1908–; m. *Beatrice Hudson.* −I

Helen Hudson [Nellie], daughter of James, 1953–. −II

Philip, the immigrant, before 1641–1675; m. *Sarah Harrison*, d. 1687. +VIII

John Chew, great-grandson of Philip, 1764–1836; m. *Mary Snowden*, 1770–1844. +IV

Eliza, daughter of John Chew, b. 1792; m. *George Gray Leiper*, 1786–1864. +III

Henrietta Maria, daughter of John Chew, 1799–1874. +III

Dr. *Richard Henry Thomas*, son of John Chew, 1805–1860; m. (1) *Martha Carey*, 1805–1835, daughter of *James* and *Hannah* (*Ellicott*) *Carey*; m. (2) *Phoebe Clapp*; m. (3) *Deborah Hinsdale*, d. 1889. +II

Dr. *James Carey*, son of Richard Henry and Martha, 1833–1897; m. *Mary Whitall* (see *Whitall*). +I

Dr. *Richard Henry, Jr.*, son of Richard Henry and Phoebe, 1854–1904; m. *Anna Braithwaite*. +I

Martha Carey, daughter of James and sister of Helen, 1857–1935.

Dr. *Henry M.*, brother of Helen, 1861–1925; m. *Josephine Gibson* (*Zoe*).

Bond Valentine, brother of Helen, 1863–1920; m. *Edith Carpenter*.

Margaret, sister of Helen, b. 1869; m. *M. Morris Carey*.

Helen Whitall, 1871–1956; m. *Simon Flexner* (offspring under *Flexner*).

Frank S., brother of Helen, 1873–1937; m. *Eleanor M. Bridgeland*.

Millicent Carey, daughter of Margaret, 1898–; m. *Rustin McIntosh*. –I

James, the immigrant, in America before 1688, d. 1714; m. *Hannah*. +VI

James, grandson of John, 1717–1788; m. *Ann Cooper*, d. 1797. +IV

Captain John Mickle Whitall, grandson of James, 1800–1877; m. *Mary Tatum*, 1803–1880. +II

Hannah, daughter of John M., 1832–1911; m. *Robert Pearsall Smith* (for offspring, see Pearsall Smith). +I

Sarah, daughter of John M., 1833–1880; m. *William Nicholson*. +I

Mary, daughter of John M., 1836–1880; m. *James Carey Thomas* (for offspring, see *Thomas*). +I

James, 1834–1892, son of John M.; m. *Mary Cope*. +I

Robert, 1827–1898; m. *Hannah Whitall*, Helen's aunt. +I

Mary (*Mariechen*), daughter of Robert; m. (1) *Frank Costelloe*, 1855–1899; m. (2) *Bernard Berenson*, 1865–1959.

Logan, son of Robert, 1865–1946.

Alys, daughter of Robert, 1867–1951; m. *Bertrand Russell,* 1872–1970.

Ray, daughter of Mary (Mariechen) and Frank Costelloe, 1887–1940; m. *Oliver Strachey* (brother of Lytton Strachey), 1874–1960. —I

Karin, daughter of Mary (Mariechen) and Frank Costelloe, 1889–1953; m. *Adrien Stephen* (brother of Virginia Wolfe), 1883–1949. —I

Barbara Strachey, daughter of Oliver Strachey, 1912–; m. (1) *Olav Hultin;* m. (2) *Wolf Halperon.* —II

Bibliography

This book is primarily grounded on manuscript material not previously utilized.

MANUSCRIPT SOURCES

FLEXNER PAPERS. Donated by my brother and myself, with the approval of the Rockefeller University where they had been stored, to the American Philosophical Society in Philadelphia, Pennsylvania. The papers, constituting the major archives preserved by both Helen Thomas Flexner and Simon Flexner, contain quantities of personal and some ancestral documents. For a partial survey of other types of papers, see Margaret Miller, "A Guide to Selected Files of the Professional Papers of Simon Flexner at the American Philosophical Society" (mimeographed; Philadelphia, 1979). The Flexner Papers are referred to in the source references as FP.

JAMES THOMAS FLEXNER COLLECTION. In New York City. Papers, artifacts, and other materials dealing with the Thomas and Whitall families as far back as the 1820's, and with the lives of Helen Thomas and Simon Flexner. Referred to in the source references as JTFC.

Autobiographical Sources
in the Above Collections

Simon Flexner's unfinished formal autobiography. In the Flexner Papers. Handwritten draft and typescript. The writing of an autobiography was an occupation, not too assiduously pursued, of Simon Flexner's last years. The narrative hardly extends beyond the period covered in this book. Since the intention was publication, the manuscript is characterized by the reserve he always maintained in his relations with the outside world. As a factual record, the manuscript is very important. Referred to in the source references as SFAu.

An earlier draft of the autobiography. Also in the Flexner Papers. Handwritten and variously dated, this draft is somewhat less inhibited than the formal manuscript and is particularly valuable for subsequently deleted discussions of Simon Flexner's scientific work. Referred to in the source references as SFAuD.

Simon Flexner's autobiographical notations. In the Flexner Papers. Over a period of some forty years he made these notations whenever the impulse struck him. Usually dated, they are distributed throughout his personal archives. Some he jotted on any paper that came most conveniently to hand; others filled spaces assigned to specific dates in the "line-a-day" books in which he wrote his diary. They are aspects of his attempt to explain to himself his own remarkable career. Since they were not intended for publication, he did not feel inhibited but applied to them, as far as his memory served him, the accuracy of his scientific reports. The little reminiscences include visual descriptions of locations and people. Accounts of the same event, even when written several decades apart, are amazingly consistent. In the preparations for his formal autobiography he did not consult these notations, perhaps because he did not wish to rummage for them in his welter of papers, perhaps because he remembered that they were too intimate for his public project. There are indications that he hoped I would ferret the notations out, as it was his desire that I should write his biography. Referred to in the source references as SFN.

Simon Flexner's oral reminiscences concerning his early years. In the James Thomas Flexner Collection. These I took down in January and February of 1936. The handwritten manuscript supplements my unrecorded memories of what my father told me as the decades passed. Referred to in the source references as SFOR.

Simon Flexner's Recollections

The autobiography, the autobiographical notations, and the oral reminiscences together form a web of recollections that are the only source (except for Abraham Flexner's *I Remember*) for the account given here of Simon Flexner's pre-Hopkins career, and also for many personal experiences thereafter. A professional biographer cannot remain unconscious of the dangers of such documentation. However, there are methods of judging reliability, and these rank the Simon Flexner recollections very high. Exterior documentation, when it makes its appearance, almost invariably corroborates. There is, furthermore, in Simon Flexner's recorded memories none of the drift towards self-justification and self-aggrandizement which usually mounts in autobiographical writings as the writer grows older.

Simon Flexner, indeed, applied to his introspective examination of his own past the same rigorous standards he applied to his scientific research, where careless observation or self-deception would destroy results. He did not, like his wife in *A Quaker Childhood*, eschew conclusions based on hindsight, but, as in a scientific paper, he kept clear the separation between his comments and the factual report.

II

Abraham Flexner Papers. In the Library of Congress. This archive should be mentioned, although Abraham Flexner seems not to have preserved a single document dealing with the period of his life covered in this book. The only relevant letters are the many preserved by Simon Flexner in the Flexner Papers.

Johns Hopkins Medical School. Volumes A and B of the "Minutes," in the Alan Mason Chesney Medical Archives, Johns Hopkins University.

Rockefeller Institute for Medical Research. Some of the documents, official and otherwise, are in the Rockefeller Archives at Pocantico Hills, New York, and others are in the library of the Rockefeller University in New York City. The latter are referred to in the source references as RUP.

Bertrand Russell Papers. In the Mills Memorial Library, McMaster University, Hamilton, Ontario. This archive represents a major effort to bring together all Bertrand Russell material. As the result of an exchange, photocopies of all Russell's letters to Helen Thomas are here, and those of Helen Thomas's letters to Russell are in the Flexner Papers. Referred to in the source references as BRP.

Logan Pearsall Smith Papers. The largest archive is in the Library of Congress but it contains little of consequence for this book. Most of the relevant documents are in the Flexner Papers; some were kindly made available to me by Smith's literary executor, John Russell. Edwin Tribble, who is preparing an edition of Smith's correspondence, wrote me (December 30, 1982): "I think it is this combination of his love for the breadth and warmth of Helen Flexner as a person and his admiration of her as an intellectual that made him write to her so warmly and spontaneously."

Barbara Strachey Collection. In Oxford, England. Some twenty thousand documents dealing with the Helen Thomas Flexner connections in England. Strongly recommended is Strachey's book *Remarkable Relations*, which is listed below.

M. Carey Thomas Papers. Documents concerning her career, her family, and her personal connections are in the library of Bryn Mawr College, Bryn Mawr, Pennsylvania. They are referred to in the source references as MCTP. A manuscript of childhood reminiscences is in the Flexner Papers.

William H. Welch Papers. In the Alan Mason Chesney Medical Archives, Johns Hopkins University, Baltimore. Correspondence with Simon Flexner and other documents. Referred to in the source references as WP. Additional source materials relevant to Simon Flexner and his career are in other of the Johns Hopkins Libraries.

PUBLISHED SOURCES

Andrews, Matthew Page. *The Founding of Maryland.* Baltimore, 1933.
———. *History of Maryland.* New York, 1929.
Armstrong, William M. "Bertrand Russell Comes to America." *Studies in History and Society* 2 (1970): 29–39.
Atkinson, Brooks. *Broadway.* New York, 1970.
Bamberger, Bernard J. *The Story of Judaism.* New York, 1957.
Barker, Lewellys F. *Time and the Physician.* New York, 1942.
Benison, Saul. "Poliomyelitis and the Rockefeller Institute." *Journal of the History of Medicine and Allied Sciences* 29 (1974): 74–92.
———. "Simon Flexner: The Evolution of a Career in Medical Science." In Rockefeller University, *Institute to University* (New York, 1976).
Binns, Archie. *Mrs. Fiske and the American Theatre.* New York, 1955.
Board of Managers of the Pennsylvania Hospital. *Annual Reports.* 1900–1904. Philadelphia, 1901–1905.
Bordley, James, III, and McGehee, Harvey. *Two Centuries of American Medicine.* Philadelphia, 1976.
Brown, E. Richard. *The Rockefeller Medicine Men.* Berkeley, 1979.
Brown, Ward. *Montpelier: The Snowden-Long House.* New York, 1930.
Bryn Mawr College, Fiftieth Anniversary. Bryn Mawr, 1889.
Carpenter, Edith. *Lorenzo de Medici: An Historical Portrait.* New York, 1893.
———. *Your Money or Your Life: A Story.* New York and London, c. 1896.
Carter, Benjamin F., and others. *History of Woodbury, N.J.* Woodbury, 1937.
Chapman, J. Wilbur. *The Life and Work of Dwight L. Moody.* Philadelphia, 1900.
Chastellux, François Jean. *Travels in North America.* Edited by Howard C. Rice, Jr. Chapel Hill, 1963.
Chesney, Alan M. *The Johns Hopkins Hospital and the Johns Hopkins University.* Vols. 1 and 2. Baltimore, 1943, 1958.
Clark, Ronald W. *The Life of Bertrand Russell.* New York, 1976.
Comfort, William Wister. *Stephen Grellet, 1773–1855.* New York, 1942.
Cooper, Howard M. *Historical Sketch of Camden.* Camden, N.J., 1909.
Corner, Geroge W. *A History of the Rockefeller Institute.* New York, 1964.
Croskey, John Welsh. *A History of Blockley . . . the Philadelphia General Hospital . . . 1731–1928.* Philadelphia, 1929.
Cushing, Harvey. *The Life of Sir William Osler.* Vol. 1. Oxford, 1925.
Decker, John Paul, "The Ayer Bequest." *Bulletin of the Ayer Clinical Laboratory,* new ser., 4 (1980): 1–2.
———. "Warfield T. Longcope and the Ayer Clinical Laboratory." *Bulletin of the Ayer Clinical Laboratory,* new ser., 3 (1977): 1–2.
Duffus, Robert L., and Holt, J. Emmett, Jr. *L. Emmett Holt.* New York, 1940.
Eckstein, Gustave. *Noguchi.* New York, 1931.
Feinberg, Barry, and Kaskils, Ronald. *Bertrand Russell's America.* London, n.d.
Finch, Edith. *Carey Thomas of Bryn Mawr.* New York and London, 1947.
Findlay, James F., Jr. *Dwight L. Moody.* Chicago, 1969.
Fleming, Donald. *William Henry Welch.* Boston, 1954.
Flexner, Abraham. *Daniel Coit Gilman.* New York, 1946.
———. *I Remember.* New York, 1940.

Although of necessity an important source, this work suffers from the autobiographer's besetting sin of molding memory and changing happenings (see the discussion in ch. 16 of the present volume). When Abraham Flexner was in his eighties, he permitted editors to recast *I Remember* to make it "more saleable." The result, *Abraham Flexner: An Autobiography* (New York, 1960), which carries its author to an older age, presents no new material concerning the period of his life here under discussion. The 1940 edition is referred to in the source references as AF, *IR*.

————. *Medical Education in the United States and Canada.* New York, 1910.

————. "The Preparatory School." *Atlantic Monthly* 94 (1904): 368–377.

Flexner, Anne Crawford. *A Man's Woman.* Louisville, 1900.

Flexner, Helen Whitall [Thomas]. *A Quaker Childhood.* New Haven, 1940.

Helen Thomas Flexner's autobiographical account of her childhood, which ends with her mother's death when Helen was seventeen, was the result of distillation so extended that, when in 1938 or 1939 she announced the completion of the manuscript, the family were as astonished as they were delighted. That at one time she contemplated including a family history in her autobiographical work was revealed by the discovery, after she had died, of a large peeling leather suitcase full of Thomas and Whitall papers. These documents, which she seems to have gathered from her brothers and sisters, now constitute a major part of the James Thomas Flexner Collection (see "Manuscript Sources," p. 457). When she changed her objective, she decided to ignore most of the documents that cast light on her childhood. They conflicted with what had become her intention: to reconstruct her early life as, from year to year, she had then experienced it. Her aim not only precluded exterior evidence not then available to her, but also all conclusions drawn by her older self. It has remained for this writer to fuse her narrative with the wider view made possible by extensive additional source materials.

————. Introduction to *Equal Suffrage . . . An Investigation in Colorado Made for the Equal Suffrage League of New York State,* by Helen Laura Sumner. New York and London, 1909.

Flexner, Jacob A. "A Vanishing Profession [pharmacist]." *Atlantic Monthly* 98 (1931): 16–23.

Flexner, James Thomas. "Mother's Important Cousins." *Blackwood's Magazine* 309 (1976): 25–31.

————. "My Father, Simon Flexner." In Rockefeller University, *Institute to University.* New York, 1976.

Flexner, Simon. *A Half Century of American Medicine.* Chicago, 1937.

————. "Hideyo Noguchi." *Science* 69 (1929): 653–660.

————. "William Henry Welch: A Biographical Sketch." In William Henry Welch, *Papers and Addresses.* Baltimore, 1920. 1:xi–xxxiv.

————. "William Henry Welch." *National Academy of Sciences: Biographical Memoirs,* 22:215–231.

Flexner, Simon, and Flexner, James Thomas. *William Henry Welch.* New York, 1941. Referred to in the source references as *Flexners, WHW.*

Fosdick, Raymond B. *John D. Rockefeller, Jr.* New York, 1956.

————. *The Story of the Rockefeller Foundation.* New York, 1952.

Fox, George. *A Journal. . . . 1694.* Preface by William Penn. London, 1765.

Fox, John. *Book of Martyrs.* Edited by Charles Goodrich. Hartford, 1830.

Franklin, Fabian. *The Life of Daniel Coit Gilman.* New York, 1910.

Gathorne-Hardy, Robert. *Recollections of Logan Pearsall Smith.* New York, 1950.

Goldstein, Jonathan. *Philadelphia and the China Trade, 1682–1846.* University Park, Pa., 1978.

Graetz, Heinrich. *History of the Jews.* Vol. 5. Philadelphia, 1895.

Grellet, Stephen. *Memoirs.* Philadelphia, 1860.

Hall, Clayton Colman. *Narratives of Early Maryland, 1633–1684.* New York, 1910.

Hammond, John. *Hammond vs. Heamans, or an answer to an audacious pamphlet published by an imprudent and ridiculous fellow named Roger Heamans.* London, 1655(?).

Harris, Michael R. *Counterrevolutionists in Higher Education.* 1979.

Hawkins, Hugh. *Pioneer: A History of the Johns Hopkins University, 1874–1889.* Ithaca, N.Y., 1960.

Heamans, Roger. *An additional brief narrative of the late bloody designs against the Protestants in Ann Arundel County.* Reprinted in *Maryland Historical Magazine* 4 (1909): 140–153.

Heston, Alfred M. *Red Bank.* Atlantic City, N.J., 1900(?).

James, Sidney W. *A People Among Peoples: Quaker Benevolence in Eighteenth-Century America.* Cambridge, Mass., 1963.

Johnston, J. Stoddard, ed. *A Memorial History of Louisville.* 2 vols. Chicago and New York, n.d.

Krows, Arthur Edwin. *Play Production in America.* New York, 1916.

Larrabee, Eric. *The Benevolent and Necessary Institution: The New York Hospital, 1871–1971.* New York, 1971.

Lossing, Benson John. *The Pictorial Field Book of the Revolution.* Vol. 2. New York, 1851.

MacCallum, W. G. *William Stewart Halsted, Surgeon.* Baltimore, 1930.

McGehee, Harvey A. "Johns Hopkins' Pioneer Venture into International Medicine." *Johns Hopkins Medical Journal* 147 (1980): 13–27.

Maiden Tribute to Modern Babylon, The: The Report of the Pall Mall Gazette's Secret Committee. London, 1883.

Mickle, Isaac. *Reminiscences of Gloucester, N.J.* Camden, N.J., 1877.

Moscow, Alvin. *The Rockefeller Inheritance.* New York, 1977.

Nevins, Allan. *John D. Rockefeller.* 2 vols. New York, 1940.

Noguchi, Hideyo. *Snake Venoms.* Washington, D.C., 1909.

Norris, Walter B. *Annapolis: Its Colonial and Naval Story.* New York, 1925.

Opie, Eugene L. "Simon Flexner, M.D." *Archives of Pathology* 42 (1946): 234–242.

Osler, William. *The Principles and Practice of Medicine.* 1892. Many subsequent editions.

Parker, Francis. "Abraham Flexner, 1866–1959." *History of Education Quarterly* 2 (1962).

Parker, Robert Allerton. *The Transatlantic Smiths.* New York, 1959.

Penn, William. *See* Fox, George.

Pepper, Adeline. *The Glass Gaffers of New Jersey.* New York, 1971.

Plesset, Isabel R. *Noguchi and His Patrons.* Rutherford, N.J., 1980.

Pomfret, John E. "West New Jersey: A Quaker Society, 1765–1775." *William and Mary Quarterly,* 3d ser., 8 (1951): 443–519.

Prudden, Lillian E., ed. *Biographical Sketches and Letters of T. Mitchell Prudden.* New Haven, 1927.

Randall, Daniel R. *A Puritan Colony in Maryland.* Baltimore, 1886.

Rice, Alice Hegan. *The Inky Way.* New York, 1941.

Rice, Caleb Young. *Bridging the Years.* New York, 1939.

R.N.T. [Bessie Taylor]. *Memoir of Mary Whitall by Her Grand-daughter, R.N.T.* Philadelphia, 1885.

Robins, Robert Patterson. *A Short Account of the First Tramway in America, to which is added a biographical sketch of its projector, Thomas Leiper.* Philadelphia, 1886.

Rockefeller Institute for Medical Research. *Memorial Meeting for Simon Flexner.* June 12, 1946.

Rous, Peyton. "Simon Flexner." *Obituary Notices of the Fellows of the Royal Society* 16 (1942): 409–445.

———. "Simon Flexner and Medical Discovery." *Science* 107 (1948): 611–613.

Russell, Bertrand. *The Autobiography of Bertrand Russell.* Vol. 1. Boston, 1967.

Russell, John. *A Portrait of Logan Pearsall Smith Drawn from His Letters and Diaries.* London, 1951.

Sabin, Florence R. *Franklin Paine Mall.* Baltimore, 1924.

Samuels, Ernest. *Bernard Berenson: The Making of a Connoisseur.* Cambridge, Mass., 1979.

Secrest, Meryle. *Being Bernard Berenson.* New York, 1979.

Silver, Rollo, ed. *The Bright Particular Star: Letters from Walt Whitman to Mary Smith Costelloe.* New York, 1937.

Smith, Hannah Whitall. "Being Personal Experiences of Religious Fanaticism." In *Group Movements of the Past,* by Ray Strachey. London, 1934. Pp. 153–270.

————. *The Christian's Secret of a Happy Life.* Many editions.

————. *John M. Whitall: The Story of His Life.* Philadelphia, 1879. Referred to in the source references as HWS, *JMW.*

————. *The Record of a Happy Life, Being Memorials of Franklin Whitall Smith . . . by His Mother.* Philadelphia, 1879.

————. *A Religious Rebel: The Letters of "HWS."* Edited by Logan Pearsall Smith, with a preface and memoir by Robert Gathorne-Hardy. London, 1949.

Smith, Logan Pearsall. *Reperusals and Recollections.* London, 1936.

————. *Trivia.* London, 1902.

————. *Unforgotten Years.* Boston, 1939.

Starr, Paul. *The Social Transformation of American Medicine.* New York, 1982.

Stein, Gertrude. "Fernhurst." In *Fernhurst, Q. E. D., and Other Early Writings.* New York, 1971. Pp. 33–49.

Steiner, Bernard C. *Maryland under the Commonwealth.* Baltimore, 1911.

Stevens, Lucinda. *Crawford Genealogy.* Macon, Ga., 1936.

Stewart, Frank H. *History of the Battle of Red Bank.* Woodbury, N.J., 1927.

————. *Notes on Old Gloucester* [N.J.]. Camden, N.J., 1917.

Strachey, Barbara. *Remarkable Relations.* London, 1980.

Strachey, Ray. *A Quaker Grandmother: Hannah Whitall Smith.* New York, 1914.

Swift, Homer F. "Simon Flexner." Reprint from *Journal of Immunology* 54 (Dec., 1946).

Thomas, John Chew. *Letter Addressed to "Dear Sir."* Fairland, Md., 1800.

Thomas, Henry M. "Some Memories of the Development of the Medical School and Osler's Advent." *Johns Hopkins Hospital Bulletin* (1919): 188 ff.

Thomas, Lawrence Buckley. *The Thomas Book.* New York, 1896. Referred to in the source references as LBT, *Thomas.*

Thomas, M. Carey. *The Making of a Feminist: Early Journals and Letters.* Edited by Marjorie Houseplan Dobkin. Kent, Ohio, 1979.

Thomas, Richard Henry, Sr. *Memoir of Martha C. Thomas.* Baltimore, 1841.

Thomas, Richard Henry, Jr. *Life and Letters.* Edited by his wife. London, 1905.

Traubel, Horace, ed. *With Walt Whitman in Camden.* Boston, 1906.

Warfield, Benjamin Breckenridge. *Perfectionism.* New York, 1931.

Watson, John Fanning, *Annals of Philadelphia.* Philadelphia, 1847.

Whitall, Tatum and Co., 1880. Reprinted catalogue with historical introduction. Princeton, 1971.

Whitman, Walt. *Correspondence.* Edited by E. H. Miller. 5 vols. New York, 1969–1978.

Wilson, Graham, Sr., and Miles, Sir Ashley. *Principles of Bacteriology, Virology, and Immunity.* Baltimore, 1973.

Winslow, C. E. A. *Herman M. Biggs.* Philadelphia, 1929.

Works Progress Administration, Kentucky Writers Project. "Biographical and Critical Materials Pertaining to Kentucky Authors." Mimeograph, 1941.

————. *A Centennial History of the University of Louisville.* 2 vols. Louisville, Ky., 1932.

SIMON FLEXNER'S SCIENTIFIC PUBLICATIONS, 1890–1903

From the list (unpublished) compiled by Hilda A. von Berg in 1937, FP. Referred to in the source references by the abbreviation SFSP and the appropriate number.

1. A report on pathological histology and urinalysis. *Am. Practitioner and News,* Louisville, 1890, ix, 342.

2. Abstract of a report on pathological histology and urinalysis. *Memphis Med. Month.,* 1980, x, 337.

3. Chemical aids to the diagnosis of diseases of the stomach. *Am. Practitioner and News,* 1890, x, No. 5, 129.

4. Remarks on the histology of the blood corpuscles. *Am. Practitioner and News,* 1891, xii, 76.

5. The diagnostic value of the diphtheritic bacillus. (Read at the May meeting of the Kentucky State Med. Soc., 1891.) *Am. Practitioner and News,* 1891, xii, 40.

6. Tuberculosis of knee. *Johns Hopkins Hosp. Bull.*, 1891, ii, 63.
7. With William H. Welch. The histological changes in experimental diphtheria. Preliminary communication. *Johns Hopkins Hosp. Bull.*, 1891, ii, 107.
8. A peculiar glioma (neuroepithelioma?) of the retina. *Johns Hopkins Hosp. Bull.*, 1891, ii, 115.
9. Tuberculosis of the aorta. *Johns Hopkins Hosp. Bull.*, 1891, ii, 120.
10. The etiology of croupous pneumonia. *Am. Practitioner and News*, 1892, n.s. xiv, 33; *Tr. Kentucky Med. Soc.*, Louisville, 1892, n.s. i, 147.
11. With William H. Welch. The histological lesions produced by the tox-albumen [sic] of diphtheria. *Johns Hopkins Hosp. Bull.*, 1892, iii, 17.
12. Lympho-sarcomata. *Johns Hopkins Hosp. Bull.*, 1892, iii, 32.
13. A case of primary carcinoma of the pancreas with multiple carcinosis. The organisms of cancer. *Johns Hopkins Hosp. Bull.*, 1892, iii, 54.
14. Amoebae in an abscess of the jaw. *Johns Hopkins Hosp. Bull.*, 1892, iii, 104.
15. Review of: "A Manual of Autopsies Designed for the Use of Hospitals for the Insane and other Public Institutions," by I. W. Blackburn, M.D., Pathologist to the Government Hospital for the Insane, Washington (Philadelphia, P. Blakiston, Son & Co., 1892). *Johns Hopkins Hosp. Bull.*, 1892, iii, 107.
16. Sarcoma of the peri-pancreatic lymph glands with miliary sarcomatosis of the peritoneum, etc. *Johns Hopkins Hosp. Bull.*, 1892, iii, 121.
17. Tuberculosis of the oesophagus. (Larvae of diptera in the ulcers.) *Johns Hopkins Hosp. Bull.*, 1893, iv, 4.
18. Remarks on aspergillus mycosis. *Johns Hopkins Hosp. Bull.*, 1893, iv, 10.
19. Peritonitis due to proteus vulgaris. *Johns Hopkins Hosp. Bull.*, 1893, iv, 12.
20. Primary tuberculosis of the intestine. *Johns Hopkins Hosp. Bull.*, 1893, iv, 13.
21. Tuberculosis of clavicle, infection of pleura and peritoneum, and general miliary tuberculosis. *Johns Hopkins Hosp. Bull.*, 1893, iv, 13.
22. Diphtheria with broncho-pneumonia. *Johns Hopkins Hosp. Bull.*, 1893, iv, 32.
23. Peritonitis caused by the proteus vulgaris. *Johns Hopkins Hosp. Bull.*, 1893, iv, 34.
24. With W. S. Thayer. Demonstration of specimen of amoebic abscess of liver. *Johns Hopkins Hosp. Bull.*, 1893, iv, 56.
25. With L. F. Barker. The recent outbreak of epidemic cerebro-spinal meningitis at Lonaconing and other places in the valley of George's Creek, Maryland. *Johns Hopkins Hosp. Bull.*, 1893, iv, 68.
26. Exhibition of specimens of cystic kidney. *Johns Hopkins Hosp. Bull.*, 1893, iv, 110.
27. A case of gas-poisoning. Notes of autopsy. *Johns Hopkins Hosp. Bull.*, 1893, iv, 128.
28. Multiple lympho-sarcomata, with a report of two cases. A contribution to the infectious nature of lympho-sarcoma. *Johns Hopkins Hosp. Rep.*, 1893, iii, 153.
29. Exhibition of specimens from a case of carcinoma of the pancreas with multiple carcinosis. *Johns Hopkins Hosp. Bull.*, 1894, v, 16.
30. Exhibition of specimens from a case of acute pericarditis, pleuritis and peritonitis, associated with contracted kidney, etc. *Johns Hopkins Hosp. Bull.*, 1894, v, 17.
31. Fatty degeneration of the heart muscle. *Johns Hopkins Hosp. Bull.*, 1894, v, 26.
32. The lesions caused by certain so-called toxalbumins. *Johns Hopkins Hosp. Bull.*, 1894, v, 83.
33. The bacillus of the plague. Abstract of report to the Journal Club of the Johns Hopkins Hospital. *Johns Hopkins Hosp. Bull.*, 1894, v, 96.
34. A case of typhoid septicaemia associated with focal abscesses in the kidneys, due to the typhoid bacillus. *Johns Hopkins Hosp. Bull.*, 1894, v, 120.
35. With L. F. Barker. A contribution to our knowledge of epidemic cerebrospinal meningitis. *Am. J. Med. Sci.*, 1894, n.s., cvii, 155 and 259.
36. The pathological changes caused by certain so-called toxalbumins. An experimental study. *Med. News*, Phila., 1894, lxv, 116.
37. With H. D. Pease. Primary diphtheria of the lips and gums. *Johns Hopkins Hosp. Bull.*, 1895, vi, 22.
38. With H. D. Pease. Difteria primitiva de los labios y encias. Trans. from *Johns Hopkins Hosp. Bull.*, 1895, vi, 22. *Arch. de ginecop.*, Barcelona, 1895, viii, 323, 589.
39. The bacteriology and pathology of diphtheria. *Johns Hopkins Hosp. Bull.*, 1895, vi, 39; *Am. J. Med. Sci.*, 1895, n.s., cix, 240.

40. Peritonitis caused by the invasion of the micrococcus lanceolatus from the intestine. *Johns Hopkins Hosp. Bull.*, 1895, vi, 64.
41. Exhibition of specimens: cases of tuberculosis. *Johns Hopkins Hosp. Bull.*, 1895, vi, 69.
42. A case of anthrax in a human being. *Johns Hopkins Hosp. Bull.*, 1895, vi, 94.
43. Bacillus pyogenes filiformis (nov. spec.). *Johns Hopkins Hosp. Bull.*, 1895, vi, 147.
44. Studies in typhoid fever. V. Certain forms of infection in typhoid fever. *Johns Hopkins Hosp. Rep.*, 1895, v, 343.
45. Diphtheria antitoxin sometimes found in the blood of horses that have not been injected with toxin. Discussion. *Tr. Assn. Am. Physn.*, 1896, xi, 64.
46. Two rare cases of diseases of the skin. Discussion. *Johns Hopkins Hosp. Bull.*, 1896, vii, 142.
47. A case of combined protozoan and bacterial infection. Amoebic dysentery, malaria, and micrococcus lanceolatus, acute fibrinopurulent peritonitis. *Johns Hopkins Hosp. Bull.*, 1896, vii, 171.
48. The bubonic plague. *Johns Hopkins Hosp. Bull.*, 1896, vii, 181.
49. Specimen of adeno-carcinoma of pancreas. Discussion. *Johns Hopkins Hosp. Bull.*, 1896, vii, 190.
50. Alveolar sarcoma of the cerebellum. Pathological report. *Johns Hopkins Hosp. Bull.*, 1896, vii, 193.
51. With William H. Welch. Observations concerning the bacillus aerogenes capsulatus. *J. Exp. Med.*, 1896, i, 5.
52. A study of the bacillus (leptothrix?) pyogenes filiformis (nov. spec.) and of its pathogenic action. *J. Exp. Med.*, 1896, i, 211.
53. A statistical and experimental study of terminal infections. *J. Exp. Med.*, 1896, i, 559; *Tr. Assn. Am. Physn.*, 1896, xi, 229.
54. Remarks on the pathology and bacteriology of typhoid fever. *Maryland Med. J.*, 1896, xxxvi, 145.
55. A case of typhoid septicaemia associated with focal abscesses in the kidneys, due to the typhoid bacillus. *J. Path. and Bact.*, 1896, iii, 202.
56. Infection and intoxication. Biological lectures, delivered at The Marine Biological Laboratory at Wood's Hole (in the summer session of 1895). Boston, Ginn and Co., 1896, First Lecture, p. 1.
57. The pathologic changes caused by certain so-called toxalbumins — an experimental study. (Read at the meeting of the Pathological Society of Philadelphia, April 26, 1894). *Tr. Path. Soc. Philadelphia*, 1896, xvii, 212.
58. Puerperal sepsis due to infection with the bacillus aerogenes capsulatus. Discussion. *Johns Hopkins Hosp. Bull.*, 1897, viii, 28.
59. Discussion of Dr. Bloch's paper on "Agglutination of typhoid bacilli, etc." *Johns Hopkins Hosp. Bull.*, 1897, viii, 54.
60. Pseudo-tuberculosis hominis streptotricha. A preliminary note. *Johns Hopkins Hosp. Bull.*, 1897, viii, 128.
61. With N. McL. Harris. Typhoid infection without intestinal lesions. *Johns Hopkins Hosp. Bull.*, 1897, viii, 259.
62. The pathology of toxalbumin intoxication. *Johns Hopkins Hosp. Rep.*, 1897, vi, 259.
63. The histological changes produced by ricin and abrin intoxications. *J. Exp. Med.*, 1897, ii, 197.
64. On the occurrence of the fat-splitting ferment in peritoneal fat necroses and the histology of these lesions. *J. Exp. Med.*, 1897, ii, 413; *Tr. Assn. Am. Physn.*, 1897, xii, 278.
65. Remarks on the etiology and pathology of acute peritonitis. *Maryland Med. J.*, 1897, xxxvii, 189.
66. Microscopic picture of leprosy. *Maryland Med. J.*, 1897, xxxvii, 419.
67. With W. H. Hudson. A case of actinomycosis hominis, involving the tissues of the back and the lungs. With pathological report. *Ann. Surg.*, 1897, xxvi, 626.
68. Perforation of the inferior vena cava in amoebic abscesses of the liver. *Am. J. Med. Sc.*, 1897, n.s., cxiii, 553.
69. Cancer of the stomach in early life. Discussion. *Tr. Assn. Am. Physn.*, 1897, xii, 167.

70. The preservation of natural colors in museum specimens. *Maryland Med. J.*, 1897–1898, xxxviii, 299.
71. The regeneration of the nervous system of planaria torva and the anatomy of the nervous system of double-headed forms. *J. Morphol.*, 1897–1898, xiv, 337.
72. Cerebro-spinal meningitis. Discussion. *Johns Hopkins Hosp. Bull.*, 1898, ix, 32.
73. Exhibition of specimen of round ulcer of the stomach. Erosion of gastric artery; post-mortem perforation. *Johns Hopkins Hosp. Bull.*, 1898, ix, 41.
74. With H. B. Anderson. The results of the intra-tracheal inoculation of the bacillus diptheriae in rabbits. *Johns Hopkins Hosp. Bull.*, 1898, ix, 72.
75. A microscopical study of the spinal cord in two cases of Pott's disease. Discussion. *Johns Hopkins Hosp. Bull.*, 1898, ix, 133.
76. Note on the osteoid tissue found in the tubercular exudate in the thoracic region of the cord. *Johns Hopkins Hosp. Bull.*, 1898, ix, 133.
77. Forty-six intubated cases of diphtheria treated with antitoxine. Discussion. *Johns Hopkins Hosp. Bull.*, 1898, ix, 147.
78. Discussion of Mr. MacCallum's paper on pathology of heart muscle. *Johns Hopkins Hosp. Bull.*, 1898, ix, 273.
79. Pseudo-tuberculosis hominis streptotricha. *J. Exp. Med.*, 1898, iii, 435.
80. Psuedo-tuberculosis hominis streptotricha. *Tr. Assn. Am. Physn.*, 1898, xiii, 31.
81. Gastric syphilis, with the report of a case of perforating syphilitic ulcer of the stomach. *Tr. Assn. Am. Physn.*, 1898, xiii, 102; *Am. J. Med. Sc.*, 1898, n.s., cxvi, 424.
82. Glia and gliomatosis. *J. Nerv. and Ment. Dis.*, 1898, xxv, 306, 339 (discussion).
83. The etiology and the classification of peritonitis. *Philadelphia Med. J.*, 1898, ii, 1019.
84. A new method of staining malarial parasites. Discussion. *Johns Hopkins Hosp. Bull.*, 1899, x, 71.
85. Aneurism of aorta, compressing and rupturing into left bronchus. *Johns Hopkins Hosp. Bull.*, 1899, x, 97.
86. Multiple metastases from pelvic sarcoma. *Johns Hopkins Hosp. Bull.*, 1899, x, 98.
87. Nodular tumors of the pancreas. *Maryland Med. J.*, 1899, xli, 107.
88. Lymphatic leukemia. *Maryland Med. J.*, 1899, xli, 107.
89. With C. Wilson. Report of a case of Hodgkin's disease, showing long periods of fever. Pathological report. *Am. J. Med. Sc.*, 1899, cxviii, n.s., 411.
90. A case of glioma of the lower cervical region of the spinal cord producing a total transverse lesion, in which there was spasticity of the lower limbs and persistence of the deep reflexes. III. Some points in the pathology of syringo-myelia. *Am. J. Med. Sc.*, 1899, n.s., cxvii, 648.
91. With L. F. Barker. On the prevalent diseases in the Philippines. A report to the Committee of the Johns Hopkins Medical School. Baltimore, 1899.
92. Medical conditions existing in the Philippines. *Tr. College Physn. Philadelphia*, 1899, 3 s., xxi, 165.
93. Experimental pancreatitis. *Proc. Path. Soc. Philadelphia*, 1899–1900, n.s., iii, 25.
94. Remarks on typhoid septicemia. *Proc. Path. Soc. Philadelphia*, 1899–1900, n.s., iii, 89.
95. Actinomycosis of the human lung. *Proc. Path. Soc. Philadelphia*, 1899–1900, n.s., iii, 141.
96. With L. F. Barker. Report of a special commission sent to the Philippines by the Johns Hopkins University to investigate the prevalent diseases of the islands. *Johns Hopkins Univ. Circular*, 1900, xix, 13.
97. With L. F. Barker. Report upon an expedition sent by the Johns Hopkins University to investigate the prevalent diseases in the Philippines. *Johns Hopkins Hosp. Bull.*, 1900, xi, 37.
98. Medical conditions existing in the Philippines. Amplification of remarks made before the College of Physicians, Philadelphia. *Internat. Clin.*, 1900, i, 10th s., 1.
99. With L. F. Barker. The prevalent diseases in the Philippines. *Science*, 1900, n.s., xi, 521.
100. Nature and distribution of the new tissue in cirrhosis of the liver. Preliminary communication. *Tr. Assn. Am. Physn.*, 1900, xv, 523.
101. Pathology of tropical dysentery. Abstract. *Brit. Med. J.*, 1900, ii, 20.

102. Nature and distribution of the new tissue in cirrhosis of the liver. *Univ. Med. Mag.*, 1900, xiii, 613.
103. A discussion on the pathology of cirrhosis of the liver in adults and young children. *Brit. Med. J.*, 1900, ii, 913.
104. On the etiology of tropical dysentery. (Middleton-Goldsmith Lecture). *Philadelphia Med. J.*, 1900, vi, 414; *Johns Hopkins Hosp. Bull.*, 1900, xi, 231.
105. The etiology of tropical dysentery. *Brit. Med. J.*, 1900, ii, 917.
106. The aetiology of tropical dysentery. *Tr. Cong. Am. Physn. and Surg.*, 1900, v, 61.
107. The etiology of tropical dysentery. *Centralbl. f. Bakt.*, I. Abt., 1900, xxviii, 625.
108. Microorganisms. *Stedman's 20th Century Practice of Med.*, New York, Wood, 1900, xix, 525.
109. Unusual forms of infection with the typhoid bacillus with especial reference to typhoid fever without intestinal lesions. *Johns Hopkins Hosp. Rep.*, 1900, viii, 241.
110. Experimental pancreatitis. In: Contributions to the Science of Medicine, dedicated by his Pupils to William Henry Welch, upon the twenty-fifth anniversary of his Doctorate, Baltimore, Johns Hopkins Press, 1900, p. 743; *Johns Hopkins Hosp. Rep.*, 1900, ix, 743.
111. Refractory subcutaneous abscesses caused by sporothrix Schenckii. A new pathogenic fungus. Discussion. *Tr. Assn. Am. Physn.*, 1900, xv, 513.
112. Yellow fever; its nature and cause. Discussion. *J. Am. Med. Assn.*, 1900, xxxv, 875.
113. Varicosity of the superficial epigastric veins. Discussion. *Univ. Med. Mag.*, 1900–1901, xiii, 61.
114. Removal of an appendix filled with oxyurides vermiculares. Discussion. *Univ. Med. Mag.*, 1900–1901, xiii, 66.
115. Nature and distribution of the new tissue in cirrhosis of the liver. Preliminary communication. *Proc. Path. Soc. Philadelphia*, 1900–1901, n.s., iv, 9.
116. Experimental dysentery in dogs, with exhibitions of microscopic specimens. Discussion. *Proc. Path. Soc. Philadelphia*, 1900–1901, n.s., iv, 194.
117. The pathology of diabetes. *Proc. Path. Soc. Philadelphia*, 1900–1901, n.s., iv, 243.
118. The etiology of tropical dysentery. *Tr. Path. Soc. London*, 1901, lii, Pt. I, 1.
119. Etiology of dysentery. *J. Am. Med Assn.*, 1901, xxxvi, 6.
120. A comparative study of dysenteric bacilli. *Univ. Pennsylvania Med. Bull.*, 1901, xiv, 190; *Centralbl. f. Bakt.*, 1901, l. Abt., xxx, 449.
121. Experimental pancreatitis. *Univ. Med. Mag.*, 1901, xiii, 780.
122. With R. M. Pearce. Experimental pancreatitis. II. *Univ. Pennsylvania Med. Bull.*, 1901, xiv, 193.
123. With R. M. Pearce. Experimental pancreatitis. Second paper. *Tr. Assn. Am. Physn.*, 1901, xvi, 348.
124. The clinical laboratory in surgical diagnosis. *N.Y. State J. Med.*, 1901, i, 330.
125. The new medical laboratories of the University of Pennsylvania. *J. Applied Microscopy*, 1901, iv, 1445.
126. The nature of internal lesions in death from superficial burns. Discussion. *Tr. Assn. Am. Physn.*, 1901, xvi, 163.
127. Abscess of the brain due to a streptothrix. Discussion. *Tr. Assn. Am. Physn.*, 1901, xvi, 215.
128. With J. K. Mitchell and D. L. Edsall. A brief report of the clinical, physiologic, and chemical study of three cases of family periodic paralysis. *Tr. Assn. Am. Physn.*, 1901, xvi, 268.
129. The pathology of bubonic plague. *Univ. Pennsylvania Med. Bull.*, 1901, xiv, 205; *Tr. Assn. Am. Physn.*, 1901, xvi, 481, 519 (discussion); *Am. J. Med. Sc.*, 1901, n.s., cxxii, 396.
130. With L. F. Barker and F. G. Novy. Report of the commission appointed by the Secretary of the Treasury for the investigation of plague in San Francisco, under instructions from the Surgeon-General, Marine-Hospital Service. Treasury Dept., U.S. Marine-Hospital Service, Washington, Government Printing Office, 1901.
131. Etiology of acute dysentery. *Pennyslvania Med. J.*, 1901–1902, v, 367.
132. Bubonic plague: its nature, mode of spread, and clinical manifestations. *Univ. Pennsylvania Med. Bull.*, 1902, xv, 278.

133. Bubonic plague, its nature, mode of spread, and clinical manifestations. *Yale Med. J.*, 1902, viii, 293.
134. With H. Noguchi. Snake venom in relation to haemolysis, bacteriolysis, and toxicity. *J. Exp. Med.*, 1902, vi, 277; *Univ. Pennsylvania Med. Bull.*, 1902, xiv, 438.
135. With H. Noguchi. The constitution of snake venom and snake sera. *Univ. Pennsylvania Med. Bull.*, 1902, xv, 345.
136. Concerning hepatic syphilis. *New York Med. J.*, 1902, lxxv, 101.
137. On thrombi composed of agglutinated red blood corpuscles. Preliminary communication. *J. Med Research*, 1902, viii, 316.
138. The pathology of diabetes. *Univ. Pennsylvania Med. Bull.*, 1902, xiv, 390.
139. The pathology of lymphotoxic and myelotoxic intoxication. *Univ. Pennsylvania Med. Bull.*, 1902, xv, 287.
140. With J. K. Mitchell and D. L. Edsall. A brief report of the clinical, physiological, and chemical study of three cases of family periodic paralysis. *Brain*, 1902, xxv, 109.
141. Dysentery in the United States. *Alumni Reg.*, Philadelphia, 1902, vi, 333.
142. Bacillary dysentery. *Therap. Gaz.*, 1902, 3rd s., xviii, 218; *Proc. Philadelphia Co. Med. Soc.*, 1902, n.s., iv, 46.
143. The etiological significance of the acid-resisting group of bacteria, and the evidence in favor of their botanical relation to bacillus tuberculosis. Discussion. *Tr. Assn. Am. Physn.*, 1902, xvii, 78.
144. A new study of snake venom. *Johns Hopkins Hosp. Bull.*, 1902, xiii, 146.
145. Thrombi composed of agglutinated red blood corpuscles. Preliminary communication. *Univ. Pennsylvania Med. Bull.*, 1902–1903, xv, 324.
146. Specimens from a case of influenzal endocarditis. *Univ. Pennsylvania Med. Bull.*, 1902–1903, xv, 451.
147. An aspect of modern pathology. *Tr. Med. and Chir. Fac. State of Maryland*, 1902–1903, p. 87; *Am. J. Med Sc.*, 1903, n.s., cxxvi, 202; *Science*, 1903, n.s., xviii, 3.
148. The pancreas and pancreatic disease. The pathology of pancreatitis, diabetes and fat necrosis. *Tr. Cong. Am. Physn. and Surg.*, 1903, vi, 18: discussion, p. 98.
149. With H. Noguchi. Upon the plurality of cytolysins in normal blood sera. *J. Med. Research*, 1903, ix, 257.
150. With H. Noguchi. On the plurality of cytolysins in normal blood serum. *Univ. Pennsylvania Med. Bull.*, 1903, xvi, 158.
151. With H. Noguchi. On the plurality of cytolysins in snake venom. *Univ. Pennsylvania Med. Bull.*, 1903, xvi, 163.
152. With H. Noguchi. The constitution of snake venom and snake sera. *J. Path. and Bact.*, 1903, viii, 379.
153. A note on autolysis in lobar and unresolved pneumonia. *Univ. Pennsylvania Med. Bull.*, 1903, xvi, 185; *Tr. Assn. Am. Physn.*, 1903, xviii, 359.
154. An experimental study of nephrotoxins. Discussion. *Tr. Assn. Am. Physn.*, 1903, xviii, 597.
155. Immunization from tuberculosis. *Philadelphia Med. J.*, 1903, xi, 284.
156. Infection with the bacillus of dysentery, with especial reference to its role in the summer diarrheas of children. *Year Book Med. Assn. Gr. N.Y.*, 1903, p. 67.
157. The bacillus of dysentery, with special reference to its etiological relationship to the summer diarrhea of children. *Bull. Johns Hopkins Hosp.*, 1903, xiv, 320.
158. Discussion on the relation of the bacillus of Shiga to the summer diarrheas of children. *Arch. Pediat.*, 1903, xx, 801; *Tr. Am. Pediat. Soc.*, 1903, xv, 89, 103.
159. Bacteriological and clinical studies of the diarrheal diseases of infancy with reference to the Bacillus dysenteriae (Shiga) from The Rockefeller Institute for Medical Research. Edited by Simon Flexner and L. Emmett Holt. Investigations during the summer of 1903. Introduction, p. 31. Discussion and conclusions, p. 121. New York, Rooney and Otten Printing Co., 1904; *Studies from The Rockefeller Institute for Medical Research*, 1904, ii, 25; 115.

Abbreviations
Used in the
Source References

AF	Abraham Flexner
AF, *IR*	Abraham Flexner, *I Remember* (1940)
BR	Bertrand Russell
BRP	Bertrand Russell Papers
DAB	*Dictionary of American Biography*
DNB	*Dictionary of National Biography*
EAF	Esther Abraham Flexner
FP	Flexner Papers
Flexners, *WHW*	Simon Flexner and James Thomas Flexner, *William Henry Welch* (1941)
HT and HTF	Helen Thomas and Helen Thomas Flexner
HT, *QC*	Helen Whitall [Thomas] Flexner, *A Quaker Childhood* (1940)
HT, VN	Helen Thomas's vellum-bound notebooks
HRC	Humanities Research Center, University of Texas, Austin, Texas
HWS	Hannah Whitall Smith
HWS, *JMW*	Hannah Whitall Smith, *John M. Whitall* (1879)
JCT	James Carey Thomas
JDR, Sr.	John D. Rockefeller, Sr.
JDR, Jr.	John D. Rockefeller, Jr.
JTF	James Thomas Flexner
JTFC	James Thomas Flexner Collection
JMW	John M. Whitall
JHU	Johns Hopkins University
LBT, *Thomas*	Lawrence Buckley Thomas, *The Thomas Book* (1894)
LC	Library of Congress
LPS	Logan Pearsall Smith
LMD	Lucy Martin Donnelly
MCT	M. Carey Thomas

MCTP	M. Carey Thomas Papers
MWT	Mary Whitall and Mary Whitall Thomas
NCAB	*National Cyclopaedia of American Biography*
RA	Rockefeller Archives
RHT, Sr.	Richard Henry Thomas, Sr., 1805–1860
RHT, Jr.	Richard Henry Thomas, Jr., 1881–1924
RI	Rockefeller Institute for Medical Research
RU	Rockefeller University
RUP	Papers of the Rockefeller Institute in the library of Rockefeller University
SF	Simon Flexner
SFAu	Simon Flexner, unfinished autobiography (see Flexner Papers, p. 457)
SFAuD	Simon Flexner, earlier draft of the autobiography (see Flexner Papers, p. 457)
SFN	Simon Flexner, autobiographical notes (see Flexner Papers, p. 457–458)
SFOR	Simon Flexner, oral reminiscences (see James Thomas Flexner Collection, p. 458)
SFSP	Simon Flexner's scientific publications through 1903 (see pp. 462–467)
SWN	Sarah Whitall Nicholson
WHW	William Henry Welch
WP	William Henry Welch Papers (see p. 459)

Source References

1. BOHEMIA — STRASBOURG — KENTUCKY

1. AF, *IR*, 5.
2. EAF, "Father," typescript, FP; SF, "Notes on the early migrations of my father dictated by my mother several years before her death," typescript, FP.
3. Rous, "Simon Flexner," 409.
4. EAF, 1.
5. Szigeti MS ("Michael Flexner"), typescript, FP.
6. EAF, 1; Szigeti MS, 1–2.
7. SFN, 7/8/1933, 7/9/1933.
8. AF, *IR*, 4.
9. SFN, 12/15/1936.
10. Mary Flexner to JTF (oral).
11. AF, *IR*, 7–8.
12. Ibid., 6.
13. EAF, 4. The subsequent account of his trip to America and his early days there are on pp. 2–4 of EAF's account.

2. GERMANY — PARIS — KENTUCKY

1. EAF, "Memories of My Youth," 1, typescript, FP.
2. SF to EAF, 5/27/1883, FP; SFN, 2/25/1945.
3. SF to JTF (oral).
4. EAF, 1–2.
5. AF, *IR*, 9–10.
6. SFOR, 29.

7. EAF, 1–3.
8. Ibid., 3–4.
9. Ibid., 5.
10. Ibid., 5–6.
11. Ibid., 7–9.
12. AF, "Father," 4–6, FP.
13. The photographs are in JTFC.
14. Bernard Flexner to JTF (oral), Mar., 1928, JTFC; SF, "Notes on early migrations of my father . . . ," FP.

3. SIMON FLEXNER, DELINQUENT

1. SFOR, 16; SFN, 7/20/1924.
2. SFOR, 7.
3. SFN, 5/18/1931, 5/30/1937.
4. SF to HT, 8/22/1901, FP.
5. SFOR, 1; SFN, July–Aug., 1930.
6. SFOR, 6.
7. Ibid., 7.
8. Ibid., 6–7.
9. SFN, 7/7/1926.
10. SFOR, 8.
11. SFN, 5/31/1931, 11/15/1932, 8/8/1943.
12. Ibid., 11/15/1932.
13. SFOR, 3–4; notebook, c. 1926, FP; loose page, FP.
14. SFN, 3/30/1931.
15. SFOR, 15.
16. SFN, July–Aug., 1930.
17. SFOR, 8–9.
18. SF to JTF (oral).
19. SFOR, 11; SFN, July–Aug., 1930, 1/22/1936.

20. SFN, 3/6/1934.
21. SFN, 4/6/1930, July–Aug., 1930.
22. SF to JTF (oral).
23. SFOR, 1, 7; SF to JTF (oral).
24. SFOR, 5, 9.
25. Ibid., 9.
26. SF to JTF (oral).
27. SF to JTF (oral).
28. SFOR, 1–2; SFN, 7/8/1930.
29. SF, notebook, c. 1930, FP; SF to JTF (oral).

4. HARD TIMES

1. SFOR, 2.
2. The portraits are in JTFC.
3. SFN, 1936.
4. SFOR, 15, 28; SFN, 3/13/1931, 3/30/1931.
5. SFOR, 14–15; SFN, 12/14/1931.
6. SFN, 12/15/1936.
7. SF to HT, 12/22/1936, FP.
8. SFN, 11/12/1932.
9. AF, *IR*, 13.
10. SFOR, 16; SFN, 7/19/1923.
11. SF to HT, 5/27/1903, FP.
12. SFOR, 10, 13–14, 35–36; SFN, 1/8/1930, 3/9/1931, 4/15/1934, 12/22/1936, 6/31/1937.
13. The photographs are in JTFC.
14. SFN, 4/12/1936.
15. SFN, 7/20/1924, 8/12/1927.
16. SFOR, 10–11; SFN, July–Aug., 1930.

5. SIMON FLEXNER, UNEMPLOYABLE

1. SFOR, 2–3; SFN, July–Aug., 1930, 7/9/1930, 7/23/1936, 12/15/1936.
2. SFN, 7/20/1924; SFOR, 12–13.
3. SFN, 1/22/1936; SFOR, 17–18.
4. SFAu, ch. 1, p. 3; SFOR, 3–4, 19–20; SFN, 7/20/1924, 8/9/1933.
5. SFAu, ch. 1, p. 3; SFOR, 20–22.
6. SFN, 1936.
7. SFOR, 17, 22–23; SFN, 7/20/1924.
8. SFOR, 23–25; SFN, 8/12/1925, 3/8/1933, 8/8/1933, 1/22/1936.

6. NEW DEPARTURES

1. SFOR, 12; SFN, July–Aug., 1930, 1/22/1936, 7/11/1936.
2. SFOR, 12; Johnston, *A Memorial History of Louisville*, 2:244.
3. SFOR, 26.

4. Ibid., 26–27; SFN, 4/12/1936.
5. SFN, 7/20/1924, 7–8, 1930, 11/22/1932; *DAB* 9:67–68; Johnston, 2:275.
6. Johnston, 2:275–276.
7. AF to Samuel Dorfman, 11/31/1944, Abraham Flexner Papers, LC.
8. SFOR, 61–62; SFN, 7/20/1924, 8/12/1925.
9. SFOR, 61.
10. Ibid., 28; SF to HT, 6/9/1903, 7/4/1903, FP.
11. SFN, 4/12/1925, 1/22/1926.
12. Ibid., 4/12/1936, 11/2/1937.
13. Ibid., 8/14/1925, 8/24/1938.
14. SFOR, 29.
15. SF to HT, 12/29/1902, FP.

7. PURITAN TO QUAKER

1. LBT, *Thomas*, 29.
2. Ibid., 2–3.
3. Ibid., 8–9.
4. "Rhys ap Thomas," *DNB*.
5. LBT, *Thomas*, xiii; HT to JTF (oral).
6. MWT to SWN, 10/3/1884, JTFC; LBT, *Thomas*, xiii.
7. See Randall, *Puritan Colony*.
8. *Archives of Maryland*, 2 (1884): 18, 318; 3 (1885): 325; LBT, *Thomas*, 29–34.
9. Hall, *Narratives;* Hammond, *Hammond vs. Heamans;* Heamans, *Additional brief narrative.*
10. Fox, *Journal*, 440; LBT, *Thomas*, 32.
11. "George Fox," *DNB;* W. Penn, Preface to Fox, *Journal*, xxvii, xxx.
12. LBT, *Thomas*, 33.

8. MANUMISSION AND AFTERMATH

1. Horatio Sharpe, "Letters," in *Archives of Maryland*, vols 6 (1888), 9 (1890), 14 (1893), 21 (1911); LBT, *Thomas*, 35–36.
2. RHT, Jr., *Life and Letters*, 46; miniature of John Chew Thomas after James Peale, JTFC; LBT, *Thomas*, 507–518.
3. W. Brown, *Montpelier;* Washington, *Diaries*, Fitzpatrick ed., 3:215.
4. RHT, Jr., 48.
5. John Chew Thomas, *Letter* . . .

6. *Annals of Congress, 1799–1801,*
1032–1033; Alexander Hamilton,
Papers, ed. by H. C. Syrett, 15:17,
n. 17.
7. RHT, Jr., 48.
8. Comfort, *Stephen Grellet;* S. Grellet, *Memoirs.*
9. RHT, Jr., 48–50.
10. Comfort, *Grellet.*
11. RHT, Jr., 50–51.
12. John Chew Thomas, deed of manumission, 4/23/1810, JTFC.
13. RHT, Jr., 50.
14. Henrietta Thomas to RHT, Sr.,
4/5/1830, JTFC.
15. Henrietta Thomas to RHT, Sr.,
4/15/1830, JTFC.
16. Henrietta Thomas to RHT, Sr.,
9/4/1826, JTFC.
17. RHT, Jr., 50–51.
18. LBT, *Thomas,* 42.
19. Henrietta Thomas to RHT, Sr.,
1/29/1830, 2/12/1830, JTFC.
20. Henrietta Thomas to RHT, Sr.,
10/5/1828, 2/18/1828, JTFC.
21. Henrietta Thomas to RHT, Sr.,
6/7/1827, 4/18/1827, JTFC.
22. "George Leiper," *DAB;* Robins,
Tramway.
23. John Chew Thomas to RHT, Sr.,
4/8/1830, JTFC.
24. John Chew Thomas, correspondence, 1822–1839, JTFC.

9. THE MIDNIGHT CRY

1. Henrietta Thomas to RHT, Sr.,
11/4/1827, JTFC.
2. RHT, Jr., *Life and Letters,* 54–55.
3. RHT, Sr., *Memoir of Martha C.
Thomas,* 10–11.
4. MCT, *The Making of a Feminist,*
290–291.
5. LBT, *Thomas,* 239–241.
6. RHT, Sr., *Memoir of Martha,*
11–13.
7. Ibid., 15–18.
8. RHT, Sr., to Galloway Cheston,
5/17/1835, JTFC.
9. RHT, Sr., and Martha to Henrietta
Thomas, 6/5/1835, JTFC.
10. RHT, Sr., *Memoir of Martha,*
18–23.
11. Ibid., 21–22.
12. Ibid., 24.
13. Ibid.
14. Ibid., 40–41.

15. Ibid., 33 ff.
16. Ibid., 35–37.
17. RHT, Jr., 56.
18. RHT, Sr., copious correspondence,
JTFC.
19. RHT, Jr., 5–6.
20. Ibid., 12–13.
21. Ibid., 13–15.

10. TESTIMONY AGAINST WAR

1. HT, *QC,* 46–47.
2. Elizabeth's story also appears in
Cooper, *Camden,* 16–17, 68–69;
HWS, *JMW,* 28–30.
3. HWS, *JMW,* 3–4.
4. For West Jersey and the Whitall
role therein, see the works by
Carter, Mickle, Pomfret, and
Stewart (*Old Gloucester*) in the
bibliography.
5. HWS, 22; LPS, "Ann Whitall," in
LPS, *Reperusals,* 334–357. Ann
Whitall's diary is in the LPS papers
in the LC.
6. HWS, 22; LPS, 357.
7. For the Battle of Red Bank, see
Heston, *Red Bank;* HWS, 8–12;
Lossing, *Field Book,* index;
Stewart, *Red Bank;* Watson,
Annals of Philadelphia, 11 ff.
8. Chastellux, *Travels,* 1:157, 159,
317.
9. HWS, 23–25.

11. PRIVATE INTERCOURSE WITH GOD

The principal source for the account of
JMW's life as presented here is HWS's
John Mickle Whitall, pp. 80–151. Other
sources are cited in the notes below.
1. HWS, *JMW,* 26–28, 38–50.
2. Ibid., 35–38.
3. Goldstein, *Philadelphia and the
China Trade,* 50.
4. HWS, 194–195.
5. HT, *QC,* 142.
6. HWS, 195.
7. Ibid., 198.
8. Ibid., 83.
9. Ibid., 192.
10. HT, *QC,* 42.
11. Pepper, *Glass Gaffers* (see index);
*Whitall, Tatum and Company,
1880* (catalogue).
12. R.N.T., *Memoirs of Mary Whitall.*

13. HWS, 167 ff.; R.N.T., 10.
14. HT, *QC*, 26.
15. HT to JTF (oral); HWS, passim.

12. A YOUNG MARRIAGE

1. Henrietta Thomas to RHT, Sr., 1/21/1824, 12/23/1824, JTFC.
2. B. L. Gildersleeve to MCT, 11/14/1897, JTFC.
3. RHT, Jr., *Life and Letters*, 7–8.
4. Henrietta Thomas to RHT, Sr., 12/18/1828, JTFC.
5. Photographs, JTFC.
6. JCT to MWT, 7/7/1854, 7/18/1854, MCTP.
7. Baltimore *Sun*, 11/10/1897; MWT to JCT, 7/9/1854, 8/18/1854, JTFC.
8. MWT to JCT, 10/6/1854, JTFC.
9. MWT to JCT, 3/29/1855, JTFC.
10. JCT to MWT, 7/3/1854, MCTP.
11. JCT to MWT, 10/12/1854, MCTP.
12. MWT to JCT, 11/9/1854, 11/25/1854, JTFC.
13. MWT to SWN, 11/2/1854, JTFC.
14. MWT to SWN, 12/1/1855, JTFC.
15. MWT to JMW, 11/6/1857, JTFC.
16. MWT to JMW, 10/16/1856, JTFC.
17. JCT to William H. Nicholson, 10/6/1860; JCT to JMW, 3/5/1861; MWT to "Parents," 4/2/1861; MWT to [?], 4/19/1865 — all in JTFC; MCT, unpaginated account of her childhood, FP.
18. MWT, correspondence beginning January, 1857, JTFC.
19. MWT to "Sister," 11/22/1861, JTFC.
20. MWT to SWN, 11/13/1871, JTFC.

13. THE GATE OPENS

1. SFOR, 32.
2. SFAu, ch. 1, p. 6; SFOR, 33; SFN, 5/3/1931, Apr., 1942, Aug., 1943.
3. SFN, 4/4/1947; Johnston, ed., *Memorial History of Louisville*, 2:55.
4. SF, "The College of Pharmacy," undated memo, FP; SFAu, ch. 1, pp. 6–7; SFOR, 33; SFN, 11/15/1932.
5. SFN, 11/15/1932, 8/9/1933.
6. SFN, 8/19/1943.

7. SFN, 8/12/1923, 12/4/1932, 7/22/1936.
8. SFAu, ch. 1, p. 4; SFN, July–Aug., 1930.
9. SFN, 8/12/1925.
10. SFN, 12/4/1932, 8/9/1943.
11. EAF to HT, n.d., JTFC.

14. JACOB'S DRUGSTORE

1. SFN, 8/16/1926.
2. SFN, 8/13/1926.
3. SFAu, ch. 1, p. 8.
4. SFAuD, ch. 1, p. 6.
5. SFN, 7/12/1931, 7/19/1937.
6. SFOR, 38A.
7. SF to JTF (oral).
8. SFN, 11/15/1932.
9. SFOR, 30–31; SFN, 6/3/1937.
10. SFN, 8/14/1920, 12/15/1931, 11/15/1932; pocket notebook, n.d., FP.
11. SFOR, 41.
12. SFN, 11/3/1937.
13. SFN, 5/25/1936.
14. SFN, 7/27/1929, 5/23/1936.

15. MICROSCOPE WITH WINGS

1. SFN, 7/7/1924, 7/29/1927, 6/3/1937, 8/6/1943.
2. SFN, 7/29/1974, 8/3/1943.
3. SFOR, 46–47.
4. SFAuD, ch. 1, p. 4; SFOR, 43–44; SFN, July, 1924; pocket notebook, n.d., FP.
5. *New York City Directory, 1883–1884*.
6. SFOR, 54–56.
7. SFN, 7/19/1937.
8. SFN, pocket notebook, n.d., FP.

16. AN UNPREPARED STUDENT AND A NEW UNIVERSITY

1. SFN, 9/25/1942; undated memo, FP.
2. AF to Eleanor Flexner, 10/3/1924, AF Papers, LC; AF, *IR*, 7.
3. AF, *IR*, 12–13.
4. Mary Flexner to JTF (oral).
5. AF, *IR*, 20.
6. Ibid., 28.
7. Ibid., 28–29; SFN, 8/31/1932; pocket notebook, n.d., FP.
8. AF, *IR*, 29.

9. Ibid., 35.
10. Ibid., 44–46.
11. "Johns Hopkins," *DAB;* AF, *Gilman*, 28–33; LBT, *Thomas*, 39, 354.
12. AF, *Gilman*, 33–37.
13. Ibid., 54.
14. JHU, *Circular* (Dec., 1897), 37.
15. AF, *Gilman*, 40.
16. Ibid., 47–51.
17. D. C. Gilman to JCT, 6/12/1886, JTFC.
18. AF, *IR*, 32. The subsequent description of AF's college years is based on ibid., 53–64.
19. Ibid., 66.
20. Ibid., 66–67.
21. Ibid., 71.

17. PATHWAYS FOR ESCAPE

1. SFAu, ch. 1, pp. 13–14; SFN, July, 1924, 7/19/1927, 8/10/1943.
2. AF, *IR*, 63–65; Flexners, *WHW*, 150 ff.
3. SF to HT, 7/15/1903, FP; SFN, 1/22/1930.
4. SF to HT, 7/15/1903, FP; SFOR, 62; SF, *A Half Century of American Medicine*, 33; SFN, 7/19/1921, 7/9/1927, 1/22/1936.
5. SFN, 7/19/1921.
6. SFN, 7/1/1924, 8/9/1943.
7. SFN, 8/19/1925; SFSP, nos. 1–3.
8. SFOR, 62.
9. SFN, 7/19/1927, 7/24/[?]
10. SFN, 11/15/1932.
11. Photographs of SF are in JTFC.
12. SFN, 7/19/1927, 3/9/1931.
13. SF to JTF (oral).
14. SFN, 6/3/1937; Flexner, *WHW*, 173.
15. SFN, 8/10/1926; notebook, July, 1924, FP.
16. SFN, 3/26/1939; notebook, July, 1924, FP.
17. SFN, 8/26/1937.
18. SF to HT, 7/15/1903, FP; SFOR, 62.

18. HELEN'S CHILDHOOD

The sources for HT's early childhood (pages 143–155) are MWT, "Journal" summary of the year 1871 and summary of the years 1872 and 1873, MCTP; and HT, *QC*, 1–20. The source for the trip to Germany and its aftermath (pages 150–155) is HT, *QC*, 57–77.

1. HWS to MWT, 8/8/1879, JTFC; HT, *QC*, 12.
2. MWT to "Sister," 8/7/1866, JTFC; HT, *QC*, 52–53.
3. MCT, unpaginated account of her childhood, FP.
4. MCT, *The Making of a Feminist*, 67.
5. HT, *QC*, 83–89.
6. Finch, *Carey Thomas*, 49.
7. MWT to HWS, 4/6/1879, JTFC.
8. MWT to MCT, 8/10/1874, 7/4/1878, MCTP.
9. MCT, 123.
10. HT, *QC*, 35–36.
11. MCT, 152.
12. Ibid., 142–143.
13. Ibid., 162.
14. MWT to HWS, 8/22/1879, JTFC.
15. MCT, correspondence and diary notes, 1879–1882, MCTP; HT, *QC*, 62.

19. EVANGELISTS

1. MWT to SWN, 4/13/1865, JTFC.
2. MWT to SWN, 12/3/1862, JTFC.
3. MWT to SWN, 9/4/1867, JTFC.
4. HT, *QC*, 250.
5. Correspondence between MWT and her sisters HWS and SWN, 1859–1871, JCTP.
6. HWS to MWT, 1/12/1872, JCTP.
7. The published sources concerning HWS and her religious experiences with Robert Pearsall Smith are voluminous, as indicated in the bibliography. See there particular writings listed under HWS, and B. Strachey's *Remarkable Relations*, R. Strachey's *A Quaker Grandmother*, and Parker's *Transatlantic Smiths*. For a discussion of the Higher Life Movement, see Warfield, *Perfectionism*.
8. HWS, "Personal Experiences of Religious Fanaticism"; B. Strachey, 35.
9. HWS, *Christian's Secret*, ch. 2.
10. BR, *Autobiography*, 1:224.
11. MWT to HWS, 7/3/1885, JTFC.
12. HWS to JCT, 2/24/1872, 7/1/1873, n.d., JTFC.
13. HWS to MWT, 5/10/1874, JTFC.

14. For biographies of Moody, see the works by Chapman and Findlay in the bibliography.
15. HWS to MWT, n.d. [1879], JTFC.
16. Chapman, *Moody*, 102.
17. MWT to HWS, 11/24/1879, JTFC.
18. MWT to HWS, n.d. [1879], JTFC.
19. MWT to HWS, 4/6/1879, JTFC.
20. MWT to "Mother," 1/23/1879, JTFC; MWT to HWS, 4/24/1879, JTFC.
21. HWS to MWT, 1/7/1879, JTFC; HWT to JCT (oral).
22. MWT to MCT, 18/19/1874, MCTP; MWT to HWS, 8/3/1885, JTFC.
23. MWT to HWS, 7/3/1885, JTFC.

20. HELEN GROWING

1. HT, *QC*, 139.
2. Ibid.
3. Ibid., 159–162.
4. Ibid., 183.
5. Ibid., 168.
6. Finch, *Carey Thomas*, 134 ff.
7. JMW to MWT, 5/3/1872, JTFC.
8. MWT to HWS, 10/3/1889, JTFC.
9. HT, *QC*, 240–241.
10. Ibid., 190, 228–229, 283.
11. MWT to "Sister," 4/2/1877, JTFC; HT, *QC*, 272.
12. MWT to SWN, 1/10/1878, JTFC.
13. HT, *QC*, 94, 302.
14. Ibid., 298.
15. Ibid., 291.

21. SEXUAL DIVISIONS

1. RHT, Jr., *Life and Letters*, 122.
2. HT, *QC*, 108.
3. Ibid.
4. Ibid., 79, 100.
5. Ibid., 33–34.
6. Ibid., 179.
7. Ibid., 81–82.
8. MWT to "Sister," 2/2/1860, JTFC.
9. HT, *QC*, 17–18.
10. Ibid., 109–111.
11. Ibid., 111–112.
12. MWT to "Sister," 1885, JTFC.

22. SEXUAL REVULSION

1. HT, *QC*, 139–142.
2. MWT to MCT, 1885[?], JTFC.

3. MWT to HWS, 8/6/1885, JTFC.
4. HT, *QC*, 244.
5. MCT, *Making*, 148–149.
6. MCT, unpaginated account of her childhood, FP.
7. MWT to SWN, 1/1/1862, 6/17/1867, JTFC.
8. HT to JTF (oral).
9. HT, *QC*, 222.
10. In all the family collections: FP, JTFC, MCTP, Strachey Papers.
11. MWT to HWS, 8/3/1885, 3/13/1886, 4/20/1886, JTFC.
12. MWT to HWS, 4/20/1886, JTFC.
13. MWT to HWS, 3/23/1886, 2/20/1887, JTFC.
14. HT, *QC*, 266.
15. Ibid., 293–294.

23. CATASTROPHE

1. MWT to HWS, 9/28/1881, JTFC.
2. MWT to HWS, 1/14/1884, 3/30/1884, JTFC; MWT, undated fragment [1885?], JTFC.
3. MWT to HWS, "First Day," [1885?], JTFC; HT to HWS, 3/23/1886, JTFC.
4. MWT to HWS, n.d. [1884?], JTFC.
5. MWT to HWS, 3/30/1884, JTFC.
6. MWT to [?], 6/6/1887, JTFC; MWT to MCT, n.d. [1887?], JTFC.
7. MWT to HWS, n.d. [1887?], JTFC.
8. HT, *QC*, 307–308.
9. RHT, Jr., *Life and Letters*, 220–221.
10. HT, *QC*, 305–306.
11. Ibid., 309.
12. E. L. Tatum to MWT, 1887; HWS to MWT, 12/26/1888, JTFC.
13. MWT to HWS, 1887, JTFC.
14. HWS to MCT, 12/6/1887, 1/30/1888, etc., JTFC; HT, *QC*, 323 ff.
15. MWT to HWS, two letters, n.d., JTFC; HT, *QC*, 327.
16. HT, *QC*, 322.
17. Ibid., 331–332.
18. Ibid., 327–328.
19. Ibid., 332.
20. Ibid., 333.
21. MCT to HWS, 7/10/1888, JTFC.
22. James Whitall to his children, 7/14/1888, JTFC.

23. MCT to HWS, 7/10/1888, 7/13/1888, JTFC.
24. MCT to HWS, 7/19/1888, JTFC.
25. John Thomas to "Ginnie," 7/6/1888, JTFC.
26. *The White Ribbon Herald, Memorial Number ... Mary Whitall Thomas*, published by the Woman's Christian Temperance Union of Baltimore (Baltimore, 1888).
27. HT, *QC*, 334-335.

24. A NEW LIFE STARTS

1. SFAu, ch. 2, p. 1; ch. 4, p. 11; SFN, 8/24/1926.
2. Flexners, *WHW*, 160.
3. SFAu, ch. 2, pp. 2-3; SFN, 7/7/1926, 7/27/1927; SF, MS headed "Edgartown," FP.
4. SFAu, ch. 2, p. 3; SF, MS headed "Councilman," FP; SF, "Edgartown" MS.
5. SFAu, ch. 2, p. 2.
6. Flexners, *WHW*, 161.
7. SF, "Councilman" MS; SFAuD, ch. 5, pp. 5-6; SFN, 8/16/1926, 7/2/1927, 11/14/1941.
8. SF to JTF (oral).
9. SFN, 7/20/1935, 11/14/1941.
10. JTF, recollections.
11. SFN, 7/19/1927.
12. SFAu, ch. 2, pp. 7-8.
13. Ibid., pp. 4-6; SF, "Councilman" MS; SFN, 7/12/1927; SFSP, nos. 6, 8.
14. Cushing, *Osler*, 1:321, 343.
15. SFAu, ch. 2, pp. 6-7; SF, "Edgartown" MS; SFSP, nos. 7, 11.
16. Benison, "Simon Flexner," 15.
17. AF to SF, 11/10/1890, FP.
18. SFAu, ch. 2, p. 8; SF, "Edgartown" MS.

25. SETTLING IN AT THE HOPKINS

1. SFAu, ch. 3, pp. 1-2; SF, "Edgartown" MS, FP; SFN, 8/14/1926.
2. JCT to Gilman, 7/26/1889, copy, WP.
3. MCT to SF, 6/23/1934, FP.
4. Flexners, *WHW*, 213.
5. Flexners, *WHW*, 219.

6. MCT to SF, 6/23/1934, FP; SFN, 8/21/1943; Flexners, *WHW*, 211-221.
7. SF, "Edgartown" MS; SFN, 7/19/1927, 1/8/1931, 8/2/1931; Flexners, *WHW*, 160 ff.; SFAu, ch. 3, pp. 3 ff.
8. *Boston Medical and Surgical Journal*, 4 (Apr., 1920).
9. SFN, 1/12/1927, 1/8/1931, 8/2/1931.
10. SFN, 7/21/1937.
11. SFN, 5/25/1936.
12. Flexners, *WHW*, 166.
13. SFSP, no. 14.
14. Barker, *Time*, 50-52; SFN, 7/7/1926, FP.
15. SFAuD, ch. 3, p. 49; SFN, 1/17/1934.
16. SFAu, ch. 2, p. 8.
17. AF to SF, 5/13/1892, 5/16/1892, FP.
18. SFAuD, ch. 3, p. 47.

26. BREAKING TRAIL

1. SFAu, ch. 3, pp. 2-3.
2. *Boston Medical and Surgical Journal* 4 (1920).
3. SFAuD, ch. 3, pp. 48-52; Flexners, *WHW*, 166; SFN, 1/17/1934.
4. SFSP, nos. 6 ff.
5. JCT to Gilman, 10/14/1889, Eisenhower Library, JHU.
6. JCT to Gilman, 8/22/1881, Eisenhower Library, JHU.
7. SF to JTF (oral).
8. JHU, *Medical Department Catalogue* (1889).
9. SFAu, ch. 4, p. 1; WHW to SF, 6/23/1893, FP.
10. SFAu, ch. 4, p. 1.
11. Ibid., 2-6.
12. SF to his family (oral).
13. SFAu, ch. 4, pp. 4-6.
14. Ibid., 7-8.

27. RISING

1. Flexners, *WHW*, 227 ff.
2. AF, *IR*, see index; SFN, 12/16/1938, 3/12/1913; SF to JTF (oral).
3. SFSP, no. 71; Rous, "Simon Flexner," 414.
4. SF, "Edgartown" MS, FP; Barker, *Time and the Physician*.

5. SFN, 12/11/1932.
6. SFAuD, ch. 5, p. 46.
7. SFN, 1930–1936, Section B.
8. SFN, 12/14/1932.
9. SFAuD, ch. 5, p. 42.
10. Ibid., pp. 51–52; SFN, 4/5/1931.
11. SF to JTF (oral).
12. SFOR, 64; SFN, "Chocorua," 1933.
13. SFAu, ch. 5, p. 5.
14. Henry M. Thomas to JCT, 6/15/1896, JTFC.
15. SFN, 8/21/1931.
16. MCT to Mary Garrett, 2/28/1890, 3/1/1890, MCTP.
17. Flexners, *WHW*, 157.
18. Ibid., 170.
19. Ibid., 167–168.
20. Ibid., 172–173.
21. SFN, 12/18/1938.
22. SFN, 8/16/1926.
23. The papers are listed in SFSP, beginning with no. 17.
24. SFAuD, ch. 4, pp. 53–55; ch. 5, pp. 10–11; ch. 6, pp. 3 ff; SFSP, nos. 57, 62, 63.
25. SFAuD, as cited in n. 24.
26. SFAuD, ch. 5, pp. 11–14; SFSP, nos. 93, 110, 121, 122, 123, 148.
27. SFSP, nos. 43, 52.
28. SFSP, nos. 60, 79, 80; SFAuD, ch. 5, pp. 11–12.
29. SFSP, no. 51.
30. SFSP, nos. 53, 58.
31. SFAuD, ch. 4, pp. 53–55; ch. 5, pp. 11–12.
32. WHW to "Sister," 7/18/1898, WP.

28. DANGER AT THE CROSSROADS

1. HT to SF, 12/3/1901, FP.
2. SFAuD, ch. 6, pp. 1–5.
3. SFN, 3/5/1949; WHW to G. H. F. Nutthall, 9/27/1895, WP; WHW to SF, 8/31/1897, FP.
4. SFN, 3/5/1945.
5. Larrabee, *Benevolent*, 288–291.
6. WHW to F. P. Mall, 6/30/1898, WP.
7. WHW to "Sister," 7/18/1898, WP.
8. WHW to SF, 7/7/1898, 7/11/1898, 7/24/1898, 8/2/1898, FP.
9. Councilman to SF, 8/9/1898, FP.
10. SFAuD, ch. 4, p. 2; SFN, 7/21/1927.

11. SFN, 7/21/1927; SFAuD, ch. 6, pp. 1–2.
12. SF, "Mall," FP.
13. F. P. Mall to A. C. Abbott, 12/31/1898, FP.
14. SFAuD, ch. 6, pp. 2, 10; SF to JTF (oral); SFN, 3/5/1947.
15. Abbott to SF, 2/27/1932, FP; SFN, Oct., 1934.
16. University of Pennsylvania Archives, "Minutes of Medical Faculty," 10:2568; "Minutes of Trustees," 13:581, 583.
17. WHW to SF, 3/17/1899, FP.

29. MISSION TO THE PHILIPPINES

1. Barker, *Time and the Physician*, 63; SF, diary, Manila, 1–2, FP.
2. SF, diary, 2–3, FP.
3. Barker, 63–64; SF, diary, 3–15, FP.
4. SF to "Dear Girls and Anne," 3/22/1899, FP; SF, diary, 20, 29, FP.
5. SF to "Dear Ones," 4/15/1899. FP.
6. SF to "My Dear Ones," 4/19/1899, FP.
7. SF, "Noguchi"; SFN, 1/1/1928; Eckstein, *Noguchi*, 59.
8. Barker, 64.
9. Ibid., 65; SF to "Dear Ones," 4/29/1889, FP.
10. SF, diary, 33, FP.
11. SF to JCT (oral).
12. SF to "Dear Ones," 6/7/1899, 6/12/1899, 6/21/1899, FP.
13. Barker, 71; SF, diary, 116–118, FP.
14. SF, diary, 121, FP.
15. Ibid., 125.
16. Ibid., 17.
17. Ibid., 149, 167; Barker, 66–70.
18. SFSP, nos. 91, 92, 96–99, 101, 104–106.
19. SF to "Dear Ones," 6/21/1899, FP; SF to "Mother," 7/25/1899, FP.
20. SF to "Mother," 8/19/1899, FP.

30. THE FURTHER ADVENTURES OF ABRAHAM

1. AF, *IR*, 74 ff.
2. AF to SF, 8/14/1893, FP; AF, *IR*, 75.
3. AF, *IR*, 67.
4. AF to SF, 5/21/1892, 2/10/1894, FP.
5. SFN, 8/8/1933.

6. AF to SF, 3/17/1894, FP.
7. AF to SF, 1/17/1894, FP.
8. SF to JTF (oral).
9. SF, "Marketing of Albuminate and Financial Failure," n.d., FP.
10. AF to SF, 9/1/1896, 9/12/1896, 9/30/1896; "Saturday" [1896], FP.
11. AF to SF, "Saturday" [1896], and "Sunday" [1896], FP.
12. SFN, 1/3/1937.
13. AF to SF, "Wednesday" [1896], and "Saturday" [1896], FP.
14. AF to SF, 9/30/1896, FP.
15. *NCAB*, LII, 161.
16. *NCAB*, XXXIV, 265.
17. "Bernard Flexner," *DAB*, Supplement, III.

31. SEESAW

1. MCT to HT, 1889, MCTP.
2. Ibid.; Edith Thomas to HT, 4/9/1889, JTFC.
3. MCT to HT, 12/1/1888, MCTP; HT to MCT, 12/19/1888, JTFC.
4. HT to MCT, 8/19/1889, MCTP.
5. HT to MCT, 1/15/1888, JTFC.
6. HT to MCT, 8/7/1889, MCTP.
7. HT to MCT, 9/19/1889, MCTP.
8. *Bryn Mawr Fiftieth Anniversary*, 8.
9. JTF recollections.
10. HT to JCT, 11/25/1889, FP.
11. *Bryn Mawr Fiftieth*, 25.
12. HT to JCT, 10/20/1889, JTFC.
13. HT to JCT, 1/14 & 24/1890, JTFC.
14. HT to JCT, 3/16 & 5/9/1890, FP.
15. HT to JTF (oral); HT to LMD, 3/26/1890, FP.
16. HT to LMD, 3/23/1890, FP.
17. HT, *QC*, 90; HT to LMD, May, 1890, FP.
18. HT to LMD, 6/13/1890, FP.
19. HT to LMD, 7/9/1890, FP.
20. HT to LMD, 5/11/1890, FP.
21. HT to LMD, 6/13/1890, FP.
22. HT to LMD, 7/9/1890, FP.
23. HT to LMD, 5/11/1890, 5/16/1890, 7/9/1890, FP.
24. HT to LMD, 6/13/1890, FP.

32. ENTRAPMENTS AND ESCAPES

1. HT to JCT, 10/26/1890, FP; "Friday morning," [1890], FP.
2. HT to JCT, 4/19/1890, FP.
3. HT to JCT, 2/15/1891, 3/15/1891, 6/8/1891, FP.

4. MCT to HT, 11/9/1891, FP.
5. HT to JCT, 6/15/1891, FP.
6. HT to LMD, 8/2/1891, FP.
7. HT to JCT, 8/1/1891, FP.
8. HT to LMD, 9/18/1891, FP.
9. Undated manuscript, JTFC.
10. HT to LMD, 9/25/1891, FP.
11. Ibid.
12. Henry M. Thomas to JCT, 5/26/1896, FP.
13. HT to LMD, 12/31/1893, FP.
14. HT to MCT, 6/11/1894, 7/30/1894, 7/17/1895, MCTP.
15. HT to MCT, 7/11/1894, 7/30/1894, MCTP.
16. HT to MCT, 8/18/1894, MCTP.

33. EXPLODING HORIZONS

1. HT, *QC*, 265–267.
2. R. A. Parker, *Transatlantic Smiths*, passim; B. Strachey, *Remarkable Relations*, 65–71; Whitman, *Correspondence*, vols. 4 and 5 (consult indexes); Traubel, ed., *With Walt Whitman in Camden*, passim; Silver, ed., *Bright Star*, passim.
3. Parker, 54 ff.
4. Strachey, 85 ff.
5. BR, *Autobiography*, 1:104; Clark, *Russell*, 36–37; Strachey, 106.
6. Samuels, *Berenson*, 106–111; Strachey, 110.
7. Strachey, 111.
8. Clark, 27 ff.
9. HT to BR, July 1901, BRP.
10. BR, 1:103–141; Clark, 36–37.
11. Clark, passim.
12. HWS to Alys, 3/7/1886, quoted in Strachey, 89.
13. BR, 1:114–115; Strachey, 127–139.
14. Strachey, 135.
15. BR, 1:116.
16. Strachey, 139 ff.
17. HT to BR, "Monday [Nov., 1894]," BRP.
18. Strachey, 112 ff.
19. Clark, 54–55; Strachey, 141–144.
20. HT to MCT, 11/7/1894, 4/26/1895, MCTP.
21. BR to Alys, 11/28/1894, SC.

34. FRIDAY'S HILL

1. MCT to HT, 1895, MCTP.
2. HT to MCT, 1895, MCTP.
3. James Whitall to JCT, 4/11/1893,

5/9/1893, JTFC; Finch, *Carey Thomas*, 209–214.
4. HT to MCT, 4/26/1895, MCTP.
5. HT to MCT, 7/7/1895, 7/17/1895, MCTP.
6. HT to MCT, 8/4/1895, MCTP.
7. HT to MCT, 7/8/1895, MCTP.
8. HT to MCT, 5/22/1896, MCTP; HT to JCT, 6/6/1896, JTFC.
9. HT to JCT, 5/18/1896, JTFC.
10. MCT to HT, 8/9/1896, FP.
11. Grace to MCT, 9/14/1896, MCTP; Grace to JCT, 9/14/1896, JTFC.
12. Henry K. Douglas to "Judge," 10/9/1896, MCTP.
13. See ch. 22.
14. HT to JCT, July, 1897, JTFC.
15. MCT to Mary Garrett, 9/28/1896, 9/29/1896, MCTP.
16. HT to JCT, 8/20/1897, JTFC.
17. JCT to Gilman, 7/7/1896, Eisenhower Library, JHU.
18. Armstrong, *Russell*, 29–34; Clark, *Russell*, 65–67; Feinberg and Kaskils, *Russell's America*, 19–97.
19. BR, *Autobiography*, 1:195, 209.
20. HT to JCT, 6/11/1897, JTFC.
21. HT to JCT, 7/13/1897, JTFC.
22. HT to JCT, 7/22/1897, JTFC.
23. HT to MCT, 7/1/1897, MCTP.
24. HT to MCT, July, 1897, MCTP.
25. HT to JCT, 7/5/1897, JTFC.
26. HT to MCT, 7/1/1897, MCTP; HT to JCT, 7/19/1897, JTFC.
27. The pamphlet is in FP.
28. HT to MCT, 7/29/1896, MCTP.
29. LPS, *Trivia*, 37.
30. LPS to HT, 7/11/1902, FP.
31. HT to JCT, 7/2/1897, 8/4/1897, JTFC.
32. HT to JCT, 8/13/1897, JTFC.

35. DEATH OF A FATHER

1. HT, VN, 1:35–36, JTFC.
2. "November, 1897," pamphlet containing clippings from Baltimore *American*, 11/10, 11/12, 11/22; Baltimore *News*, 11/10, 11/12; Baltimore *Sun*, 11/10, 11/12; in Eisenhower Library, JHU. "A Finished Life," *The American Friend*, 11/18/1897.
3. HT, VN, 1:36.
4. HT to Grace Worthington, 11/10/1897, JCTP; MCT to HWS, 11/11/1897, JCTP.
5. HT to Grace Worthington, 11/10/1897, JCTP.
6. Ibid.; MCT to HWS, 11/11/1897, JCTP.
7. MCT to HWS, 11/19/1897, JTFC; MCT to Grace Worthington, 11/26/1897, JTFC.
8. "The Death of Dr. James Carey Thomas," *University Circular, Johns Hopkins University* (Dec., 1897), 37.
9. HT to LMD, 11/10/1897, 11/11/1897, FP.
10. MCT to HWS, 11/19/1897, JTFC.
11. HT to Grace Worthington, 11/10/1897, JCTP.

36. THE VELLUM SANCTUARY

1. MCT to Grace Thomas Worthington, 1/26/1897, JTFC.
2. HT to MCT, n.d. [1898], MCTP.
3. HT to MCT, 8/23/1898, MCTP.
4. MCT to HT, 11/23/1898, FP.
5. LPS to HT, 10/14/1899, FP.
6. Ibid.
7. HT, VN, 1:2–4, JTFC. The quotations that follow this one are also from v. 1, pp. 6, 11–12, 23–24, 30–31, 34, 52–53 respectively.
8. HT, undated notation on a single sheet, JCTP.
9. HT, VN, 1:72–76.
10. Ibid., 40.
11. Ibid., 77–90.
12. Ibid., 81–83.

37. SETTLING IN AT PHILADELPHIA

1. SFAuD, ch. 5, p. 13.
2. SF to "Family," 9/15/1899, FP; WHW to SF, 9/15/1899, Eisenhower Library, JHU.
3. SFAu, ch. 7, p. 1.
4. WHW to SF, 9/15/1899, FP.
5. SF to "My Dear Ones," 9/12/1899, FP; SFN, 7/19/1935.
6. WHW to SF, 11/9/1899, FP.
7. SF to "My Dear Ones," Dec., 1899, FP.
8. SFAu, ch. 7, p. 1.
9. SFN, 7/19/1937.
10. SFAu, ch. 7, pp. 4–5.
11. SF, "Hideyo Noguchi," *Science* 69 (1929): 653–660; SFN 1/1/1928,

6/22/1928, 7/12/1931; SF, "Early
November," 1944, FP; Plesset, *Noguchi*, 72 ff.; Noguchi to SF,
5/24/1899, 5/30/1899, FP; Kita-
zato to SF, 11/7/1900, FP.
12. SFN, 1/1/1928, 7/12/1931.
13. SFN, Nov.,1944.
14. SFAuD, ch. 5, p. 13.
15. SF, "Noguchi."
16. SFN, July, 1943; SFAu, ch. 7, p. 3;
SFAuD.
17. SF to EAF, 1/21/1900, FP.
18. SF to his sons (oral).

38. HELEN THOMAS AND
BERTRAND RUSSELL

1. HT to SF, 1/22/1900, FP.
2. HT to SF, 2/6/1900, FP.
3. HT to SF, 3/3/1900, FP.
4. HT, VN, 1:96, JTFC
5. LMD to HT, 3/7/1900, FP.
6. BR, *Autobiography*, 1:314.
7. BR, handwritten introduction to a
packet of HT's letters, BRP; BR,
Autobiography, 1:195.
8. BR, *Autobiography*, 1:199–200.
9. HT to SF, 4/27/1903, FP.
10. HT, VN, 1:111–118.
11. HT to MCT, 3/30/1900, MCTP.
12. Alys Russell to HT, 1900 and
thereafter, FP.
13. BR to HT, 12/31/1900, FP; BR,
Autobiography, 1:219.
14. BR to Lady Ottoline Morrell, nos.
392, 572 HRC.
15. BR to Lady Ottoline, no. 354 HRC.
16. BR to Lady Ottoline, no. 232 HRC.
17. JTF recollections.
18. JTF recollections.

39. A LION IN PHILADELPHIA

1. SFAuD, ch. 7, p. 104.
2. SF to Barker, 2/27/1900, Chesney
Medical Archives, JHU.
3. Croskey, *History of Blockley*,
82–83; Philadelphia Department of
Charities and Corrections, *Annual
Report for 1900;* SFN, 3/13/1923.
4. SFAu, ch. 5, p. 5; SFN, 3/26/1927.
5. Pennsylvania Hospital Board of
Managers, *150th Annual Report*
(1900–1901), 7, 13, 93; idem, *151st
Annual Report* (1901–1902), 10;
Pennsylvania Hospital Board of
Managers, "Minutes," microfilm

ed., 1/28/1901, 4/27/1901, Pennsylvania Hospital.
6. SFN, 2 (or 7?)/9/1931.
7. SFAu, ch. 7, p. 9.
8. Ibid., 9–10.
9. SF to WHW, 5/8/1900, WP.
10. SFAuD, ch. 7, p. 20.
11. Ibid., pp. 97–100; SFSP, no. 139.

40. THE BLACK DEATH

1. SFAuD, ch. 7, p. 9.
2. Barker, *Time and the Physician*,
109–110.
3. SFSP, nos. 130, 132, 133.
4. Barker, 111.
5. WHW to SF, 2/7/1901, FP.
6. SFAuD, ch. 7, p. 9.
7. Barker, 112–113; SFSP, no. 130.
8. Ibid.
9. SFAuD, ch. 7, pp. 9–10.
10. Barker, 113–115; SFAuD, ch. 7, p.
10; SFSP, nos. 130, 132, 133.
11. SFSP, no. 130.
12. Barker, 115; SFAuD, ch. 7, p. 10.
13. SFSP, no. 130.
14. Barker, 115.
15. WHW to SF, 3/26/1901, FP.

41. THE VALLEY OF DESPAIR

1. HT to MCT, 3/30/1900, MCTP.
2. HT, VN, 1:102–103, JTFC.
3. Ibid., 163–167.
4. Ibid., 177–178.
5. LMD to HT, 1/1 to 5/15, 1900, FP.
6. HT to SF, 11/26/1900, FP; LMD
to HT, 9/24/1900, 9/28/1900,
10/6/1900, 10/8/1900, 1900, FP.
7. HT to MCT, Dec., 1900, MCTP.
8. HT, VN, 2:27–28.
9. LMD to HT, 11/18/1900,
11/22/1900, etc., FP.
10. BR to HT, 12/31/1900, BRP.
11. HT to BR, 1/21/1901, FP.
12. HT, VN, 2:35–36.
13. HT to SF, "Wednesday" [1901],
FP.
14. HT to SF, 6/8/1901, FP.
15. HT to SF, 6/17/1901, FP.
16. HT to her sons (oral).
17. HT to MCT, 3/30/1901, MCTP.
18. HT to BR, 7/2/1901, BRP.
19. HT to SF, 9/6/1901, FP.
20. LMD to HT, 8/11/1901, 9/1/1901,
FP.

21. LPS to HWS, 9/13/1901, John Russell Collection, New York City.
22. HT to SF, 10/12/1901, FP.
23. HT to SF, 11/5/1901, FP.
24. LMD to HT, 10/6/1901, FP.
25. HT to BR, 12/10/1901, BRP.
26. HT, VN, 2:108–109.
27. Ibid., 62–63, 66.
28. Ibid., 66–68.

42. ENTER THE ROCKEFELLER INSTITUTE

1. Corner, *History of the Rockefeller Institute*, 16, 576–579.
2. Ibid., 17–19.
3. Ibid., 18–22, 580–581.
4. Gates, "The Memories of Frederick T. Gates," *American Heritage* 6 (Apr., 1955).
5. Corner, 580–583.
6. Ibid., 25.
7. G. H. F. Nuttall to Starr J. Murphy, 1/21/1901, RUP; Seth Low to WHW, 9/8/1900, WP; WHW to Low, 11/5/1900, RUP; Low to Prudden, 9/8/1900, in L. E. Prudden, ed., *Prudden*, 280–281; WHW to Theobald Smith, 5/5/1901, WP.
8. Duffus and Holt, *L. Emmett Holt*, passim.
9. L. Emmett Holt, memo, 3/9/1921, RUP.
10. *DAB*; W. G. N., *Christian Herter* n.p., n.d.
11. *DAB*; Duffus and Holt, 112–113; *Bio-chemical Journal* (Liverpool) 5 (1911): xxi; *Johns Hopkins Hospital Bulletin*, May, 1911.
12. Holt, memo, 3/9/1921.
13. Herter to WHW, 3/15/1901, WP.
14. WHW to Herter, 3/21/1901 (copy), WP.
15. JDR, Jr., to Holt, 4/29/1901 (copy), WP.
16. RI, "Minutes," 5/1/1901, RUP.
17. WHW to Theobald Smith, 5/5/1901 (copy), WP.
18. RI, "Minutes," 5/10/1901; Corner, 45.
19. RI, "Minutes," 5/26/1901, RUP.
20. Ibid., 10/2/1901.
21. Summarized in JDR, Jr., to WHW, 1/17/1902, WP.
22. WHW to JDR, Jr., 1/13/1902, RUP.

23. Smith to WHW, 2/11/1902, RUP.
24. WHW to Herter, 1/30/1902, RUP.
25. Smith to WHW, 2/11/1902, WP.
26. SF to WHW, 6/16/1902, WP.
27. AF to SF, 2/26/1902, FP.
28. SF to Barker, 2/29/1902, Chesney Medical Archives, JHU.
29. Barker to SF, 4/12/1902, FP.
30. WHW to Prudden, 3/5/1902, RUP.
31. Prudden to Herter, Prudden to Biggs, Prudden to Holt, 3/6/1902, RUP.
32. SF to WHW 4/8/1902, WP; RI, "Minutes," 3/8/1902, RUP.
33. SF to JTF (oral).

43. AN OFFER AND A REFUSAL

1. HT, VN, 2:68–69, JTFC.
2. Ibid., 83, 86–87.
3. SF to WHW, 4/8/1902 (copy), WP.
4. RI, "Minutes," 31–37, RUP.
5. Herter to SF, 5/15/1902, FP.
6. HT to SF, 5/14?/1902, FP.
7. SF to HT, 5/16?/1902, FP.
8. HT to SF, May, 1902, FP.
9. SF to HT, 5/19/1902, FP.
10. HT to SF, 5/20/1902, FP.
11. SF to HT, 12/25/1902, FP.
12. What was said in their conversation, on May 27, 1902, was gleaned from their subsequent correspondence.
13. HT to SF, 5/28/1902, FP.
14. SF to HT, 5/31/1902, FP.
15. SF to HT, 12/31/1902, FP; HT to SF, 2/7/1902, FP.

44. ABRAHAM AND ANNE

1. AF, *IR*, 83–84.
2. *DAB*.
3. AF, *IR*, 87; Stevens, *Crawford Genealogy*, 176–178.
4. AF, *IR*, 87.
5. Works Progress Administration, Kentucky Writers Project, "Biographical and Critical Materials. . . ."
6. Hayden Calhoun, "A Few Minutes with Anne Crawford Flexner," New York *Telegraph*, 1/13/1914.
7. AF, *IR*, 84–85.
8. *Theatre Magazine* 4 (1940): 298; WPA, "Biographical and Critical Materials."

9. AF, *IR*, 84.
10. Ibid., 89.
11. Calhoun, "A Few Minutes . . ."
12. *NCAB*, 17:333.
13. Calhoun, "A Few Minutes . . ."
14. AF, *IR*, 81-82.
15. AF, "A Freshman at Nineteen," *Educational Review* (Nov. 1899): 353-356.
16. AF to SF, 12/13/1899, FP; AF, *IR*, 82.
17. Atkinson, *Broadway*, 33-35; Kraus, *Play Production*, 265.
18. AF to SF, 1/5/1901, 2/2/1901, FP.
19. AF to SF, "Saturday" [1910], FP.
20. Binns, *Fiske*, 119-121, 407.
21. New York *Tribune*, 10/25/1901.
22. AF to SF, 10/4/1902, "Saturday" [1902], FP.
23. New York *Post*, 11/[?]/1903, 11/24/1903, clippings, FP.
24. AF to SF, 7/8/1903, FP; AF, "The Preparatory School," *Atlantic Monthly* 94 (1904): 368-377.
25. AF to SF, 7/6/1903, FP.
26. SF to HT, 7/21/1903, FP.
27. C. Y. Rice, *Bridging the Years*, see index; Hagen, *Inky*, 45, 172 ff.
28. London *Daily News*, 4/29/[?], clipping in the Library of Performing Arts, New York City.
29. New York *Times*, 10/23/1959.

45. CONSUMMATIONS

1. JDR, Jr., to JDR, Sr., 6/13/1902 (copy), WP.
2. JDR, Sr., to JDR, Jr., 6/14/1902 (copy), WP.
3. RI, "Minutes," 41, RUP.
4. SF to WHW, 6/16/1902 (copy), WP.
5. Prudden to WHW, 6/17/1902 (copy), WP.
6. Prudden to WHW, 6/20/1902 (copy), WP.
7. AF to SF, 6/21/1902, FP.
8. WHW to JDR, Jr., 6/21/1902 (copy), WP.
9. SF to WHW, undated draft, FP.
10. SF to Herter, 1/6/1902, RUP.
11. RI, "Minutes," 10/25/1902, RUP.
12. SF to HT, 11/4/1902, FP.
13. BR to HT, 3/3/1902, FP.
14. BR to HT, 6/10/1902, FP.
15. BR to HT, 6/27/1902, FP.
16. HT to Br, 7/20/1902, BRP.

17. LPS to HT, 7/12/1902, FP.
18. LPS to HT, 7/11/1902, FP.
19. HT to BR, 10/4/1902, BRP. HT, VN, v. 2, 10/9/1902, JTFC.
20. SF to HT, 11/3/1902, 11/4/1902, FP.
21. HT to SF, 11/4/1902, FP.
22. SF to HT, 11/9/1902, FP.
23. HT to Alys and BR, 1/25/1903, BRP.
24. HT to SF, 11/30/1902, FP.
25. SF to HT, 12/1/1902 (two letters), FP.
26. SF to HT, 12/2/1902, FP.

46. GREAT CHANGES

1. SF to HT, 12/2/1902, FP.
2. HT to Alys and BR, 1/25/1903, JTFC.
3. BR to HT, 2/7/1903, BRP.
4. LPS to HT, 4/15/1903, FP.
5. HT to SF, 12/20/1902, FP.
6. SF to HT, 12/20/1902, FP.
7. HT to SF, 12/28/1902, FP.
8. SF to HT, 1/7/1902, FP.
9. HT to SF, 1/5/1902, FP.
10. HT to SF, 2/8/1903, FP.
11. HT to SF, 12/31/1902, FP.
12. HT to SF, 1/17/1903, FP.
13. HT to SF, 1/18/1903, FP.
14. MWT to Mary Garrett, 1/18/1903, MCTP.
15. SF to HT, 1/7/1903, FP.
16. HWS to Mary Berenson, 5/8/1903, Strachey Papers.
17. New York *World*, late February, 1903, clipping, FP.
18. HT to SF, 3/2/1903, FP.
19. Barker to SF, 1/28/1903, FP.

47. LUCY AND OTHER TROUBLES

1. SF to his sons (oral).
2. HT to SF, 5/4/1903, FP.
3. HT to SF, 5/[?]/1903, FP.
4. SF to HT, 3/19/1903, FP.
5. SF to HT, 12/29/1902, 1/19/1903, FP.
6. Mildred Minton to HT, 6/12/1903, FP.
7. BR, *Autobiography*, 1:194.
8. MCT, *Making*, 82-85.
9. HT to SF, 6/10/1903, 6/12/1903, FP.

10. SF to HT, 6/16/1903, FP.
11. SF to HT, 6/18/1903, FP.
12. *NCAB*, 18:21–22.
13. *Notable American Women*, 2:197–199.
14. Ellen Giler to HT, 6/21/1903, 3/8/1907, FP.
15. HT to SF, 6/14/1903, FP.
16. SF to HT, June, 1903, FP.
17. HT to SF, 8/20/1903, FP.
18. SF to HT, 5/6/1903 (two letters), FP.
19. SF to HT, 12/12/1902, FP.
20. HT to SF, 3/11/1903, FP.

48. A HECTIC DEPARTURE

1. SF to Herter, 1/6/1902 (actually 1903), RUP.
2. SF to HT, 7/5/1903, FP.
3. SF to HT, 7/18/1903, FP.
4. Souvenir menu, 4/16/1903, JTFC.
5. H. A. Hare, poem (copy), FP.
6. SF to HT, 7/18/1903, FP.
7. SFOR, 61.
8. SF to JTF (oral).
9. SF to HT, 7/14/1903, FP.
10. SFAuD, ch. 7, p. 101; SFSP, no. 153.
11. SFSP, nos. 134, 135, 144, 149, 150, 151, 152.
12. SF to HT, 7/14/1903, FP.
13. SFSP, nos. 120, 131.
14. SFSP, no. 159, pp. 131–133.
15. SFN, 7/19/1927.
16. WHW to Herter, 9/6/1901, WP; WHW to JDR, Jr., 9/9/1901, WP; JDR, Jr., to WHW, 9/10/1901, WP.
17. SFSP, no. 159, p. 35.
18. Milton Campbell to SF, 10/20/1902, RUP; RI, "Minutes," 10/25/1902, RUP; SF to Prudden, 10/27/1902, 11/4/1902, RUP; Prudden to SF, 10/29/1902, 11/11/1902, 11/12/1902, RUP; SF to Mulford, 11/14/1902, RUP; SF to HT, 7/6/1903, FP.

19. RI, "Minutes," 4/11/1903, RUP; SFSP, no. 159, pp. 32–41.
20. SFSP, no. 159, pp. 31–41, 131–136.
21. SF to HT, 7/6/1903, FP.
22. SF to HT, 7/24/1903, FP.
23. SF to HT, 8/20/1903, 8/22/1903, FP.
24. Wilson and Miles, *Principles*, 901 ff.

49. THE MILDNESS OF A STRONG LOVE

1. Marriage certificate, FP.
2. HT to her family (oral).
3. HT to SF, 6/11/1903, FP.
4. HT to SF, 6/17/1903, FP.
5. HT to SF, 5/11/1903, FP.
6. SF to HT, 5/12/1903, FP.
7. HT to SF, 1/8/1903, FP; SF to HT, 1/13/1903, FP.
8. SF to HT, 7/16/1903, FP.
9. HT to SF, 12/3/1902, FP.
10. HT to SF, 1/7/1903, FP.
11. SF to HT, 2/22/1903, FP.
12. SF to HT, 7/12/1903, FP.
13. SF to HT, 6/9/1903, FP.
14. SF to HT, 2/22/1903, FP.
15. SF to HT, 8/23/1903, FP.

50. THE LATER YEARS

1. LPS to Kenneth Clark, 10/5/1936, courtesy, Edwin Tribble.
2. Corner, *History of the Rockefeller Institute*, 245.
3. Rous, "Simon Flexner," *Obituary Notices . . .*, 414.
4. Corner, 156.
5. Rous, 420.
6. Ibid., 420–421.
7. Corner, 323–324.
8. Fosdick, *John D. Rockefeller, Jr.*, 122–123.
9. RI, *Memorial Meeting*, 36.
10. Rous, "Simon Flexner and Medical Discovery," *Science* 107 (1948): 613.

Index